THE MARKETING OF LIBRARY AND INFORMATION SERVICES 2

Aslib, The Association for Information Management has some two thousand corporate members worldwide. It actively promotes better management of information resources.

Aslib lobbies on all aspects of the management of and legislation concerning information. It provides consultancy and information services, professional development training, specialist recruitment and publishes primary and secondary journals, conference proceedings, directories and monographs.

Further information about Aslib can be obtained from:
Aslib, The Association for Information Management,
Information House, 20–24 Old Street, London EC1V 9AP
Tel: 071 253 4488

The Marketing of Library and Information Services 2

Edited by Blaise Cronin
Indiana University

First published in 1992 by
Aslib, The Association for Information Management
Information House
20–24 Old Street
London EC1V 9AP

© Contributors

Previously published titles in the *Aslib Reader Series*
Volume 1. *National Libraries* M. B. Line and J. Line
Volume 2. *The Scientific Journal* A. J. Meadows
Volume 3. *The Professional Development of the Librarian and Information Worker* P. Layzell Ward
Volume 4. *The Marketing of Library and Information Services 1* B. Cronin
Volume 5. *Costing and the Economics of Library and Information Services* M. B. Line and J. Line
Volume 6. *Natioal Libraries 2, 1975–1986*

British Library Cataloguing in Publication Data
A Catalogue record for this book is available from the British Library

ISBN: 0–85142–278–0

Typeset by Megaron, Cardiff
Printed and Bound in Great Britain by
Bell & Bain Ltd, Glasgow

Contents

vii

The Marketing of Library and Information Services 2

edited by Blaise Cronin

Indiana University

Introduction

Blaise Cronin

Indiana University

It is ten years since the first edition of *The marketing of libraries and information services* appeared. The world has moved on and the time is right for an update. For instance, since publication of the first edition, the idea of applying marketing to not–for–profit institutions, which first emerged during the early 1970s, has become universally accepted:

a virtual stampede of marketing scholars and professionals has come forward to show that marketing principles are indeed of productive value to an expanding and amazingly diverse set of situations and organizations . . . Driven partly by cost and competitive pressures and partly by the exciting promise marketing has to offer, practitioners in health care, education, and the arts rushed to embrace the new discipline and explore its possibilities. They were followed very shortly by the librarians, recreation specialists, politicians, and leaders of social service organizations and major charities.[1]

The present volume does not supersede the first edition, rather is it intended as a complement and extension. The four anchor papers in the 1981 compilation are as worthy and pertinent as they were then: more than once I have had occasion to refer to Levitt's classic *Marketing myopia*[2] and the trio of papers by Kotler,[3] Shapiro[4] and Kotler and Levy[5] on the marketing of non–business organisations. They remain benchmarks. But there have been some conceptual advances in mainstream marketing theory and research since then: niche marketing, customisation, global advertising, megamarketing, and quality assurance are now rooted firmly in the professional lexicon. And thanks largely to the work of Porter[6, 7, 8,] the relationship between strategic marketing and competitive advantage has been rediscovered (and popularised as marketing warfare by Ries and Trout).[9]

In their standard textbook, *Strategic marketing for nonprofit organizations*, Kotler and Andreasen note that librarians have 'joined the marketing bandwagon'.[10] Even in 1980, there was a considerable pool from which to select papers dealing specifically with the application of marketing principles to the operations of libraries and information services, though the quality of the corpus left something to be desired. Trawling through the bloated library and information science literature of the 1980s was not a rewarding experience. The quality of papers, in

terms of analytic power, conceptualisation and methodological sophistication, remains low, while the majority of practitioner accounts of
market planning, research and audits do little to fire enthusiasm.[11] Yet,
virtually every library/ information science school pays lip service to the
marketing credo, and the practitioner is faced with an *embarras du choix* in
terms of marketing–related conferences, workshops, journal articles,
textbooks and DIY manuals. Certainly, attitudes changed markedly
during the 1980s, and now marketing is recognised as an integral part of
library management, even if amateurism remains the order of the day.[12, 13]
We have lived through a decade in which marketeers have applied their
skills to a dazzlingly diverse range of products, personalities, services,
experiences, constructs and situations; from prophylactics to presidents;
from charities to chips; from Bradford to Bros. Librarianship has not
been slow to see the potential of marketing, but looking back over the last
twenty years, it is debatable whether progress has been as rapid or
convincing as might have been expected: much chattering and scribbling,
to be sure, but few landmark successes.

The purpose of this book is to illustrate how marketing can be applied
to libraries and information services, both commercial and not–for–
profit. It is aimed at students on library and information science courses,
entry–level practitioners, and individuals charged for the first time with
producing a marketing plan, or carrying out market research, for their
unit or institution. The structure is similar to that of the 1981 edition,
though there is now a section of the marketing of electronic services and
products, reflecting developments in the information industry over the
last ten years. The chapter on cooperation and coordination, which
focused on publicity, promotion and PR, has been dropped, since little of
note or originality seems to have happened of late in these areas.

The forty one articles which make up the volume range in style from
the scholarly to the folksy. The majority come from the USA (19) and the
UK (14), with two each from Australia and Finland, and one each from
Canada, Sweden, Norway and Denmark. The mixture of styles, topics
and contexts is intentional. Whether you work in a rural public library,
for a database vendor, in a major research library, or as a freelance
information broker, there should be something for you.

REFERENCES

1. KOTLER, P. and ANDREASEN, A. R. *Strategic marketing for nonprofit organizations.* 3rd.ed. Englewood Cliffs: Prentice–Hall, 1987.
2. LEVITT, T. Marketing myopia. *Harvard Business Review*, 38(4), 1960, 45–56.
3. KOTLER, P. Strategies for introducing marketing into nonprofit organizations. *Journal of Marketing*, 43, January 1979, 37–44.
4. SHAPIRO, B. P. Marketing for nonprofit organizations. *Harvard Business Review*, 51(5), 1973, 123–132.
5. KOTLER, P. and LEVY, S. J. Broadening the concept of marketing.

Journal of Marketing, 33(1), 1969, 10–15.

6. PORTER, M. E. *Competitive strategy: techniques for analyzing industries and competitors.* New York: Free Press, 1980.

7. PORTER, M. E. *Competitive advantage: creating and sustaining superior performance.* New York: Free Press, 1985.

8. PORTER, M. E. *The competitive advantage of nations.* London: Macmillan, 1990.

9. RIES, A. and TROUT, J. *Marketing warfare.* New York: MacGraw–Hill, 1986.

10. KOTLER and ANDREASEN, op. cit., 5.

11. ARNOLD, S. E. Marketing electronic information: theory, practice, and challenges, 1980–1990. In: WILLIAMS, M. E. (ed.). *Annual Review of Information Science and Technology*, 25, 1990, 87–144.

12. CRONIN, B. *Library orthodoxies: a decade of change.* London: Taylor Graham, 1991.

13. CRONIN, B. and DAVENPORT, E. *Post–professionalism: transforming the information heartland.* London: Taylor Graham, 1988.

Mainstream Marketing

Mainstream Marketing – Introductory Notes

Blaise Cronin

Indiana University

The customer may not always be right, but it pays to operate on the principle that he is.[1,2] Henry T. Ford's approach to marketing ('Any color, so long as it's black') is unlikely to go down well with today's discerning buyer. Nor, for that matter, with Jan Carlzon (*Putting the customer first: the key to service strategy*), the charismatic CEO of SAS, whose commitment to customer care and quality is legendary. Customisation is *à la mode*: if you want a Trabant with tail fins, then that's what you'll get. Today's flexible design and manufacturing technologies allow mass production and individualization to be combined in a way that was unimaginable in Ford's time or under Honecker's regime in East Germany. Customisation and choice (designer jeans or designer genes), deregulation and competitive diversity became hallmarks of the eighties, from telecommunications to travel.

The volume opens with McKenna's 1988 article, *Marketing in an age of competitive diversity*, which analyses the implications of fractured markets. Marketing in an age of diversity means more options for the consumer, increased competition in the marketplace (quality of service sets SAS apart from other carriers in the airline industry), low perceived product differentiation, debasement of language (as advertisers bend and abuse language in an effort to grab the consumer's attention), corporate refocusing (downsizing, networking, partnerships), and changes in leverage criteria, as economies of scale give way to economies of knowledge, that is, 'knowledge of the customer's business, of current and likely future technology trends, and of the competitive environment . . . '. Much of this in fact describes recent trends in the electronic information services marketplace, where niched products, boutique services, customised software, value–added features and inflated rhetoric have become the norm.[3,4] In the light of recurrent poor quality reference service performance and lukewarm customer satisfaction ratings (see, for example, the *Which?* report in the *Market Research* section)[5,6] there is much that libraries could learn from SAS and other industry leaders about the bottom line value of quality assurance and customer care. If SAS can allow customers' preferences to govern business decisions, why should the sampe principle not be applied to the management of library services?

Public sector library and information services do not exist in a competitive vacuum. They compete for custom with a wide variety of agencies, organisations and media. Competition comes in many shapes and forms: from satellite TV through leisure facilities, to direct competition from brokers, commercial information providers and informal exchange networks. Every other contender for funds from the public purse (health, education, social services, recreation) is also a competitor. If the 'marketing is war' metaphor is valid, then the logic which holds for General Motors can be applied across the board:

In the marketing plan of the future, many more pages will be dedicated to the competition. This plan will carefully dissect each participant in the marketplace. It will develop a list of competitive weaknesses and strengths as well as a plan of action to either exploit or defend against them . . . who are General Motor's competitors? There is the Justice Department, the Federal Trade Commission, and the US Congress (both houses).[7]

Until recently this kind of language and thinking was anathema to librarians. But there are heartening signs of change[8], and indications that the ostrich mentality is on the wane. Take for example the *Situation audit* chapter in Bryson's 1990 book *Effective library and information centre management*. This was written as a text book for library school students and beginning professionals, yet it makes liberal and unselfconscious use of the language of competition thoughout:

The situation audit provides library and information centre managers with important background information which is used in strategic management. After scanning the external and internal environments of the library or information centre and carrying out some analyses, the librarian or information centre manager should be able to determine the role of the library in its environment, its influence and image, and the service which it provides. The situation audit should also provide information on existing and potential users of the library, stakeholders and other influences found in the environment, and competitors of the library.[9]

This is the message behind Bergsma's scene–setting paper (*From market research to business research*) which stresses that 'understanding market segments (i.e. where to compete) is critical for identifying opportunities to establish a competitive advantage or, more basically, for determining whether you have one in the first place'. In addition, however, you need to figure out the rules of the game, the strengths of other players and how best to compete. To do this, Bergsma devised an easy–to–use forcing device called the strategic gameboard.[10] It does not require a great deal of imagination to see the connection between his ideas and the challenge thrown down by Woodsworth and her co–authors ('strategic directions need to be articulated now') in their article *The model research library: planning for the future* which is included in the section on *Applying the Principles of Marketing*.

Perhaps the most celebrated marketing neologism of the decade was Kotler's 'megamarketing', which takes us beyond the classic four Ps (product, price, place, promotion) to power and public relations. Increasingly, marketers have to function as political strategists, lobbying, lubricating and leveraging their organisation into a position where trade becomes possible. Marketing has become 'the art of managing power', opening doors, winning over opponents, sceptics, regulators and politicians and at the same time harnessing public opinion to 'pull the company into the market'. More than ever, these skills are required of senior librarians and information managers, be they in the public or private sector. Marketing services to end–users is not enough; what is needed is macro user education, or getting the message across to those who control the purse strings.[11] Marketing is a two–fold process which involves the attraction *and* allocation of resources. A simple but often overlooked fact.

REFERENCES

1. GARVIN, D. A. *Managing quality*. New York: Free Press, 1988.
2. PETERS, T. J. and WATERMAN, R. H. *In search of excellence: lessons from America's best–run companies*. New York: Harper & Row, 1982.
3. OPPENHEIM, C. Why is online bibliographic information so unimportant? *International Journal of Information Management*, 7(4), 1987, pp. 197–204.
4. RAFFERTY, P., CRONIN, B. and DAVENPORT, L. The rhetoric of promise: advertising in the information industry. *Aslib Proceedings*, 40(11/12), 1988, pp. 295–301.
5. CRONIN, B. Libraries AD2000: the skills requirement. In: MILLERCHIP, J. J. G. (ed.). *Personal management skills*. London: LA/CoFHE, 1991, pp. 1–12.
6. BURTON, P. F. Accuracy of information: the need for client–centred service. *Journal of Librarianship*, 22(4), 1990, pp. 201–215.
7. RIES, A. and TROUT, J. *Marketing warfare*. New York: McGraw–Hill, 1986, p. 5, p. 51.
8. CRONIN, B. New horizons for the information profession: strategic intelligence and competitive advantage. In: DYER, G. and TSENG, G. (eds.). *New horizons for the information profession*. London: Taylor Graham, 1988, pp. 3–22.
9. BRYSON, J. *Effective library and information centre management*. Aldershot: Gower, 1990, p. 22.
10. CRONIN, B. From vertical to horizontal resource management. In: GENT, R. P. (ed.). *Public library resources – getting the return*. London: LA/PLG, 1986, pp.3–8.
11. CRONIN, B. Macro user education – sensitizing management to the value of information. *South African Journal of Library and Information Science*, 53(3), 1985, pp. 120–123.

Marketing in an Age of Diversity

Regis McKenna

Regis McKenna Inc., Palo Alto, California

Spreading east from California, a new individualism has taken root across the United States. Gone is the convenient fiction of a single, homogeneous market. The days of a uniformly accepted view of the world are over. Today diversity exerts tremendous influence, both economically and politically Technology and social change are interdependent. Companies are using new flexible technology, like computer-aided design and manufacturing and software customization to create astonishing diversity in the marketplace and society. And individuals temporarily coalescing into 'micromajorities' are making use of platforms – media, education, and the law – to express their desires.

In the marketing world, for example, the protests of thousands of consumers, broadcast by the media as an event of cultural significance, was enough to force Coca-Cola to reverse its decision to do away with 'classic' Coke. On the political scene, vociferous minorities, sophisticated in using communication technology, exert influence greatly disproportionate to their numbers: the Moral Majority is really just another minority – but focused and amplified. When we see wealthy people driving Volkswagens and pickup trucks, it becomes clear that this is a society where individual tastes are no longer predictable; marketers cannot easily and neatly categorize their customer base.

Over the last 15 years, new technology has spawned products aimed at diverse, new sectors and market niches. Computer-aided technologies now allow companies to customize virtually any product, from designer jeans to designer genes, serving ever narrower customer needs. With this newfound technology, manufacturers are making more and more high-quality products in smaller and smaller batches; today 75 per cent of all machined parts are produced in batches of 50 or fewer.

Consumers demand – and get – more variety and options in all kinds of products, from cars to clothes. Auto buyers, for example, can choose from 300 different types of cars and light trucks, domestic and imported, and get variations within each of those lines. Beer drinkers now have 400 brands to sample. The number of products in supermarkets has soared from 13,000 in 1981 to 21,000 in 1987. There are so many new items that stores can demand hefty fees from packaged-foods manufacturers just for displaying new items on grocery shelves.

Deregulation has also increased the number of choices – from a flurry of competing airfares to automated banking to single-premium life insurance that you can buy at Sears. The government has even adapted antitrust laws to permit companies to serve emerging micromarkets: the Orphan Drug Act of 1983, for instance, gives pharmaceutical companies tax breaks and a seven-year monopoly on any drugs that serve fewer than 200,000 people.

Diversity and niches create tough problems for old-line companies more accustomed to mass markets. Sears, the country's largest retailer, is trying to reposition its products, which traditionally have appealed to older middle-class and blue-collar customers. To lure younger, style-minded buyers, Sears has come up with celebrity-signature lines, fashion boutiques, and a new line of children's clothing, McKids, playing off McDonald's draw. New, smaller stores, specialty catalogs, and merchandise tailored to regional tastes are all part of Sears's effort to reach a new clientele – and without alienating its old one.

Faced with slimmer profits from staples like detergents, diapers, and toothpaste, and lackluster results from new food and beverage products, Procter & Gamble, the world's largest marketer, is rethinking what it should sell and how to sell it. The company is now concentrating on health products; it has high hopes for a fat substitute called 'olestra', which may take some of the junk out of junk food. At the same time that P&G is shifting its product thinking, it also is changing its organization, opening up and streamlining its highly insular pyramidal management structure as part of a larger effort to listen and respond to customers. Small groups that include both factory workers and executives work on cutting costs, while other teams look for new ways to speed products to market.

In trying to respond to the new demands of a diverse market, the problem that giants like Sears and P&G face is not fundamental change, not a total turnabout in what an entire nation of consumers wants. Rather, it is the fracturing of mass markets. To contend with diversity, managers must drastically alter how they design, manufacture, market, and sell their products.

Marketing in the age of diversity means:

More options for goods producers and more choices for consumers.

Less perceived differentiation among similar products.

Intensified competition, with promotional efforts sounding more and more alike, approaching 'white noise' in the marketplace.

Newly minted meanings for words and phrases as marketers try to 'invent' differentiation.

Disposable information as consumers try to cope with information deluge from print, television, computer terminal, telephone, fax, satellite dish.

Customization by users as flexible manufacturing makes niche production every bit as economic as mass production.

Changing leverage criteria as economies of scale give way to economies of knowledge – knowledge of the customer's business, of current and likely future technology trends, and of the competitive environment that allows the rapid development of new products and services.

Changing company structure as large corporations continue to down-size to compete with smaller niche players that nibble at their markets.

Smaller wins – fewer chances for gigantic wins in mass markets, but more opportunities for healthy profits in smaller markets.

THE DECLINE OF BRANDING, THE RISE OF 'OTHER'

In today's fractured marketplace, tried-and-true marketing techniques from the past no longer work for most products – particularly for complex ones based on new technology. Branding products and seizing market share, for instance, no longer guarantee loyal customers. In one case after another, the old, established brands have been supplanted by the rise of 'other.'

Television viewers in 1983 and 1984, for instance, tuned out the big three broadcasters to watch cable and independent 'narrowcast' stations. Last year, the trend continued as the big three networks lost 9 per cent of their viewers – more than six million people. Small companies appealing to niche-oriented viewers attacked the majority market share. NBC responded by buying a cable television company for $20 million.

No single brand can claim the largest share of the gate array, integrated circuit, or computer market. Even IBM has lost its reign over the personal computer field – not to one fast-charging competitor but to an assortment of smaller producers. Tropicana, Minute Maid, and Citrus Hill actually account for less than half the frozen orange juice market. A full 56 per cent belongs to hundreds of mostly small private labels. In one area after another, 'other' has become the major market holder.

IBM's story of lost market share bears elaboration, in large part because of the company's almost legendary position in the US business pantheon. After its rise in the personal computer market through 1984, IBM found its stronghold eroding – but not to just one, huge competitor that could be identified and stalked methodically. IBM could no longer rely on tracking the dozen or so companies that had been its steady competition for almost two decades. Instead, more than 300 clone producers worldwide intruded on Big Blue's territory. Moreover, IBM has faced the same competitive challenge in one product area after another, from supercomputers to networks. In response, IBM has changed how it does business. In the past, IBM wouldn't even bother to enter a market lacking a value of at least $100 million. But today, as customer groups diversify and markets splinter, that criterion is obsolete. The shift in competition has also prompted IBM to reorganize, decentralizing the company into five autonomous groups so decisions can be made closer to customers.

Similar stories abound in other industries. Kodak dominated film processing in the United States until little kiosks sprang up in shopping centers and ate up that market. Twenty years ago, the US semiconductor industry consisted of 100 companies; today there are more than 300. In fact, practically every industry has more of every kind of company catering to the consumer's love of diversity – more ice cream companies, more cookie companies, more weight loss and exercise companies. Last year, enterprising managers started 233,000 new businesses of all types to offer customers their choice of 'other.'

THE FALSE SECURITY OF MARKET SHARE

The proliferation of successful small companies dramatizes how the security of majority market share – seized by a large corporation and held unchallenged for decades – is now a dangerous anachronism. In the past, the dominant marketing models drew on the measurement and control notions embedded in engineering and manufacturing. The underlying mechanistic logic was that companies could measure everything, and anything they could measure, they could control – including customers. Market-share measurements became a way to understand the market-place and thus to control it. For example, marketers used to be able to pin down a target customer with relative ease: if it were a man, he was between 25 and 35 years old, married, with two-and a-half children, and half a dog. Since he was one of so many measurable men in a mass society, marketers assumed that they could manipulate the market just by knowing the demographic characteristics.

But we don't live in that world anymore, and those kinds of measurements are meaningless. Marketers trying to measure that same 'ideal' customer today would discover that the pattern no longer holds; that married fellow with two-and-a-half kids could now be divorced, situated in New York instead of Minnesota, and living in a condo instead of a brick colonial. These days, the idea of market share is a trap that can lull business people into a false sense of security.

Managers should wake up every morning uncertain about the market-place, because it is invariably changing. That's why five-year plans are dangerous: Who can pinpoint what the market will be five years from now? The president of one large industrial corporation recently told me, 'The only thing we know about our business plan is that it's wrong. It's either too high or too low – but we never know which.'

In the old days, mass marketing offered an easy solution: 'just run some ads'. Not today. IBM tried that approach with the PC Jr., laying out an estimated $100 million on advertising – before the product failed. AT&T spent tens of millions of dollars running ads for its computer products.

In sharp contrast, Digital Equipment Corporation spent very little on expensive national television advertising and managed to wrest a healthy market position. Skipping the expensive mass-advertising campaigns, DEC concentrated on developing its reputation in the computer business by solving problems for niche markets. Word of mouth sold DEC products. The company focused its marketing and sales staffs where they already had business and aimed its message at people who actually make the decision on what machines to buy. DEC clearly understood that no one buys a complex product like a computer without a reliable outside reference however elaborate the company's promotion.

NICHE MARKETING: SELLING BIG BY SELLING SMALL

Intel was in the personal computer business two years before Apple started in Steve Jobs's garage. The company produced the first micro-processor chip and subsequently developed an early version of what became known as the hobby computer, sold in electronics hobby stores. An early Intel advertisement in *Scientific American* showed a junior high school student using the product. Intel's market research, however, revealed that the market for hobbyists was quite small and it abandoned the project. Two years later, Apple built itself on the hobbyist market. As it turned out, many of the early users of personal computers in education, small business, and the professional markets came from hobbyists or enthusiasts.

I recently looked at several market forecasts made by research organizations in 1978 projecting the size of the personal computer market in 1985. The most optimistic forecast looked for a $2 billion market. It exceeded $25 billion.

Most large markets evolve from niche markets. That's because niche marketing teaches many important lessons about customers – in particular, to think of them as individuals and to respond to their special needs. Niche marketing depends on word of mouth references and infrastructure development, a broadening of people in related industries whose opinions are crucial to the product's success.

Infrastructure marketing can be applied to almost all markets. In the medical area, for example, recognized research gurus in a given field – diabetes, cancer, heart disease – will first experiment with new devices or drugs at research institutions. Universities and research institutions become identified by their specialties. Experts in a particular area talk to each other, read the same journals, and attend the same conferences. Many companies form their own scientific advisory boards designed to tap into the members' expertise and to build credibility for new technology and products. The word of mouth created by infrastructure marketing can make or break a new drug or a new supplier. Conductus, a new superconductor company in Palo Alto, is building its business around an advisory board of seven top scientists from Stanford University and Berkeley.

Represented graphically, infrastructure development would look like an inverted pyramid. So, Apple's pyramid, for instance, would include the references of influential users, software designers who create programs, dealers, industry consultants, analysts, the press, and, most important, customers.

Customer focus derived from niche marketing helps companies respond faster to demand changes. That is the meaning of today's most critical requirement – that companies become market driven. From the board of directors down through the ranks, company leaders must educate everyone to the singular importance of the customer, who is no longer a faceless, abstract entity or a mass statistic.

Many electronics companies have developed teams consisting of software and hardware development engineers, quality control and manufacturingple, as well as marketing and sales – who all visit customers or play key roles in dealing with customers. Convex Computer and Tandem use this approach. Whatever method a company may use, the purpose is the same: to get the entire company to focus on the fragmented, ever-evolving customer base as if it were an integral part of the organization.

Because niche markets are not easily identified in their infancy, managers must keep one foot in the technology to know its potential and one foot in the market to see opportunity Tandem Computers built its solid customer base by adapting its products to the emerging on-line transaction market. Jimmy Treybig, president and CEO, told me that the company had to learn the market's language. Bankers don't talk about MIPS (millions of instructions per second) the way computer people do, he said; they talk about transactions. So Tandem built its products and marketing position to become the leading computer in the transaction market. Not long ago, Treybig was on a nationwide tour visiting key customers. 'Guess who was calling on my customers just a few days ahead of me', he said. 'John Akers' – chairman of IBM.

THE INTEGRATED PRODUCT

Competition from small companies in fractured markets has even produced dramatic changes in how companies define their products. The product is no longer just the thing itself; it includes service, word of mouth references, company financial reports, the technology, and even the personal image of the CEO.

As a result, product marketing and service marketing, formerly two distinct fields, have become a single hybrid. For example, Genentech, which manufactures a growth hormone, arms its sales force with lap-top computers. When a Genentech salesperson visits an endocrinologist, the physician can tie into a database of all the tests run on people with characteristics similar to his or her patients. The computer represents an extended set of services married to the original product.

Or take the example of Apple Computer and Quantum Corporation, which recently announced a joint venture offering online interactive computer services for Apple Computer users. In addition to a long list of transaction services that reads like a television programming guide, Apple product service, support, and even simple maintenance will be integrated into the product itself. Prodigy, a joint venture between IBM and Sears, will soon offer IBM and Apple users access to banking, shopping, the stock market, regional weather forecasts, sports statistics, encyclopedias of all kinds – and even direct advice from Sylvia Porter, Howard Cosell, or Ask Beth.

In consumer products, service has become the predominant distinguishing feature. Lands' End promotes its catalog-marketed outdoorsy clothes by guaranteeing products unconditionally and promising to ship orders within 24 to 48 hours. Carport, near Atlanta, offers air travelers an ultradeluxe parking service: it drives customers to their gates, checks their bags, and, while they are airborne, services, washes, and waxes their cars. 'Macy's by Appointment' is a free shopping service for customers who are too busy or too baffled to make their own selections.

With so much choice backed by service, customers can afford to be fickle. As a result, references have become vital to product marketing. And the more complex the product, the more complex the supporting references. After all, customers who switch toothpaste risk losing only a dollar or so if the new choice is a dud. But consumers buying a complete phone system or a computer system or any other costly, long-term and pervasive product, cannot afford to take their investments lightly. References become a part of the product – and they come in all kinds of forms. Company financial reports are a kind of reference. A person shopping for an expensive computer wants to see how profitable the company is; how can the company promise maintenance service if it's about to fold? Even the CEO's personality can make a sale. Customers who see Don Petersen of Ford splashed across a magazine cover – or Apple's John Sculley or Hewlett-Packard's John Young – feel reassured that a real person stands behind the complex and expensive product.

In this complicated world, customers weigh all these factors to winnow out the products they want from those they don't. Now more than ever, marketers must sell every aspect of their businesses as important elements of the products themselves.

THE CUSTOMER AS CUSTOMIZER

Customer involvement in product design has become an accepted part of the development and marketing processes in many industries. In technologically driven products, which often evolve slowly as discoveries percolate to the surface, the customer can practically invent the market for a company

Apple's experience with desktop publishing shows how companies and customers work together to create new applications – and new markets. Apple entered the field with the Macintosh personal computer, which offered good graphics and easy-to-use features. But desktop publishing didn't even exist then; it wasn't on anyone's pie chart as a defined market niche, and no one had predicted its emergence.

Apple's customers made it happen; newspapers and research organizations simply started using Macintosh's unique graphics capability to create charts and graphs. Early users made do with primitive software and printers, but that was enough to spark the imagination of other developers. Other hardware and software companies began developing products that could be combined with the Macintosh to enhance the user's publishing power. By visiting and talking to customers and other players in the marketplace, Apple began to realize desktop publishing's potential.

As customers explored the possibilities presented by the technology, the technology, in turn, developed to fit the customers' needs. The improved software evolved from a dynamic working relationship between company and customers, not from a rigid, bureaucratic headquarters determination of where Apple could find an extra slice of the marketing pie.

Technological innovation makes it easier to involve customers in design. For example, Milliken, the textile manufacturer, provides customers with computer terminals where they can select their own carpet designs from thousands of colors and patterns. Electronics customers, too, have assumed the role of product designer. New design tools allow companies like Tandem and Convex to design their own specialty chips, which the integrated-circuit suppliers then manufacture according to their specifications. Similarly, American Airlines designs its own computer systems. In cases like these, the design and manufacturing processes have been completely separated. So semiconductor companies – and many computer companies – have become raw-materials producers, with integration occurring all the way up the supply line.

The fact that customers have taken charge of design opens the door for value-added resellers, who integrate different materials and processes. These people are the essence of new-age marketers: they add value by understanding what happens in a doctor's office or a travel agency or a machine-tool plant and customize that service or product to the customer's needs. To capitalize on market changes, companies should follow these examples and work directly with customers – even before products hit the drawing boards.

THE EVOLUTION OF DISTRIBUTION

It is nearly impossible to make a prediction on the basis of past patterns. Perhaps many big institutions founded on assumptions of mass marketing and market share will disappear like dinosaurs. Or they'll evolve into closely integrated service and distribution organizations.

In fact, tremendous innovation in distribution channels has already begun in nearly every industry. Distribution channels have to be flexible to survive. As more flows into them, they have to change. Grocery stores sell flowers and cameras. Convenience stores rent out videos. And television offers viewers direct purchasing access to everything from diamonds to snowblowers to a decent funeral.

To get products closer to customers, marketers are distributing more and more samples in more ways. Today laundry detergent arrives in the mail, magazines enfold perfume-doused tear-outs, and department stores offer chocolate samples. Software companies bind floppy disk samples into magazines or mail out diskettes that work only until a certain date, giving customers the chance to test a product before buying.

Every successful computer retailer has not only a showroom but also a classroom. The large computer retailers are not selling to just off-the-street traffic. Most of their volume now comes from a direct sales force calling on corporate America. In addition, all have application-development labs, extensive user-training programs and service centers – and some have recently experimented with private labeling their own computer product brands. The electronics community talks more and more about design centers – places where customers can get help customizing products and applications.

Today the product is an experience. As customers use it, they grow to trust it – and distribution represents the beginning of that evolving relationship. That's why computer companies donate their systems to elementary schools: schools are now a distribution channel for product experience.

GOLIATH PLUS DAVID

Besides making changes in distribution channels, big corporations will also have to forge new partnerships with smaller companies. IBM, for example, already has ties to 1,500 small computer-service companies nationwide, offering help for IBM midsized machine owners. Olivetti makes personal computers for AT&T. All over the world, manufacturers are producing generic computer platforms; larger companies buy these, then add their own service-oriented, value-adding applications.

This approach seems almost inevitable considering what we know about patterns of research and development. Technological developments typically originate with basic research, move to applied research, to development, then to manufacturing and marketing. Very few US companies do basic research; universities and various public and private labs generally shoulder that burden. Many big companies do applied R&D while small companies concentrate on development. Basic and applied research means time and money. Consider the cases of two seminal inventions – antibiotics and television, the first of which took 30 years and the second 63 years from idea to the market.

Perhaps because of their narrow focus, small companies realize more development breakthroughs than larger ones. For example, the origins of recombinant DNA technology go back to the mid-1950s; it took Genentech only about six years to bring the world's first recombinant DNA commercial product to market.

A 1986 study by the Small Business Administration showed that 55 per cent of innovations have come from companies with fewer than 500 employees, and twice as many innovations per employee come from small companies than from large ones. This finding, however, does not indicate that large companies are completely ineffective developers. Rather, the data suggest that small, venture-capitalized companies will scramble to invent a product that the market does not yet want, need, or perhaps even recognize; big companies will wait patiently for the market to develop so they can enter later with their strong manufacturing and marketing organizations.

The Japanese have shown us that it is wise to let small companies handle development – but only if large companies can somehow share that wisdom before the product reaches the market. From 1950 to 1978, Japanese companies held 32,000 licensing agreements to acquire foreign technology – mostly from the United States – for about $9 billion. In essence, the Japanese simply subcontracted out for R&D – and then used that investment in US knowledge to dominate one market after another.

If orchestrated properly, agreements between large and small companies can prove mutually beneficial. When Genentech developed its first product, recombinant DNA insulin, the company chose not to compete against Eli Lilly, which held over 70% of the insulin market. Instead Genentech entered into a licensing agreement with Lilly that put the larger company in charge of manufacturing and marketing the products developed by the smaller company. Over time, Genentech built its own manufacturing company while maintaining its proprietary product.

. This model worked so well that it has shaped the fortunes of Silicon Valley. Of the 3,000 companies there, only a dozen hold places on the lists of America's largest corporations. Most of the companies are small developers of new products. Like the Japanese, large US companies are now subcontracting development to these mostly high-tech startups. In the process, they are securing a critical resource, an ongoing relationship with a small, innovative enterprise.

Giant companies can compete in the newly diversifying markets if they recognize the importance of relationships – with small companies, within then own organizations, with their customers. Becoming market driven means abandoning old-style marketshare thinking and instead tying the uniqueness of any product to the unique needs of the customer. This approach to marketing demands a revolution in how business people act – and even more important, in how they think. These changes are critical to success, but they can come only gradually, as managers and organizations adapt to the new rules of marketing in the age of diversity. As any good marketer knows, even instant success takes time.

Megamarketing

Philip Kotler

Kellogg Graduate School of Management,
Northwestern University, Illinois

Successful marketing is increasingly becoming a political exercise, as two recent episodes – one international and the other domestic – illustrate:

- Pepsi-Cola outwitted its arch rival, Coca-Cola, by striking a deal to gain entry into India's huge consumer market of 730 million people. Coca-Cola had dominated the Indian soft drink market until it abruptly withdrew from India in 1978 in protest over Indian government policies. Coca-Cola, along with Seven-Up, tried to reenter, but hard work and effective political marketing gave Pepsi the prize.

Pepsi worked with an Indian group to form a joint venture with terms designed to win government approval over the opposition of both domestic soft drink companies and anti-MNC legislators. Pepsi offered to help India export its agro-based products in a volume that would more than cover the cost of importing soft drink concentrate. Furthermore, Pepsi promised to focus considerable selling effort on rural areas as well as major urban markets. Pepsi also offered to bring new food processing, packaging, and water treatment technology to India. Clearly, Pepsi-Cola orchestrated a set of benefits that would win over various interest groups in India.

- Citicorp, the US banking giant, had been trying for years to start full-service banking in Maryland. It had only credit card and small service operations in the state. Under Maryland law, out-of-state banks could provide only certain services and were barred from advertising, setting up branches, and other types of marketing efforts.

In March 1985, Citicorp offered to build a major credit card center in Maryland that would create 1,000 white-collar jobs and further offered the state $1 million in cash for the property where it would locate. By imaginatively designing a proposal to benefit Maryland, Citicorp will become the first out-of-state bank to provide full banking services there.

These two instances demonstrate the growing need for companies that want to operate in certain markets to master the art of supplying benefits to parties other than target consumers. This need extends beyond the requirements to serve and satisfy normal intermediaries like agents, distributors, and dealers. I am talking about third parties – governments, labor unions, and other interest groups – that, singly or collectively, can block profitable entry into a market. These groups act as gatekeepers, and they are growing in importance.

Markets characterized by high entry barriers can be called *blocked* or *protected* markets. In addition to the four Ps of marketing strategy – product, price, place, and promotion – executives must add two more – power and public relations. I call such strategic thinking *megamarketing*.

Marketing is the task of arranging need-satisfying and profitable offers to target buyers. Sometimes, however, it is necessary to create additional incentives and pressures at the right times and in the right amounts for noncustomers. Megamarketing thus takes an enlarged view of the skills and resources needed to enter and operate in certain markets. In addition to preparing attractive offers for customers, megamarketers may use inducements and sanctions to gain the desired responses from gate-keepers. I define megamarketing as the strategically coordinated application of economic, psychological, political, and public relations skills to gain the cooperation of a number of parties in order to enter and/or operate in a given market. Megamarketing challenges are found in both domestic and international situations.

This article describes marketing situations that call for megamarketing strategies and shows how companies can organize their power and public relations resources to achieve entry and operating success in blocked markets.

STRATEGIES FOR ENTRY

As they mature, markets acquire a fixed set of suppliers, competitors, distributors, and customers. These players develop a vested interest in preserving the market's closed system and seek to protect it against intruders. They are often supported by government regulatory agencies, labor unions, banks, and other institutions. They may erect visible and invisible barriers to entry: taxes, tariffs, quotas, and compliance re-quirements.

Examples of such closed markets abound. A long-standing complaint against Japan concerns the visible and invisible barriers that protect many of its markets. Besides facing high tariffs, foreign companies encounter difficulty in signing up good Japanese distributors and dealers, even when the non-Japanese companies offer superior products and better margins. Motorola, for example, fought for years to sell its telecommunications equipment in Japan. It succeeded only by influencing Washington to apply pressure on Japan and by redesigning its equipment to comply with Japan's tough and sometimes arbitrary standards.

Other countries as well are erecting barriers to the free entry of foreign competitors to protect their manufacturers, suppliers, distributors, and dealers. France, for example, has adopted a number of official and unofficial measures to hit the number of Japanese cars and consumer electronics products entering its market. France for a time routed Japanese videocassette recorders into Poitiers, a medium-sized inland town, for record keeping and inspection purposes; only two inspectors were assigned to handle the mounting volume of Japanese goods. The goods sat in customs for so long that Japan's market share and profits were severely restricted.

The British and French developers of the Concorde airplane encountered obstacles in their efforts to obtain landing rights to serve a number of cities; most prominent among the opposition were entrenched airlines and protesters against noise. The Concorde group, which needed to sell 64 planes to break even, sold only 16; the result was the costliest new product failure in history.

Of course, companies that have trouble breaking into new markets aren't always victims of blocked markets. The problem may be inferior products, overpricing, financing difficulties, unwillingness to pay taxes or tariffs that other companies pay, or protection of the market by a legitimate patent. By blocked markets, I mean markets in which the established participants or approvers have made it difficult for companies with similar or even better marketing offers to enter or operate. The barriers may include discriminatory legal requirements, political favoritism, cartel agreements, social or cultural biases, unfriendly distribution channels, and refusals to cooperate. These create the challenge that megamarketing has to overcome.

How can companies break into blocked markets? There is usually an easy way and a hard way. The easy way is to offer many concessions, thus making it almost unprofitable to enter the market. Japan recently won a coveted contract in Turkey to build a 3,576-foot suspension bridge spanning the Bosporus Strait. Its bid was so low that both the competitors and the Turks were startled; the rivals were left grumbling about unfair competition. Complained the manager of Cleveland Bridge & Engineering, 'It would be cheaper [for Japan] to go to the Turks and say, 'We'll give you the bridge!' '

The hard way is to formulate a strategy for entry, a task calling for skills never acquired by most marketers through normal training and experience. Marketers are trained primarily in the use of the four Ps: product, price, place, and promotion. They know how to create a cost-effective marketing mix that appeals to customers and end users. But customers and end users are not always the main problem. When a huge gate blocks the company's path into the market, it needs to blast the gate open, or at least find the key so that its goods can be offered to potential customers.

To further complicate matters, not one but several gates must be opened for the company to reach its goal of selling in the blocked market. The company must identify each gatekeeper and convert it by applying influence or power.

B

Moreover, the strategic marketing effort does not end with successful entry into the protected market. The company must know how to stay in as well as break in. Indian government regulations forced Coca-Cola and IBM to leave the country after many years of operating there. Today, IBM in France is doing its best to withstand French protectionist sentiment; its program includes political and public opinion strategies.

MEGAMARKETING SKILLS

The following two examples help illustrate megamarketing problems and the skills needed to cope successfully.

Freshtaste & the Japanese market

Freshtaste, a U.S. manufacturer of milk-sterilising equipment, wants to introduce its equipment into Japan but has encountered numerous problems.[1] Sterilized milk is a recent innovation that offers two main advantages over fresh milk: it can be stored at room temperature for up to three months and has twice the refrigerated shelf life of ordinary milk after the package is opened. Freshtaste has developed superior equipment for sterilizing milk that avoids the unpleasant side effects of sterilization – a cooked and slightly burnt taste, and a filminess that lingers in the mouth after the milk is swallowed.

In searching for new markets for its equipment, the company sees Japan as a good candidate. Japan has a huge population, a low but growing rate of per capita milk consumption, and a limited availability of fresh milk. As Freshtaste sets out to sell its equipment to large Japanese dairies, it encounters the following obstacles:

1 It has to develop an advertising campaign to change Japanese milk consumption habits and convince Japanese consumers of the advantages of buying and drinking sterilized milk.
2 The Consumers' Union of Japan opposes the product because of concernns about sterilized milk's safety.
3 Dairy farmers located near large cities oppose the distribution of sterilized milk. They fear competition from faraway dairies, since sterilized milk has a long inventory life and can be shipped long distances.
4 Several large retailers say they will not carry sterilized milk because of interest-group pressure. Milk specialty stores, which thrive on home deliveries, also oppose the introduction of sterilized milk.
5 The Health and Welfare Ministry and the Ministry of Agriculture and Forestry have indicated they will wait and gauge consumer acceptance of sterilized milk before taking action to approve or disapprove general distribution.

Freshtaste must thus undertake campaigns tailored to each barrier, as shown in Figure 1. It must seek cooperation from the ministry of health;

FIGURE 1 FRESHTASTE'S MEGAMARKETING CHALLENGE

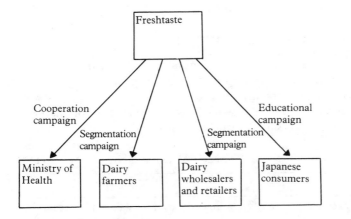

attract support from favorable segments of dairy farmers, wholesalers, and retailers; and educate Japanese consumers. The company faces a formidable megamarketing problem calling for adroit political and public relations skills as well as normal commercial ones. It must be sure that the Japanese market is large enough, and the probability of successful entry high enough, to justify the cost and time involved in trying to enter this market.

Japanese consumer electronics in India

Japanese companies have coped with blocked markets in ingenious ways. India, for example, banned the import of luxury consumer electronics products in a drive to conserve its foreign hard currency and protect its fledgling home consumer electronics industry. Yet Japanese companies like Sony, Panasonic, and Toshiba have taken steps to pry open the Indian market, however slightly, to its brands of televisions, video-cassette recorders, and stereos.[2]

Although many Japanese consumer electronics products are not officially available in India, several Japanese companies advertise their products in Indian newspapers and magazines in order to build preference for them should they become available at a later date. In the meantime, this advertising influences the selection of Japanese products by Indian tourists in Sri Lanka, Singapore, and other free markets as well as by Indian workers laboring in other countries. Furthermore, some Japanese products enter the Indian market unofficially and are immediately purchased by consumers.

In addition, the Japanese government supports Japanese companies by lobbying the Indian government for a relaxation of the ban or for its transformation into quotas or normal tariffs. In return, Japan offers to buy more Indian goods and services.

Thus, although Japanese businesses cannot export certain products to India, they have pursued megamarketing actions on several fronts to gain access to this vast and fertile market.

MEGAMARKETING VS. MARKETING

Although companies face a growing number of blocked markets, they are rarely organized to develop or execute megamarketing strategies. By comparing megamarketing with marketing, Figure 2 suggests why. The comparison means reviewing elementary aspects of marketing, but the review is necessary to evaluate megamarketing effectively.

FIGURE 2 MARKETING AND MEGAMARKETING CONTRASTED

	Marketing	Megamarketing
Marketing objective	To satisfy consumer demand	To gain market access in order to satisfy consumer demand or to create or alter consumer demand
Parties involved	Consumers, distributors, dealers, suppliers, marketing firms, banks	Normal parties plus legislators, government agencies, labor unions, reform groups, general public
Marketing tools	Market research, product development, pricing, distribution planning, promotion	Normal tools plus the use of power and public relations
Type of inducement	Positive and official inducements	Positive inducements (official and unofficial) and negative inducements (threats)
Time frame	Short	Much longer
Investment cost	Low	Much higher
Personnel involved	Marketers	Marketers plus company officers, lawyers, public relations and public affairs staff

Marketing objective

In normal marketing situations, a market already exists for a given product category. Consumers understand that category and simply choose among a set of brands and suppliers. A company entering the market will define a target need or customer group, design the appropriate product, set up distribution, and establish a marketing communications program. On the other hand, megamarketers face the problem of first gaining market access. If the product is quite new, they must also be skilled in creating or altering demand. This requires more skill and time than simply meeting existing demand.

Parties involved

Marketers routinely deal with several parties: customers, suppliers, distributors, dealers, advertising agencies, market research firms, and others. Megamarketing situations involve even more parties: legislators, government agencies, political parties, public-interest groups, unions, and churches, among others. Each party has an interest in the company's activity and must be sold on supporting, or at least not blocking, the company Megamarketing is thus a greater multiparty marketing problem than marketing.

Marketing tools

Megamarketing involves the normal tools of marketing (the four Ps) plus two others: power and public relations.

1 Power

The megamarketer must often win the support of influential industry officials, legislators, and government bureaucrats to enter and operate in the target market. A pharmaceutical company, for example, that is trying to introduce a new birth control pill into a country will have to obtain the approval of the country's ministry of health. Thus the megamarketer needs political skills and a political strategy.

The company must identify the people with the power to open the gate. It must determine the right mix of incentives to offer. Under what circumstances will the gatekeepers acquiesce? Is legislator X primarily seeking fame, fortune, or power? How can the company induce this legislator to cooperate? In some countries, the answer may be with a cash payoff (a hidden P). Elsewhere, a payoff in entertainment, travel, or campaign contributions may work. Essentially, the megamarketer must have sophisticated lobbying and negotiating skills in order to achieve the desired response from the other party without giving away the house.

2 Public relations

Whereas power is a push strategy, public relations is a pull strategy. Public opinion takes longer to cultivate, but when generalized, it can help pull the company into the market.

Indeed, power alone may not get a company into a market or keep it there. In the late 1960s, for example, Japanese chemical companies received permission to open chemical factories in Korea by exploiting Korea's desperate need to expand its heavy industry. They played the power game with the Korean government by offering technological assistance, new jobs, and side payments to government officials. In the early 1970s, however, the Korean media accused Japanese factories of exposing young female workers to toxic chemicals; most of them became barren. The Japanese companies tried to pay government officials to quiet the media but they couldn't silence public opinion. They should have paid more attention to establishing responsible production methods and cultivating the public's goodwill.

Before entering a market, companies must understand the community's beliefs, attitudes, and values. After entering, they need to play the role of good citizen by contributing to public causes, sponsoring civic and cultural events, and working effectively with the media. Olivetti, for example, has won a good name in many markets by making large contributions to worthwhile causes in host countries. It has shown skill in the strategic management of its corporate public image.

Type of inducement

Marketers are trained primarily in the art of using positive inducements to persuade other parties to cooperate. They believe in the voluntary exchange principle: each party should offer sufficient benefits to the other to motivate voluntary exchanges.

Megamarketers, however, often find that conventional inducements are insufficient. The other party either wants more than is reasonable or refuses to accept any positive inducement at all. Thus the company may have to add unofficial payments to speed the approval process. Or it may threaten to withdraw support or mobilize opposition to the other party. The relationships of auto manufacturers with their franchised dealers and of drugstore chains with some pharmaceutical manufacturers demonstrate how companies use raw power from time to time to gain their ends.[3]

Although companies occasionally use negative as well as positive inducements, most experts believe that positive inducements are better in the long run.[4] Negative inducements are ethically questionable and may produce resentment that can backfire on the marketer.

Time frame

Most product introductions take only a few years. Megamarketing challenges, on the other hand, usually require much more time. Numerous gates have to be opened, and if the product is new to the public, much work has to be done to educate the target market.

Investment cost

Because the effort must be sustained over a long period and may entail side payments to secure the cooperation of various parties, megamarketing involves higher costs as well as more time.

Personnel involved

Marketing problems are normally handled by a product manager, who draws on the services of advertising specialists, market researchers, and other professionals. Megamarketing problems require additional skilled personnel, both inside and outside the company: top managers, lawyers, public relations and public affairs professionals. Megamarketing planning and implementation teams are large and require much coordination. For example, when KLM, the Dutch airline, sought landing rights in Taiwan, the company's president participated, its international department exploited its contacts with Taiwan officials, its public relations department put out favorable news stories and arranged news conferences, and its lawyers participated in the negotiations to make sure the contracts were sound.

Although new skills are required to enter blocked markets, marketing professionals need not be specially trained in the additional skills. Rather, they need to broaden their view of what it takes to enter these markets and to coordinate various specialists to achieve the desired goals.

MARKETERS AS POLITICAL STRATEGISTS

Few marketers are trained in the art of politics and are thus unaccustomed to using power to achieve favorable transactions. Most marketers think that value, not power, wins in the marketplace.

The growth of protected markets, however, requires marketers to incorporate the notion of power into their strategies. Marketing is increasingly becoming the art of managing power. What do they need to know about power? They need to know that power is the ability of one party (A) to get another party (B) to do what it might not otherwise have done. It is A's ability to increase the probability of B's taking an action. A can draw on at least five bases of power to influence B.[5]

Rewards

A offers to reward B for engaging in the desired behavior. The reward might be recognition, entertainment, gifts, or payments. Marketers are expert in the use of rewards.

Coercion

A threatens to harm B in the absence of compliant behavior. A may threaten physical, social, or financial harm. Marketers have been loath to use coercive power because of its doubtful ethical status, because it doesn't square with the marketing concept, and because it can create hostility that can backfire on the marketer.

Expertise or information

A offers B special expertise, such as technical assistance or access to special information, in exchange for B's compliance.

Legitimacy

A is seen to have a legitimate right to make certain requests of B. An example would be the Japanese premier asking Nippon Electric Company to put Motorola on its approved supplier list.

Prestige

A has prestige in B's mind and draws on this to request Bs compliance. An example would be Chrysler president Lee Iacocca requesting a meeting with officials in a foreign country to present arguments for opening a Chrysler plant in that country.

Power is the key to megamarketers. Companies that find themselves blocked from a market must undertake a three-step process for creating an entry strategy: mapping the power structure, forging a grand strategy, and developing a tactical implementation plan.

MAPPING THE POWER STRUCTURE

Executives must first understand how power is distributed in the particular target community (city, state, nation). Political scientists identify three types of power structures.[6] The first type is a pyramidal power structure in which power is invested in a ruling élite, which may be an individual, a family, a company, an industry, or a clique. The élite carries out its wishes through a layer of lieutenants, who in turn manage a layer of doers. The marketing strategist who wants to operate in such a community can get in only if the ruling élite approves or is neutral.

The second type is a factional power structure in which two or more factions (power blocs, pressure groups, special-interest groups) compete for power in the community. Political parties are an example. The competing parties represent different constituencies – labor, business, ethnic minorities, or farmers. Here the company's strategists must decide with which factions they want to work. In allying with certain factions, the company usually loses the goodwill of others.

The third type is a coalitional power structure in which influential parties from various power blocs form temporary coalitions. When power is in the hands of a coalition, however temporarily, the company has to work through the coalition to secure its objectives. Or the company can form a counter-coalition to support its cause.

Identifying the power structure as pyramidal, factional, or coalitional is only the first step of the analysis. Executives next have to assess the relative power of various parties. A's power over B is directly related to B's dependence on A. B's dependence on A is directly proportional to B's interest in goals controlled by A and inversely proportional to B's chance of achieving the goals without A. In other words, A has power over B to the extent that A can directly affect B's goal attainment and B has few alternatives.[7]

FORGING A GRAND STRATEGY

In planning entry into a blocked market, the company must identify opponents, allies, and neutral groups. Its aim is to overcome the opposition, and it can choose from three broad strategies:

1 Neutralize opponents by offering to compensate them for any losses. The theory of welfare economics holds that a proposed action will generally be supported if everyone benefits, or if those who benefit can satisfactorily compensate those who are hurt. Compensation costs should be included as part of the total cost when determining whether it pays to go forward with the project.

2 Organize allies into a coalition. The company's potential supporters may be scattered in the community, and their individual power is less than their potential collective power. Thus the company can further its cause by creating a coalition of allies.

3 Turn neutral groups into allies. Most groups in a community will be unaffected by the company's entry and thus indifferent. The company can use influence and rewards to convert these groups into supporters.

A growing number of companies are forming strategic alliances – licensing arrangements, joint ventures, management contracts, and consortia – to overcome blocked markets. Examples of strategic partnering in the automobile industry include General Motors-Toyota, Ford-Mazda, and Renault-AMC. In other industries, we have such examples as Honeywell-Ericsson in communications, Sharp-Olivetti in office automation equipment, and Philips-Siemens in voice-synthesis technology.[8] Intercompany networking offers a superior means for securing entry and operating clout in otherwise blocked markets.

Still another approach is to harness the power of one's government to aid in opening another country's market. This calls for effective 'at home' lobbying of the sort Motorola did in getting the U.S. government to pressure Japan into opening its telecommunications market. Similarly, American computer companies lobbied in Washington to get President Reagan to threaten banning various Brazilian exports to the United States if Brazil did not rescind its bill banning the sale of foreign-made computers in Brazil.

DEVELOPING A TACTICAL IMPLEMENTATION PLAN

Once a company has chosen a broad strategy, it must create an implementation plan that spells out who does what, when, where, and how. Activities can be sequenced in two broad ways: in linear or multilinear fashion (Figure 3). Adopting a linear approach, Freshtaste (described earlier) can try first to win the approval of Japan's Minister of Health to market its product because, without that approval, the

TWO WAYS TO IMPLEMENT A TACTICAL PLAN

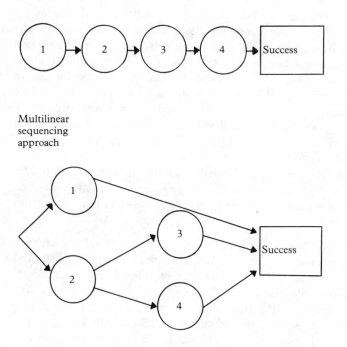

Linear
sequencing
approach

Multilinear
sequencing
approach

1 Contact Minister of Health and Welfare.
2 Contact a few large supermarket chains.
3 Contact some key diaries.
4 Run an educational campaign for consumers.

Figure 3

company cannot succeed. If it gets the approval, Freshtaste might then try to convince one or more large retailers to carry sterilized milk. Again, if it cannot accomplish this, it will withdraw. In this way, Freshtaste accumulates successive commitments before entering the market.

Multilinear sequencing will shorten the time required for accomplishing the project. Freshtaste executives could contact the minister and the supermarket chains simultaneously If some supermarket chains sign up, Freshtaste can then contact some dairies and start a consumer education campaign. If, however, some crucial commitment is not forthcoming, Freshtaste will withdraw. This approach may lose more money but settle the issues earlier.

IMPLICATIONS OF MEGAMARKETING

Megamarketing broadens the thinking of marketers in three ways:

1 Enlarging the multiparty marketing concept. Marketers spend much time analyzing how to create preference and satisfaction in target buyers. Because other parties – governments, labor unions, banks, reform groups – can block the path to the target buyers, marketers must also study the obstacles these parties create and develop strategies for attracting their support or at least neutralizing their opposition.

2 Blurring the distinction between environmental and controllable variables. Marketers have traditionally defined the environment as those outside forces that cannot be controlled by the business. But megamarketing argues that some environmental forces can be changed through lobbying, legal action, negotiation, issue advertising, public relations, and strategic partnering.[9]

3 Broadening the understanding of how markets work. Most market thinkers assume that demand creates its own supply. Ideally, companies discover a market need and rush to satisfy that need. But real markets are often blocked, and the best marketer doesn't always win. We have seen that foreign competitors with offers comparable or superior to those of local companies can't always enter the market. The result is a lower level of consumer satisfaction and producer innovation than would otherwise result.

Some may oppose the enlarged view of marketing proposed here. After all, megamarketing impinges on the responsibilities of some non-marketing executives and argues that marketers should feel comfortable using power to accomplish their purposes. Marketers normally deal with other parties in the most courteous manner; many will suffer image shock in adopting the megamarketing approach. Yet this innocence has led companies to fail in both international and home markets where transactions are marked by tough bargaining, side payments, and various complexities. Megamarketing offers executives an approach to dealing with rising international and domestic competition for large-scale and long-term sales.

REFERENCES

1 Philip R. Cateora and John M. Hess, *International Marketing* (Homewood, Ill.: Richard D. Irwin, 1979), p. 234.

2 P. Rajan Varsdarajan, 'A Strategy for Penetrating Third World Markets with High Entry Barriers: An Exposition of the Japanese Approach,' unpublished paper, Texas A&M University 1984.

3 Valentine F. Ridgway, 'Administration of Manufacturer-Dealer Systems,' *Administrative Science Quarterly,* March 1957, p. 464; Joseph C. Palamountain, *The Politics of Distribution* (Cambridge: Harvard University Press, 1955).

4   See, for example, B.F. Skinner, *Beyond Freedom and Dignity* (New York: Alfred A. Knopf, 1971).

5   John R.P. French, Jr. and Bertram Raven, 'The Bases of Social Power,' in *Studies in Social Power,* ed. Dorwin Cartwright (Ann Arbor, Mich.: Institute for Social Research, 1959), p. 118.

6   John B. Mitchell and Sheldon C. Lowry, *Power Structure, Community Leadership and Social Action* (Columbus: Ohio State University Cooperative Extension Service, 1973).

7   Richard M. Emerson, 'Power-Dependence Relations,' *American Sociological Review,* February 1962, p. 31.

8   Robert J. Conrads, 'Strategic Partnering: A New Formula to Crack New Markets in the 80s,' *Electronic Business Management,* March 1983, p. 23.

9   Carl P. Zeithaml and Valarie A. Zeithaml, 'Environmental Management: Revising the Marketing Perspective,' *Journal of Marketing,* Spring 1984, p. 47.

From market research to business research

Ennius Bergsma

A. C. Nielsen Company, New York

ABSTRACT

Large corporate planning staffs will become a thing of the past as the responsibility for strategic initiative is laid once again in the laps of the line managers who must implement it, the author argues. Yet there will still be a demand for the environmental data on which to base strategic decisions. In this article he looks at the way companies develop their strategic capabilities and suggests that the role of market research will necessarily broaden as the strategic sophistication of top management grows.

To corporate managements seeking to steer a steady course through the choppy waters of economic change and the cross-currents of evolving consumer needs and tastes, the guidance of market research has long since become indispensable. But despite their skill at detecting discontinuities in the business environment, few market researchers have yet sensed the approach of a groundswell of change that may transform the very nature of their work. For in the years just ahead, traditional market research will almost certainly be challenged to broaden its scope and begin to extend its activities across the whole business spectrum. It will have to start looking not only at marketing issues, but also at competitors' actions and industry economics.

To some degree marketing research will be moving into this broader role by default. because the groups that used to do the other research are disappearing. Over the past few years we have seen a trend away from large planning staffs. Responsibility for planning and the plan is moving back to line management where it belongs. But though planning staffs disappear, the need for data on which to base plans does not; if anything, that need is expanding. Unless market research takes over the data generation and synthesis that have been performed by strategic planning staffs (though often not very well), the support for line management is likely to become very minimal indeed.

There is, however, another and more important reason why the role of corporate market research staffs must broaden: namely, the serious side effects of a pure marketing focus. Over the years, the marketing concept has made many consumer goods companies masters of the art of creating and targeting products for specific customer needs. But as they have focused on 'where to compete,' they have paid much less attention to 'how to compete' – that is, how to operate *successfully* in the markets they are going after. Successful competitors are those that have sustainable competitive advantages built on superior management of the other functions of the enterprise, such as raw materials sourcing, manufacturing, or distribution. Others are based on better linkages between functions. Companies that have focused on the marketing concept have often given only secondary attention to these other functions, and as a result have missed significant opportunities to capture competitive advantages.

But capitalizing on functional strength will not be enough, especially in mature markets. In many of these the overall profitability of the industry is constrained by structural factors that transcend the competitive positions of industry competitors, such as the bargaining power of suppliers, the threat of substitute products, or industry barriers to exit. To change these structural factors to one's advantage and thus create a new economic equilibrium requires a much deeper understanding of total industry dynamics than most companies have today. They need to understand the nature and impact of these structural factors in order to be able to formulate strategies that neutralize their negative consequences or create a unique capability to exploit them.

So where does this leave marketing research? In a critical position, really. If it provides the right kind of balanced, competitively oriented data to line management, a research department can itself constitute a strategic advantage. If it continues to focus on marketing alone, the skewed data it provides to line management could amount to a strategic handicap. Consider some of the factors at work affecting the kinds of data a company needs from its market researchers.

LOOKING AT 'HOW TO COMPETE'

Most consumer-oriented industries have focused heavily on where to compete, and it has paid off. Over the years, the ability to segment the market, i.e. to identify consumer needs and tailor products to those needs, has become an important factor in developing competitive advantages. Successful companies have been able to offer their customer segments better value than competitors, at lower cost or with less investment than competitors. Indeed, unless a company is very clear about the market segment in which it operates, it is often difficult for management to tell whether it has a competitive advantage or not.

Consider, for example, two producers of small electrical motors that are sold to household appliance manufacturers. If Competitor A has a technical service force and Competitor B does not, Competitor A has higher costs and needs to charge higher prices. For small customers, however, technical service backup is probably a key element in the total product package, while it is of no value to large customers with comprehensive in-house technical service capabilities. They don't need technical service and probably don't want to pay for it. Therefore, the competitor with the technical service force probably has a competitive advantage in the small assembler segment, and a competitive disadvantage in the large assembler segment.

Clearly, then, a thorough understanding of market segments (i.e. where to compete) is critical for identifying opportunities to establish a competitive advantage or, more basically, for determining whether you have one in the first place. But it is not enough. Unless serious attention is also given to the how to compete side, important opportunities are likely to be missed.

In balancing these two sets of considerations, it is helpful to use a forcing device like the so-called 'strategic gameboard' shown in Exhibit I, which lays out the alternative kinds of action associated with different 'where to compete' and 'how to compete' choices. As the Exhibit shows, 'where to compete' can mean going after either the core market or a niche. The 'how to compete' dimension splits between 'old rules' (i.e. the way things have always been done), and 'new rules' (i.e. challenging the conventional wisdom that has traditionally defined the rules of competition).

EXHIBIT I THE STRATEGIC GAMEBOARD

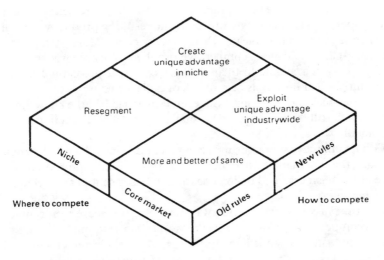

The odds are heavily against any competitor who tries to win by going after the core market with the old rules. Such a competitor can succeed only by consistently outperforming the market leader on cost and/or value – and that will be possible only if the leader is sluggish or too complacent to respond to the challenge and mount an effective response. The point may seem obvious, yet scores of companies still behave as though challenging Goliath with his own weapons made some kind of strategic sense.

A good many consumer-oriented companies have recognized this problem and gone to great lengths to resegment the market and go for a niche. This approach can be quite successful, at least in the short run. But if a niche marketer's success becomes too conspicuous, at some point the market leader typically invades the niche with the power of its larger resources. In most cases, therefore, to be an effective niche competitor, you have to be big enough to have a meaningful business, but small enough to escape the attention of the market leader.

So if you are not the market leader and seek to establish sustainable competitive advantage, you need to pay a lot more attention to the question of how to compete. You must try to create a unique advantage by redefining the rules of competition in a niche or across the industry.

CHANGING THE RULES

Consider two examples, the first a consummate marketing company that found a competitive advantage in its R&D and manufacturing functions. The product was toilet tissue. Conventional wisdom in this business held that you always faced a fundamental tradeoff: the paper was either strong or soft, not both. Obviously, neither option really satisfied the consumer. Along came Procter & Gamble (P&G), which developed a new process to lay the fibers and dry the paper, replacing the rolls that pressed water out of the paper with an air-drying process. The resulting product was both strong and soft. That meant that P&G's competitors, Scott and Kimberly-Clark, had a real competitive problem. Not only was the new P&G process unavailable to them because of patent protection, but in addition they had hundreds of millions of dollars tied up in the old wet crepe paper-making technology. So, even if they had had the know-how, they would still have had to take major write-offs on their current equipment.

With its unique manufacturing advantage, P&G introduced Charmin, attacking the core market with a new-rules strategy that captured a major share of the business. Today P&G has about 25 per cent of the US toilet tissue market.

Sometimes a company can find a way not merely to secure an advantage over its competitors, but also to affect the forces constraining the profits of a whole industry – defined by Professor Michael Porter of Harvard Business School as the bargaining power of suppliers and customers, barriers to exit and entry, and substitute products. My second example, drawn from the American blue jeans industry (Exhibit II), shows how this broader perspective can help redefine how to compete.

With the exception of two companies – Levi Strauss and Blue Bell, the makers of Wranglers – industry profits were low during the 1970s, largely as a result of extremely low barriers to entry. If an entrepreneur had some

EXHIBIT II STRUCTURAL DYNAMICS OF THE US BLUE JEANS
INDUSTRY

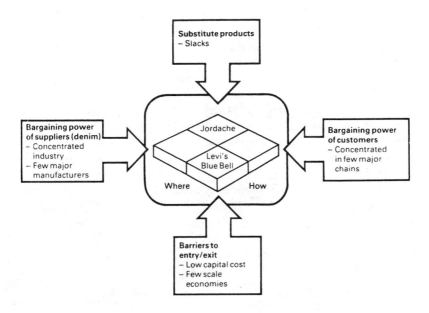

equipment, an empty warehouse and some semi-skilled labor, he was in
business. As a result almost a hundred small jeans manufacturers had
joined the fray, all competing aggressively on price.

These small manufacturers, moreover, had very little control over raw
materials pricing. The production of denim is in the hands of about four
major textile companies, so no one small manufacturer was important to
them – jeans makers had to take their price or leave it. In addition, most of
the jeans sold in the United States are handled by relatively few buyers in
major store chains. If one small manufacturer won't sell for the price they
want to pay, they will soon find another who will.

Along came Jordache with its new concept of designer jeans, supported
by heavy up-front advertising. They designed a new way to compete that
changed the industry forces. To begin with, Jordache reduced the
bargaining power of their customers (the store buyers) by creating strong
consumer preference. The buyer had to meet Jordache's price, rather
than the other way round. In addition, the success of their approach
depended on considerable advertising investment, which created significant entry barriers to participating in this new game. Inevitably,
Jordache's success attracted imitators, but the competitive field in this
designer jeans segment has remained significantly less crowded.

In short, Jordache initiated a new-game niche strategy that neutralized
many of the structural forces surrounding the industry – forces that had
made the industry quite unattractive, up to that point, to the smaller

competitors. Today, as a $500-million company, Jordache is no longer a small competitor.

SUPPLY AND DEMAND

But even strategies based on keen insight into the nature of competition and the structural forces surrounding the industry can backfire, if the designers of 'how to compete' don't understand how their actions are going to affect the basic economics of supply and demand. This is especially important in an industry that is undergoing, or likely to undergo, structural change as a result of someone's new-game initiative. Anyone who redefines 'how to compete' runs a real strategic risk unless he has taken the trouble to analyze and understand how the interdependent dynamics of capacity, cost and demand operate in the industry over time.

Consider an example from the US brewing industry. In 1969 and 1970 Philip Morris acquired the Miller Brewing Company, a small brewer holding 4 per cent of the fragmented beer market in the United States. Philip Morris brought its marketing expertise to the party, as well as substantial sums of money for both media spending and capital investment.

Over the course of the decade Miller, quickly followed by Anheuser-Busch (AB), the leader in the industry with a 23 per cent share in 1970, set out to restructure what up till that time had been largely a regional business. Miller and AB achieved significant cost efficiency advantages over the regional brewers by shifting to large, automated breweries and network advertising, rather than the less efficient spot television. As they drove for share, adding low-cost capacity to the industry, the regional brewers were forced out. In the early 1970s there were more than 100 independent beer producers in the country; within a decade this number had been pared down to 40. Over the same period Miller captured a market share of 23 per cent and AB drove its own share up to 33 per cent. In effect, Miller and AB drove the marginal regional competitors out of business.

If economic theory is right, it would be reasonable to expect that the elimination of high-cost producers would result in price declines, because prices reach their equilibrium where the supply curve and demand curve intersect. As the supply curve shifts downward, the new price equilibrium will be at a point of the demand curve where volume is higher and prices are lower. And that is exactly what happened. Between 1970 and 1980, prices for the largest market segment – regular premium beer – fell in constant dollars from $69 to $59 per barrel (Exhibit III). If these retrospectively obvious industry dynamics were not anticipated in advance of this new-game strategy the financial results can hardly have lived up to the original projections. And we find that industry cost-curve dynamics hold up in most industries we have studied, including shipping, banking, paper, steel, grocery distribution and packaged goods.

EXHIBIT III US BEER INDUSTRY COST CURVES, 1971 VS. 1980

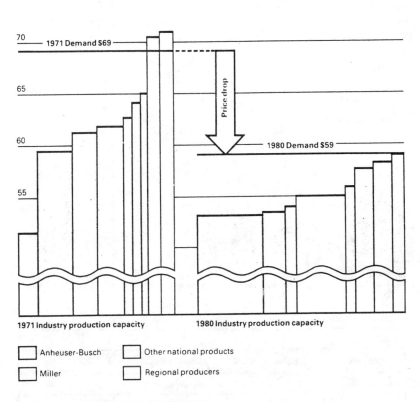

75 (1980 dollars) Cost per barrel of regular premium beer

70 ── 1971 Demand $69

Price drop

1980 Demand $59

65

60

55

1971 Industry production capacity   1980 Industry production capacity

☐ Anheuser-Busch   ☐ Other national products

☐ Miller   ☐ Regional producers

RESEARCH IMPLICATIONS

In identifying options for changing the rules of the game and creating advantages that are not necessarily marketing-based, thorough competitive research, leading to a detailed understanding of the competitor's cost structure and value added, is an essential prerequisite. But the strategist's field of vision needs to be further broadened to identify the structural and microeconomic forces that will affect profitability, for which industry research is required.

As strategic planning staffs are trimmed and responsibility for planning is put back in the lap of line management, it will be largely up to the market research department to supply them with the data needed to play tomorrow's increasingly intricate and demanding marketing game. Many corporate market research staffs, of course, are not yet in a position to assume this broad strategic role. For most, it is likely to be a process of evolution, which is likely to closely mirror the evolution of strategic decision making in his or her company.

The effectiveness of strategic decision making tends to evolve in stages. Each of the four stages shown in Exhibit IV represents a clear advance over its predecessor, in terms of how well issues are defined and alternatives formulated, how good preparatory data analysis and synthesis are, how ready top management is to participate in and guide the process, and how effective implementation is.

EXHIBIT IV EVOLUTION OF PLANNING: HOW RESEARCH FITS IN

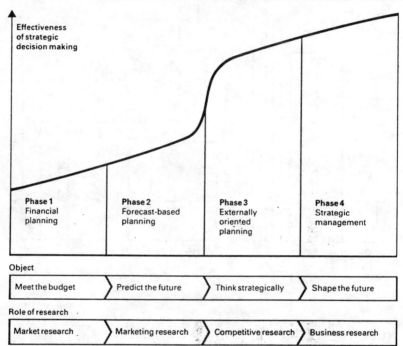

Most companies start with *financial planning*. The focus is on the annual budget and the company's primary goal is to 'meet the budget.' Typically, the planning and organization have a functional focus. The second stage is *forecast-based planning*. Here, the company does multi-year budgets, and analyzes the gaps in revenues or profits that are uncovered by these forecasts. The company's objective in this stage is to optimize its current businesses – that is, by competing in the context of the conventional industry wisdoms.

As managers gain experience with forecast-based planning, and feel increasingly frustrated because they cannot see opportunities that will allow them to meet their financial objectives, they begin to dig deeper for alternatives that may not be so readily apparent. This usually leads to a third phase, which we call *externally oriented planning*. Here, preoccupation with internal financial measures and further refinements in 'the way we do things' begins to be replaced by an overriding concern to understand competitors and the wider context of the forces at work in the industry. In our observation, this phase represents a quantum leap in the quality of strategic plans and alternatives, and often leads to an allocation of resources to businesses where potential is seen for changing the conventional wisdoms to the new rules, resulting in a sustainable competitive advantage.

Beyond this third phase, some observers pose a fourth. It is called *strategic management*. Much has been said about strategic management, but few companies can claim to be fully into it – although Procter & Gamble, General Electric, Mitsubishi, and a few others may be knocking on its door. The value systems of these companies are driven by their confidence that they can actually shape, not merely predict, the future.

A CHANGING ROLE

This four-phase evolution is closely parallelled by changes in the role of the research function. Phase 1 is typified by what I would call *market research*. If any department exists at all, it typically consists of one coordinator whose responsibility is to survey trade press and government sources to answer such questions as: 'How big is the market?' 'How is it growing and why?' 'What are our and competitors' shares?' Basically, the role is to find the best answer to the question of where to compete.

In the next phase this market research broadens into *marketing research*. Companies are introducing the marketing concept and a real marketing research department emerges with a substantial budget. This is the phase where advertising testing is introduced, attitude and usage studies are conducted, new product testing takes place, and the typical consumer goods company becomes a customer of A.C. Nielsen or some other continuous market research agency. The value system has evolved from 'Where do we compete?' to 'Where *should* we compete?' Market segmentation studies become an important element of the department's output.

In Phase 3, externally oriented planning, the company's focus broadens from almost exclusively on 'where to compete' to include 'how to compete' considerations. In my observation only a handful of companies have made this transition fully, though many are in the process. The major challenge, they have found, is to collect and synthesize the information that they must have to define how to compete. That means they need *competitive research* as well as marketing research, and that need creates a major opportunity for the marketing research department. Not to supplant the disappearing planners, but to provide substantive support – in the form of the right information presented in the most helpful way – to line managers as they need it.

One company I know has instituted a 'competitive library.' Marketing research is responsible for developing data files on each of the company's competitors. Information for these files is collected from published sources – e.g. newspaper announcements and magazine articles, as well as surveys and analysis. For example, marketing research developed a sales force questionnaire by which the company's own sales force was surveyed to piece together the organization structure, size, coverage, call frequencies, and similar items for competitors' sales forces. In a similar vein, accounts were surveyed to establish how often and from what distribution points competitive products were received. This information was fed back to the logistics department, which was thus able to put together the logistics networks for these competitors.

Particularly in light of the frequent turnover in product management ranks, where typical tenure on a brand is less than two years, a centralized competitive database, maintained by a competitive research group, ensures continuity in providing the factual underpinnings for new-game initiatives.

Finally, in Phase 4 competitive research becomes *industry research,* where the full integration of 'where' and 'how' takes place in the context of an evolving industry structure. It is at this stage that the company understands how its strategy and those of its competitors will affect the industry's supply and demand, as well as market price levels and profitability.

PROFESSIONAL INITIATIVES

Whether market research will be allowed to assume these broader responsibilities is very much in the hands of market researchers themselves. They will have to show line management through their own initiatives that their role can add significantly more value than it has done to date.

Today there is one critical area where a beginning is waiting to be made. Using industry cost-curve analysis, it is now possible to determine with reasonable accuracy, from available data, the cost and capacity situations of many industries. That establishes the supply side of the equation. But when you begin looking at the demand side – for example, the issues of elasticity and cross-elasticity of demand – remarkably little practical work appears to have been done. Many companies operating in low-growth categories take market stagnation as a given and worry only about getting a bigger slice of the pie. Too few are thinking about what it might take to pull customers in from other categories. For example, if you are in beer, should you worry about the prices of wine?

In some respects, market research is still an infant science; its tools and methodologies are not yet developed to their full potential. But rapid changes are taking place. The advent of the Universal Product Code and supermarket scanners is creating opportunities for exploring actual consumer behavior that have been unavailable to date. The ability to keep track of consumer panel members' purchases through scanners allows marketing researchers to develop new insights into the effects of advertising, promotion and pricing. In consequence, it is possible today to explore the phenomena of demand elasticity and product-substitute behavior at less cost and with greater accuracy than ever before.

By bringing their professional know-how to bear on these demand curve issues, corporate marketing researchers can put a powerful tool in the hands of line management. By combining demand curves with supply curves, they can lay the groundwork for a much fuller understanding of the factors that drive the profitability of an industry and that of individual competitors within it. It is this understanding that will give management the basis for developing integrated strategies to change the competitive dynamics to their advantage – a priceless capability in mature industries.

It is the need for supply inputs as well as for demand inputs that poses the immediate challenge. Supply curves can be constructed only when competitive capacities and cost structures are known. As the starting point toward full integration of supply and demand dynamics, therefore, marketing research must broaden its scope to include competitive research. Only then will industry research in the fullest sense become possible.

Putting the customer first: the key to service strategy

Jan Carlzon

Chief executive of Scandinavian Airlines System

ABSTRACT

A service company must decide who it wants to serve, discover what those customers want, and set a strategy that single-mindedly provides that service to those customers. With such clearly-articulated goals, top management can give front-line employees responsibility for responding instantly to customer needs in those 'moments of truth' that determine a company's success or failure. In this excerpt from his recent book, the CEO of SAS shares the secrets of a customer-oriented approach that has turned around the Scandinavian airline's faltering fortunes.

Rudy Peterson was an American businessman staying at the Grand Hotel in Stockholm. Arriving at Stockholm's Arlanda airport for an important day trip with a colleague to Copenhagen on a Scandinavian Airlines (SAS) flight, he realized he'd left his ticket in his hotel room.

Everyone knows you can't board an airplane without a ticket, so Rudy Peterson resigned himself to missing the flight and his business meeting in Copenhagen. But when he explained his dilemma to the ticket agent, he got a pleasant surprise. 'Don't worry, Mr Peterson,' she said with a smile. 'Here's your boarding card. I'll insert a temporary ticket in here. If you just tell me your room number at the Grand Hotel and your destination in Copenhagen, I'll take care of the rest'.

While Rudy and his colleague waited in the passenger lounge, the ticket agent dialed the hotel. A bellhop checked the room and found the ticket. The ticket agent then sent an SAS limo to retrieve it from the hotel and bring it directly to her. They moved so quickly that the ticket arrived before the Copenhagen flight departed. No one was more surprised than Rudy Peterson when the flight attendant approached him and said calmly, 'Mr Peterson? Here's your ticket'.

What would have happened at a more traditional airline? Most airline manuals are clear: 'No ticket, no flight'. At best, the ticket agent would have informed her supervisor of the problem, but Rudy Peterson almost certainly would have missed his flight. Instead, because of the way SAS handled his situation, he was both impressed and on time for his meeting.

MOMENTS OF TRUTH

I'm very proud of the Rudy Peterson story because it reflects what we have been able to achieve in the past six years. We have reoriented ourselves to become a customer-driven company – a company that recognizes that its only true assets are satisfied customers, all of whom expect to be treated as individuals and who won't select us as their airline unless we do just that.

We used to think of ourselves as the sum total of our aircraft, our maintenance bases, our offices and our administrative procedures. But if you ask our customers about us, they won't tell you about our planes or our offices or the way we finance our capital investments. Instead, they'll talk about their experiences with the people at SAS. The company is not just a collection of material assets but also, and even more importantly, the quality of the contact between an individual customer and the employees who serve the customer directly (or, as we refer to them, our 'front line').

Last year, each of our 10 million customers came in contact with approximately five of our employees, and this contact lasted an average of 15 seconds each time. Thus, the company is 'created' in the minds of our customers 50 million times a year, 15 seconds at a time. These 50 million 'moments of truth' are the moments that ultimately determine whether the company will succeed or fail. They are the moments when we must prove to our customers that SAS is their best alternative.

If we are truly dedicated to orienting our company toward each customer's individual needs, then we cannot rely on rule books and instructions from distant corporate offices. We have to place responsibility for ideas, decisions and actions with the people who *are* SAS during those 15 seconds: ticket agents, flight attendants, baggage handlers, and all the other frontline employees. If they have to go up the organizational chain of command for a decision on an individual problem, then those 15 golden seconds will elapse without a response, and we will have lost an opportunity to earn a loyal customer.

BREAKING WITH TRADITION

This approach may seem to turn the traditional corporation upside down. It does, and I believe that is necessary. The traditional corporate structure resembles a layered pyramid with a pointed top, several intermediate levels, and a base connected with the market. At the top of the company sit the chief executive and a number of highly qualified vice presidents – well-educated, skilled specialists in finance, production, exports and sales. The task of this top management group is to control operations by making all the decisions necessary to run the company.

The sheer number of decisions that must be made keeps them occupied with the decision-making process, necessitating that intermediaries convey these decisions throughout the company. So a large corps of people in middle management converts top management's decisions into instructions, rules, policies and orders for the workers at the bottom level to follow. Although these people are called 'middle management,' they are actually not managers at all if by 'manager' we mean someone who makes his own decisions within a sphere of responsibility. In reality, they are just messengers who relay decisions made higher up in the corporate pyramid.

At the bottom of the pyramid are the foot-soldiers, which include both blue- and white-collar workers. These are the people who have daily contact with the customers and who know the most about the company's frontline operations. Ironically, however, they are typically powerless to respond to the individual situations that constantly arise.

Yet the business environment upon which this hierarchical corporate structure was based has changed. In today's global economy, Western industrialized nations are no longer protected by their traditional competitive advantages, which once allowed Europeans and North Americans to produce and sell their goods exclusively in local markets. Cheap raw materials, cheap labor and advanced technological developments are now found in the Third World. Today cows are slaughtered in Texas and the hides are sent to Argentina for tanning and on to Korea to be made into baseball gloves. The gloves come full circle when they are shipped back to Texas and sold to local sporting goods shops.

Increasingly unable to compete from a product-oriented advantage, the Western economies are being transformed into 'service' economies. We are at an historic crossroad where the age of customer orientation has arrived, even for businesses that have never before viewed themselves as service businesses.

In a customer-driven company, the distribution of roles is radically different. The organization is decentralized, with responsibility delegated to those who until now have comprised the order-obeying bottom level of the pyramid. The traditional, hierarchical corporate structure, in other words, is beginning to give way to a flattened, more horizontal, structure. This is particularly true in service businesses that begin not with the product but with the customer.

CHANGES AT THE TOP

In order to become a customer-oriented company, extensive changes will be required on the part of frontline employees. Yet, the initiative for those changes must originate in the executive suite. It is up to the top executive to become a true leader, devoted to creating an environment in which employees can accept and execute their responsibilities with confidence and finesse. He must communicate with his employees, imparting the company's vision and listening to what they need to make that vision a reality. To succeed he can no longer be an isolated and autocratic decision maker. Instead, he must be a visionary, a strategist, an informer, a teacher and an inspirer.

To middle managers he must delegate responsibility for analyzing problems, managing resources and, most importantly, supporting the needs of the frontline employees. In fact, there is tremendous opportunity to be found in a new breed of highly capable and well-educated young people who are eager to accept the challenges of responsible management. We must give this new breed an active role in modern business, charging them with real responsibility and showing them respect and trust.

To frontline employees the leader must pass along the authority to respond to the needs and problems of individual customers. Like the agent who arranged to pick up Rudy Peterson's forgotten ticket, frontline employees must be trained properly so they become empowered to respond to customers' unique needs with speed and courtesy.

By reapportioning responsibility in this way, companies can maximize their 'moments of truth'. They will multiply their happy, satisfied customers and, thereby, secure an important competitive advantage.

THE SERVICE STRATEGY

Remarkably, many business executives begin by devising goals and strategies, and only later come back to an examination of the business climate and the customers' needs. Obviously, this is proceeding in the wrong order. How can you know what your goals or strategies should be if you don't have a clear picture of the environment you're working in or of what your customers want? Sadly, by the time many businesses recognize they should have planned the other way around, it is too late.

Given today's increased competitiveness and emphasis on service, the first step must be to acquire a customer orientation. To a certain extent, this means looking at your company and deciding, from the customer's point of view, what business you're really in. For example, is SAS in the airline business? Or is it really in the business of transporting people from one place to another in the safest and most efficient way possible? I think it is obvious that the answer is the latter.

The response to that question will go a long way toward determining how you will organize your company to provide the best service. Are Ford and General Motors in the automobile business? Or are they really in the business of providing people with the means to transport themselves from one place to another overland? If they decide they are in the automobile business, then naturally they should concentrate their efforts on state-of-the-art design and aerodynamics and fuel economy – on the car itself.

But let us say they decide they are in the ground transport services business. Should they sell only cars? Wouldn't it also make sense – from the customer's point of view – to sell a plastic card guaranteeing that a car would be made available to you immediately, wherever and whenever you want to drive somewhere? After all, when you call for a taxi, you don't specify a Ford or Chevrolet taxi. You're ordering a transportation service.

I am not suggesting that Ford and General Motors ought to stop concentrating on cars. But I think the point is clear: when you are oriented toward your customers, you are probably in the business of providing them with a service in addition to the 'hardware' itself. Similarly, banks are no longer in the business of handling coins and notes alone. Now their business centers on managing the information flow about economic transactions. I suspect that any banker who has not redefined his services accordingly will soon be out of business.

Once you decide what business you're really in, you must determine exactly who your customers are. This sounds easy, but for those sitting at the top of the pyramid – and not working on the front lines, in day to day contact with the customers – it can be tricky.

After you discover what your customers really want, you can turn to establishing your business goals and a strategy to achieve them. These goals needn't be complicated. But whatever they are, they should be oriented toward the customer, and you should use them as a yardstick against which to measure your strategy and results.

THE BUSINESS TRAVELER

When I came to SAS in 1981, we decided that our goal was to become the world's best airline for the business traveler. At the time, SAS had just taken delivery of four Airbuses – large, shorthaul planes that were technologically modern and had bright, spacious interiors. The four Airbuses alone had cost $120 million and we had ordered another eight.

Such a large purchase was not unusual for a major airline. Since the beginning of commercial aviation, SAS and all of its counterparts had regularly replaced their aircraft with newer, more technologically advanced models that could fly passengers at a lower cost to the airlines. It was an article of faith among airline executives that new aircraft should be purchased as soon as they were available.

The Airbuses could be operated 6 per cent more cheaply per passenger mile than the DC–9, our workhorse aircraft. But the Airbuses were also bigger than the DC–9s (240 seats vs. 110 seats), so no savings could be realized unless the Airbuses flew with a full passenger load. And after making the purchase, SAS discovered that its passenger base was too small.

The Airbuses had been purchased on the basis of forecasts that our passenger load would increase some 7 to 9 per cent annually and that cargo would increase rapidly as well. But, with the onslaught of the oil crisis, the market had stagnated. The only economical way for SAS to fly

Airbuses from Stockholm to major cities in continental Europe was to fill them up in Copenhagen. They were too big to provide nonstop service from other Scandinavian cities to continental Europe – a service our customers were demanding.

To airline executives who assumed that their passenger market would grow steadily each year the approach of constantly investing in new aircraft made sense – and, indeed, it had helped SAS chalk up 17 consecutive profitable years. But we could no longer afford that kind of thinking now that the market had plateaued. We had to start taking the point of view of our customers, the business travelers. And seen from their perspective, the picture looked very different.

We saw that the only way SAS could use the Airbus economically was to provide poor service to the very customers we were working to attract. How would business executives in Stockholm and elsewhere in Scandinavia prefer to organize their travels? Would they want to fly in our roomy, new Airbus, even if they would have few flights to choose from and required stops in Copenhagen? Or would they prefer traveling in ordinary DC–9s on frequent, nonstop flights from Stockholm, Oslo, or elsewhere directly to major cities in continental Europe?

To me, the answer was obvious. 'Put the Airbuses in mothballs', I said. 'Use the DC–9s instead'. Many people at SAS were aghast; it was as if a company had built a brand new factory, only to have the president close it down on dedication day. But it was the decision that made the most sense. I wasn't saying Airbuses aren't fine aircraft; they are. In fact, we have leased them for charter excursions since we stopped using them on our own routes. But to remain competitive in attracting the limited market of Scandinavian business travelers, we had to offer frequent, nonstop flights. And we couldn't do that using the Airbuses.

PRODUCTS AND CUSTOMERS

The Airbus story illustrates the difference between a product-oriented philosophy and a customer-driven philosophy. The classic product-oriented company produces or invests – in this case by purchasing an aircraft – and adapts its operations to the equipment.

In the early days of air travel, there was nothing wrong with orientation. Flying was still an event that people considered worth some inconvenience; they weren't seeking good service as much as a novel experience. And it was genuinely important for airlines to keep up with aircraft development because each new model represented enormous productivity gains. During this period the 'flag carrier' concept emerged. Airlines from each nation flew to as many destinations as possible just to put their country's flag there, even if they scheduled only one flight a week.

If a Scandinavian business executive wanted to fly on SAS to Chicago or Rio in 1960, for example, he would plan his trip around our available flights. A loyal SAS customer was perfectly willing to defer to our schedules. The alternative modes of transportation took much longer, and some national pride was involved in his choice of airlines.

Today it works the other way around. When a business traveler plans a trip, he arranges his meetings and then books a flight on the airline that best suits his timetable. If SAS has a convenient flight, he'll buy a ticket from us; otherwise, he won't. That is why SAS now focuses on those destinations that have enough passengers to support frequent flights – and why we cannot use large planes like the Airbus or the 747, for that matter, unless we are able to fill them every day. Our new customer-oriented perspective begins out in the market rather than with the product. Then we adapt the means of production to achieve the best possible product for our customers.

GOING AGAINST CONVENTION

For the same reason that we mothballed the Airbuses we also decided not to replace our fleet of DC–9s when a new generation of aircraft came on the market. We had made all sorts of calculations, but no new airplane was better suited for our business travelers, and thus more profitable for SAS, than the DC–9s we were already using. Our decision was, nevertheless, so unconventional that I myself felt a little uncertain. While visiting another airline, I asked its executives straight out, 'How do you arrive at a decision to buy new planes? Is it really more profitable than using the planes you already have? Or does it make your service better?'

A bit puzzled by my question, they replied, 'Well, we never made those analyses. It was so obvious that We should buy new planes. We've always done it that way'.

Once we had decided not to buy new planes, we knew that we had plenty of time before we would need to replace our fleet. When we began to study the available planes, we noticed that there had been some dazzling technical advances, yet there were surprisingly few refinements in the cabin where the passengers were located. We had the time to develop a new plane that would really be right for us and our customers.

Although well into the 1970s a plane's economic lifetime was much shorter than its technical lifetime (in other words, it was profitable to replace planes long before they wore out), in the 1980s it is the other way around: a plane's economic lifetime is longer than its technical lifetime, and so there are seldom any economic reasons to replace planes.

A PASSENGER PLEASER

Knowing that our DC–9s would be in operation for a few more years, we realized that we had time to design an airplane with something really new in terms of passenger comfort – something that would give us a competitive advantage over other airlines. Obviously, we wanted the best technological equipment too, but what we were really looking for was what we called the 'Passenger-Pleasing Plane', or the 'Three-P Plane' for short. Top management proposed that our goal should be to build an aircraft that, for the first time since the DC–3, would feature genuine innovations in the passenger compartment, such as more space to store carry-on luggage, wider twin aisles and doors for easier mobility within the plane and during disembarking, no middle seats, and reduced cabin noise.

The SAS board agreed, and three of us – Curt Nicolin, our chairman; Frede Ahlgreen Eriksen, our executive vice president; and I – made the rounds of aircraft manufacturers to discuss the matter. We soon realized why the Three-P plane had never been produced. Like any other business, airplane manufacturers had to please their customers – the airlines. And airline executives were so caught up in technological innovations that they hardly gave a thought to making the passenger's ride more comfortable.

One of the plants we visited was Boeing in Seattle, where we met with the entire top management group. They had orchestrated a slick presentation, including color pictures of new planes with the SAS insignia already emblazoned on them. We listened politely, then informed Boeing that we were not interested in their current planes. We wanted something else. We wanted a plane that for the first time ever would be tailored to the needs of the passenger. After all, that is who pays to fly in the plane.

They listened to us, but I suspected that they didn't take us seriously. Finally, they asked what we 'really' meant. At that point, Curt Nicolin, an engineer by training, sketched a traditional airplane on a napkin. He drew a cross-section of the oval-shaped fuselage. The floor of the cabin is located at the widest part of the oval – the midpoint. That means only 50 percent of the fuselage space is used for passengers.

'Turn the oval on its side', Nicolin said. 'Then put the floor on the bottom, not halfway up. That way you can use 80 per cent of the space for passengers'. 'Interesting', our hosts politely responded. Then they talked about air resistance and enumerated all the other technical reasons it couldn't be done.

A NEW REALISM

But a few weeks later the chairman of Boeing phoned to say that he absolutely had to meet with me in Paris during the biennial air show there. When I saw him, he eagerly pulled a huge stack of drawings out of his briefcase. After our visit to Seattle, he explained, the Boeing executives had told their designers about our fuzzy and somewhat naive ideas for building an airplane. The designers immediately opened their file drawers and hauled out one drawing after another showing fascinating ideas for improving the passenger environment.

'Why haven't you shown these to us before?' the executives asked. 'No one asked for them,' the designers replied. In fact, they had sketched their ideas on their own time, more or less covertly, because they too believed the development of a better passenger environment had been neglected.

In 1985 we joined Boeing in a project to develop new, passenger-oriented aircraft for use in the 1990s – just about the time when our DC–9s will finally reach the end of their useful life. By now, the Three-P Plane concept is familiar throughout the airline industry and is sure to leave its mark on the next generation of airplanes.

This story again illustrates the gap between a customer-driven and a product-oriented approach. Manufacturers have long talked technology with technicians. Every design change has centered on achieving the lowest possible operating cost per seat per mile. It had not occurred to anyone that a change in the shape of the product might generate new revenue, even if the unit cost were not the lowest in absolute terms.

I am not saying that Boeing's top management team was obdurate. They had done their best to meet their clients' demands. Nor had these clients – the airline executives – done their job incorrectly. They had become accustomed to working in a market where growth was rapid and competition was limited. But today the situation is different, so we must think along new lines.

WHEN THE TAIL WAGS THE DOG

As I learned more about SAS, I was amazed at how many of its policies and procedures catered to the equipment or the employees, even if they inconvenienced the passengers. Equally amazing was how easy these practices were to spot – and to rectify – by looking at them from the point of view of our target customer, the frequent business traveler.

Early one morning I arrived at Copenhagen Airport on the flight from New York and had to change planes to get to Stockholm. I had plenty of hand baggage, and I was tired from flying all night. Once inside the terminal, I looked around the concourse for the Stockholm gate. There were planes bound for Los Angeles, Chicago and Rio, but none for my destination.

So I asked an SAS employee where the Stockholm gate was. He said that it was in Concourse A – a half mile away. 'But why isn't it right here?' I asked. 'All of us are going on to Stockholm'. Eyeing me with a slight air of superiority he retorted, 'Only wide-body planes park here'. 'I see', I said. 'You mean to say there are a lot of passengers here in Copenhagen who get off the plane from New York and then immediately board the plane to Chicago? Is that why all the wide-bodies are next to each other?' 'No, no', he answered. 'They're here because they're all serviced at the hangar right over there'. 'But why is my plane at the other end of the airport?' I asked. 'Well, that's because it was operating on Danish domestic routes in the morning and Concourse A is closest to the domestic terminal'.

I tried to explain to him that I was standing here right now, not in Concourse A, and it would be nice if my plane were here too. The problem was that the planes were being positioned at the departure gate. that was most convenient for the planes! The ground handlers chose the departure gate closest to the hangar or the gate where the plane had arrived.

Now, I've heard many a business traveler swear up and down about having to rush around between the concourses at Copenhagen Airport – but I've never heard an airplane complain about being dragged a couple of hundred yards. Today at Copenhagen we tow more planes from concourse to concourse. Whereas once two-thirds of our passengers in transit had to change concourses at Copenhagen, that figure is down to one-third. Not only are our passengers less harried but we've minimized delays caused by waiting for passengers who needed a few extra minutes to dash from one concourse to another.

Another example of how we allowed customers' preferences to guide our decisions was when we established a nonstop route from Stockholm to New York, even though we couldn't use our most impressive airliner for the flight.

For years, SAS had flown to New York two ways: from Stockholm via Oslo, using a Boeing 747, and nonstop from Copenhagen. When we reoriented the company toward the business traveler – whose highest priority is convenience, not price – we added a nonstop Stockholm to New York flight using the DC–10. We decided to try two such flights a week, though on paper such a route looked unprofitable. Within two months, however, the Stockholm-New York nonstop had become the most profitable route in our longhaul network. We were determined to find out why.

It turned out that on the days when Stockholm-New York travelers would have had to change in Copenhagen or stop in Oslo on SAS, they took another airline instead. They flew from Stockholm to London or Amsterdam and changed there – particularly if their ultimate US destination was other than New York and they could get a direct flight from continental Europe. But on the days when SAS flew nonstop from Stockholm to New York in the smaller DC–10, not a single Scandinavian business traveler was abandoning SAS.

FOCUSING THE BUSINESS

One often neglected challenge of developing a business strategy is knowing when to say no to good ideas that don't fit. I remember once asking the late Simon Spies, a sage of the Scandinavian package tour business, why he didn't offer any attractive vacation discounts or special services for children.

C

'There's nothing wrong with kiddie clubs and all that sort of thing', he said. 'But the point is that, in this company, we've decided that what we're selling is vacations for grown-ups – good, simple tour packages for individuals or couples. Childrens' clubs don't fit into that strategy'. Raising his forefinger, he continued: 'Jan, never forget that the hardest part of making good business deals is to resist making bad business deals. I don't care about all the families with children who pass us by, as long as we've decided that we want to do business with another category of customer and are willing to go the extra mile for them'.

SAS receives a hundred business offers and proposals a month, many of them quite good. But only a fraction fit in with our goal of providing the best possible service for the frequent business traveler. The rest would require us to dissipate our energy after we have worked so hard to focus it on our goal. For example, when we received permission to fly our Scandinavia-Tokyo route over Siberia, we were quite excited because it meant cutting five hours off the trip, which we anticipated would attract more business travelers. Then someone suggested that the return trip should take the longer route, with a stopover in Anchorage. His argument was that the plane could then arrive in Scandinavia in the early morning. That way, Japanese tourist groups could begin their first day with sightseeing and save the first night's hotel expenses.

This was actually a very good idea, except for one thing: it had nothing to do with our strategy of targeting business travelers. In fact, it was detrimental to it. Business executives don't want to spend five unnecessary hours in an airplane and arrive wrinkled and tired just when they have to rush off to a business meeting. They would much rather fly the shortest route, arrive in the evening, and pay for a good night's sleep in a hotel.

In contrast to a product-oriented company, where decisions are motivated by product and technology considerations, the customer-oriented company begins with the market and lets *it* guide every decision, every investment, every change.

If we had chosen to be 'The Tourist Airline', we would never have mothballed the Airbuses or kept our DC–9s or introduced the DC–10 nonstop service from Stockholm to New York or frowned on the idea of a stopover in Anchorage. We would have bought new and larger planes, scheduled fewer departures, and attracted more Japanese tourists – all of which would have given us lower costs per passenger mile and, therefore, lower fares. Tourists are perfectly willing to wait a day or two as long as the price is low enough. But we had targeted business travelers, and they would rather pay than be inconvenienced. Having targeted them, giving them what they wanted enabled us to remain clearly focused on our chosen strategy.

Our concentration on the business travel market does not mean that we have forgotten or disregarded the tourist market. Just the opposite, in fact. There is an important paradox here: the more we do for business travelers, the easier it becomes to offer low prices to tourist travelers.

The more full-fare business passengers we have, the higher the revenue per flight. Invariably, however, there are empty seats on flights that, due to the day of travel or departure time, are not attractive to business travelers. Since we generally have a high percentage of full-fare travelers, and those full fares have paid what it actually costs to operate a flight, we can afford to 'dump' prices on the empty seats. By selling at a substantial discount what would otherwise have been empty seats, we make even more money per flight. With more money per flight since every seat is sold, our overall revenue is greater and we can then pass the extra earnings on to the business travelers in the form of lower fares for them as well.

That's just what we've done. SAS has the lowest tourist-class fares in Europe today. And the benefits ultimately circle back to our primary market, the business traveler.

Value-Based Management

Value-Based Management
Introductory Notes

Blaise Cronin

Indiana University

The rash of hostile take–over bids and leveraged buy–outs which characterised corporate life in the 1980s was fuelled, in part, by managers' failure to maximise shareholder value. One consequence was the emergence of a business approach known as value–based strategic management (VSM) which seeks to combine strategic business planning with financially oriented techniques designed to create long–term shareholder value. This approach encourages managers to develop a "raider's sense' for spotting real value creation opportunities.'[1] Libraries do not have shareholders in the literal sense of the word, but there are multiple stakeholders, who may not always feel that optimal value is being extruded from the library's assets, and whose view of satisfactory rates of return on investment may differ from those of the professional management:

Research library directors take the long view: the materials they acquire are intended to serve successive generations of scholars. Collections are developed (just like collections of Sèvres porcelain or Victorian postage stamps), balanced, managed, ranked and assessed in terms of scope and depth . . . Stakeholders, particularly those in ground–breaking research fields where competition and rewards are high, will not be happy with disguised dilettantism and deferred returns on investment.[2]

Though the terminology of VSM is neither explictly nor rigorously applied, the papers in this section have as their theme value–based management. One admires Cropley's bullishness (*As you sow, so shall you reap: understanding the value of information*), but doubts whether 'Librarians do have a unique and powerful role in their organisations, either in their own eyes or those of their paymasters.' Still, the general points she makes deserve an airing, even if they fall into the Motherhood and Apple Pie category. She is spot on, however, in noting that in evaluating services 'We need to examine the impact on the whole community, not just the enthusiastic'.

My own paper (*Value for money: finding and taking fresh opportunities*) argues for a conscious shift from a functionalist to an asset–based management approach to library and information services. It offers two tools: one, an asset management matrix which combines six generic assets with a range of managerial options; the other is Porter's value chain, which we have elsewhere attempted to apply to academic information services and activities.[3] Tools of this kind are easy to apply and can be extremely useful as a means of clarifying options and identifying opportunities for value enhancement.

Information may be an important asset, but its value is often unrecognised or underestimated. This point emerges clearly from the Maguire/Lovelace sectoral study (*Marketing in the Australian food industry: the information base*). Across firms there are wide variations in (a) information awareness and (b) information–related expenditures in support of the marketing function,[4] though the authors do not feel able to infer relationships between information propensity and key organisational characteristics or indicators. Ginman (*Information culture and business performance*) is, however, prepared to assert a relationship between the information culture or style of CEOs and their company's life cycle phase, and neatly encapsulates her ideas in a reworking of the Boston Consulting Group (BCG) market share/growth rate portfolio matrix.

Demonstrating the value of information is not a straightforward matter, given the slippery nature of the concept and the associated terminological confusion. We have suggested that there are seven, though not necessarily mutually exclusive, types of information value (value–in–use; exchange value; option value; insurable value; latent value; covert value; integrative value) which, inevitably, creates problems as far as metrication and quantification are concerned.[5] Value remains an elusive concept in the information domain, but the quite different kinds of investigative approaches used by Strassmann[6] and King[7,8] deserve close attention and suggest that progress can be made.[9]

REFERENCES

1. REIMANN, B. C. *Managing for value: a guide to value–based strategic management*. Oxford: Blackwell/Planning Forum, 1989.
2. CRONIN, B. Research libraries: an agenda for change. *British Journal of Academic Librarianship*, 4(1), 1989, pp. 19–26.
3. CRONIN, B. and DAVENPORT, L. Libraries and the university value chain. *British Journal of Academic Librarianship*, 2(2), 1987, pp. 85–90.
4. ROBERTS, N. and WILSON, T. D. Information resources management: a question of attitudes? *International Journal of Information Management*, 7(2), 1987, pp. 67–75.
5. CRONIN, B. and DAVENPORT, E. *Elements of information management*. Metuchen, New Jersey: Scarecrow Press, 1991, Chapter 3.
6. STRASSMANN, P. A. *Information payoff: the transformation of work in the electronic age*. New York: Free Press, 1985.
7. KING, D. W. et al. *The value of the energy data base*. Report submitted to the Department of Energy. Rockville: King Research, 1982.
8. KING, D. W. and GRIFFITHS, J–M. The information advantage. In CRONIN, B. and TUDOR–SILOVIC, N. (eds.). *Information resource*

management: concepts, strategies, applications. London: Taylor Graham, 1989, pp. 56–68.
9. KOENIG, M. E. D. Information services and downstream productivity. In: WILLIAMS, M. E. (ed.). *Annual Review of Information Science and Technology*, 25, 1990, pp. 55–86.

As you sow, so shall you reap: understanding the value of information

Jacqueline Cropley

Manager, Information Services, The Royal Bank of Canada

Paper presented at the Third Asian Pacific Special and Law Librarians Conference on 6–10 August 1989 at the Adelaide Convention Centre, South Australia

It should be plain to all how important a role the librarian plays within the organisation. The value of the information services should be clear. There is a need to concentrate on the impact and significance of the librarian's activities, in situations where there would be visible deficiencies without them. The identification of the organisation's concerns is essential, so that the service can be constantly measured against them. Evaluation must be objective. Constant monitoring of activities can be used to develop awareness of trends in requirements, and changes should be quickly and correctly responded to. The librarian must be imaginative in developing resources that serve genuine needs rather than popular demand. Information should not just be supplied; there is an obligation to ensure that it is used properly. The assessment of value must be directed towards developing the significance of the library services to the user, so that they will be seen as a worthy investment. Much that is currently done may be questioned and rejected. Information is vital to any organisation. It is the librarian's duty to ensure that its provision leads to growth and added value.

How many librarians feel that they hold a privileged position in their organisation? How many feel they are so valuable that their organisation cannot function adequately without them? How often is it clear that information is a fundamental, vital resource, which forms the basis of every decision taken? How many information departments are used at every level of their organisation and at every stage? Librarians do have a unique and powerful role within their organisation. Yet is is probably true that a large number would find little to recognise in these opening questions.

Perhaps some of the following questions seem more familiar. How many feel they are in a perpetual state of siege? How many services are cut back or closed down with little prior warning or concern for the consequences? Who feels excluded from the management discussions about the future of the service? How many of you find annual budgeting a huge and soul-destroying task? Who believes they would have more time to get on with their work if they did not have to expend so much energy on resource justification and fire fighting? In short, how many of you feel that you have control over what happens to your service? Can you sow your seeds with a reasonable hope of reaping a good harvest? How do you get from the second set of questions to the first?

COMMONLY REPORTED PROBLEMS

Most of us consider that we are providing valuable services. We believe we are doing all we can to give the organisation what it wants. Often the first realisation that all is not well occurs as responsiveness to library needs diminishes over time, or a major change of policy is announced. Librarians are usually good problem-solvers. So let us look at some of the issues where some people feel out of control, and try to move beyond them to what can be achieved.

Libraries are the first to be cut when times are bad

Most professions think that when something bad happens to them that it is unfair. This is not unique to librarians. Are they the first to go? In the City of London over the last couple of years, the financial institutions have undergone a huge restructuring process. Hundreds of people have lost their jobs. Whole departments have been closed down because they are no longer required. Gilts traders, futures salesmen, eurobond dealers, economists, research analysts, stockbrokers, all core departments, high spenders and high achievers, who probably never gave a thought to a less than rosy future. Support staff went too. Operating and back office staff, accountants, administration managers, personnel and training departments, caterers, computer support. There are simply less people around. So can we be surprised if some librarians went too? This is just part of a process. We need to be aware of what is happening all around us, and position ourselves accordingly.

Does this mean that we are powerless to affect our fate? Not at all. If you look at the same City organisations, you will find that there are many information departments still around. Few are totally unscathed, but why is it that they survived, when others, which may even have seemed better off, did not? It is not entirely chance, it is certainly not that they have not yet been scrutinised. It must be something that they do right. Somehow they have turned the situation so that their value is recognised. They have received adequate investment, and they do control their fate.

Every year we get less money than last year

Less money, less staff, less resources. Again this is not unique. No one has enough. Marketing departments cannot get funds to attend exhibitions or advertise, research & development departments cannot afford to replace scientists who are bought up by the competition. There are two aspects to the money and resources situation.

You have to increase the value of what you have

Look at the resources available. How much is genuinely needed? What alternative methods of provision are there? Your management will expect you to know the cost of getting material elsewhere. Changing priorities as a result of reduced funds may make it worthwhile to explore other options seriously. Look at the objectives for the service. This does not mean cutting anything that looks convenient, but making sure that expenditure is not diluted. Put your money where it does the most good. Can you make more of the skills of your staff? Most people feel that they are overworked, but professionally underused. Less material on the shelves means less time spent ordering, classifying, and filing, and more time free for research and presentation. Less money spent on books may bring more effort in pursuing the value added. Concentration on improving the results at the user end may show what is less necessary on the supply side.

If you genuinely need more, you will have to find ways of getting it

If the user is getting better value, then there is a better case for requesting more money. There is a finite amount that can be spent, and there will be many competing claims on the organisation's resources. Librarians who herald standards and quality in general terms will get nowhere. Making the service invaluable to the right people, and demonstrating that you know what you are doing, are the only real hopes. This means being sure of what is genuinely required right now, and determining to satisfy that need, however difficult. Most library users would confess if pressed that they could still function if the service did not exist. Services which are efficient are still deemed to be expendable. Services which feed vital information into every stage of the decision-making process are the ones which a user will have to support, even when funds are low. Commercial services will also increase revenue by giving additional value.

We give a marvellous service. All our users say so. Yet we get no credit for it.

There are lots of quantitative and qualitative measures for evaluating the service. Cost benefit analysis, management by objectives, shadow valuation, value added assessment, market needs, comparative studies, relative costs, and all the attendant surveys, statistics, and testing, can give a reasonable picture of what is going on. So why are the results unsatisfactory?

The main danger is in having tunnel vision. The librarian sees the library full of people working busily away. The telephone never stops ringing. Issue statistics are high. The information provided is exactly what was asked for, and was supplied in good time. What is wrong? How representative of the organisation as a whole are the people who use the library? Are they important? Do they bring prosperity or esteem to the organisation? Does the management think they are useful? Who never uses the library at all? Are they important? What do they use for information, if anything? Does the librarian know? Perhaps the library is missing a service which should be provided, or its products are not properly advertised? Is information handling controlled or haphazard? We need to examine the impact on the whole community, not just the enthusiastic.

What is the significance of the information provided? The sole measure of the value of information is the effect that it produces. Most librarians forget how skilled they are at judging, evaluating, and interpreting information. It is easy to assume that everyone else can also assess how good one source may be in relation to another, or what may be missing from a particular story, or what may be significant about the timing. In some organisations it may be appropriate to carry out the analysis and commentary. In others, all that may be possible is to highlight and signpost, or to teach users what to look for. If the service is to have real value, the librarian must make sure that the information can be used. This goes a long way beyond a simple direction to the appropriate books or database, or presenting a batch of relevant articles or facts. In the old days when we had large intakes of management recruits coming into the company, they used to attend a training programme. As well as partaking in the basic lectures about our services, each trainee in turn would spend a week in the information department, so that we could really introduce them to proper information handling and its advantages and pitfalls. Now without this luxury the approach is more piecemeal, but the principles still apply.

The management prefers to rely on external consultants rather than to listen to us

Look around you. Is this standard policy? Does it happen to every department? Try to work out why the consultants have been brought in. What is their brief? They are always expensive. What is management trying to achieve? They are certainly checking for value for money. Use the consultants as your allies. Ask them questions constantly. You may not be able to get to the bottom of what they want to do. Too often they prefer to work in an atmosphere of secrecy. If you know your organisation well you have the advantage. They will not reach sensible conclusions without your input, so make sure that you give the right information. Feed them with as many of your plans and hopes as you can. If they are well thought out their implementation may be accelerated by impartial acknowledgement. You can use the consultants' time to carry out the reviews and investigations you might not have found time for. Tell them what you want to know.

If there is enough interest in your department to call in consultants, this is a good time to put forward a report of your own assessments and ideas. This way you should not be afraid that they will get the credit for all your ideas. Equally, if the consultants' report is not all you hoped for, your own views are already there for consideration. It may be that the consultants have been brought in because it is thought that the librarian's views about the service will be biased. Clearly, you will have your own preferences. There are times when the management wants real objectivity. They want to be able to evaluate the service without taking into account vested interests. They want to explore hypotheses which may be unpalatable. They may want to implement sensitive changes. You can choose whether you want to become part of the discussion team or not. To join them you have to be visibly capable of supplying undistorted facts, and of radical thinking, and unemotive consideration. You need to be able to look at the whole situation, and all the implications of change. This can be hard to come to terms with, but such a display of your professionalism will serve you and your management well. If you are objective enough, and visibly so, the production of your own consultative study may prevent the summoning of external investigators in the first place.

Nothing I do or say seems to make any difference. No one asks what I think

This happens in most occupations most of the time. The one weapon librarians have, which no one else does, is information. Most librarians can find out all manner of things for everyone else, but do very little for themselves. Library managers have been given resources to run a service. They have a duty to establish the framework in which they are expected to operate. This means the regular passage of information up, down, and all around the organisation. Do not wait to be asked. Do not wait to be told. Go out and discover what is going on. Identify the key people. Get your message across to everyone who might be useful. Be selective, and consider the potential value. Find out what is significant and of interest to the important parties, and keep them informed. Establish yourself as someone who should be consulted and who can be trusted, and the information will begin to come to you. Once you begin to find out what is going on, you can start to input your views, and become involved.

How can we plan, when no one will tell us what is going on?

Nothing is stable any more. Most occupations are experiencing enormous changes. It may not be possible to communicate every consideration to the staff. The librarian has to recognise this situation and operate within it. Look at what forecasters do. They work out various scenarios, based on worst and best case analysis, and appropriate levels in between. Plan for the most likely situation and be realistic, but have alternatives already calculated for other possibilities. Whatever happens you will have made some level of preparation for it. Watch for the clues and signs which may point the way. Know what your organisation is doing, and what it considers important. Examine what is happening with its competitors and its market, or its environment. The ability to anticipate potential change and to respond quickly and appropriately are the new requirements for all.

THE RECOGNITION OF VALUE

There are many similar difficulties which could be cited. Most have been met and dealt with through thought and application. There is always scope for imagination to bring about further improvements. It is not so much innovation as perception and understanding that is required. Each of the above situations demonstrates that the value of the information service can be increased.

- Libraries are not always cut – by establishing their value, they can become essential.
- Funding is reduced – it is not funding, but value, which is significant. The money is only one means to this end. Increased esteem may even bring in more funds.
- The service looks good, but is unrecognised – credit will only be given for real value, and we need to learn to assess this.
- Our direction is controlled by consultants – the librarian should know where the value of the service lies, and be able to present the case to invest in it.
- Our views are never considered – the librarian's information handling skills have real professional value, and no one should be shy about finding out what is going on and getting a hearing.
- Planning is hard in a vacuum – services must be responsive to change. This forces a consideration of effectiveness. Looking at alternatives will bring decisions on priorities and where the real worth lies.

UNDERSTANDING THE VALUE OF INFORMATION

Having moved on from the problems which many librarians identify, we can see as a key issue the ability to establish where and how the information service can be of real value to the organisation. Now that the requirement for libraries and services is not taken as a matter of course, this is the main factor that has to be taken into account. If the library provides just marginal benefits then its loss would only be marginal. Certain things would go wrong, but nothing would be affected too seriously. If, on the other hand, there is genuine value provided to people who have real significance to the organisation, then the question becomes one of assessing the level of funding that is appropriate.

The managing body may be looking at value and worth as an end product, but it is up to the librarian as a professional to supply the products which create that value. It is here that a real understanding of the skill requirements is necessary.

Objectives

Librarians need to question and re-evaluate their objectives constantly in order to ensure that they are really contributing to the organisational goals. This means clear awareness of the strategy and decision-making processes. Is the service relevant to these aims? What is needed, and how can this be achieved?

Information targeting

Do the decision makers use the information from the service, or is it only provided to the lower levels of staff? Often the library deals with junior executives. Is the information actually for them, or are they processing it to give to senior people? Better presentation to the juniors may tempt them to pass material up the line intact, so that the library's involvement is clearer.

Executive targeting

Executives who have learnt to respect the library's information handling will call direct with enquiries, and spend time discussing their requirements, provided that the material is of significant use to them. This is a relationship built on trust and effort spent on learning their particular preferences. Librarians are often distracted by their organisation's products and services, and forget that there is a need for management and strategic information too. If management sees its own needs neglected, it will be unsure about successes elsewhere. Keep the possibilities in mind, and determine where direct contact is appropriate.

Service effectiveness

Most librarians are good at meeting the objectives for running their services. It is a useful exercise to stand back at regular intervals to try to see the library through the eyes of a newcomer. What are the first impressions? Is it a service which looks useful and usable? Is the material on the shelves relevant and current? Are the database resources a mystery or an attraction? Does the user get what he wants, or does he confess the opposite as soon as he is out of earshot? Do not allow any area of dissatisfaction to be unattended for too long. Develop plans to deal with it and implement them as soon as possible. Anything that you forget may be used to condemn you at a later date.

Service measurement

How much does the librarian know about what is going on? How quickly can changing usage patterns and trends be picked up? Can monitoring data be produced regularly, or does any simple performance measurement question produce a blank look and a panic attack? Data collection should become a way of life, but it should be collected unobtrusively and with a real purpose in mind. To say that issue or enquiry statistics are up or down is not helpful unless there are implications which need addressing. These too have to be looked at objectively. Increases do not mean more staff are required, if the activity is unnecessary or low value in the first place. The data may show a trend and pose a question, but it is not of value in itself.

The more complex issues can be covered by surveys, which concentrate on specific points for a limited period of time. Wider questions can be introduced which place little demand on the user if they are posed when assessing the next budget. This should encourage the user to focus on value, and help him to understand the investment that may be needed to enable him to achieve his own aims. A regular review will ensure that the service is kept current, and that the librarian is not justifying the service by reference to a user group which no longer needs it.

Value assessment

Where is the value of the library to the organisation? Probably, there is no simple answer. It will be providing significant input into a number of unrelated areas. The librarian must be aware of what all these requirements are, and how well they are being met. Any change needs immediate attention. The perception of value is fundamental to the existence of the service. The ability to bring these different value strands together to give a concise and objective overview is vital. It is even more important to ensure that this is seen by the decision makers at the right time. An explanatory note appended to the budget statement means that the information is available, when the question is being asked about how much funding is appropriate. If it seems hard to do, there are many departments for whom it is even harder. Those who succeed are likely to receive favourable attention.

CONCLUSION

We all want the value of our services to be recognised. Yet to a large extent librarians are content to rest on their laurels. If a service looks good, and it has some keen supporters, everything must be all right. But there are many occasions when a nasty surprise is waiting round the corner. We need to take stock of the whole situation, to be sure that everything is under control.

How sure are we of the value of our services? Are there things we should or should not be doing? If we cannot give clear answers to these questions, it is naive to expect that others will do our selling for us. The understanding of value and its potential, and the effective provision of information, are our responsibility and ours only. We need to know our user base, and provide whatever they require for their own effective performance. Get the right information to the right person at the right time, in the right format and for the right price, and the value will not only be evident, but it will grow. Investment in information is planning for growth in achievement. The aim of this conference is to show us how it might be done. It is then our duty to go back and build in value at every stage.

BIBLIOGRAPHY

BARTKOVICH, J.P. (1979) Student use and perception of value of IRC resources and services. ERIC ED 211 041, p.p. 35.

BECKMAN, M. (1987) The importance of measuring library effectiveness. *Bibliotecha medica Canadiana, 8,* (4), p.p. 180–189.

BIGELOW, L. (1985) Indicators of need, costs and quality in LRC program evaluation. *Community and junior college libraries, 4,* (1), p.p. 43–48.

BIRD, J. (1 98 1) *Assessing effectiveness: a preliminary study of the views of public librarians, September 1979–May 1980. British Library R & D Report 5632.* London: Polytechnic of North London.

BLAGDEN, J. (1980) *Do we really need libraries?* London: Clive Bingley.

BLAGDEN, J. (1982) Financial management. In Ashworth, W. *Handbook of special librarianship.* 5th rev. ed. London: Aslib.

BLAGDEN, J. and HARRISON, J. (1989) *How good is your library? draft report.* Cranfield: Cranfield Institute.

BUCKLAND, M.K. (1982) Concepts of library goodness. *Canadian library journal, 39,* (2), p.p. 63–66.

CHILDERS, T. (1987) The quality of reference: still moot after twenty years. *Journal of academic librarianship, 13,* (2), p.p. 73–74.

CHRISTOU, C. (1988) Marketing the information centre: a blueprint for action *Wilson library bulletin, 62,* (8), p.p. 35–37.

CRONIN, B. (1982) Performance measurement and information management. *Aslib proceedings, 34,* (5), p.p. 227–236.

CRONIN, B. (1988) Value chains, pogo sticks and competitive edge. *Aslib proceedings, 40,* (7/8), p.p. 217–228.

CROPLEY, J. (1988) Budgeting. In Wood, L. (editor) *Resource allocation in industrial and commercial libraries: optimising new technology and new services.* London: Taylor Graham.

CROWE, L. *and* ANTHES, S.H. (1988) The academic librarian and information technology: ethical issues. *College and research libraries, 49,* (2), p.p. 123–130.

DAVENPORT, L. *and* CRONIN, B. (1988) Strategic information management; forging the value chain. *International journal of information management, 8,* (1), p.p. 25–34.

DRIELS, J. (ed.) (1986) *Circle of State Libraries Conference on what we are worth: assessing the value of library and information services. Kew,* 8 October 1985.

DOUGHERTY, R.M. *and* HEINRITZ, F.J. (1982) *Scientific management of library operations.* Metuchen, N.J. Scarecrow Press.

DURRANCE, J.C. (1986) Knowing the cost of everything and the value of nothing. *Collection building, 8,* (1), p.p. 35–36.

EVANS, G.E. (1983) *Management techniques for librarians.* 2nd ed. New York: Academic Press.

HANNABUSS, S. (1983) Measuring the value and marketing the service: an approach to library benefit. *Aslib proceedings, 35,* (10), p.p. 418–427.

IFIDON, S.E. (1986) The evaluation of performance. *Libri,* 36, (3), p.p. 224–229.

KELLY, L. (1985) Budgeting in non-profit organisations. *Drexel library quarterly,* 21, (3), p.p. 3–18.

KING, D.W. (1983a) Putting value into evaluation. *Chemical information bulletin, 35,* (1), p.15.

KING, D.W. (1983b) Recognizing and getting the recognition of the value of information and the value added of our services and products. *Chemical information bulletin,* 35, (2), p.13.

KING, J.L. *and* SCHREMS, E.L. (1983) Cost benefit analysis in information systems development and operation. In Matthews, J.R. (editor) *A reader on choosing an automated library system.* White Plains, NY: Knowledge Industry Publications, p.p. 70–90.

KOENIG, M.E.D. *and* ALPERIN, V. (1985) ZBB and PPBS: what's left now that the trendiness has gone? *Drexel library quarterly,* 21, (3), p.p. 19–38.

MASON, D. (1976) Management techniques applied to the operation of information services. In Shimmon R. (editor) *A reader in library management.* London: Clive Bingley.

McDONALD, I.D. (1976) Role of information in planning industrial investment. *Aslib proceedings,* 28, (2), p.p. 96–101.

OLDMAN, C. (1982) Demonstrating library value: a report of a research investigation. In Vaughan, A. (editor) *Studies in library management. 7.* London: Clive Bingley.

ORR, R.H. (1973) et al Measuring the goodness of library services: a general framework for considering quantitative measures. *Journal of documentation,* 29, p.p. 315–332.

PORTER, M.E. *and* MILLAR, V.E. (1985) How information gives you competitive advantage. *Harvard business review,* 63, (4), p.p. 149–160.

RAMSING, K.D. *and* WISH, J.R. (1982) What do library users want? A conjoint measurement technique may yield the answer. *Information processing and management,* 18, (5), p.p. 237–242.

REPPO, A.J. (1986) The dual approach to the value of information: an appraisal of use and exchange values. *Information processing and management,* 22, (5), p.p. 373–383.

ROBERTS, S.A. (1984) *Costing and the economics of library and information services.* London: Aslib, p.p. 347.

ROBERTS, S.A. (1985) *Cost management for library and information services.* London: Butterworths; p.p. 181.

SETTANI, J.A. (1986) Information value: managing records as a viable resource. *Journal of information and image management,* 19, (2), p.p. 10–13.

SMITH, B.B. (1983) Marketing strategies for libraries. *Library management, 4,* (1), p.p. 1–52.

WHITE, H.S. (1985) Cost benefit analysis and other fun and games. *Library journal,* p.p. 118–121.

WILDE, D.U. *and* COOPER, N.R. (1988) Justifying your information center's budget. In *Proceedings of the 9th National Online Meeting,* New York, p.p. 421–427.

WOOD, L. (ed.) (1988) *Resource allocation in industrial and commercial libraries: optimising new technology and new services.* London: Taylor Graham.

Value for Money. Finding and taking fresh opportunities

Blaise Cronin

Head of Department, Strathclyde University Business School, Department of Information Science

Actually I wanted to call this paper *'Rolling out the Renoirs'*, but that would have vulgarized the proceedings. You can just see the headline – *'Impoverished Pensioner Finds Picasso in her Attic'*. I began to think about what might be stored in the attics of Libraryland, and that is what I want to talk about today.

I am going to talk not about asset-stripping but asset management. There is a subtle and very significant distinction. Assets of course come in various shapes and sizes; some are tangible and some not. It is not a case of flogging off the Mappa Mundi, or pawning the family silver. We want to look rather carefully at what can be done with what is there. There are two viewpoints. One we know and love, and it is an approach which I would describe as 'the management of functions'. We acquire information, we process information, we store it, we retrieve it, and we pass it on to people. So we think the management of libraries is the management of a suite of functions.

We could look at it differently, in terms of the management of a portfolio of assets. This is not meant to be a definitive list, but these are some of the assets that one immediately thinks of:

the current stock, which is turned over on a daily basis;
property, discussed at some length this morning by Idris Pearce;
professional skills, which may not always be utilized as much as they
    might;
goodwill, an intangible par excellence;
the installed base – the hardware and communications systems which
    are in place;
and then another sort of stock, the cultural or intellectual heritage of
    the nation; the rarer, more valuable bits and pieces that we find in
    the attics of Libraryland.

So I began to think at a very elementary text book level about how you might relate the various assets I have just run through with various managerial options. With assets you could dispose of them, you could lease them – sell them on a lease-back basis perhaps. You could franchise them. How could you improve the return on your investment? How could you better manage your resources? How can you identify fresh markets?

Look at assets in terms of their power to do something that is terribly important, namely differentiate. To give you something that others have not. To give you something that you can exploit more effectively than somebody else. And then you look at the cost to obtain them. In the ideal world a library would use the matrix below (*Figure 1*) to identify an asset which is low cost to obtain and then move it across to the top right-hand quadrant where it has got power to differentiate, and where it becomes extremely expensive for somebody else to copy, imitate or acquire (a patent is a classic means of achieving this effect).

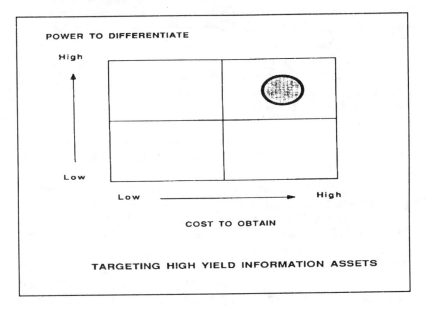

Figure 1

Think about it in terms of public libraries; they often have unique collections of local history material. I was in Grenoble two weeks ago. The public library there has a unique collection of sepia coloured photographs on Grenoble from the turn of the century. It is not replicated anywhere else; it is not available anywhere else. How can they activate that, bring it to life? They went out and sought some marketing and technical expertise in the form of an interactive video company. That resource which had lain dormant is now being brought into the light of day through an effective joint venture between the Grenoble public library service and an interactive video disc company. A resource, an asset, has come out of the dust-laden attic into the glare of sunlight, and into the hands of the public. The aim is to identify something that you have got, or something that is not going to cost you a lot to get and bring to life, and to make it work as effectively as possible – squeezing your assets till the pips squeak.

Take one of the six assets (*Figure 2*) I have identified, property, and look at the various strategies for dealing with property, and then the possible benefits which flow as a result of applying a particular option. We could dispose of the property outright; sell it, get a capital sum. What does that do? Well, it puts pennies in your pocket, it gives you an option to relocate, to rebuild or to invest the money elsewhere in your service. Lease-back on a 99 year basis – you sell and get a capital sum. You have the building effectively, but not quite, in perpetuity. You still have your premises, but you have your hands on some working capital to allow you to develop new services. You might decide to franchise some of the space, one of the ideas that John Myers proposed this morning. This improves your revenue flow and it may allow you to achieve a more interesting mix of services and vendors on the library site. This has an overall positive impact upon patron attitudes and relationships.

When I was thinking about this talk, my eye fell upon a piece in the *Financial Times* a couple of weeks ago about the airline industry. We live in an era when people talk a great deal about vertical integration. One sees it in the media industry, in broadcasting. But it made me think in terms of vertical disintegration. Look at the airline industry. There are many airlines that actually think it is not important to own their central business asset; they sub-contract the maintenance; they lease aircraft; baggage-handling is done by a third party; reservations are handled by systems like Galileo, Apollo and Sabre. Sometimes they actually charter in – and I have been on flights where this has happened – the entire crew from a competitor. So you are left asking, '*What is the essence, what is at the heart, what is the core of the airline business?*' Taken to its logical extreme what you are left with is a clutch of management techniques, a brand image and scheduling. Now it does not take a great deal of imagination to see that the concept of vertical disintegration could be applied to libraries; contracting out, decentralizing, eliminating fixed costs and ending up with a virtual library which hires, buys in and manages on an 'as-the-need-arises' basis. Flexibility and responsiveness par excellence.

Once-upon-a-time I would have called the *figure 2* below a product mix, but today it is an asset mix comprising the six major assets I identified, stock, property, professional skills, goodwill, the installed computer and systems base and this fuzzy called heritage. Under each of these generic headings we have a list of specifics.

Take goodwill. All the market research in this country, in Australia, Canada, United States, wherever, comes up with the conclusion that people rather like libraries, notwithstanding their limitations, their

	Stock	Property	Prof.Skills	Goodwill	IS/IT Base	Heritage
D e p t h	Books Journals Tapes Records Software Art works Databases etc.	H.Q. Branches Public halls Stores Mobiles etc.	Info. mang/ analysis Bibliog. searching D/base creation Info. broking etc.	General public Political Opinion leaders	Micros/ minis/ m/frames Viewdata MIS E-mail IR Networks etc.	MSS Local history Rare/op items Genealogy etc.

Breadth

ASSET MIX

Figure 2

shortcomings. They are warm, friendly, and appreciated. Whether it is the MORI Research that John quoted today, or the studies that my own students do, the public impression is, by and large, favourable and positive. This makes it difficult for libraries to be closed down. The power of the electorate comes into play. You have got leverage, now the question is, are you getting maximum return from that goodwill with the public at large, with your political paymasters, the movers and shakers, the opinion leaders in the local community?

The question of under-exploited assets reminds me of a paper which popped up recently in the *British Journal of Academic Librarianship* on *'Life-Cycle Costing'*. Here we are looking at all the costs associated with acquiring, stocking, controlling and disposing of physical assets, in this case the materials a library typically requires. We are looking for hidden costs, the long run costs, the indirect costs, so that you can work towards a picture of the aggregate costs of acquiring, handling and managing a particular asset. It is an interesting paper; it claims to be the first, or one of the first, *'to apply Life-Cycle Costing techniques to library materials'*. It is important to remember that when you subscribe to a journal, a lot of things happen downstream. It is not just those frozen moments in time when you fill in an order form and the thing arrives and you stamp it into your collection, or log it into the system. It is the cost of selecting it; of managing the subscription, and actually paying for it across whatever number of years. There is the cost of cataloguing, indexing and recording it. There is the cost of physically accessioning the material. There are handling costs and preservation costs in relation to the number of years you retain the item. Then there is the individual storage cost per issue, per volume. I suspect that those who handle this sort of material could probably add other elements. So the actual cost is a summation of these, some of which are variable, some of which fixed. The cost is not the subscription price that you pay to the publisher, it is much more complex and much higher.

The next diagram is, as I recall, from a study done by one of the big eight management consultants for one of the State libraries in Australia. (*Figure 3*) It was looking at the use made of the State library, the relevance of its holdings, and levels of consumer satisfaction with the services provided by that State library. You find there, a simple inverse law coming into effect. The stronger the collection, the lower its perceived value; the weaker the collection the greater the potential demand. Assets, in other words, are being misused and the result is value loss. This, I think, reinforces John Myers' observations on the importance of taking into account consumer needs and requirements.

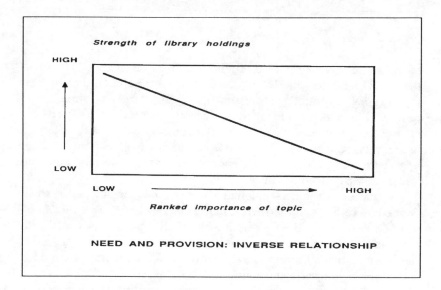

Figure 3

Listening to Royston Brown this morning I recalled the days when the FD/3 committee was conceiving the concept of LIPS. It is interesting to find that he used the phrase '*information map*'. My mind then went back to the work done by McLaughlin and others at Harvard in mapping the information industry. Now we are mapping information assets on the ground, in the community, and looking for synergies, looking for ways of rationalising expenditure, of optimising resources . . . of making our assets sweat.

The idea of mapping resources to identify what is there, where connections are not being made, where duplication is occurring, where potential synergies could be made, where overlap exists, where blockages occur can be a very useful approach. The Value Chain is currently one of my favourite tools (it is a technique developed by Michael Porter of Harvard Business School), and I have written elsewhere about how it might be used in the management of university libraries and I shall try to show how the concept can be applied to public libraries.

The Value Chain (*Figure 4*) disaggregates the functions of a firm into five primary activities (inbound logistics; operations; outbound logistics; marketing and sales; service). Here we have a tool which can be used to identify areas where value loss is occurring, where synergies are not being capitalised on, and ways of achieving value acceleration, value restructuring, or value amplification. To try to translate it into terminology that is familiar to librarians, I have listed some of the functions which one would array under the five primary activities.

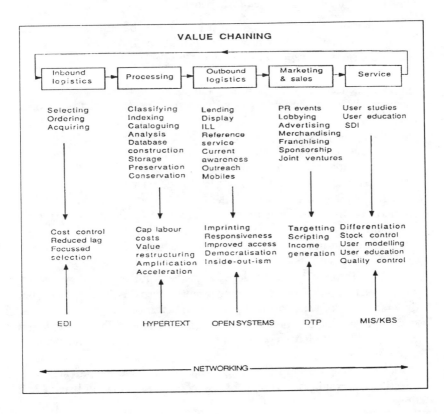

Figure 4

The processes of selecting books or materials, ordering and actually acquiring them, is what we mean by inbound logistics.

Processing could mean anything from classifying materials, indexing them, creating a database, to the processes of conservation and preservation.

Outbound logistics means getting the material from the back room into the hands of the user. So it is lending, displaying, etc.

Marketing and sales, translated into the language of Libraryland, is PR events, lobbying merchandising; it is advertising, franchising, and it is seeking sponsorship or setting up joint ventures.

And finally, service. When my freezer breaks down I ring and an engineer comes. How, can this possibly apply to libraries? But we like to know what our consumers are doing. Are they getting what they want, or are they disaffected? So, user studies gathering feedback from users, or providing SDI services, are examples of what can be done.

Now let's try to itemize some of the benefits:

Information technology might be used to create benefits under each of these five primary activity headings. You might try to reduce cost, to reduce the time between ordering a book and getting into the hands of the customer. In processing terms you might create a very simple expert system which does not replace the catalogue or indexer, but is a sort of intellectual aide-de-camp which reduces the time it takes to catalogue new material.

Outbound logistics. Imprinting – the next generation computer which can actually fashion an intellectual profile of a person's interests. Somehow that is embedded in the system and it runs this against material as acquired and provides perfectly customized output.

Marketing and sales. I would like to see the idea of the scriptorium reemerging, and libraries being transmogrified into electronic scriptoria and a blurring of the division between author and reader. Libraries are not just repositories, or take away centres, but places where there is intellectual activity.

Service. Information technology, as it does with any turnkey system, allows you to monitor borrowing and usage patterns. You can get a deeper understanding of your consumers through better profiling.

What I have tried to do below is illustrate those enabling technologies which are likely to have a significant impact on each of the five primary activities.

EDI, Electronic Data Interchange – so that we have efficient and cost-effective electronic ordering between book suppliers, publishers and libraries.

Hypertext – the next generation of catalogues will make effective use of hypertext systems.

Open Systems Interconnection to ensure greater ease in communicating information from within the four walls of the physical library, or from the virtual library to its user constituencies.

Desktop Publishing – a technology which will improve the quality of presentational materials produced by a library service.

Management Information Systems – if you want to get better management information then start to develop effective knowledge-based systems.

The envelope or environment which will enable all this to happen is a wide area network; the sort of developments that are happening at Aston University in this country or in the States at Columbia, Maryland, MIT, Stanford.

Earlier John Myers talked about Hyperlibraries and I would simply conclude by taking a 20/20 vision. There is a man called Ted Nelson, known to some of you. He is a visionary, and he has had the same vision for 29 years. *Xanadu*. It is *'the ultimate global publishing system'*. It will be a democratic, universal hypertext system, in which every piece of recorded information, graphic, textable, numeric, will be stored and accessible. It is a vision which he thinks will come to pass in 2020.

If Nelson's vision comes to pass, as Nelson undoubtedly believes, and as I am sneakingly beginning to, we will live in a world where all the distinguishing lines between author and reader will disappear. Where the library is a system called *Xanadu*. Where hidden assets come to life and connections between ideas and nuggets of knowledge are made explicit. Where new, unthought of, values are discovered.

Marketing in the Australian food industry: the information base

Carmel Maguire and Eugenia Lovelace

School of Librarianship, University of New South Wales, Sydney, Australia

ABSTRACT

Marketing staff in Australian food manufacturing firms were questioned on use of and expenditure on advertising and marketing information services, on the sources from which they derive new ideas, and on favoured strategies for different aspects of their work. The thirty replies are presented in the framework of marketing theory and of Australian food marketing practice. Some clear contrasts arise between high and low information users though the sample is too small to reveal systematic variations according to size of firm, type of industry, etc. The most striking findings are the high value placed by the marketers on product movement data, the difficulty in getting expenditure data, and the lack of use of formal external information sources, especially the online databases, whether those specialising in marketing data or those with demographic and general economic data of relevance.

ORIGINS OF THE STUDY

Innovation is seen in most Western countries as the key to renewed industrial prosperity and governments go to great lengths to encourage it. In an attempt to stimulate the search for new products and processes, the Australian Government has since 1986 offered Australian firms a 150 per cent taxation concession on the amount which they spend on research and development. In fact Australian industry is constantly admonished to innovate, by ministers of state, politicians, public [civil] servants, academics and journalists. Not all of these admonitions are well-informed and very few venture any practical advice. There has, however, recently been a contribution from an economist, Schedvin,[1] who dares to look at the whole problem in the perspective of history rather than in either the dim light of economic dogma or the glare of economic crisis.

After a masterly summary of how the Australian economy got to be the way it is, Schedvin argues strongly that 'the future must lie in heavier and sharply focused investment in science and technology based on detailed knowledge of particular markets'.[1] Investment in science and technology is, of course, investment in the creation and dissemination of information, as Schedvin realises. He argues that the ratio of Australian exports to imports must be improved and the move from exports of commodities to exports of manufactures accelerated, and that 'sustained growth in exports of manufactures will require prolonged and systematic exploitation of science and technology, more efficient use and dissemination of information including information about export market potential'.[1] Unlike a good many commentators, and not a few researchers and managers in universities and government research laboratories, Schedvin is well aware that scientific and technical information is not all you need to make viable technologies and saleable products. He concludes that 'what needs to be done in present circumstances is for commercial and technical information to be brought into closer proximity'.[1]

Studies of Australian industry at the micro level confirm the existence of this combination of need for technical and commercial information in industrial decisions about whether to introduce new products or processes.[2,3] These studies also point up the difficulties experienced by Australian manufacturers in obtaining information about markets. If more effective use of information is necessary, as Schedvin has cogently argued, then it seems that more attention ought to be paid to the ways in which information is obtained and used by those who make marketing decisions in companies. This article reports on one such attempt: namely, a study of the sources of information used by some marketing staff in the Australian food industry. A full report on the study, which was funded by the Australian Research Grants Scheme, is also available.[4]

In order to place the study and its results in context, the theory and practice of marketing in general and conditions prevailing in the Australian food manufacturing industry and marketing are first briefly explored.

THE MARKETING CONTEXT: THE THEORETICAL HIGH GROUND

No body of data comparable to that accumulated in studies of use and users of scientific and technological information has been assembled for marketers and marketing information. On the other hand, marketing presents a rich and intriguing theoretical literature which has been built largely over the past four decades. In fact a survey of the contents of the *Journal of Marketing*[5] from 1945 to 1985, reveals complexities of issues and conflicts of world view which are familiar in the theoretical literature of library and information science, as in that of the social sciences generally.

The search for a unifying theory and the inevitable debate on whether marketing is a science has led, as in all other social science fields, to debates on empiricism and relativism, on the relevance of the scientific method to the study of human behaviour, and on the relative validity of quantitative and qualitative approaches to inquiry. Peter and Olson, in a brilliant variation on 'is marketing science?', argue rather that science is marketing.[6] They illuminate the complex process by which scientific theories are 'priced' and they conclude that since much of science is concerned with the exchange of ideas, and since exchange processes are the core of the discipline of marketing that a marketing perspective can lead to a better understanding of science. This extended connotation of 'price', to include all the effort and inconvenience involved in the 'purchase' or adoption of a theory, may offer new insights to students of the sociology of science and of the industrial innovation process. In particular, excessive 'price' may explain why what is best scientifically and technically in discovery and invention is not necessarily readily or indeed ever adopted. Ability to calculate 'price' may also allow better prediction and development of winners among scientific and technological innovations.

Debates between the logical positivists and the adherents of basically relativistic approaches have led the peacemakers among marketing theorists like Leong to advocate 'a sophisticated methodological pluralism'[7] and Arndt to urge 'paradigmatic ecumenism'.[8] Such truce overtures could be overdue in library and information science research! To decide whether marketing theorists have made more progress than information researchers on the road to theoretical enlightenment would require much more searching analysis. The research literature of marketing certainly provides insights into the nature of research. Kotler, for example, in 1972 wrote that in studying marketing behaviour, as in all human inquiry, 'the phenomena do not create the questions to be asked; rather the questions are suggested by the disciplined view brought to the phenomena'.[9] Understanding that all research is a human artefact could hardly be conveyed more succinctly.

Naturally, marketing theorists and practitioners do not suffer from the inadequate concept of 'marketing' held by many librarians and other information practitioners. Especially to many employed in the public sector, *marketing* means *promotion* and remains faintly disreputable, despite several brave attempts in the library and information science literature, notably by Cronin,[10] Jennings[11] and Condous,[12] to expound the nature and purpose of marketing as an exchange process.

Whether the theoretical insights in the marketing literature are reflected in the practice of marketing is another issue. Fennell, writing in 1982, claimed that 'the outlook for an early end to the academic-practitioner divide is not promising'.[13] One of the factors contributing to the gap she described as follows:

Because of the public nature of science, the constructs of the sciences are accessible to anyone who wants to study the literature. The marketing practitioner's constructs are not public in this sense and practitioners sometimes may not make them explicit, even to themselves.[13]

Evidence collected from the Australian food industry confirms that the high ground of marketing theory is not the ground on which marketing is practised.

THE MARKETING CONTEXT: THE BATTLEGROUND OF PRACTICE

The five major features of the environment in which food is manufactured and marketed in Australia can be quickly identified.

1. The stakes are high. Australians spend almost 20 per cent of their incomes on food and non-alcoholic drinks, according to the latest published figures.[14]

2. Distributors are few. The 'trade' consists of warehouses and supermarket chains which are in the control of a few companies. In 1985 just three retailers accounted for more than half of the Australian food trade.[15] Some consumer food products, such as some ice creams, breads and other bakery products, go directly from the supplier or manufacturer to the final retail outlet. The majority, however, go from the supplier to warehouses, and the larger supermarket chains, such as Coles and Woolworths, have their own warehouses. In the State of New South Wales, in which this research is based, the smaller chains including the cooperatives to which individual grocery shop owners belong, are supplied by one other company, which provides them with supplies from its warehouses.

3. Product movement information is power. The 'trade' accumulates information on which commodities and brands people are buying, which is vital to food manufacturers. These 'product movement data' come in two broad categories, warehouse withdrawals and store (or retail) audit information. Data on warehouse withdrawals are sold to the suppliers by the warehouse owners, and are usually made available every four weeks. The various supermarket and wholesaler warehouses do not present the data in a standardised form, hence most suppliers employ market research companies to analyse and interpret the data. The 'trade' will not allow market research companies to purchase data directly and imposes stiff conditions on transfer of data. Suppliers are also interested in how their products fare, once in the stores, in comparison with their competitors' products. Market research companies provide services like *Nielsen Grocery Index* based on invoice and stock data, reports of consumer sales, and so on.

In Australia, many manufacturers spend tens of thousands of dollars on the purchase and analysis of product movement data. With the widespread adoption of product barcodes and point-of-sale scanners at supermarket checkouts, new electronic data services can be created which are at once more complete, better segmented, more up to date, and of course more expensive. In the United States the availability of these services is alleged to be driving out of business many smaller market research companies and causing rapid consolidation of many of the larger. Dun and Bradstreet bought Information Resources Inc. in August 1987 and Control Data Corporation announced in October 1987 that it would buy SAM I, Time Inc's market research arm which bought up Burke Marketing a few years ago. According to a recent analyst, the market research companies which will survive in the United States will do so in 'special niches – for example, working with manufacturers whose products are not sold in supermarkets or with small manufacturers who cannot afford to subscribe to electronic data services that can cost upwards of $500,000 a year'.[16]

4. The 'trade' must be wooed. There is strong competition among suppliers to obtain and retain 'facings', that is the amount of space occupied by their products on supermarket shelves. Some supermarket chains require that the supplier advertise products before they are placed on the shelves to promote product awareness, and afterwards to maintain sales. Some suppliers allege that the supermarkets demand large fees before they will place a new product on their shelves. In-store pro-motions, often called 'cooperative advertising', usually take the form of displays of the product at the end of supermarket bays along with price reductions. The supplier is generally responsible for arranging the display and is charged a fee for the use of the 'gondola' as the containers which fit at the ends of the aisles are called. If there is a price reduction this is often borne by the supplier. As well as being in competition with other manufacturers' branded products, suppliers are faced with competition from house brands and generics; the house brands do not identify the manufacturer and neither do the generics which carry names of proud anonymity, 'No Frills', 'Plain Wrap', and so on. The suppliers who will pack neither house brands nor generics are known as generic virgins.

In such a competitive atmosphere the food manufacturers have to market their products to the 'trade' as well as to consumers. Many examples of the efforts of suppliers to urge the 'trade' to stock their products are available in the trade magazine *Retail World*.[17] Subtlety seems to play no part in any of it. One taste may be enough. In recommending 'Jelly Things' to the 'trade', the manufacturers pointed out that:

Over 82 per cent of all children aged 5–14 will see the 'Jelly Things' animated TV commercial more than 19 times during the launch campaign. With tremendous heavyweight TV support like this and eye-catching point-of-sale, be prepared for the rush and stock up now!

After disclosing the schedule for the TV campaign, the advertisement concludes:

Stock your shelves now and don't let 'Jelly Things' extra profits wobble through your fingers.[18]

5. A state of war exists. In a 1985 article, Arndt described marketing practice as dominated by the logical empiricist world view, in which instrumental man manipulated the 4 Ps (Product, Price, Place, Promotion) which formed the marketing mix, in order to win the marketing war.[8] Arndt also pointed out the unabashed use of militaristic terms. The 'marketing warfare' metaphor to which he referred[8] is very evident in the Australian food trade magazine *Foodweek*. Captions such as 'Brand leaders hold their ground',[19] and 'The daunting battles of food manufacturers'[20] abound. Rumours are rife. One propounded in 1986 was that 'Some retailers even orchestrated seasonal deletions to get new line fees next season'.[21] Moreover war news from other fronts is reported, presumably to maintain local morale. In one example of this, *Foodweek* quotes from an annual report on the United States food industry that:

The belief that retailers hold the most muscle in the food industry power struggle is held by the majority of both wholesalers and retailers and the belief is 6 per cent more widespread than it was last year.[22]

The two armies engaged in this state of war appear to be the suppliers and the distributors, although the 'targets' are often the consumers. Much of the intelligence gathered in this research came from food manufacturers and no doubt distributors would choose to emphasise different aspects of the conflict and would have their own accusations of foul play to make. There seems no doubt however that any report on marketing in the food industry anywhere would be of battles in a continuing war.

THE STUDY

Aim, method and sample

The aim of the study was to elicit information from marketing staff in food manufacturing companies which would provide baseline data about their information sources and strategies. It was also designed to complement an earlier study which examined the industry's access to new technological information, mainly by means of a mail questionnaire.[23] The drawbacks of applying this method to the study of marketing staff were obvious: the researchers' knowledge of the conventions and vocabulary of the marketing arm of the industry was limited: the warning given by Fennell that marketing is a private activity has already been cited.[13] Furthermore, as soon as the researchers began to talk to marketing people in the food industry it became obvious that their verbal fluency would make them very good subjects for personal interview, a method not within the limited resources available for the study. In order to mitigate some of the drawbacks of the method, lengthy and minimally-structured

D

interviews were held with six marketing staff still active in or recently retired from the food industry and with one academic from the Australian Graduate School of Management who specialises in marketing.

In these preliminary conversations insights were gained into the complexities of consumer marketing. The differences between brand, product and concept marketing were highlighted, and so were the difficulties of evaluating the effects of both marketing and market research. There were also examples of the communication failures which can occur between technical and marketing people. A former marketing manager in the industry told it this way:

The problem with technical people is that they often want to improve the product, without recognising the fact that consumers may prefer the 'worse' product. For example, the technical people managed to make a chicken noodle soup without MSG (monosodium glutamate) but the public didn't like it. The technical people actually slipped the change in without telling marketing!

The researchers also soon learned that a considerable divide separates consumer from industrial food marketing. One industrial marketer said that he would never go back to consumer marketing because 'it is just so complex'. He saw the two main advantages of industrial marketing as follows:

. . . on the one hand you can communicate personally with all your customers and on the other hand there is the advantage that your customers are informed about what they want and why – no impulse buyers!

This is not to suggest that industrial marketing is an open book. Our informant went on to explain that in gaining access to marketing information in general, 'the best way of getting information is just ringing up other people – you soon work out who knows what, or who knows who knows what – and who'll tell'.

In the pilot interviews there were no problems in contacting people who would tell! As well as providing information about marketing practices they made valuable suggestions regarding the questionnaire survey, stressing the need to distinguish not only between consumer and industrial marketing but also between marketing and sales activities. They also stressed the necessity for a personal approach to the sample and the need to 'sell' the request for completion of the questionnaire by offering something in return.

On the basis of help obtained in the pilot interviews the questionnaire was structured to elicit:

1 level of internal marketing information activity;
2 use of external marketing and advertising services;
3 cost of information purchased externally;
4 sources of new information and ideas.

Background data were also sought on the nature of the marketing activity in which each respondent was engaged; whether the reply was to apply to the whole company or a part thereof; whether the company or division engaged in consumer or industrial marketing or a mixture of both, whether marketing was organisationally separate from sales and how many people were engaged in it. An open question was also included to give respondents the opportunity to suggest ways in which access to reliable marketing information might be improved. A final section asked the name of the company, total employees and expenditure on marketing as a percentage of sales turnover. The cover letter offered respondents a summary of the broad quantitative data collected.

The sampling frame was provided by the *Foodweek directory of manufacturers*,[24] and the food products section of the *Kompass directory*[25] as well as the food manufacturing companies in the earlier study of sources of technical information in the industry.[23] Companies had to be operating from headquarters in New South Wales, and food manufacture had to be a major focus of their business. Thus distributors, wholesalers and agents were excluded. From the sample sources and personal contacts, 94 names of marketing staff were ascertained in 87 companies. Again heeding the advice of the pilot interviews, the researchers telephoned all 94 people to explain the nature of the survey and to attempt to obtain their agreement to participate. Various factors, including company mergers, led to the refinement of this list to 70 people in 66 companies. In only one case, however, was a refusal received on the basis of company policy. In later negotiation two large companies which had opted for multiple questionnaires cut down their requirements, and, in all, questionnaires were accepted by 68 people in 66 companies.

The response was disappointing, especially since all 68 people had agreed to participate in the study. The final yield was 30 usable responses to the questionnaire; 22 others gave reasons for not completing it, five said that they had returned it although only two anonymous replies were received and 13 people who continued in a number of follow-up phone calls to say that they would return it never did so. The reasons for refusal included eight cases where it was claimed that lack of marketing activity made the questionnaire inappropriate; seven cases where company policy was reported to prohibit disclosure of the information requested; and five cases where lack of time was claimed to preclude a reply in companies involved in takeovers and other forms of merger. The final response rate was therefore 44 per cent (30 out of 68), or 50 per cent (30 out of 60) if the eight companies who deemed the questionnaire inappropriate to them are excluded. Another limitation of the data is that not all respondents answered all questions. Many were reluctant to divulge information on what was spent on various activities.

It is of no great comfort that some other mail questionnaire surveys of marketing activity reported in the literature appear to have fared no better. A survey of international marketing senior executives in 250 of the Fortune 500 United States companies received a 20 per cent response rate.[26] A survey of business and industrial marketers' advertising and promotions budget plans received an 11 per cent response.[27]

The 30 responses to this study represent companies which manufacture food in 15 different product categories, in which number of employees ranges from six to 1,600 (with a mean of 443 and a median of 218) and number of full time marketing staff from zero to 20 (with a mean of 4.2 and a median of 2.5), and with a sales staff ranging from zero to 1,250 (with a mean of 91.1 and a median of 29). There is, as one would expect, a statistically significant relationship between marketing expenditure and the percentage of total staff engaged in marketing and the number of marketing staff, according to Pearson product moment coefficients derived from the data. The numbers are far too small to try to explore some of the other variables likely to affect both the scale and style of marketing in a company: are there, for example, significant differences according to the particular products, whether company ownership is private, public or multinational, and indeed the management style adopted? Probably all this study can do is to provide a thin base line of measures of some of the characteristics of the 30 respondents. So far as the researchers are aware, there are no comparative data on which they could, for example, have rated as under- or over-staffed the marketing operations in the respondents' firms. But there are other questions for which the data contribute at least some opportunities for analysis.

THE STUDY RESULTS

The level of internal marketing information activity

The concept of internal marketing information activity was operationalised along four dimensions, namely:

staffing and expenditure on marketing;
frequency of regularly scheduled and needs-based meetings;
interaction between marketing and sales staff;
maintenance of internal databases.

The positive correlation between amount spent on marketing and numbers of marketing staff and percentage of total staff engaged in marketing has already been mentioned above. From the data, speculation at least may be entered that the level of marketing activity – in terms of staff and expenditure may be a function of particular markets. For example, of the five companies which reported highest expenditure on marketing, four were companies whose products are very well represented in supermarkets. The five companies with lowest expenditure included three which processed meat and poultry, and the nine companies in the middle range included all the five dairy product producers in the sample. Variation in the size of the sales force seems, on the other hand, to relate directly to distribution methods. One bread company, for example, had a sales force of 1,250 in a total staff of 1,600. Sales force numbers may be product specific as well as industry specific.

Respondents were asked how frequently they held scheduled meetings with R&D (or product development), production, sales and distribution staff. In 28 responses, five reported holding no regularly scheduled meetings with any of these sections. Most other respondents met regularly, usually at least monthly, with R&D, production and sales staff, but there were fewer meetings with distribution staff with whom twelve companies held none at all. Data from this question are presented-in Table 1 below.

TABLE 1. *Frequency of regularly scheduled meetings of markeing staff and staff of other departments (N = 28) *N = 27. One respondent put 'Not applicable' for meetings with R&D or Product Development; another had no meetings with Sales because Sales and Marketing were combined*

Frequency	Department			
	R & D*	Production	Sales*	Distribution
Daily	0	2	1	1
2–3 per week	1	0	0	0
Weekly	3	6	7	4
Two-weekly	2	2	1	1
Monthly	11	6	6	5
Quarterly	0	0	4	0
Six-monthly	0	0	1	0
Yearly	0	0	1	0
None scheduled	10	12	6	17

Respondents were also asked when their latest needs-based meetings had been held with other departments. Unfortunately nearly all respondents answered 'as required' to all or part of this question, and not enough data were provided to be useful.

Further analysis of the data on regularly scheduled meetings, however, proved interesting. A division was made between the six respondents who reported most frequent meetings and the five respondents who reported that they held no regularly scheduled meetings. A comparison was then made between the two groups, according to the percentage of sales turnover spent on marketing, the number of employees and the number of marketing staff. The results are shown in Table 2.

Small numbers and incomplete data again make more precise measurement impossible, but the trend seems to be that the smaller companies with fewer marketing staff which spend lesser proportions of their total sales turnover on marketing will be less likely to schedule regular meetings with other sections, though there appears to be no necessary connection between number of employees and number of marketing staff.

TABLE 2. *Comparison of respondents who held frequent regularly scheduled meetings (N = 6) and those who held no regularaly scheduled meetings (N = 5)*

	% of Sales turnover spent on marketing	Number of employees	Number of marketing staff
Frequent	11	300	8
meeters	9	70	5
	7	900	6
	4.5	98	2
	n.d.	1600	8
	n.d.	n.d.	0
No regularly	5	45	1
scheduled	1	300	2
meetings	0.3	36	2
	n.d.	250	0
	n.d.	n.d.	3

In the 27 respondent companies in which marketing was organisationally separate from sales, 23 reported 35 ways other than meetings in which communication took place between the two departments. Of these 18 were written and 17 were face to face. Telex and facsimile were each mentioned only once and only one respondent reported planning to introduce electronic mail.

All 30 respondents answered the questions relating to whether their company or division maintained internal computer databases which included marketing information. Only six reported that they had no access to such databases; the remaining 24 provided 62 examples of the types of data collected. Sales data were reported by all 24 positive respondents, and the next most frequently reported content was pricing data (reported by eleven). Less frequently held were data on customers (six), market share (five), competitive activity (four), forecasting (four), costs (three), stock (three) and general financial data (two).

The variables measured make it possible to discriminate at least roughly between respondents reporting high and low levels of internal marketing information activity. These measures will be combined later with those taken in the other major areas explored.

The use of external advertising and other marketing information services

This area of questioning included the services of public relations companies but only eight respondents reported ever having used them, and this source of information was not further explored. In contrast advertising services were used by 26 of the 30 respondents. The numbers of respondents who reported using the different types of advertising services are shown in Table 3.

TABLE 3. *Use of external advertising services (N = 30)*

Type of advertising service	Number of respondents
Media advertising, including production	21
Direct marketing services	4
Point of sale advertising	21
Other advertising services	15
No advertising services used	4

As Table 3 shows, media advertising and point of sale advertising were the services most frequently reported. Direct marketing services, on the other hand, were reported as being used by only four respondents. The numbers who used two or fewer services (16) are almost equalled by those who used three or more (14). At the extremes of the scale only four respondents reported not using any advertising agency services at all and only three reported using all of the services listed, including some in the 'other' category wherein were mentioned consumer-oriented and trade-oriented services, such as demonstrations, cooperative advertising and sales promotions. The four respondents who reported not using any advertising agency services included two whose companies produced industrial products only, together with a manufacturer of processed meats and a manufacturer of icing [powdered] sugar. The three respondents who used all the advertising services listed included a manufacturer of bakery products, a manufacturer of canned vegetables and sauces, and a manufacturer of breakfast cereals. All of these firms distribute through supermarket chains.

Respondents were also asked about their purchases of external marketing information services. A summary of the 29 usable responses is presented in Table 4.

Especially commissioned consumer research (19 reports) and retail sales warehouse withdrawals (18 reports) were the services most frequently reported as purchased, followed by store audit information (eleven). Regularly produced media and consumer surveys were purchased by a minority and the least used service was the especially commissioned media survey. On the other hand, only two respondents reported using neither store audit nor retail sales withdrawals, and nine respondents reported that they used both these services.

Data presented in Tables 3 and 4 indicate that while four firms use no external advertising services, seven use no external marketing information services. In an attempt to get a better overall understanding of these data, the seven firms which used no marketing information services (non-users) were compared with the eight which used both store audit and warehouse withdrawal data (high users), according to their use of advertising services. The results are presented in Table 5.

TABLE 4. *Use of various external marketing information services (N = 29). In this Table consumer surveys include, for example, surveys where people are asked about eating and buying habits. Media surveys include, for example, surveys where people are asked which television programmes they watch, which magazines they read and so on*

External marketing information service	Number of respondents
Store audit information, e.g. from Nielsen	11
Retail sales warehouse withdrawals, e.g. from Gallo	18
Consumer surveys produced regularly by marketing research companies for several clients, e.g. from Morgan Gallup	6
Consumer surveys produced by marketing research companies for the company or division exclusively (Quantitative and qualitative research included)	19
Media surveys produced regularly by marketing research companies for several clients, e.g. McNair Anderson	9
Media surveys produced by marketing research companies for the company or division exclusively	3
Other	2
No marketing information services used	7

TABLE 5. *Comparative use of advertising services by non-users and high-users of marketing information services*

Category of respondent	Number of advertising services used, by type		
	Media advertising	Point of sale	Other
Non-users of marketing information services (N = 7)	0	3	1
High users of marketing information services (N = 8)	8	7	6

(Note. Direct marketing, which was reported used by only four of the thirty respondents, has been excluded from this analysis.)

In some cases the correlation is complete: the four respondents who did not use any advertising services did not use any of the marketing information services either. Their products included icing sugar, processed meats and industrial products only. On the positive side, among other firms marketing all or mostly differentiated consumer products there is apparently a strong association between use of advertising and of marketing information services.

Questioning on use of external services also covered respondents' use of external online databases, whether of numeric data (such as warehouse withdrawals) or textual data (such as citations and full text of journal articles). Apparently almost no use is made of these services. One of the respondents referred elliptically to 'digital data received through the Head Office Library', and of the other 29 respondents one reported using

SAMI, an online database containing warehouse withdrawal data, which the respondent reported accessing using a terminal in the Sydney office connected to the database in Melbourne, 500 miles away. This apparent ignorance of the wealth of commercial information now available online, which includes demographic and market research data, is discussed in the final section of this article.

Cost of information purchased externally

Respondents were especially reluctant to divulge their spending on the different types of advertising services purchased externally. Whether this reticence was due to the confidential nature of the information or to difficulties in acquiring it remains of course unknown. Comments in a recent bestseller on innovation in US business point to the ignorance of costs which has been detected in even the largest manufacturing enterprises.[28] Suspicions also arise that the breakdown of costs sought in this study may not have been so much well-guarded as well-buried in aggregates of expenditure. Nineteen of the total 25 respondents, however, did report their total expenditures on external advertising services. The mean expenditure of these respondents was $2.4 million with a median of $2 million and a range of $30,000 to $10 million. From the figures given for spending on media advertising, direct marketing service, point of sale advertising and other services, because of low response rates, little can be deduced other than that, as might have been expected, media advertising appears to account for the bulk of moneys spent on advertising agency services.

Again in the questions relating to amounts spent on marketing information services, there was more reluctance to give figures for the different types of service than to give totals. The 17 respondents who revealed total spending on marketing information services reported a mean expenditure of $131,800, with a median of $100,000 and a range from $1,800 to $382,000. According to the figures reported, most companies incurred most costs in buying data on retail sales warehouse withdrawals, but many companies incurred as high or higher costs in the purchase of consumer surveys produced by marketing research companies for them exclusively. The third most likely expenditure was on store audit information and the fourth was on consumer surveys produced regularly by marketing research companies for several clients. Not only did fewer companies spend on media surveys, but lesser sums were spent by those who did buy them.

The figures reported also make it evident that less is spent on external marketing information services than is spent on advertising agency services. The fragmented answers are disappointing, and neither is any ready explanation available of the fact that, asked whether they had ever had to forego obtaining available marketing information because of its cost, 13 of the 24 respondents claimed that they had, but more than half of them (seven) made comments critical of the quality of the sources they had not been able to buy. On these inconclusive data, whether costs of marketing information data are a major deterrent to use remains a moot point.

Sources of new information and ideas

The fourth aim of the questionnaire was to explore the sources from which marketing staff derived new information and ideas, in general and in particular aspects of their work. They were asked to indicate, on a five-point scale ranging from 'Never' to 'Very often', which of 20 possible sources they had found fruitful as sources of new marketing ideas. There were two reasons for selecting the particular range of sources listed. One was the desire to maintain comparability with the information known from earlier research about the sources of technological information used in the food industry[23] and in high technology enterprise.[29] Thus, for example, suppliers were listed because they were known to be an important source of new technological information for many firms in the industry. Similarly, personal contacts in the major government research organisation, the Commonwealth Scientific and Industrial Research Organisation (CSIRO), in universities and in government departments were included because these were known to be important sources of information for entrepreneurs in high technology firms, even though the researchers did not think that they would be a significant source of marketing information in traditional food manufacturing. Other sources were included because they had been mentioned in the preliminary interviews and in the results of other studies. Such sources included the sales force and brainstorming.

Many potential sources, such as public or academic libraries, had to be omitted for the sake of practicality. The researchers are also aware of the dangers of equating frequency of reported use with usefulness of a source. Accessibility has long been proven a more important determinant of use of an information source than any other attribute. A source may be rarely used but essential on the occasions on which it is needed. Respondents were offered an 'Other, please specify' option at the end of the list, in case a source which they found fruitful had been omitted. In fact respondents volunteered no other sources.

Some analysis of the answers on frequency of use of the suggested sources of new information is presented in Tables 6 and 7. The 'middle of the road' answers, that is, those who marked 'sometimes' on the five-point scale, have been removed from both tables in order to sharpen the contrasts. (The numbers of respondents who gave this reply may, of course, be easily calculated by addition of the numbers shown and subtraction from the number of respondents). Table 6 shows the sources most frequently and least frequently reported by the marketers as sources of new information.

TABLE 6. *Sources of new information most frequently and least frequently reported used by marketing staff (N = 30)*

Information sources	Number of respondents by frequenty of use	
	Very often/Often	Hardly ever/Never
Frequently used:		
Sales force	18	3
Brainstorming	15	6
Infrequently used:		
Printed reports	0	26
CSIRO, university and		
similar contacts	2	24
Trade exhibits	0	22
Trade and industry associations	0	22
Seminars, etc.	0	21
Statistical data	1	21
Innovative customers		
and customers	4	18
Personal contacts in		
other companies in Australia	5	13
New employees with		
experience in other companies	4	10

TABLE 7. *Sources of new marketing information apparently equally likely to be used often or rarely. (N = 30) *N = 29: one respondent did not answer. **N = 23: not applicable to 7 respondents. ***N = 27: not applicable to 3 respondents*

Information sources	Number of respondents by frequency of use	
	Very often/Often	Rarely/Never
Overseas travel/		
conferences	10	10
Retailers of your products	10	11
Competitors	10	9
Personal contacts in		
other companies overseas	10	9
Suppliers	8	7
Trade & marketing journals	12	9
Market research and		
advertising companies*	11	14
Overseas parent company**	7	11
Companies in same		
corporate family***	9	13

Overall it appears that there was more agreement on what was not used than on what was used. The frequent use of the sales force and of brainstorming as sources of new marketing information and ideas is confirmed, and so is the infrequent use of government research bodies, trade exhibits, trade and industry associations, seminars and continuing education activities. Perhaps more surprising is the lack of use of statistical data such as those provided by the Australian Bureau of Statistics. There is also apparently little use of innovative consumers and customers: this is probably better interpreted as little direct use, as undoubtedly the sales force filters knowledge of consumer and customer behaviour to marketing staff.

The rest of the possible sources of new information presented to marketing staff were apparently just as likely to be reported by the respondents as used 'often' of 'very often' as 'rarely' or 'never'. These are set out in Table 7.

Some of the causes of the unpredictability of use of sources suggested in Table 7 can be readily hypothesised. Whether, for example, trade and marketing journals are fruitful sources of new marketing ideas could be expected to depend largely on the quality and relevance of available publications for the particular products being marketed. On the other hand whether overseas travel and conferences and personal contacts in other companies overseas had proved fruitful sources could also depend on the stage of the marketer's career and on company policy. Rather more surprising is how little agreement there appears to be about overseas parents and related companies as sources of marketing ideas. If these sources could have been expected to have brought reports of frequent use, so perhaps could market research and advertising companies and retailers of the company's products. In contrast, perhaps the apparently equal likelihood that suppliers and competitors will or will not be fruitful sources of new ideas could stem from inherent qualities of the product and the way in which it is distributed.

A larger sample and a less structured research instrument could afford opportunity of analysis of these and other factors affecting the frequency with which particular firms use particular sources of new marketing ideas and even if causality was still elusive, at least coexisting characteristics of the frequent and rare users of the same sources could be elicited.

Sources for particular aspects of marketers' work

In an attempt to overcome the limitations of the question which had prompted respondents with the names of possible sources, immediately after it a series of questions was presented asking the respondents to volunteer the sources which they used in particular aspects of their work. Thus respondents were asked to indicate the sources of information they had found more fruitful in trying to find information on market share, consumer attitudes, product information, potential markets and in getting marketing advice.

Market share information

This was reported as overwhelmingly derived from product movement data. Of the 26 respondents who volunteered sources, 19 mentioned warehouse withdrawals data and two referred to store audit information.

Consumer attitudes

21 out of 28 respondents named market research information sources, referring variously to 'market research', 'consumer research', 'qualitative surveys', 'omnibus surveys', and so on. Of the remaining seven, two mentioned trade associations.

Product information

The question relating to fruitful sources of product information brought a far greater range of replies with in many cases several sources listed per respondent. Internal technical sections of the companies were mentioned nine times by the 25 respondents; journals, trade magazines and so on were mentioned eight times; suppliers and manufacturers' representatives three times, market research three times and trade associations twice. 14 other sources were mentioned once.

Potential markets

The question on sources of information on potential markets brought forth a similar dispersion of answers. Among the 23 respondents, the sources most frequently mentioned were product movement data (by eight people) and market research (by seven). The only other sources mentioned more than once were retail trade contacts (three), and personal contacts and advertising agencies which were mentioned twice each.

Marketing advice

Respondents were also asked their most important sources of marketing advice, such as how much it would cost to break into a particular market. Three respondents, producers of industrial or bulk products, saw no relevance to them in the question. The other 19 respondents offered a varied list of sources in which the largest single category was the company's own experience, mentioned by five respondents, followed by advice from advertising agencies and internal company sources (each mentioned by three respondents) as well as warehouse withdrawals and market research data (each mentioned twice). Twelve other sources were each mentioned once.

Looking overall at the responses regarding sources of information for these particular aspects of marketing work, it appears that where to go for data about the present, that is, market share and consumer attitudes is fairly clear. To ascertain their market share position food marketers appear to turn predominantly to product movement data, and to ascertain the attitudes of their consumers they use consumer surveys, either commissioned from market research companies or conducted in-house. For product information some emphasis appears to be placed on internal technical expertise and on literature based sources. When it comes to finding out information about the future, that is, potential markets and marketing advice, there is far less agreement on the most useful sources of information.

Market planning

The most important sources of information reported by respondents for market planning, both long and short range, were diverse. For long range planning, 26 respondents mentioned 29 sources. The most frequently mentioned of them were overseas trends (mentioned by eight respondents) and statistical data (mentioned by seven). Market research and observing local trends were each mentioned by five respondents, and product movement data by four. Sales history and forecasting were each mentioned twice, with eight other sources each mentioned once. Two respondents offered the pessimistic if not defeatist opinion that long range planning was simply not possible in the prevailing economic climate.

Short range planning elicited another diverse range of sources: 36 were mentioned by 26 respondents. Overall product movement data were mentioned eight times and market research five times. Four respondents suggested a close 'watch' on the market, presumably by being alert for data from a variety of sources including market share information (which three others mentioned) and trade magazines and competitors' activities each mentioned twice. Twelve other sources were each mentioned once.

Long and short range planning share some characteristics with other future oriented activities in that a variety of sources of information is used with, at best, moderate agreement on the most pertinent sources.

In Table 8 the sources most often named as used for information about present and future markets are shown with the percentage of the sample by which they were acknowledged. This seems the most economical way to give at once the most frequently reported sources for various aspects of marketing work and to indicate, albeit roughly, the degree of consensus which seems to exist about the centrality of certain types of data to certain activities.

Asked whether they marketed their products overseas, 18 of the 30 respondents reported that they did, and 16 gave details about the sources of information used on the latest occasion on which information about overseas markets had been sought. The most frequently mentioned sources were overseas travel and visits (six) and government trade bodies (five). Two respondents volunteered the information that they exported only through agents and so did not actively seek markets themselves.

TABLE 8. *Sources most often named as used for information about present and future markets*

Information area	Source most often named	Percentage of sample
Market share	Product movement data	70
Consumer attitudes	Market research	75
Product information	Internal technical	36
Potential markets	Product movement data	35
Marketing advice	Own experience	23
Long range planning	Overseas trends	31
Short range planning	Product movement data	31

Improvements

Respondents were invited to volunteer suggestions for improving access to reliable marketing information. They were asked to suggest initiatives which could be taken by five categories of players: government, the 'trade', customers, their own companies, and by marketing information services.

Eighteen respondents had suggestions for government. More than half of them related to improvements in statistical data services, while four others made terse suggestions that government should take no initiatives at all. Of the 16 respondents who had suggestions for the 'trade', nine wanted improved provision of product movement data. Suggestions for initiatives by customers (nine), their own companies (nine) and marketing information services (five) were much more diverse, and in some cases contradictory. One respondent would have customers 'answer research questions truthfully': another praised customers for their 'excellent feedback – could not better it'. Within their own companies, three respondents suggested more use of computers. In the 'Other' category provided, one respondent claimed that 'Marketing information is not a limiting factor in sales expansion – capital availability is the limiting factor for sales both local and overseas'.

Overall results

In the responses relating to sources of information there are consistent patterns. There appears throughout to be little dependence on formal sources of information, especially formal external sources except for product movement data and market research data.

At the same time there appears to be less communication with other parts of the companies than may have been expected. The most frequently reported meetings were with sales, R & D and production departments, but indications of the effectiveness of communication were not sought. There is some independent evidence of the isolation of marketing from financial departments in the Australian food industry.

Ratnatunga's study offers strong evidence that marketing activities in Australian food manufacturing companies are pursued with little input, influence or understanding from the companies' accountants.[30] In a recent US study, Ruekert and Walker identify a shortage of theoretical and empirical work on the relationships between marketing and other functional areas.[31] At the same time the results of their study point up 'the importance of such interaction to the effective implementation of marketing programs and to the performance of organisations as a whole'.[31] Replication within the Australian food industry of their study of the social system constituted by interactions of marketing staff with those in production, R & D and accounts departments could be very interesting. There are marked differences in the usage of external online databases by marketing staff contacted in the study reported in this paper and by food technologists in the Australian industry contacted in an earlier study.[32] These differences suggest a fairly low *domain similarity*, a concept defined as 'the degree to which two different individuals or departments share the same goals, skills, or tasks'.[31] Ruekert and Walker's empirical study supports their hypothesis that 'The amount of transaction flows between marketing personnel and people in other functional areas is related positively to the degree of domain similarity between them'.[31]

The study reported in this paper offers some opportunity for discrimination between marketing staff who are heavy and those who are light users and transmitters of information. A scale was constructed according to whether respondents had: 1, regularly scheduled meetings at least every two weeks with two other sections; 2, held a needs-based meeting with two other sections in the past week; 3, used an internal database of sales and/or pricing data and at least one additional application; 4, used both warehouse withdrawal and store audit information; 5, used three or more advertising services; 6, used a written system of communicating with sales staff; 7, used more suggested sources of new ideas 'often/very often' than the mean. A positive score on each of these characteristics was represented by one, and a negative by zero. On this rough scale 18 companies scored between zero and two points and 12 companies scored between three and six points. In comparison with other characteristics high scores on this scale tend to be associated with larger companies, more marketing staff and more expenditure on marketing. Since it is self-evident that expenditure on marketing will be higher in those companies which use more advertising and marketing research services, criteria 4 and 5 above were deleted. In the ensuing analysis, 23 companies scored between zero to two points and seven scored between three and five points. In both calculations nine companies were in common in the top ten highest scorers and eight out of the bottom ten were also in common.

Whether the nature and mix of products and the methods of distribution correlate with information use and level of marketing information activity is not clear. On the one hand, all of the six companies which answered positively on five or more or the original seven dimensions produce well known brand names in breakfast foods, canned vegetables, salamis and smallgoods, tea and coffee, dairy products and confectionery. All their products are highly visible in both supermarkets and independent stores. On the other hand, when looking at the lowest scoring companies, those who scored zero or one on the seven dimensions, three do not distribute through supermarket chains but the remaining six do and their products include icing sugar, frozen meals, fruit juices, soft drinks, salamis and smallgoods, and tea and coffee. So whether it is the nature of the product, the degree of market competition, the method of distribution, the marketing approach of the company or some more elusive corporate or personal factors that most influence information use by marketers is not yet clear. But even from the thin baseline established in this study some implications can be seen both for information services and for innovation.

IMPLICATIONS FOR INFORMATION SERVICES AND INNOVATION

There are at least two useful lessons that managers of libraries and other information services could draw from the behaviour of the food marketers studied. One is their reliance on product movement data and the effort and resources they put into deriving and interpreting these data for feedback into their operations. If librarians had been so motivated to gather data on the operation of the systems which they manage, discussion of core collections and the factors which influence the composition of the core might have progressed to useful guidelines for collection building and management. In fact few libraries appear to have followed up the insights offered many years ago by the work at the University of Lancaster, the theory of which was usefully set out by Buckland.[33] Questions may be asked of companies which have designed operationally sophisticated integrated automated systems for libraries about the relative lack of development of management information systems capable, for example, of identifying both individual titles and categories of high use items and of reporting needs for changes in loan periods. Answers so far collected by the authors of this paper are that there is virtually no demand for such facilities from librarians, in either their requests for proposal or in their less formal statements of systems desiderata.

A second lesson for information service managers may lie in the importance which marketers place on advertising and promotion of their products. This is a lesson already assimilated by many librarians in the public as well as the private sector. But there remain at least in many Australian libraries managers who could well find useful metaphors in the supermarket, especially in the concepts of 'facings' and 'shelf life'.

On the findings of this study, one benefit which the information managers have to offer the marketers is knowledge of and access to the external online databases. The ambivalence of Australian food marketers about the usefulness of overseas sources of information might be resolved if they knew and had access to specialised marketing databases of high quality such as MARS (Predicasts Marketing and Advertising Reference Service) from the United States and MAID (the Market Analysis and Information Database) from the United Kingdom. In addition to such specialised sources there is an apparent lack of knowledge of the information on demographics and general economic indicators for Australia which is scattered in the international databases as well as those compiled locally. The nearest link to this study found in the literature, in which media companies in Britain were found similarly innocent of knowledge of the online databases,[34] suggests that such ignorance may not be peculiar either to Australia or to the food industry.

Some preliminary work is likely to be necessary, however, in order for the marketers to be attracted to seek help from traditional information services such as university, college or public libraries. Those information service managers anxious to attract the custom of marketing staff in industry have some new vocabulary and attitudes to learn. The authors of this paper were interested to find that the library of their own university, which houses a School of Marketing, does not hold *Foodweek* or *Retail World*. It seems likely that the trade literature, which is very important to marketing and technical staff in industry, is poorly represented in most academic and public libraries.

Apart from the need for advertisement and promotion in order to have innovations adopted, including innovations in information services, there is also evidence, however fragmentary, in this study of the difficulties that lie in the path of getting innovative consumer products to market. This may serve to reinforce the message for information managers about the need to promote services. At least among the subjects of this study online information services seem to have poor market penetration. With this goes a final *caveat emptor*. The authors have put before you a very small picture, made of data structured on their concepts, set in the frame which they built. If marketers could be induced to participate in the design of future studies of what they need to know, then the proprietors of information services might gain some really useful data on how to manufacture better products.

REFERENCES

1.   SCHEDVIN, C.B. The Australian economy on the hinge of history. *Australian Economic Review*, 77, 1987, 20–30.

2. MAGUIRE, C., WEIR, A.D. *and* WOOD, L. *Scientific and technological information: its use and supply in Australia.* Canberra: Department of Science, 1987.

3. MAGUIRE, C. *and* KENCH, R. Sources of ideas for applied university research, and their effect on the applications of findings in Australian industry. *Social Studies of science, 14,* 1984, 371–397.

4. MAGUIRE, C. *and* LOVELACE, E. *Marketing in the Australian food industry: information sources and strategies.* Sydney: School of Librarianship, University of New South Wales, 1987.

5. *Journal of Marketing.* Chicago: American Marketing Association.

6. PETER, J. *and* OLSON, J. Is science marketing? *Journal of Marketing, 47,* 1983, 111–125.

7. LEONG, S. Metatheory and metamethodology in marketing: a Lakatosian reconstruction. *Journal of Marketing, 49,* 1985, 23–40.

8. ARNDT, J. On making marketing more scientific: role of orientations, paradigms, metaphors and puzzle solving. *Journal of Marketing, 49,* 1985, 11–23.

9. KOTLER, P. A generic concept of marketing. *Journal of Marketing, 36,* 1972, 48.

10. CRONIN, B., ed. *The marketing of library and information services.* London: Aslib, 1981.

11. JENNINGS, L. Marketing for non-market transactions: problems and issues for librarians. *Australian Library Journal, 33*(2), 1984, 10–17.

12. CONDOUS, C. Non-profit marketing–libraries' future? *Aslib Proceedings, 35*(10), 1983, 407–417.

13. FENNELL, G. Terms v. concepts: market segmentation, brand positioning and other aspects of the academic-practitioner gap. *In:* BUSH, R. *and* HUNT, S., eds. *Marketing theory: philosophy of science perspectives.* Chicago: American Marketing Association, 1982, 97–102.

14. AUSTRALIAN BUREAU OF STATISTICS. *Household expenditure survey, 1984.* Canberra: 1986.

15. The food trade's roundabouts and swings. *Foodweek,* (907), 1986, 8–9.

16. DEUTSCH, C.H. What do people want anyway? *New York Times,* November 8, 1987.

17. *Retail World.* Sydney: Retail World Pty. Ltd.

18. [Advertisement for Jelly Things] *Retail World, 39*(19), 1986, 26.

19. *Foodweek,* (893), 1986, 16.

20. *Foodweek,* (905), 1986, 8–9.

21. LUKER, P. The food industry is screwing itself. *Foodweek,*(893), 1986, 8–9.

22. How American food industry faced the music in 1985. *Foodweek,* (902), 1986, 8–9.

23. MAGUIRE, C. *and* KENCH, R. The access of Australian manufacturing industry to information about new technology. *Lasie, 15,* 1984, 15–21.

24. *Foodweek directory of manufacturers.* Sydney: Foodweek, 1985.

25. *Kompass Australia, 1985–1986.* Prahan, Victoria: Peter Isaacson, 1986.

26. RYAN, J. *and* MITCHELL, L. Survey methodology. *Business Marketing, 71,* 1986, 67.

27. FINCH, P. Survey: '86 ad/promotion budgets to climb 10%. *Business Marketing, 71,* 1986, 22.

28. WATERMAN, R.H. *The renewal factor.* Toronto: Bantam Books, 1987.

29. MAGUIRE, C. *and* KENCH, R. *Information and high technology companies.* Unpublished. 1985.

30. RATNATUNGA, J. *Financial controls in the Australian food marketing*

industry: a qualitative study. Canberra: International Fellowship for Social and Economic Development, 1985.

31.   RUEKERT, R.W. *and* WALKER, O.C. Marketing's interaction with other functional units: a conceptual framework and empirical evidence. *Journal of Marketing, 51,* 1987, 1–19.

32.   MAGUIRE, C. *and* KENCH, R. Use of new information technology by food and chemical companies. *Food Technology in Australia,* 37, 1985, 204–206.

33.   BUCKLAND, M.K. *Book availability and the library user.* New York: Pergamon, 1975.

34.   HARRIS, K., NICHOLAS, D. *and* ERBACH, G. Online use and end-users in media and advertising: an overview. *Aslib Proceedings, 38*(11/12), 1986, 389–397.

Information culture and business performance

Mariam Ginman

Department of Library and Information Science, The Swedish University of Finland, SF-20500 Åbo, Finland

THE PROJECT

A market-geared company thrives through the transformation of its resources. These resources can be either primary or secondary. Primary resources are essential for the acquisition and utilization of other kinds of resources. In many companies, the main primary resources are the momentary ones. Inflow of capital into the organization is a prerequisite for the acquisition of other resources needed for its activities, such as employees, raw materials, and technological production facilities. Together, these components constitute the basis of the company's material resource transformations (Fig. 1).

A company possessing these funds and supplies is not yet productive, unless a transformation of intellectual resources is maintained alongside the transformation of material resources. The primary resources for this transformation are varying kinds of knowledge and information. The output achieved is a processed intellectual product which is necessary for the material activities to function and develop positively (Fig. 2). At present, companies are investing heavily in optimizing the transformation of material resources. Training, computerization, administration, target-orientation, strategic planning, and rationalization are the means by which basic resources achieve optimally efficient production. But whatever happened to the intellectual transformation process? Some companies have started regarding it as essential and worth investing in, while others have developed it only very little or not at all. In the former case, information is used as a resource; in the latter, rather as a product'.

In early 1986, the Department of Library and Information Science of The Swedish University of Finland launched a project investigating these questions. A specific aim of the project is the analysis of the factors determining information culture in a business environment. The target groups chosen were on the one hand the small and medium-sized metalworking companies and, on the other hand, the giants of the field. 39 Chief Executive Officers (CEOs) were interviewed. The technique

FIG 1. MATERIAL RESOURCE TRANSFORMATIONS

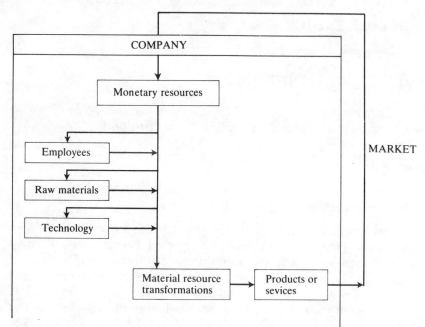

applied was a semi-structured thematic interview lasting for several hours per interviewee. Every interview was tape-recorded and transcribed. Responses were graded with a view to obtaining total scores for the various theme headings. The results were evaluated mainly according to soft methods, and they were further supported by the results of combined factor and regression analysis.

RESULTS

The aspects investigated can be grouped under three main headings:

(a) *The CEOs' approach to information* was described in terms of six variables, namely:
1. Use of internal information
2. Use of external information
3. Use of oral information
4. Use of written information
5. Quantity of information used
6. Attitudes towards information.

(b) *Company characteristics* included the following variables:
1. Size and age
2. Efficiency
3. Level of research, know-how, and knowledge

FIG 2. INTELLECTUAL RESOURCE TRANSFORMATIONS

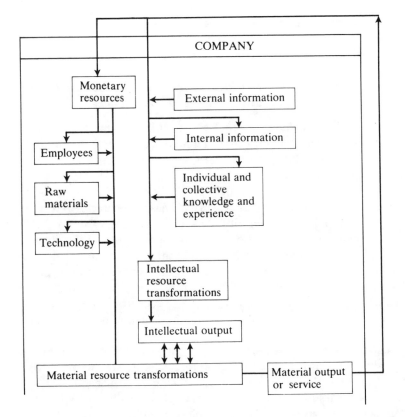

4. Internal communication level
5. External communication level
6. Problem level (development phase, life cycle, and culture).

(c) *Personal characteristics of the CEOs* included the following variables:
1. Age, training, and work experience
2. Experiential orientation
3. Market orientation
4. Production orientation
5. Approach to administration and management.

All the variables within these three main sections comprise a large number of different questions, grouped and graded so that higher scores reflect a higher degree of orientation. The analysis of the approach to information in relation to sections (b) and (c) revealed interesting links, which were further corroborated by subsequent factor and regression analysis. These links were also used to establish different characteristic company blocks. Inter-relations between CEO information culture, company life cycle, company culture, and product market success are discussed in this paper.

An SAS programme with varimax factor rotation and stepwise regression procedure was used for the factor and regression analyses. The results included, among other things, the correlations shown in Fig. 3 and Fig. 4.

Correlations between CEO information culture, company life cycle, company culture, and product market success

During their lifespan, companies go through two interesting development phenomena. One concerns different phases of their chronological development,[2,5,6,8] and the other is an evolutionary cycle, also referred to as the company life cycle.[4,7]

The individual phases of chronological development are initiated by the company's problems and crises. Each phase is characterized by its own specific problems, which ultimately bring about a crisis. It can be said that a company develops from one crisis to another and that its need for knowledge and information is rooted in this very characteristic. The number of crises (and phases), as defined by different researchers, varies, but a summary might comprise five different phases, which are: (1) the initial phase, (2) the functional phase, (3) the decentralization phase, (4) the official supervision phase, and (5) the information phase. To put it briefly, in the first phase, activities are set up (Fig. 5). In the second phase various functions diversify and a formal structure and hierarchy are established. During the third phase tasks are delegated to the appropriate levels. In the fourth phase the CEO starts losing control of activities, and a need for official supervision arises. In the fifth phase the company enters a stage where it strives to achieve complete integration of activities and diversified information. For the first time, information becomes a need recognized by the CEO in phase 4.[1]

In each development phase, companies may be at different stages of their life cycles. The life cycle is the phenomenon which, in conjunction with the development phase, determines company ideologies, norms, attitudes to problems, and the nature of the problems themselves. Initially, the life cycle phases coincide with the stages of chronological development, but may later develop independently within the various development phases, or as partial functions of company activities, e.g. within different strategic business units (SBUs). The company life cycle is generally divided into five phases:[4,7]

Birth Phase I

The company is young, lacks experience, is extrovert, audacious and
informal.

Growth Phase II

Attention focuses on output and growth, the company adopts a more
cautious approach and is reluctant to make dramatic investments.

The decision-making process becomes more complex, CEOs pay more attention to employee demands and thereby become more aware of internal company matters.

Maturity Phase III

Companies are older and bigger, the market is heterogeneous, bureaucracy increases, internal achievements assume more and more significance, company history and culture are important.

Revival Phase IV

Old traditions are abolished, employees dismissed, the company looks for new knowledge and expertise, fresh ideas and innovation. Attention focuses maximally on external matters.

Decline Phase V

This phase may start at any point and is characterized by falling profitability, emphasis on cost-cutting, rigorous control of internal activities, low morale, scepticism, maximal fixation on internal matters by the CEO.

The different phases of company life cycles are thus characterized by different attitudes and problems. A matter of particular interest, therefore, is that the factor analysis of characteristic company problems established two new variables, S15P1 and S15P2 (see Figs. 3 and 4). S15P1 showed high loadings for problems pertaining to task allocation, coordination, cooperation, and unnecessary organizational complexity. It has been shown that such problems are typical of companies that have become sufficiently large, complex, and difficult to manage, i.e. show characteristics impeding rational, efficient, and up-to-date activities and development'. Facing such problems compels the CEO to turn his interest to internal factors. He becomes introvert and runs the risk of not finding sufficient time or interest to keep up with developments in the external environment. Consequently, he (and the company) will start falling behind and development will stagnate more and more. Considering these problems and the CEO's 'introvert-extrovert' orientation in different life cycle phases, it may be said that the behavioural pattern comes rather close to that observed in the maturity phase, which (especially if it extends over a longer period) may imply stagnation and subsequent decline. Companies showing this problem profile are therefore in the present context referred to as being in a 'stagnation phase' of their life cycle.

S15P2 was obtained as a second factor in the factor analysis of company problem profiles. It showed high loadings for recognized lack of expertise in a company (Fig. 3). Miller and Friesen' demonstrated that such an expertise-oriented way of thinking is typical of a company moving through the revival phase. There is a strong demand for new know-how as well as development and restructuring of all company activities. Experts are called in, employees replaced, new strategies devised, and established

FIG 3

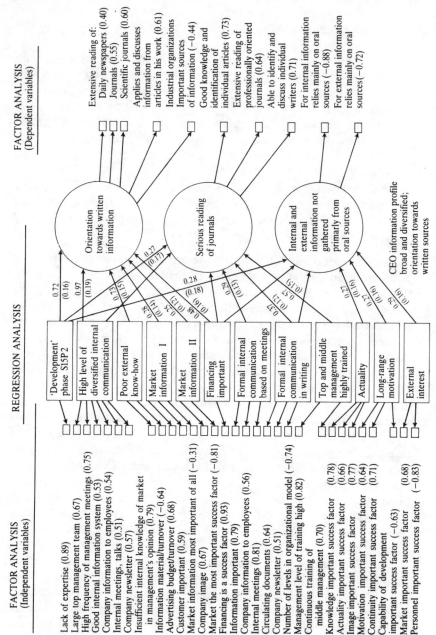

FIG 4

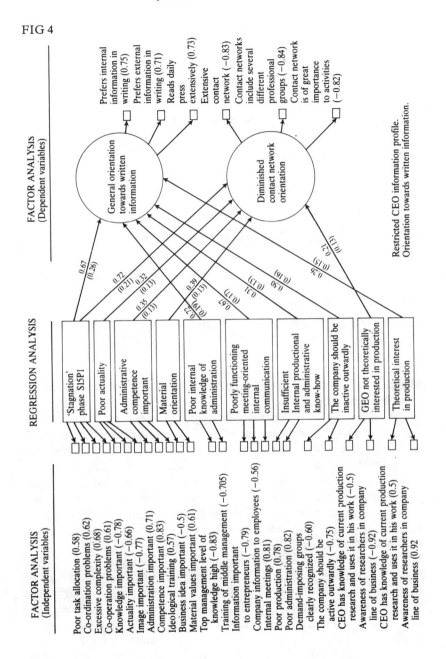

FIG 5. THE CHRONOLOGICAL DEVELOPMENT OF A COMPANY

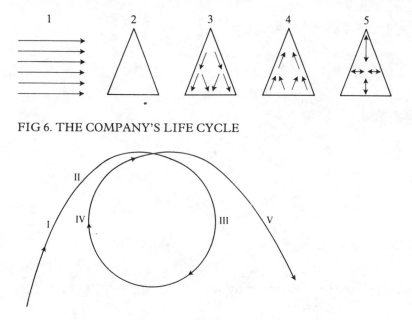

FIG 6. THE COMPANY'S LIFE CYCLE

attitudes scrutinized. In the present study, companies facing these problems will therefore be referred to as being in the 'revival phase' of their life cycle.

The regression analysis revealed that in organizations going through 'the revival phase of their life cycle', the CEOs' information culture has both width and depth (Fig. 3). They read and communicate extensively, taking their reading seriously. The fact that they are able to discuss individual writers and articles implies that they memorize and analyse what they read. Their extensive active use of external information in their work indicates an information culture resembling that of Gatekeepers. This seems to take place at the expense of an extremely pronounced oral orientation in their ways of gathering information.

In the same way, a specific approach to information can be observed for CEOs of companies in a 'stagnation phase'. Internal exchange of information is mainly in writing (Fig. 4). However, written information lacks the social and other aspects which would produce a rewarding exchange of knowledge and ideas. The marked orientation towards written information therefore supports the notion that internal infor-mation serves these CEOs mainly as a formal control instrument. Their need for external information is satisfied by extensive reading of the daily press. It can be observed that the reading of newspapers increasingly seems to substitute for communication with their contact networks as the extent of current problems grows. The CEO's 'introvert' orientation becomes increasingly pronounced. Serious journals do not seem to interest CEOs of 'stagnating companies'. They do read journals, but at the same time belong to the category unable to specify individual authors or articles they have read. 'I read journals like women read women's magazines' is a statement very typical of this group. Nor do these CEOs normally discuss acquired information with their colleagues in the company.

Figures 3 and 4 further indicate that CEOs with a broad and deep personal information profile work in companies with a high level of diversified internal communication. In the case of CEOs with little interest in information, the level of oral communication is downright poor. It is also noticeable that CEOs of the former category do not rank the market as the foremost element of success, although they emphasize its importance alongside that of other aspects. Material resources, such as employees, are not regarded as primary success initiators, but long-term motivation is put forward as an essential success factor. This factor is based on concepts such as motivation and continuity (Fig. 3), which in present personnel research are seen as essential to successful personnel management. These CEOs also stress the importance of actuality as an essential element in success. This factor encompasses concepts such as knowledge, actuality and image (Fig. 3). CEOs with a highly developed serious interest in information thus seem prepared to invest in expertise, internal communication, knowledge, 'extrovert orientation', actuality, motivation, and continuity, i.e. factors also found to be characteristic of companies moving through the development phase. CEOs with a restricted information profile manifest an 'introvert' orientation in regard to all these factors. In their opinion, the company's expertise in production and administration is inferior, in comparison with the competition. They do not think their companies ought to be actively outwardly oriented. This, to them, justifies focusing their attention 'inwards'. They regard internal administrative competence as an important prerequisite for success, but actuality, knowledge, and image as less significant.

CEOs with a narrow information profile mainly rely on internal reports and, as regards external information, restrict themselves to reading the daily press. Their companies, too, show poor formal information systems as well as friction in administrative cooperation, CEOs of this type attach importance to administrative competence and monitored development of material resources. These factors fit the generally accepted description of stagnating companies.

Each development phase thus seems to be characterized by its own specific company culture, which moulds the common norms and attitudes.

If the Birth phase and the Growth phase are combined into one, the Development phase, the company cultures put forward by Deal and

Kennedy[3] can be applied to the various phases as follows:[4]

1. The Development phase has a Tough Guy/Macho culture, characterized by a high degree of financial risk-taking and rapid feedback to investments and described as the 'find a mountain and climb it' ideology.
2. The Maturity phase has a Work Hard/Play Hard culture with a low degree of risk and rapid feedback to investments, referred to as the 'find a need and fill it' ideology.
3. The Revival phase has a Bet Your Company culture, which is the opposite of the Work Hard/Play Hard culture.
4. The Decline phase has a Process culture, characterized by low risks, slow feedback to investments and a high degree of bureaucracy. Attention focuses 'on how something is done rather than on what is being done'.

The linkage to the market will be examined by plotting the company products in a market growth share matrix (Fig. 7). A company's position, which can be any one of four, is determined by two coordinates: the relative market share of its products and market growth rate. The top right field contains 'question marks', products with low shares of a fast-growing market.

Investments in these may produce a product belonging in the top left field, i.e. a 'star' with a high share of a rapidly growing market. The products in the bottom left corner have high market shares in a stabilized

FIG 7. MARKET GROWTH SHARE MATRIX (THE BOSTON CONSULTING GROUPS MODEL[4]

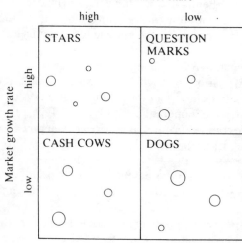

market and consequently are the real 'cash cows' continuously supplying the company with capital to be used, e.g. for the transformation of 'question marks' into 'stars'. Just before a product disappears completely from the market, it usually turns into a 'dog', i.e. has a small share of a market characterized by a low growth rate.

If one relates the links between life cycle, culture, and market success, as proved by Deshpandé *et al.*,[4] to the results of the comparison between information cultures at different development stages, in different life cycle phases, and as determined by different approaches to information, this produces four blocks of characteristic connections (Fig. 8). The criteria used to define information culture were the degree of interest in information and the attitude to factors in the external company environment.

Fig. 8 demonstrates four different blocks, each with a specific CEO information culture.

FIG 8. LINKAGES BETWEEN CEO INFORMATION CULTURE, COMPANY CULTURE, LIFE CYCLE AND BUSINESS PERFORMANCE.

Degree of interest in information,
Relative market share, Rate of feedback ·

		high	low
Interest in external matters, Market growth rate, Risk-taking	high	B Intense interest in information Revival phase Bet Your Company culture 'STAR' products	A Casual attitude to information Development phase Tough Guy/Macho culture. 'QUESTION MARK' products
	low	C Stable interest in information Maturity phase Work Hard / Play Hard culture 'CASH COW' products	D Hostile attitude to information Decline phase Process culture 'DOGS' products

Block A represents a company with a casual attitude to information. With regard to the introduction of its products in the market, the company is at an initial stage. Its culture is Tough Guy/Macho. Its products are still 'question marks'. Marketing is essential. Investments in advertising and sales promotion are substantial. Cost and risks are high, return on investment is slow, market shares are small, but there is clear market growth. The companies are bold and confident. Investing in making the market aware of the company is a far more important issue than adapting the company to the market. There is little concern for information from outside. Certainly, the company is extrovert, but this applies mainly to the distribution of sales and advertising information.

Block B. A company with an intense interest in information has a Bet Your Company culture. There is market growth, and market shares are substantial. The company's products are 'stars'. Investments in marketing and production are heavy. Risks are high. Keen competition in the market and the fast feedback to strategies necessitate a constant active gathering and in-house dissemination of information. Investments are geared to the future. Management and the whole company become very aware of information. The CEO has a broad information profile, i.e. he makes abundant use of internal and external information. He consciously endeavours to create a social environment that will facilitate the flow of information at all levels in the company. He devotes himself to serious reading of both professional and scientific journals and appreciates expertise. He insists on long-term motivation and continuity. Internal communication is at a high level, and the CEO is well aware of the significance of current information in relation to the history and traditions of the company. Continuous efforts are made to up-date knowledge and expertise.

Block C. A company with a stable interest in information maintains a Work Hard/Play Hard culture. Its products are so-called 'cash cows'. The sales curve becomes horizontal, growth declines, and the market stabilizes. Risks are low and feedback to investment is rapid. Since there is no further market growth, companies can increase their shares only by taking over markets from each other. This, however, only rarely happens as a result of advertising. More frequently, methods such as price competition or customer service are applied. This tends to cut profit margins and compels companies to rely on volume. Small companies founder, the giants sail through. In this phase, internal functions assume great significance. All transformations of material resources must yield optimal profits. The production process is analysed with a view to initiating cost-cutting improvements. Internal control becomes prominent. The CEO becomes more and more internally oriented, often at the expense of external information. Complex bureaucracy and supervision, however, impede the flow of internal information. Employee expertise declines, and so does external know-how. The CEO assumes a bureaucratic and defensive attitude towards his environment, relying on formal, written, internal information and information acquired through extensive reading of daily newspapers. The contact network orientation gradually becomes weaker.

Block D. A company with a hostile attitude to information has a Process culture. Its products are 'dogs' and the company is in the decline phase. The characteristic features of this phase are almost identical with those of the maturity phase, only much more accentuated. Market shares are shrinking and investments decline. Risk-taking is low and feedback to possible investments is slow. The CEO becomes more internally oriented, the Board assumes a more prominent position, news is often negative and tends to be shunned by the CEO, who communicates less and less, both internally and externally.

DISCUSSION

It can be concluded that a highly developed information culture correlates positively with successful business performance and is closely connected with activities, attitudes, and business cultures initiating successful results.

The adaptation of a company's business culture, its characteristic problems as determined by the life cycle, its approach to the market and its information culture emerge as the result of internal interaction and as a rule finally reach an optimal mode within a block. This state of harmony is not easily disturbed. It has proved difficult and often impossible to implement a business or information culture typical of one block in another without modifying the other functions. To mention the extreme cases: introducing a Bet Your Company culture in the maturity phase or a Tough Guy culture in the decline phase is inconceivable. Attempts to make a CEO change his approach to information to one of intense interest in an environment hostile to that kind of culture will hardly succeed. Consequently, the supply of information to companies must be designed to comply with their prevailing culture and requirements.

A company may decide actively and deliberately to modify the current behavioural patterns within its block. To facilitate such change, all the different factors, i.e. the company's culture, approach to information, etc. must be kept flexible. If a company can move painlessly from one block to another during its life cycle, it is in a position to achieve greater success more smoothly and with a minimum of conflict. Quite often very successful companies have deliberately maintained a flexible approach in order to avoid being restricted by one particular culture at a certain stage of their life cycle. IBM is often mentioned as an example of cultural flexibility.

Obviously, an information culture characterized by intense interest creates prospects for successful business performance; in other words, there seems to be a strong connection between intellectual and material resource transformations. It is not sufficient to change one of the factors in a block unless the others have been modified to allow for the change. Consequently, intellectual resource transformations must be incorporated in strategic planning on an equal footing with the planning of material resources. This is the only way of ensuring that various future information needs are recognized in time and that the company is sufficiently prepared to meet them as well as capable of optimizing both the form and the quality of its intellectual output to provide a maximally efficient service to the material resource transformations.

REFERENCES

1   AALTO, P. and JARENKO, L-M. Tieto yrityksen voimavarana. *Ekonomia-sarja,* Weilin - Goos, 1984.
2.   BHASKER, M. *Tietohallinnan kehitys organisaatiokehityksen osana.* Helsinki Business School (Mast. thesis), Helsinki, 1985.
3.   DEAL, E. and KENNEDY, A. A. *Corporate cultures.* Reading, Mass., Addison Wesley, 1982.
4.   DESHPANDE, R. and PARASURAMAN, A. Linking corporate culture to strategic planning. *Business Horizons* **29** (3) 1986: pp. 28–37.
5.   GRFINER, L. E. Evaluation and revolution as organizations grow. *Harvard Business Review,* **50** (4) 1972: pp 37–46.
6.   LIEVEGOED, B. C. J. *The developing organization.* London, 1973.
7.   MILLER, D. and FRIESEN, P. M. A longitudinal study of corporate life cycle. *Management Science,* **30** (10) 1984: 1161–1183.
8.   PULKKINEN, K. *The premises of decision support systems.* Helsinki, Helsinki Business School Publications, 1982.

Applying the Principles of Marketing

Applying the Principles of Marketing – Introductory Notes

Blaise Cronin

Indiana University

The papers in this section are designed to show how textbook theory can be applied at grassroots level. Roy Smith (*Marketing the library*) is a born-again marketing man, one of the most successful of his kind in contemporary public librarianship. A British pragmatist, with little time for baroque conceptualisation or paradigm peddling, he describes the snowballing success of Sutton library in a language that is nothing if not accessible: 'Our relationship with the press is a busy strand of our marketing plan . . . We know where their staff drink, and their particular fancies, and we trust them to do a good reporting job. Consequently, we are rarely out of the headlines – for the nicest of reasons'. Megamarketing comes down to earth in suburban Sutton: 'The information needs of Councillors receive high priority . . . I defend myself against accusations of favouritism by asserting that *they* can influence for good or ill the distribution of resources . . . '. What works in the suburbs can also work in rural contexts, as Leah Griffiths (*Political marketing of the rural library*) observes: 'Knowing that Councilor C is a teacher and values the library's children's program, the library can emphasize those services in discussions with that individual'.

Alec Gallimore (*Marketing a public sector business library: developing a strategy*) gives a straighforward account of how a marketing plan was developed and implemented in a business library. This kind of approach cannot really be considered an optional extra when government (in the form of the Audit Commission, for example, in the UK) is increasingly conscious of the three Es (economy, efficiency and effectiveness) and keen for demonstrable evidence of satisfactory performance. Similar expectations have long been the norm in industry, though, as Zachert and Williams (*Marketing measures for information services*) recount, many special librarians experience frustration when it comes to the evaluation of marketing initiatives. Their paper provides a simple introduction to some of the techiques which could be used to assess the value and impact of a strategic marketing programme.

The development of a strategic marketing thrust for academic libraries is explored by Blunden–Ellis (*Services marketing and the academic library*) who speculates that there will a drift from the comfortable world of the professional bureaucracy to more adhocratic organisational forms. This theme is picked up in Don Schauder's investigation of staff attitudes and organisational structures (*Entrepreneurship and the academic library: insights from organization theory*), which concludes that professional bureaucracies (in case we did not already know)[2,3] do not stimulate innovation. Libraries are not the natural habitat of intrapreneurs; in Schauder's phraseology 'an uninhibited *prospector* or *promoter* strategy does not work'. In general terms, reactivism, risk–aversion, equivocation, and maintenance of the status–quo are characteristics of library personnel. Adhocracy may not be so easily achieved.

The boundary conditions and transitional steps which will change the face of research libraries are speculated upon by Anne Woodsworth and colleagues (*The model research library: planning for the future*). Their 2020 vision sees new forms of governance, campus alignments and fiscal pressures. Tomorrow's research library can be understood in terms of three interconnected activities: (a) information handling; (b) information access; (c) evaluating user needs and delivering services. Each of these is linked in turn to six key elements (focus, function, resources, staffing, knowledge/skills, results) to produce an information activity matrix. Their outlook is fresh and open–minded, if at times naively optimistic.[4,5,6,7] One point stands out: by 2020 staffing will be the major issue: 'On the whole, future research library staff will be better educated; also a greater percentage will have degrees in disciplines other than librarianship'. And 30 years from now, the skills of the 'electronic librarian' will be supplemented (if not supplanted) by 'knowbots'.[8]

Patricia Hämäläinen takes us from the world of large research libraries to a special library in ALKO Ltd, Finland's state alcohol monopoly. This is a crisply written account of how business planning and information planning should be linked. Her approach, which uses CSFs (critical success factors), seeks 'to develop and market information niche products and services for managers on the business unit level. The main task is to find the niche and service it'. Find and serve could be the motto behind AT&T's information access station, a demountable unit (small footprint; easy assembly; mobile; attractive to patrons; low cost) which is located close to customers, providing access to both local and remote materials: 'We expect service to move away from the bricks–and–mortar concept and go where our employees are . . . This will be accomplished first by access stations and ultimately by direct delivery to the workplace (desk) and home via electronic searching and document'. What Penniman (*Tomorrow's library today*) is describing is phase one of the deinstitutionalisation, or 'libraries without walls', process.

REFERENCES

1.   See the special issue of *European Journal of Marketing*, 18(2), 1984 devoted to the marketing of local authority services.

2. PETERS, T. *Thriving on chaos: handbook for a management revolution.* London: Macmillan, 1988.
3. KANTER, R. M. *The change masters: corporate entrepreneurs at work.* London: Unwin, 1985.
4. MURR, L. E. and WILLIAMS, J. B. The roles of the future library. *Library Hi-Tech*, 19, 1987, pp. 7–23.
5. WEISKEL, T. C. University libraries, integrated scholarly information systems (ISIS) and the changing character of academic research. *Library Hi–Tech*, 24, 1989, pp. 7–27.
6. ARMS, C. (ed.). *Campus networking strategies.* Bedford, MA: Digital Press, 1988.
7. BRINDLEY, L. (ed.). *The electronic campus: an information strategy.* London: British Library, 1989.
8. See for example INCE, M. A country switched on to thinking big. *Times Higher Education Supplement*, 23 March, 1991, p. 15.

Marketing the Library

Roy Smith

Central Library, London Borough of Sutton

Paper presented at the 59th Aslib Annual Conference, 'The Adaptive Information Manager', University of Sussex, 17–20 March 1987.

I have a confession to make. I wrote a paper, *The marketing of libraries,* which turned out to be a poor man's Blaise Cronin. My sin was not to ask the elementary questions of the Aslib request for my presence – namely: 'What, when, where and why?' Had I done so I would have got to 'Why' and saved myself some hours of writing and research. Why then did Aslib ask me? The answer must be that Sutton has succeeded in crashing the normally impenetrable barrier between public and special libraries. Possibly its razzmatazz, its well-oiled publicity machine – even its maverick temerity to accept that libraries are not, and probably cannot be, 'open and free', may have struck a spark in your conference organising committee's consciousness.

So, my paper will be embellished with experiences and activities from the first and only public library to have been awarded the Library Association Robinson Medal for significant advances in marketing techniques, and is annual winner of some aspect of the Library Association T C Ferries Publicity Awards – yes, it's Sutton! It is for you to accept or reject our experiences and views or, more likely, to adapt some of them to your own requirements.

In the early 1970s the senior management made the obvious but nonetheless significant decision to go all out to inform, cultivate and therefore influence the elected members of Sutton. They are the policy-makers and hold the purse strings, yet they knew very little about libraries and the arts. I formed the view that my predecessors had worked on the Will Hay principle of 'treat them rough and tell them nothing'. In contrast we have worked for 20 years at interesting and informing our Council. Every week three or four selected press releases are also relayed to members. Details of our successes are written-up in the Council newsletter. The information needs of Councillors receive high priority. Invitations to private views; publishing launches; celebrity lectures are not stinted and we always attempt to make ourselves useful. I defend myself against accusations of favouritism by asserting that *they* can influence for good or ill the distribution of resources, *they* need to know about our activities and *they* therefore deserve this kind of special attention.

Our application to the task was early rewarded when we were fortunate to get indications that Sutton Council was, at long last, seriously contemplating a new Central Library. We formulated a marketing strategy that has stood the test of time:

1) Our library is 'user centred' and is organised to this end over administrative ease. Not for us separate reference and lending libraries but *subject* libraries with teams qualified professionally, academically and by experience to promote their subjects throughout the town. That is their remit – they buy and organise stock, answer questions, give advice and do the traditional work of a librarian and information officer, but they also organise lectures, seminars and other live activities relating to their subject; they conceive and organise exhibitions; they write press releases; they compose advertising copy; they vie with each other to produce stimulating activities to persuade the community to use library facilities. They are so successful that we claim to be the busiest library system in London.

2) This kind of motivation and lively atmosphere has several spin offs. First, it attracts good staff from a wide variety of libraries. We have reversed the normal 'brain drain' from public libraries to other kinds of libraries and have recruited staff from special, academic and university libraries. Second, our staff tend to stay and develop a great loyalty to the underlying philosophy. Third, we have succeeded in developing hidden talents in a gratifying number of staff. My favourite success story in this respect was a 'put-upon' reference assistant, plodding away adequately but without much enthusiasm on the day-to-day routine of the reference desk. His real love was local history. Now he is a well regarded heritage officer, responsible for publishing over 30 works of local history; the developer of two magnificent historic houses; the originator of an air show to celebrate the 50th anniversary of Amy Johnson's famous flight and organiser of several influential local societies; the Croydon Airport Society, the Wandle Group, the Carew Manor Group, Friends of Whitehall, East Surrey Family History Society, to name but a few!

We spent time in the early days analysing what we had to do and how. The 1964 Public Libraries Act placed on us two particular duties 'to provide a comprehensive and efficient service' and to encourage use. The comprehensive and efficient service has been achieved by persuading a fairly hard-nosed Tory administration of that time (remember we are now one of the South West London 'progressive' Alliance League) of the value of libraries and securing, with their approval, a generous share of capital and revenue resources. The encouragement of use brought into play another distinctive organisation method which, starting from small beginnings, has grown to be a central tenet of policy. We decided to 'bring the library into the marketplace'. Not for us the off-putting image of a reserved academic backwater – although there are quiet places of study, and our subject departments serve our users in depth. Rather, we have embraced the decor of a good department store embellished with the exciting but paradoxical ordinariness of a street market. We actually use market stalls and our gallery display space is filled with a succession of ever-changing activities – art exhibitions, booksales, computer fairs, craft demonstrations, jazz concerts, music recitals, etc. We have let the space for the sale of encyclopaedias, gas stoves, showers, timeshares and holidays.

Our coffee shop is never empty and our book, jigsaw and souvenir sales produce a healthy profit and add to the spirit of the place. We attract people and we pride ourselves in catering for their needs. My staff are always searching for new and improved services, ranging from major activities like online services, compact discs and machines for hire, and videos, to small but still important adjuncts to the service such as umbrella loans (good advertising); the Domesday Discs; facilities for nursing mothers, etc. You can buy a ticket for a show; hire a typewriter or a market stall; consult a book or periodical or listen to records and cassettes. We are in the world of communicating in ways suiting our public.

This all needs publicising and selling, in an area where the stereotyped, introverted, intellectually superior library staff, it is alleged, will fail. Don't you believe it. My staff are brilliant at marketing. Press releases are sent out by the dozen; a 12/16 page bi-monthly *What's On,* with stories, pictures and promotional gimmicks. Talks to some kind of local society are a weekly occurrence. Posters advertising our activities are every-where. Our relationship with the press is a busy strand of our marketing plan. We are blessed with four very good series of local newspapers and we certainly cultivate them. We know where their staff drink, and their particular fancies, and we trust them to do a good reporting job. Consequently, we are rarely out of the headlines – for the nicest of reasons.

We excel ourselves from time-to-time. One of our best stunts was to so publicise *The First Writer in Residence in a Library Anywhere in the World* that the story made such august newspapers as *The Independance Journal* and the *Woga Woga Times;* the *South China Morning Post* and the *Calgary Herald.* We never decline an opportunity to blow our own trumpet – and why not? We are confident of the value of our services we wish to proselytise whenever we can.

Some of you may be thinking that what I have said is a far cry from the world of the professional librarian and information worker. If so, you are wrong and it is only by using and adapting such devices to one's own library environment that you will achieve the recognition needed from your masters, and gain the resources you require in order to achieve maximum service. Whether you are Peter Hall directing the National Theatre; a Henry Wrong running the Barbican or Roy Smith promoting Sutton Libraries you will only succeed by persuasion, flair and constant application to the business of *marketing*. It matters not that the prime activities are different. All will be applying techniques to secure resources, enjoy public recognition and thus get their facilities used. That, colleagues, is the name of the game.

Marketing a public sector business library: developing a strategy

Alec Gallimore

Manchester Public Libraries

BACKGROUND

Manchester Commercial Library is one of the main public sector business libraries in the UK. The demand for its services is high. In a typical year almost 35,000 telephone inquiries for information are answered. Many more inquiries from visitors to the library are dealt with. It is known that many telephone callers fail to get through at peak periods because of the volume of calls received. When the library was closed to visitors for one week recently, for recarpeting, staff were able to concentrate solely on telephone inquiries. The result was that 50 per cent more inquiries were dealt with, few of which seemed to be from people who would normally have visited the library.

A recent survey of users of the library[1] showed that 60 per cent of telephone inquirers were calling from outside the City of Manchester and 50 per cent of visitors to the library either lived or worked outside Manchester. The summary of the survey[2] – which was carried out by the Consultancy and Research Unit (CRUS) of Sheffield University – showed that 30 per cent of telephone inquiries were for personal rather than work-related information needs and 50 per cent of visitors to the library were seeking information for personal use rather than work-related use.

WHY MARKETING?

In the face of the demands on the service, and the heavy use by 'outsiders' who make no direct contribution to the financial support of the service – it is funded entirely by Manchester City Council – it is legitimate to ask why marketing should be undertaken at all.

Marketing is not simply a matter of promoting a service. It is an essential management activity for both public and private sector organizations. A marketing strategy must be developed in accordance with the objectives of the organization. Public libraries have become increasingly aware of the need to market their services effectively in a period when funding has been reduced, demand has increased and new services are being introduced which, in their start-up phase, can absorb a disproportionate amount of the total budget.

The Audit Commission's requirements for economy, efficiency and effectiveness in the public sector have important implications for marketing. Since the services offered by public libraries have already been paid for, the aim must be to maximize the take-up of those services to ensure the greatest cost-effectiveness. Maximum effectiveness also means serving those with the greatest need. Even without the promptings of the Audit Commission it should be a fundamental management objective to continue to improve existing services.

In order to meet its objectives a public sector organization must convert its resources into an offering relevant to its market. Maximum take-up is encouraged by planned promotional activities.

As far as public sector business libraries are concerned, the main reasons for having a marketing strategy are:

1 The market is constantly changing. There are changes taking place in business locations and personnel, in student populations and in the population generally. Many users are only occasional users.
2 The potential market for business information is very large and has only been partially tapped by public sector business libraries.
3 There is a need to inform existing and potential users of the totality of information available. Also many new sources of information are becoming available. Business information is probably growing faster than information in any other sector.
4 Competition for attention in the marketplace is high. Public sector services may be overlooked by potential users.

The main aim in marketing the services of Manchester Commercial Library is to concentrate the effort on the individuals and organizations within the City of Manchester in order to attract more of those who do not yet use the service. The intention is to increase the percentage of Manchester users and to squeeze out some of the non-Manchester users in the process. Any marketing effort would need to be low-key, to limit the response to what could be coped with. It should persuade more people to visit the library, where they can help themselves to information, rather than encourage more telephone inquiries which would require more staff to deal with them.

MARKETING MODEL

Marketing is not simply a matter of promoting the service to potential users, it is part of the management process. In practice, marketing activities tend to develop in an unplanned way – a little bit of PR here, a user survey there, the introduction of a new service because everyone else is doing it. If resources are to be fully exploited and the needs of legitimate users of the service met in the most effective way then a proper strategy must be developed.

A firm rationale is needed upon which the strategy can be based. The following model of the marketing process owes much to the rational decision-making model proposed by Simon[3] for applications in policy planning and strategic management. Kotler[4] proposed an organizational analysis in preparation for the development of a marketing strategy. There were three elements in this: mission analysis, market analysis and resource analysis. These elements fit easily into the first stages of the model, which has a total of seven stages:

1 *Mission analysis* Analysing objectives.
2 *Market analysis* Defining the market.
3 *Market analysis* Assessing the needs of users and potential users.
4 *Resource analysis/offering mix* Providing the resources and services to meet those needs.
5 *Promotion* Informing users and potential users about the offering.
6 *Evaluation* Measuring the degree of take-up of the offering.
7 *Feedback* Modifying the strategy in the light of evaluation.

This model is most suitable for starting up a new service or radically restructuring an old one. For a mature, established service, some modification may be needed, although it is legitimate to question established services from time to time. Some of the offerings may be well established but under-promoted. The aim should be to maximize the take-up of services to ensure the greatest degree of cost-effectiveness.

The stages outlined in the model can be examined in turn in relation to Manchester Commercial Library.

MISSION ANALYSIS

Kotler's list of questions is useful in analysing the objectives of the service.

What business are we in?

This is the most important question. In the case of Manchester Commercial Library, it is to make a positive contribution to the local economy and to the needs of people in Manchester by providing and promoting the use of information about business and commerce. The fact that it is a free public service casts it in a particular mould and presents a particular image to potential users.

Who are the customers?

Individuals and organizations in the City of Manchester. Since the service is funded entirely by Manchester City Council the primary market must be confined to the local authority area. However, it is known that significant numbers of users come from outside the City of Manchester. This has important implications for the marketing strategy.

Which needs are we trying to satisfy?

A wide variety of needs were identified in user surveys in 1972[5] and 1986.[2] Details of these are given in other parts of this article.

Which segments do we want to focus on?

Different user groups have been identified in the 1972 and 1986 surveys, during research into the use of statistical publications,[6] from contact with groups of users touring the library and from frequent contact with users by staff on the inquiry desk. It would be impossible to focus on every identifiable segment. Choices have to be made when the resources available for marketing are limited.

Among the groups singled out recently for targeting have been ethnic groups, small firms and trade unionists, all of which represent potential users in market segments which have been untapped in the past.

Who are the main competitors?

This is an important question for a public sector organization. There is little point in trying to duplicate services already provided elsewhere, by organizations which have far more resources available for marketing. However, other information services often require a more rigid qualification from users than public libraries, and this may indicate a gap in the market.

There is no publicly available service in the Manchester area with the range and depth of resources offered by Manchester Commercial Library. Within the City of Manchester there are other information services which cover different market segments, such as the Small Firms Service. In fact, Manchester is a regional centre for such services and there are many of them. These services generally have different offering mixes from Manchester Commercial Library. Many, for example, provide business advice and counselling dealing mainly with questions connected with finance. Some information services undertake research for a fee but do not have access to the range of published materials which is maintained by Manchester Commercial Library.

Specialist government bodies help firms with grants and advice and may provide information occasionally. Business clubs provide contact points for individuals, thus encouraging informal information transfer. Specialist firms such as credit agencies have their exclusive information resources to which they offer access, at a price. Educational institutions with business information resources, such as Manchester Business School, have their own well-defined markets. Although there may be some overlap in information provision between Manchester Commercial Library and other services, there is little competition in the type of service offered.

The presence of other organizations, the images they have of themselves and the way they market their services do have implications for the way in which Manchester Commercial Library markets its own services. This is especially true in an area such as information for small firms which other organizations may feel is exclusively their own territory.

What advantages do we offer the target market?

1　The service is free of charge.
2　There are no restrictions on who can use the service and no qualification is required to use the service, i.e. there are no formalities.
3　Most information is on open access and users are encouraged to help themselves to it.
4　The wide range and depth of resources means that most users can find what they require in one place. Local users do not need to travel to London to find important business information.
5　Information can be supplied on the spot for telephone inquirers.
6　There are facilities in the library for study and research.
7　The library is conveniently situated in the city centre.
8　The library either supplies information directly or guides users to sources which they can consult themselves on the premises. The service is thus an information resource, not an agency for referral, as many business advisory or counselling services are.

It is important that any marketing effort should avoid creating unrealistic expectations in the minds of users by clearly indicating that the service is not a business advisory or counselling service but is an information resource centre.

What are the objectives?

Although parts of the marketing strategy might be concerned with short-term goals – e.g. a promotion campaign – the main objectives are longer term. These are:

1　To improve awareness of Manchester Commercial Library and of the value of business information to people and organizations in Manchester.
2　To increase the number of users who visit the library to find information for themselves.
3　To promote more effectively those resources in the library which have potential for greater use.
4　To concentrate on specific groups of potential users who, at present, make little or no use of the library.

MARKET ANALYSIS

Trends (environmental analysis)

Even in an established service provision must be made for the changing needs of users. A comparison of the 1972 and 1986 surveys showed several changes in the composition of users over time, reflecting changes in the local economy. It was found, for example, that the proportion of users from manufacturing firms had declined from 42 per cent in 1972 to 14 per cent in 1986, whereas the proportion of users from financial companies had increased from 10 to 20 per cent. Such changes have implications for stock selection and for marketing.

Developments in industry, commerce and the economy must be constantly monitored so that future needs can be predicted. Provision can then be made in anticipation of future demands. Such provision may, in turn, need to be promoted to bring it to the attention of potential users. A recent example of this was the introduction of the Data Protection Register.

Primary market

The primary market for Manchester Commercial Library is defined largely in terms of geography since the service is financed by the local authority. The library has no justification for providing a service nationally or regionally although the 1986 survey showed that telephone inquiries were regularly received from as far away as Edinburgh, Plymouth, Newcastle, Blackpool, Birmingham, Hull and Wrexham. The marketing effort should be restricted to the City of Manchester to encourage as many people as possible in the area to use the service.

As part of the public library service in Manchester, the Commercial Library has a statutory duty to provide for the information needs of the general public, not just for one particular group. To some extent the specialized nature of business information restricts its appeal but, as has been pointed out, there are many needs besides those of private companies which can be met by business information.

Market Segmentation

The major market segments are companies, both large and medium sized – and the individuals who work for them – engaged in a variety of activities including manufacturing, finance, services and distribution. There are also many individuals who use the library for personal rather than work-related reasons. These include people wanting consumer information, small investors, those who are preparing for job interviews, and people using maps and timetables. Other users identified are local and national government departments, journalists, consultants, marketing managers, other information and advice agencies, students, lecturers and researchers.

This variety of types of users who form separate market segments presents an interesting marketing challenge.

Needs assessment

The most valuable form of market research is that conducted among non-users of the service in order to find out the needs of potential users. Unfortunatelv this type of research is expensive and time consuming to carry out. It is best done by professional market researchers or researchers from universities, polytechnics, etc.

It is possible to glean information from published research which has application to a local service. Several useful reports have been published in recent years, notably by Backhouse on information for trade unionists,[7] and by Capital Planning Information on information for small firms[8] and for retailers.[9]

Needs which are expressed as demands in the library can be uncovered by surveys of users and by monitoring inquiries. Although these do not provide a complete picture of needs they can be a valuable indicator.

Local demographic data are of limited use to a specialized business information service. Data on local companies and industries are often only available in forms which do not lend themselves to easy analysis. Yellow pages and local directories may be suitable for constructing mailing lists, but they do not give enough information to provide an analysis of local industry. Recently, an in-house database has been established in Manchester Commercial Library containing details of over 7,500 local companies. Companies can be listed by size or by SIC code and, although the database was established for the benefit of library users, it should be possible to use it as a marketing tool for the library in future.

In assessing needs it is useful to keep an ear to the ground for suggestions from users, though there are dangers in relying too much upon subjective demands for specialized items with only limited appeal to other users. The business information needs of different segments show considerable overlap. The same information can be used by different people. What is different is the way the information is perceived and used. The promotion of business information to different market segments must take these differences into account.

Awareness

The wide range of business publications and electronic databases presents a problem for the user and also for the librarian who is marketing the service. Even regular users of a library service may only be aware of a few well-known sources of information in their own field of interest. First-time users may be aware only of an information need without knowing the type of information source which can help them. Potential users (i.e. non-users with a need for business information) may not be aware of the existence of the library, may not be aware that an answer to their problem exists in published form, or may not even be aware that problems which manifest themselves in their jobs or private lives are information problems. Small firms, especially one-man outfits in which an individual is struggling to deal with all the different problems of running a business, often have no time to search for information even if it is realized that information is needed. Part of the marketing effort should be to raise awareness of the usefulness of business information.

Some segments of the market have a high degree of awareness, usually gained after years of experience in seeking and using information. These tend to be the larger firms, and individuals in the information or education world, such as journalists, advertising agents, consultants, lecturers and researchers. Part of the marketing effort should be devoted to raising the level of awareness of business information among those market segments which, for various reasons, are only partially aware, or are unaware, of the advantages they might obtain from using business information. If these segments can be reached then the marketing effort will be most effective because there will be a tendency for them to associate useful information with Manchester Commercial Library rather than with other agencies.

Among the segments which have been identified for awareness marketing are trade unionists, small firms and ethnic minority businesses. Different marketing techniques are obviously necessary if these different market segments are to be reached.

Some regular users only use a narrow range of information in the library, such as company information, and may not be aware of other sources or of other areas of business information which could also be of use to them. Part of the marketing effort, therefore, should be to increase awareness of the range of information sources which are being offered. This applies to the whole of the offering mix. Visitors leaving the Commercial Library were asked in the CRUS survey whether they knew that the library operated a telephone inquiry service. Less than 40 per cent said that they were aware of it.

Image

This is probably one of the most important aspects of marketing and one of the most difficult to deal with. There are many factors affecting the image of Manchester Commercial Library. For instance, the library is funded by Manchester City Council and is therefore affected by the image which the council has among local organizations.

The library is part of the public library service which generates its own image in the minds of users and non-users. The library does not make a charge for its services, which is unusual for an organization working in a business environment. The location of the library and the type of building it is situated in affect the preconceptions of those who have not yet visited the library. The internal design of the library, its fixtures and fittings and the overall arrangement of stock generate an image in the minds of visitors. The guiding and display of stock, the staff at the inquiry desk, the atmosphere within the library also contribute to its image.

Different types of users form different preconceptions of the library and these images may prevent take-up by some groups. Trade unionists, for example, may feel uncomfortable about using a library which they believe to be exclusively for businessmen. Some companies place little value upon services which are provided free of charge or which are provided by a council with which they have no political sympathies. The individual who simply wants an address of a company in order to make a consumer complaint may feel intimidated about using a service which is quite different from the local lending library.

It is unlikely that the adoption and promotion of one single image would satisfy all the different people who use the service. Different images may have to be projected to different market segments in order to encourage take-up of the library's offerings. Where the same type of information may serve different segments, it may have to be packaged and promoted differently to present the images which will encourage greatest take-up.

User satisfaction

The CRUS survey attempted to evaluate user satisfaction by asking departing users to rate the stock of Manchester Commercial Library on a scale ranging from poor to excellent. Some 90 per cent of those interviewed rated the stock from good to excellent and none thought that it was poor. In response to a further question, 80 per cent claimed to have found what they wanted during their visit and a further 10 per cent found part of what they wanted. Users were also asked to rate the importance of the service to them. Altogether 90 per cent regarded the service as important. In fact, 17 per cent said that it was vital and another 40 per cent said that it was very important.

These results indicate that Manchester Commercial Library is providing a service which meets most of the needs of current users and is an important resource in the City of Manchester. Most users have a positive image of the service. This suggests that the main marketing effort should be less concerned with trying to maintain the existing base but should concentrate on making non-users aware of the value the service could have to them.

RESOURCE ANALYSIS

Offering mix

The Appendix shows a breakdown of the offering mix of Manchester Commercial Library. Business information does not have precise boundaries. When the library first opened in 1919, the official opening programme defined its aim as 'the provision of any and every kind of commercial information which may be obtained from printed matter, and such additional information as it may be possible to procure from public or private sources'. There are virtually no limits to the type of information required to meet the needs of users of the library. The stock thus includes directories, company information, market research reports, statistics, economic information, periodicals and newspapers, maps and travel information, EC legislation, export/import regulations, and trade names.

Online access to business databases is now an essential element in the provision of business information. As already mentioned Manchester Commercial Library has also developed its own internal database on local companies to fill an important gap in provision. The marketing of these services presents a separate challenge.

The only constant factor among these varied sources of information, and the one thing which limits the scope of the Commercial Library and prevents it from becoming an all-devouring cuckoo in the public library nest, is that the information must be current. Only the latest editions of directories, up-to-the-minute news and the most recent statistics are required. Keeping stock up to date requires a continuing organizational effort and the strength of the service lies in successful stock maintenance. Without up-to-date materials the service would not be viable.

The wide range of publications listed is of interest to a range of people and organizations besides those in business. Statistical publications, for example, as a recent in-house survey has shown,[6] are used by schoolchildren, students, journalists, importers, local councillors, consultants, trade unionists, marketing managers and psychologists.

An important part of the offering mix is facilities for study and research. Seating was increased by 20 per cent recently during refurbishment of the library. A separate browsing area for periodicals was established, with easy chairs, to take some of the pressure away from crowded tables.

An on-the-spot photocopying service is crucial for visitors who are in a hurry and wish to obtain information in the shortest possible time and with the minimum of effort.

The telephone inquiry service caters for those who are unable to visit the library. No business information service would have credibility in the business world if it did not use the telephone, one of its main channels of communication. Although it is staff-intensive and expensive to operate, it provides information in the most direct way and at the same time it effectively promotes the service.

Talks to groups of users and potential users and tours of the library are given both to instruct users and to raise their level of awareness of the service. Such activities have proved very effective, e.g. as part of short courses for people starting up in business.

Facilitation

Facilitation is the establishment of an organized system to enable take-up of services. One important aspect of this is the location of the library. Manchester Commercial Library benefits from its easily accessible position close to the commercial centre of the city. Opening hours must match the requirements of users. The library is open during business hours (from 9 to 6 o'clock, Monday to Friday) and from 9 to 5 o'clock on Saturday for the benefit of those who cannot visit the library during the working week.

Telephones are an essential part of the facilitation system. The library has five outside telephone lines, one of which is dedicated to the small firms liaison officer. A telex machine is also available. The possibility of using electronic mail has been considered but it is unlikely that this would facilitate many more users in Manchester.

The organization of the library is important if people who are in a hurry are to find the information they want quickly and efficiently. With this in mind, the library was recently reorganized with a plan of the room placed at the entrance, and more visual guiding and instructions for finding different types of information prominently displayed. Extra shelving was put into the library during refurbishment so that more material could be put on open access. The speed and ease with which people can find the information they want helps to create an efficient, business-like atmosphere which gives a positive image of the service to users.

Staff guidance and help is still an essential requirement if the library is to be exploited effectively. Therefore, the inquiry desk is permanently manned by training and willing staff during all the hours that the library is open.

PROMOTION

Constraints

The promotion of Manchester Commercial Library is subject to a number of constraints, as has been mentioned earlier. These help to define the context in which the promotional effort can take place and the form it can take.

  1 *Demand* Existing demand for the service is high and the telephone inquiry service is subject, at peak periods, to over-demand. Marketing must, therefore, be directed in such a way as to encourage users to visit the library and help themselves to information, preferably without adding to the pressure on the inquiry desk. This is why great attention was given to reorganizing and refurbishing the library, improving the layout and providing better guiding and instructions, before any promotion was undertaken.

  2 *Geography* It has already been mentioned that many users, particularly of the telephone inquiry service, are from outside the City

of Manchester and make no contribution to the running costs of the service. The library does have a duty to provide a service for people who live, work or study in Manchester but this should not be extended further afield. Broadcasting a message to Greater Manchester and beyond would be detrimental to the library's objective. Promotion should, therefore, be restricted to Manchester alone.

3 *Time* Promotion can be a time-consuming activity with uncertain results. Time must be found, but there are shifting priorities when one is acting both as a business information specialist and as a library manager. Lack of expertise in some marketing activities means that learning must precede practice and this lengthens the time taken for each activity.

4 *Money* Few local authorities, especially those which have been forced in recent years to trim budgets and cut back services, are prepared to devote the same proportion of their budgets to marketing as similar sized organizations in the private sector. Promotion budgets in public libraries are small and quickly exhausted. Cheap alternatives to standard methods of publicity and promotion have to be found.

5 *Diversity* The wide range of information available in Manchester Commercial Library and the different identifiable groups of users present a problem.

It is not possible to promote all the information available to everyone who might use it. The aim of any marketing strategy should be to achieve maximum return for the effort employed. This can be done in a number of ways. First, information which has a wide appeal, such as company information, can be promoted without reference to particular groups of users. Second, information which has potential for greater use if awareness is increased can be promoted separately, e.g. business travel and tourist information. Third, a service or type of information which has been introduced for the first time can be highlighted to make more people aware of it, e.g. a collection of market research reports. Fourth, an effort should be made to target identifiable groups of potential users to encourage more of them to use the library, e.g. small firms.

Care must be taken to ensure that these diverse activities are fully integrated into an overall marketing strategy so that neither users nor staff are confused by what might seem to be, at times, divergent aims. A balance must also be achieved so that one aspect of the service does not become over-promoted with respect to others to produce a demand which occupies staff or resources to the detriment of other activities.

Activities

A wide range of activities has been undertaken to promote Manchester

Commercial Library to the targeted individuals and organizations.

Improving awareness

Contact has been made with the local press which has resulted in articles about the library services appearing in the *Manchester Evening News* and the *Manchester Magazine*. Contact with bodies such as the Greater Manchester Economic Development Corporation resulted in the inclusion of details of the library service in their promotional packs.

The development of an extensive network of contacts among organizations in Manchester is essential for the successful promotion of the service. The advantages are free publicity, distribution of promotional leaflets and the display of posters, feedback and suggestions about the service, and the development of a higher profile in the community for the library service. Leaflets and posters have been displayed by, for example, the Northern Stock Exchange, the Small Firms Service, the Department of Trade and Industry North West and the Manchester Chamber of Commerce. Selective mailings have been made to relevant organizations in Manchester, which is a regional centre for many large commercial organizations, government bodies, foreign consulates and trade centres. All the leaflets were designed in the same house style with a recognizable image on the front which incorporates the distinctive Central Library building, a major architectural landmark in the city centre.

Promotional talks have been a useful means of reaching potential users directly, providing the opportunity for a more detailed description of the advantages of using the library and encouraging dialogue with the public. When combined with tours of the library these talks can be very productive, allowing individual users to discuss their particular information needs. Such talks have been arranged, for example, for local businessmen's clubs, Small Firms Service counsellors and groups of people attending business start-up courses.

Increasing self-help use of the library

Improvements in guiding and layout of the library have already been mentioned, as has the aim of putting more material on open access. The eventual aim is to put all materials on open access and to provide more detailed instructions for problem marterials. It is hoped that further progress will be made in this direction when the new Central Library security system becomes operational.

Some of the leaflets produced for promotional purposes serve also as guides to finding information, such as those on company information and market research information. Displays have been placed in each separate information section in the library with search strategies outlined for directories, company information, statistics, maps, etc.

Promoting specific types of information

In any library with large information resources it is inevitable that some will be relatively under-used, overlooked or used only occasionally. Where this information has potential for greater exploitation it should be given more promotion. Travel and tourist information, for example, although used by some visitors for business purposes and by others incidentally to their main purpose of using other types of business information, obviously has a wider appeal. A leaflet has been designed about this type of material and distributed to, for example, all the travel agencies in Manchester, to the geography departments of local colleges and the university and to local tourist offices.

Targeting: ethnic groups

Leaflets have been produced, in conjunction with ethnic services librarians from the district libraries, in Chinese, Urdu, Gujarati and Bengali, the main ethnic languages in Manchester. These have been distributed to ethnic businesses and organizations in Manchester by ethnic services librarians on behalf of the Commercial Library. A talk at a recent Asian Business Seminar at Manchester Town Hall drew positive responses from the audience, most of whom were unaware of the extensive holdings of overseas trade directories or of the information on exporting and importing. Generally speaking, the ethnic services librarians are likely to be more successful in promoting the services of the Commercial Library to opinion leaders in the different ethnic communities than staff in the Commercial Library who have less knowledge of those communities and less time to develop contacts.

Targeting: trade unionists

A leaflet on information for trade unionists was produced in an attempt to outline the usefulness of business information from the trade union point of view. Trade union liaison officers from the City Council have helped in the distribution of the leaflet. The leaflet was featured in a local trade union magazine with a circlation of over 10,000, and it has been sent to local trade union offices and colleges which offer trade union studies courses. Some students from these courses have been given a tour of the library as a follow-up to this. A small exhibition has been mounted at local trade union weeks and leaflets given to visitors to the seminars, etc.

The problem of reaching this particular group is not likely to be surmounted by leaflets alone. There is an obvious need for coaching in the use of the library and of business information. A proposal for a trade union liaison officer to be based in Manchester Commercial Library was accepted in principle by the Leisure Services Committee but still awaits funding.

Targeting: small firms

A more concerted effort has been made to promote the service to small firms in the City of Manchester. A small firms liaison officer was appointed in 1984 to make personal calls on small firms in the inner-city areas of Manchester, with two main aims: to try to raise the awareness of small firms of the information available to them which could help them in their business, and to inform them about the free services of Manchester Commercial Library which, as ratepayers, they are helping to fund. The project was funded by the Department of the Environment for three years but at a lower level than originally envisaged, and was then taken over by Manchester City Council for a further year.

During the project the small firms liaison officer developed extensive contacts with all organizations concerned with small firms in Manchester. Leaflets and posters were produced and distributed. About 800 firms were visited in the second phase of the project and an exclusive telephone number was set aside for priority inquiries from those firms.

Concentration on very small firms, often one-man outfits in inner-city areas, has revealed a range of information problems which the library is only partially capable of dealing with. Research on behalf of small firms can be very staff-intensive and would command far more resources than the library is able to commit at present. In marketing the library to small firms care has been taken to avoid raising expectations unrealistically by concentrating on the role of the library as a business information resource and not an advice and counselling agency.

The targeting of specific groups is best done by specialists who have a more detailed knowledge of those groups, can move freely within them and are aware of their needs.

EVALUATION AND FEEDBACK

Unlike an organization in the private sector which can measure the success of a marketing strategy in terms of increased sales and profits, a library service has no simple method of evaluating its marketing efforts.

Numbers of inquiries dealt with by the library are monitored both for telephone callers and visitors to the library. However, when the service is already working to meet a high level of demand, a plateau is reached which represents the limit to the number of inquiries which a fixed number of staff can cope with. New inquiries generated by promoting the service are unlikely to show up clearly during regular monitoring. Overall, however, inquiries have continued to grow every year for the last five years. Other services, such as the supply of photocopies to readers, also show steady growth.

A new service can be monitored for take-up. This was done recently when a comprehensive collection of market research reports was established and a leaflet and posters were used to promote awareness of this new facility. The results of the monitoring provided full justification for the introduction of the collection, which undoubtedly helped to generate more use of the library and attracted new users who had a specific need for this type of information.

Detailed records of visitors to the library have never been kept, although occasional samples have been taken and estimates made. It is apparent that overall use of the library has increased in the last couple of years. Although seating and study space was increased by 20 per cent during refurbishment, this still does not meet the demand at peak periods.

Promotional activities directed at non-users is bound to increase awareness of Manchester Commercial Library but there is no guarantee of subsequent take-up of the offerings. Some indications of take-up due to marketing might be obtained in future by asking users where and how they first heard of the library's services. Surveys of users will be undertaken at intervals in order to see if any further changes have occurred in users and user needs. In particular, evicence will be sought for an increase in the proportion of Manchester-based users who make use of the telephone inquiry service since marketing has been confined entirely within Manchester.

Any increase in the use of the service by targeted groups would be difficult to measure against a background of existing high demand. Some indications may be noticed by staff on the inquiry desk, e.g. an increase in demand for information of interest to trade unionists, but this is not always obvious. Requests for tours of the library are often an indication that awareness has been stimulated by promotional activities. Reports of referrals from outside bodies with which publicity materials have been lodged also indicate an increase in awareness.

One area where a detailed evaluation can be made is that of small firms. Detailed records were kept of all those visited and a follow-up sample telephone survey has been planned to find out how many have subsequently used the service. It was found during the visits that about 31 per cent had been aware of the existence of the service and 25 per cent had already used it. Most of the users were firms close to the city centre. This, together with other information gleaned, leads to the conclusion that those in small firms are unlikely to visit the library unless they are in close proximity to it. The greatest need is for market and financial information, but direct assistance in the research and gathering of such information is needed. This is a need which cannot be met at present with existing staffing levels but it has prompted discussions with other City Council departments with a view to a joint effort in this area.

Feedback from users during the marketing effort provides useful information for tailoring the service more closely to user needs. The marketing strategy can in turn be modified and refined in the light of this information.

CONCLUSION

Marketing is not a short-term exercise but is part of the continuous management of the library service. The aim of the marketing strategy is not to seek short-term increases in use but to develop and consolidate a sound user base, by assessing the needs of users, providing for those needs and ensuring that all potential users are aware of the services on offer.

The marketing strategy model developed here has proved useful for clarifying the marketing effort in Manchester Commercial Library but it could be applied to any library service.

APPENDIX: MANCHESTER COMMERCIAL LIBRARY – OFFERING MIX

Materials for information and research

Directories: UK and foreign, trade, telephone, telex, Fax
Company information
Market research, statistics
Product/industry/economy news and background
Periodicals and newspapers plus indexes/abstracts
Maps and travel information
EC legislation
Export/import information
Trade names and marks
Local and tourist information
Electoral registers

Accommodation

Study facilities: tables and chairs, map tables, etc.

Reprographic facilities

Photocopying
Copying from microform

Advice/expertise

Telephone inquiries
Postal inquiries
Visitor inquiries
Library instruction
Instructional displays and information sheets
Small firms liaison officer

Electronic services

Online information retrieval access to 300 databases
In-house database of local companies

REFERENCES

1   Gallimore, A, and Owen, D. Surveys of the use of the Commercial Library. Report prepared for Leisure Services Committee, Manchester City Council, 10 December 1986.

2   Roberts, N, Clarke, D, Craghill, D, and White, D. *Uses and users of public sector business libraries*. CRUS Occasional Paper no. 14. Consultancy and Research Unit, Department of Information Studies, University of Sheffield, 1987.

3   Simon, H A. *Administrative Behavior*, 3rd edn. Free Press, 1976.

4   Kotler, Philip. Strageties for introducing marketing into nonprofit organizations *Journal of Marketing*, January 1979, **43**, 37–44.

5   Osborn, A, and Smythy, L. Public use of business and commercial information: a pilot study at the Commercial Library, Manchester City Library. *Aslib Proceedings*, 1973, **25** (7), 243–51.

6   Gallimore, A. The use of statistical publications in the public library. *Statistical News*, November 1985 (71), 16–18.

7   Backhouse, Roger. *Information services for trade unionists*. BLR&D Report no. 5695. Elm Publications, 1982.

8   Capital Planning Information. *Information and the small manufacturing firm*. BLR&D Report No. 5729. British Library, 1982.

9   Capital Planning Information. *Retailing and services: information for the small firm*. Capital Planning Information, 1985.

Political Marketing of the Rural Library

Leah Griffith

Cornelius Public Library, Oregon

WANTED: POLITICIAN/LIBRARIAN FOR SMALL, RURAL PUBLIC LIBRARY.

While a want ad as direct as this will probably never appear in the library press or on a job-line, the realization is growing that a library, even a small one, requires a director with political savvy and advertisements are appearing for candidates with that ability. The library director plays a key role in the political process and libraries, regardless of size, are a part of that process. The players and stakes may vary depending on the population and form of governance, but any publicly supported library will have some type of governing board or individual with whom it works as well as a community it is mandated to serve. The experienced librarian will recognize the necessity of being an active participant in the political arena, but those new to the managing of small or rural libraries may be surprised by the extent of political involvement. And while it may seem overwhelming for the director of a small rural library to be a cataloger, circulation clerk, storyteller, bookkeeper, janitor, *and* politician, it is possible.

MARKETING IN THE POLITICAL ARENA

One activity that can assist the small/rural librarian is marketing. While usually associated with the selling of a product, marketing can be very effective in the political arena. Many marketing techniques, as well as the philosophy of marketing, can be incorporated into everyday library activities. For the director of a small/rural library, acquiring a marketing orientation can make participation in the political scene easier and can benefit the library.

Marketing goes far beyond the posters and commercials that many people associate with it. Public relations is, in fact, only one segment of the overall marketing process. The marketing concept is based on the principle of an exchange occurring between two parties. Each group that is identified has something that the other wants, and the purpose of marketing is to facilitate an exchange of these values. This can be done by developing a marketing plan, whose four key components are the following:

Analysis is the step that sets marketing apart from public relations. The target group is studied to determine its needs and how they can best be met. Methods can include conducting a survey, interviewing individuals, studying demographic statistics, and other research activities. With this process the exchange relationship is determined, and a coordinated marketing effort is developed.

Planning involves setting the objectives for the marketing effort. The objectives should be challenging but attainable. The activities, the participants, and the time frame of the marketing plan are also determined at this stage. The result is a detailed description of what will actually be done, when, and by whom.

Implementation of the marketing plan is next. As the plan is carried out, adjustments will most likely need to be made, but the overall objectives should always be kept in mind whenever modifications are necessary.

Evaluation is the final, and usually the most forgotten, component in the marketing plan, but it is vital to future marketing efforts. By evaluating the plan, the most effective activities can be determined and the reasons for failures pinpointed. Without this step, mistakes could be repeated in future marketing endeavours, and other more productive activities could be forgotten. Evaluation should occur throughout the length of the plan as well as at the end.

TARGETS

In order for marketing to succeed, effective communication between the library and its targets must occur. A marketing plan will include methods allowing the library director to determine the message about the library that goes out into the community, whether it is a written press release, a speech to the Booster Club, or a new sign at the library's entrance.

A formalized process is very valid and should be utilized when seeking a specific objective such as passing a budget or getting a library built. But the reality of operating a small/rural library can mean that procedures have to be modified to fit the time and budget that is available. When the library director is the 1 of a 1.8 FTE staff, there is little time to develop a full-fledged marketing plan. But even with time constraints, many of the techniques of marketing can be incorporated into everyday activities and philosophies. Analysis is of prime importance as it enables one to determine the library's targets and their needs. The concept of satisfying the targets' needs in exchange for support of one kind or another forms the backbone of a marketing orientation. This orientation can be of valuable assistance in the political process and while it does not replace carrying out a complete marketing plan, for those with limited time and resources, it sometimes is all that can be done. Identifying targets is the first step in any marketing effort, whether formal or informal. In the political arena three groups that are appropriate targets are those that make the decisions (governing boards), control the funds (taxpayers/ voters), and compete with the library (other local government units).

Decision makers

The primary target for the library's political marketing effort is the decision makers: the groups, such as governing boards, city councils, county commissions, and the individuals, such as mayors, city managers, and board chairs, who have control over the funding, policies, and activities of the library. They are faced with providing for mandated services, such as police and fire, at the same time the taxpayer is protesting tax increases. A smaller community can also be very hard hit by the closure of a single plant or factory, or when the taxes collected are much lower than anticipated. The library must be able to present its case to the decision makers in such a way as to maintain or increase its support in these times.

In marketing to governing boards, they should be approached like any other target group; thus, the first step is to analyze them, both as a group and as individuals. A good way to start is by reading campaign literature that is disseminated during elections to find out why board members ran for office and what promises they may have made. If they were elected on a platform of cutting government services, this will greatly affect how they treat the library and what approach the librarian should take with them. Local newspapers can provide current information about the politicians and their concerns; many times a small-town newspaper will even run editorials written by local officials.

Another source of information on incumbent officials is the minutes of past meetings, which can provide insights into how they have treated the library in the past. Another value of examining these records is that they can provide a clue as to the alliances that exist among the members. It may be that Councilor A always votes with Councilor B on issues concerning the library, police, and public works, but almost never on issues concerning land use planning or social services. The librarian may only need to convince Councilor B of the value of the library's proposal, as Councilor A will usually follow B's lead.

One should also gather personal information about these people. Their occupation may affect their method of governing. Are they managers in their jobs or blue-collar workers? If being on the city council is their only managerial position, they may react differently to situations than would others with more managerial experience. Their educational level can also affect how they perceive the library and its role in the community. The librarian should also be aware whether the decision makers or their families are library users. No special treatment should necessarily be given, but it is good to know that the parent with the five children at storytime is married to a city councilor.

If the decision makers have been researched thoroughly, one should be able to determine their needs and be able to deal with them more productively. Knowing that Councilor C is a teacher and values the library's children's program, the librarian can emphasize those services in discussions with that individual. On the other hand, the councilor who sees children's services as simply a baby-sitting service will need a different approach. When governing board members are polarized, the librarian will need to be aware of those opposing values and work to keep both parties content while furthering the cause of the library.

Most governing groups prefer for things to remain noncontroversial. This cannot always be controlled, but if the librarian can handle difficult situations effectively and buffer the governing authority from controversy, it will usually be appreciated. Another concern of governing boards is the quality of fiscal management under their authority. They have a responsibility to the taxpayers to see that tax monies are appropriately and wisely spent, and if the librarian displays competence as a manager, their job is made easier. Most governing authorities feel the need to build a good image in the community; the librarian can provide public relations opportunities such as giving board members appropriate credit for special programs or activities and inviting them to cut ribbons or to participate in other library events.

The beginner to the political arena may believe that all decisions are made during public meetings, but in reality many decisions are made behind the scenes. During discussions in the hallway or over coffee is when councilors or board members are really making up their mind. The questions that are asked during a coffee break may very likely be ones that wouldn't be voiced during an open meeting. The answer given informally might be the one thing that convinces the board member or councilor of the merit of the library's proposal. This personal touch is especially important in a small community where informal contact is part of everyday life.

Governing authorities should not be expected to understand how libraries operate, just as they do not need to understand how the sewer treatment facility operates in order to fulfill their role as policy makers. The librarian is responsible for providing them with the information they need to make decisions. And while this may require answering a few inane, as well as basic, questions, the answer delivered with tact may be just what is needed to get the library's proposal approved.

There is another kind of decision maker, however, and that is the person who, while not formally an office holder, has very real influence over those who are. Edward Howard, in *Local Power and the Community Library*, defines these people as interorganizational leaders.[1] They are leaders in a variety of organizations in a community and have a wide-ranging sphere of influence. It is important to identify these people and work towards developing a good relationship between them and the library.

F

Taxpayers

In addition to the decision makers, one of the most important target groups that can affect a library is the taxpayer/voter. This group ultimately provides the funding for almost all public libraries. It is not enough to think of taxpayers only at elections; one must be aware of and concerned with this market continuously. Librarians should remember that usually only a small segment of the taxpayer/voter market are library users; a large number of the people who financially support the library never cross its threshold.

Assessing the needs of the taxpayer/voter target is vital. A survey of the constituents of the library to reveal their opinions, what they want from a library, and how much they are willing to pay for it should be conducted regularly. Even the small library with limited funds should survey the needs of its constituents. A local college may be a good source for assistance with this project; many business classes would welcome the chance to conduct a marketing survey.

Other departments

A third target for a library's marketing effort is the other departments in the governmental organization, such as the police department or public works. If the library is asking for money that comes from a common source these departments are the competition. Even if the library is not competing for funds, it is competing for the attention and favorable decisions of the same decision makers. This does not mean one should establish a competitive relationship with these departments; in fact, librarians who work in concert with the other chief executives will probably achieve their objectives sooner than those who adopt an adversarial attitude. Interest should be shown in the broader issues that affect the entire organization and in the activities and concerns of the other departments, as these can ultimately affect the entire governmental structure and consequently the library as well. Librarians can also improve their standing with other department heads by remembering they can also be patrons and providing them with library service. If the library purchases something of interest to them, it can be sent over to their office first. This effort may not cause them to join the Friends of the Library, but if they have benefitted from library service, they can appreciate its value to the community.

Another way to show the library's importance to other governmental agencies is to become a local version of the Library of Congress. Just as its primary role is to provide for the research needs of Congress, a local version would similarly tend to the needs of the governing authorities and their departments. One library that has taken on this role is the Tucson (Ariz.) Public Library. Essentially, a special library of government information has been established in city hall. Special indexes, government publications, and online searching are all a part of this library's services. But just as important as the service rendered is the role this facility and its staff play as public relations agents for the library.[2] This idea is not a new one, however; Robert Leigh in the 1950 publication *The Public Library in the United States* discussed the role of a municipal reference division and its ability to 'offer a strategic opportunity to demonstrate the value of public library service to the people most influential in providing the library's financial support'.[3]

A small library usually can't afford to establish a branch for city hall, but the basic idea is not beyond its reach. Some libraries already have an advantage in that they share a building with city hall, but a local government center can be established by any library by pulling together the items of interest to government administrators. By combining input from the departments and the librarian's knowledge of selection and organization,the center can become a viable library service and marketing tool.

COMMUNICATING AN IMAGE

After the targets and their needs have been identified, an exchange relationship is established through marketing communication. This communication is not just verbal and written, but it includes all messages that are transmitted about the library. Many of these messages are conveyed by the images the library and its staff have in the community.

The library has an image whether or not one wants to admit it. In a small community with a stable population, the library's image may be the same today as it was 20 years ago, even if today's library is very different. If little effort has been made to update the community members about the library, they may not realize that it has changed. Rather than letting the library's image develop haphazardly, the librarian with a marketing orientation will want to control as much as possible the image that is presented. Three key elements of a library's image include the building, the staff, and the library director.

The building

An image check of the library building itself should be undertaken periodically and especially before a marketing plan is developed. Look at the library the way a stranger would. Can the library easily be found, or are there no signs on the main street indicating where the library is located or that there is even a library in the community? Are there signs on the library building itself indicating it houses a library? Sometimes in a small town it seems that everyone knows where everything is, but that is not always true, and even if it were, good signage serves to remind people about the library. Once the library is found, is the entrance well defined and welcoming or hard to find and forbidding? Have weeds overtaken the landscaping? These factors all reflect on the library's image before a person even steps inside. And as stated earlier, since a vast majority of the taxpayer/voter market will never use the library, this outside image is all they may ever see.

Inside the library, is the atmosphere friendly or cold? Are the signs faded and illegible? Are there signs at all? Signs do not need to be expensive; stationery stores carry vinyl or transfer lettering that can make attractive inside or even outside signs. Cheap-looking hand-lettered signs convey a non professional and ineffective image.

The overall appearance of the library also affects its image. Is the circulation desk so cluttered it looks as if little work could be accomplished there? Are books falling over in the stacks? Is there a dead coffee tree in the children's area? All this adds up to a look of inefficiency and incompetence.

Once the general image factors mentioned above are dealt with, the librarian should look at the values and needs of the target groups to determine the specific image the library should project. One library may promote itself as a community building while another may be viewed as primarily a place to study. While both libraries would provide general services, each would emphasize the characteristic that is viewed as important by the particular target.

Staff

The building itself, however, does not totally determine the image the library has in the community. The staff can affect that image greatly. An architect can design a warm, friendly, open building, but if the staff is unhelpful, surly, and gruff, the library might as well be in a dungeon because the attitude of the staff will overwhelm any appealing physical appearance. A small library especially needs to maintain the friendliness of the staff. In a large facility the patrons will deal with many different staff members and one antagonistic individual will be only a minor annoyance. But with a staff of two or three, that individual will have a bigger impact since patrons have more contact with each staff member. Some patrons may quit using the library completely or at least complain to their neighbors, both of which will affect the status of the library in the community. The library's procedures and policies also need to reflect a friendly attitude. The staff may be amiable and helpful, but if patrons receive an overdue notice within seventy-two hours that threatens them with $50 fines, the library's policies defeat the staff's friendly attitude.

The library director needs to work with all staff members to help them acquire a patron-oriented attitude. This involves the philosophy that the library is there to serve the needs of the patrons, not the needs of the staff. The result of this philosophy can range from making a procedure easier for patrons to simply listening attentively when a patron asks a question.

In any marketing effort, whether it is a formal plan or simply a marketing orientation, it is vital to have the staff understand and support the effort, for they are the library to the public. These frontline employees can make or break a marketing program. Staff should be involved in the market planning and execution and fully understand the reasoning behind the program.

Library director

The key staff member in all of this, however, is the library director. 'The popular image of the librarian has direct effect upon the degree of support given his library in book funds, salaries, housing, equipment . . . .'[4]

Although this statement was written in 1960 it still holds true today. Librarians need to take charge of their own image rather than to allow a stereotype to prevail. This is especially important in a small town where the image of the library will very often be a direct reflection of the image of the librarian.

Librarians can take charge of their image in a variety of ways. Many have scoffed and made jokes about the IBM uniform or the yellow power tie, but the 'dress for success' idea does make sense. If one dresses in a professional manner, one will more likely be treated as a professional. This does not mean, however, that everyone needs to wear a navy three-piece suit; in fact, an individual's personality should show through or the image may be more forbidding than impressive. In a small community, the librarian should observe the attire of other professionals and dress in a similar fashion. This will usually be on the casual side, but it will vary by community.

Dressing for success is not enough, however; librarians must also be able to conduct themselves in a professional manner. This includes formal presentations to community groups and informal one-on-one discussions. Librarians must be able to present their case for the library clearly and concisely without fumbling or appearing not to know what is going on. The political arena requires one to be an able communicator and the politician/librarian should be skilled as a public speaker.

Additionally, it is important for the librarian to be a part of the community. Blythe Jorgenson of the Toledo (Oreg.) Public Library, for example, has served as president of the Toledo Chamber of Commerce. In this town of 3,500 the library is a valued part of the community and is supported accordingly. It has one of the highest budgets per capita and one of the highest circulations per capita of any public library in Oregon. The time and effort that Jorgenson has put into her community involvement has paid off in a well-supported and well-used library. While this doesn't mean every library director should run for chamber president, it would be appropriate to join and participate in the chamber's activities. Other staff members should also be encouraged to participate in the community's activities. The time spent should be recognized as vital to the library as cataloging or reference work, and accordingly, released time should be granted, if possible.

The varied demands placed upon those charged with the administration of small/rural libraries require them to develop creative ways of management. The small/rural librarian who acquires a marketing orientation in lieu of conducting a full marketing plan will find it provides a method of operating in the political arena that is both effective and efficient in the use of time. The marketing concepts presented in this article can be adapted to create a personalised marketing orientation. Awareness of a library's targets and their needs as well as awareness of the library's image is the key; the small/rural librarian can utilize this knowledge in everyday activities and become a skillful participant in the local political process.

NOTES

1. Edward Howard, *Local Power and the Community Library* (Chicago: American Library Association, 1978), 29.
2. Will Manley, 'Facing the Public,' *Wilson Library Bulletin* 57 (November 1982): 228-29.
3. Robert Leigh, *The Public Library in the United States* (New York: Columbia University Press, 1950), 97.
4. Robert Leigh and Kathryn Sewny, 'The Popular Image of the Library and the Librarian,' *Library Journal* 85 (1 June 1960): 2089.

Services Marketing and the Academic Library

John Blunden-Ellis

University of Salford

INTRODUCTION

There is a growing body of literature that explores the special character-istics of services marketing, although this is a relatively new field and the ground rules are still being laid.[1] Enough work has been done, however, to emphasise the complexities of marketing in a noncommercial en-vironment, and as the service sector of the total marketplace is growing, it is important to address the problems in an effort to understand the underlying dynamics of the various service sectors.

The key ideas that emerge from the services marketing literature may be summarised as follows:

- The service 'product' tends towards intangibility.[2-5] The customer does not always take a physical object away with him at the end of the transaction. He does not own the service that is provided for him, or the expertise of the service provider. However, the customer does seek to benefit from the process, which indicates not only the importance of how the service is delivered, but also the immediate impact of the 'image' being created.
- Production is often inseparable from consumption.[6-8] This means that the customer experiences (benefits from) the service as it is delivered to him. This simultaneous production and consumption shows how important the service provider is in the overall quality of the service.
- Because of this dependence on the service provider, another character-istic of services is that of heterogeneity, or variability of performance.[9,10] Standardisation and quality control become extremely difficult to calibrate, which leads to problems of costing and pricing.
- Some services are strongly experiential, which makes them difficult to store or preserve in the same way that a physical product may be stored. This characteristic has been called perishability.[11,12] Work is being done in areas such as service classification[13] and position-ing[14,15] in order to gain an insight into differences among service

organisations and an appreciation of the overall complexity of the subject. The problem with the term 'services marketing' is that it is too narrow to embrace the variety of problems confronting the manager of a service. Compounding the difficulties for the library manager are: a vagueness about 'mission', an apparent lack of direct competition, a (more-or-less) captive clientele, and funding which is rarely related to performance on an annual basis. Within this environment, strategic planning loses a lot of its effectiveness.

A SERVICES MARKETING MODEL

In marketing a service, certain principles apply:

- The quality of the actual service is inseparable from the quality of the service provider, (e.g. lawyers, doctors).
- The customer is strongly influenced by the image of the service. – The quality of the actual service is strongly dependent on the manner and form of delivery.
- Service marketing and service operations must be closely interrelated.
- The closer the integration between service and customer, the more effective the service becomes.
- The quality of the actual service may sometimes be measured by the amount of competitive advantage it gives the client and/or parent organisation.

The above principles are an attempt to embrace most of the ideas which are of current concern in the services marketing literature, and these have been used as the basis for a model (Fig. 1) for studying marketing in an academic library context. The model uses a number of key terms which cover the important aspects of the subject; each will be discussed in turn. These key terms are: Image, Service Delivery/Technology, Management Structure/Environment, and Resources/Finance.

Image

Quality is in the eye of the beholder. The service customer will, in part, judge the quality and nature of the service he is using by its outward appearance; he is affected and influenced by his immediate environment, and first impressions rapidly become fixed. The work of both Gronroos[16–18] and Gummesson[19] in the field of service quality control focuses strongly on image, which is regarded as of 'the utmost importance to most service firms'.[20] Corporate image is seen to be the result of the customer's perceptions built up over time, and reflects the technical quality and functional quality of the services. Image is also seen to be influenced by ideology, word-of-mouth, advertising, pricing and public relations. Gummesson's research concluded that functional quality (how a service is delivered) is more important to the perceived service than is technical

FIG. 1: SERVICES MARKETING MODEL FOR ACADEMIC LIBRARIES

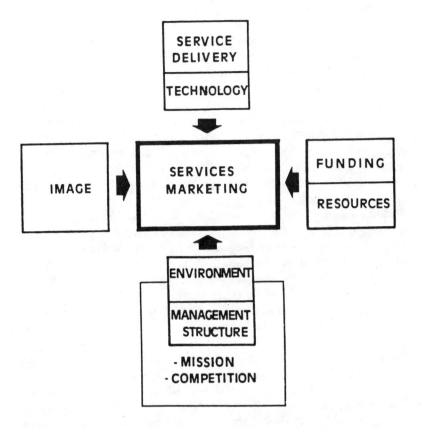

quality – provided that technical quality is at an acceptable level. Functional quality is a clear method of differentiating a particular service and enhancing image, and depends almost entirely on 'contact personnel' – the staff. To quote Esteve-Coll: 'The Library is not an abstraction. It has an identity, an identity created by the staff contact with the users. The quality of the Library's service is judged by the user's perception of an individual member of staff.'[21]

Library personnel themselves are vital to image, and this should be acknowledged in staff training. 'PR', telephone manner, personality, and individual attitude are all-important here, which means that staff motivation must be high. Successful commercial organisations attach great importance to their reception areas, and the appearance and quality of their 'up-front' staff. Scruffy interiors with dirty walls, noise, litter, etc. (and, in libraries, unshelved or untidy books) immediately create a poor impression, and do not foster confidence in the service itself.

The intimate relationship between the client and the service personnel is a key factor in services marketing – albeit inconveniently woolly and difficult to act upon strategically. For example, Grove and Fisk[22] talk of the importance of 'impression management'. The concepts surrounding image are regarded as vital topics by many writers on marketing theory. Shostack[23] notes that service realities appear to be shaped to a large extent by the things that the customer immediately experiences. Thus, the idea that services are generally experiential in nature means that management of the physical environment should be one of the service marketer's highest priorities. For example, Berry[24] has described the emergence of 'relationship marketing' which consists of the following: devising a core service strategy, customizing the service to individuals, augmenting the service (building in extras as a means of differentiation), pricing incentives, and finally, internal marketing (market research, segment-ation, product modification, etc.). The aim is to attract, maintain, and build customer relationships.

The library image, of course, must be enhanced throughout the parent institution by the use of stylishly presented literature with, perhaps, a library logo and specially designed glossy covers attached to all bulletins, SDI products, literature searches, newsletters, memoranda, etc. If the product (information being disseminated) is good, then the packaging should shout the fact. Additional opportunities for promoting the library image may be developed within the context of service delivery. Fur-thermore, the more closely the library staff are involved in the day-to-day activities of the institution, the better.

Institutions of higher education will increasingly have to operate in an aggressive competitive environment; they will have to market, advertise and promote themselves. The library is one of their central resources and will be used as one of the selling points of the institution. Line[25] sums it up well: 'A positive library should also be a visibly good library. It's no good being good if we don't make it obvious to everybody . . . We also need to have much more aggressive public relations than we do at present.'

Service delivery

According to Laver: 'The greatest problem for libraries is how to connect the inarticulate with the incomprehensible, how to bring the silent needs of their readers into communication with the voluble capabilities of information technologists. It is exactly here that librarians have a vital, interpretive role to play.'[26] Raw data is only transmuted into useful information in the minds of users. The librarian's job is to assist in this conversion process, which essentially consists of filtering out the relevant from the obviously irrelevant data, packaging the data in a way that makes it attractive and easy to use, and delivering it in a way that is convenient for the client.

Service delivery and technology

It is now common knowledge that new technology does not necessarily save either expenditure or manpower. Furthermore, it has been confirmed[27] that in badly managed organisations, the introduction of new technology will not convert them into successes; it will merely act as an additional burden. In other words, it is pointless to attempt to automate your way out of failure. In marketing terms, technology should be judged on the basis of how it will affect the delivery of the service. Does it bring the service closer to the user? Is access easier? Does it make the information simpler to use? How quickly is the information made available to the user? What opportunities are there for adding value to the information? etc. If the benefits are unclear, or the technology is insufficiently developed to explore practical applications, then it is a waste of time to consider it further.

Too often in the past, the user has had to come physically to the library. Technology can bring the library to the user. Library information units (see below) that deliver a range of services to departments and offices indicate the importance – in marketing terms – of integrating the service with the customer; it is the first step in using the campus computer network for marketing purposes. (the Library Information Unit (LIU) discussed here is the front end of the marketing effort. Essentially it is the packaging which surrounds the information delivery point, ideally an online public access catalogue. The LIU may, for example, consist of a set of display boards for library literature, bulletins, notices, new book information, etc., a headboard displaying the library logo and name, and a table for the online public access catalogue (OPAC). This aims to advertise the library, act as a platform for library desktop publishing ventures, and deliver the information attractively within the department).

If technology obstructs the process of delivery, it is useless; systems the users will not or cannot use do not help the customer-service interface. Ultimately technology should enable the user to retrieve information in his own way rather than in a way dictated by someone else's rules. Historically, the conventional library catalogue with long involved classmarks has proved useful for librarians, but a disaster in marketing and PR, because from the user's point of view it inhibits service delivery. OPACs with keyword searching therefore have obvious advantages; CD-ROM and CD-I have attractions with regard to service delivery because of large storage capacities, multi-media information, unlimited access to databases, etc. Local area networks also help to deliver information exactly where it is required. Technology facilitates the combination of data from a variety of different sources and media to form single packages created by the LIS (or the user himself) for use via information workstations. An important point to mention here, however, is that service delivery must where necessary be followed up by personal contact to establish customer satisfaction.

Increasingly, IT will be used as the method of choice for product delivery, and substantial capital expenditure is likely to be involved.

Many libraries (and commercial organisations) have introduced technology in a piecemeal fashion in an attempt to offset the impact of such scales of expenditure. There is evidence to suggest[28] that this method is counterproductive and inefficient in the long run. What is required is coherent institution-wide IT strategy planning before any thought of implementation within departments. This has implications for resources and finance.

Service delivery and competition

Potential competition exists for all services. If information needs are not satisfied by the library, alternative means of provision will automatically develop within the institution itself.

Some academic disciplines (e.g. Arts, Humanities) traditionally make more extensive use of the library than others (e.g. Engineering). Those that use the library do so because, on the whole, it is able to deliver information in a form convenient to them. If members of a department or faculty are non-users or occasional users it may be because they have developed their own information channels to satisfy needs unsatisfied by the library. These channels, similar to distribution channels in commercial marketing, constitute dangerous competition and can be extremely difficult to compete against once established. Generally, they include invisible colleges, professional grapevine, word-of-mouth, correspondence, conferences, etc., or any information service with which the library has not been involved. If non-users of the library are politically powerful, it is important to tackle these channels, the existence of which reflects an absence of 'good will' towards the library service. How can the library compete? Here, the important principle of bringing the service to the user – service penetration applies.

Service delivery planning process

There are two techniques which may be useful in designing an appropriate strategy for library service delivery; one operates mainly at the departmental level and the other at the institutional level. Kotler[29] has described the strategic marketing planning process (SMPP), which may be modified to suit service design at the departmental level. An example is given below of how the logic of the process may be adapted to an hypothetical situation:

- *SWOT analysis* (Strengths/Weaknesses/Opportunities/Threats)
  1. General analysis. Determine departmental objectives, mission, and specific goals. Identify departmental research activities that attract the most outside funding. Identify sites of influence and political power.
  2. Competition. How are departmental information channels used? What do they consist of? How did they evolve? How efficiently/

effectively do they deliver? How is the information packaged? Is the arrangement appropriate for the department?

3. Opportunity analysis. Compile a list of research publications of all members of departmental academic staff over the last five years. Check library records for use/nonuse of library.

- *Formulation*
  4. Focus. Create research profiles for each individual, with levels of external funding obtained. Together with the opportunity analysis assess individual needs for information.

- *Implementation*
  5. Target. Compile a highly focussed literature survey, attractively printed and packaged, listing the most up-to-date references for chosen individuals who are highly active in research. Target individual research students by offering an initial free online search.

- *Assessment*
  6. Follow up. Personal interviews to assess impact. (Relevance of information. Presentation. How will the information be used? Required frequency of updates, etc.)
  7. Review. Evaluate/modify strategy on the basis of experience.

The above is a simple example of adapting a well-tried stepwise process to a possible problem situation in service delivery. The sequence of activities is important at the implementation stage, where questions arise such as: do we provide a new image with bulletins, Library Information Units, information packs, circulars, etc. before or after targetting key personnel for specialist information services?

At the institutional level, windows of opportunity may be discovered by means of Porter's value chain model[30] which may be used to uncover competitive advantage in commercially driven organisations. This model has been applied to information services within universities in an important paper by Cronin and Davenport.[31] They suggest that the strategic operations undertaken by a university can be reduced to a three-tiered value chain consisting of People, Information and Management. This chain is disaggregated into a 15-cell matrix, and the activities within these cells are used to identify windows of opportunity for the university library sector. These opportunities are: prospecting, intelligence, impact assessment, marketing and megamarketing. Examples of each are provided.

Environment and management structure

Mission and environment

A clearly conceived mission is only possible in an institution which possesses a strong corporate identity. Many well-known Japanese organisations have this powerful sense of identity arising from a combination of employee loyalty, motivation and dedication. Whatever the method used, institutions of higher education must aim to establish individual corporate identities as a first step in differentiating themselves from the competition, and in formulating a mission.

The Jarratt report on efficiency studies in universities observed that 'Objectives and aims in universities are defined only in very broad terms. They usually take the form of general statements of intent . . .'[32] The nature of competition in higher education in the 1990s will require something rather more from universities than general statements of intent. The possible stratification of universities into research, in-termediate, and teaching institutions, together with the incipient independence of polytechnics in April 1989, will force these institutions to think about precisely defined aims and objectives. This precision will be necessary in order to compete successfully in the changing market-place.

With properly defined aims and objectives established, efficient man-agement information networks throughout the institution become vital. Jarratt recognises this importance and recommends the use of depart-mental profiles which include a mixture of facts and indicators of performance over time.[33] Apart from financial allocations, these 'profiles' include A-level scores, applications/place, unit costs, etc. If institutions are to compete for intake of high quality and research funding along the lines of commercial competition, then these input measures become vital, and should be extended to include such topics as competitor profiles. This sort of information resembles the strategic information so valued in the commercial marketplace. The library/information service should come to be regarded as the prime source for this form of 'hot' data, and such a service can only be created through dedicated service links with the departments. One of the vital roles that a library should adopt is to act as a strategic information service to the central administration, implementing and supporting strategies that help the institution's external marketing effort.

With aims and objectives and management information support in place, the next step is to target selected market segments. It has been predicted that the main growth area in the higher education market in the next decade will be continuing education, particularly for professional development. A recent report concludes that 'Britain's managers want to see work experience as a compulsory element in both schools and HE Institutions. And one in three recognises the need for continuing education to update and retrain their own generation.'[34] As part of its strategic information service the library can, using its resources and expertise, compile detailed market reports on potential target segments. All this would have to be undertaken at the same time as serving the academic needs of individuals and departments within the institution.

This in turn may require a review of the existing management structure within the library.

Management structure

Theories about management structure – or 'organisational design'[35] – are largely concerned with efficiency (doing things right) and effectiveness (doing the right things).[36] The challenge is to do both at the same time. There is a great deal of debate in the literature about what is actually meant by efficiency and effectiveness and how to model them.[37] A common sense approach suggests that you should concentrate first on identifying the right things to do, and then worry about how to do them right. Marketing is the key to understanding effectiveness, firstly by means of a sophisticated knowledge of current consumer needs, and secondly by a predictive knowledge of future needs through a pro-active management structure.

Mintzberg[38] has worked extensively in the field of management structure and concludes that, broadly speaking, every organisation falls into one of five structures; the simple structure, the machine bureaucracy, the professional bureaucracy, the decentralised form, and the adhocracy.[39] Each of these structures consists of a 'strategic apex' (top management), a 'middle line' (senior middle management), the 'operating core' (the people who do the basic work of the organisation), the 'technostructure' (systems design; computers, etc.), and the 'support staff'.

Many academic libraries function at present as 'professional bureaucracies'. (Fig. 2). This organisational design relies for its operating tasks on trained professionals – skilled people who have substantial control over their own work. These skills, however, tend to become standardised over a period of time due to the stable environment. The structure is usually very decentralised; power flows from the apex to the operating core. In a professional bureaucracy the support staff is typically very large. Mintzberg points out the interesting fact that in the professional bureaucracy parallel hierarchies emerge – one democratic with bottom-up power for the professionals, another autocratic with top-down control for the support staff. This is a familiar situation in many academic libraries.

The professional bureaucracy is a comfortable arrangement for a comfortable environment. Standardisation of skills raises problems of adaptability. This structure does not foster innovation, but is highly effective at running tried and tested systems. When the environment is predictable and stable, the professional bureaucracy works well. It identifies the needs of the clients and generally provides standardised solutions. In a fluid competitive environment, however, this structure is not very helpful. Furthermore Mintzberg says that 'Professional

FIG. 2: PROFESSIONAL BUREAUCRACY

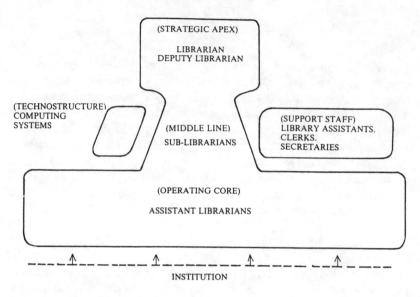

bureaucracy offers (professional workers) considerable autonomy, freeing them even of the need to coordinate closely with each other'.[40] This coordination of professional activity is, however, vital for corporate image and also for effectiveness in the innovative service environment that academic libraries will face in the future. Consequently a more flexible management structure needs to be devised, and this flexibility is found in 'Adhocracy'.

The Adhocracy is a management structure for the IT age – the so-called 'Third Wave' which will be full of surprises for both commercial and service organisations. This environment requires organisations with 'project structures' which absorb experts from differing specialities into creative forward-looking groups.[41] This structure is highly flexible and management control is by liaison via integrating managers who coordinate the task forces and establish a reporting structure for senior management. However, managers in an adhocracy do not control in the sense of direct supervision; instead they act as experts whose function is to link the different teams together. Power is based on expertise and not on authority. The whole arrangement is pro-active because power is distributed throughout the organisational structure; broad strategy is planned from above, but evolves and is refined in response to the variety of decisions made by the project groups. Consequently, the Adhocracy is 'continually developing its strategy as it accepts and works out new projects.'[42]

A Central Information Service (formerly the Library) based on the adhocratic structure would need to be able to target, retrieve, package and deliver information as one operation. (Fig. 3). This will involve expertise

FIG. 3: ADHOCRACY

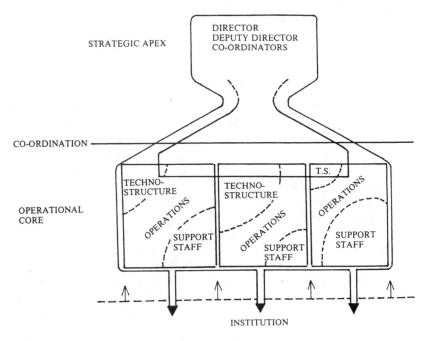

STRATEGIC APEX — DIRECTOR / DEPUTY DIRECTOR / CO-ORDINATORS

CO-ORDINATION

OPERATIONAL CORE

TECHNO-STRUCTURE — OPERATIONS — SUPPORT STAFF

TECHNO-STRUCTURE — OPERATIONS — SUPPORT STAFF

T.S. — OPERATIONS — SUPPORT STAFF

INSTITUTION

in computer software, hardware, networks, etc. at a level not generally found in library staff alone. Consequently a very close cooperation with Computing Services is needed. At the University of Salford, this is being achieved by the amalgamation of the Library, Computing Services, and Audio-Visual Media into one central information service. Faculty or even departmental teams can be developed that possess extensive specialist information skills together with the technical ability to package and deliver information in a form convenient to the users. Furthermore, new developments in IT can be more rigorously evaluated and costed for possible deployment in the information delivery process. The specialist groups could also provide, as a matter of course, management and marketing information to the institution/faculty/department, and a general information service to library users. The whole structure will depend upon efficient liaison management, nurturing and maintaining the links between the groups, and from the groups to senior management by written and verbal reporting structures via group coordinators. Group identity should be enhanced by formal minuted meetings chaired by the individual coordinators.

In this form of adhocracy a close working relationship between project groups and departments is essential and may take a great deal of time and effort to achieve. Ultimately, departments should come to regard the project groups virtually as members of their own staff. This intimate linkage – the 'customer/service interface' – once fully operational, eases the flow of management information from departments to the Central Information Service, which in turn enables opportunities for more efficient strategic information to be created for central administration.

Resources and finance

Marketing is not about selling; it is about understanding needs and environments in order to allocate resources more effectively. This effective resource allocation is, of course, part of the internal marketing process of persuading the institution to make available the necessary funds. Much of this paper has been concerned with the library's relationship with its institution in a changing environment; consequently the 'customer/service' interface is important not only at the individual level but at the library/institution level.

The parent institution must provide future funding for IT projects, not just because it may think it has a good library, but because the library is the key element (the central exchange if you like) in the institution's overall IT strategy for information dissemination. Funding this strategy is also funding the library, and any institution that does not develop such a coherent standardisation policy will find itself at a disadvantage in head-to-head competition. The academic library, therefore, must be an initiator and a springboard in this information planning process; it must come to be regarded as a source of expertise and, consequently, as indispensable. Hence the importance of the adhocratic management structure in the process of services marketing. This is why thinking about methods of charging for photocopying, interloans, online searches, etc. is appropriate at the operational level, but it does not begin to tackle financing and resource planning at the strategic level, and it is at the strategic level that the ever-present problems of funding are to be solved. Services marketing plays its part in this process by creating the environment in which corporate planning can flourish. The library is in a unique position, by virtue of being a central resource, in pioneering the necessary changes.

CONCLUSIONS

This paper has attempted to focus on some of the key issues connected with marketing an information service in an academic environment; an environment which is increasingly subject to change. The pace of this change and the implications surrounding information transmission and manipulation are having a profound effect not only on our own profession, but in the economy as a whole (e.g. increasing skill obsolescence). It is important that we appreciate the nature of the market forces that will, with increasing power, affect our future working lives and the stature of our profession.

REFERENCES

1. ZEITHAML, V.A., PARASURAMEN, A. *and* BERRY, L.L. Problems and strategies in service marketing. *Journal of Marketing, 49,* Spring 1985, 33–46.
2. BERRY, L.L. Services marketing is different. *Business, 30,* 1980, 24–29.
3. LOVELOCK, C.H. Why marketing management needs to be different for services. *In:* J.H. Donnelly *and* W.R. George, *eds. Marketing of services.* American Marketing Association, 1981. 5–9.
4. SHOSTACK, G.L. Breaking free from product marketing. *Journal of Marketing, 41,* 1977, 73–80.
5. DONNELLY, J.H. Service delivery strategies in the 1980's – academic perspective. In: *Financial institution marketing strategies in the 1980s.* L.L. Berry *and* J.H. Donnelly, *eds.* Consumer Bankers Assoc., 1980. 143–150.
6. REGAN, W.J. The service revolution. *Journal of Marketing, 47,* 1963, 57–62.
7. CARMEN, J.M. *and* LANGEARD, E. Growth strategies for service firms. *Strategic Management Journal 1,* 1980, 7–22.
8. GRONROOS, C. A service oriented approach to marketing of services. *European Journal of Marketing, 12,* 1978, 588–601.
9. LANGEARD, E. *Service marketing: new insights from consumers and managers.* Marketing Science Institute, 1981.
10. KNISELY, G. Financial Services marketers must learn packaged goods selling tools. *Advertising Age, 50,* 1979, 58–62.
11. THOMAS, D.R.E. Strategy is different in service business. *Harvard Business Review, 56,* 1978, 158–165.
12. BESSOM, R.M. *and* JACKSON, D.W. Service retailing – a strategic marketing approach. *Journal of Retailing, 8,* 1975, 137–149.
13. LOVELOCK, C.H. Classifying services to gain strategic marketing insights. *Journal of Marketing, 47,* 1983, 9–20.
14. WYCKHAM, R.G., FITZROY, P.T. *and* MANDRY, G.D. Marketing of services; an evaluation of the theory. *European Journal of Marketing, 9(1),* 1975, 59–67.
15. SHOSTACK, G.L. *op.cit.*
16. GRONROOS, C. *op.cit.*
17. GRONROOS, C. An applied theory for marketing industrial services. *Industrial Marketing Management, 8,* 1979, 45–50.
18. GRONROOS, C. Innovative marketing strategies and organisational structures for service firms. *In:* L. Berry *and* G.L. Shostack, *eds.* Emerging perspectives in service firms. American Marketing Association, 1983. 9–21.
19. GUMMESSON, E. The marketing of professional services – an organisational dilemma. *Industrial Marketing Management, 5,* 1979.
20. GRONROOS, C. Innovative marketing strategies. *op.cit.*
21. ESTEVE-COLL, E. Marketing and the academic library. *Information and Library Manager, 5 (3),* 1985, 1–7.
22. GROVE, S.J. *and* FISK, R.P. The dramaturgy of service exchange: an analytical framework for services marketing. *In:* L. Berry *et al., eds. Emerging perspectives on services marketing.* American Marketing Association, 1983. 45–50.
23. SHOSTACK, G.L. Service positioning through structural change. *Journal of Marketing, 51,* 1987, 34–43.
24. BERRY, L.M. Relationship marketing. *In: Emerging perspectives on services marketing, op.cit.* 25–29.
25. LINE, M. Library goodness. *UC & R Newsletter, 20,* November 1986, 3–8.

26.   LAVER, F.J.M. *Information, technology and libraries*, First British Library Annual Research Lecture, London: British Library, 1983, 2.

27.   *Does information technology slow you down?* Report prepared by the Kobler Unit for the Management of Information Technology (Reporter: Beat Hochstrasser). Kobler Unit, Imperial College, London, 1987.

28.   *ibid.*

29.   KOTLER, P. *and* ANDERSON, A.R. *(eds.) Strategic marketing for non-profit organisations.* 3rd ed. Prentice Hall, 1987, 159.

30.   PORTER, M. *Competitive advantage: creating and sustaining superior performance.* New York: Free Press, 1985.

31.   CRONIN, B. *and* DAVENPORT, L. Libraries and the university value chain. *British Journal of Academic Librarianship, 2(2),* 1987, 85–90.

32.   *Steering Committee for efficiency studies in universities. Report.* London: Committee of Vice-Chancellors and Principals, 1985. (Jarratt Report).

33.   *ibid.*

34.   Report cited by the *Times Higher Education Supplement*, January 8th, 1988, p. 1.

35.   For example, CHILD, J. Organisational structure, environment and performance: the role of strategic choice. *Sociology, 6,* 1972, 1–22.

36.   DRUCKER, P.F. *Management tasks, responsibilities, practices.* New York: Harper and Row, 1973. 45.

37.   MINTZBERG, H. *Power in and around organizations,* Prentice Hall, 1983, 269.

38.   MINTZBERG, H. *The structuring of organisations.* Prentice Hall, 1979.

39.   MINTZBERG, H. Organisation design: fashion or fit. *Harvard Business Review, 59,* 1981, 103–116.

40.   *ibid,* 110.

41.   *ibid,* 111.

42.   *ibid,* 112.

Entrepreneurship and The Academic Library: Insights from Organization Theory

Don Schauder

Institute Librarian, Chisholm Institute of Technology, Box 197, Caulfield East, Victoria 3145, Australia.

ISSUES AND DEFINITIONS

An urgent issue of the financially austere late 1980s is the extent to which academic libraries can diversify and increase their funding base, or obtain more productivity from their existing resources.

There is a widespread belief that more use could be made of the considerable expertise which exists in academic libraries to provide specialized information services to business, government and community groups.[1] Examples of innovative ventures that could be undertaken by academic libraries are highly customized information services; publishing projects in print or in electronic form; the creation and marketing of new databases; the development and marketing of new devices or equipment relevant to information technology; and active, flexible consultancy services. Such products and services might be sold, or funded out of grant money. They would be sold to the education and research community, or to the wider information marketplace, namely industry, commerce, the professions, non-profit service organizations, and government.

The theme explored in this paper is whether academic libraries as organizations have the capacity to adopt entrepreneurship as a feature of their strategy and management style.

An *academic library* is a library that belongs to an institution of higher education, and whose primary role is to support the educational programmes and research activities of its parent institution. Academic staff and students are its primary clientele.

Entrepreneurs have been defined as 'dreamers who do'.[2] The entrepreneur is a person with a vision, and the commitment to make that vision a reality. The specific tool of entrepreneurship is innovation.[3] The term *intrapreneur* has been coined for entrepreneurs who work within organizations rather than independently.[4] Entrepreneurship is not an all-

or-none trait, but rather a range of behaviours.[5] In her studies of innovative managers and innovative companies, Kanter has distinguished two clusters or categories of accomplishments: *basic and innovative*. *Basic* accomplishments are done solely within the organization's existing framework, and do not affect its longer term capacity. Basic accomplishments include: working effectively within the bounds of one's job (e.g. keeping services functioning normally during reorganization or rebuilding); achieving effectiveness in the deployment of staff (e.g. transferring a subordinate to a more suitable job); and advancing incrementally within one's job (e.g. handling higher volumes of work than in the past). *Innovative* accomplishments include effecting a new policy, or creating a change of orientation or direction; finding a new opportunity, developing a new product or service, or opening a new market; devising a fresh method, or introducing a new process, procedure or technology for continued use; and making structural changes – changing the formal structure, re-organizing or introducing a new structure, or forging a different link among units.[6]

Judgment and decision lie at the heart of entrepreneurship. In the context of economic theory, Casson defines an entrepreneur as 'someone who specializes in taking judgmental decisions about the coordination of scarce resources'. The entrepreneur is 'not concerned merely with the perpetuation of the existing allocation of resources, but with improving upon it'.[7]

For this paper, entrepreneurship in academic libraries means the provision of innovative products and/or services: a) to clientele outside the parent institution (i.e. institution of higher eduication) with a view to generating profit either in the form of money or other new resources, and/ or b) to clientele inside the parent institution, but without requiring major new (as opposed to re-allocated) resource inputs.

Organization theory can help to answer the question: 'Are academic libraries, as organizations, suited to entrepreneurship?' Etymologically, the word *theory* is concerned with *seeing* (c.f. 'theatre'), and the word organization derives from the term for an implement or tool. An *organization* can therefore be defined as *a social group formed and sustained by people as a device or tool to help them do particular things, and organization theory as a discipline that provides ways of looking at organizations in order to gain an understanding of them*.[8] The fields of business, public administration and education, and the disciplines of anthropology, psychology, social psychology, political science, and economics have all contributed to the development of organization theory.[9] The feasibility of entrepreneurship on the part of academic libraries exemplifies a practical problem to which organization theory can potentially be applied.

The ways in which academic libraries can participate in the information marketplace within and outside their parent institutions depend heavily on their organizational characteristics, and their developmental strategies. The decision on whether, and how far, to commit a library to relatively high-risk new ventures requires sound judgment, based on a deep understanding of the potentialities and limitations of that library as an organization.

Organization theory is important because all the people who are involved in the library, particularly in situations of change, need a framework of ideas to help them to understand the significance of their own roles within the organization, and to assess whether they are succeeding in what they are doing. They need to understand the organization in order to focus their advice and criticism about policies and practices, and to participate in planning for the future. It is possible that their behaviour and attitudes are already substantially influenced, whether consciously or not, by theories of organization, both in the way that they comprehend their organization, and in the extent to which they can predict or foresee the possible consequences of decisions or actions they may take, or fail to take. Entrepreneurial activity involves not merely change, but change with risk. Under such circumstances a more deliberate and systematic application of organization theory can help all persons involved to achieve better understanding of the issues and the options.

There are several possible reasons for undertaking entrepreneurial activities, in addition to that of increasing the financial resources available to the library. Entrepreneurial activities might increase the professional experience, and also possibly the financial rewards of individual library staff. Such activities might enhance the library's reputation within the parent institution, giving the library more influence, and a higher priority in the allocation of institutional funds and resources. Intrapreneurial activities might also highlight the potential of academic libraries to contribute to economic prosperity and to meeting the needs of the wider community, thereby improving the chances of community support for future government funding to academic libraries.

THEORETICAL FRAMEWORKS

Since the early 1970s a vigorous debate has taken place in the field of educational administration about the appropriate focus of organization theory. Two major viewpoints have dominated the debate. The question at issue between them is how organizations, and educational organizations in particular, should be thought about and studied. The mainstream viewpoint, which follows the positivist tradition of Simon is concerned primarily with *facts* – with questions of 'What is?'[10] The dissenting viewpoint, initiated by Greenfield, is concerned primarily with *values* – with questions of 'What ought to be?'.[11] The emphasis of the mainstream viewpoint is *objective*, while that of the dissenting viewpoint is *subjective*. The emphasis of the mainstream viewpoint stresses the collectivity, while that of the dissenting viewpoint stresses the individual.

FIG. 1. TWO THEORIES OF ORGANIZATION: A RESEARCH
FRAMEWORK

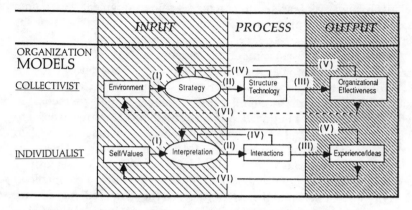

The two viewpoints can be presented in parallel by means of two
systems models (Fig. 1).[12] It can be argued that the two theoretical
viewpoints are complementary rather than contradictory. When the
models derived from the two theories are overlaid with one another, the
effect is to re-unite the realms of *facts* and *values*, providing a single,
powerful framework for understanding and inquiry. At the same time,
the two viewpoints considered separately provide valuable critiques of
each other's conceptual and practical pitfalls.

In Fig. 1, the *collectivist* model shows how opportunities and constraints from outside the organization (*environment*) are responded to
(linkage I) by means of decision-making (*strategy*), resulting (linkage II)
in activities which are allocated among people in the organization
(*structure*) and carried out in ways that seem appropriate (*technology*).
The organization's activities produce (linkage III) results which are
assessed by various criteria (*organizational effectiveness*). Problems or
unintended consequences encountered when *strategy* is applied by means
of *structure* and *technology* result (linkage IV) in adjustments to *strategy*.
Results which fail to meet effectiveness criteria result (linkage V) in
adjustments to *strategy*. Where environmental factors are identified as the
cause of failure to meet effectiveness criteria, attempts may be made
(linkage VI) to change those conditions rather than adjust *strategy*.

The *individualist* model in Fig. 1 shows how the individual characteristics of people (*self/values*) are selectively applied (linkage 1) by those
people to the way (*interpretation*) in which they participate in the
organization, resulting (linkage II) in collaboration or conflict with other
people (*interactions*) in the organization. The *interactions* produce
(linkage III) outcomes (*experience/ideas*) for the people concerned.
Unforeseen consequences encountered during *interactions* may result
(linkage IV) in adjustments to *interpretation*. Outcomes in the form of

positive or negative *experience* or *ideas* may result (linkages V and VI) in adjustments to *interpretation* and/or to *self/values*.

The two models have thus been combined in a single framework through the systems approach of input-process-output. The intention is to illustrate, in a way that is hopefully more effective than many chapters of exposition, that greater understanding of organizations is likely to be achieved by participants at all levels if both sets of factors and relationships are considered.

The perspective of the theoretical framework in Fig. 1 could usefully be applied to a variety of organizational problems affecting academic libraries, both in terms of their internal administration and their relationships with their parent institutions or the external world. Problems that could be considered might be the impact of the increasing unionization of staff on the administration of libraries, the relationship between the organizational characteristics of the academic departments of the institution and those of the library, and indeed any issue where predictions need to be made on the likely impact of environmental or institutional change on library staff, users, and funding authorities. The theoretical framework in Fig. 1 is useful in a study of entrepreneurship and the academic library. The *collectivist* model can help to answer questions about whether academic libraries as organizations are congenial settings for entrepreneurs, and whether they have the potential to become entrepreneurial organizations. The *individualist* model can help to answer questions about how entrepreneurship can be identified, developed and encouraged among library staff.

Stevenson and Gumpert have developed two further models which relate particularly to entrepreneurship.[13] The model entitled 'Corporate opportunity matrix' (see Fig. 2) can be used in conjunction with the *collectivist* model in Fig. 1. The model entitled 'Manager opportunity matrix' (see Fig. 3) can be used in conjunction with the *individualist* model in Fig. 1. The 'Corporate opportunity matrix' and the 'Manager opportunity matrix' are based on a typology of behaviours that range from *promotor* at one end of the scale to *trustee* on the other. The *promotor* type of manager is confident of his or her ability to seize opportunity. The *promotor* expects surprises, and expects not only to adjust to change but also to capitalize on it and make things happen. In contrast the *trustee* type of manager prefers to rely on the status quo and:

> . . . feels threatened by change and the unknown . . . To the trustee type, predictability fosters effective management of existing resources while unpredictability endangers them.[14]

As is common with typologies, most people fall between the two extremes. However, managers who move closer to the *promotor* end are predicted to be more entrepreneurial, and those who move closer to the trustee end, less so. The two matrix models in Figs 2 and 3 portray the

FIG. 2.

CORPORATE OPPORTUNITY MATRIX		Desired future state characterized by growth or change	
		Yes	No
Self-perceived power and ability to realize goals	Yes	Adaptive, entrepreneurial organization	Complacent, though successful, market leaders
	No	Reactive planners	Bureaucratic and lethargic organization

FIG. 3.

MANAGER'S OPPORTUNITY MATRIX		Desired future state characterized by growth or change	
		Yes	No
Self-perceived power and ability to realize goals	Yes	Entrepreneur	Satisfied manager
	No	Frustrated potential entrepreneur	Consummate bureaucratic functionary

implications of the *trustee-promotor* typology for individual managers and their organizations. The entrepreneurial manager, and the adaptive entrepreneurial organization, are predicted to desire and envision a future state of affairs that is characterized by growth or change. The entrepreneurial manager and the entrepreneurial organization are both predicted to perceive that they have the power and ability to achieve their goals within that changing future.

APPLYING THE MODELS TO ACADEMIC LIBRARIES

Theories, and models derived from them, become stronger each time they are subjected to empirical test. In the context of academic libraries the models outlined above have hardly been tested at all.

However, in 1986 a study of academic libraries was undertaken in the state of Victoria, Australia. It was based primarily on the *collectivist* model in Fig. 1 (henceforth referred to as 'the Victorian study'). Hypotheses and propositions concerning the relationship among the factors of the model, namely *environment, strategy, structure, technology,* and *organizational effectiveness* were formulated, and were largely supported by the survey results. Respondents to the survey were 17 of the 21 chief librarians of universities and colleges of advanced education in Victoria, or their representatives. The methods, results, and interpretation of the survey have been reported.[15]

Typological sub-models were used for measurement of all the factors in the *collectivist* model. The sub-model used in the survey to categorize the *factor strategy* had much in common with the *trustee-prospector* typology of Stevenson and Gumpert.

The themes of leadership, decision making, change and innovation broadly cover the concerns included in definitions of organizational strategy. For example, Robbins gives the following definition of *strategy*:

> The determination of the basic long-term goals of the organization and the adoption of courses of action and the allocation of resources necessary for carrying out these goals.[16]

The sub-model of strategy used in the Victorian study was that of Miles *et al.*[17] It provides a typology which characterizes the strategies which decision makers can adopt for their organizations. The categories are those of *defender, analyzer* and *prospector*. These categories are described in Table 1.

TABLE 1. *Typology of strategic possibilities for organizations (after Miles et al.)*[18]

	Types	Descriptions	Flexibility/Control
1.	Defenders	These allow little change to occur.	Low flexibility (high control)
2.	Analyzers	These perceive change but wait for competing organizations to develop responses and then adapt to them.	Medium flexibility (medium control)
3.	Prospectors	These perceive opportunities for change and want to create change and to experiment.	High flexibility (low control)

NOTE: There is a fourth category, that of *Reactor*, which characterizes organizations wholly at the mercy of forces in their environment, and usually in a state of decay. It is a residual category which, following Robbins' example in his Table 6–1[19] will be excluded for purposes of the present discussion.

It will readily be seen that Miles' *defender* strategy is closely aligned to Stevenson and Gumpert's category of *trustee*, and the *prospector* strategy with that of *promotor*. It follows, then, that the category of analyzer corresponds to a position on Stevenson and Gumpert's typology midway between *trustee* and *promotor*.

The respondents in the Victorian study were given a series of forced-choice questions which were intended to identify the strategy most closely approximating that desired for their own library.

As shown in Table 2 below, the results indicated that the respondents were strongly agreed on their most preferred strategy. The *analyzer* strategy was clearly the most strongly preferred option for both colleges and universities. For the universities the *defender* strategy ran second, while for the colleges it was the third preference. The *prospector* category (which is most characteristic of successful entrepreneurial organizations in new fields of endeavour) was ranked third by the universities, but second by the colleges. The difference between the college and university patterns of support for the *prospector* strategy was found to be statistically significant at the 5 per cent level.

TABLE 2. *Preferred strategies*

Scores each type of strategy	DEFENDER	ANALYZER	PROSPECTOR
COLLEGES			
Scores	18/76	60/75	35/75
Per cent	23.7%	80.0%	46.7%
Ranking	3	1	2
UNIVERSITIES			
Scores	8/23	22/23	5/24
Per cent	34.8%	91.7%	21.7%
Ranking	2	1	3
ALL			
Total scores	26/99	82/98	40/99
Per cent	26.3%	82.8%	40.4%
Ranking	3	1	2

QUESTIONS ON STRATEGY

Scoring: For each forced-choice option ticked by respondents, one point was assigned to the relevant strategy, and for each strategy the total of the points is shown as a fraction of the possible maximum for that strategy. No points were assigned for non-responses, and the maximum total points attainable were reduced accordingly.

When all results were aggregated the *analyzer* strategy emerged very strongly as the most preferred option.

The very strong and unified response on *strategy* was particularly striking. Academic libraries have emerged as *analyzers,* i.e. as organizations which consistently seek the conflicting aims of both preserving their present characteristics, as well as introducing changes seen as beneficial, as long as these do not pose any significant threat to the status quo.[20]

BARRIERS TO ENTREPRENEURSHIP IN LIBRARIES AND OTHER SERVICE INSTITUTIONS

Entrepreneurship in the academic library presents several problems. In order to develop new activities, staff must be diverted wholly or partially from what is regarded as their 'real' job (namely serving the students and staff of the institution) hence disadvantaging the library's operation in the short or medium term, on the chance that advantages will accrue in the long term. For some activities hard decisions also need to be made about who has first call on services and materials – students of the institution, or external paying customers. A further problem is that the parent institution might see externally-raised funds as a substitute for internal funding, instead of as a supplement to the library's regular grant.

Drucker believes that public service institutions such as government agencies, schools, hospitals, charitable organizations and labour unions need to be as innovative and entrepreneurial as any business, because such organizations are faced with conspicuous threats, as well as great opportunities, in to-day's world. However public service organizations find innovation more difficult than businesses because:

The 'existing' seems to be even more of an obstacle . . . stopping what has 'always been' and doing something new are equally anathema to service institutions, or at least excruciatingly painful to them.[21]

The Victorian study, which identified the dominant strategy of the libraries surveyed as *analyzer,* also found good and consistent reasons why an uninhibited *prospector* or *promotor* strategy does not prevail. It is not because chief librarians are 'timid bureaucrats', although obviously in any group the element of risk would be more acceptable to some than to others. The results of the Victorian study were consistent with the three obstacles to innovation in public service institutions identified by Drucker, namely: 'budget' versus results-based funding, multiple constituencies, and the fact that public service institutions exist to 'do good'. These barriers to innovation each warrant brief discussion.

'Budget' versus results-based finding

The budgets received by academic libraries are often only indirectly linked to their performance. The responses in the Victorian study showed that decisions in the institutional and wider environment of the academic libraries were made more 'on the influence of powerful groups or individuals' than 'on the strengths of the arguments',[22] and this means that a reliable nexus between organizational performance and funding level is very difficult to achieve. The result can be the so-called 'freeway effect', where the library's very success in providing a service creates a demand which is too great to be adequately met without increased resources, and the library then needs to adopt a defensive posture to ration the service. Success thus becomes failure. Conversely, success in attracting more resources through political means unconnected with performance, remains success, because these new resources need not be fully stretched. Finally, as mentioned before, there is the ever-present danger than the library's basic grant might be cut by whatever amount is earned as profit or saved through efficiency.

Multiple constituents

Drucker observes that in a business that sells its products on the market, one constituent, the consumer, eventually overrides all the others. Academic libraries have many constituents. The Victorian study showed that the staff of the library would be among the most important of these.[23] It is understandable that staff should be an important constituency because their livelihood and professional identity depend on its welfare, and they can be depended on to defend its resource base. Also where permanent appointments are a feature of staffing policy, the long-term staff are in a position to make new initiatives unworkable if they oppose them. Other people or groups in the institution, or in government, responsible for making funding or other decisions about academic libraries, might seldom or never use the services of academic libraries. The 'consumer' is by no means the ultimate arbiter of the academic library's destiny.

Public-service institutions exist to 'do good'

The ideology of the free library with a mission to provide everyone with all the information they require is one which most librarians have helped to promote, but it has perilous consequences when libraries try to engage in commercial activities. Giving service priority to those who can afford to, or are prepared to, pay is generally unacceptable, even if ultimately this approach might benefit all users in the form of enriched bibliographic resources and more powerful information technology. The academic libraries have a clearly identified primary clientele – the staff and students of the institution – but to the extent that academic libraries are supported by tax-revenue they are regarded like public libraries, as resources which should be freely available to the community at large.

There are thus many justifications for the dominance of the *analyzer* strategy among Victorian chief librarians. Nevertheless, a choice is involved, and it is probable that the middle ground between *defender* and *prospector,* between *trustee* and *promotor* is chosen because achievable alternatives are difficult to envisage, or because there are no obvious rewards, and many risks, in making the shift towards a *prospector* or *promotor* strategy. There is still sufficient security in the library's 'stable product and market' areas to discourage major commitment to entrepreneurial strategies.

EXAMPLES OF ENTREPRENEURSHIP IN VICTORIAN ACADEMIC LIBRARIES

Notwithstanding the general situation that has been described, some notable entrepreneurial achievements have been initiated or fostered in Victorian academic libraries.

Supermap

Supermap, a highly innovative application of CD-ROM technology was the initiative of two staff members of the University of Melbourne: Jack Massey of the Department of Geography and Jeff Leeuwenburg, Information Services Librarian of Baillieu Library – the University's central library. The sponsor of the project was Dennis Richardson, University Librarian of the University of Melbourne.

Massey and Leeuwenburg recognised that there was a high demand for mapped and unmapped statistics. Available on-line services were very expensive to use. Accordingly they developed a system covering census data from the Australian Bureau of Statistics and map boundary information from the Division of National Mapping. Dennis Richardson realised that the cost of sponsoring the project was reasonable compared to the costs which his library was accustomed to paying for on-line access to statistical and mapping information. The library provided necessary equipment, paid for CD-ROM mastering costs, provided support in the form of telex and fax facilities, and obtained data sets not yet available on campus.

The result is a product that enables desk-top production of colour maps of virtually any combination of social data in Australia, down to the level of individual Census Collectors Districts.

Perhaps sadly, when the product reached maturity at the end of 1986, it moved out of the Library and the University, and is now being developed and marketed by a private company, Space-Time Research, in which both Massey and Leeuwenburg are principals. The University of Melbourne Library will receive free copies of its products for some time to come, and the Library has had its already considerable prestige enhanced by its part in the development of Supermap. Massey and Leeuwenburg intend to publish in the same format as Supermap the census and mapping data of other countries.[24]

AMIC – The Australian Microcomputer Industry Clearinghouse

AMIC was the idea of Don Schauder, then Associate Librarian at the Royal Melbourne Institute of Technology. In 1983, when an explosive growth in microcomputer hardware and software products was taking place, Schauder recognized that neither the RMIT Libraries nor RMIT as a whole, could hope to make available a wide range of hardware and software to students and staff without either a massive increase in funding or the active collaboration of the microcomputer industry.

Conceived originally as a library of computer hardware and software, the concept was initially canvassed within the RMIT Libraries Committee structure, but was judged too big for the Libraries alone to handle. Much hard work was required to persuade computer companies of the merits of AMIC. After all, there wasn't an AMIC elsewhere in Australia or in the United States. However, they were finally persuaded to deposit hundreds of thousands of dollars worth of equipment and software, and to pay substantial fees to cover AMIC's costs, including rental of prestige accommodation adjacent to the RMIT campus.

AMIC has gone from strength to strength as a demonstration and training centre. It was recently recognised by *Australian PC World* as 'tops among computer training centres headquartered in Melbourne'.[25] It is used as a training centre on a fee-paying basis by many of Australia's most distinguished companies, large and small. AMIC is a rewarding venture for the computer companies who display their products; for the RMIT staff who teach its fee-for-service courses and undertake consultancies for commerce and industries; for RMIT as a whole, which has access to a constantly updated and renewed collection of hardware and software; for the national and state governments who use it as a launching pad for Australian information technology; and for its customers who have access to a range of equipment, software and expertise which few if any other organisations can offer.

As with Supermap, the concept was nurtured in a library, but reached maturity outside the library organization. In contrast to Supermap, however, it remains a part of its parent institution, RMIT.

INFORMIT

INFORMIT is another example of library entrepreneurship at RMIT which, in contrast to AMIC, has remained within RMIT Libraries. It provides a vehicle for a range of services which RMIT Libraries offer to commerce, industry and the community, including on-line searching and bibliographic work. INFORMIT is an example of collective entrepreneurship by RMIT Libraries senior management, led by the Institute Librarian, Barrie Mitcheson.

WESTDOC

WESTDOC, a collaborative project with the municipalities in the western region of Melbourne, is a bibliographic database on the history and development of the western region. WESTDOC has diversified into additional services such as statistical information and a current information service on Telecom's VIATEL Videotex system.

WESTDOC has received funding from several sources, but its main funding has come from federal government employment creation programs. Dozens of long-term unemployed people have worked on the project and left with marketable skills in information work.

WESTDOC has been replicated and extended at Chisholm Institute of Technology under the name SOUTHGUIDE. Another replicative project, EASTDOC has started in the outer eastern region, with collaboration from the library of Victoria College.

The databases on the WESTDOC model provide substantial help to planners in the private and public sector, and to numerous community groups. They also serve as a resource for education and research in the academic institutions with which they are connected, and other educational organizations.

HITS

HITS – the Hargrave Information Technology Service – was established in 1985, to provide a fee-based information service to industry. The entrepreneurs involved were Marta Chiba, the Hargrave Librarian, and Leigh Oldmeadow, her deputy, who developed and now market the service. The Hargrave Library is part of the library system of Monash University and specialises in science and technology.

HITS was designed and targeted with great care. Its clientele are limited to a manageable number of firms within a 20 km radius of Monash. The concept was promoted by means of seminars. Pricing is set to cover all direct costs, overheads, salaries and includes a profit margin.

It is the stated intention of HITS that revenue earned should benefit the primary clientele of Hargrave Library, namely the staff and students of Monash University, through the provision of enriched facilities. From the viewpoint of the library staff, HITS provides an opportunity to broaden their experience, and to 'gain an idea of the information services undergraduates will require as professionals once they join the workforce'.[26]

ENTREPRENEURSHIP AND ACADEMIC LIBRARIES–THE NEXT PHASE

The examples of entrepreneurship given above are impressive, and are by no means exhaustive for Australian, or even for Victorian, academic libraries. However, they are no more than a beginning. Two of the examples – AMIC and Supermap – left the orbit of the library, and even the parent institution, at an early stage; the WESTDOC style projects operate alongside rather than within their library organizations. HITS and INFORMIT represent concepts which have been carefully integrated into the mainstream work of its library, but the price of this achievement is that the projects must proceed cautiously and on a small scale.

Lennart Bokajo of the Foresight Group of Sweden and USA has outlined the differences in management techniques required between 'traditional' and 'entrepreneurial' organizations. Essentially he recommends that organizations be flexible, that internal competition be tolerated, that managers should share their vision of the future, and that mistakes should be tolerated.[27] The Victorian study showed that the organizational characteristics of academic libraries had much in common with the 'traditional' paradigm described by Bokajo in that they use a fairly high degree of *formalization* of structure, or control of work patterns through rules and procedures. They were also resistant to the concept of split reporting lines.[28] Kanter provides a similar list to that of Bokajo of organizational characteristics that support creativity. It includes multiple reporting relationships, overlapping managerial territories, a free and 'somewhat random' flow of information, multiple centres of power with some budgetary flexibility, loose definition of managerial positions, an emphasis on lateral or cross-functional contact, and a system of rewards 'that emphasizes investment in people and projects rather than payment for past services (i.e. move successful entrepreneurs into more challenging jobs, and give them the chance to take on even bigger projects).[29]

Developing an entrepreneurial library clearly involves a difficult trade-off between the flexibility needed for innovators to prosper and the control needed to keep a library running efficiently in the short to medium term. This conflict between flexibility and control is the key tension that library managers need to contend with in promoting innovation. There is no guarantee that greater flexibility will improve morale among all staff members. For the manager personally there remains the apparent problem that public sector organizations have a skewed reward system which tends to penalize failure but not to reward success. The first step is simply to acknowledge this fact, and then proceed to limit the risks by handling the decision processes carefully, achieving some notable short term successes, and building political support.[30] Returning to the organization theory models in Figs. 1, 2 and 3, there is room for optimism about the future of entrepreneurship in academic libraries.

It must be remembered that the typologies which furnish the conceptual frameworks for organizational analysis are 'ideal types' – they are never fully encountered in the real world. The findings of the Victorian study show that while the organizational characteristics of Victorian academic libraries are not those of Miles' *prospector* or Stevenson and Gumpert's *promotor*, neither are they those of *defender* and *trustee*. Within the dominant *analyzer* strategy revealed by the Victorian study, there is a basic capacity for, and interest in, innovation and entrepreneurship. While it is true that 'one swallow does not make a summer', the examples of entrepreneurship given above seem to indicate, however tentatively, the potential for a more entrepreneurial future for academic libraries.

REFERENCES

1.   REID, B. J., ed. *Science parks and academic library services to business and*

industry. Papers of an ASCIS Seminar held in Aston Science Park, November 11th 1983. London, SCONUL, 1984.

BROADBENT, M. Academic library services – what is their market? *Australian Academic and Research Libraries,* **17**(3), 1986: pp. 105–109.

STALL, R. Subject – the bleeding obvious. *Incite,* 7(18) October, 1986: p. 1.

2.   PINCHOT, GIFFORD. *Intrapreneuring: why you don't have to leave the corporation to become an entrepreneur.* New York, Harper and Row, 1986. 368p. (Perennial Library), p. ix.

3.   DRUCKER, PETER F. *Innovation and entrepreneurship: practice and principles.* New York, Harper and Row, 1985, 277p. p. 19.

4.   DELIN, GUSTAF. Rewiring corporate thinking. *Public Relations Journal,* August 1983: pp. 12–13, 15.

BEECHEY, ANN. How to develop intrapreneurs inside your corporation, or how to hold on to people with good ideas. *Link,* 3(1) October 1985: p. 66.

BAILEY, JOHN E. *Entrepreneurship, intrapreneurship and organizational futures.* Caulfield East, Victoria, Centre for the Development of Entrepreneurs, Chisholm Institute of Technology, 1986. 18p

PINCHOT, *op. cit.*

5.   STEVENSON, HOWARD H. and GUMPERT, DAVID E. The heart of entrepreneurship. *Harvard Business Review,* **85**(2) 1985: pp. 85–94.

6.   KANTER, ROSABETH MOSS. The middle manager as innovator. *Harvard Business Review,* July-August, 1982: pp. 95–105. p. 99.

7.   CASSON, MARK. *The entrepreneur: an economic theory.* Oxford. Martin Robertson, 1982. 418 p. pp. 23–25.

8.   SCHAUDER, DONALD E. *Organization theory and academic libraries.* Unpublished thesis submitted for M.Ed. degree, University of Melbourne, 1987. 188p. p. 129.

9.   HOWARD, H. Organization theory. *Library Trends,* **32**(4) Spring, 1984: pp. 477–496.

10. SIMON, H. A. *Administrative behavior: a study of decision-making processes in administrative organizations.* 2nd edn. New York, Free Press, 1965.

11. GREENFIELD, T. B. Organization theory as ideology. *Curriculum Inquiry,* **9**(2), 1979: pp. 97–112.

GREENFIELD, T. B. The man who comes back through the door in the wall: discovering truth, discovering self, discovering organizations. *Educational Administration Quarterly,* **16**(3) Fall, 1980: pp. 26–59.

GREENFIELD, T. B. Against group mind: an anarchist theory of organization. In: *Reflective readings in educational administration.* Geelong, Victoria, Deakin University Press, 1983. pp. 293–301).

GREENFIELD, T. B. Theories of educational organization: a critical perspective. [Photocopy of manuscript for publication]. In: *International encyclopedia of education: research and studies,* Oxford, Pergamon Press, 1985. 30p.

12. SCHAUDER, *op cit.* p. 34.

13. STEVENSON and GUMPERT, *op. cit.* pp. 86, 93.

14. *Ibid.* p. 86.

15. SCHAUDER, DON. The technology of wisdom: applying organization theory to academic libraries. *Australian Academic Research Libraries,* **17**(30), 1986: pp. 126–147.

SCHAUDER, *Organization theory and academic libraries, op. cit.*

16. ROBBINS, S. P. *Organization theory.* Englewood Cliffs, N. J., Prentice Hall, 1983. p. 423.

17. MILES, R. E., SNOW, C. C., MEYER, A. D. & COLEMAN, H. J.

Organizational strategy, structure, and process. *Academy of Management Review,* July 1978: pp. 546–562.

18.   *Ibid.*
19.   ROBBINS, *op. cit.* p. 103.
20.   *Ibid,* p. 102.
21.   DRUCKER, *op. cit.* p. 177.
22.   SCHAUDER, The technology of wisdom, *op. cit.* p. 129.
23.   *Ibid.* pp. 139–140.
24.   Australian library tests new approach to mapping with CD-ROM. *CD Data Report,* 2(7) May 1986: p. 1.
       LEEUWENBuRG, JEFF. SUPERMAP I: the census on CD-ROM. In: *Information online 87: worldwide information at your fingertips: preprints: second Australian Online Conference and Exhibition,* 27–29 January 1987, Hilton International, Sydney. Sponsored by the Information Science Section of the Library Association of Australia. Sydney, The Section, 1986. 299p. pp. 106–108.
25.   Recognition. *AMIC News Digest,* March 1987: p. 6.
26.   OLDMEADOW, LEICH. HITS: a university based information service to industry. In: *Information online 87: worldwide information at your fingertips: preprints: second australian Online Conference and Exhibition,* 27–29 January 1987, Hilton International, Sydney. Sponsored by the Information Science Section of the Library Association of Australia. Sydney, The Section, 1986. 299p. pp. 232–237.
27.   BEECHEY, *op. cit.*
28.   SCHAUDER, The technology of widom, *op. cit.* p. 137.
29.   KANTER, *op. cit.* pp. 104–105.
30.   RAMAMURTI, RAVI. Public entrepreneurs: who they are and how they operate. *California Management Review,* xxviii (3) Spring 1986: p. 150.

ACKNOWLEDGEMENTS

The help given by Dr John Bailey, Executive Director, Centre for the Development of Entrepreneurs, Chisholm Institute of Technology, Victoria, Australia; and by my friend and mentor Dr Pierre Gorman, Visiting Fellow, Chisholm Institute of Technology, in the preparation of this paper, is gratefully acknowledged.

The Model Research Library: Planning for the Future

by *Anne Woodsworth, Nancy Allen, Irene Hoadley, June Lester, Pat Molholt, Danuta Nitecki, and Lou Wetherbee*

ABSTRACT

Scholars, academic administrators, and librarians have expressed differing views on the shape and function of the research library of the 21st century. This group of library professionals offers one plausible vision. As the participants underscore: 'While not all members of the group accepted all of the details, or even agreed to all of the underlying premises, there was enough unanimity about the model to generate a sense of urgency and excitement about sharing it beyond the conference and its participants.' With the publication of this article, we hope to stimulate further thought and discussion on this important issue. In fact, the next issue of JAL will feature reactions to this article – and the future research library model it proposes – from professionals with a variety of perspectives.

In publishing an article listing more than three authors, JAL has broken a long-standing policy for the first (and perhaps last) time. We felt that this essay merited an exception to our three-author limit because the ideas expressed here are truly the product of a collaborative effort. Although Anne Woodsworth gathered together and synthesized the group's ideas, she did this with the acknowledged assistance of all those involved in generating them.

MISSION STATEMENT

The future mission of the research library will be:

to ensure that a ready and free flow of information-based services, collections, and library services are integrated into the research, teaching, and administrative functions of the university. To pursue this mission the library must assume a central and integral role in formulating policy, and in fostering collaborative activities within the university and with other actors in the scholarly communication process.[1]

To describe the future is speculative and risky. To articulate what the future *should* hold, however, is another matter and requires more insight than foresight. To influence the shape of libraries in the future, not only is it desirable to describe what the future should be – to outline a vision or an ideal – but doing so is a first step in ensuring that the vision becomes reality.

The above mission statement differs from most others because it asserts a more integral and primary role for research libraries in educational and research processes than they currently have. It assumes that libraries will become more active participants in the scholarly communication process as information technologies and information resources converge and become inseparable parts of all functions within the university. The mission statement and the resultant model of the future research library presented here were developed by participants at a 1988 conference 'Options for the Future,' sponsored by the Council on Library Resources.[2]

The conceptual model shows how the research library of the future will operate, and is followed by the transitional steps needed to build a sound foundation for it. As the model and transition steps are outlined in the following pages, it should become apparent that flexibility, collaboration, diversity, and fluidity will become key attributes of all those involved in the future of North American research libraries.

THE CONCEPTUAL MODEL

The components and categories of information activities in the research library of the year 2020 are best depicted as a tripartite and interconnected system (see Figure 1). Each of the three components of the system has a set of characteristics that distinguishes one from the others. The elements of this set, displayed in Figure 1, consist of:

- focus for its activities,
- functions,
- a set of primary resources with which it deals,
- appropriate groups with which it communicates,
- staffing patterns and expertise, *and*
- distinctive results for which it is accountable.

The arrows in Figure 1 show communication among the three components to be multi-directional within the system. Externally, all components have two-way interaction with users and others engaged in the scholarly communication process. Although all three components communicate externally, each component has a different set of primary external connections. For example, component 1, which handles information in various formats, will deal with the external information environment from which the information products and services are acquired. At the same time, the information access system designers (component 2) will be communicating with individuals and groups on campus, at other institutions, and in industry who are working to improve or design access systems and networks. Component 3, the group that delivers and evaluates programs and services, will deal most often with the users of information such as faculty, researchers, and students.

FIG. 1. INFORMATION ACTIVITIES OF THE RESEARCH LIBRARY OF THE FUTURE

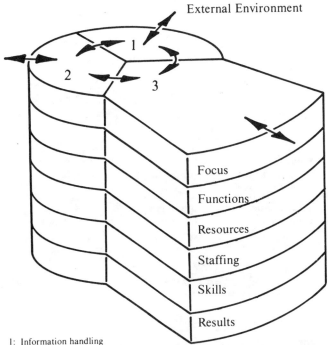

1: Information handling
2: Designing access systems
3: Evaluating user needs and delivering services and programs

However, the third component will not be the exclusive point of contact for users since the staff who are expert in organizing, acquiring, and packaging information will also be working directly with users – e.g. advising them how to structure personal information files.

As shown in Table 1, each component has a distinctive character that stems from its primary responsibility or focus.

Component 1 handles information in various formats; it will deal with greatly diversified collections and other physical expressions of information. Although most of its activities will focus on traditional printed materials, it will handle information available online, on microfiche, on CD-ROM, and in other formats as well. Component 2 designs access systems; it will be concerned with files related to the information carriers, including the structure of electronic information files, and with establishing electronic connections among objects and files.

The functional component that evaluates needs and delivers programs and services, component 3, will have the most user interaction on a day-to-day basis and will have information users as its primary focus. This component, for example, will develop the user profiles that

TABLE 1. *Information Activities of the Research Library of the Future*

Elements	Component 1	Component 2	Component 3
Focus	Handle information in various formats	Design access systems	Recognize and provide for user needs
Function	Acquisition Organization Preservation	Design and maintain access systems	Evaluate user needs Deliver user programs and services
Resources	Objects Collections	Objects Files	People
Staffing	Centralized High-level support staff	Centralized Information professionals	Dispersed Library professionals
Knowledge/Skills	Preservation techniques Collection organization and development	Artificial intelligence uses Information structures User support systems	Subject orientation and knowledge Interpersonal skills Technological and information literacy
Results	Objects are organized and presented	Access systems are user-sensitive	User needs are met

are integrated into information retrieval systems and will provide the data and analyses needed to develop AI applications for libraries. Most of the library's professional staff will be deployed in this area of the operation.

Generally, staff who are involved in handling information in various formats and in designing access systems will be centralized, while those involved in delivering and evaluating programs and services will be dispersed, functioning in 'service clusters' close to their main user groups. The results of this more user-sensitive information 'system' will be products and services that are more readily measurable and highly visible since they will be targeted at specific groups of users.

The following sections expand on the nature of the programmatic and service changes in the research library and illustrate in more detail the functions of the three primary components. To facilitate understanding and to link the components to current concepts, they are grouped under terms that are in common use at present.

User services. Future user services will be characterized by:

- proactive identification or anticipation of user needs;

- provision of access to almost all information at the level of the user's workstation;
- collaboration with faculty in developing new and customized services; *and*
- delivery of faster, more convenient access to bibliographic information and physical forms of information, irrespective of location.

In the main, the library's human resources will focus on service to users and will have a high level of interaction with other information providers on campus. The library will be a more integral part of the teaching, learning and research processes in the university and, as a result, will lose some of its current insularity.

In this environment, the library staff will carry out functions that are presently only ideas or, at best, in nascent or experimental form. They will:

- create databases and other information products for both individuals and groups of users;
- work with others in the institution to make these databases commercially available beyond the university;
- deliver documents in many formats;
- transform information from one format to another;
- evaluate the validity and relevance of information;
- package information to suit the user, including conversion of format or 'container' when needed; *and*
- provide instruction to ensure information literacy.

The library's staff will work as partners in the research process with discipline-based scholars; serve as consultants on the design of databases and the management of information files and resources; and identify and adapt external information services to meet local needs. Staff from all three components of the system will be needed to provide these kinds of responsive services.

Collections

The value of a library will not be measured by the size, depth, or breadth of the collections owned but rather by its ability to provide access to information in all formats. Bibliographic access systems and digitization will continue to improve, expanded by wholetext retrieval and in-depth access to materials not in machine-readable form. This improved access will permit more on-demand acquisitions, dispersed access to primary and secondary sources in different formats, and, last but not least, widespread realization of coordinated collections and preservation efforts among institutions. Organization and preservation functions will rely heavily on shared expertise, networked systems, and cooperative efforts. Acquisitions, except in the largest research libraries, will be demand driven.

Facilities

Although materials will continue to be produced in print and paper format, new functions for library and information services will dictate changes in the use of existing facilities. With the exception of a small number of research libraries that will continue to maintain large collections of record, most capital expenditures will go toward the construction of storage and preservation facilities that are separate from 'use' facilities. Each campus will resolve the offsite-onsite and local-regional debates relating to storage, but materials will not necessarily be housed permanently in the facilities used to deliver service.

Existing library and campus facilities will be adapted to function as service nodes, close to user groups. These service points will have less staff work space and more user space; will be secure and easily accessible; and will have warm, friendly interiors conducive to research and scholarship. Somewhere on campus, perhaps in the library, facilities will exist that can transform information from one format to another, according to user need, and can arrange for delivery to the user or the user's service cluster. The amount and configuration of library space will be determined to a large extent by institutional values and the degree of emphasis on ownership of materials versus access to information.

Staffing

Staffing configurations for the three components will vary due to the different functions and concerns of each (see Table 1). The capabilities and skills possessed by the composite research library staff will include, along with an understanding of libraries and librarianship:

- knowledge of cognitive and disciplinary research processes and of psychology;
- technological sophistication;
- well-developed interpersonal skills;
- knowledge of information policy development and analysis;
- political acumen, and planning skills.

In addition, librarians will be assertive risk-takers and synthesizers and have the ability to function in an atmosphere of ambiguity and change.

On the whole, future research library staff will be better educated; also, a greater percentage will have degrees in disciplines other than librarianship. All library personnel will perform a higher level of work and have more responsibility than they do in current staffing configurations. Staff skills will be supplemented by 'knowbots' – expert systems that help define needs, facilitate information access, and tailor the information packages to suit individuals or groups of people.[3] There will be a need for discipline-based subject expertise, specific to the character of the institution, that will permit a more successful integration of the library into the research and scholarly processes on campus. Many routine operations will be handled by external contractors. Decisions to contract out will be made by careful examination of make-or-buy benefits/drawbacks as determined by the character of the institution and needs of the users.

Administration

The relationship of service clusters to each other and to the administration of the library will be fluid and complex. The shape and composition of service clusters will vary over time and among institutions, depending on the needs of users and on the characteristics of information generation, production, and use within the discipline and/or group being served. Groups will be formed to work together across the three categories as needed; their group affiliations will range from very short term to semi-permanent. To pool more narrow expertise, some support will be centralized, with personnel perhaps flowing in and out of the clusters as required in a manner similar to the formation of mission-based research groups.

Due to dispersal of staff into user-oriented clusters, the administration of the library will become more complex than it has been to date. In order to maintain their user-driven service orientation, administrators will be increasingly accountable and sensitive to market needs. Library administrators will also participate to a greater extent in the development of information policy on campus. Similarly, more time and effort will be spent on interinstitutional cooperation, consortia, and nationally coordinated efforts, as well as on external development of information policies at regional, national, and international levels.

Internally, the role of the administration in this model will be to facilitate, coordinate, and orchestrate the work of each component. The functions of the library administration will vary with the mission of the institution and will change in response to changing environmental conditions. This organizational concept is radically different from today's hierarchical library structures, but it is common in organizations operating under matrix management principles. The construct is also consistent with a trend observed in highly automated corporate environments where one of the impacts of technology has been the flattening of organizational structures through the elimination of middle management. In order to respond quickly to changing user needs, budget control, decision making, and accountability will reside at the level of the service cluster.

BOUNDARY CONDITIONS

The above model of the future research library did not develop quixotically. It was derived after consideration of future boundary conditions and premises about the university, the information industry, technological developments, and governmental priorities. Premises and assumptions that form the boundary conditions for research libraries in the future range from local, university-based factors to broad societal trends.

The university

The university will not change significantly over the next 20 or 30 years in mission, character, or organizational structure. It will remain essentially a medieval institution. However, some of the inner workings that will change include the following.

Instructional delivery will be more geographically decentralized. The student body will be more diverse in age and ethnicity, will be multilingual and multinational, and will come to the university with more divergent technical and academic preparations. While the role of faculty governance will remain the same, the nature of the faculty will undergo changes.

- Both greater interdisciplinary alliances and greater divergence in research patterns and information needs of scientists and humanists will take shape.
- Because of a continuing brain drain to the private commercial sector, the overall quality of the faculty may be less consistent.
- More funding will come from the private sector, with one result being more effort directed to applied research.
- More researchers will be trained outside the university, in corporate or private educational settings.
- The gap between research and instructional missions of the university will have widened.
- The faculty in most disciplines will measure excellence of the library and the university in new ways, focusing on excellence in technological support services (computing and electronic information access) rather than on the size of the library's book collection.

The administration of the university will assume a corporate decision-making approach or attitude, expecting more accountability from divisions and units in the institution. Competing forces within universities will seek control of information policies and funds.

The library

While the character of the library's services and operations will change, not all future research libraries will be identical in scope, structure, and service emphasis. Some will be funded to retain their national resource mission, and remain relatively unchanged in continuing to focus on the acquisition of comprehensive collections. At the opposite end of the spectrum, some will dedicate most of their efforts and funds to providing electronic access to information resources. Common characteristics will include the following:

- Collections will include data files and resources in electronic form;
- Libraries will be packaging information and services with the convenience of users in mind;
- Librarians will take an increasingly proactive role in advising individuals and departments on information processing for both research purposes and the operation of the university;
- Library staff will include subject specialists, technicians, and professionals from other information fields – e.g., programmer/ analysts, network designers and managers, marketing specialists, and experts in artificial intelligence and the cognitive sciences;
- Fund reallocation decisions within each library will become key factors in engendering diversity among academic libraries;
- Because of increasingly diverse student bodies, librarians will support and participate in general education programs to create a base of information skills. One of their primary roles will be teaching, including serving in an advisory capacity for faculty and graduate students;
- The number of routine, clerical tasks will decrease in libraries and be performed elsewhere or by computers (e.g. as in present technical services), enabling more of the library's human resources to engage in direct user services; *and*
- Training and recruitment for the library of the future will be critical.

The government

It is assumed that governments at all levels will have increasing influence on higher education, be it through priorities for research and development, information policies such as privatization, or financial support. Several assumptions about the future have influenced the formation of our conceptual model of tomorrow's research library.

- Universities and libraries will face more accountability from sources of funding for services and programs.
- More restrictions will be placed on the flow of information; this will mean that libraries will have to deal with classified materials.
- Although no single government agency is now responsible for information policy, a new over-arching policy agency may be put in place to coordinate policies and to reemphasize the international position of the USA
- Because information has unusual properties as a commodity (e.g. is procurable, shareable, transportable), libraries will need to take a vigorous role in developing new intellectual property policies,

particularly since they will be producing and/ or marketing information as well as acquiring it for dissemination to users.

Information industry

Underlying all of the assumptions made about information products and technology is a tacit acceptance that the publishing industry will change more slowly from print to electronic publication outputs than has been previously envisioned. Nevertheless, the following factors are some that win influence research libraries.

- Standardization of information products and technology will occur of necessity, and libraries must put forth effort to influence the development of standards for both products and services.
- Because of competition with and within the private-sector portion of the information market place, the 'bestseller' (commercially successful) products and technologies will end up as the property of the private sector. Because libraries will control esoteric, unusual, or rare information, they may lose power and influence in the commercial market place, but might gain them in the scholarly communication process since they will have control of specialized files and resources.
- The general availability and value of information as a commodity will influence libraries to sell information systems and access, and will lead them to package information for the academic market, and possibly for the general public.
- There will be more offshore ownership of information by multi-national corporations with holdings portfolios of a very broad nature. Hence, the content and accessibility of information products and services may be shaped by vendors with economic, social, and cultural values that differ from those held in an open democratic society.
- The information industry will work more closely with the information producers such as scholarly societies and libraries. For example, faculty working with libraries will be producing specialized, marketable databases and coordinating access and distribution of them with information vendors.

Fiscal factors

While sources of funding and choices in the reallocation of expenditures have already been mentioned, it is recognized that decisions about capital versus operational investment and related priority questions will usually be made on an institution-by-institution basis. Nevertheless, there will be some basic fiscal issues that will face all universities in the information age with respect to research libraries.

For instance, marketing of information products and services is a potential source of revenue. The university's role could be one of developing databases that could either be sold directly or contracted out to the private sector for marketing or sale. Also, libraries will, of necessity, move toward a commercial, private-sector attitude about their collections – that is, they will act on the premise that collections are not only assets to be guarded but also properties to be exploited in order to support the mission of the library.

The philosophy of keeping library services and collections as free goods may be at risk, and this tenet must be examined. The current fee-or-free duality that plagues the issue of information access must be recognized, and decisions must be made about the extent to which a revenue-producing approach will be carried into the new information environment.

To illustrate, the following questions must be answered by each academic community: Should traditional library services and collections continue to be funded as university overhead? Should new services, including new information technologies, and especially customized/tailored services, be funded by users/departments and developed as self-supporting services?

New definitions of the base-line information services that will be made available free of charge will have to be developed, with greater clarification of funding and support for value-added information services. The changed needs inherent in a swing from ownership to access can be funded in part from the sales of information from locally produced databases. This source of revenue, however, will not fully support either the continuation of traditional and existing library services or the newer, access-oriented library services.

Information technology

Information technology, which is continuing to develop at an exponential rate, will provide universities and libraries with unforeseeable opportunities for the creation, storage, and transmission of information. With respect to information handling in and for research libraries in the future, the following assumptions are made.

- Technology will be transparent to the user and therefore will be of less concern than the content of the information access systems.
- Telecommunications and standards will provide the backbone for connectivity sufficient to support campus information needs and for interinstitutional coordination of library/information services.
- Appropriate hardware and software will permit shared use of systems and resources, exchange of information in various formats, access to remote and distributed databases, and shared development of systems that provide information access and delivery, both

among libraries and directly to users. Satisfactory models for local, regional, and state consortia and networks will have developed for multitype and multipurpose cooperation among libraries and information agencies.

TURNING THE MODEL INTO REALITY

Some library leaders have already started to make the changes that will enable research libraries to incorporate the concepts presented in this paper. Over the next 20 to 30 years, many steps will have to be taken to enable the research library of the future to serve increasingly divergent needs of faculty and students; to establish the appropriately flexible, fluid, and responsive organizations; and to foster a climate of cooperation with and among librarians, scholars, researchers, publishers, others in the information industry, and key government agencies. What follows is a selection of some of the transitional steps that must be pursued in order to successfully position research libraries in the coming decades of societal, economic, and technological changes.

Facilities

Some building blocks are relatively easy to identify and put into place. For example, to ensure that physical facilities are planned and built to meet (not impede) future needs, several steps can be taken in the near future. At the local level, each campus can articulate a strategic direction for its library and information services and then build and renovate physical facilities in the coming decades based on its long-range plan. Nationally, agencies such as the Council on Library Resources and the Association of Research Libraries can conduct space inventories and, as they have done with preservation, assist with the design and implement-ation of national and international strategies to deal with a shortage of space for research library collections.

On campus

There are other, broader transitions that are more difficult to implement, since they call for modification (at best) or total transformation (at worst) of attitudes and skills. Consider, for example, the changes needed to achieve the following states:

- Diversity in the services, programs, and collections of research libraries is recognized and appreciated.
- Differing measures of effectiveness, specific to the nature of the individual research library, are the norm.
- The role of librarians is broadly seen as that of a partner with faculty and researchers in the generation, production, and management of information.

- Units and specialists within the library function in a highly collaborative mode in order to meet users needs.
- The campus community perceives the library as the facilitator of access to information, rather than as a repository of information containers and artifacts.
- Administration of the library is highly complex as a result of (1) the centralization of university-wide information technology decisions and related policies, and (2) the increased significance of interinstitutional systems and relationships in the provision of access to information.
- Librarians are accepted as having key local, national, and international roles in determining information policy at all levels.

In these areas, as in all the transitional steps mentioned, librarians must first and foremost prepare themselves to change – to begin making moves toward realizing their vision of the research library 30 years hence. Outside the library, other key players need to shift their perceptions and attitudes. Students, faculty, and researchers, who form the primary groups of information users; campus administrators, who control the planning mechanisms, academic programs, and other intersecting interests; those running bibliographic utilities and other components of the information industry; those involved in scholarly associations and foundations; and government officials at various levels – all will have to recognize and support the new role for the research library of the future.

At first glance the task seems awesome. On college and university campuses alone, however, some initial steps may be taken.

- Articulate and promote on campus a concept or vision of the library that better defines its unique role as an information provider.
- Experiment with new or enhanced services to special target groups in order to gain experience in evaluating user needs and to build credibility in functioning as part of the team that generates/produces/manages information.
- Foster more informal contacts for librarians with faculty and administrators.
- Establish mechanisms and funding sources for research, development, and implementation of new services as the information technologies evolve. In so doing, ensure that the experience is widely shared and that these new concepts are incorporated into ongoing decision making and planning.
- Begin offering new services on campus by identifying campus data files and data resources that could be campus-wide resources. Promote access to these faculty/research files through the campus online public access catalog.
- Develop and implement services tailored to student needs.
- Incorporate information literacy into the curriculum by (1) establishing informal and formal contacts with academic program

decision makers, and (2) educating faculty about the importance of information literacy.

- Focus the planning activities of the university on information needs and information management.
- Establish campus policies that will govern access to and control of information services. Begin to develop cost and funding structures that will endure and build a foundation for the future research library.
- Ensure that librarians are involved in information technology decisions on campus.
- Change the mandate and scope of the library advisory committee to encompass management of and access to information resources throughout the university.

Inside the library

Inside the library, transitional steps will have to lead toward acceptance of more proactive and diverse roles for staff and more frequent and diverse organizational changes. As pointed out, the skills and attitudes of library staff will need to shift dramatically. Some ways to foster these needed changes follow.

- Articulate and broadcast a vision of the future within the library itself.
- Educate existing staff, both attitudinally and technologically, to work in a more collaborative manner with users and to promote the use of information technologies. Accomplishing such change will require that staff throughout the organization, at all working levels, be given greater responsibility and decision-making power. It also will demand that educational opportunities be provided for staff to develop subject expertise, interpersonal skills, technological competency, and leadership ability.
- Use performance expectations and reward systems to reinforce and encourage changes that mesh with the future vision of the library.
- Experiment; take risks with organizational structures.
- Recruit library staff from a broader base of education and experience, e.g. from nonresearch libraries and other professions.
- Adopt an attitude of partnership with library schools in responsibility for the preparation of librarians through (1) the redesign of library education or creation of alternatives, (2) the provision of more in-house training and education, and (3) increased practitioner interaction with library educators.
- Actively recruit 'the brightest and the best' into the library and information science professions.

Beyond the library

Beyond the library there are many steps that must be taken for the concepts outlined in this paper to materialize. Outside of a single institutional boundary, there are several that are seen as key to a successful transition.

- Librarians must become active partners in the scholarly process and in discussions pertaining to the generation, production, and access of information, including those on archival and preservation needs in the electronic environment.
- Librarians must be increasingly involved with those responsible for the development of information technology for the university and the information industry.
- Librarians must influence information policy as it affects information use and technology by collaborating with other stakeholders, especially in the political arena, at various governmental levels, and in scholarly associations.

In all of these efforts, librarians must take responsibility for positioning themselves in the appropriate groups and situations; they must not sit and wait to be noticed. Key actors with whom research librarians should establish ongoing contact include faculty involved in information research, computing center staff, publishers, information producers and vendors, those involved in telecommunications networks, and state and government librarians.

Finally and more broadly, there must be discussion and reconceptualization of the research library in light of forthcoming technological, societal, and economic changes. The model presented here is not intended to be ideal or definitive. Since there will be more, not less, diversity among research libraries in the future, the spectrum along which research libraries will develop will require elaboration of more transitional steps and continual reviews of boundary conditions.

However, no matter how a given research library defines its future, collaboration, flexibility, and fluidity will be the key attributes that characterize its operations and services. No research library can afford to drift toward the turn of the century without a vision for the future. Strategic directions need to be articulated *now* so that resources and efforts in the intervening years are most effectively deployed. Only with a clear vision of its future mission and a strategy for navigating the transition can a research library retain and improve both relevance and support on campus.

REFERENCES

1   From the mission statement produced by conference participants at 'Options for the Future,' UCLA, August 20–23, 1988.
2   Participating in the conference were representatives from the Council on Library Resources and its Research Library Committee; the Dean and Assistant Dean of UCLA's Graduate School of Library and Information Science; and librarians who had participated in UCLA's Senior Fellows

Program (a leadership development program also sponsored by CLR) between 1982 and 1987. For the three days of the conference, 36 Senior Fellow participants were divided into four groups, each charged with the following goals: describe the ideal research library; clarify the assumptions, including the predicted environmental conditions, upon which the ideal is based; and identify the transition steps needed to achieve the ideal. One of the groups developed the vision that is presented in this paper. While not all members of the group accepted all of the details, or even agreed to all of the underlying premises, there was enough unanimity about the model to generate a sense of urgency and excitement about sharing it beyond the conference and its participants. The group that developed the concepts in this paper from August 20–23, 1988, included Nancy Allen (Colorado State), Irene Hoadley (Texas A & M), June Lester (ALA), Pat Molholt (Rensselaer), Danuta Nitecki (Maryland), Richard Talbot (Massachusetts), Louella Wetherbee (AMIGOS), and Anne Woodsworth (Pittsburgh).

3   The 'Knowbot' concept was developed by Robert Kahn of the Corporation for Research Initiatives. A similar concept, the 'Knowledge Navigator,' was presented by John Scully at EDUCOM in 1987.

Niche products for the manager

Patricia Hämäläinen

Senior Information Officer, ALKO Ltd., Helsinki, Finland

ABSTRACT

Changing business environments are challenging managers to play and to succeed in a new game. The rules, the players, the boundaries, and the potential for success are in the process of rapid development. How are managers preparing themselves to participate in the new arena? How can Information Services located in a corporate setting support management in this effort? One strategy is to produce niche products that fit the managers' developing global orientation.

A problem that many managers face is how to follow global changes which impact on their business interests. New trade boundaries are emerging in Europe, in North America and in the Far East. Traditional corporate relationships, ownerships, and country affiliation are evolving into new patterns. Companies are seeing new competitors enter home markets in greater numbers at the same time as they are looking for market expansion outside their home areas. There are political implications developing in Eastern Europe as well as a shifting of economic strength to the Pacific Rim countries.

Many corporate decisions depend on management being knowledgeable about conditions outside their traditional market area. In order to assess their company's longterm goals and objectives, managers increasingly need to be aware of developments in terms of the global situation.

INFORMATION TASK

ALKO Ltd in Finland, which holds the state monopoly for producing and selling alcoholic beverages, also exports both its products and technical know-how. The company's turnover in 1988 was FIM 4.7 billion. Employees number about 2,800.

The problem for Information Services located in a corporate situation, such as ALKO's for example, is to develop information products and services that fit this emerging need. One strategy ALKO's Information Services Unit has developed to meet this need is to develop and market information niche products and services for managers on the business unit level. The main task is to find the niche and service it.

In developing information products inside a corporation, there are important questions such as:

- Who are the customers?
- What information do they need?
- What are they willing to pay for information products?
- What are service expectations?

These questions are often answered in part in terms of 'quality'. This means quality in terms of the customer perception, quality in terms of pricing, and quality in terms of service expectations met.

But what exactly is perceived as 'quality' in information products? And more specifically, what does the business unit manager perceive as quality in information products that are designed to help him or her compete internationally?

The following describes the development of a method that ties the definition of the information product and service directly to the customer at the planning stages. In other words, the customer sculpts his or her own product. This process tends to build quality aspects into the product as the product is being designed, and tends to address the issue of service expectations. The result of the process leads to business-driven information products and services that are perceived by the customer as high quality. The customer is satisfied, the price is weighed against the quality aspects as well as sensitivity to service expectations.

MODEL FOR NICHE PRODUCTS

As a guide to finding the information niche a working model was developed. The model for development of products and services is designed to link business objectives to information planning. The end result is products and services driven by customer need and expectations. They become tools which offer information that management can factor into decision-making on the business unit level.

The steps in the model are the following:

- assess the corporate mission of the business unit
- define the critical success factors of the unit
- develop information strategy
- produce products and services

The method of using CSFs was developed by a research team at the MIT Sloan School of Management.

CORPORATE MISSION

The first step in determining the internal market information needs and expectations is to assess the corporate mission of the business unit. One way to do this is to use already developed systems for analysis of a company's portfolio of businesses. For example, the Boston Consulting Group's model (Dogs, Cash Cows, Question Marks or Stars) or Michael Porter's model (Divest, Leadership, Harvest or Niche) would be well-known systems. Both provide a marketing view of a company's business unit's corporate mission.

Knowing the corporate role of the business unit helps in information planning in several ways. Priority units can be identified for action. The allocation of time and money can be concentrated where it matters. Using the Boston model, it is easy to see that a unit that plays a Star role will require different information initiatives and support than one which is in a Dog role.

CRITICAL SUCCESS FACTORS

The next step is a key area. This step involves determining the critical success factors (CSF) of the unit. This step further sharpens the focus for defining your customer specific needs. The manager becomes the central figure and co-producer in the information process. He or she defines those factors that are essential and critical for the success of the unit. For example, 'market success for product X in Denmark' might be one CSF. Another CSF might be 'good contacts in government regulation offices'. Most companies have at least several CSFs.

The role of the information officer in collaboration with the manager then is to address the issues presented in the CSFs of the business unit. The initial step is to ask: 'What information is needed to match the unit's CSFs?' Key questions are formulated that highlight the critical issues and whose answers would provide a picture of what is happening in that area.

INFORMATION STRATEGY

At this next step in the model, business planning and information planning are linked together and the information becomes business driven. Using the mentioned CSFs 'market success' and 'good contacts', the information needed might be defined in the following way:

For 'market success', typical questions might be:
- Who are the major players in the Danish market?
- What are the recent acquisition patterns of the major players?
- What trends are developing in x product area in the EC?

For 'good contracts', typical questions might be:

- Who runs the regulation office?
- What are recent decisions from the office?
- What are recent regulation trends in the EC?

The information questions are directly related to critical issues for the business unit or corporation as defined by the manager. As the CSFs change, the information question changes in tandem. Therefore, this step involves continual servicing by re-defining and re-formulating the questions to fit the critical issues in the unit. The process of adapting to change creates sensitivity to customer needs and builds flexibility into product development.

An information plan is developed that matches business planning efforts and the role of the business unit in the company. The plan is specific and identifies information objectives, timetable, service options, core products, and spin-off products. This information planning stage also includes household tasks such as identifying reliable sources of information, calculating the costs and exploiting available technical tools to process the information.

The result at this stage will be a working framework and schedule for production of the products or services. Effort and detail at this stage also contribute to later evaluation of a project. If the product is not successful, re-evaluation at this stage may help in identifying the part that should be changed.

ISSUE: DECISION-MAKING PROCESS

At this stage in finding the niche, it is important to have some understanding of the decision-making process of the manager and the role the information is to play in the process.

Many managers build a unique system over the years for obtaining reliable information which they factor into their decisions. The sources are varied – from personal contacts to international databases. Each is valued and plays a role at different times in the decision-making process from the definition of a problem to the final decision. Also, it seems clear that in the process of reaching a conclusion, managers will tend to link their sources at different stages of the process. It is also likely that the closer the manager moves to the point of decision, the more targeted and valued the information.

One consideration is that managers often develop decision processes which have a certain pattern depending on the type of the decision to be made. Another consideration is that they all have a pattern of seeking information at various stages along the way. The process tends to be unique with each person.

For the information officer, knowing how the manager thinks and assessing his or her decision patterns is important. Also, knowing how critical an issue is to a unit or at what stage the information-seeking process is, will aid in determining more exactly what products or services are required. With cooperative planning and trust between manager and information officer, each question answered fits in the manager's thinking process and moves the manager toward his or her objectives.

PRODUCTS AND SERVICES

The last step then is to produce and take to the marketplace the core products and services that fit your customer's needs and expectations. The production process includes exploiting business information resources, formatting, testing, packaging, quality control measures and transfer.

ISSUE: COMMUNICATION STYLES

An important issue at this final production stage is communication styles. Successful communication of messages is of central concern to product and service development.

Different people have different styles of communicating, both in verbal and in written form. For simplicity, common characteristics can be identified. For example, an action-oriented person tends to focus on results, likes to have brief accounts, practical suggestions and appreciates visual aids. In contrast, a people-oriented person may prefer to emphasise the relationships between a product and the people concerned. Also they are concerned with past precedent and tend to prefer informal writing or speaking styles.

Recognising that there are different styles, and matching products communication style with the customers' communication style is appreciated, and will bring return customers.

EXAMPLES

End products groups might fall under such descriptive titles as:
Corporate Profiles, Management Briefs, Company Analysis, Cross-border Monitor, Tracking Industry Movers or News Update.

The possibilities for services are quite broad. To illustrate, a bundle of services available for a core product might be a mix of several elements. For example, News Update Products could include high level services such as quick delivery; short, clear statements; brief documents; sharp or narrow focus; and as-it-happens supply.

Or, as a low end variation of service options, News Updates might simply be abstracts taken from international databases, supplied at regular, preplanned intervals and serviced once a year for changes in topic area.

Tracking Industry Mover Products might be serviced in another way. For example, a verbal person-to-person summary might accompany each Brief to the manager. This high-level customer contact service gives the customer the opportunity to ask questions and. get immediate, critical feedback.

Reports supplied incrementally as Briefs, instead of in one big batch, might also be a valued service. A special notebook organiser for paper editions, or electronic file system, might be another service option.

CHARACTERISTICS OF THE NICHE SERVICE

From the company's point of view, the framework for product development can be used across different product lines or business units. This builds synergy among units by sharing activities and expertise company-wide. This is cost effective. Also, the information production process becomes less labour-intensive in planned and sharply focused services than in services that are *ad hoc*. Additionally, less resources are accessed and analysed. Labour and resource costs are controlled.

From the manager's viewpoint, the niche service is customised. The end product is personal and confidential. Additionally, the information is linked to business objectives. It is a useful tool that can be readily used in day-to-day decision making.

It is also a responsive service. Products and services quickly adjust to changes in the business unit's critical success factors. Other characteristics include flexibility. CSFs and information questions are highly individualised and subject to continual change.

Chances of a successful product are enhanced when the manager becomes a co-producer in the information process. There is a vested interest in creating a useful and valuable product. From the information officer's viewpoint, the steps in the working model are defined. It is easy to follow and effective. The model also allows and requires creativity both on the part of the manager and the information officer. Also, the process is clearly business-driven. Time is used efficiently and effectively. A major effort is concentrated on creating quality.

CONCLUSION

This niche product and service model is applicable in both large and small enterprises. In large companies, the niche product strategy might be used to supplement the company-wide generalised products and services, such as resource development, inhouse materials circulation, internal database development or reference services. In small companies, the strategy could be altered to fit a one-unit situation. For example, instead of beginning with the step 'Identifying the corporate role of the unit', it might begin with 'Identify strategic product groups'. The niche product model might in this case be the major activity of an in-house information unit.

BACKGROUND READING

1.   ANSOFF, H.I. Managing strategic surprise by response to weak signals. *California Management Review*, Vol.XVII. No.2. Winter, 1975.
2.   ETZIONI, A. Humble decision making. *Harvard Business Review*. July-August 1989.
3.   MINTZBERG, H. *The nature of managerial work*. New York: Harper & Row, 1973.
4.   MINTZBERG, H. Crafting strategy. *Harvard Business Review*, July-August 1987.

5. PORTER, M.E. *Competitive strategy: techniques for analysing industries and competitors*. New York: The Free Press, 1980.
6. PORTER, M.E. From competitive advantage to corporate strategy. *Harvard Business Review*, May-June 1987.
7. ROCKART, J.F. Chief Executives define their own data needs. *Harvard Business Review*, March-April 1979.

Tomorrow's Library Today

W. David Penniman

Director of the Libraries and Information Center at AT&T Bell Laboratories

ABSTRACT

Libraries are challenged on a variety of fronts in terms of their role and function. While technology is advancing at an incredible pace, our ability to absorb and use the technology in an essentially human endeavor, i.e. information transfer, is still limited. The library as an institution is on the brink of becoming either crucial or superfluous, depending upon strategies selected by library leaders within the very near future. Strategies for extending library services without creating more 'bricks and mortar' are presented based on a government/industry cooperative project involving the National Commission on Libraries and Information Science and direct experience with the Library Network at AT&T Bell Laboratories.

INTRODUCTION

This paper covers four major topics. In it I describe what I see as the current environment for libraries in business as well as in the public sector. I describe a model or structure for looking at the future and influencing that future. To do so, I talk about the past. I describe how the Library Network operated by AT&T Bell Laboratories has responded to a changing environment, not only with the aid of electronic technology, but also with other tools from the business world. Finally, I characterize the challenge we all face as a response to the real crisis for most institutions today, i.e. a changing environment.

CURRENT LIBRARY ENVIRONMENT

When technologists discuss 'the future,' we invariably hear about cost per chip or bit capacity of a communication channel and the fact that the capacities are rising and costs are dropping exponentially. Discussion may extend to artificial intelligence, expert systems, and the potential onslaught of fifth-generation computing from 'Japan, Inc.'

We also hear about 'courses on a chip, schools on a wafer and libraries on a disc,' which will be part of our solid state culture. In his article on future libraries in the *Wilson Library Bulletin*, Suprenant raises the question as to 'whether or not we can manage to merge the information and electronic revolution with essential humanitarian and humanistic values.'[1] There is an equally fundamental and related issue: How do we absorb the technologies now available to libraries in a useful way and contain the rising costs of staff and the bricks and mortar in which they are housed?

Pat Batten[2] has described three generations of library computing:

- *First generation* – automation of processing activities (i.e., backroom functions plus circulation control).
- *Second generation* – development and installation of integrated systems including online catalogs.
- *Third generation* – local area networks with computing/ communication capacities moved to the individual's workstation.

Within many settings, including some academic and industrial, the third stage presents a major challenge by potentially merging the computing center and library functions. Far more prevalent a challenge, however, is that of introducing most libraries to the first stage. There are significant differences between what is technically possible and what is widely successful or even economically acceptable. Witness the painfully slow growth of online catalogs within the library community. Predictions of a 'tidal wave' involving the replacement of traditional card catalogs with online terminals have not been realized. The realities of cost have prevented most libraries from embracing technology already well understood, let alone breaking new ground with 'state-of-the-art' technologies.

Even in cases where significant commitment has been made and resources invested, the human aspects of information processing and delivery have continued to limit the full utilization of available technology. A library is essentially a labor-intensive institution because information transfer relies in a large part on human-to-human communication. Finding methods for making this process more efficient and effective is the real challenge facing librarians today.

Bridging the Gap

With that as a backup, I would like to present a problem and challenge not limited to libraries – that is, how to bridge the gap between what is technically possible (which drives our predictions of the future) and what we ultimately realize (which is often far less than we have predicted).

In this second area, I describe a model of how to bridge the gap between prediction and realization, and I use some examples from the past to help make my case.

But first, some definitions[3] according to the dictionary:

Prediction: To make known in advance
(Can also be the statement of a goal)

Realization: To make actual
To comprehend completely

I will go back over a decade to give a case in point; I want to talk about interactive cable television, the technology of the early 1970s that was to change the way we worked, played, and learned. It was closely related to widely held concepts and libraries of the future at that time, because the kinds of services that this technology was to deliver overlapped with those that libraries already provided or hoped to provide.

In the early 1970s, predictions were widely enthusiastic. Paul Baran, writing in the *Futurist*,[4] identified 30 services to be provided by this technology and, via the Delphi forecasting process,[5] zeroed in on 16 services to be in place by 1980.

The services included:

- Video Library of Plays and Movies
- Cashless Transactions
- Computer Tutor
- Adult Evening Courses
- Answering Services
- Computer Assisted Meetings
- Secretarial Assistance
- Banking Services
- Grocery Price List, Information and Ordering
- Consumer Advisory Service
- Weather Bureau
- Fares and Ticket Reservations
- Message Recording
- Index of All Serviced by Terminals
- Bus, Air, Train Scheduling *and*
- Restaurants.

One of the dangers of publishing predictions is that they can be referred to in the future and that introduces an element of feedback between prediction and realization. This element could also be considered accountability. How did Paul Baran do in his predictions? Not one of the services in his list is available today via interactive cable television. There were some skeptics – even in the 1970s. One article in the August 1974 issue of *Datamation*[6] pointed out weaknesses due to capitalization requirements and (even more critical) a lack of understanding of the social impacts of this technology.

Referring to figure 1, the first connection between prediction and realization is a simple bridge accomplished by a retrospective feedback loop.

Next, I would like to add a new element to the model in figure 1. That element is intervention. It is not enough to predict and get feedback (though we do need to look back); we also need a forward acting

FIGURE 1. MODEL FOR REALIZING PREDICTIONS

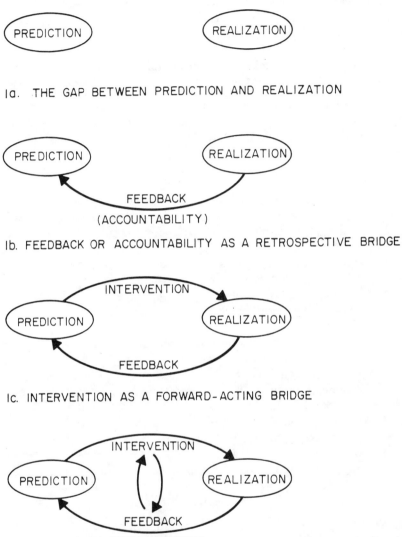

Ia. THE GAP BETWEEN PREDICTION AND REALIZATION

Ib. FEEDBACK OR ACCOUNTABILITY AS A RETROSPECTIVE BRIDGE

Ic. INTERVENTION AS A FORWARD-ACTING BRIDGE

Id. REFINEMENT OF FEEDBACK TO INCLUDE ANALYSIS

acting device. Let us look at some interventions in the 1970s for interactive cable TV. There were at least nine experiments in interactive cable[7] ranging from California to South Carolina and from Florida to Pennsylvania. Many were funded by the federal government. By the early 1980s, there was one barely surviving commercial venture in Columbus, Ohio.[8]

How does this relate to the challenges facing the library profession? The answer lies in a closer look at the intervention phase of the model.

Intervention is more than experiments. It is successfully moving an idea from creation to application, and that is a key factor in the future for libraries. What do we know about that process of successfully moving ideas from creation to application? We know from past studies[9,10] that there must be certain factors for success. These factors are summarized here:

- There must be an understanding of the technology in terms of its advantages over other technologies already available. This understanding must include a thorough knowledge of costs and the relation to processes already in use.
- Feasibility demonstrations are necessary, but not sufficient. Such demonstrations help to identify shortcomings and give early warning signals where improvements are needed.
- Advocates or champions are needed among both the producers and user groups to assure that early obstacles do not become permanent barriers.
- External pressures, such as competition and other threats, help to stimulate the implementation process.
- Joint programs involving multiple organizations provide a broader base of support for the innovation in its early stages.
- Availability of adequate capital is essential and must not be taken for granted. Ideas do not sell themselves; they require constant attention, and that requires capital.
- Visibility of consequences is a strong motivator to avoid failure. Announcing publicly an objective makes it more difficult to turn away from that objective.
- Social support is often a key element and may involve organizations that can provide moral, if not financial, support.
- Promotional agents, such as the press, or other public relations groups can help to assure that all affected parties understand the technology and how it will benefit them. Such agents also help to elevate the visibility of consequences (see above).

We also know from past research[11] a fair amount about reasons for failure in the information arena. In a study of over 100 information innovations that did not succeed in the marketplace, an interesting pattern emerged regarding reasons for failure. Over 70 per cent of the failures were due to nontechnical reasons. Marketing, management, capitalization, and organizational issues caused the demise most often. It is not adequate to have the right technology; the rest of the environment must be correct as well.

My model is almost complete; you can see its complete structure at the bottom of figure 1. I have identified intervention and feedback (or account-ability) as crucial elements in bridging the gap; now I would like to go back and elaborate on the feedback component. This element should contain an analysis element. In our context this means not only *analysis of technologies* but also *analysis of markets and services*. We must determine how markets, services, and technologies fit together in the current social/political/economic environment. For *libraries* we must be willing to do hard-nosed analysis of the *value* of our services. We must not delude ourselves. It is not enough to ask for better libraries or more money for our services because 'it is the right thing to do'. We must provide strategies that demonstrate our ability and innovativeness to expand library services while containing costs. We must be innovators, as well as interveners and analyzers. We cannot be merely managers. Further, we must look at libraries as *business ventures,* as well as social institutions, because we operate in a competitive arena, competing for limited resources. This is true for public libraries, university libraries, and special libraries equally.

We must understand in a business-like manner our costs, services, and markets, as well as our technologies, and we must lead our libraries as if we were new venture entrepreneurs *because we are.*

Now I am going to make a prediction. I am going to paint a scenario for you that has 100 per cent probability of realization.

I see an important social institution (and corporate resource) in the following way:

- This institution is caught in the trap of rising costs of bricks and mortar.
- Automation, while used, is mostly in backroom operations; service is still labor intensive.
- Changing social patterns and competition from service providers threaten its status.
- The institution responds by using current technology and techniques to deliver service without expensive additions of bricks and mortar and enters a new era.

Why am I willing to say this prediction has 100 per cent probability of happening? Because I am not referring, in this case, to libraries today. I am referring to the banking industry of over a decade ago. Banks responded to their changing environment with low-cost structures that were portable and easily erected. They went to where the customers were – in suburban shopping malls and parking lots of shopping centers. They supported these units with minimal staff and relied on 24-hour automated teller machines to deliver basic service to a new generation of computer-friendly users. They revolutionized the image and service delivery concept of their institution.

LIBRARY SERVICES IN AT&T'S CHANGING ENVIRONMENT

The Library Network operated by AT&T Bell Laboratories is responding to a changing environment. In January 1984, when I joined the Laboratories, the organization was just beginning to realize the true impact of the divestiture it had been preparing for. I arrived at the Library Network as a messenger with an unpleasant message. As an outsider, I was preaching change to the premier private-industry library network in the country. I started preaching a paradox. And the paradox is – if you have something good and you are in a changing environment, you must change to hold your position, otherwise your position will degrade. At AT&T Bell Laboratories, we are radically revising our view of library service delivery mechanisms while moving to expand our services and reduce our per patron cost. We are doing this with the concept of an information access station. This concept builds on the existing backbone of libraries already in place in the Library Network. (The Library Network, operated by AT&T Bell Laboratories, consists of 35 libraries and 19 specialized service units linked electronically and by a common set of procedures and databases within AT&T.) The access station concept combines the physical, electronic, and human elements of information delivery.

The access station uses only proven off-the-shelf technologies and draws upon resources already available elsewhere in the network. It is a means of moving service closer to the patron's workplace. If this sounds familiar, it should. The banking scenario I painted earlier is a direct model for the information access station concept. The information access station provides the following functions:

- Access to current journals in hard-copy on site.
- Access to key works including reference material and selected books for local circulation only.
- Access to local databases by terminals or microcomputers with user friendly front-end software.
- Access to remote databases offered by commercial vendors as well as central AT&T databases with user friendly front-end software and downloading software.
- Access to backcopies of journals and other normally space-intensive material stored on high-density storage media. Currently this media is microform, but will soon include optical disc technology.
- Access to holdings of other sources via bibliographic utilities, such as OCLC, and via a union catalog of holdings within AT&T. Access in this sense includes the ability to transmit facsimiles or request hard-copies via slower delivery mechanisms.
- Access to human interaction with an onsite staff member who is a trained generalist in the areas of marketing or cross-selling of services, training of users, and generalized reference service.
- Access to expert assistance by means of telephone or electronic mail in specialized reference areas.
- Access from the client's own workstation by means of electronic mail and specialized UNIX™ command functions for selected

functions listed above (e.g. local and remote database access, expert reference assistance).

The access station is housed in a small footprint facility (less than 400 square feet), and is easy to assemble, easy to move, and requires low initial investment and maintenance cost. It is designed to attract patrons in terms of its location and arrangement so as to be visually attractive. See figure 2 for the 'free-standing' access station and refer to the appendix for a more detailed, top-level, functional description. Like banking institutions, we expect service to move away from the bricks-and-mortar concept and go where our employees are regardless of size or austerity of the facility. This will be accomplished first by access stations and ultimately by direct delivery to the workplace (desk) and home via electronic searching and document delivery.

FIGURE 2. FREE-STANDING ACCESS STATION

Some reasons to expect success in our current efforts to place information access stations include the following:

- The concept is market driven, where the market consists of our current users who indicated in focus interviews and surveys that they wanted onsite access to resources and reference help, even if a full-scale library was not economically possible.
- The access station uses understood technologies selected from off the shelf. New technologies are incorporated only after being proven in the market.
- The design is in response to external pressures: AT&T has made it clear that services previously taken for granted must prove their cost effectiveness against competitive external services available from the marketplace.
- The design was prepared as part of a joint program that included NCLIS and the 1985 IFLA show, and, thus, the project had initial high visibility.

- The project had champions in its early stages. Besides my support, we had the strong backing of Dr. Toni Bearman, then executive director of NCLIS and now dean of the School of Library and Information Science at the University of Pittsburgh.

These factors fit the elements for success described in my model when I discussed intervention and what has been learned from previous research in moving ideas successfully through the implementation stage.

IMPLICATIONS FOR LIBRARIES AND LIBRARIANSHIP

How does this help institutions to respond to the challenge regarding expanding information services while containing cost? It provides one example of how libraries can extend their reach via low-cost network nodes, where once only more or bigger libraries were thought to be acceptable. It is only an example. As interveners, librarians must find other innovative means to revolutionize their operations. Lew Branscomb has stated:

If *libraries* are to play a creative role in this period of experimentation, they must again become teachers and innovators, and not custodians, lest the treasures in their custody are made obsolete by alternative services that fail to serve humanity as imaginatively and profoundly as they could.[12]

What is needed in the library profession is education in ways of business as well as librarianship. This includes such areas as marketing and technology, but, most important, librarians must be educated in the ways of change.

While Wilf Lancaster has stated that 'the survival of the library profession depends on its ability and willingness to change its emphasis and image',[13] Pat Battin has pointed out that 'one of the most powerful deterrents to change in conservative institutions is the existence of strong autonomous vested interests and the fear of losing one's empire'.[14] While she was talking specifically about academic institutions, I can assure you that the statement holds true for other institutions as well. In a recent article in the *Journal of the American Society for Information Science*, there appeared a concise statement of what is needed:

Library administrators have the responsibility to create organizational climates that encourage and promote change. Traditional committee structures are an insufficient approach to anticipate and meet the challenges. Experimentation is essential, improvisation inevitable, and the sharing of both successes and failures a professional and organizational imperative. The great responsibility, however, rests with the individual who must adapt, and adopt the idea of continual change as a goal and mode of both personal and organizational operation'.[15]

Remember my model and the key role of intervention. I do not believe the future 'unfolds' as some forecasters would have us believe. That implies a technological predestination for which little evidence exists. I believe we must shape our future. A new technology will neither do us in nor save us. Our failure to respond will. It is appropriate to conclude this message with two brief quotes. The first is from former Librarian of Congress Daniel Boorstin:

Libraries remain the meccas of self-help, the most open of open universities . . . where there are no entrance examinations and no diplomas, and where one can enter at any age.[16]

The second quote is from a novel about the romantic possibilities of a public library in California:

We don't use the Dewey decimal classification or any index system to keep track of our books. We record their entrance into the Library in the Library Contents Ledger and then we give the book back to its author who is free to place it anywhere he wants in the library, on whatever shelf catches his fancy.

It doesn't make any difference where a book is placed because nobody ever checks them out and nobody ever comes here to read them. This is not that kind of library. This is another kind of library.[17]

To remain the meccas that Boorstin speaks of, we must change. If we do not change, we risk becoming the other kind of library that Brautigan describes. That is the paradox.

APPENDIX

Functional Description of the AT&T Library Network Information Access Station

This appendix provides a top-level functional description of an information access station such as used as a node in the Library Network operated by AT&T Bell Laboratories where modular, small footprint (less than 400 square feet of floor space), current technology capabilities are helping to offset the rising cost of information service delivery.

The access station is the development of the Libraries and Information Systems Center of AT&T Bell Laboratories, and was shown publicly in August 1985 in Chicago at the annual meeting of the International Federation of Library Associations and Institutions (IFLA) in conjunction with the National Commission on Libraries and Information Science (NCLIS).

The approach described accommodates three means of information packaging and delivery – physical, electronic, and human. Further, it recognizes that these three means are merging, and any system must acknowledge and encourage the rapid and easy migration of information from one of these domains to another.

The following paragraphs identify the necessary functions, describe those functions, and provide guidelines for housing the functions.

FUNCTIONS FOR THE LIBRARY OF THE FUTURE

A. Access to current journal literature in hardcopy for browsing (and distribution).

B. Access to selected reference and key works in hardcopy for browsing (and distribution).

C. Access to local databases in interactive mode with ability to produce hardcopy and to download and massage output. Local update must also be available in a protected fashion.

D. Access to remote databases in interactive mode with ability to produce hardcopy and to download and massage output.

E. Access to the content of back copies of journals on site with the ability to produce hardcopy.

F. Access to holdings of other libraries and information sources with electronic delivery for brief material and delayed delivery for lengthier material.

G. Access to human interaction and assistance in locating information. Access to expert assistance in locating/interpreting/analyzing specialized information.

I. Access to local and remote databases and expert assistance from the patron's workstation located in an office or at home.

FUNCTIONAL DESCRIPTIONS

For each function identified in Section 1, a brief description is provided here along with identification of the technologies currently available to provide this function. The intention here is to use readily available technology and not require significant development of new systems.

The structure in which to house the access station should also be based on current technology, and should incorporate low first-cost and low maintenance-cost design techniques. The structure should attract patrons into the access station. These characteristics are further described in Section III.

A. *Access to Current Journal Literature in Hardcopy for Browsing (and distribution)*

This function is provided by shelving for the organization and display of current printed material. The shelving should be located so that the material is prominent and readily accessible to patrons passing by the Access Station.

The shelving should accommodate the storage of recent back copies of journals so that recent issues not being routed are also available for browsing.

The distribution aspect of this function should be accommodated by a local charge-out mechanism.

B. *Access to Selected Reference and Key Works in Hardcopy for Browsing (and distribution)*

This function is provided by book shelving for the organization and display of book material. The shelving should be located so that patrons have access to the material for browsing.

The distribution aspect of this function should be accommodated by a local charge-out mechanism.

C. *Access to Local Databases in Interactive Mode with Ability to Produce Hardcopy and Download and Massage Output. Local Update Must be Available in a Protected Fashion.*

This function is provided by an online information storage and retrieval system running on a local computer with storage capable of accommodating multiple databases of 5,000 to 10,000 records of 500 bytes each. Access to these records should be via search keys built from selected fields within each record, and search strategies should be accommodated which involve multiple fields. Online update/addition of records by selected users must be possible. At least two terminals capable of querying these databases should be available in the access station, one for patrons and one for staff, and a hardcopy printer should be accessible from either terminal. These terminals should have enough intelligence to allow for reformatting, duplicate elimination, and data manipulation of output.

D. *Access to Remote Databases in Interactive Mode with Ability to Produce Hardcopy and to Download and Massage Output*

This function should be available from the terminals in the access station and provide access to databases not residing at the local host, including central Library Network Databases as well as commercially available databases. The function should incorporate currently available software that simplifies searching of commercially available databases. Output should be available for massaging of the type described in 'C' prior to dispatching to the printer. In addition, there should be the potential for downloading records to the local databases described in 'C.'

E. *Access to the Content of Back Copies of Journals Onsite*

This function must be provided by compact equipment that stores page images of journal articles and retrieves/displays page contents for patron access. Hardcopy of the page images should be available on demand.

Current technology to perform this function includes microfilm and videodisc with microfilm more readily available. While videodisc is promising, the necessary databases are not yet available in this media.

F. *Access to Holdings of Other Libraries and Information Resources with Rapid Delivery of Brief Material*

There are two aspects to this function. The first is to provide access to the holdings within the Library Network and provide rapid delivery of that material to the requester. The second is to provide access to material held outside of the Library Network.

The internal aspect of this function is provided by access to the online catalog of the Library Network in conjunction with the circulation control system so that the location of desired material can be identified, and the material can be requested and circulated to the requester.

The external aspect of this function is provided by gaining access to one or more of the existing bibliographic utilities. Dial-up access must be available from at least one of the existing terminals in the access station. The utility should be used to identify sources of material not held by the organization and to execute interlibrary loan requests.

In the cases where material is brief in nature and lends itself to photocopying, the option to transmit material directly to the access station by facsimile transmission should be available. At a minimum, the access station should be capable of receiving facsimile copies from one external 'super' source (e.g. UMI, Information Store, or ISI), as well as other traditional libraries within and outside of AT&T. The facsimile transmission feature must be capable of full node-to-node transmission within the Library Network.

G. *Access to Human Interactions and Assistance in Locating Information*

This function is provided by an onsite trained generalist (i.e. reference librarian or information specialist). One generalist is located at each access station site and serves as the human interface to all information services. As such, this generalist must be capable of promoting as well as delivering such services and training patrons to use these services.

H. *Access to Expert Assistance in Locating/Interpreting/Analyzing Specialized Information*

This function is provided by access to remotely located reference specialists who are skilled in selected areas (e.g. marketplace information).

Access could be by both telephone and terminal and should be invoked by either the access station staff or the patron directly.

I. *Access to Local and Remote Databases and Expert Assistance from the Patron's Workstation Located in an Office or at Home*

This function is provided by electronic mail and specialized 'library' commands as part of the UNIX(TM) system in place at AT&T Bell Laboratories. These functions allow for direct searching of Library Network database, including the book catalog and other specialized collection databases. In addition, documents can be ordered directly via these commands and reference questions can be submitted. Commercial databases can be searched via a front-end software package.

HOUSING THE FUNCTIONS

The functions described in the previous section of this appendix must be packaged in an efficient manner that: a) uses a small footprint (less than 400 square feet of floor space); b) is easy to assemble, disassemble, and move; c) requires small initial investment and small maintenance cost; and d) attracts patrons to use all of the available functions.

Commercially available, prefabricated library structures can satisfy these requirements and lend themselves to installation in atriums and other areas where heavy staff traffic would assure wide exposure to the information services. Where more austere environments are required, there are packaged designs developed to place an access station within an existing room of 300 to 400 square feet.

REFERENCES

1. Suprenant, Tom. 'Future Libraries.' *Wilson Library Bulletin,* May 1983, p. 765.
2. Battin, Patricia. 'National and International Perspectives,' presented at the Library and Information Resources for the Northwest (LIRN) Advisory Committee Meeting of July 31, 1984, and appearing in Minutes of that Meeting dated October 2, 1984, p. 3.
3. *The American Heritage Dictionary of the English Language,* William Morris, Editor. New York: American Heritage Publishing Co., Inc., 1970.
4. Baran, Paul. '30 Services that Two-Way Television Can Provide.' *The Futurist 7* (no. 5): 202–210 (October 1973).
5. Linstone, Harold A., and Murray Turoff (editors). *The Delphi Method: Techniques and Applications.* Reading, Mass.: Addison-Wesley Publishing Company, 1975.
6. Buckelew, Donald P. and W. David Penniman. 'The Outlook for Interactive Television.' *Datamation,* August 1974, pp. 54–58.
7. Cable Television Information Center (CTIC). Internal Memorandum on Status of Two-Way Cable Experiments, April 1973.
8. 'Warner Cable Venture Drops 'Qube' Programming in 6 Cities.' *The Wall Street Journal,* January 19, 1984, p. 3.
9. Cohen, Kirsch; Seymour Keller; and Donald Streeter. 'The Transfer of Technology from Research to Development.' *Research Management 22:* 11–17 (May 1979).
10. Dutton, J. M. and W. H. Starbuck. 'Diffusion of an Intellectual Technology,' presented at the Conference on Communication and Control in Social Processes sponsored by the American Society for Cybernetics and the University of Pennsylvania, November 1, 1974.
11. Sweezy, E. E. and J. H. Hopper. 'Obstacles to Innovation in the Scientific and Technical Information Services Industry,' Final Report prepared for the U.S. National Science Foundation by the Institute for Public Administration, Washington, D.C. (IPA Monograph 76–2), October 1975.
12. Bramscomb, Lewis M. 'The Electronic Library.' *Journal of Communication 31* (no. 1): 150 (Winter 1981).
13. Lancaster, F. W. *Libraries and Librarians in the Age of Electronics.* Info Resources Press, 1982, p. 150.
14. Battin, Patricia. 'The Library: Center of the Restructured University.' *Current Issues In Higher Education.* 1983–1984 (no.1):25.
15. Lucier, Richard E. and James F. Dooley. 'Cosmology and the Changing Role of Libraries: An Analogy and Reflections.' *journal of the American Society for Information Science 36* (no. 1): 47 (January 1985).
16. *Alliance for Excellence: Librarians Respond to a Nation At Risk.* U.S. Department of Education, available from U.S. Government Printing Office, July 1984, p. 45.
17. Brautigan, Richard. *The Abortion: An Historical Romance 1966.* New York: Simon and Schuster, 1971, p. 20.

Marketing Measures for Information Services

Martha Jane Zachert

Health Sciences Libraries, Library Education Projects, Tallahassee, FL

Robert V. Williams

College of Library and Information Science, University of South Carolina, Columbia, SC

ABSTRACT

Despite their leadership in developing information services, special librarians often express frustration with the design and evaluation of the programs by which they market these services. This paper explores the problem by analyzing and synthesizing ideas from the literature of marketing and performance evaluation. Potentially useful approaches and quantifiable measures for market structure analysis, design decision-making, and marketing program evaluation are identified.

INTRODUCTION

The marketing of information services has been a popular topic in the library profession in recent years. For special librarians, neither the concept nor the practice of marketing is new; both have been part of the special library idea for a long time.[1] This 'special library idea' maintains that the manager of information services must be *proactive* rather than *reactive* to user information needs and demands. The basic idea of marketing is that *responsiveness* to client needs and demands is the key to success in the marketplace.[2] Actually, both ideas speak to an understanding of needs and preferences and to meeting them in advance of extensive demands.

The telling characteristic of a responsive organization (in marketing terms) has two sides. On one side, the organization encourages its clients to participate outspokenly in its activities. On the other side, the organization wholeheartedly accepts these needs and demands, as stated, in the design and delivery of products or services. Open, personal communication is the key.

The opposite kind of organization is the bureaucracy, routinized in its operations, delivering services according to its own version of need, carrying out impersonal policies through a rigid hierarchy of command – a truly unresponsive organization. A bureaucracy makes it difficult for its clients to voice their opinions, and it takes no initiative in finding out the precise needs or preferences of these clients.[2] Such unresponsive, bureaucratic organizations are the antithesis of 'the special library idea.' As would-be service organizations, they fail in both the profit and the nonprofit sectors. The organization that succeeds is 'responsive' in marketing terms, 'proactive' in the thinking of special librarians.

Despite their belief in the special library idea and despite the relationship between this concept and current marketing beliefs, many special librarians have expressed frustration in their efforts to apply the basics of marketing as it is practiced in the for-profit sector to their own not-for-profit information agencies. This frustration reaches acute levels when it comes to the evaluation of the marketing programs they design and mount. (Note that we describe special libraries and information centers as 'not-for-profit' even when they are located in commercial organizations. We do so because this is the traditional management view on which corporate accounting rationale is so often based.)

We believe that an examination of key marketing concepts and of selected evaluation techniques currently in use by some special librarians will show a convergence that would be helpful to others who attempt to increase the responsiveness of their information agencies through marketing programs. We also believe that the suggestions we will make at the conclusion of this paper will, if acted on by special librarians, lead to a new rationale for accounting the value of special libraries, information centers, and information services. Although we are presenting this trend in terms of corporate libraries, it will be evident that it also has potential for information agencies in government, academe and other locales.

KEY MARKETING CONCEPTS

Basic to all of the marketing is the idea of 'responsive organization' just described. Given an organization that is open to personal suggestions from its clients and that is flexible and creative enough to adapt itself or its services to meet the changing needs and demands of these clients, certain questions face the organization. Five key marketing concepts relate to these questions. All five concepts are in use, in greater or lesser degree, by some special librarians.

Market Segmentation is the name of the concept which states that a marketplace is comprised of individuals, some of whom will have a need for your organization's services, though in varying degrees; some, of course, will be uninterested in your offerings. No organization can be successful by treating the entire marketplace as if it will show equal interest in the organization's products or services. The process of determining the proportion of individuals already demanding your service, and the proportion that will never be interested, is called 'market segmentation'. It answers the following questions: Who, exactly, are your clients? To what extent are they similar, to what extent different in their needs and demands? Which groups, among your clients, are your most intensive users? Least intensive users?[2] Segmentation is a marketing measure that holds considerable significance for special librarian managers.

Public libraries have traditionally segmented their clients on the basis of demographic characteristics. Academic libraries have segmented their markets by academic factors. Special librarians must use factors such as internal structure of the company, the organizational position and mission of the information service and the division of work responsibilities within the parent company's total work force. Geographical relationships between the information service and the company units it is assigned to serve, as well as selected demographic characteristics of the work force, may also be important. A graphic design of the library's marketplace for a given special library results from a market analysis – a measure already somewhat in use by many special librarians, probably under another name.

FIGURE 1. *Key Marketing Concepts, Their Nature and Significance*

Key Concepts	Nature/Significance of Concepts
1. *Market Segmentation*	Identification of actual and potential markets and nonmarkets within company. *Information gathering. Quantification.*
2. *Market Positioning*	Prioritizing clients, groups and information services. *Policy Making.*
3. *Consumer Analysis*	Determination of needs and preferences. *Information gathering. Quantification.*
4. *Marketing Program*	Determination of optimum mix of product, price, delivery mode (place, promotion. *Planning. Customization. Coordination.*
5. *Marketing Audit*	Evaluation of plan and implementation. *Information gathering. Quantification. Making Judgements. Reporting.*

N.B. Marketing is a cyclical process, comprised of five major steps, represented by the five concepts above. Each of these five concepts includes secondary concepts, thus each step in the process includes secondary steps. "Secondary" does not mean less important, but rather hierarchical in relation to the five key concepts/steps shown here.

Given such a graphic design which identifies markets and their size, with supplemental data about total information resources within and available to the company, a special librarian would then be able to move on to answering questions about prioritizing groups of clients and types of services. This is the process of *market positioning*. It results in policy statements about who are the primary client groups, about the expenditure of library resources in relation to each group, who pays for service to each, even what proportion of cost must come from what sources, and possibly policies about what services shall be left to the competition.[2] Having arrived at these policies, the librarian will be able to establish both short- and long-range goals, and state these goals in such a way that quantitative measures can be used to determine the extent to which each is achieved.

From analysis of market segments and choice of a market position, the special librarian who is implementing marketing concepts will move on to *consumer analysis*. This process answers questions about the extent of the need for homogenous subgroups, even individual clients, the significance of each need in relation to company objectives, the preference for delivery of information products or services, the perceptions of members of client groups about library/information center service. Measures used in consumer analysis concentrate on obtaining detailed quantitative data. Information gained provides the foundation for planning a marketing program.[2]

The concept of a *marketing program* underlies the coordinated effort which utilizes information gained and policies established in the interests of the parent company. The purpose of this step is to arrive at a customized plan for the optimum mix of product or service, price and cost, place or mode of delivery, and promotion of the products or services within your company.[2] Without such an inclusive customized plan, with its own built-in goals and measures for defining success, libraries and other information agencies cannot be said to be truly engaged in marketing. Although they may be using some marketing concepts, without well-defined marketing *programs,* much of the potential impact of market segmentation, positioning and consumer analysis will be lost.

Finally, a *marketing audit* completes the cycle and sets the stage for the next cycle of planning, implementation and review. Such an audit, or evaluation, uses multiple measures to quantitatively study the results of the marketing program. It answers questions about the effectiveness of marketing programs and sets the stage for expansion or retraction, continuance of discontinuance of specific parts of the program. If there have been changes in the parent company or in the library's professional environment outside the company, additional studies relative to revised market segmentation and positioning may be needed as part of the audit. High turnover or new work assignments to significant portions of the client groups may call for new consumer analyses.[2] The marketing audit sets the stage for the next phase of library/information agency service.

MEASURES USED IN THE IMPLEMENTATION OF KEY MARKETING CONCEPTS/STEPS

Of the key concepts just identified, three require the use of measures for quantification in their information gathering. (Several utilize other kinds of information as well; we are concerned here only with measures for quantification.) We'll look at these in the order of their usage in marketing.

Market Segmentation

Market segmentation is based on descriptive data such as the total number of individuals in each category under study. For interpretation, these data are often converted to proportions. When studying an individual library market, it is critical to identify categories that are meaningful in relation to company structure, nature of the work performed by each company unit, and company priorities.

Company structure comes straight from the organization chart and, since most companies are structured functionally, the chart tells you a good bit (but not all) about the work performed in each unit. Your company personnel office can supply you with the numbers.

For example, an initial market segmentation chart might look like Figure 2, in a Hypothetical Company in which the information service is assigned the responsibility for meeting the needs of company management, research and development, and sales.

This kind of information tells you how many individuals you have in your total market, and it gives you the broad dimensions of your subject coverage and your services. You also need to know the intensity of interest in these market segments at the beginning of your planning. This information is available to you from library records or from your users. The picture might look like Figure 3.

Now you know, by company units, where the intense segments of interest are. In corporate management, for instance, your officers, marketing and financial executives and your computer managers are heavy users. Similarly, you would have the picture for research and development and sales. Your mission is to serve all of these units, so you have question marks in your mind beside the non-intensive user units, to call them to your attention later in the marketing process. Some of these work units are potential markets. Some may be nonmarkets, depending on company priorities, alternative information sources available to the workers, limitations of library resources, or for other reasons. All of this information helps you in the key step called market positioning, in which library priorities are determined and service policies are formulated in relation to your own users and to other suppliers.

FIGURE 2. *Hypothetical Company in Which Library is Assigned Responsibility to Company Management, R/D, & Sales*

Work Units by Structure	No./Sub-Unit	No./Major Unit
Corporate Management		100
Officers	5	
Personnel	20	
Marketing	10	
Legal	5	
Finance	5	
Non-exempt personnel:		
Office management	10	
Computer operations	20	
Other support	25	
Research/Development		50
Unit Managers	5	
Unit 1	5	
Unit 2	10	
Unit 3	15	
Non-exempt personnel	15	
Sales		350
Regional Managers	20	
Account Executives	200	
Advertising	20	
Non-exempt personnel	110	

FIGURE 3. *Intensity of Current Library Usage by Work Units*

Company Work Units	% of Unit Workers Using Library			
	1/week	*1/month*	*1/3 months*	*1/6 months*
Corporate Mngt (N = 100)				
Officers (n = 5)	90	10		
Personnel (n = 20)	10	10	30	10
Marketing (n = 10)	80	10	10	
Legal (n = 5)	10	10	20	30
Finance (n = 5)	90	10		
Office Mngt (n = 10)	30	10		
Computer Mngt (n = 20)	80	10	10	
Support Staff (n = 25)		10	20	10
Research/Development				
Sales				

Consumer Analysis

Consumer analysis is the detailed study of the characteristics and information-seeking behavior of your users. Data collection techniques include direct and indirect (unobtrusive) observation as well as the collection of user-supplied data. The latter, familiarly known as 'surveys,' are by far the most often used, and the name covers a broad range of more or less formal, more or less rigorous activities. The results are, therefore, more or less valid and reliable. This is not the place to go into the nature or mechanics of a good study, as numerous textbooks are available.[3]

Examples of survey instruments abound in the literature. One bibliography, covering the literature from 1965–1982, identified 57 studies in which instruments used in special libraries and information centers are reproduced.[4] This bibliography has been updated as part of our work. Selected examples are listed in an appendix to this paper.

Results of a consumer analysis survey might look like Figures 4 and 5 (plus, of course, considerable additional data).

FIGURE 4. *Levels of Information Used Regularly in R/D Unit*

| *R/D Units* | *Percent of Sample Giving Highest Priority to and Using at Least Once per Week* | | | | |
	News/ Update	*Research Reports*	*Manuals*	*Govt Regs*	*Secondary Reference*
Unit Managers (n = 5)	60	20		20	
Unit 1 (n = 5)	20	80			
Unit 2 (n = 1)				100	
Unit 3 (n = 2)		50		50	
Non-exempt (n = 2)			50		50

FIGURE 5. *Delivery Preference for Selected Services by R/D Units*

| *R/D Units* | *News/Update* | | | | *Research Reports** | | | |
	(1)	*(2)*	*(3)*	*(4)*	*(1)*	*(2)*	*(3)*	*(4)*
Unit Managers (n = 5)		80	20				90	10
Unit 1 (n = 5)		20		20	60	20	20	
Unit 2 (n = 1)							100	
Unit 3 (n = 2)							100	
Non-exempt (n = 2)								

*Numbers 1–4 represent alternative kinds of delivery, such as: routing, notifying with request capability, notifying without request capability, SDI, on-demand searches.

Consumer analysis surveys will provide information for choosing between optional designs of the same service, especially when the options represent different cost levels. Consumer analysis surveys can also provide information about how to customize the delivery and promotion of your services. In short, consumer analysis is a *sine qua non* of marketing. It provides you with specifics on which to base your decisions about each of the four Ps of marketing: products, place or methods of dissemination of your products, price or cost of products, and methods of promotion of your products. Without consumer analysis, you simply are not into marketing.

Marketing Audit

Now we move to measures used during the marketing audit. The audit is the evaluation step, used after the marketing plan (based on information gained in the previous steps) has been implemented. A critical part of that plan consists in the setting of measurable goals.

It is our belief, based on the literature, that a new understanding of goals needs to be developed among special librarians. Cost-effectiveness goals have been emphasized in the past. Performance goals are currently popular. However, these kinds of goals result in measurement categories that speak more to cost containment of the work done in the library than to successful marketing or the impact of the library on the parent agency. Failure to differentiate between administrative goals for the operation of the library and marketing goals for getting services and products out of the library may well be the cause of the frustration special librarians voice about the evaluation of their marketing efforts.

This is not to say that cost containment is unimportant. For routine internal administrative purposes, budget justification, and in periods of company retrenchment it is critical to have such information and be able to present it convincingly. Marketing measures, however, have a different purpose and require a different rationale.

Remember that marketing is a process for determining what information services are needed by company personnel and customizing those services in such a way as to get the company's work done effectively in the marketplace. The marketing audit is the evaluation of how well one has accomplished that purpose during a specific promotion or over a given period of time. The measures used during your audit must relate specifically to the goals of your customized program. They can never exclude the users of the offered information services. Top management is interested in the worth – to the users and therefore to the company – of specific services or products. Thus cost-*benefit* measures speak with greatest power in marketing audits.

Cost-benefit analysis answers the question: Is the benefit, in dollar value, more or less than the cost, in dollar value? A particular activity in the company is considered worthwhile when its benefits exceed its costs. Benefits are all of the contributions the particular activity makes to the company's objectives, just as costs are all of the resources the activity will divert from alternative objectives.[2]

This rationale (which is standard business usage) places critical importance on the parent organization's objectives – not only on its long-range objectives but also, perhaps more importantly, on its immediate objectives. It places emphasis on company values which are the philosophic foundation for management of the company. Among the values expressed by top management, and used for operational decision-making, are:

- To be first in the marketplace with new products on a regular basis;
- To be competitive by economic marketing of existing products;
- To turn the company away from declining markets for once standard products toward expanding markets for what will become enduring new products; *and*
- To maintain a specific company image in the local community.

From these and other kinds of values, top management derives company goals related to sales volume, profit level, return on investment, level of market share, company image, company resource accumulation, and social goals.[5]

Special librarians need to study their own company's values and objectives in order to determine the market positioning of their information services and to develop customized programs for marketing these services. We need to develop measurable goals for our marketing programs in *company terms*. It will be especially helpful if those who do carry through on this will publish their experiences so that other special librarians can begin to identify commonalities and to draw generalizations. Commonalities and working generalizations can in turn become the basis for the assumptions and hypotheses of needed research.

Measures used in the past to describe special libraries to top management, as reported in the literature,[6,7] have been about 99 per cent oriented to internal management, i.e. staff activities (e.g. circulation and reference transactions, each more or less subdivided in different libraries). There has been little effort that we can find to convert these data to terms of impact on company goals, of impact on profit centers and revenue earning programs, and on the perception of this impact by profit center managers. It is in these terms that we must describe our benefit to the company if we are to impress top management.[8]

The problem is that we do not need reports of staff activities, per se, nor reports of self-justification of library budgets. What we need are reports that show the *impact* of the library on company goals. One group of special libraries has been very concerned on this point: hospital libraries. There a concerted effort is being made to demonstrate a strong positive relationship between high quality library service and high quality patient care.[9] It is essential that hospital libraries be able to do so because of their need to demonstrate this relationship to third party payers for hospital care. Unfortunately, no convincing measure has yet emerged.

One additional difficulty in developing and using marketing measures in special libraries stems from the emphasis in our literature, and in the minds of many librarians, on a need for performance standards against which the activity in an individual library may be described and evaluated. These standards are conceived as being industry-wide, or at least applicable to broad segments of the world of special libraries. Such standards, were they available, might be very useful to library managers; however, few have been developed and virtually none have been validated.

Instead of continuing the search for the unicorns of performance standards, special librarians should adopt the attitude of Brown: the idiosyncratic nature of performance measurement and the relation of such measures to the specific objectives of individual special libraries preclude standard performance measures.[7] Rather, we should be trying to identify to which of those company goals of sales volume, profit level, return on investment, level of market share, company image, company resource accumulation and social goals the library *does* make a high quality, essential contribution. Then we should find measures that will express, in company terms, what that contribution is.

The measure with the greatest potential that we have seen reported is that of 'return on investment'. In a 1982 study of the Department of Energy Technical Information Center and its Energy Data Base, King Research used sophisticated economic modeling methodologies to determine costs and values of specific services and products and of the data base.[10] Return on investment for the Energy Data Base, for example, was determined by comparing its overall production costs to its value to users. Value was determined by surveying users regarding their time and effort saved by using the database. Application of the economic model to survey responses showed that reading a periodical article was worth $590, and reading a technical report was worth $1,280. The overall return on investment for the Energy Data Base was about 220 per cent or 2.2 to 1. Similar savings and return were calculated for online searches, printed indexes, specific areas of Department of Energy funding. Consequences that would occur if the services were not available were also projected.

Manning has used a different way to convert the measure of time saved for researchers by library activities to a return on investment figure which is very impressive to top management.[11] She assumes that the amount of dollars saved the company when the library does an hour's work for an engineer is the amount of an engineer's salary for that hour, using an average supplied by the personnel department. That is, of course, the gross saving, or benefit. The net benefit is the amount of the engineer's salary less the library's cost in substituting for the engineer during a specific period of time. Subtleties (such as the value of the work done by the engineer while the is engaged in doing work formerly done by the engineer, or allowing for same library work being used by more than one engineer) are not included in the formula at present. The net benefit divided by the company investment in library services equals the percentage or proportion called 'return on investment'.

In Manning's usage, the total amount of time saved is calculated from the average of the responses to the question 'How much time do you estimate that library services save you per month?' The formula shown in

FIGURE 6. *Manning's Formula for Return on Investment*

Step 1.   (average hours per month saved)(number of responses) = total hours
per month saved

Step 2.   (total hours per month saved)(average $ per engineer hour)(12 months)
= gross benefit in dollars

Step 3.   (gross benefit) − (cost of library services) = net benefit in dollars

Step 4. $$\frac{\text{net benefit}}{\text{total cost of library services}} = \text{return on investment (\%)}$$

N.B. Manning used this formula to obtain a return on investment in total library services. To use it in a marketing audit one would substitute cost of the specific marketing plan, or even cost of one or more specific products or services

Figure 6 was used to convert data obtained in surveys to a return on investment figure which ranged, in different years of an annual survey and on different groups of employees, from 400 per cent to 1,200 per cent. The use of measures such as those of King Research and Manning, some complex but some fairly simple, will enable special librarians not only to calculate a variety of general and specific returns on investment but also to evaluate specific marketing strategies.

CONCLUSIONS

As in business ventures, market segmentation, consumer analysis, and the marketing audit call for the use of quantitative measures. Market segmentation and consumer analysis utilize measures well-known to special librarians, though marketing effort will be best served if librarians now move away from mere opinion surveys to new levels of sophistication in their data gathering and, as a consequence, in their interpretations of market needs, demands and usage of information products.

Evaluation of marketing plans (the marketing audit) is the most difficult step for special librarians for several reasons:

1. The lack of quantitative measures that are being widely used, and thereby tested and reported.

2. A dearth of critical examination of the assumptions underlying those evaluation measures that are being tried. Many of these assumptions are researchable questions themselves, but one cannot expect busy practitioners to undertake this research.

3. Failure of special librarians to relate the measureable objectives of their marketing programs to company objectives and to carry out and report their audits in terms meaningful to top management. Return on investment is one such measure which has been reported in the literature.

Marketing is planning that focuses on products, place or mode of delivery, adjustment of cost/price to the market, and promotion to specifically targeted segments of the special librarian's market. As such, marketing is in its infancy in application by special librarians. Marketing is, however, a logical extension of our historically valued and highly successful proactive style of information service, worthy of continuing application and critical discussion.

REFERENCES

1. Woods, Bill M. 'Two Decisive Decades: The Special Library Concept of Service.' *American Libraries,* Vol. 3, January 1972, pp. 759–768.
2. Kotler, Philip. *Marketing for Nonprofit Organizations.* 2d ed. Englewood Cliffs, NJ: Prentice-Hall, 1982.
3. Dillman, Don A. *Mail and Telephone Surveys: The Total Design Method.* New York: Wiley, 1978.
4. Craven, Trudy W. and Robert V. Williams. *Library and Information Center Use/User Survey Instruments: A Bibliography, 1964–1982.* Columbia, S.C.: College of Library and Information Science, University of South Carolina, 1982. (mimeographed)
5. Lipson, Harry A. and John R. Darling. *Marketing Fundamentals.* New York: Wiley, 1974. Chapter 17, 'Appraisals of Marketing Performance,' pp. 503–525.
6. Wallace, Danny P. *Performance Measures in Illinois Special Libraries.* Springfield: Illinois State Library, 1983. (Illinois Library Statistical Report No. 8)
7. Brown, Maryann Kevin. 'Library Data, Statistics and Information.' *Special Libraries,* Vol. 71, November 1980, pp. 475–484.
8. White, Herbert S. 'Cost-effectiveness and Cost-benefit Determination in Special Libraries.' *Special Libraries,* Vol. 70, April 1979, pp. 163–69.
9. Bradley, Jana et al. *Hospital Library Management.* Chicago: Medical Library Association, 1983.
10. U.S. Department of Energy. *Value of the Energy Data Base.* King Research, Inc., National Technical Information Center, March 1, 1982. 81pp. (DoE/OR/112321; DE 82014240)
11. Manning, Helen. "Application of Data from a User Survey" in *Online Age: Assessment and Directions.* Collected Papers Presented at the 12th ASIS Mid-Year Meeting. ASIS, 1983. pp. 2–3

APPENDIX

Bibliography of Selected Use Studies That Include Survey Instruments

Bayer, Alan E, and Jahoda, Gerald. 'Back-ground Characteristics of Industrial and Academic Users and Nonusers of Online Bibliographic Search Services,' *Online Review,* Vol. 3, March 1979, pp. 95–105.

Bakin, Dottie; Jackson, Sara Jane; and Hannigan, Gale G. 'Consumer Health Information: Libraries as Partners,' *Medical Library Association Bulletin,* Vol. 68, April 1980, pp. 220–229.

Fosdick, Howard. 'An SDG-based On-line Search Service: A Patron Evaluation Survey and Implications,' *Special Libraries* Vol. 68, September 1977, pp. 305–312.

Greenberg, B. et al. 'Evaluation of a Clinical Librarian Program at the Yale Medical Library,' *Medical Library Association Bulletin,* Vol. 66, July 1978, pp. 319–326.

Helm, Kathleen M. 'Social Science Data Archives: A User Study.' Ph.D. Thesis. University of Wisconsin (Madison), 1980.

Tagliacozzo, R. 'Consumers of New Information Technology: A Survey of the Utilization of MEDLINE,' *American Society of Information Science Journal*, Vol. 26, September 1975, pp. 294–304.

U.S. Department of Energy, *Value of the Energy Data Bases*, King Research Inc.: Rockville, MD., 1982. 79pp. (DOE/OR/11232–1:–DE82–014290).

Warden, C. L. 'Industrial Current Awareness Service: A User Evaluation Study,' *Special Libraries*, Vol. 69, December 1978, pp. 459–467.

Warden, C. L. 'User Evaluation of a Corporate Library Online Search Service,' *Special Libraries*, Vol. 72, April 1981, pp. 113–17.

Pricing and Charging

Pricing and Charging – Introductory Notes

The issue which generated most animated discussion throughout the 1980s undoubtedly was that of charging for library and information services. Even after a decade of debate, the topic remains powerfully emotive for many in the public sector, who at times seem unwilling or unable to move beyond polemic to reasoned analysis and remain locked into the 'moneylenders in the temple' interpretation of recent developments. White's 1980 study remains one of the few to examine the economic foundations and assumptions underpinning public sector librarianship. It is a model of clarity and reason, yet, paradoxically, it has been largely ignored by the library and information profession:

> . . . the case for a tax–supported public library that provides services to users at zero cost is not a strong one. The strongest arguments are for public–library services for children and students; the educational benefits of these services appear to provide adequate justification. The case is much weaker for adult services . . . The positive externalities from adult use are not substantial or pervasive. The institution does not meet the standard criteria of a public good. In the end one can only fall back on the notion that library use is a good thing and on the library community's assurance of just how good a thing it is. That notion is not a solid foundation for a public institution.[1]

The eight contributions which make up this section address pricing strategies, information broking, charge back mechanisms, contracting out and privatisation. None could be described as polemical. Each, it is hoped, will provide a little illumination and help clarify the interlocking strands of the debate.[2,3]

Olaisen (*Pricing strategies for library and information services*) provides a fairly comprehensive tutorial *cum* review essay on the rationale for, and approaches to, pricing, recognising at the outset that 'organizations operate according to many different objectives' and that these will influence attitudes to charging policies and practices. Julie Virgo's paper (*Costing and pricing information services*) is complementary in character, though it concentrates primarily on the calculation of costs: 'Library cost data are critical in order to accurately and fairly set prices for services, to make informed management decisions, and to communicate effectively with funding bodies or those upon whom the library is dependent for dollar allocations'.

Costing and pricing are crucial activities for anyone contemplating a career in information brokerage. The pioneering Alice Sizer Warner (*Information brokering: the state of the art*) reckons that a one–time investment of $80,000 with additional start–up costs of $20,000 (at 1989 prices) will be required to launch your business. Her advice is worth heeding: 'Stay away from entrepreneuring unless you like thinking about and working with money . . . , like to sell, like to fiddle with spreadsheets'.

Pricing is a topical and contentious issue in the electronic information services industry. In his paper (*In search of ideal information pricing*), Donald Hawkins looks at the various bases for pricing online services: connect time, resource unit, flat rate, baud rate, hit rate, unlimited rate. This is a highly volatile area, but Hawkins' article is an extremely lucid and useful starting point for anyone wishing to make sense of current developments in the industry.

How to respond to organisational policy changes which call for the introduction of charges, moving, in other words, from an overhead expense to a cost–recovery mode of operation, is the subject of Lawraine Wood's highly practical and readable paper (*Running a library as a profit–making business*) which describes her experiences with the British Hydromechanics Research Association. She outlines the advantages and disadvantages of running a library as a business, and overall favours the commercial approach as it puts control in the hands of those who run and manage the service. It also engenders an interesting change in perceptions and attitudes: 'The 'library pest' . . . suddenly becomes a valued customer'.

The selective introduction of charges in an academic library setting is described in H. B. Josephine's paper (*University libraries and information services for the business community*). This became something of a *cause célèbre* in the library profession, when a freelance information broker filed an action against Arizona State University for unfair competition. The full story has been recounted elsewhere by Josephine.[4]

Amid the shrill response from the library community which greeted the publication in 1988 of the Government's Green Paper on public library financing,[5] Bailey's (*Charging for public library services*) cooly argued contributions came as a breath of fresh air.[6,7,8] Like White, he challenges some of the profession's cherished assumptions and exposes the weakness of the underlying logic: 'Without an accurate account of public, as well as private, benefits it is not possible to determine how much library users should be subsidised from tax revenues. Whilst it may be argued that external benefits do exist, and therefore library users should be encouraged by subsidy, it is not possible to conclude that the service should be completely financed through subsidy'.

The concluding paper (*The privatizing of government information: economic consideration*) by Calvin Kent, despite its US focus, is a thoroughgoing analysis of the central issues in the privatisation debate. The logic is rigorous, the tone measured, the conclusions fair: 'There is a case for government intervention in the market for information, but economics alone cannot define the justifiable scope of that intervention'.

REFERENCES

1. WHITE, L. J. *The public library in the 1980s: the problems of choice.* Lexington: Lexington Books, 1980.
2. See Directions of the information industry. *Bulletin of the American Society for Information Science,* 15(4), 1989, pp. 26–28.
3. NATIONAL COMMISSION ON LIBRARIES AND INFOR-MATION SCIENCE. *Public sector/ private sector interaction in providing information services.* Washington, DC: NCLIS, 1982.
4. JOSEPHINE, H. B. Fee–based information services in academic libraries: competitors in the private sector? In *National Online Meeting, Proceedings of the Tenth National Online Meeting,* New York, May 9–11, 1989. Medford: Learned Information Inc., 1989, pp. 213–218.
5. HMSO. *Financing our public library service: four subjects for debate: a consultative paper.* London: HMSO, 1988.
6. BAILEY, S. J. Financing the public library service. *Public Money & Management,* Spring/Summer 1988, pp. 19–21.
7. BAILEY, S. J. The economics of public library charges. *New Library World,* November 1988, pp. 203–205.
8. BAILEY, S. J. *Practical charging policies for local government.* Report to the Public Finance Foundation, London, 1988.

Pricing Strategies for Library and Information Services

Johan L. Olaisen

The Norwegian School of Management, Sandvika, Norway

INTRODUCTION

Traditionally, library services are provided to users without charge. Presumably this is done because library services benefit the community more than they benefit the individual user. Rapidly rising costs together with a political philosophy that favours privatization have forced administrators, funders and policy-makers to re-examine the policy of free public services. For their part, the users question the quality of the services and the function of the service delivery system. The whole organization of public services is a matter of debate in Western Europe today. One of the most frequently recurring suggestions in the debate has been the imposition of user fees, but the public services have for different reasons avoided a feedback mechanism such as pricing.

A unit of library service is not easily identifiable or measurable for the purpose of apportioning charges, but a public information service will always have a price for the customer: the time and trouble it takes to acquire the service. The customer may find it cheaper to buy a paperback at a bookstore than to borrow it 'free' from the nearest public library. The libraries are mostly interested in storing information and less interested in a service-oriented distribution of information. We would probably get more efficient and business-like information services for the users by charging for them.

THE OBJECTIVES OF PUBLIC SERVICES AND PRICING

Any economic system must solve the problem of how to use scarce resources. The charging system is the vehicle by which economic units are evaluated in a market context. When the units have been evaluated the strategy of allocating resources to those willing to pay the highest price ensures the maximization of total unity realized by use of these resources. It is also widely accepted that organizations operate according to many different objectives, be they stated explicitly or not. The pricing policy must relate to these objectives. The objectives of a library are to provide:

(a) the user with the right information in the right form at the right time (the user perspective); *and*

(b) society with a large accessible collection of documents (the storage perspective).

The belief that no one should be excluded from access to information is fundamental to our democratic society. This belief is fundamental to the library identity. Libraries, like other public services, must be able to differentiate between core services which meet the need of an informed society and more peripheral services. In our opinion it will not be possible to offer all the information services information technology makes it possible to offer if these services are going to be paid only through taxation.

Libraries must be able to define those services that derive from the core services. Use of user fees to finance selected services leads neither to the salvation of public information services nor to its demise. Charging is an economically viable, socially sound way to expand some services and improve others. Both private business and many private persons would be happy to pay if the libraries could meet objective (a). This would make the libraries aware of their own costs and what the market can bear. Fees should be used only to support general tax revenue, not to supplant it.

Should libraries and other public institutions decide to adopt a strict no fee policy, it will undoubtedly be necessary to limit services. This may mean excluding new and expensive media, since society is unwilling to accept an increase in taxes to pay for them.

It is imperative that libraries and other public institutions distinguish clearly between those activities which are fundamental to the institutions for all citizens and those services (for instance on-line document searches) that derive from it. These services could very well be priced at marginal cost. We may assume that the more users or usage of a computerized system, the lower the cost per minute of use. If we encourage channelling all use of and access to the database through one computer system so as to take advantage of the declining costs, we are encouraging a monopoly.

It is always important to remember that in the non-profit sector one will be saddled with the public interest centred around the taxation. There are in other words, no simple solutions. *Zais* (1977) has in addition to this given an appropriate warning: 'Flexibility be maintained when approaching the issue of pricing information services and products. There are many models of pricing behavior that can be exploited for their applicability . . .' To create successful pricing policies, management needs knowledge of the organization's costs and some knowledge of the market in which the organization operates. Research is needed to learn who purchases information services and products and their sensibility to price. More purposeful cost data gathering is needed – not only effects to improve accounting data or historic cost data but also research that takes up such issues as joint costs, avoidable costs and correct allocation of overhead'. The discussion of charging is centered around the question of whether it is a mechanism for the recovery of costs (including profit) or a mechanism for allocating resources. *Singer, Kanter* and *Moore* (1968) are quite clear: 'This point should be stressed: prices are a rationing device, not a mechanism for recovering cost'. In our opinion any price mechanism will function as an allocation mechanism. Pricing will have the dual role of functioning as a market price (i.e. demanding what the market is willing to pay) or recovering some or all of the cost. The criticism of the cost-recovery policy is that it is short-term and not oriented towards the future and long-termed planning. This is an important criticism since information services are changing so fast. As *Cotton* (1974) noted: 'It is necessary to establish a pricing policy which considers both objectives of price. The overall result of the policy must be to achieve some cost-recovery objective as well as to allocate resources on an equitable basis'. In libraries, cost recovery often implies recovery of the fee the online database vendor charges the library. This is, for example, the way The Norwegian School of Technology charges *Lamvik* (1986).

ALTERNATIVE PRICING STRATEGIES

We will examine the pricing strategies that can be assumed to apply to a public service characterized by economies of scale. Economies of scale arise when the average cost per unit of output declines as output is increased. Scale analysis has three possible outcomes depending on whether long-term cost increases, more than proportionate to size and diseconomies of scale, are present. Should average costs decrease economies of scale exist. When the relationship remains the same, returns to scale are constant.

Ross (1977) used the Cobb-Douglas form of production function to ascertain the existence of scale economics in the journal publishing industry. The authors analyzed data from 1 to 36 journals each, and found that the average costs of the largest publisher were about 75 per cent of those of the smallest.

Clark (1977) undertook an empirical investigation to determine whether economies or diseconomies of scale existed in Californian public libraries from 1974 to 1976, and found that scale economies were observed in the average and that marginal cost and average cost decreased, ending up almost constant.

Using scale economics as a base line there will be five interesting pricing models:

1. Optimal pricing where substantial profit is made ·
2. Pricing according to value allowing both profit and loss
3. Full cost recovery where all costs are covered
4. Marginal cost pricing where subsidies are needed *and*
5. Free distribution of services where full subsidies are needed.

We have illustrated these five alternatives in Figure 1.

FIGURE 1. ALTERNATIVE PRICING STRATEGIES

The Alternatives:
1. Optimal pricing – for p_1 for k_1
2. Full cost recovery – p_2 for k_2
3. Marginal cost pricing – p_3 for k_3
4. Free distribution – p_4 for k_4
5. Price according to value – p_5, p_6, p_7, p_8 for q_5, q_6, q_7, q_8 (segmented market)

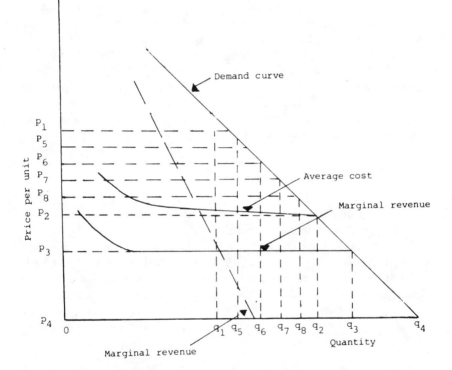

OPTIMAL PRICING

Optimal pricing occurs in the cross-point between marginal revenue and marginal cost (see figure 1). The quantity may be relatively small and the price relatively high. This is also called profit maximation. It requires a monopoly situation or a situation where the information services offered are of a better quality than the competitors can offer. For public information services like libraries, the bulk of short-term costs are fixed, so that virtually all marginal revenue represents a contribution to 'profit'. Total short-term profits are then maximized by increasing production up to the point where marginal costs just equal marginal revenue. This could be done by selling all available time (i.e. using the full capacity of a service) and by setting the price according to the average demand. There are two important shortcomings of optimal pricing:

(1) it ignores temporal variations in demand. This may result in all prime time being sold, but no sales for night time use.
(2) by selling to capacity during the peak hours, the quality of the service may become substantially degraded, which may result in a loss of both paying and non-paying customers if they grow dissatisfied with the service they are receiving.

The goal for a private information broker will be profit maximization. Many database vendors are trying to maximize the profit by charging the highest possible average price during peak hours while they offer substantial rebates during off-peak hours. They are using advanced statistical software programs to find the highest possible price both for the 'business class' and 'tourist class'. Some database vendors (Finsbury, for instance) have found that the best pricing policy is to charge an average price during all hours. Finsbury is maximizing long-term profit by working continuously towards maximizing short-term profits. Finsbury has found that by offering their services at NOK 800 per hour they will be working very near their capacity. If Finsbury experiences stiffer competition they can either lower their prices or differentiate their services (i.e. still try to get optimal price).

In our opinion it is not normal for public information services such as libraries to charge only an optimal price. The libraries are not in the information business to maximize their profit. Pricing is a supplement to allow improvement of services for all their customers. One may ask whether some customers are willing to pay a high price for premium quality. It may be the case for business information or for well-funded research projects and this will be the subject for discussion in the section below. The library may create a single department where profit maximization is the goal.

PRICING ACCORDING TO VALUE

The characteristic negative slope of an aggregate demand curve arises, in part from the fact that the value of service may vary substantially from one buyer to another, and in part from the decreasing marginal utility of additional quantities of the service to a single user. Price discrimination is a technique by which groups of users are isolated and charged prices that are closer to the maximum price which they would be willing to pay. Price discrimination may be accomplished by segregating users into groups defined according to their demand schedules, and charging the groups different prices. This can also be done by offering all groups the same core services but in a different wrapping (i.e. peripheral services). This is done by the airline companies for instance. Scandinavian Airline System (SAS) does it by offering different prices according to the demand and by offering a quite large business class with special services and a tourist class with substantial price savings, but not such service. The requirements for price discrimination are that it be possible (legally and practically) to segment the market, and that users in low-cost segments should not be able to resell services to users in higher-cost segments.

It should be possible to offer segmentation in a public, college or university library in this way:

1. Segmentation by the type of user:
   Employees (for instance free for own research work)
   Students (for instance free for the less expensive services)
   Consultant work done by employees
   Research funded by external public sources done by employees
   Research funded by external private sources done by employees
   Private business customers

2. Segmentation by type of application (may be combined with segmentation by type of user and/or segmentation by time):
   Public national databases
   Private national databases
   Public Nordic databases
   Private Nordic databases
   Public Non-Nordic databases
   Private Non-Nordic databases

3. Segmentation by time (may be combined with segmentation by type of user and/or segmentation by type of application):
   By time of day during the semester (spreading the overall load)
   By period (for instance cheaper when the semester is over to be able to spread the work over the working year)

Segmentation in a library will help the library to:

(a) understand better how the users value different services and then to be more user-oriented (e.g. market-oriented).
(b) be able to spread the overall working load over the day and the working year (i.e. to influence users to adjust their demands to that most beneficial to the capacity of the library)
(c) understand where and how the costs occur
(d) to get an economical supplement to public-provided money which can be used to improve old services and/or to offer new services.

Birks (1978) argues in his large British study for pricing according to value. Birks found charging for information services according to segmentation of users to be the most equitable solution.

PRICING FOR COST RECOVERY

To cover all costs of operation, excluding profit, in the case of public information services sounds like a sensible proposal. Ideally there would be no need for public subsidies and there would be no profit. Use is estimated over a given period and the prices are set so that they will cover all costs. The latter require the prices to be completely inelastic.

The discussion of pricing is centred around the question of whether it is a mechanism for the recovery of costs (including profit for commercial organizations) or a mechanism for allocating resources. Singer, Kanter and Moore (1968) are quite clear: 'This point should be stressed: prices are a rationing device, not a mechanism for recovering cost'. In our opinion any price mechanism will function as an allocation mechanism. Pricing will have the dual role of functioning as a market price (i.e. demanding what the market is willing to pay) or recovering the cost or some of the cost. The criticism of the cost-recovery policy is that it is short-termed and fast-oriented. It is not oriented towards the future and long-term planning. This is an important criticism since information services are changing so fast. As *Cotton* (1974) noted: 'It is necessary to establish a pricing policy which considers both objectives of price. The overall result of the policy must be to achieve some cost-recovery objective as well as to allocate resources on an equitable basis'. In libraries, cost recovery often implies recovery of the fee the online database vendor charges the library. It thus excludes staff time and implicit overhead costs. In short, the library passes on the vendor charges directly to the user. If a library buys a computer it is clearly advisable to encourage the users to make full use of the capacity early in the life of the computer when excess capacity exists and to discourage use when usage approaches the capacity of the system. However, if the library wants to charge according to cost over a given time interval (for instance five years) the charges will provide incentives that are exactly the opposite of what is desired. When the computer is new and fixed and variable costs are allocated to few users the cost per unit of work will be very high and prohibit further use and new users. The only way out of this dilemma, in our opinion, is to recognize that the price at any point in time need not bear any relation to the costs of the services at that time. It is very difficult for a library to charge for the cost of providing a large and good collection of documents when they offer one or several documents to a customer. The customer's willingness to pay will have nothing to do with the size of the collection, but with whether the documents solve an urgent and important problem. Pricing for cost recovery will be very difficult for libraries since it will be perfectly inelastic to the demand for the services. In as far as the pricing mechanism is static, it will provide the feedback mechanism the libraries need.

We will advocate flexible pricing schemes where the price is allowed to vary in order to adjust to demand at any given time.

MARGINAL COST PRICING

Marginal cost is defined as the incremental cost of another unit of output. The argument for marginal cost pricing of some public goods and services rests on the theories of welfare economics and monopolistic pricing. These theories maintain that once a capital intensive facility operating over a range of decreasing costs is installed, the general welfare goal should be to maximize the use of the facility. When we start to charge for a service, or when we increase the price, we usually find that the quantity used tends to drop.

We want welfare economics to minimize the sum of these quantity effects. Economic efficiency is attained when there is no unsatisfied demand and this happens when the price equals marginal costs. We have assumed that information services follow the rules of economies of scale (i.e. the cost per unit declines when heavily used). In a declining cost industry, such as the information industry, the marginal price will be smaller than the average cost, resulting in a deficit. The goal of economic efficiency will here conflict with the goal of financial sufficiency. The allocation of the subsidies needed will be dependent on how important the service is for society.

Marginal cost pricing will prevent spillovers since the price is less than a profit-oriented company will offer, but still high enough to prevent overuse of the goods. If the marginal cost gets too high then the public services exercise competition from private information services. It will, in other words, function to keep the public information services cost-effective.

We may assume that the more users or usage of a computerized system, the lower the cost per minute of use. If we encourage all of the usage and access to the database to be channelled through one computer system so as to take advantage of the declining costs, we are encouraging a monopoly. A state monopoly in national information databases might be beneficial in the Scandinavian countries. We could then have an integrated national system where we might catalogue each document only once and where the resources could be better shared and used than today. However, in the Scandinavian countries, the state will still have to maintain the collections.

FREE DISTRIBUTION OF INFORMATION SERVICES

This is also a pricing alternative. Society would pay all costs through taxation and services would be free. This is done to get an equal distribution of services to all the citizens in what is often described as the welfare state. The ideal situation, according to Marx, will be when everybody demands according to their needs. The fee services will anyhow have a price for the users: the time and trouble it takes to acquire them. We may very well consider it less expensive to buy a paperback at the book store than to borrow it at the public library.

We must consider if society can offer all information services free of charge. The benefits must then be greater than the costs, thus yielding a net gain to the society. We must consider to whom additional benefits from a governmental policy like this are likely to go and who will pay for the cost. As *Machlup* (1979) phrased the vital questions:

'If we are convinced that the benefits would accrue almost entirely to a small group of people while the cost would have to be borne by other groups, large or small, should we endorse such a measure with the same enthusiasm than if the benefits were widely diffused? Or should we examine the worthiness of the special interest group favoured by the program?'

If the beneficiaries are sick or handicapped persons we do not mind at all that other people have to bear the cost. But would we feel the same way if the beneficiaries of online information services were a privileged well-off small group? An informed society requires free distribution of core information services, but free distribution of all information services is more questionable. It is possible, as shown in this article, to do a market segmentation for a university library. It is, for instance, questionable whether society should pay for the information services to small and medium-sized enterprises.

Free use of an integrated national bibliographical database (for instance) might be beneficial to society, since we may assume that the more users of usage of a computerized system, the lower the cost per minute of use. If we encourage all of the use of and access to the database to be channelled through one computer system so as to take advantage of the declining costs, we may be a encouraging a monopoly. A state monopoly for national information databases is also questionable in a free society.

BREAK-EVEN ANALYSIS

Any library will have considerable fixed costs. These costs will occur whether the library is used or not. These costs are the costs to provide the library facilities, the administration costs, the salaries and the costs to provide a minimum selection of documents and services. Once on the shelves there is little addition fixed cost for increased use. The fixed costs may be divided into those that are direct (e.g. salaries) and those that are indirect (e.g. rent). It would be very difficult to allocate the fixed costs to individual uses because of the uncertainty of amount of use. Any library will have smaller variable costs. Variable costs are related to each use of library materials and services. For instance, online services costs will be heavily dependent on use since the database hosts charge for connection time.

When one adds either the fixed or indirect costs associated with materials and services, the average unit cost per use decreases as the number of units used increases. This decrease may be substantial over a small number of uses, but it ultimately approaches the variable cost. The average fixed and indirect cost per use begins, however, to increase at some point because of large incremental increases, e.g. when additional space and copies are needed.

Break-even analysis assumes that all costs can be represented as either fixed or variable costs, and that all units are sold at the same price so that marginal revenue is the same for each. The break-even analysis gives us the price to be able to cover the total costs. We can, however, also get breakeven for variable costs or fixed costs. The following factors are taken into consideration:

BEP = Break-Even-Point
TFC = Total Fixed Costs
SP = Selling Price
AVC = Average Variable Cost

$$BEP = \frac{TFC}{SP-AVC}$$

The break-even analysis illustrates only how many units a library must sell to cover the costs. Whether quantity can be sold on the open market at all is another story. Most costs in a library are fixed costs and this makes it difficult to calculate the costs for each service the library offers. Figure 2 illustrates break-even points at four different prices.

This analysis has two shortcomings. First the break-even level of production may exceed capacity. If this is the case, cost recovery is impossible at the given price. The immediate temptation is to raise the price, but this gives rise to the second shortcoming: the analysis ignores supply-demand considerations.

PROBLEMS ASSOCIATED WITH INTERLIBRARY LOANS – AN EXAMPLE OF A BREAK-EVEN ANALYSIS

A library service that may involve charging is photocopying done for another library as an inter-library service. Many Scandinavian research libraries have, as a result of smaller budgets, sought ways to reduce costs through such means as not subscribing to new periodicals and not renewing subscriptions. Reduction in periodical subscriptions is likely to result in increased interlibrary lending and photocopying, which shifts some of the cost burden from the borrowing library to the lending library. Most journals also have a short life-span (i.e. it is only the latest volumes which are in demand). *Rugaas* (1987) has found this cost burden too heavy for the Royal University Library in Oslo and wants the smaller research libraries to pay for the interlibrary services. They may then have to charge their users. The alternative is to give the university libraries in Norway more public money.

FIGURE 2. BREAK-EVEN POINTS AT DIFFERENT PRICES.

Total Fixed Costs: NOK 3000
Variable Costs Per Unit: NOK 200
B^1, B^2, B^3 and B^4 = Break Even Points

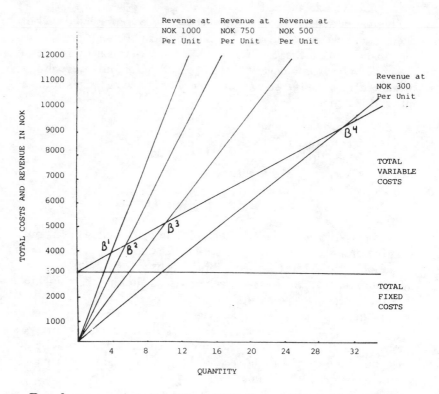

Data from several studies (King, 1978; Kent, 1978) yield the following typical costs to borrowing and lending libraries:

Borrowing Library:
Average annual subscription price:	$37.72
Annual maintenance and storage:	$37.92
Total average fixed costs:	$75.64
Variable costs per use internal circulation:	$ 2.00
Variable cost per interlibrary loan:	$11.60
Lending Library:	
Variable cost per use interlibrary loan:	$ 8.40

A library must decide (periodically) whether to renew a journal subscription or rely on interlibrary loan to fulfil the demands from the users. If the periodical is used once, the cost per use will be $77.64. This cost is much higher than borrowing a photocopy, which is $11.60. For four uses the average cost will be $20.79, which is substantially higher than the average cost of borrowing a copy. The break-even point is nine uses, at which point it becomes less expensive to purchase.

The interesting question is: what would be the effect if the lending library charged the borrowing library $8.40 for its loan?

This may be answered by a table using data provided by a University of Pittsburgh study in which the number of uses of scientific journals in several university libraries was estimated. The journals are within physics, chemistry and life sciences subject areas.

We can see from the table that free interlibrary loans yields considerable savings to the borrowing library at the expense of the lending library. If the lending library charged $8.40 per use, the total cost for the borrowing library would be $20 per use. The break-even point would now be between four and five uses. A total of 363 journals have 4 or fewer uses accounting for 753 uses. There would be a decrease of 1,418 interlibrary loans due to the charge of variable costs. However, if the lending library also charged an administrative fee for handling let us say $3 – then the break-even point would drop to between three and four uses.

TABLE 1. *Cost of the use of journals in academic libraries by number of uses*

Number of Uses	Number of Journals	Total Number of Uses	Total Cost $	Cost Per Use $
0	49	0	3750	
1	86	86	6754	78.50
2	84	168	6765	40.30
3	77	231	6320	27.40
4	67	268	5664	21.10
5	63	315	5452	17.30
6	58	348	5135	14.80
7	53	371	4799	12.90
8	48	384	4442	11.60
9	44	396	4160	10.50
10	41	410	3958	9.60
10 +	975	38601	151829	3.90
Total	1645	41578	209028	5.00

Note that break even with charge is 4 Number of Uses and that break even with no change is 8 Number of Uses.
Uses here are defined as readings. There could be other uses as well.
Source: Kent, A. et al.: *A Cost-Benefit Model of Some Critical Library Operations in Terms of Use of Materials.*
(Pittsburgh, Pa: Pittsburgh U. Press, 1978.)

To use charges is an effective way to get the interlibrary circulation to drop. Thus, the usual practice of not charging ordinary users should continue. It is important to get an optimal use of journals. The savings for society as a whole will be very modest. Society should increase the budgets of the large interlibrary lending libraries. The libraries should however charge private companies and professionals using the interlibrary services. The essence of this analysis is that it will pay for a library to use interlibrary loans if a journal has eight or less uses per year. The money saved could be used to increase the number of subscriptions of the most-used journals. This would increase the total circulation of journals and the benefits for most of the users.

ELASTICITY ANALYSIS

Libraries or other public services should never establish a pricing mechanism without first determining the implications that a such a policy would have on performance and utilization of the library services. The effect of lowering or raising prices depends, of course, on the price elasticity of the information services. For information services with a high price elasticity a small change in the price will result in a large change in the quantity demanded. This may be the situation if libraries started to charge fees for the circulation of books. If the elasticity is high then pricing will be a mechanism directed more at controlling budgets and restricting usage. This is the situation if the libraries do not want certain groups to use the services. For example, UC Berkeley are charging all groups other than the students and employees a fee of $25 for the circulation of documents to restrict the usage for all people other than their own students and employees. For information services with a low elasticities, raising prices may, indeed, aid in recovering cost and making a profit. Cost recovery and the possibility of earning excess profits will normally be accomplished through information services with low price elasticity. We believe this will be the case in all business-oriented information found in bibliographical databases, full text databases and fact databases. These are the services offered by private information brokers today. The libraries may also offer a combination of the above-mentioned online services and circulation of documents. If the two services are combined, then the price elasticity may be low. Most often, however, differentiated services tend to have lower price elasticities. This is reason why service companies are dividing up service packages.

To be able to use a successful pricing strategy any library or public institution must have some knowledge about:

(a) its objectives;
(b) its own cost functions; *and*
(c) the nature of the market in which it is dealing.

Any library needs to consider these factors to be able to offer adequate services to society. The library must then decide what services it wants to sell and how to price these services.

THE WELFARE LOSS

We will examine here what the welfare loss would be if we started to price some public information services. We have used the marginal pricing alternative as a basis for presenting a model which illustrates the welfare loss (i.e. the loss for the consumer having to pay a marginal price instead of getting universal free distribution of information services).

FIGURE 3. THE WELFARE LOSS

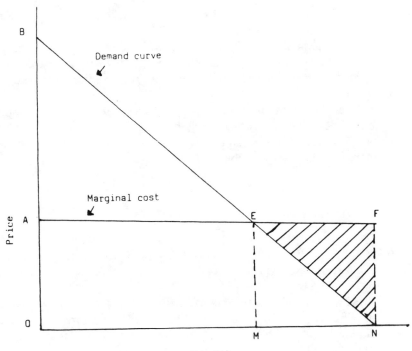

This model gives the following advantages and costs:

1. The consumer advantage by marginal cost pricing = ABE
2. The cost for the consumer by marginal cost pricing = OAEM
3. The total free distribution advantage = OBN
4. The increased cost for the society by using free distribution = EFNM
5. The welfare loss by using marginal cost pricing = OAEN − OAEM = EMN = EFN

Equity is a concept concerned with fairness. It, too, derives from the 'benefit received' principle and rests on the belief that in cases where individual benefits are paramount, the individuals receiving the benefit should bear the costs. One of the perversions of tax support of some public institutions is a redistribution of effective income from lower to higher income groups. An investigation done in Norway in 1978 showed that it is the higher income groups which tend to use publicly subsidized cultural services. *Cooper's* (1978) argument is that these higher income groups are well-placed to pay for new expensive online literature searching in public libraries. Some economists maintain that equity would best be served by the use of charging policy together with an income subsidy. Briefly, the theory is that individuals should be guaranteed an income floor and permitted to make their own decisions about services they wish to purchase.

Other economists maintain that equity would be best served by the use of full cost recovery pricing or marginal cost pricing where the users who can prove they cannot pay for the services are subsidized according to their needs.

It is not the intention of this paper to digress into another economic treatise, but only to stress that it is difficult to divide apparent from real equality. Marginal pricing and/or full cost recovery may, in some cases, be more just than free distribution.

CASE STUDIES

A Historical Case

The public library services in Volda and Ørsta in Norway were from 1852 to 1874 priced that the taxable part of the population (i.e. those with a certain fortune and income) paid a special tax for library services (*Olaisen* 1978, 1979, 1980).

Those who did not pay this tax had to prove that they were too poor to pay it. This was done by application to the board of the library and had to be done each year. The practical function was that very few from the lower class used the library services, as few of them wanted to prove their poverty to be able to use the library. Those who were exempted from the tax clearly used the library more than the average user. The special tax served the function of keeping the library as a middle class library. The selection policy of books were also clearly middle class dominated. It is difficult to make historical cases valid for today's society, but the fee policy in these Norwegian communities prohibited certain groups from using the public library services.

Four Californian Public Libraries

Cooper and DeWath (1977) compared the differences of providing free online information searching and marginal cost pricing in four public libraries in California. The services were free for six months but not for the next six months. Their main findings were:

1. The number of enquiries increased by 12.7 per cent in the period with marginal cost pricing.
2. The librarians were more careful about accepting searches for which they expected to find a fair amount of information once user fees were instituted.
3. The average time used for each search increased from 49 minutes in the free period to 55 minutes in the pay period owing to the fact that the librarians used more time to determine the users needs in the pay period. The librarians felt more strongly that the users had to get value for what they paid.
4. The librarians got a bonus up to 10 per cent in the pay period. This made the librarians more 'businesslike' in the pay period. This makes it however more difficult to compare the two periods.
5. The total cost per request decreased from $28.78 in the free period to $26.73 in the pay period (where the users paid approximately half of the total cost). The net result was that the librarians could extend other services.

The users were more satisfied with the service in the pay period. This might also be owing to the fact that the librarians had had more training in online searching and had avoided some of the mistakes made in the first period. Cooper and DeWath (1977) concluded: 'It is not argued that the use of information is not beneficial to the society, but rather that this segment of the population would probably use online searches with or without charge'. This study showed that charging for a specific service in a public library did not prevent people from using it.

Aarhus School of Business and Administration

The library at Aarhus School of Business and Administration charges for its services. Researchers, professors and students ordering photocopies from external institutions have to pay the library costs. Private industry has to pay DKK 1.50 for each page and a fee of DKK 10 if they are ordered from domestic institutions and DKK 25 if they are from foreign institutions.

Online searching is free for researchers and professors without external financial support for their projects, and for students working with papers recommended by a professor. Professors working with external financial support have to pay DKK 275 for each 15 minute searching period, DKK 4.50 for each off-line reference and DKK 3 for each online reference. Private industry and researchers with financial support from private industry (for instance consultants) have to pay DKK 400 for each started 15 minutes period, DKK 4.50 for each offline reference, and DKK 3 for each online reference.

Online searching in the Nordic databases SCANP and SCIMP is less expensive, while searches on the most expensive US databases are charged at substantially higher rates (1986).

This is a kind of marginal cost pricing. The prices are expected to cover the variable online searching costs for the library. The library would not be able to offer online literature searching if its were not able to charge a fee. In our opinion the fee charged makes it possible to offer free online searching for the researchers and professors at this institution.

Private information broking

Axess is the leading information broker company in Norway. They sell information services and regard themselves as specialists in information databases (telephone conversation with information broker 1986).

It is possible to get anything from a list of references to a complete consultant report. The average price for each commission is between NOK 3,000 and 5,000 for database literature searching. The rate per hour for an information broker (for instance a librarian) is NOK 500. This is, according to Eilertsen, what the Norwegian market is willing to pay. The company does not set the price according to costs, but according to the market value. It started out with an average price around NOK 2,000, but found that the quality of the information delivery services were much more important than the price. None of the customers has reacted on the higher price. Demand increased during the first half of 1986. Only 15 per cent of the company's sale in 1985 came from online literature searching. The company expects the Norwegian market to 'take off' in 1992. The main income source so far has derived from offering courses for information officers. Axess has tried to estimate the size of the Norwegian online market. They have estimated it to be about 80 million NOK in 1986. 65 per cent of the market is financial information, 12 per cent is medical information services, 8 per cent is scientific information and 7 per cent is marketing information. They concluded that nobody earns any money yet by selling information. The important thing is to get a position on the market to be able to meet the demand in the 1990s. The pricing strategy of this company illustrates the difficulties involved in pricing information services. The company is unsure about how much the market is willing to pay and starts with a low price. In our opinion the reverse would be a better solution. We think the company should have started with a minimum price of NOK 10,000 and offered high quality information services (i.e. better information services than they offer to day).

A private company – Norsk Hydro

The library at the largest industrial company in Norway, Norsk Hydro, had to price its services more cost-effectively from 1987. It had to try to estimate the price according to the use of the services in 1986. Each department is charged according to their use of the services. The library charges NOK per use of a journal. In the beginning many of the departments believed they could do this more cheaply than the library and wanted to subscribe to and circulate the journals themselves. All of the departments trying this found, however, that the central library could take care of this service in a much more cost-effective way.

The library tried to divide the level of services into three classes, from basic level to premium service. It found that the demand for premium services or the gold class was too small to offer the service at all. The internal pricing of the services has forced the library to be more cost-effective and more businesslike and, interestingly enough, the employees do understand better the value of the services when they are internally invoiced for them. The use of the services decreased in the beginning, but six months later was slowly increasing.

CONCLUSION

The growth of large databanks is one of the most interesting aspects of the Information Society. Whether private or government owned, data banks have the convenience of remote access at locations of choice via data communication lines. But with convenience has come the tying up of vital information which used to be available in printed form. Ease of use is increasing the tempo of information consumption. The market is expanding at an exponential rate, with the result that well-designed and marketed data are guaranteed acceptance. Databanks have become highly commercialized and, as a result, information tied up in databanks often is not available to users of public information centres or libraries because of the cost. It is important that researchers and students who genuinely cannot pay, have access to publicly available databanks. It is also important that these databanks are designed to be truly user-friendly.

At the present time, when most information is still available in printed form, charging fees is not a major deterrent to bona fide information seekers. This will not be true in the 1990s. In a few years time we will see the use of library catalogues as remotely accessible databases, the electronic transmission of printed material, automatic preparation of information retrieval and current awareness requests and the provision within libraries of workstations linked to national and international networks. Bringing these services into general use will not be cheap; the costs will moreover be not only for research but also for upkeep. The libraries are therefore likely to be under increasing pressure to recoup some of these costs through charging for at least some of their services.

In this paper we have identified five pricing alternatives for public information services: *optimal pricing, pricing according to value, full cost recovery, marginal cost pricing and 'free' distribution.* These may all be used on their own or combined. We have mainly discussed marginal cost pricing for public information services and have presented a model which identifies the welfare loss by changing from free universal distribution to marginal cost pricing. Marginal cost pricing of public services may reduce the spillovers and may increase public efficiency. It may also enable public institutions to offer new services and to maintain their old services.

Should public research libraries decide to adopt a strict no-fee policy it will undoubtedly be necessary to limit services. The addition of expensive private databases is probably out of the question for most public institutions resolved to resist public charging. Public charging in itself should not be seen as a first step towards either dismantling of our public institutions or the disenfranchisement of our (information) poor. We have also discussed the problem of regarding information as one regards other goods or services. To our knowledge there has so far been no satisfactory cost-benefit study. Finally, it should be pointed out that measurement of cost or benefit need not be in financial terms, but when an important resource like information is not valued, there is always the danger that decision-makers will tend to underestimate its importance.

REFERENCES

1. Aarhus, Handelshojskolens Bibliotek: *Bibliotekets Politik pa[p10] Informationsomrddet*. Aarhus (Aarhus: Handelshojskolens Bibliotek 1986).
2. Arrow, K. J.: 'Economic Welfare and the Allocation of Resources for Invention'. In: *The Rate and Direction of Inventive Activity,* p. 609–625. Princeton, N. J.: (Princeton University Press, 1962), p. 609–625, p. 616.
3. Barro, R. and H. Grossman: 'A General Disequilibrium Model of Income and Employment'. *American Economic Review* 61,1 (March, 1971): 82–93.
4. Birks, C. I.: *Information Services in the Market Place*. (London: British Library Research Report, 1978).
5. Boulding, K. E.: 'The Economics of Knowledge and the Knowledge of Economics'. *American Economic Review* 56,3 (1966): 1–13.
6. Casper, C. A.: 'Pricing Policy for Library Services'. *JASIS* (September, 1979): 304–309.
7. Clark, C., ed.: *California Library Statistics and Directory 1976*. (Sacramento: California State Library, 1977).
8. Cooper, M.: 'Charging Users for Library Services'. *Information Processing & Management* 14 (1978):419–427.
9. Cooper, M. and N. DeWath: 'The Effects of User Fees on the Cost of On-line Searching in Libraries'. *Journal of Library Automation* (December, 1977): 304–319.
10. Cotton, I.: *Network Management Survey*. Note 805. (Washington DC: National Bureau of Standards, 1974).
11. Demsetz, H.: 'Information and Efficiency: Another Viewpoint'. *Journal of Law and Economics* 12, 1 (April, 1969): 1–22.
12. DFI.: *Allmanna Rad och Rekommendationer*. *Dnr. 26186–28*. (Stockholm: DFI, 1986).
13. Eilertsen, T.: *Private telephone interview* (Oslo: July 4, 1986).
14. Feltham, G. A. 1968. 'The Value of Information'. *Accounting Review* (October, 1968): 684–696.

15. Geers, C.: *Local Knowledge*. (New York: Basic Books, 1983).
16. Gell, M. K.: 'User Fees: The Economic Argument'. *Library Journal* 104 (1979): 19–23.
17. Hayek, F. A.: 'The Use of Knowledge in the Society'. *American Economic Review* 35,4 (September, 1945): 519–530.
18. Hicks, J. R.: *Value and Capital*. (Oxford: Clarendon Press, 1946).
19. Hunstad, S.: *Prissetting av EDB-Baserte Bibliotekstjenester*. (Oslo: Norsk Dokumentdata, 1981).
20. Jorgensen, A. and H. K. Hogas: *Markedsokonomiske Modeller passer darlig pa Bibliotekssektoren*. Unpublished thesis. (Oslo: Statens bibliotekshogskole, 1985), p. 27.
21. Kent, A.: *A Cost benefit Model of Some Critical Library Operations in Terms of Use of Materials*. Pittsburgh, Pa.: Pittsburgh University Press, 1978.
22. King, D. W.: A *Study of Pricing Policies for Information Products and Services*. (Rockville, Md.: King Research, 1978).
23. Lamvik, A.: *Private telephone communication*. (June 4, 1986).
24. Lejonhufud, A.: *On Keynesian Economics and the Economics of Keynes*. (New York: Oxford University Press, 1968).
25. Machlup, E: *Knowledge: Its Creation. Distribution and Economic Significance*. (Los Angeles: Sage Publications, 1979), p. 64.
26. Machlup, E: *The Production and Distribution of Knowledge in the United States*. (Princeton, N.J.: Princeton University Press, 1962).
27. Marchack et al.: *Strategy for R and D*. (New York: Springer Verlag, 1967).
28. Normann, R.: *Service Management*. (Oslo: Bedriftsokonomens Forlag, 1984).
29. OECD.: *Trends in Information Technology Statistics*. Report No. 17. (Geneve: OECD, 1987).
30. Olafsen, T. and L. Vokac.: 'Optimal Values of Recall and Precision'. *Journal of the American Society for Information Science* (March, 1982): 92–96, p. 94.
31. Olaisen, J. L.: *Eit litteratursosiologisk perspektiv pa bibliotekshistoria til Volda og Orsta*. (Rena: Hedmark DH, 1980).
32. Olaisen, J. L.: *Volda folkebibliotek 1797–1900. Lokalkulturhistorisk samanheng, organisasjon, okonomi og utlan*. Unpublished thesis. (Trondheim: Universitetet i Trondheim, 1978).
33. Olaisen, J. L.: *Orsta folkebibliotek 1797–1900*. Unpublished thesis. (Oslo: Statens bibliotekshogskole, 1979).
34. Porat, M.: *The Information Economy: Definition and Measurement*. (Washington D.C.: US Government Printing Office, 1977).
35. Pratt, V.: *Private interview* (Berkeley: November, 6, 1984).
36. Ross, M.: 'Accountability, Productivity and the Impeding Crisis in the Public Library'. *The Journal of Economic* 3 (1977): 165–168.
37. Rugaas, B.: 'Om a sette Pris pa Informasjon'. *Synopsis* 18,2 (1987): 57–59.
38. Samuelsson, P. A. 1947. *Foundation of Economic Analysis*. (Cambridge, Mass.: Harvard University Press, 1947).
39. Schwuchow, W.: 'Fundamental Aspects of the Financing of Information Centres'. *Information Storage and Retrieval* 9 (1973): 569–575.
40. Shackle, G. L. S.: *Epistemics and Economics: A Critique of Economic Doctrines*. (Cambridge: Cambridge University Press, 1973).
41. Singer, N. M.; H. Kanter and A. Moore: 'Prices and the Allocations of Computer Time'. *Proceedings. AFIPS Fall JF. Computer Conf*. 1968: 493–498.
42. SSB.: *Bruk av Kulturtjenester*. (Oslo: Statistisk Sentralbyra, 1978).

43.   Steen, J. E. *Private Communication.* (Bergen: The Norwegian School of Business Administration, February 13, 1987).
44.   Thue, B. and P. E. Hovelsen.: *Private communication.* (Sundvoll: May 13, 1987).
45.   Zais, H. W.: 'Economic Modeling: An Aid to the Pricing of Information Information Services'. *Journal of the American Society for Information Science* 28 (March, 1977): 88–95, p. 95.

Costing and Pricing Information Services

Julie A. C. Virgo

College of Information Studies, Drexel University

As surely as a store sells a product at a particular cost to the buyer, a library provides a product that also has a cost. The cost of library service is not readily observable to the customer because, at the point of using the product, there is [usually] no charge.[1]

INTRODUCTION

Costing a library service, program, or activity and setting a price for that service or activity are two separate and distinct steps and serve separate and distinct purposes. Traditionally, libraries have generally not charged for their services and as a consequence have not needed to establish prices. But the need to set a price is not the only reason for determining library costs – in fact in making pricing decisions, cost is only one element in deciding how much to charge. Other considerations in setting prices might include the intrinsic value of the service to the potential buyer, what the market will bear, what the competition is charging, and even whether you are trying to get people to use a new product or service and are therefore willing initially to price it at below cost.

This paper focuses on costing services, rather than pricing services, since one must know costs prior to making pricing decisions, and because once costs are known they can be used for a variety of other library purposes. Library cost data are critical in order to accurately and fairly set prices for services, to make informed management decisions, and to communicate effectively with funding bodies or those upon whom the library is dependent for dollar allocations.

CHARGING FOR SERVICES

Information centers and libraries exist in both the for-profit and not-for-profit (including government) worlds. Yet libraries in either environment may be called upon to provide data on the costs of their services, and in some environments to set a price for selling the service.

Some libraries are required (or permitted) to charge back to other departments of the organisation the cost of the library service being provided to them. In law, management consulting, and executive search firms the cost may be charged directly to the client. In corporations some or all of the costs may be charged back to the department using the library. In government agencies and local municipalities the cost of providing service or library facilities may be refunded to the library in the form of an intergovernmental chargeback.

As financial resources become constrained, some organizations are providing certain basic library services at no direct cost to the user, and then offering specific supplemental services at cost (or more). These services might include, for example, photocopying, online searches, interlibrary loans, and long distance telephone calls for reference work.

For information brokers and other forms of library entrepreneurship, knowing costs is critical to establishing pricing structures if, in the long run, the venture is to survive.

Libraries are increasingly being called upon to demonstrate cost-effectiveness in the way they provide their services. The federal government has targeted libraries as one type of unit that must demonstrate that it is cheaper to provide library services in-house, or have that service contracted out to a cheaper outside vendor (as described in OMB Circular A 76). In order to make the comparison, one obviously needs to know the existing costs.

For those libraries that receive grant moneys from federal government agencies, for which indirect costs can be claimed, it is to their advantage to know their costs in order to negotiate a federal indirect cost rate.

Each of these situations calls for the library to know what its costs are in order to charge for a service at cost, to set a price on a service, or to decide whether it is cheaper to do an activity in-house or to contract it out.

MANAGEMENT DECISION MAKING

To improve the quality of management decision making, it is necessary to have basic cost data that can be factored into choosing from alternatives and making other types of management decisions. Cost data on services and programs provide the building blocks that can be used in a variety of ways for making decisions on the effective allocation of resources. Such data put into perspective the financial resources necessary to provide library and information services and demonstrate how the library is using its financial resources in performing various activities.

For budget preparation, cost data supply useful information for forecasting the financial impact of maintaining, expanding, replacing or curtailing service delivery. The data can be used to determine the costs of specific products and services when making decisions on pricing, the continuation of a service, or the extent to which a service or activity will be subsidized.

As a result, one can project the impact on a budget of adding a specific service, dropping a service (how many dollars will be freed up to provide another service), or if faced with a budget cut, what services will need to be modified or dropped to absorb the dollar amount of the cut.

By knowing the cost of specific activities and tasks, one can compare different ways of achieving a particular goal, to determine the most cost-effective way of achieving that goal or performing that service. The result may be to modify an existing practice, or even to contract the activity out if that is the least expensive way of accomplishing the task or goal.

When costs (particularly staff time costs translated into dollars) are monitored over time, changes in them can be readily recognized and can be used to flag the need to examine the underlying cause of the change. It may be that staff are doing a task more efficiently, more quickly, or too well. By having cost data available one can look at what is contributing to the change in costs. If the change is in the area of personnel costs, one can consider how staff time is being utilized and how staff costs are being allocated. It may be that too many highly paid personnel are spending too much time on routine functions, that a staff member is doing a task in more depth than it needs to be done, or that someone misunderstands a procedure or needs more training.

By monitoring costs and tying them to the unit-production for various activities, the efficiency of services can be determined. If cost reduction targets are set, the cost analysis data will provide an ongoing mechanism for providing feedback on the extent to which the targets are being met. Such feedback can be critical to motivating and modifying employee's performance behavior.

Cost analysis data, tied to performance measures, can be used as one source of data to evaluate employee performance, and to reward those who are able to accomplish tasks or responsibilities at a lower unit cost. This approach takes objective data as one basis for factoring into the appraisal process; it can also be used as a vehicle for negotiating performance expectations for the year ahead.

Oftentimes managers and boards think that certain activities or programs have a high priority in their organization's overall plan. It can be most revealing to compare the extent to which the actual budget allocation (including staff costs) does in fact reflect the planned priorities of the organization. Cost analysis, by providing data on the cost of specific services and activities, permits such a check to be made.

As a tool for improving management decision making, cost data is invaluable. As with most other management tools, though, one must be sure to remember that the data do not make decisions – it is the manager's informed use of the data, within the broad context of other institutional considerations, that results in quality management decisions.

FUNDING SUPPORT

In order to get the necessary support to provide library and information services, the funding body or community group needs to have a clear picture of what is necessary, why it costs what it does, and how it contributes to the overall program of service of the larger community. It is critical to communicate effectively with funding groups, and in a language that has meaning to them, to get their continued support.

Organizations, including not-for-profits and governmental agencies, are being called upon for greater fiscal accountability. Cost data enable the library or information center to communicate how resources are being used by describing the components of the library budget in a programmatic way.

When tied to library performance units, the library is able to more meaningfully report on its accomplishments. Increases in the library budget can, one hopes, be shown to be tied to increases in service levels on a per-unit basis, rather than simply an increase in cost. An example of this might be to show that: although circulation costs increased 11 per cent, only 2 per cent of this was an increase in staffing costs; the remaining 9 per cent occurred because of a 14 per cent increase in the number of items circulated; and, in fact, the cost per item circulated dropped from $2.16 to $2.05.

Similarly, one can show more persuasively the effect of increases, decreases, or the maintenance of existing budget levels, on the next year's program if the building block cost data have been systematically collected and used.

Competence as a manager is projected when you know your costs and are able to articulate them. Funding groups have confidence in the person who has a handle on costs, on the impact of projected programmatic changes on the budget, and who can explain clearly and factually what specific elements have contributed to those changed costs. As Johnson writes 'Cost allocation is very valuable in making appeals for revenues – legislators derive a sense of well-being and confidence if they can know the exact costs for units of service.'[2]

If you are asked to justify specific items in the budget, or to contract out certain services, you will be able to pinpoint clearly the impact on other parts of the library's budget; for example, whether some of the fixed costs will still remain after the service has been contracted out, or whether a new service may be instituted at little incremental cost to the total budget because of existing capabilities the library or information center already has.

Most important, the value of cost analysis data lies in the increased understanding it provides the manager of his operations, and the ability to communicate with outside funding groups in an effective and persuasive manner, based on facts rather than emotions.

HOW TO COST SERVICES

Having by now been persuaded of the value of knowing the cost of your various services and programs, we turn to the process of how these costs can be calculated. This is an extensive topic; for more detailed descriptions the reader is referred to the publications of Johnson,[3] Mitchell,[4] Smith,[5] and Rosenberg.[6]

Types of Costs

The total cost of an activity is composed of its direct costs, its indirect costs, and in some instances an additional allocated overhead cost.

The *direct costs* are all the costs that can be specifically identified with a project or activity. Examples of direct costs might include personnel, equipment, travel, materials, and some telephone and supplies costs. The *indirect costs* are those costs that are not readily assignable to a specific project or activity. Examples of these might include administration and bookkeeping expenses, heat, janitorial service, stationery, insurance, and utilities, as well as library support services such as cataloging, binding, and acquisitions. Some specific cost categories may have both a direct and an indirect component to them. For example, a unit may have direct telephone costs (for the long distance and local calls made) and indirect telephone costs (to cover the telephone equipment and maintenance costs).

There may sometimes be a third layer of cost imposed by the parent body, an indirect cost that a university or local government charges the library for services it performs that indirectly benefit the library. The total cost of a project or activity is therefore composed of:

Direct Cost + Indirect Cost = Total Cost

The cost accounting process

The first step in the cost accounting process is to *define the unit of measurement,* that is, the unit of product or service for which the cost is to be determined. This might be the cost of circulating an item, answering a reference question, processing a book, or of serving a borrower. For example, perhaps you want to know the cost of acquiring and processing a book. The tasks you would need to perform, and their associated costs, would be the relevant costs associated with the number of books processed.

The second step is to *specify the cost centers* for each of the functions in the library. Cost centers are usually broken down into two categories: direct mission or program centers and support service centers. The mission or program centers provide direct services to the library's users. The support services (e.g. acquisitions, administration, and facilities) provide services that enable the direct program services to happen.

The third step is to collect *the cost data* for each cost center and its activity. The fourth step is to *allocate the indirect or service center costs* to the program or mission cost centers, and then the final step is to *determine* the unit cost by dividing the total cost of a cost center by its appropriate unit of measurement.

As a simple example, let us assume that our library provides three services – circulation, reference assistance, and programs, for example, instruction in database sources. In order to provide these services, the library has identified five cost centers:

- Circulation
- Reference
- Programs
- Technical processes
- Administration.

Note that the first three of these are program cost centers; the last two are service cost centers and these costs will ultimately be allocated back to the three program centers.

In order to perform the tasks associated with each cost center, we need to spend money on personnel, library materials, supplies and services, equipment, arid overhead or indirect expenditures. So our cost matrix might look like figure 1.

FIGURE 1

	DIRECT COSTS			INDIRECT COSTS	
	Circulation	Reference	Programs	Technical Processes	Administration
Salaries Fringe Travel Materials Insurance Facilities Supplies Equipment					
Total Cost					

As we record data on where the money is being spent, we will also record data on the units of measurement or the outputs – that is, the number of circulations, the number of reference questions answered, the number of programs presented, and the number of people who attended them. With these data we can then calculate the following unit costs:

$$\text{Cost per circulation} = \frac{\text{Total cost of circulation}}{\text{Number of circulations}}$$

$$\text{Cost per reference questions} = \frac{\text{Total cost of reference}}{\text{Number of reference questions}}$$

$$\text{Cost per program attendance hours} = \frac{\text{Total cost of programs}}{\text{Program attendance hours}}$$

Or, we might want to have data collected at a more detailed level than the cost center level. For the circulation cost center, we could collect data at a series of activity levels, for example, overdues or, for each activity, at a series of task levels, for example, identifying overdue materials, preparing overdue notices. By collecting units of measurement data appropriate to each of these levels we can determine the average cost of each activity. The relationship between cost centers, activities and tasks can be shown graphically in figure 2, taken from Rosenberg.[7]

FIGURE 2. RELATIONSHIP OF COST CENTERS TO ACTIVITIES AND TASKS

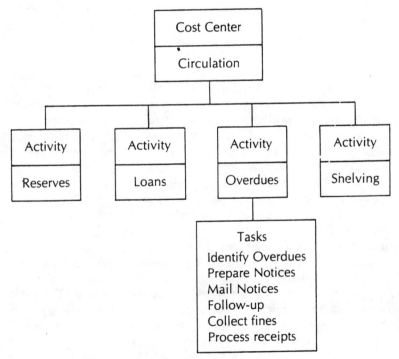

Collecting the data

There are two approaches to cost allocation. The preferred approach is to allocate costs for the whole organization on a continuous, systematic basis. Persuasive arguments for this approach have been made by Mitchell,[8] Hayes,[9] and Johnson.[10]

Mitchell says that some might wonder why they (Mitchell et al.) felt it necessary to undertake such a large-scale study instead of using sampling techniques to identify costs. They believed that sampling techniques were less accurate than a continuing cost accounting program, partly because of seasonal and other fluctuations within a library. She states that 'limited, one-shot studies and other sampling methods are known to introduce larger error factors in the data than do total data collection studies'.[11] Johnson also bases his argument for collecting data year round on seasonality issues.

In Mitchell's study, she stressed the importance of recording *all* staff time, including such things as sick leave and vacation, because true costs vary significantly depending upon how much non-unit-producing time is paid for by the library. If only unit-producing time is accounted for, the library that one way or another reduces non-unit-producing time would possibly not appear to be more effective. If administration and other non-unit producing costs are not accounted for, costs would be spuriously low. Mitchell makes another point that when all time of an individual is recorded, rather than only time spent on specific activities, it is more possible to check the accuracy of the recording.

A third argument for looking at total system costs relates to the desire to be able to measure the effects of procedural and other changes upon library productivity and effectiveness over time. By collecting the data daily, one can monitor changes and draw conclusions about the effectiveness of various ways of conducting the library's business. When few or no procedural changes are made, it is possible to use the data to pinpoint otherwise unexplained variations from time period to time period.[12]

This author's experience has been that it is easier to get people to follow systematic data gathering when it is a part of the normal work routine. Performed daily, it becomes a non-event. New people entering the work force accept the idea more readily when the reasons for the data gathering are explained and they can see that everyone else is doing it. At the end of the month, when each person summarizes his/her data, employees often show considerable interest in examining where they spent their time and what they accomplished.

This points to an important factor in cost allocation studies – the attitudes of staff to the process. If the study is an ongoing event, people will be less likely to be threatened by it. If it is implemented for the first time or done on a sampling basis, great care must be taken to introduce it in such a way that the staff do not feel threatened by it – that big brother is watching over their shoulders. Employees, when asked to keep track of their time and activities, have a tendency to fear that the data will be used against them. To the extent that the study is presented in the spirit of inquiry, curiosity, and data gathering within a positive outcome, people will more readily accept it. And to the extent that they see their supervisors also keeping track of *their* time, they will also more willingly accept the data gathering and analysis. Wherever possible, employees should tabulate their own data – this gives them an opportunity to see how the data is interesting and useful, and the end results will therefore have more credibility in their eyes.

In order to do a cost analysis while looking at the total library's costs, the following steps are necessary:

1 Identify cost centers and break them down into as many sub-cost centers as the library demands. Be sure that everything that is done in the library (either staff-related or other costs) fits into these cost centers.

2 For each employee, construct a list of activities and tasks that person spends time performing. This should also include non-unit-producing time such as coffee breaks, sick leave, vacation, committee meetings, travel, and personal phone calls.

3 For each employee, select the unit measures that describe that employee's outputs, if applicable.

4 On a daily basis, have each employee keep track of how many minutes are spent on each of the tasks, and how many units they produced or performed, if applicable.

5 At the end of the month, for each employee, summarize the time data and the 'units produced' data.

6 At the end of the year, summarize the total time data for each employee and multiply the proportion of time spent on each task or activity by the salary, including fringe benefits, for that employee, to determine how to allocate the employee's salary for the task and activities.

7 Consolidate data for all employees by task, activity, and cost center at the end of the year.

8 Allocate non-personnel expenses to each task, activity and cost center at the end of the year.

9 Allocate indirect costs (both operating expenses and support service cost centers) to the program cost centers.

10 Determine appropriate average costs for each unit of measurement (e.g. books cataloged, searches performed, telephone inquiries answered).

Allocating indirect costs

When allocating indirect operating expenses and support center costs to the direct programs, the 'step down' method is the one most commonly used. This is basically a method of 'trickling down' sequentially the costs of the service centers to the other service centers and finally to the program cost centers.

The first step is to identify those indirect operating expenses and service center costs that need to be allocated. For each of these, there needs to be some basis for allocation, e.g. building depreciation expense to be allocated on the basis of the percentage of square feet used for that activity, or accounting department to be allocated on the basis of the proportion of expenses each unit incurs compared to the expenses of all units.

The next step is to list the cost centers and program centers so that the costs of the first expense category, for example, maintenance, are distributed over the remaining unallocated expense categories and program units. Then the second expense category is distributed, and so on. An important feature of the step-down method, is that no reverse allocation ever takes place. Once an operating expense or service center's costs have been allocated, that service center receives no additional allocations from other service centers. Service center costs are allocated to both other service centers and to program centers, but program center costs are not allocated to other program centers.

Because no reverse allocation takes place, the sequence in which costs are allocated, or 'stepped-down,' first is an important cost accounting decision. In some instances the choice of order can have a significant influence on the costs allocated to the various program centers. The total cost of the program centers includes their direct costs, plus the indirect costs assigned to them, plus the service costs allocated to them. An example of a 'step-down' cost allocation is shown in Table 1. For illustration purposes, we will consider that the library has the following expenses:

The task is to allocate the service center costs to the program cost centers. The table shows the direct expenses for each service cost center and program cost center, then it allocates the direct expense for each of the three service cost centers, one center at a time, to the other cost centers to the right of the one being allocated. Note that program costs are not allocated to other program costs. From the table it can be seen, for example, that circulation had direct costs of $85,000 and allocated indirect costs of $65,431 ($9,967 + $22,123 + $33,341) for a total program cost of $150,931. Figures in the table that are in parentheses are negative figures – those amounts have been canceled out or done away with, by allocating them to the other cost centers.

A second approach

Many directors may feel overwhelmed by the prospect of doing a total cost analysis on a regular basis for their information centers or libraries. They may feel that the problem of 'selling' the data gathering to all their staff would be insurmountable, or they may not feel they have the resources to train a large staff to conduct the effort and analyze the results. Or, a person who is not at the director level may want to do a cost analysis of his/her own work or unit of responsibility, even though the library or information center as a whole is not involved in a cost analysis study. For

Table 1
Example of Step-Down Cost Allocation

	Maintenance	Administration	Technical Services	Circulation	Reference	Programs	Total Cost
Direct expenses to be allocated Maintenance	$18,000 (18,000)	$66,000 368	$33,000 258	$ 85,500 9,967	$48,000 2,561	$37,500 4,846	$288,000 18,000
Administration		66,368 (66,368)	18,437	22,123	11,061	14,747	66,368
Technical services			51,695 (51,695)	33,341	7,241	11,113	51,695
Full cost of programs				$150,931	$68,863	$68,206	$288,000

these people the desired approach may be that outlined in the Public Library Association's manual *Cost Finding for Public Libraries*.[13] Cost finding is defined as:

> . . . a less formal method of cost determination or estimation on an irregular basis. There may be no formal accounting entries during the year to record costs in specific costs accounts. Instead, cost finding usually involves taking available fund financial accounting data and recasting and adjusting it to derive the cost data or estimate needed.[14]

Cost finding is the process of using available financial data, or 'finding' costs, from budget details, the budgetary accounting system, analysis of detailed transactions (such as payroll records, contracts, invoices, and stores requisitions), and interviews with staff.[15] Work sampling forms the basis for determining staff time spent on activities and tasks, and for measuring units of work performed, in order that costs can be related to activities.

The steps followed in the cost finding approach are similar to those followed in the more generalized approach. The five cost findings steps are:

1 Identify the cost center to be examined. (Remember that a cost center is a grouping of activities as a responsibility area, for which costs can be reasonably accumulated and related to output).
2 Determine the activities and tasks related to the cost center e.g. circulation → overdues → preparing overdue notices.
3 Select the unit cost measures appropriate to the cost center, activity, or task being examined.
4 Capture the unit cost information. This is done by looking at existing financial reports, supplemented by the following nine steps.[16]
   - Determine the full hourly cost of time spent by library personnel, by developing a factor that reflects fringe benefits and the cost of actual hours worked as opposed to hours paid.
   - Record actual time staff spends on the activity or task.
   - Record direct supplies, materials, and capital outlays.
   - Record other direct expenses such as travel, facilities, etc., if necessary.
   - Determine total direct activity cost.
   - Determine indirect operating expenses (e.g. utilities, insurance, memberships, etc.), and allocate to direct cost of activity.
   - Determine indirect service costs (e.g. administration, personnel, binding and repair, etc.), and allocate to direct cost of activity.
   - Determine total activity cost.
   - Calculate unit cost information.
5 Analyze the data.

Sources of cost data

In addition to keeping track of staff time (either routinely or on a sampling basis) and of units of measurement, the person or institution doing a cost study will want to have access to actual accounting data. This will probably be in the form of the library's list of expenditures by operating unit, cost center and/or activity. Salary data will also be needed.

Depreciation data will be needed to determine how much of a capital asset (equipment, building) was 'used up' in carrying out the library's work during the year. Therefore it is necessary to have information on the major capital items that the library owns, how much they cost, and what their useful life is. For example, a photocopier may have cost $5,000 and be estimated to have a useful life of five years after which time it will be 'junked' (no salvage value). The depreciation expense for the photocopier on an annual basis would be calculated as $5,000 ÷ 5 or $1,000. The same kind of calculation would need to be done for the building, too. The parent body usually has schedules for determining the estimated life of buildings and equipment, or you can obtain commonly-used figures from your accountant and modify them if necessary to your local conditions.

A common rule of thumb for determining which items (otherwise known as the fixed assets) should be depreciated is that the item must be tangible in nature (can you kick it or thump it?), have a useful life longer than one year (you would simply expense it if it had a useful life that would all be used up during the year of the cost study) and it must have significant value (usually $500 or more).

The actual line item budget for the previous year, together with the supporting worksheets used during the budget preparation will provide important information. In service industries, as opposed to routine manufacturing operations, cost allocation studies are generally done on retrospective data. When done prospectively (to forecast future costs based on projected future demand levels), one can use estimated expenses but must recognize that these may or may not be close to the actual expenses.

Expenditure vs. expense

In using data from existing budget reports, an important distinction needs to be noted between an *expenditure* and an *expense*. The annual budget may show an expenditure of $5,000 for the photocopying machine described above. However, you are planning to 'use up' only $1,000 of it for this year, so you would need to adjust your budget figure so that the $5,000 did not appear in your calculations, but rather just the $1,000 depreciation expense for the photocopier.

Another example would be if you were to place a large order for stationery for your organization. You order enough to last you for two years because you can achieve a significant cost savings by ordering the larger quantity. The total cost was the expenditure, but the expense figure you would use for the cost study would be for the amount of stationery you used in one year.

For those readers who are familiar with basic financial accounting concepts, the conversion of expenditure data to expense data is like making adjusting entries at the end of a period. An expenditure is more of a balance sheet item, and an expense an income statement item.

Using Cost Analysis Data

Costs may be categorized in a number of different ways. The same cost element may be categorized in more than one way, depending on how you are looking at it. We have already seen how telephone expenses can be both a direct cost (long distance costs) and an indirect cost (the basic cost of the equipment and service up to the point that you make the first phone call).

Cost data are building blocks that can be used in a variety of ways, depending on the idea you are presenting or the point you want to make. Cost analysis to this extent can be viewed as an art, not a science. Two people can look at the same data and arrive at dissimilar conclusions, depending on which part of the data they have chosen to highlight.

For example, suppose that you identify the cost of the janitorial services in your library as being $4.75 a square foot. A member of your library board says that his firm pays only $4.25 a square foot to an outside firm for the same level of cleaning service. At first glance it would appear that perhaps you should fire the library maintenance staff and contract out the service at a savings of $.50 a square foot. However, on looking at the elements that make up the library's figure of $4.75 you determine that $3.50 is directly attributable to janitorial staff time and supplies. The remaining $1.25 per square foot is the library overhead (indirect cost) assigned to the maintenance function (the indirect cost in this instance includes the director, bookkeeper, insurance, secretarial support, a portion of the building space, etc.). Regardless of whether or not the library continues to provide its own janitorial services, these indirect costs will remain (they will just be reallocated over the rest of the library's program). Therefore, if the janitorial services are contracted out, the actual cost to the library will be the $1.25 indirect cost plus the $4.25 contract price; that is, $5.50 per square foot instead of the present library cost of $4.75 (this example has been adapted from Rosenberg).

The point is that by knowing the elements that make up the janitorial costs, we can evaluate the impact of a specific decision (should we contract out the maintenance service?) on the library's total fiscal picture.

This example also points to different kinds of costs in identifying the total cost of a service or program. We have already discussed the difference between direct and indirect costs. There are other useful distinctions in explaining or considering cost structures. In our example above we could view the indirect or overhead cost as a *fixed cost*, a cost that will be there even if we fire all the maintenance staff and don't clean or maintain the library. If you rent the space you are in, the rent is another example of a fixed cost – it doesn't matter if the library is closed, open 20 hours a week or 80 hours a week, the rent is a fixed cost. Graphically, a fixed cost can be represented in figure 3. Fixed costs are often called *non-controllable costs* because, for the period of the lease, or in the short run, there is nothing the manager can do to change the cost. The janitorial staff has no control over the overhead allocated to its unit.

FIGURE 3.

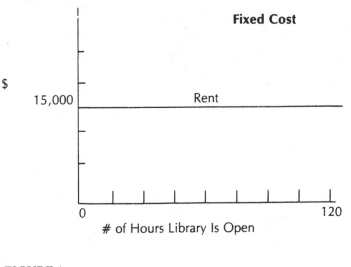

FIGURE 4.

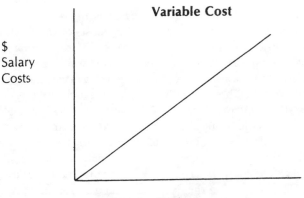

A *variable cost* is one which changes as the activity level changes. An example of this might be the relationship between the cost of staffing a reference desk and the number of hours the reference desk is open. As the number of hours increases, so does the salary cost increase proportionately. Graphically, a strictly variable cost function would look like figure 4.

Certain costs are *semi-fixed or step costs*. If in our library we were permitted to hire librarians not on an hourly basis but only in increments of one-half full-time equivalents each day (i.e. we can hire half a reference librarian, one reference librarian, or one and a half reference librarians) our cost structure would have a fixed component to it (our costs would be fixed for each four periods) but would vary as we added each four-hour-a-day reference librarian. Graphically, our costs would look like figure 5.

FIGURE 5

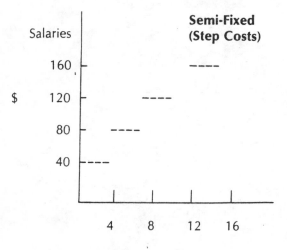

# of Hours Library Is Open

Most costs in a library are *semi-variable costs*. (See figure 6.) They have a fixed cost component (the equipment and service costs of the OCLC terminal) and a variable cost component (the time spent on the terminal). Or, in the example previously given, the overhead cost was a fixed cost, and the hours the janitorial staff worked could be viewed as a variable cost. Even if the janitors worked 0 hours (on the horizontal axis) the janitorial service still incurred the overhead cost (on the vertical axis). As noted earlier, cost centers, activities or tasks that are semi-variable in their cost structure, have important implications for management decision making; if you delete the service, the fixed cost component will not necessarily disappear. Conversely, you may be able to achieve economies of scale by increasing the service, amortizing the fixed cost over a larger number of units, and thereby reducing the average cost per unit.

FIGURE 6

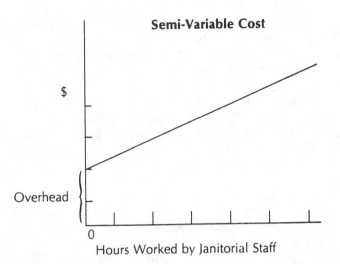

This fact can sometimes be a powerful argument for getting budget increases for specific programs. For example, lets say you want to get additional staffing for the bookmobile so that it can travel the same distance but make twice as many stops. You currently have the bookmobile operating 20 hours a week (5 hours traveling, 15 hours for the service stops). You describe to your funding body that for an additional 15 hours of staff time a week you can increase your user coverage by more than 100 per cent. At the same time you would only be increasing the total cost of the bookmobile service by the additional cost of the staff, and an increased administration and technical services allocation. Your average circulation cost would come down because you would have (hypothetically) twice as many circulations over which to amortize the fixed costs (bookmobile depreciation, gas, maintenance, insurance, and promotion). Your users would feel they were getting a 100 per cent increase in the amount of service, whereas your funding body only has to make an incremental increase to your budget of say, 35 per cent.

Another pitfall for the unwary is the consideration of *joint costs*. Joint costs are like indirect costs in that they cannot be unambiguously and economically separated. The cost for acquiring, organizing and maintaining a collection may be viewed as a joint cost. if you acquire journals, indexes, and reference works for use by the general public and the reference staff, you need to be able to allocate the cost to the different functions for which they will be used. Now, what happens when you stop providing one particular function? You still need the collection for other purposes, and the cost does not go away. In making management decisions, one needs to be watchful for joint cost considerations.

In considering which units of measurement to report, consider your purposes. Just because you collect data, doesn't mean you have to provide your enemies with ammunition to use against you. Cost analysis data are for internal use. Be selective as to which data you report externally. If you have data on the cost per user and the cost per circulation, and your library tends to have a small number of users but they use the library heavily, you will likely want to report externally on only the cost per circulation. If you are making a case for additional book-mobile stops, and you have data that show that most users come from a three block radius of the bookmobile stop, you may want to show the likely positive effects of reducing the cost-per-user if you add more stops. Consider the purpose you are trying to accomplish and use your data accordingly.

One of the problems in using cost data externally is that it can be taken out of context by others who are not familiar with the underlying assumptions, and misused or misquoted. This is another reason for viewing cost analysis as primarily an in-house tool.

Sometimes cost data are compared across libraries when quite different elements may go into the cost calculations. One library may report its costs without having to include a parent body overhead while another has to include it. One library may report on its average variable cost per unit of work performed (known as direct or variable costing), and another unit might include direct and indirect costs (known as full costing). One library may have a manual circulation system or catalog and another library's may be automated. One library may use a large number of volunteers or student assistants. Always consider cost data with a healthy degree of scepticism until you understand the costing principles, environment, and assumptions used to arrive at the data.

Cost analysis is best viewed as an internal tool for monitoring costs and productivity, detecting unexpected variations, and as a planning tool for budget preparation. External use of cost data can be very effective if you take into account the pitfalls outlined above.

At a library and at an institutional level, there is value in knowing the costs of services and programs, even if you do not follow the ideal and tie costs to performance measures. To know what one service costs compared to another, to identify variations in cost levels, to see an explicit statement of service priorities (expressed in dollars), to understand the cost structure of a program or service, have value in and of themselves in promoting budget support from funding bodies and in management decision making.

Even though you may not be able to capture 100 per cent accurate data (particularly on personnel costs), the data you do capture will provide a considerably better picture of your organization's operations and priorities than intuitive guesses. Don't delay doing cost analysis simply because you cannot achieve perfection in your data gathering efforts. And don't aim for perfection to the extent that the time and effort spent on calculating each element of cost outweighs the likely impact of that component on the total cost of the activity analyzed.

Remember the limitations of cost data. Cost data yield 'hard' numbers, and once an item is quantified, no matter how 'soft' the underlying basis, there are some who would regard the data as totally scientific. Remember the admonition, cost accounting is an art, not a science. Cost analysis yields data, but it does not evaluate the quality of a service, the staff, or the collections. Cost analysis reveals cost information, but it does not on its own tell if a cost is too high or too low. Cost analysis can be a useful tool, when used by an effective, thoughtful manager.

CONCLUSION

Cost analysis is an appropriate and necessary concept that can be usefully applied to libraries and other not-for-profit organizations. The principles that have been developed to apply to the for-profit environment can be adapted to the not-for-profit world. Although cost analysis in its purest form ties costs to related outputs, it can be an effective tool even when outputs are difficult to quantify. The ability to see patterns in total cost data by program over time can yield important insights to employees, supervisors, directors and funding agencies. Cost data are the key to knowing the costs of services. By knowing the costs of services, and the elements that form those costs, management is positioned to make better decisions about the present and future operations of the library.

REFERENCES

1   William W. Johnson and Ed Sayre, *Cost Accounting Procedures for Public Libraries: A Model* (Aurora, CO: Central Colorado Library System,, 1975), p. 3.
2   Ibid., p. 23.
3   Ibid.
4   Betty Jo Mitchell, Norman E. Tanis, and Jack Jaffe, *Cost Analysis of Library Functions: A Total System Approach* (Greenwich, CT: JAI Press, 1978).
5   G. Stevenson Smith, *Accounting for Librarians and Other Not-for-Profit Managers* (Chicago: American Library Association, 1983).
6   Philip Rosenberg, *Cost Finding for Public Libraries: A Manager's Handbook* (Chicago: American Library Association, 1985).
7   Ibid., p. 15.
8   Mitchell.
9   Robert M. Hayes and Joseph Becker, *Handbook of Data Processing for Libraries* (Los Angeles: Melville Publishing Co., 1974), p. 103.
10 Johnson, p. 4.
11 Mitchell, p. 5.
12 Ibid., p. 35.
13 Rosenberg.

14   William W. Holder, Robert J. Freeman, and Harold H. Hensold, Jr., 'Cost Accounting and Analysis in State and Local Government,' *Cost and Managerial Accountant's Handbook* (New York: Dow Jones-Irwin, 1979), p. 9 7.
15   Rosenberg, p. 9.
16   Ibid., p. 27.

Information brokering: the state of the art

Alice Sizer Warner

Information Guild, Lexington, Mass.

Entrepreneurs in today's library world are individuals who operate enterprises that charge fees for information-related services and products. Intrapreneurs do the same thing but they do it within an already-existing institution, such as a public, university, or special library or an association.

ENTREPRENEURS

Fifteen years ago, Betty Eddison, a Simmons classmate, and I thought we had personally invented the idea of setting up an information company.

We soon found we weren't unique at all: we identified twenty-odd other North American information entrepreneurships. Today there are at least 800 fee-based enterprises located in North America.

What do these information entrepreneurs do? They develop specialized libraries from scratch, clip newspapers, compile directories, consult on everything from computers to construction. They create archives and software, develop vocabularies, do chores (moving, bar coding, shelf reading), help libraries write RFPS. They index manuals and books and documents, they organize conferences and prepare proceedings, they organize files and plan paper flow. They provide alerting services, publish books and newsletters, retrieve documents, search online, substitute for librarians who are having babies. They teach. They travel as couriers. They write abstracts, they write computer instruction manuals.

As has been said, 'Where there is confusion, there is opportunity for a librarian,' and our librarians-turned-entrepreneurs are taking advantage of confusion wherever they find it. At last count, the service most frequently offered by information entrepreneurs was online searching followed closely by document delivery. Consulting in its various guises and 'research' (however defined) came next.

What we do not know, and probably won't know, is how profitable the types of entrepreneurial services are. There may well be regional differences; for instance, the business of providing substitute librarians goes well in some parts of the country and doesn't in others. In general, those entrepreneurs who do best know exactly what it is they are selling and to whom, can explain what they sell in words a nine-year-old would understand, and are more interested in their clients than in what they themselves do. Generalist entrepreneurs who try to be all things to all customers (which is essentially what is taught in library school) have a harder time.

Many information entrepreneurs, in my opinion, fit into one or more of the following unfortunate categories: they think they're doing well because they're very, very busy and confuse volume with profit; they won't tell you whether or not they are profitable and some actually throw up smoke screens so as to seem more successful than they are; and they really don't know whether they are profitable or not, so they couldn't tell you even if they wanted to. Many who work at home think they are being profitable when they really are not – they forget that the business should bear part of the cost of running the household (or the 'apartmenthold' as one person called it).

Some figures that are available are from the American Entrepreneurs Association. It reports that for the business called 'information broker' (a popular generic term):

The high net profit before taxes is upwards of $175,000 and the average net profit before taxes is $60,000

Minimum start-up investment is $8,000 with average start-up costing $20,000

Industry growth prospects are good, stability is increasing, and risk factors are moderate.

Business is getting your hands on someone else's money. Stay away from entrepreneuring unless you like thinking about and working with money (including collecting it), like to sell, like to fiddle with spread-sheets. Doing the information work itself is the easy part: you can hire people to do it for you. Finding customers and managing cash flow and running the business are what the entrepreneur must have firmly in control. Being an entrepreneur can be glorious fun. Just be certain you do it with your eyes open.

INTRAPRENEURS

The current wave of fee-based, in-house library services began at about the same time the information entrepreneurs began to organize them-selves. In examining fee-based services in libraries, be careful of the phrases 'profit center' (profit for whom, and who gets to keep the money?) and 'cost recovery' (specifically, what costs?). These phrases carry different meanings for different people and each meaning is just as correct as another, so beware!

Most academic libraries offer online searching for students and faculty at little more than out-of-pocket cost. However, between 80 and 200 (maybe many more – no one is sure of the exact number) academic libraries have established fee-based services for customers from outside the academic community. Most commonly offered are online and manual research services, providing copies of articles and other documents, and lending books from the library's collections.

The largest, oldest university fee-based services are fielding about 20,000 requests a year: 120 requests each business day, almost 15 requests an hour with a new request coming in every four minutes. The smallest, low-key fee-based services have one or two customers a week.

Some universities have multiple fee-based services. One big quasi-public university has at least three different fee-based research services, each with a different hourly rate: $25, $55, and $90. The $90-an-hour library was at last report about to raise prices.

A few universities charge for membership, usually $1,000 or more a year, and then have two fee scales: a lower one for members, who get priority service, and a higher scale for nonmembers who must wait their turn. At one university, the members pay $40 an hour, nonmembers pay $80.

Some prices are set with specific cost recovery goals in mind – recovery, for instance, of one librarian's salary and benefits. One university charges $70 an hour, and librarians are expected to bill at least 2.5 hours per day as contribution to total cost recovery (heat, light, university overhead) of the fee-based division.

Other fees seem less logical. For instance, one university fee-based service charges $60 an hour. The librarian doesn't know how that price was arrived at: she inherited it.

In theory, guidelines on charging for information services reflect the goals of the institution. A university may have as a goal for a fee-based service that of maintaining good town-gown relationships; the fee-based service allows nonaffiliated people to use the library, and this is good public relations. A university may also use its fee-based service as a way to keep alumni, especially rich alumni, in contact with the university: smart move.

Although public library fees are an extremely hot political topic, a few public libraries offer fee-based research services. Hourly charges vary hugely ($15 to $85 an hour at last count) as do the goals of the services. A typical financial goal is that of one of the older public library fee-based services: to recover salaries (three people) plus benefits (30 per cent of salary) but not to recover cost of physical space. At least one public library charges $30 an hour because 'that's what other libraries in the consortium charge'.

Medical libraries, like virtually all other libraries, are inventing their own fee-charging wheels. Hourly rates seem lower than in other kinds of libraries and one sees set rates, such as a $27.50 surcharge for nonaffiliated outsiders, or flat fees, such as $40 per search.

Association libraries tend to charge information fees to nonmembers at an exorbitant rate and to members at an affordable rate (definitions of 'exorbitant' and 'affordable' vary, of course) with the goal to convert nonmembers to membership. Association librarians in Washington, D.C. have created an ad hoc support group, and hold brown-bag lunch meetings to discuss mutual problems, including fee setting.

CHARGING BACK, CHARGING OUT

Charging back is another fees mechanism, used primarily in special libraries. Services are charged back to departments, to projects, to jobs: the accounting department debits money from the appropriate department account, or project account, or job account, and credits that money to the library's account.

There is much variety in how companies with special libraries manage charge backs. It is common, but by no means universal, to charge back out-of-pocket costs, such as costs of doing an online search, to the individual or department ordering the search; some libraries charge back for the librarian's time spent on a search as well. Some company libraries charge back for out-of-pocket costs and beyond that charge back to departments on a head-count basis, regardless of how often which department asks for what services.

Costs of space, usually expressed in terms of dollars per square foot per year, often must be accounted for. When one librarian joined a company, the library had 10,000 square feet. Within a year, she had cut back to 7,600 square feet and, at last report, was hoping to knock off more square footage, all in an effort to 'pay' less for the space her library encumbers.

Accounting methods, such as charging back for library services, can change rapidly. One beleaguered publishing company library that had never had to charge back anything (it had always functioned as overhead) was asked in mid-August to start charging back immediately, and would that please be retroactive to July 1? (You can guess when that company's new treasurer came on board!)

No one has counted how many special libraries charge back. A guess might be 600 to 1,200, between 5 per cent and 10 per cent of 12,000-odd special libraries.

Charging out is a variation of charging back, and again occurs primarily in special libraries. Charging out happens when a fee for library/information service is added to the fee that is already being charged to a customer for the primary service of the parent institution, such as law, accounting, or advertising. The library is not functioning directly as a fee-based service, but a fee for library service is passed on to clients of the firm.

TALKING TO EACH OTHER

Entrepreneurs have, at last, learned how to talk to each other. There are national groups for library entrepreneurs and increasing numbers of local groups. Longtime information entrepreneurs are still asked how-to-do-it questions by the newcomers, but not as many or as often: there is more written on the subject now, there are courses and workshops, there are more role models.

There is not as much easy communication among library intrapreneurs as there is among the entrepreneurs. Much communication that exists consists of calling each other up to ask for price lists. Fee-based services in libraries are only beginning to receive the cool-headed analysis that entrepreneurships have received. 'Fee', of course, can be a passionately dirty word, and librarians operating intrapreneurships find few willing role models or support groups. Decisions are more political for those working in institutions than for entrepreneurs, and bureaucracies can move slowly.

The older, more established fee-based service librarians are getting tired of being asked how to set up a fee-based service (some now charge consultation fees: entrepreneurism within an intrapreneurship?). There is little how-to material written and most support groups are informal.

Special librarians, many of whom work in one-person libraries, seem to feel that they must figure out all charge back and charge out answers by themselves and tend to forget to ask for help from the treasurer's office, the accountant, the bookkeeping department. Special librarians do, however, conspicuously help each other with meetings, workshops, discussion groups.

In the late 1980s, the state of the art is that there are multifaceted variations of charging fees for library and information service. There is controversy, confusion, and misunderstanding, and yet there is activity, lots and lots of activity, and from this activity we are gradually developing experience and guideposts to help librarians in the 1990s and beyond.

ASSOCIATIONS FOR ENTREPRENEURS

Association of Independent Information Professionals, Box 71053, Milwaukee, WI 53211. 800/545-4141, ext. 389. Annual conference, usually in June.

Consultants' Section Library Management Division, Special Libraries Association, 1700 18th St., NW, Washington, DC 20009. 202/234-4700. Meets at and sponsors programs at SLA annual conferences; publishes membership directory.

Independent Librarians Exchange Round Table, American Library Association, 50 E. Huron St., Chicago, IL 60611. 800/545-2433. Meets at both annual and midwinter ALA conferences; publishes membership directory.

FOR INTRAPRENEURS

Fee-Based Information Service Centers in Academic Libraries Discussion Group (FISCAL), Association of College and Research Libraries,

American Library Association. Meets at both annual and midwinter ALA conferences; publishes membership directory.

PUBLICATIONS

Directory of Fee-Based Information Services, Burwell Enterprises (5106 F.M. 1960 W., #349, Houston, TX 77069), 1978–. Annual. ISSN 0147-1678. Lists both entrepreneurs and selected intrapreneurships.
Information Broker. Houston, TX: Burwell Enterprises, 1978–. Bi-monthly. Articles on entrepreneurship and on fee-based services in institutions.

WORKSHOPS

Ackerman Associates, Box 1707, East Lansing, MI 48823. 517/332-6818. "The Ins and Outs of Information Brokering".
Information Guild, Box 254, Lexington, MA 02173. 617/862-9278. Workshops on intrapreneuring, entrepreneuring.
The Rugge Group, 1626 Chestnut St., Berkeley, CA 94702. 415/524-3212. "The Information Broker's Seminar"

SELECTED READINGS

General Overview

Kinder, Robin and Bill Katz, eds. *Information Brokers and Reference Services.* New York: Haworth Press, 1988. Also published as v.22 (1988) of *Reference Librarian.*
Warner, Alice Sizer. "Fees for Information Service". In *The Information Profession: Facing Future Challenges,* proceedings of 1987. Special Libraries Association State-of-the-Art Institute. Washington, DC: SLA, 1988.

Intrapreneurship

Curley, Arthur, ed. "Fees for Library Service: Current Practice & Future Policy." *Collection Building* 8, no. 4 (1986).
Dubberly, Ronald. "Managing NOT to Charge Fees." *American Libraries* 17 (October 1986): 670–76.
Fee-Based Services: Issues & Answers, proceedings of the Second Conference on Fee-Based Research in College and University Libraries, 10–12 May 1987, at Ann Arbor, Michigan. Ann Arbor, MI: Michigan Information Transfer Source, University of Michigan, 1987.
Stump, Barbara. *Opening and Marketing Fee-Based Services in Academic Libraries—A Small Business Approach.* Chicago: ALA, 1983.
Warner, Alice Sizer. *Making Money: Fees for Library Services* NY: Neal-Schuman, 1989.

Entrepreneurship

Everett, John and Elizabeth Powell Crowe. *The Information Broker's Handbook: How to Start and Operate Your Own Data Research Service.* Blue Ridge Summit, PA: Tab Books, 1988.
Warner, Alice Sizer. *Mind Your Own Business: A Guide for the Information Entrepreneur.* New York: Neal-Schuman, 1987.

Running the library as a profit making business

Lawraine Wood

Deputy Librarian, Royal Military College of Science, Shrivenham, Swindon, Wilts., SN6 8LA

INTRODUCTION

In my last job, I had the opportunity of running a technical library in an RA (Research Association). During my time there, the Association made the transition from quasi civil service/government funded organisation, to independent commercially run company. During the same period, the library went through a similar transition. This is an account of that experience.

In this paper I will give an overview of the organisation, the changes in the last few years that affected its development, and how those changes affected the Information Group, in particular the library, and how we arrived at the point of considering the introduction of charges.

I will then examine how we approach the subject of charging, by asking the following questions:

What do we have to sell?
Who are our customers?
How do we pay for parts of the service which do not generate income?
How much do we charge?

A BRIEF HISTORY OF THE RA

The RA was one of about twenty similar bodies set up in a period of post war reconstruction for the purpose of disseminating technological innovation to industry. The central pool of expertise would research the problems of industry, which were too costly for an individual company to solve, but which could be cost effectively dealt with by a single body working for more than one client. The government supported these RAs by awarding grants, which I believe originally made up in the region of 75 per cent of the total income, the rest coming from industry.

The policies of the current government have not been kind to research in general. It is an easy task to trace through the pages of the popular scientific press the effects of those policies, on science in particular. The government has stated that it believes that industry should fund its own research. This policy has had far reaching effects on the research community as a whole. My organisation was no exception. In a period of three years the RA moved from a position of about one third of its income being derived from grants from the DTI, matched by income from industry, to a position where hidden bureaucratic holdups made this form of income so unreliable that the organisation was forced to prepare budgets which took no account of any income from government sources. Any money received from the government was treated as an unexpected bonus. Other RAs have undergone parallel kinds of transformations to become much more hard nosed and commercial. This was not easy in an organisation where for many years there was an atmosphere of cosy security and 'profit' was a dirty word. Some drastic measures were required, including some redundancies and sell offs.

THE INFORMATION GROUP

The Information Group reflects these changes. The provision of information as everyone knows, is a highly expensive business, and if profits are made, the margins are slender. In the early days, the efforts of the Information Group were an integral part of the organisation, and were directed towards keeping member companies, who paid subscriptions, informed of the latest developments. Through the provision of an online database and abstract journals, it alerted them to these new trends and to others working in similar fields, thus providing them with opportunities to keep development costs to a minimum.

In 1982 the Information Group consisted of the Library and Reports Production, an Information Section populated by Information Scientists who scanned the literature, wrote abstracts, edited the journals, and produced bibliographies and literature searches, a Conference Section which ran something like 10 conferences every year in subjects closely aligned to our subject matter, a Graphics Section and Print Room (all publications were produced in-house) and a Publications Sales Department. A total of 48 people worked in the Information Group.

The group was financed partly by sales of publications, including conference proceeding volumes, the attendance of the conferences, and the whole of the membership income, part of which was used to finance the Library. Unfortunately the mastermind of this highly profitable business, and his deputy, left the company within a short time of each other, leaving the business vulnerable. There followed a succession of different managers, none of whom seemed to appreciate the importance of membership income to the health of the group. At the same time, the cost of staff was increasing, yet the services were not reviewed or prices increased to reflect those increases. More staff changes elsewhere in the company meant that membership was allowed to decline to a point where it was no longer providing the group with a sufficient income. Suddenly the Information Group was sustaining large losses which were affecting the rest of the RA's business. Some drastic action was required. A new manager, this time a publisher, (we had previously had a computer buff and an engineer trying to run the business) was recruited to get the whole show back on the road.

Along with these changes, other changes were occurring at corporate level. The previous fashion of income generating activities paying for the overhead activities has become outmoded. There was a move towards eliminating overheads completely, and establishing each Group of the newly formed company as a separate identity. This is partly a result of the fact that the organisation's overheads were enormous – test rigs use enormous amounts of electricity, for example, and there were arguments about whether a Group such as the Information Group should bear the cost of that bill. New arrangements introduced the idea of Inter-Group Trading: if a Group wanted some electrical work doing, it paid the Technical Services Department for doing the work, rather than just phoning them up and asking them to do it and the cost being absorbed invisibly. Similarly, the Information Group paid the Computer Department for the use of computer time. It is against this background that the idea of charging for library services first arose.

I would like to digress briefly to give you a view of the kind of work with which the Information Group was involved. It produced an online database, which contains about 250,000 references and is available commercially through Dialog and ESA-IRS. There were also twelve abstract journal titles, which represented the hard copy of the material on the database. Four newsletters, occasional bibliographies and the proceedings of the RA's conferences completed the publishing activity.

The Library, as well as existing to serve the needs of the RA's research staff, was responsible for obtaining the source material needed for abstracting purposes. The core material was purchased and became part of the library stock. More ephemeral material was borrowed, largely from the British Library. The Library subscribed to around 600 current journal titles, another 2,300 were borrowed regularly. About 11,500 books, 12,000 technical reports and about 5,000 standards and patents were held.

I personally find it easy to be ideologically opposed to the idea of charges for library services. However, it is my belief that in certain circumstances charges are justified and indeed, necessary to avoid imminent death to an information unit. The specific situation that I faced at that time, where change was happening all around me convinced me that it was necessary to 'go with the flow'.

THE INFORMATION BUSINESS

In 1989, the business of the Information Group was as follows. It produced the online database, which contains some 250,000 references to the literature in the RA's subject area. The Group published 12 abstract journal titles, these being the hard copy of material on the database. Bibliographies, four newsletters and the proceedings of conferences which were organised by the Conference Section completed the published output.

The Graphics Section and the Print Room had been closed down, the Publications Sales section was in severe retraction and eventually was contracted out. The Reports Production section (for internally produced reports) had been moved to the Administration Section.

The Library, operating as a section within the Information Group, had two functions. Firstly it existed to provide library services to research scientists and member companies. This had not included the provision of online searches of the database, which was always the preserve of Information Scientists, (but latterly became a library responsibility.) Secondly, its job was to obtain the source material for scanning and abstracting purposes by the Information Scientists. An analysis of the way library staff spent their time revealed that approximately 70 per cent was spent serving the needs of the Information Group, and about 30 per cent serving the interests of staff and members.

Below are a few figures on the size of operations to give a little perspective:

600 current periodical titles subscribed to
200 borrowed on a regular basis
11,500 books in stock
12,000 technical reports
6,000 standards and patents

In the three years that I worked for the RA, I think that it is probably fair comment that I suffered all of the usual pressures which special librarians currently are having to face. There was pressure on the space that we occupied. I had to employ all of the usual tactics of subterfuge to reduce my expenditure – hiding costs on other people's budgets, begging free copies of material and so on. Inevitably there came a point in time when there arose a conflict of interests between our service to the Information Group, and that to the staff. So when my boss started to ask whether I thought we could sell our services, it suddenly seemed like a remarkably good opportunity to seize control of our destiny, instead of being the political football of the RA's managers. Surely, if I had my own budget, and was allowed to sell my services to the users, this meant that any profits I made could be ploughed back in to improve the services. Suddenly I had great visions of more staff, improved computer equipment and so on. The problem was, could it be done?

Like all good researchers, the first thing I did was to take a look at the literature, to see if any one else had done it before. Although I found quite a lot of articles entitled 'How to make a profit out of information', they all seemed to concentrate on selling online services, or enquiries or so on. I could not find anything on charging for library use. However, at about the same time LAIG ran a seminar on charging for services. One of our number had managed to track down someone who was already running a successful business to talk to the meeting. My newly found 'expert' fired me with enthusiasm, so I returned to the problem with renewed vigour, after close consultations with 'how she did it good'.

THE LIBRARY AS A BUSINESS

The profitability of any business is recorded on a balance sheet, so this was how I started. I worked out how much money would be desirable for the forthcoming year to enable me to provide an acceptable service. This included inflation on the cost of materials, staff salary increases, capital equipment costs and an extra member of staff. I arrived at the figure of £92,000, so I called it £100,000 to allow for a margin of error. This is about £25,000 more than I currently had at my disposal.

Before going on to work out what income I thought I could generate, I felt that it was important to get an up to date analysis of library use by the various publics we served. I have always felt it important to keep accurate statistics of library work, since this is often the only measure of the work we actually do. In my library we kept loans statistics, inter-library loans statistics, enquiries statistics and acquisitions statistics. Also, my computer software enabled me to analyse journal use. These figures, although tedious and time consuming to keep, were invaluable to me in this analysis of use.

Using these analysis figures, I was able to come up with the figures for the level of use for each part of the service. My two best sources of information, which gave me a general pattern which could be applied to other parts of the service, were inter-library loans and journal circulation. Breakdown of the inter-library loans showed that 70 per cent of the total loans received were source material for the abstract journals. The remaining 30 per cent were distributed as at Fig. 1.

As for the journals use, a handy piece of software distributed the cost of a journal amongst the users whose names appeared on the circulation slip. As every user was assigned a cost code, we were able to arrive at total figures charged against each cost code. Those figures I was able to translate into percentages, and as you can see, they bear quite a similarity to the inter-library loan figures. 70 per cent of the total is again set against the abstracting budget as above. (Fig.2) The breakdown in the table represents 30 per cent of the total.

FIG. 1: PERCENTAGE USE OF THE INTER-LIBRARY LOAN SERVICE BY BUSINESS GROUP.

Business Group	Use of ILL service
Sealing technology	27.8
Processing	24.2
Oil and Gas	37.8
Software engineering	9.7
Management	0.5
Total	100.0

FIG. 2. BUSINESS GROUP SHARE OF THE COST OF THE JOURNALS (FROM ANALYSIS OF CIRCULATION DATA).

Business Group	% of total journal costs
Sealing technology	22
Processing	37
Oil and gas	34
Software engineering	6
Management	1
Total	100

Now comes the bit which is probably most unscientific. I have added together the results of my two service analyses and averaged the result to arrive at a figure which I am going to use in my future calculations to represent the Business Group share of use of the library services. At best, this is only an approximate calculation, and is unfair to some. However, my feeling is that the overall result would not be dissimilar if I were to take more time to make more accurate calculations. So you have to start somewhere (Fig.3).

FIG. 3. BUSINESS GROUP SHARE OF USE OF LIBRARY SERVICES

Business Group	Av % use of library services
Sealing technology	24
Processing	30.5
Oil and gas	36
Software engineering	8
Technical Services	1
Management	0.5
Total	100

INCOME

So far, I have worked out how much money I need, and identified the spread of use amongst our customers. The next thing to do is to fill in the other half of the balance sheet, our income. Those of you who have been around for a while will know that providing a library service is an expensive commitment, and that the income that can be made is apparently small. Libraries which have had to cover the costs of services are used to passing on the costs of services such as photocopies, inter-library loans and online searches. This is easily done, since there is a clearly identifiable cost which the library has to pay. If we want to make a profit, then obviously we have to add on a bit to the cost of an item, which becomes the handling charge. In the absence of any other information about what might be an appropriate level for such a charge, I decided on 18 per cent as a temporary figure for my calculations, which was what my 'expert' was charging in her £3 million business. (Fig. 4)

So to my items against income. I calculated the income I would have made if we had been charging for services in the last full year for which I had complete statistics.

In the table below (Fig. 4) the income from photocopies is the actual income we made from the sale of photocopy coupons (The RA operated a system similar to the BLDSC).

FIG. 4. BALANCE SHEET (1)

Income	£1,000	
Photocopy sales	2.0	
Contents Pages sales	2.0	
Bookshop service	0.5	
Enquiries	15.4	
Inter-library loan sales	1.8	
Online search sales	5.0	
		26.7
Expenditure		
Library materials	43.5	
On-line costs	10.9	
Software support	2.0	
		56.4
		−29.7
Gross Margin		
Staff	52.2	
Travel and entertainment	2.0	
		56.2
Operating Income		−85.9

Contents Pages is a service which had been recently launched and the figure represents the income I was hoping to make in the first year. Since I had not been in the position of launching a product and selling it before, I was deliberately conservative in this figure. I have learnt that it is prudent not to be over optimistic when estimating potential income.

Books were purchased for (1) library stock and (2) in response to research staff requests. Those bought in response to specific requests were always charged back to job numbers, that is, paid for by clients, though they eventually ended up as library stock. My records were able to tell me what had been bought in this way. It seemed to me that it would be easy to continue to recoup the costs of books, but I was concerned that nowhere was there any account taken of the time we actually spent in processing and receiving an order. This was an obvious case for levying a handling charge, so the figure her represents actual orders plus 18 per cent.

The next item I had to think about was enquiries. As with all libraries, we spent huge amounts of our time answering telephone enquiries and helping users in the library. This is an area of our work that is always difficult to explain to the accountants, because it is invisible. How is it possible to pay for this? The answer is is charging for the time we actually spend on an enquiry. The Science Reference and Information Service at that time were charging £60 per hour, in minimum units of 15 minutes. I made enquiries elsewhere and came up with very similar figures. My 'expert' charged £16 per 15 minute unit or part thereof. I decided to go for this higher figure. Using this figure I was at last able to quantify our time spent on enquiries. My manager showed puzzlement and surprise when I showed him these figures – like many managers, he was not a library user, and found it hard to imagine why anyone else should find it useful.

This brings me to inter-library loans, which again we had been in the habit of charging back to the job numbers. I was unsure how to treat these. There have been a number of studies over the years to try to establish the unit cost of an inter-library loan to include processing time. I found some recent references to figures around the £5 mark. My own staff carried out their own calculations, by measuring length of time taken, including the bibliographic and catalogue checking. Then we worked out the unit cost based upon the £64 per hour charge. To my surprise, the figure we arrived at was £8.70, which seemed rather high, but on checking with my 'expert', I was pleased to note that her organisation charged £8, so we were not that far out. It seemed appropriate that we use the time charge for this calculation, since the units that you are actually dealing with are so small and are constant. With books, the price is sometimes high and there is a huge variation, so it is impossible to work out a unit cost.

The exercise for inter-library loans got me thinking about unit costs for photocopies. The price of our photocopy coupons had not been increased for years, so my staff did the same sum they had done for inter-library loans. The result showed that the cost of the coupons was ludicrously low, so I pointed this out to my management, who increased these fees to be sufficient to cover the cost of providing inter-library loans.

The final item on the income side is for database income. As mentioned earlier, the RA was in the middle of some reorganisation, which included the Information Group. It was eventually decided to set up discrete parts of the total business as subsidiary companies, and the Information Group was one of those affected. Since publishing was the main operation involved, it was decided to move that part of the business to Oxford in order to maximise opportunities for expansion and development. Obviously this was not without its problems, because of the interdependent nature of the Library and the rest of the Information Group. The Library of course stayed behind, and with it one of the Information Scientists who was responsible for access to online searching and developments in that area. The figure that appears on the table is the actual income from sales of database searches. This figure was preset at £150 for a basic search; we decided to keep it at this for the future, but for anything more complicated then the time fee would also apply.

So we now have a complete balance sheet, with all my income, or as much as I can think of, and all of my expenditure. As you can see the whole thing looks like a thoroughly bad business venture! Of course, what I have left out of the balance sheet is all of the work that the Library does in support of the Information Group, which as I mentioned earlier represents about 70 per cent of our total effort. I went back to my calculator and worked out the Information Group share of the cost of the journals, and added on my 18 per cent handling charge. I costed out the inter-library loans and the cost of any searches we did for them, and it came to a staggering £33,400, which made the balance altogether better, but we were still short of £52,500, and the question was, how could this be made up, and in fact why was there such a large deficit? The reason is that running a library is a people intensive business, because of all the things you have have to do to make it work, such as cataloguing and classification, shelving, writing overdue notices, filing, etc. This is the crux of the matter: how do we actually pay for the staff and the books on the shelves? The answer lay in the dim and distant memories of my library history paper lectures. Do you remember subscription libraries? This revelation hit me with such surprise, I could not think why I had not thought of it earlier.

I now had to tackle the thorny problem of how much to charge in membership fees. I went back to my deficit. £52,500 was the amount I needed to make up. It is interesting perhaps to note that the cost of the restaffed library is £52,200. I decided that the easiest way of making up the deficit was to distribute the cost between user groups using the percentage figures I had calculated earlier. In order to end up with a small profit at the end of the day I called the figure £54,000. So the Business Group contribution looked like this.

FIG. 5. BUSINESS GROUP CONTRIBUTION TO THE COST OF THE LIBRARY

Business Group	£
Sealing technology	12,960
Processing technology	16,470
Oil and gas	19,440
Software engineering	4,320
Technical services	540
Management	270
Total	54,000

The question was, would they wear it? I discussed it with my manager. He was adamant that if the Business Groups wanted a Library then they had to be prepared to pay for it. Of course, they always had been paying through the levy of corporate overheads, it is just that none of them had any idea of what their contribution to information services was worth. The manager of the Oil and Gas Group certainly went a bit pale when I showed him the figures, but grudgingly realised he had no alternative but to pay up. After all, you can't carry out research unless you have access to literature, at least not very easily. The whole proposals were aired by my manager at the board meetings and eventually accepted.

My final balance sheet looked a lot healthier! (Fig. 6.)

FIG. 6. BALANCE SHEET (2)

Income	£1,000	
Photocopy sales	2.0	
Contents Pages sales	2.0	
Bookshop service	0.5	
Enquiries	15.4	
Inter-library loan sales	1.8	
Online search sales	5.0	
Services to Information Group	33.4	
Business Group subscriptions	54.0	
		114.1
Expenditure		
Library materials	43.5	
Online costs	10.9	
Software support	2.0	
		56.4
Gross Margin		57.7
Staff	52.2	
Travel and entertainment	2.0	
		56.2
Operating Income		1.5

CONCLUSION

So what of the advantages?

1. Firstly there was a personal benefit to me. In having to do this exercise, I believe I have gained a much greater insight into the realities of a balance sheet and the economics of running a business. It has certainly brought home to me why management always cuts costs by reducing staff.

2. In theory, running your section as a business enables you to determine your own future by having direct control over the income you do or don't make. Instead of working very hard in an atmosphere of struggling against the odds, you have targets to meet. It changes your

motivation. The 'Library Pest' who is too busy to see if the books he wants are in stock himself, suddenly becomes a valued customer, because he represents a lucrative source of income!

3. In doing this exercise you are re-evaluating everything you do. For us, it drew attention to the fact that we needed to charge more realistic rates for photocopies. It also meant that I took a second look at the statistics we keep. Now we only keep those which are useful; we have stopped collecting those that are, 'interesting but so what?'

4. It restores a correct set of priorities. Any unnecessary procedures can be reduced or cut out altogether, and you become much more aware of how you spend your time. You make sure that your time is spent productively.

And the disadvantages?

1. You are competing with other libraries that provide their services free.

2. You are always subject to the whims of management. I was fortunate that my managers accepted their share of the costs. But they could just as easily have decided that they didn't want a library and closed us down. Equally your business is vulnerable if you are dependent on subscription income for your success. If one group decides to bow out, the whole business collapses. The aim is to increase your income from saleable products so that you are less reliant on the subscription income.

3. If one group elects not to subscribe to library and information services how do you stop them from using your collection. If you're on the fire escape route, as we were, and can't lock the doors, there is no way to police it. The reality is that people sneak in after hours and pinch the stuff they want anyway.

4. Internal administration increases. We had to start keeping detailed records about who had what and when, so that periodically our accounts department could be informed about money to be transferred internally, or clients invoiced externally. I believe that half of my and my staff's time was spent collecting figures – time taken away from giving service to the users.

5. Even if you are reporting to the Managing Director, your profits are by no means sacrosanct. They may be creamed off to finance another ailing section.

6. This way of operating can only succeed if the company ethos supports it, and that all sections operate in a similar manner.

On the whole I welcomed this move towards charging, because of the feeling that your work generates its own reward.

POSTSCRIPT

Shortly after setting up this new system, I made a career move. About six months after that the Library staff was reduced even further from 4 to

$1\frac{1}{2}$. The Information Group made the move to Oxford and fairly soon afterwards the business was sold off. Through these actions, the library, which had once been an essential, vibrant and useful part of the organisation has become marginalised. The break in the link between the Information Group and the library means that the library's stock is no longer being improved by receiving the journals and books which were used for abstracting. It has been progressively starved of resources and so has got into the downward spiral of outdated stock – marginal use – less resources.

In retrospect, my main concern should have been that management didn't use the library's facilities. Although I put a lot of effort into converting them, I never quite succeeded, since they preferred to use their colleagues and friends in the CBI as sources of information. Also I have concluded that the only possible way for a library to operate as a profit centre is if it is a large organisation with a lot of staff. The collection of statistics and the maintenance of accounts justifies a complete member of staff. In a small unit where your time is under pressure anyway, you cannot afford to take a member of staff away from serving the readers to do the administration.

Perhaps a final point to be made is the fact that the events as they unfolded for me have happened in other ways in other RAs. One day it may be realised that the nation's specialised resources have been dispersed due to lack of understanding or care, but by that time it will be too late. I am also left wondering what quality of research is being conducted, if no use is being made of recent literature.

In search of ideal information pricing

Donald T. Hawkins

AT&T, Room 6233F3, 295 N. Maple Ave.,
Basking Ridge, NJ 07920

Information pricing has vaulted into prominence during the past year. People have always been interested in costs, of course, but in information circles, pricing has again come to the fore as a discussion topic after a prominent online database producer and information service host made some fundamental changes to its pricing algorithm. (Indeed, both the Spring and Fall 1988 meetings of the Association of Information and Dissemination Centers (ASIDIC) concentrated on the pricing issue.) Adding impetus to the discussion was the order issued by Judge Harold Greene on March 7, 1988, allowing the Regional Bell Operating Companies (RBOCS) a limited entry into the information gateway market. Judge Greene believes that information services have a large potential value for the American public, and in his order he discusses several issues relating to information services, including pricing. This article reviews some of the models used for pricing online information services and discusses some of the implications of these pricing algorithms.

The concept of paying for information is not new. Information has been widely disseminated in the form of books since the Middle Ages, and there has long been a willingness to pay for books and the information they contain. Publishers and bookstores continue to do a brisk business. Nevertheless, we have become accustomed to having free access to the information collected in libraries, so that when online services appeared and began charging users for information, the question of how, or whether, to pass the costs on to users arose. (See 'The Fee vs. Free Debate – Why Charge for Information?' Appendix 1, for historical background on some of these issues and how they were treated.)

Changes continue to occur all through the information business, and pricing is not exempt. An examination of information pricing is therefore of interest to a wider audience than just those concerned with 'traditional' online information retrieval. New entrants into the information business, such as the RBOCS, will need to consider the issues discussed here as they develop their own pricing strategies.

ONLINE INFORMATION PRICING ... THE OPPOSITE OF PRINT PRICING

There is a fundamental difference between pricing online information and pricing printed information: printed information is paid for in advance; online information is usually paid for as it is retrieved, or afterwards. One pays for a book before reading it, but one does not incur the cost for an online search until it is finished and the information has been delivered.

Figure 1 shows a general overview of the information revenue stream. The top portion illustrates the revenue flow if the user connects to a gateway to access a databank. In that case, the gateway provider arranges and pays for the telecommunications links between itself and the online databank. If the user connects to the databank through a packet-switched network, as shown in the lower portion of Figure 1, the databank collects all the revenue from the user and then disperses it to the database provider and packet network provider. Prices for online services generally fall into three areas:

- Charges for the Retrieval Process
- Charges for the Retrieved Information
- Telecommunications Charges

FIGURE 1. THE INFORMATION REVENUE STREAM

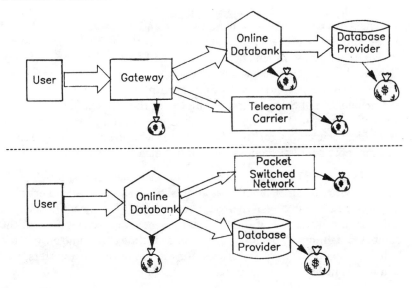

CHARGES FOR THE RETRIEVAL PROCESS: CONNECT TIME

The major online searching databanks price their service as a function of the length of time the user is connected to the system: the connect hour, or 'taxi meter' approach. Connect hour pricing began in 1971 when two information pioneers, Roger Summit (President, Dialog Information Services) and Dick Kollin (now President, Telebase Development Corp.), met at an annual conference of the American Society for Information Science to explore ways to price searches of the Pandex database then being prepared for searching on the infant DIALOG system.[1] (In an interesting and historic coincidence, their meeting occurred in the same exhibit hall in New York now used by the National Online Meeting.) Summit and Kollin saw several advantages in putting users under pressure to conduct their searches and leave the system as quickly as possible:

> In those early days of time sharing systems, too many simultaneous users degraded response times
>
> The number of ports available on the DIALOG system was much lower than it is today, limiting the number of searchers that could use the system

Summit and Kollin therefore decided to use the connect hour as the unit for pricing information retrieval. Connect hour pricing was soon adopted by other databanks (ORBIT, NLM, and BRS, for example). Since then, it has become a *de facto* standard in the online information industry.

Connect hour pricing has the advantage that it is simple. Intermediary searchers can easily explain it to end-users, and the users can understand it. Search costs are easy to calculate and estimate, so users know approximately how much their searches will cost before they are run. Connect hour pricing also accommodates a wide range of databases, so special database-dependent charging algorithms are not needed.

The decision of Summit and Kollin to use the connect hour as a basis for pricing admirably achieved its end. Connect hour pricing seemed to be an ideal charging algorithm, but as time went on and online searchers became more sophisticated, some serious deficiencies surfaced:

The length of time one is connected to a system does not relate well to the resources used nor to the amount of information retrieved. Searchers have become used to thinking of their searches in units of connect time instead of in terms of the value of the information they have retrieved from the databases. Dunn and Boyle[2] feel that connect time is of value only to the online databanks as a way of pricing for the use of their computers, and that it is of little or no value to database producers.

Search costs vary depending on the load on the online system. Indeed, DIALOG formerly published plots of system load versus time of day so that searchers could, if they wished, schedule searches when the system was likely to have a lighter load, thereby lowering their costs. (This disadvantage for searchers is an advantage to the service provider because it tends to even the load by forcing some searches into the lighter times of the day.)

Searchers spend more time studying thesauri and structuring searches in advance, rather than using the online thesauri. Online connect time and cost is therefore lowered, so searchers (or their management) may think they have cut costs. Such savings are probably an illusion because the total time spent on a search tends to be lengthened and labor cost (i.e. overhead) is increased.

Connect time pricing discourages maximum use of the interactive nature of the system. By stimulating searchers to use the system for as short a time as possible, browsing and interaction are discouraged. Much of the power and usefulness of online information systems lies in the ability to interact with a database by performing a search, then browsing the results, and revising the strategy to obtain the optimum retrieval. Connect time pricing encourages 'remote-batch' searching, in which users structure their searches before logging on, enter them as quickly as possible, print the results, and log off. Little or no interaction with the system occurs, which is a distinct disadvantage.

Connect time pricing severely penalizes slow typists

Because of hardware or software inefficiencies, computer systems often do not operate at their full potential speed, thus lengthening connect times and artificially increasing search costs

Despite the above disadvantages to connect time pricing, it has endured as a standard method of pricing information retrieval services. Due to its wide use, there was little motivation to develop alternative pricing methods until technological advances began to highlight major shortcomings in connect time pricing.

THE FAILURE OF CONNECT TIME CHARGING

Two technological advances that had great effects on information pricing are higher baud rates and the microcomputer. When online retrieval first began, most searches were conducted at 300 baud. As better quality voice grade lines and higher speed modems were developed, the public packet-switched networks installed 1200 baud nodes. Searchers happily began enjoying 1200 baud for searching, and its use grew rapidly. Recently, 2400 baud nodes on the networks have begun to appear, and when ISDN(Integrated Services Digital Network) technology becomes widespread, much higher baud rates will be possible. Some online databanks are warily eyeing the specter of higher baud rates because, of course, connect times (and revenues) will decrease as baud rates increase. Should speeds of 9600 baud or higher become widespread, connect time pricing may well be doomed to failure and go the way of the dinosaurs.

Another technology contributing to the failure of connect time charging is the microcomputer. Online searchers quickly learned to use the powerful features of their microcomputers and software packages to speed up their searches. Standard features of commercial software (for example, Pro-Search distributed by Personal Bibliographic Software, Inc.) include offline preparation of search strategies and rapid uploading of them to the online system. Using such software, there is no longer any penalty for slow and error-prone typing; the searcher can get the strategy letter perfect before connecting to the online system, and can then upload it as fast as the communications network will allow. Output can be rapidly downloaded to the user's microcomputer, and stored, browsed, and manipulated locally with no cost to the user (and no revenue to the databank and database producer).

The effect of these technological advances has already been felt by online information service organizations. A speaker from Chemical Abstracts Service (CAS) reported at a recent conference that, although the number of searches done on their system continues to increase, connect times and associated revenues have become flat.[3] Since connect time pricing is not technology-independent, this trend identified by CAS will only become further exacerbated by future developments. CAS therefore made significant changes in their pricing structure. As Jeff Pemberton pointed out in an *ONLINE* editorial last year, CAS's changes are more than a simple pricing change; they portend an entirely new relationship between online databanks and database producers.[4]

Even before the CAS changes, connect time was under attack as a valid way to charge for information retrieval. Carol Tenopir[5] questioned whether connect time pricing had become obsolete. P.L. Holmes, a long time opponent of connect time pricing, mentioned it again at the 1986 International Online Meeting,[6] and suggested a metered 'pay-as-you-use' approach, where the user would pay a small fixed fee to cover basic access plus a higher charge for each item retrieved. An earlier experiment conducted by Holmes,[7] in which the charges for use of the British Library's BLAISE system were mostly based on the retrieved items, raised concern with users, even though it had been shown that total search costs would not increase. In that experiment, Holmes noted that users spent 70 per cent of their time either idle (reading output from the screen) or keying in search commands: a basis for his opposition to connect time charging.

Jarvelin[8] remarks that what is being sold is *information,* not computer processing or computer time (as in a conventional timesharing service). He has developed a complex mathematical model for estimating of charges for using numeric databanks, where not only retrieval is being done, but also extensive manipulation and postprocessing of the infor-mation. As Jarvelin notes, the viability and acceptance of any charging scheme depends largely on the user's ability to estimate charges in advance. Finally, Tanghe[9] feels that other methods of charging (subscription fees, output volume charges, or search strategy-oriented charges) are not superior to connect time.

Connect time pricing has been discussed here in considerable detail because it is so prominent in information pricing. However, there are other ways to price information that do not have some of the problems associated with connect time.

CHARGES FOR THE RETRIEVAL PROCESS: RESOURCE UNIT PRICING

With varying degrees of success, purveyors of online information have experimented with pricing their product based on the number of 'computer resource units' used in the retrieval process. Usually such pricing schemes embody a low connect hour rate as well as a resource unit charge. A major problem that users have with resource pricing is, of course, understanding exactly what a 'computer resource unit' is. In the online retrieval world, two prominent databanks using a form of this type of pricing are Mead Data Central (MDC) and CAS.

Mead Data Central

MDC has long attempted to introduce some dependence on computer resources into the charging structure for searching their LEXIS and NEXIS databases. Unfortunately for searchers, the main effect has been one of considerable uncertainty. MDC's past charging algorithms have been criticized as complicated and difficult to understand. In addition to the usual connect time charges, there were charges for using various highly posted terms or for modifications to searches. The net result was that it was virtually impossible to estimate the cost of a search in advance, and reconciling an invoice with the searcher's personal log was an exercise in frustration. Costs tended to be high because searchers did not realize the charges they were incurring for search terms. Several articles decrying high NEXIS costs and incomprehensible invoices can be found in the literature.[10]

Faced with widespread criticism of its pricing structure, MDC has made several simplifications during recent years. Their latest price summary lists charges of $4.00 to $35.00 per search, with the explanatory note: 'Search prices vary according to the file or combined group of files selected. The average charge per search is $10.00 to $19.00'. Presumably this 'search charge' represents resources used by the searcher in retrieving the information. The controversial and distasteful search modification charge was removed in 1988, but it is still listed on the price summary as a 'no charge' item.

MDC's charging algorithm has the advantage over straight connect time pricing in that those who use few resources to do a search are not subsidizing heavier users. However, the additional charging elements are disliked by searchers because they are a source of confusion and uncertainty, and because they do not correlate well with the information retrieved.

Chemical Abstracts Service

When it first introduced its CAS ONLINE and STN International services, CAS followed the standard connect time pricing structure discussed above. As the effects of advancing technology began to be felt, CAS took a lead by making significant changes and introducing new elements into the pricing structure. In mid-1987, CAS announced that, as of January 1, 1988, it would introduce a fee for search terms (initially 10cts for textual terms and $20 for molecular structures), a 'record extraction fee' (initially 1 ct) for each CAS record extracted from a file for use as a search term, and a 'use charge' (initially 5 cts) for each partial record used in browsing the output. (The record extraction fee is applied when commands such as DIALOG's MAP or ORBIT's SELECT are used to form a list of searchable terms from fields in a record.) CAS's stated motivation for the changes was to reduce the dependence of prices on information technology by moving away from connect time as a pricing method. They stated[11] that, over time, they intend to reduce connect time fees, and increase search term and record extraction fees. So far, however, users have seen only the imposition of new fees and no reduction in connect time rates. (CAS's 1989 price list, however, does reflect a reduction in connect time rates, as well as an increase in search term fees. In their cover letter accompanying the price list, CAS stated '...The 1989 prices reflect CAS's continuing effort to base charges on the value of the information retrieved; therefore, we continue to place less emphasis on connect-hour pricing, because that method focuses on the speed of searching rather than the results delivered.')

CAS did not require its licensees to adopt the new fee structure. The licensees were only required to calculate royalties based on it. It is interesting to note that several of the major online searching databanks chose not to implement the new CAS pricing, but instead continued to use connect time pricing, raising their rates to cover the new CAS fees. CAS also estimated that the net effect on search costs would be small: about a 10 per cent increase.

CAS's new pricing scheme has been hotly debated and criticized in the online retrieval world. Jeff Pemberton,[12] in a wide-ranging and frank ONLINE interview with Harry Boyle, CAS's Manager of Marketing Services, explored many of the issues surrounding the changes in pricing and the reasons for them. In that interview, Boyle stated that CAS feels 'very comfortable with the new pricing because it neither hinders nor enhances any particular technology'. According to Boyle, several online databanks welcomed CAS's move away from connect time pricing; one databank even said that connect time is no longer workable for them.

Roger Summit voiced the concern that the move towards pricing by search terms might cause searchers to attempt to save money by using as few search terms as possible, thus degrading the quality of their searches.[13]

An early user reaction to the CAS pricing came from Joanne Witiak,[14] who suggests that the tempest will soon die down because many of the online databanks have opted for the status quo and have simply absorbed the new CAS charges into higher connect hour rates. Patrick Tanghe[15] tends to agree and thinks that CAS's pricing scheme will not be able to displace connect time as a basis for charging. Much of the opposition to the CAS fee structure came from some of the online databanks who protested that the lead time of only five months would not give them time to reprogram their complex accounting systems. Some users also protested that the new cost items would make it more difficult to estimate search costs in advance. CAS replied[12] that it should be *easier* to estimate costs because one could simply count search terms.

The CAS pricing scheme is a significant change in the way online information is priced. It is still too soon to gauge the reaction of users to it. One thing is certain, though: CAS's experiences will be closely watched by other databanks to see if the new pricing produces a substantial increase in revenues. If it does, it may be a bellwether of future information pricing.

CHARGES FOR THE RETRIEVAL PROCESS: FLAT RATE PRICING

Telebase Systems pioneered flat rate pricing with the introduction of its EasyNet service in 1985. EasyNet users pay a single fee per search (currently $10), where a 'search' is defined as one to ten items retrieved. If nothing is retrieved, the user pays nothing. If more than ten items are retrieved and displayed by the user, another search cost is incurred for each group of one to ten items displayed.

Up to the point of connection to the online databank, the EasyNet user is not charged. Initial browsing of the system menus leading to selection of the database is free. Telebase's pricing in this area is unique to the online information industry, since most connect time-based systems charge the user from the point of first contact. EasyNet is thus like a bookstore: browsing the books is free, but one must pay a price to take a book home.

Flat rate pricing works for Telebase because it has negotiated large volume discounts from the databanks and is able to minimize its connect time by preparing searches offline, then dialing up, uploading the strategy, downloading the results as rapidly as possible on high-speed lines, and disconnecting while the user peruses the output. (The search strategy is stored so it does not have to be re-entered on the keyboard by the user if additional output is desired.) The no-retrieval, no-charge pricing is unique in the online retrieval world, and it appeals psychologically to novice users because it removes an element of risk from searching. In its user surveys, Telebase regularly finds that the most attractive feature of its system is its flat rate pricing.[16] However, the degree of acceptability of flat rate pricing varies directly with the sophistication of the user: naive users like it better than sophisticated ones.

Telebase, of course, has to pay connect time charges even for those searches that fail. Obviously the search price was set high enough to include costs of the zero-hit searches and other 'free' system features such as the SOS service (real-time communication with an expert for search assistance), and therefore ensure overall profitability. The search price is the same (except for a surcharge on a few of the higher priced databases) whether a low-cost database (i.e. ERIC) or a high-cost database (i.e. Chemical Abstracts) is being accessed.

Telebase therefore makes more profit on some searches than on others. The flat rate pricing algorithm is a step function: users are charged for ten items even if they only retrieve and look at one. According to Telebase user surveys, sophisticated EasyNet users find search prices high, especially after they realize that actual database prices vary widely. Telebase also attempts to recoup losses from no-hit searches by displaying a message after every such search referring users to the SOS service for help. The hope, of course, is that the user will get help and then return to the system and do a successful search.

Flat rate priced searching has many advantages for users. It is easy for end-users to understand, and easy for intermediary searchers to explain to their customers. It removes the dependence on connect time, promotes more interaction with the system (thereby improving search quality), and generally makes for more relaxed searching. Costs are predictable in advance, and there are no extra hidden costs.

UNLIMITED ACCESS: A VARIATION OF FLAT RATE PRICING

In their quest for simpler pricing schemes, searchers, particularly those doing a high volume of searching, have expressed interest in paying a single price for unlimited access to an online searching system – a form of flat rate pricing. Few unlimited searching arrangements have been announced yet, but most of the online databanks are studying the idea.

Recently, BRS introduced BRS/After Dark Unlimited under which a user may purchase six months of access to seven databases on the BRS/After Dark system for $13,500. Purchasers receive copy-protected telecommunications software in which is embedded a BRS/After Dark password. The user does not know the password and cannot access the system without this software. BRS/After Dark Unlimited is innovative in the online information industry, and is an advance towards simple easily defined and easily understood information pricing.

To establish unlimited access pricing, the cooperation of the database producers must be obtained because their present arrangements largely depend upon current connect time-based pricing. Unlimited access and flat rate pricing represent new charging practices for producers. Although they are not usage-sensitive, these pricing methods have the advantage that the database producers know the revenue they will receive from the contract, and they receive it up front, in advance of usage. Some producers may therefore welcome this method of charging and may encourage the databanks to offer it to users.

CHARGES FOR THE RETRIEVAL PROCESS: TIME-DIFFERENTIAL CHARGING

It is common in standard time-sharing services to charge lower rates at off-peak hours, when the system load is lower. Only two of the major online databanks currently have such a policy. Both NewsNet and Dow Jones charge less for searches done during night and weekend hours. These two databanks view time-differential charging as an important part of their marketing strategy to target individual users. Since the reduced prices are offered outside of normal working hours, end-users are more able to take advantage of them rather than searchers in business environments. MDC used to offer time-differential pricing, and many searchers followed the advice of Paul Lomio[10] and took advantage of it to reduce their search costs. Unfortunately, MDC recently discarded their reduced rates and now charges the same prices regardless of the time of day the search is done.

In past years, time-differential charging might have been useful in stimulating a leveling of system loads, but with technological advances in the areas of scheduling and load balancing, the point at which high loads degrade system performance is high enough that such leveling of the load is hardly needed now. System response times have been greatly improved and are not as load-dependent as they were in the past.

CHARGES FOR THE RETRIEVAL PROCESS: BAUD RATE PRICING

Given their dependence on connect time, it is surprising that more of the major databanks do not charge different rates for different baud rate access. Three who do are NewsNet, VU/TEXT, and Dow Jones. (NewsNet doubles its base connect hour rate, and VU/TEXT adds 50 per cent for access rates of 1200 baud or higher). Several database producers have expressed a desire for baud rate pricing,[17] but so far none of the databanks seems inclined to provide it.

CHARGES FOR THE RETRIEVED INFORMATION: HIT CHARGES

In addition to charges for the retrieval process, many systems require the user to pay for the information retrieved from a database. Many database

L

producers charge searchers for such information as 'hit charges,' which are a form of output pricing and are levied in addition to other search charges. 'Hit charges' are charges for each item printed either online, at the user's workstation, or offline, at the databank's site. Most of the hit charge revenue is remitted by the databank to the database producer and represents the database producer's royalty. Hit charges were introduced in 1979, well after online searching services began operations. The first database producers to do so were Commonwealth Agricultural Bureaux (CAB) Abstracts and Engineering Information, Inc.[1] At that time, there was some resistance from searchers to databases with hit charges; if they could, they would use an alternate. Today, however, hit charges are the norm rather than the exception, and most searchers have become accustomed to them.

Most online databanks establish a standard charge for printing a full record from each database. Print formats containing less information than a full record are charged some fraction of the full record cost. Hit charges therefore have the advantage that they are easily adapted to many formats, even when the searcher defines the format, as can be done on most of today's major searching systems.

CHARGES FOR THE RETRIEVED INFORMATION: FREE FORMATS

To facilitate browsing and modifying search results, most database producers provide a 'free format', which allows the searcher to display titles and index terms of items, but no bibliographic information, free of charge. By using the 'free format', searchers are not penalized when taking advantage of the interactive nature of online systems to browse and improve their searches. In his interview with *ONLINE*, Boyle[12] discusses some ramifications of free formats, and some of the reasons that CAS has imposed a charge for their formerly free 'trial format' on the STN system. (CAS still allows its licensees to offer a free format, but the citations must be presented in random order and no display of accession numbers is permitted.)

CHARGES FOR THE RETRIEVED INFORMATION: DOWNLOADING

Downloading (capturing search output in machine-readable form for later editing, formatting, and distribution) raised much concern several years ago; among the issues was its pricing. Downloading was originally feared to be a threat to revenues, but many database producers found that their fears were unfounded, and downloading became a market opportunity. Several database producers instituted special contracts for downloading; others simply assumed that it would become widespread and raised their prices to cover it. In the latter situation, all users pay the higher prices, and those not downloading search output are subsidizing those who do. One system (the European system ESA-IRS) has a special downloading format, and database producers can define special features, such as field tags, that can only be obtained using this format. The special format has the advantages that a (presumably higher) price can be charged for downloaded output, and only those who use it incur the additional costs.

TELECOMMUNICATIONS CHARGES

In addition to paying for the information retrieval process and the information retrieved from databases, searchers must also pay for telecommunications from their workstation to the databank's remote site. The charges follow the basic charging practices of the telecommunications services in the searcher's home country. In the USA searchers have the choice of using public packet-switched networks (TYMNET, Telenet, etc.), or of dialing directly to the online host.

Most searchers opt to use a packet network because the cost of doing so is usually less than using the public direct-dial network. In this scenario, the user pays for the call to the nearest packet network node, then pays the packet network's charge for connection to the desired databank. Since many network nodes are located in large metropolitan areas with a high concentration of searchers, this mode of operation appeals to many people; access to a distant host is only a local call away. Local calls are included in a subscriber's normal monthly telephone charges, either as a flat rate or as small per-call ('message unit') use charges. In engineering their networks, telephone operating companies provide facilities based on the average number of calls per line and the length of an average call. As noted previously, as online searching spreads into the end-user market (via information gateways, for example), average call times will lengthen because searches (data calls) tend to be longer than typical voice calls. Operating companies will need to recognize this effect and adjust their facilities planning and charging methods accordingly.

Packet network charges (typically in the neighborhood of $10/hour) are lower than direct-dialed long distance calls because packet network charges are based on either the connect time or the number of packets transmitted, or both. Calling distance is ignored in the charging algorithm. The billing arrangement between the databank and telecommunications carrier is like the databank-database producer arrangement: the databank is an agent for the communications carrier and adds the communications cost to the searcher's bill (usually with a small markup). If the searcher uses the long distance public network to access an online service, he/she pays the communications costs directly on his/her monthly telephone bill.

DIALOG has its own network, DIALNET, providing searchers with an alternate access route to it. DIALNET costs tend to be slightly lower than TYMNET's or Telenet's. For remotely located searchers, a disadvantage of using a packet network is that packet nodes tend to be in areas of high usage; searchers distant from a node must pay telephone toll charges to the nearest node. For those searchers, DIALOG provides an In-WATS number (1–800–DIALNET) costing less than a direct-dial call but more than TYMNET or Telenet. (US telephone subscribers have grown accustomed to 800 numbers being reverse billed and without cost to the calling party. DIALNET's number is one of the few 800 numbers that the user pays to use.) DIALNET usage is billed to the user by DIALOG in the same way as TYMNET's or Telenet's charges.

Outside the USA, the telecommunications picture is much different. The telecommunications component of the typical online searching bill in the USA is small. This fact is not lost on searchers in other countries where telecommunications costs are significantly higher, and searchers face not only high costs but difficulties in installing data lines, etc. (For a first-hand account of these difficulties, see the brief article by Meeks.)[18] Users are charged not only for connect time but also for the number of characters transmitted and received, making accurate estimation of search costs difficult if not impossible. For these reasons, some search services have established their own satellite links to provide easier and lower cost access to their systems.

UP-FRONT FEES

From the beginning, the major online databanks have followed a pay-as-you-go policy in pricing their services. Users were not charged any fees for establishing an account or for obtaining access. This policy was a significant reason for the growth and market penetration of online services. End-users and budget-poor libraries are not fond of making major commitments of their precious resources on the speculation that a service will be used heavily. Indeed, many smaller, numeric databank services have high up-front fees (sometimes $10,000 or more), and it is no surprise that their user base is small compared to the bibliographic services. An early example of an attempt to levy up-front usage fees was the Predicasts databases. When they first became available online, users were charged an annual access fee. When several organizations did not subscribe because of the fee, or because the file was not central to their interests and they could not predict future usage levels, the fee was dropped. Evidently, Predicasts decided that some revenues were better than no revenues.

MINIMUM SERVICE REQUIREMENTS

The major online databanks do not impose any minimum usage fees on their standard (pay-as-you-go) contracts. Nevertheless, they have re-curring costs associated with maintaining customer records, mailing newsletters, maintaining help desks, etc. These costs of doing business are usually considered in setting the rates for service. During the past few years, however, several of the online services have begun charging a nominal annual service fee (not based on usage) on their standard contracts to help recover these fixed costs. DIALOG's annual fee of $25 is typical.

DISCOUNT PLANS

We have not yet seen the inauguration of 'frequent searcher' plans similar to the highly successful frequent flyer programs of the airlines. However, heavy users of online services are rewarded with a plethora of discount and contract options. The details of each databank's plan vary considerably, but in general, they offer discounts on searching costs with volume usage. Since most of the databank's revenue comes from connect hour charges, only connect hours are discounted: Hit charges and telecommunications costs are not lowered because the databank is usually acting only as an agent for the database producer or telecommunications carrier. If a user is willing to guarantee and prepay a certain volume of usage, higher discounts are usually granted. Typical discounts range from $3 to $15 per connect hour.

These discount plans have fostered the spread of consortia of small users banding together to take advantage of higher discount rates. Some libraries have had problems fitting large onetime advance payments into their budgets. The databanks have been innovative in adapting to these requirements and have even called their contracts 'subscriptions' to cast them in the familiar terms of book and journal subscriptions that libraries are used to dealing with. Discount plans can be complex, and Brian Williams[19] notes that the BRS service's pricing schedule has no less than 17 levels of searching rates.

Discounts on online searching are often offered to special groups of users. Academic discounts are common. The databanks offer them to universities in the hope that students will become dependent upon or proficient in searching and will use it heavily after they leave their studies and enter the workplace. CAS's academic discount program is well-known: Academic institutions can qualify for a discount of as much as 90 per cent. Other groups, such as searchers employed by the US government, are also eligible for discounts on usage.

Most databanks offer training discounts in the form of low-cost files available to all their customers. These training files are restricted to online searching and display only: no offline printing is possible. Typically, training files carry only a low connect hour charge with no hit charges, and they contain only one or two back updates of the database – not enough to perform any useful or comprehensive searches.

CREDIT CARD BILLING

Most online searching is governed by contracts with clearly stated payment terms, following established business practices. However, casual users, infrequent users, and consumers are not used to dealing with contracts tend to find them onerous. The EasyNet system's billing methods are therefore noteworthy because they appeal to a wide spectrum of the end-user or consumer markets which the databanks have only recently begun to enter. With its easy free telephone access using an 800 number and its ability to process credit card billings, EasyNet is truly aimed at a broad and diverse end-user market. One needs no contract with any online retrieval service (nor with EasyNet for that matter) to conduct online searches. Simply by dialing 1–800–EASYNET and entering a major credit card number, one can access over 1,000 databases. EasyNet takes care of all contractual arrangements with the databanks and the search charge appears on the user's monthly credit card statement in the familiar manner. The billing is simple, straightforward, and easily understandable by users. (The end-user services of the major databanks, such as BRS's After Dark and DIALOG's Knowledge Index, also use credit card billing.) In many respects, the EasyNet service resembles the gateway services that the RBOCs are planning to offer, and its pricing strategy may therefore provide an insight into the course the RBOCs will decide to follow. (See Appendix 2, 'Kiosk Billing: Applications For The RBOCS,' that accompanies this article.)

TWO-TIER PRICING

To counter the phenomenon of migration or the cancellation of subscriptions to printed products in favor of online access, some database producers have established two-tier pricing. Upon registration of their user numbers, subscribers to the hard-copy publications are provided with online access at a reduced rate, while non-subscribers pay the full price. The difference between subscriber and nonsubscriber rates can be substantial. The Institute for Scientific Information (ISI) is an example. According to DIALOG's latest price schedule, subscribers to ISI's printed *Science Citation Index* were charged $57 per hour connect time and 46 cts per item printed for the SCISEARCH database; non-subscribers paid $153 per hour and 46 cts per item.

DATABASE LEASING OPTIONS

Some organizations that use a few databases heavily have developed programs to lease them, process them in-house, and make them available to their own user community for searching or for other specialized uses. [20,21] Frequently, the information obtained from commercial databases is combined with in-house information to provide a single database for all types of information. Because of the substantial financial and computing resources needed to process and maintain large bibliographic databases, most searchers have not been concerned with database lease pricing, and lease contracts are negotiated individually, as circumstances dictate.

To meet the needs of users who do not wish to undertake the extensive software development needed to establish local database searching, BRS offers its On-Site service, a turnkey system allowing users to mount, maintain, and search databases locally. BRS has contracted with several large database producers to make their databases available under the On-Site program. The On-Site service includes a tape copy of the database and regular updates in the proper format, ready to add to the system. BRS provides extensive support and help to purchasers of On-Site databases. The price is in the neighborhood of $40,000 for the system and varies depending on the databases included.

The recent emergence of databases stored locally on optical media such as CD-ROMs has brought database leasing and its associated pricing issues to the attention of many searchers. (One might consider CD-ROMs as simply a new medium to contain the information that books presently contain. However, CD-ROM databases are meant to be searched. Most come packaged with search software, and some have a built-in link to an existing online service. Mention of them is, therefore, relevant here.) Subscribers to databases on optical media usually pay a single price, in advance, for their subscription and can then search the database as much as they wish without further payments. Database leasing is, therefore, another form of flat rate pricing for information. The difference between database leasing and EasyNet's flat rate pricing is that in the case of leasing, the database resides on the user's premises, and payment is usually made in advance, when the leasing arrangement begins. EasyNet is a dial-up service for which users only incur charges as they use it.

In leasing a database, only one payment has to be made, eliminating the substantial recurring bureaucratic procedures and costs involved in processing periodic invoices and remitting payments. The disadvantage is that the advance payment is likely to be sizeable, and some users may have difficulty raising a large amount of cash in advance. If the database is to be used in an organization that charges back information costs to end-users based on their usage, apportioning up-front costs to a body of users in advance of their use is difficult. The costs may have to be absorbed in the information center's budget, or, if this is impossible, they may have to be charged to the users arbitrarily as an overhead charge. Infrequent users, especially, may object to such a scheme.

WHAT NOW? – CONCLUSIONS

Information pricing is a complex issue; Nancy Garman[22] has called it a 'complex maze.' As Art Elias has noted,[23] three parties must be satisfied:

the information user, the database producer, and the databank. Each of these parties has different motives, different needs, and different goals. Conflicting interests are therefore inevitable. The literature contains numerous suggestions for changes to existing pricing structures. Jansen's[24] is typical. He notes that search techniques are changing and proposes six different ways that charging could be done (plus a seventh which is a combination of the preceding six). Most of Jansen's suggestions involve moving away from connect time and towards output pricing, a trend implemented by the CAS scheme. However, as noted in the sidebar about the RBOCS, their influence has not yet been felt in the information arena. Their need for usage-sensitive pricing may temper the trend away from connect time charging.

It is remarkable that some of the pricing methods existing today have endured since the inception of online searching and have worked reasonably well despite all the other changes and advances that have occurred. Nevertheless, changes are clearly needed. What are the characteristics of the ideal pricing scheme? We cannot recommend a specific algorithm here; too many variables are involved. However, here are some points to be recognized as factors governing all pricing decisions.

While no one likes high prices, most users recognize that database producers and databanks are providing valuable service and must make a profit to stay in business. Prices for computing hardware and storage are decreasing, so some users may expect online retrieval prices to decrease also. Users must recognize that database indexing and production are labor-intensive, and labor costs continue to rise. Some information providers have encountered unexpectedly strong resistance to price increases and have learned to set initial prices higher to avoid the need for frequent increases.

Databanks have long been in the key position in setting online pricing strategies, as the early decision to use connect time shows. The recent CAS decisions show that database producers also can now have a major impact on pricing decisions. Pricing decisions must consider the needs of all parties in the information retrieval chain.

Information pricing is complex and variable. A major need of users is consistency and predictability. Searchers need to be able to estimate search costs accurately and quickly in advance. The pricing scheme should therefore be easy to understand, easy to explain to end-users, and it should be stable. As Nancy Garman[22] aptly asked: 'No wonder searchers are confused and frustrated. No wonder there are so few end-users. Who can sort through the maze of costs, and who cannot resist a feeling of persecution when loopholes, once found, are closed?'

Technology will continue to advance. Pricing structures should be technology-independent so that they do not have to be adjusted with each technological change.

Pricing strategies need to be flexible so that they can address the needs of both casual and high-volume users. This can be done by simple and effective discounting schemes.

Pricing should encourage interaction with the system and should maximize the use of the system's powerful features. Searchers should be motivated by the pricing to use good searching techniques to obtain the highest quality retrieval. Databanks and producers should realize that user behavior is strongly motivated by pricing decisions. New users must not be discouraged by complicated pricing schemes.

Pricing should be readily correlated with the value of the product: the retrieved information. Those who set prices must remember they are selling bits and bytes of information, and not time units or computing power.

With the above in mind, it seems clear that the days of heavy reliance on connect time pricing may be numbered, although connect time will undoubtedly have some role in future pricing schemes. (Note: At press time the November 1988 issue of *Monitor* reports that the European system ESA-IRS plans to abolish connect hour charges early in 1989 (except for a nominal 'housekeeping' charge) and substitute a 'session fee' of $1 to $6 plus a charge for displaying retrieved records (2 cts to 40cts/record) depending on the format and the database. *Monitor* points out that ESA's pricing scheme is unfair to users; a searcher doing a lengthy null search will have a low bill while another searcher printing out many items will be heavily charged. The *Monitor* article comments that an essential element of growth is simple and easily understood pricing policies.) This article has discussed several elements of pricing, many of which have been tried in various forms.

This article was titled 'In Search of Ideal Information Pricing' since the ideal pricing has not yet been developed. Does it exist? Can it be developed so that everyone involved in the information retrieval process is at least reasonably well satisfied? The problem is complex and multidimensional. Online retrieval has surmounted many hurdles in its brief existence. The pricing issue has far-reaching implications, but it is no more difficult than other issues that have been solved. Only with cooperation between users, database producers, and databanks will we arrive at a satisfactory pricing scheme.

REFERENCES

1   Meadow, Charles T. 'Online Database Industry Timeline.' *DATABASE* 11, No. 5 (October 1988): pp 23–31.
2   Dunn, Ronald G. and Boyle, Harry F. 'Online Searching: Costly or Cost-Effective? A Marketing Perspective.' *Journal of Chemical Information and Computer Science* 24 (1984): pp. 51–54.
3   Seals, James. Presentation at the Fall 1987 ASIDIC Meeting, San Antonio, TX.

4   Pemberton, Jeffery K. 'Winds of Change in the Online World.' (Editorial) *ONLINE* 12, No. 2 (March 1988): pp. 7–9.

5   Tenopir, Carol. 'Is Connect Time Pricing Obsolete?' *Library Journal* 113, No. 4 (March 1, 1988): pp. 48–49.

6   Holmes, P.L. 'Is There Life Beyond Online?' *Proceedings of the 10th International Online Information Meeting,* London, 1986, Learned Information, Ltd., Oxford, England, pp. 385–393.

7   Holmes, P.L. 'An Experiment in Pricing Mechanisms for Online Information Retrieval.' *Information Services & Use* 5 (1985): pp. 269–275.

8   Jarvelin, Kalervo. 'A Straightforward Method for Advance Estimation of User Charges for Information in Numeric Databases.' *Journal of Documentation* 42, No. 2 (June 1986): pp. 65–83.

9   Tanghe, Patrick. 'Why in Online Searching Connect Time and Not Information Results is Paid For – An Economic Explanation.' *Nachrichten für Dokumentation* 38 (1987): pp. 263269. (In German)

10   Lomio, J. Paul. 'The High Cost of NEXIS and What a Searcher Can Do About It.' *ONLINE* 9, No. 5 (September 1985): pp. 54–56.

11   'CAS to Change Fee Basis for Accessing Online Databases.' *Chemical & Engineering News* 65, No. 39 (September 28,1987): p. 44.

12   Pemberton, Jeffery K. '*ONLINE* Interviews Harry Boyle on CAS's New License Policy.. Effects on Searching/Prices.' *ONLINE* 12, No. 2 (March 1988): pp. 19–25.

13   Summit, Roger K., quoted in Ref. 3.

14   Witiak, Joanne. 'It's All A Question of Price: An Expert Searcher Looks at the New CAS Pricing Scheme.' *DATABASE* 11, No. 2 (April 1988): pp. 95–96.

15   Tanghe, Patrick. 'Against Confusing Online Charging – A Critical Note on the New CAS Pricing Scheme.' *Nachrichten für Dokumentation* 39 (1988): pp. 77–81. (In German)

16   Kollin, Richard, private communication.

17   O'Leary, Mick. 'Price Versus Value for Online Data.' *ONLINE* 12, No. 2 (March 1988): pp. 26–30.

18   Meeks, Brock N. 'Life at 300 Baud: An Innocent Abroad.' *Profiles* 5, No. 11 (June 1988): pp. 54–55.

19   Williams, Brian. 'A Comparison of the New and the Old BRS Prices.' *ONLINE* 11, No. 4 (July 1987): pp. 65–68.

20   Hawkins, Donald T. 'Use of Machine-Readable Databases to Support a Large SDI Service.' *Information Processing & Management* 21, No. 3 (1985): pp. 187–204.

21   Kostenbauder, Scott 1. 'Overview of IBM's Technical Information Retrieval Services.' *Information Services & Use* 5, No. 2 (April 1985): pp. 93–100.

22   Garman, Nancy. 'Online Pricing: A Complex Maze Not For Timid Mice.' (Editorial). *DATABASE* 11 No. 2 (April 1988): pp. 6–7.

23   Elias, A.W. 'Pricing Strategies and Impacts on Producers, Vendors, and Users.' *Information Services & Use 1* (1982): pp. 351–357.

24   Jansen, Arnold A.J. 'Towards a New Pricing Structure for Online Databases.' *Journal of Information Science* 10 (1985): pp. 125–30.

APPENDIX 1

THE FEE VS. FREE DEBATE –
WHY CHARGE FOR INFORMATION?

Free access to information has been a basic principle in the USA ever since Andrew Carnegie began his philanthropic bequests to libraries.

Anyone can walk into a public library in virtually any city or town in the USA and browse the shelves, use the reference tools, read the periodicals, and ask questions of the staff. The concept of charging for on-site use of the library is foreign.

On the other hand, of course, libraries have costs that must be paid; these are generally passed back to the users in their taxes or, in the corporate world, as overhead. All taxpayers pay for the library regardless of whether it benefits them or whether they use it or not.

FEES FOR ONLINE RETRIEVAL? – THE GREAT DEBATE

For many years, the concept of unlimited free access to information worked well, but during the 1970s, two major trends seriously challenged it. The first trend was the introduction of online retrieval services and their tremendous surge in popularity. The second was the severe stresses and strains libraries experienced on their budgets as cutbacks were mandated. Many libraries could not meet the demand for the new online services. Some therefore took the unprecedented, unfamiliar, and unpalatable step of charging users for online searches. Other libraries decided to cut some services so that they could offer online retrieval instead.

A great 'fee or free' debate raged, with proponents of free service arguing that access to information was a fundamental right for all, and proponents of charging maintaining that those who used specialized services were in the minority and should pay for their usage. The debate has largely subsided with time. Those interested in the details should consult the articles and bibliography listed below. Of particular note is Burgess' summary[3] of the points on both sides of the question. Burgess comes down squarely on the side of free access to databases for all:

All library services should be free. If you believe this and cannot afford the database then admit the planning tool of the budget has not proved the need and don't buy it.

WHY CHARGE FOR ONLINE SEARCHES?

There were several reasons why online searching raised the 'fee or free' debate and caused information centers to consider charging for searches:

Real dollars were expended. Online searching charges were new direct costs and new items in many budgets for which no plans had been made. Many managers did not know where to put searching costs in the budget because they did not fit into previously established budget lines.

Pricing for online services is usage-sensitive, in contrast to overhead items such as book and periodical subscriptions, which are paid (indirectly) by all users. Users doing searches incurred the search costs, while others did not.

Database producers and online databanks were also new on the scene, did not have large customer bases, and could not discount prices for libraries.

Initiation of online services invariably generated additional costs for training, equipment, documentation, etc.

Searching costs are highly visible. Most of the major online retrieval systems display them on the terminal at the end of the search. Searchers are continually reminded that searching is a costly activity.

Some search services emphasized the cost issue in their advertising by positioning themselves as lower cost providers.

The growth of online services fueled the emergence of information brokers who made a business of selling information for profit.

Both information centers and end-users of information are therefore sensitive to pricing. Recent changes in pricing strategies have increased this sensitivity.

REFERENCES

1   Stieg, Margaret F. 'Fee vs. Free in Historical Perspective.' *Reference Librarian*, No. 12 (Spring-Summer 1985): pp. 93–103.
2   Hawkins, Donald T. *Online Information Retrieval Bibliography*. Learned Information, Inc., Medford, NJ., 1983, 1986.
3   Burgess, Dean. 'Fee or Free: The Database Access Controversy.' *Reference Librarian*, No. 12 (Spring-Summer 1985): pp. 105–115.

APPENDIX 2

KIOSK BILLING: APPLICATIONS FOR THE RBOCs

The Regional Bell Operating Companies (RBOCs) were interested in providing information gateway services even before Judge Greene's March 7, 1988 ruling gave them permission to enter the fledgling marketplace. In the ruling, Judge Greene describes the billing mechanism of the French Teletel system, calling it 'kiosk billing'.[1] Under the kiosk system, the service provider (in this case, the telephone company) bills the user a flat rate per minute. (Originally, the French system rate was database independent, but in 1987, multirate billing was instituted to accommodate a wider range of database producers.)

In the context of this article, kiosk billing is equivalent to connect time pricing without any additional charging elements. Judge Greene attributes the success of the Teletel system in France in part to its simple, nondiscriminatory billing system. He also remarks that this type of billing 'involves a measure of revenue sharing: as service providers' revenue increases, the telephone company's income from the network rises.' Although the modified final judgement generally prohibits revenue sharing between the telephone companies (RBOCS) and information providers, on March 7, Judge Greene ruled that kiosk billing is not a form of prohibited revenue sharing; saying that in a gateway service, billing that does not discriminate among information providers (database producers) is now permitted.

HOW WILL THE RBOCs PRICE THEIR INFORMATION GATEWAYS?

Greene's order has unleashed a strong interest on the part of the RBOCs in entering the information gateway market. Most of them have either filed plans with the FCC detailing their intentions or will do so soon. Pricing, of course, will have to be developed, and it appears that we can expect to see a variety of pricing schemes emerge, and so history may well repeat itself! In a recent presentation at an Information Industry Association conference, Winston Himsworth,[2] (President of Tel/Logic, Inc., a telecommunications interconnect firm) stated that the RBOCs see the information gateway market as a way to enhance their revenues by stimulating telephone network usage. Therefore, he feels that the RBOCs should not use flat rate pricing for their gateway services, but should implement usage-sensitive pricing algorithms.

Three suggested options for the RBOCs are:

1. A low monthly rate plus a per call charge
2. Measured service (i.e., connect time)
3. High threshold measured service

Option 1 is similar to the way much telephone service is charged today and has the advantage that the RBOCs are familiar with it. The monthly rate covers the fixed charges of maintaining the account, etc., and the per call charge is directly proportional to the subscriber's usage. Option 2 has the advantage that customers can subscribe without cost and become aware of the service, but it could suffer from the disadvantages of connect time pricing discussed above. Option 3 permits subscribers to use the gateway up to the threshold level without additional charges, thus encouraging browsing and familiarization. Above the threshold, measured service takes over, so that high volume users pay in proportion to their usage. Himsworth feels that high threshold measured service is the best charging method for the RBOCs to use.

FLAT VERSUS MEASURED RATES

The information provision business is a new one for the RBOCs and portends many changes for them in areas of pricing and relationships with rate-setting regulatory bodies. Central is the issue of flat rate vs. measured rates for local service. The vast majority of US telephone users pay a flat rate for their local telephone service, and rates are set based on statistics derived from average call duration measurements. As the direct use of information systems by end-users grows, average call lengths will increase because data calls are usually longer than voice calls. The

RBOCs may therefore press public utility commissions to allow them to implement usage sensitive (i.e. measured) pricing for local service. Gateways will spur this move regardless of who provides them, whether it be the RBOCs or other organizations.

When this article was written (November, 1988), few RBOC pricing plans had been announced, so it is too early to determine what pricing strategies they will follow. Bell Atlantic plans a trial in Pennsylvania in which menu browsing will be free, and there will be no subscription fee at least for the first six months (originally a $10 fee was planned, but it has been waived). Bell-South has announced a gateway trial in the Atlanta area for which connect time costs will be $3/hour during the day and $1.50/hour at night. There will also be a resource unit charge of $1.20 per 'kilosegment' (64,000 bytes) of data sent or received. These costs are in addition to those levied by the online host or database producer. The RBOCs are newcomers to the information provision business and are feeling their way in this area; they can learn much from experiences of the online information industry.

REFERENCES

1   Greene, Judge Harold H. *U.S. v. Western Electric Co., et al.* Civil Action No. 82–0192. U.S. District Court for the District of Columbia. Order filed March 7,1988.
2   Himsworth, Winston. Speech at 'Revolution in Voice Services' Conference. (Sponsored by the Information Industry Association), Washington, DC, September 26–28, 1988.

University Libraries and Information Services for the Business Community

H. B. Josephine

Arizona State University, USA

The 1980s have seen an increase in the number of specialized units within US university libraries that provide information services to the business community. A successful service at a public university is used as a case study to explore the rationales for starting these units, the types of services offered, the client base served, the marketing techniques used, the budgeting requirements needed, and the organizational model in place. A discussion of how university libraries are evolving to be more pro-active in economic development and business information services is also included.

INTRODUCTION

During the 1970s and 1980s academic libraries have increased the number of specialized information services offered to both their primary and non-primary clientele. Today, faculty, staff and students have immediate access to online catalogs with keyword or boolean searching, CD-ROM workstations with user-friendly menus, and hundreds of online databases through both US and European-based vendors. Sometimes overlooked are the information needs of the non-primary clientele – the small businessman, attorney, consultant, special librarian – all of whom look to the university library and its in-depth resources for answers to their research needs. While most academic institutions have always provided some services for off-campus clients with, perhaps, an additional user fee or service charge added, it has only been recently that separate cost-recovery units have been created specifically to meet the information needs of these unique users.

FEE-BASED INFORMATION SERVICES

Information service agencies fall within several distinct groups; among these are database producers, database vendors, publishers, document suppliers, and information brokers. Many academic and research libraries, professional societies and private companies are document suppliers. For example, the John Crerar Library in Chicago, Illinois, the Linda Hall Library in Kansas City, Missouri, the British Lending Library at Boston Spa, University Microfilms International in Ann Arbor, Michigan, and the Engineering Societies Library in New York are some of the most well-known. These services offer photocopies of articles, reports, theses, dissertations that are held in house.

Other companies and academic institutions do online searching or research for the client to identify articles to be ordered. Most private information brokers do not have their own journal collections to support document retrieval. They rely instead on academic libraries and some of the document suppliers listed above.

FULL-SERVICE ACADEMIC LIBRARY INFORMATION SERVICES

An information service within an academic institution has the advantage of access to locally-mounted databases, a variety of vendors for online searching, trained professional searchers, and most importantly a journal, report, book, and government document collection that can support almost all research requests.

Characteristics

A full-service information agency in an academic library has all of the following characteristics:

1. They provide expedited interlibrary loan or document retrieval and delivery to off-campus clientele for a fee; for an additional fee they can provide same-day or rush service.
2. They perform online database searches or custom research, and charge a research fee plus direct costs (telephone calls, photocopying, and online charges for computer database inquiries).
3. They provide other services as requested by clients including training, library research skills seminars, verifications, consultations, and translation.
4. They use marketing techniques to assess client needs and to increase their client base.
5. They are expected to operate on a full or partial cost recovery basis.

Services

Although almost 80 fee-based services in US and Canadian libraries are listed in the *1988 F.I.S.C.A.L. Directory of Fee-based Information Service Centers in Academic Libraries,* less than 20 of these have specially dedicated departments designed to meet the information needs of business and industry. Listed below are a few of these full-service fee-based information centers along with their institutional affiliation and the year they were created.

1. Arizona State University, Tempe. AZ
    Fee-based Information and Research Service Team
    F.I.R.S.T. (1987)

2. Georgia Institute of Technology
   Research Information Services
   R.I.S. (1968)
3. George Washington University, Washington D.C.
   The Gelman Library Information Service (1986)
4. Long Island University, Brookville. NY
   Center for Business Research (1979)
5. Purdue University, West Lafayette. IN Technical Information
   Service T.I.S. (1987)
6. Rice University, Houston, TX
   Regional Information and Communication Exchange
   R.I.C.E. (1967)
7. University of Colorado, Boulder, Co
   Colorado Technical Reference Center
   C.T.R.C (1967)
8. University of Michigan
   Michigan Information Transfer Source
   M.I.T.S. (1980)
9. University of Minnestoa, Minneapolis, MN
   Biological and Agricultural Sciences Information Service
   B.A.S.I.S. (1983)
   Biomedical Information Service
   B.I.S. (1981)
   Engineering, Science and Technology Information Service
   E.S.T.I.S. (1983)
   Inform (1973)
10. University of Waterloo, Waterloo, Ontario
    Industrial and Business Information Service
    I.B.I.S. (1985)
    Specialised Information Retrieval and Library Services
    S.I.R.L.S. (1985)
11. University of Wisconsin, Madison WI
    Information Services Division
    I.S.D. (1963)

Revenues

While all of these services offer both online searching or research and document retrieval, most revenues are generated from the document supply portion of the service. At Arizona State University 40 per cent of revenues for 1988-89 came from online searching or research, while 60 per cent came from document delivery. At most institutions these services are expected to be cost-recovery units – generating sufficient income to cover staff salaries and benefits, general operating expenses, and overheads. Most services take from three to five years to break even and are subsidized initially by grant funds or library funding. Other services may share facilities with existing library departments, such as interlibrary loan or reference, until revenues are sufficient to support separate staff.

Rates set by these information services vary based on local costs (student wages, photocopy contracts, university indirect charges) and the marketplace. The cost of an article ranges from $6.00 to $10.00 with additional charges added for rush services – telefacsimile, express delivery, same-day turnaround. Hourly research fees vary from $30 per hour to $70 per hour. Some services charge clients a fixed subscription rate for a year while others invoice on a per item charge for each request.

Marketing

In order to determine clients' needs and levels of service, managers of fee-based information services are responsible for marketing. This includes:

1. developing a business plan or planning document;
2. selecting target markets based on the community and the resources of the academic institution;
3. determining a pricing structure based on institutional costs and the marketplace;
4. promoting the service by designing brochures and newsletters and through public speaking engagements; and
5. developing a method for evaluating the planning and marketing efforts to determine the success or failure of the service.

Planning and budgeting for a fee-based service is a continuous process. New databases and services may be added and new client groups targeted based on the expertise of the staff and the information needs of the community.

For example, at F.I.R.S.T., we added access to the NASA databases by becoming an associate member of the NASA Industrial Application Center in Los Angeles, California. This additional service can provide citations to articles and technical reports for our clients in the aerospace and defense industry.

The service must also reflect the goals, strategic planning and mission of the university and the university library. The mission of Arizona State University is to provide 'outstanding programs instruction, research and creative activity, and service appropriate for the nation, the state of Arizona, and the state's major metropolitan area'. Universities and their libraries are being recognized as a central force in attracting business and industry and promoting economic development through their many research institutes and service programs.

CASE HISTORY

At Arizona State University, the increasing demands of off-campus users for specialized research assistance, online searching and expedited interlibrary loan led to the development of a separate library unit that would provide these services for a fee.

As the only research library in a metropolitan area of more than 2 million people with a projected growth rate of 40 per cent by the year 1990, the information resources of the ASU libraries are vital to more than just the 40,000 enrolled students and 7,000 faculty and staff members. The Phoenix metropolitan area is known for its clusters of high tech firms and growing service industries all of whom rely on the resources of the ASU libraries.

Planning and Marketing

The information service at Arizona State University began in January 1987 when a full-time librarian was hired to assess the information needs of the off-campus community and develop a business plan for the service. During the initial six month planning stage, a policy statement was written, a name for the service was chosen, brochures were designed, equipment was ordered, database vendors were contacted, and key staff positions were determined.

When the service opened in July 1987, it had a name F.I.R.S.T. (Fee- based Information and Research Service Team) and a growing client base. Initial marketing efforts were aimed at local groups of professional librarians in corporate, medical and legal offices. In addition all of the off-campus requests for online research were referred to the F.I.R.S.T. office. In the year previous to the creation of F.I.R.S.T. the ASU Libraries had performed 153 searches for off-campus patrons. During the 1987/88 fiscal year F.I.R.S.T. handled 289 research requests and in 1988/89, 400.

To develop the document retrieval portion of the service, companies in Arizona with on-going research needs which required copies of articles were contacted and given information about the new service. Additionally, the librarian developing the service gave talks to the various special library groups in the Phoenix metropolitan area informing them of the creation of the new service at Arizona State University. After one year of operation, F.I.R.S.T. had 457 clients and by June of 1989 the client base had expanded to 857.

Staffing

The initial staff for the service included one professional librarian (manager) and one student assistant at 25 hours per week. Within three months an half-time accounting clerk was hired to handle all billing, accounts receivable and accounts payable for the department. As business increased, a half-time professional librarian was added along with additional student assistants.

The manager of the service is responsible for the overall day to day operations of the service as well as for marketing, planning, and client research projects. As a university library department head, the manager reports to the Associate Dean for Library Services and participates in administrative meetings and strategic planning task forces of the University Libraries. Additional tasks include learning the university financial accounting system and keeping university-wide administration informed of the progress of the service.

Revenue and Expenses

During the first full year of operation the salary of the professional librarian-in-charge (manager) and the half-time accounting clerk were supported by the University Library. Revenues collected in the 1987/88 fiscal year covered student assistant hours, a 75 per cent time professional librarian, database vendor charges, photocopies, telephone, postage, delivery charges, printing of the brochure, letterhead, business cards, envelopes, and database training.

For the second year of operation, additional expenses were added to the budget, 75 per cent of the manager's salary plus benefits and 30 per cent indirect cost recovery divided between the library (15.64 per cent) and the university (14.36 per cent). Indirect cost is structured to cover general administration by the university, facility maintenance and operation, building use allowance, library administration, and equipment use allowance. Current revenues are sufficient to cover these added costs. As the service increases, additional staff may be added based on an annual review of the business plan and projected revenues.

Questions and Answers

Clients over the past two years have varied widely. The majority of our searches are business related although a few are in the humanities or social sciences. The ASU science library is a US Patent Depository site with microfilm copies of every US patent. Previous to the creation of F.I.R.S.T. clients with patent requests would have to come to the library. Now F.I.R.S.T. handles a number of requests for patent searches and for copies of patents over the phone and will also request copies of non-US patents from Derwent and Patent Express in Britain. This is an example of how F.I.R.S.T. has been able to make a specialized library resource more widely available.

Some of our requests have been for specific information – currency exchange data for 131 countries, planning and development documents for several US cities, the pest control properties of Boric Acid. Others have been more general – a bibliography of articles on intrapreneuring, uses of fiber optics on aircraft carriers, a review of the literature on conductive polyanilines.

Although F.I.R.S.T. has access to hundreds of databases through a variety of vendors – DIALOG, DRI, NEWSNET, NEXIS/LEXIS, ORBIT, STN International, VU/TEXT – but we often find the need to contact trade associations or experts in the field to find the answers for our clients. F.I.R.S.T. also uses the full resources of the ASU libraries' 2.5 million volumes, 32,000 serial subscriptions, and specialized collections such as solar energy and government publications to answer our clients' requests.

CONCLUSION

Growth of Services

The 1980s have seen a dramatic increase in the number of fee-based information services in academic libraries – from 1976 to 1988, 53 services were created. This is due to several factors:

1. Increased number of online services available as well as the marketing efforts of the vendors to potential end users in business and industry who then ask the library for help with online searching or for copies of articles identified by online searches

2. Increased networking among libraries through OCLC and RLIN so that holdings information for both books and journals have become instantly available.

3. Increased awareness of the role of the university and the university library in state-wide economic development.

4. Increased awareness by academic library administrators that services to the non-primary clientele can be offered only a cost recovery basis.

5. Increased availability of the academic library resources to the community as a whole via dial-in access to online public access catalogs (OPACs).

Changing Demands

In the 1990s universities and their libraries will have additional demands for service beyond the traditional mission of teaching, research and public service. Increasingly state governments are looking to their universities to provide research and information sources as part of the economic development of the state. In Pennsylvania, Indiana and Virginia the university libraries have special information services funded to provide online searching, research, and document retrieval in support of state-wide economic development for business and industry. Both Georgia Institute of Technology and the Massachusetts Institute of Technology have very successful university-industry liaison programs that, for a generous donation, give companies access to research expertise, laboratories and library resources. Other universities are considering similar projects.

While the public at large may continue to think of libraries as warehouses, libraries are confidently moving toward the model of the information supermarket with a variety of services and levels of assistance to meet the information needs of all users – on-site or remote.

Benefits

Libraries and the services they offer are changing rapidly. The new technologies that fee-based information services use to meet the information needs of their clients can also be incorporated into the services offered to the primary clientele of the library. Bulletin boards, electronic mail, telefacsimile, pc scanners, telephone answering software are all new technologies currently being investigated or in use at fee-based information centers that could have a positive impact on public service units in the library. The additional specialized reference tools and databases utilized by fee-based information services increase the resources available to all patrons of the library. The improved relationship of the library to an external community, which can now utilize a service created specifically to meet its needs, can mean increased donations to library friends programs or increased cooperation in multi-type library ventures such as the creation of union lists or online catalog networks. Finally, a fee-based information service will increase the community's awareness of both the value of the university library and the value of the information it contains.

ADDITIONAL READING

Two conferences have been held on the topic of fee-based information services in academic libraries and proceedings from both are available for purchase. They contain articles on specific issues – marketing, copyright, quality control – as well as case study examples of services currently in operation. The 1988 directory of fee-based information centers is available from Rice University. Any library considering starting a service or wanting to promote existing library services should subscribe to the bi-monthly newsletter, *Marketing Library Services*.

1. Association of Research Libraries. Office of Management Studies. Systems and Procedures Exchange Center. *Corporate Use of Research Libraries*. Kit 88. Washington DC: ARL. 1982.

2. *Conference on Fee-Based Research in College and University Libraries*. Proceedings of the meeting at the C.W. Post Center of Long Island University, June 17-18, 1982. Greenvale NY: The Center for Business Research, Long Island University, 1983. 155 p $28.50.

3. *Fee-Based Services: Issues and Answers*. Second Conference on Fee-Based Research in College and University Libraries. Compiled by Anne K. Beaubien. Ann Arbor: Michigan Information Transfer Source (MITS), The University of Michigan, 1988. 82 p $28.

4. *Marketing Library Services* (a bi-monthly newsletter). Sharon La Rosa. editor. PO Box 2286, Abington, MA 02351. Subscription $49/year.

5. *1988 F.I.S.C.A.L. Directory: Fee-Based Information Service Centers in Academic Libraries.* Compiled by Kathleen Prendergast.

Evanston: NQUERY, Northwestern University, 1988. 55p. $10.

Available from R.I.C.E., Rice University, P O Box 1892, Houston, TX, 77251 – 1892.

Descriptions of specific university programs can be found in these articles:

Center for Business Research, Long Island University

Mary McNierney Grant and Donald L. Ungarelli. 'Fee-Based Business Research in an Academic Library,' *The Reference Librarian*, n.19:239–255, 1987. Donald L. Ungarelli and Mary McNierney Grant. 'A Fee-Based Model: Administrative Considerations in an Academic Library', Drexel Library Quarterly, 19 (4): 4–12, Fall 1983.

Information Services Division (I.S.D), University of Wisconsin, Madison

Frances K. Wood. 'When do Dollars for Information Service Make Sense?' *The Bottom Line*, 1 (4): 25–27, 1987.

Lehigh University

Susan A. Cady and Berry G. Richards. 'The One-Thousand Dollar Alternative.' *American Libraries*, 13:175–176, March 1982.

Michigan Information Transfer Source (M.I.T.S.), University of Michigan

Anne K. Beaubien. 'Fees or Free', in: *Reference Service: A Perspective* edited by Sul H. Lee. Ann Arbor: Pierian Press, 1983 p.99–112.

Research information service (R.I.S.),

G Julia W. Hornbeck. 'An Academic Library's Experience with Fee-Based Services,' *Drexel Library Quarterly*. 19(4): 23-26, Fall 1983.

Charging for public library services

Stephen J. Bailey

Lecturer in Economics, Glasgow College

In February 1988, the UK government published a consultative document *Financing our Public Library Service: four subjects for debate* (Cm 324, HMSO). Whilst the government is committed to the continued provision of a free basic public library service to individuals, the Green Paper seeks to promote discussion about the increased use of library charges. This paper is an attempt to widen the debate, taking not just a financial/economic focus but also providing a review of the long-lived and rather extensive debate within the librarianship profession itself.

INTRODUCTION

Libraries are an integral part of the cultural, recreational, educational, business and government milieu in modern societies. Any discussion of library financing, including user charges, must recognise the diverse nature of modern public libraries ranging from major research libraries, like the Bodleian (Oxford University) and major municipal reference libraries, to modest local lending libraries. Recent government proposals to increase the role of charging must therefore be discussed in the context of the wider aspirations of the library service.

Historically, the objectives of public library provision have been concerned with both educational and recreational aspects of literature whether in print or such non print formats as records, film, audio tape, etc. The emphasis has traditionally been on serving the community through individual library users who use those services on a purely voluntary basis. Hence a public library has to provide for a wide range of demands from the community and its service objectives are accordingly wide-ranging, diffuse and rather vague.

Holdings of library materials are not solely dictated by the current demands of a majority of library users. Public libraries usually maintain a broadbased, balanced collection of library materials, some of which may be used very infrequently or not at all, but the librarian may be judging future as well as current needs or deciding what ought to be available in the interests of the community. The range and diversity of material will vary from branch to branch within a public library system. This paper refers to the system as a whole, including the main or central reference and lending libraries and their branch networks, and is specifically concerned with local authority library systems to the exclusion of academic and other publicly supported libraries.

THE ECONOMIC RATIONALE FOR SUBSIDISED LIBRARY SERVICES

Reference has already been made to the community aspects of library provision. It is generally argued that in providing a service to the individual, library provision also benefits the community as well. In the words of the Library Association:

It is generally accepted that information in published material made accessible to the right person at the right time in the right place has beneficial effects, whether cultural, economic or social, much greater than the cost of its provision and therefore is in the interest of a democratic society (Library Association, 1987, p. 142).

Hence library usage has external benefits (referred to as externalities) whereby the library contributes to the education of individuals which, in turn, benefits society. The magnitude of these externalities is subject to dispute, given the difficulty of measuring them in practice. Indeed, some library use will have little if any external benefit, e.g. use of library fiction books for light reading (recreation) or consulting 'Do it yourself' type materials. The nature and size of any externalities will vary depending on the user and the type of material used. However, it is not possible to predict the use to which information will be put and therefore its level of external benefits.

Indeed, the foregoing statement concerning the recreational use of books having little if any external benefit is open to dispute. For example, in response to the question 'why should recreational reading of, say, Agatha Christie be financed from the local property tax?' it has been argued that reading Agatha Christie is not merely recreational but also an exercise in developing literacy and an appreciation of a work of art, much in the same way as reading classics such as Jane Austen, etc. (Smith, 1981).

Without an accurate account of public, as well as private, benefits it is not possible to determine by how much public library users should be subsidised from tax revenues. Whilst it may be argued that external benefits do exist, and therefore library users should be encouraged by subsidy, it is not possible to conclude that the service should be completely financed through subsidy.

Other supposed justifications for subsidising library services include the low incomes of users, public good, merit good and economies of scale characteristics. Not all library users have low incomes so that the 'low incomes' argument would not necessarily justify complete subsidisation. Library services do not have the public good characteristics of non-exclusion and non-rivalry in consumption. It is possible to exclude nonmembers (e.g. as done by private libraries) and use of, say, a book precludes another person's use of that book at that time. However, information in its broadest sense does display characteristics of non-exclusion and non-rivalry so that it may be a public good:

Once in place the information in books, documents, other media and electronic sources can be perused many times during its useful lifespan without any significant diminution in its value to the user . . . the economic characteristic of 'non-depletability' (Library Association, 1987, p. 142).

Hence some aspects of library services may have public good characteristics, which means that they cannot be efficiently provided by the private sector and therefore subsidy is required. Again, however, this does not provide a rationale for the complete subsidation of *all* library services. Similarly, information may be a 'merit good' whereby the individual undervalues the benefit of consumption of that library service, i.e. one does not appreciate the true value of information needed to make rational decisions until one has it. Hence consumption should be encouraged through subsidy. Once more, however, it should be noted that this does not justify complete subsidation of all library services (see Figure 1 and Table 1).

If library provision demonstrates economies of scale (i.e. the average unit cost falls as the scale of output increases) then an economically efficient pricing policy (based on price equal to incremental cost) will fail to generate sufficient revenue to cover total costs. Hence subsidy would be required. However, it is difficult to determine to what extent economies of

FIGURE 1. DIFFERENCES BETWEEN SERVICES EXHIBITING PUBLIC MERIT, AND PRIVATE CHARACTERISTICS

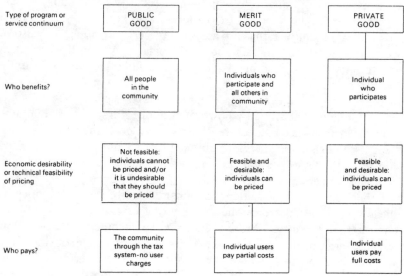

Type of program or service continuum	PUBLIC GOOD	MERIT GOOD	PRIVATE GOOD
Who benefits?	All people in the community	Individuals who participate and all others in community	Individual who participates
Economic desirability or technical feasibility of pricing	Not feasible: individuals cannot be priced and/or it is undesirable that they should be priced	Feasible and desirable: individuals can be priced	Feasible and desirable: individuals can be priced
Who pays?	The community through the tax system-no user charges	Individual users pay partial costs	Individual users pay full costs

TABLE 1. *The differences between private and public goods*

	Private good	Public good
1. Exclusion of someone who does not pay	Easy	Difficult
2. Impact of use on supply	Depletes supply	Does not deplete supply
3. Individual's choice of consumption	Choice	No choice
4. Individual's choice of kind and quality of services	Choice	No choice
5. Payment relationship to demand and consumption	Close relationship	Distant relationship
6. Mode of allocation decisions	By market mechanism	By political process

Source: Crompton and Bonk (1980).

scale exist in the provision of library services. First, output is difficult to measure (it could be books issued, answers provided to library users' enquiries, etc.) and, second, larger libraries offer different services (and therefore a different output), for example, holdings of reference and archival materials, bibliographic services, etc. (Van House, 1983, pp, 32–38). By way of repetition, any economies of scale would not justify complete subsidisation of library services.

A final argument for subsidy is that of 'option value'. Provision of library services allows everyone the option of using those services at some future time. In holding a store of information (e.g. archives) a library maintains the option for future users to use that information and hence is of value to them even if they do not currently make use of the service. Option value would apply to other public services such as fire protection, health, transit, etc. However, it could also be claimed for private services, e.g. scheduled airlines, so, once again, it cannot justify full subsidisation of library services.

THE LIBRARIANS' AVERSION TO USER CHARGES

The introduction of direct charges would have an irreparably damaging effect on public libraries and their users, and consequently on the educational and cultural development of society (Library Association, 1979, p. 431).

According to this view charges would narrow the concept of the public library (Koefoed, 1981), discourage intellectual curiosity, cause excessive dependence upon chargeable stock for library financing, seriously undermine the complex network of inter-library cooperation (because charge and exemption criteria would differ between libraries), and lead to widespread proxy borrowing (on-lending from exempt to chargeable groups or within chargeable groups to avoid charges). Charges might, also, actively discourage the infrequent and reluctant user (particularly illiterate adults), deter chargeable adults from using the library and so effectively reducing access to their young children (who need accompanying to the library), cause manifold administrative problems in deciding eligibility for exemptions (e.g. how is a student defined and what about individuals undertaking informal self-study programmes?), exacerbate the current problems of the publishing industry (in reducing demand for books) and reduce returns to authors.

More forthright views expressed by some librarians are that 'charges are as reprehensible as political censorship'; 'freedom of access to information and ideas and the culture should be regarded as a right in a mature society'; 'the role of the professional librarian is to make (access available to all) and not to concentrate on raising resources' (Smith, 1981, pp.5–7). 'The temptation to apply business thinking to the administration of libraries has led to a mindless imitation of business procedures and analyses which distort what does and can happen in libraries' (Blake and Perlmutter, 1977, pp. 2005–2006). Raising finance is seen as anti-professional. It has also been argued that as library users are being asked to pay twice, both through the local property tax and through user charges, that this represents double taxation (Berry, 1976; Stoakley, 1977). Others argue that free libraries are a highly political issue and that the declared intention to introduce library charges can lose elections (Berry, 1982). Increased revenue from charges may lead to a withdrawal of tax financed support in the future so that there is no long term financial gain to the library. Every citizen has a right to information regardless of ability to pay. In reducing library usage whilst library costs remain largely fixed, charges will lead to a loss of social benefits so that the social costs of charges are greater than the social benefits (Waldhart and Bellardo, 1979, p. 47; and Rice, 1979, p. 658). This is also said to apply to charges for non residents' use of services (Hicks, 1980).

Charges could lead to a situation where authors' claims for a proportion of income from book rental charges would be irresistible and would open the door (in the UK) to the operation of a public lending right entirely funded by local authorities. Together with reduced usage, the possible offsetting loss of intergovernmental grant, etc: 'it is highly questionable whether there would in practice be any financial benefit resulting from the imposition of a charging system on libraries, but there is little doubt that such action would undermine this service which is an integral part of the fabric of community life' (Taylor, 1980, p. 429). Finally, others argue that the cost of the library service is so small that there is little case for charging for library services, especially given the risk of deleterious effects (Stoakley, 1977).

THE GROWING MOVEMENT TOWARDS LIBRARY USER CHARGES

The foregoing criticisms of library user charges assumed a charge-for-everything approach. It has already been noted that there are valid grounds for a mixture of charging and subsidies. The policy problem is to determine the correct balance between both sources of revenue and librarians should avoid locking themselves into dogmatic or inflexible positions on user charges based on professional principle or political ideology (DeGennaro, 1975). It is possible to adopt charges for certain special services to meet the special and legitimate needs of industry, commerce and other users who are willing and able to pay for them. An eclectic approach to user fees would weigh the advantages and disadvantages *for each particular service* as suggested by Casper (1978, 1979).

By way of comparison, small scale charges have existed for more than the last century in American libraries (McMullen, 1978). The recently increased American interest in library user charges is due to a variety of factors. First, computer-based information retrieval services are increasing library costs very sharply. Second, libraries are attempting to change the nature and orientation of services increasingly towards the specific needs of individual users. Third, the traditional tax-financed funding is in decline or at least heavily constrained. Fourth, the growth of the private sector information industry, based on user charges, has close parallels with developments in public libraries. Librarians are finding it increasingly difficult to maintain existing funding levels let alone expand them, and hence they are looking to user charges as a source of supplemental revenue. Unless they do this their range and level of information services offered must necessarily be limited.

The decision not to offer a service unless it can be provided free may effectively deny the public access to the service because of lack of an alternative private supplier or because of the higher user charges in the private sector. Hence, the opposition to user charges on 'morality' or 'right of access to information' grounds is viewed with scepticism (Rettig, 1981). In practice a blanket non-charging policy may be worse than a selective charges policy on precisely these grounds.

The point we want to emphasise is that slowly, by accretion, fees are becoming an accepted fact in the library world. It will become gradually very difficult for librarians to hide from the truth: library services are not free . . .. If fees are viewed as undesirable by the profession, then we must work to convince legislators that it is in the public interest to subsidise selected services (Dougherty, 1979, p. 123).

Faced with the competing demands on public funds by other local authority services, libraries are likely to be lower down the list of spending priorities than other municipal services such as law and order, fire protection, etc. Even the argument that user charges discriminate against low income library users has come into disrepute. It is argued that libraries redistribute income, or income in kind, from the poorest to the more affluent people in the community (Skrzeszewski, 1985, p. 139; and

Gell, 1979b). Library users are predominantly the educated middle class, middle income people in white collar, professional and managerial occupations and so it is unfair to ask all residents to pay through local taxes.

With regard to the 'maintaining freedom of access' argument it is argued that 'access to or availability of services should not be confused with usage. The act of supplying a service does not mean that the service will be used' (Drake, 1984, p. 632). 'Freedom of access' has become confused with free provision. For example, an American study showed that only 3 per cent of respondents used a library to obtain information on their most important problems (Crompton and Bonk, 1980) and another study ranked libraries ninth among a variety of information sources (Drake, 1984). The main problem here is seen as the amount of time that must be expended in the library seeking out the desired information and it is the time input, rather than any charge, which serves to inhibit use of library facilities. Hence a faster customised library service with a charge may be more attractive than a free but slower self-service system.

Even for basic book borrowing 'if adequate duplication is not possible, titles may recur so seldom on the shelves that their availability free of charge is scarcely real' (Ronnie, 1984, p. 99). In this case charging a book rental for popular titles would finance not just increased duplication of titles and therefore increased accessibility but also, in reducing financial constraints, facilitate provision of a full range of quality material. Furthermore 'assumptions that the population's need for library services must be fully satisfied . . . is completely inconsistent with the way we view other goods and services in the economy, even food' (Crompton and Bonk, 1980, p. 17). 'What the library community needs to develop is an economically viable theory of access' (Prentice, 1979, p. 133). 'Rather than opposing all user fees in principle, a more appropriate and productive course of action for the profession would be to seek a better understanding of the impact of fees on the users' access to information' (Waldhart and Bellardo, 1979, p. 57).

COMMENTS ON THE LIBRARIANS' DEBATE

The foregoing text summarised the debate within the library profession itself. There are a few points which need to be commented upon. First, the claim that levying charges on users who have already contributed to library finances through tax revenues constitutes double taxation or paying twice for the service. This illustrates a misunderstanding of the economic rationale for subsidies. Tax revenues should be used to subsidise those library services generating external benefits or where the service is seen to be a merit good. But the subsidy is meant to encourage consumption at optimal levels (where the marginal social benefit equals the marginal social cost) and this will usually only require a partial (rather than full) subsidy. The subsidy will be lower where benefits occur in the predominantly private (rather than social) form and, hence, the user charge will be higher. Subsidy and charge are complementary rather than inherently exclusive. Only pure public goods require 100 per cent subsidy on efficiency grounds (Figure 1).

Second, the claim that libraries would tend to concentrate provision on those services generating income from user charges is a management problem, distinct from policy decisions about the appropriate array of library services and their financing. It should not be used as an excuse to prevent further consideration of charges and it displays a misunderstanding of the (limited) role of charged-for services within the totality of library services.

Third, the argument that it is unfair to ask all residents to contribute to the costs of a service used by a minority of the population again illustrates a lack of understanding of the nature of externalities. Difficult though it may be to quantify, library use raises the level of literacy and knowledge of users which in turn benefits society in providing a better educated labour force required for modern productive activity. Whilst there are limits to these external benefits, so that they cannot be used to justify total subsidy of all library services, nonetheless there is a clear rationale to justify some general support from the populace quite independently from any option value characteristics.

Fourth, regarding concern with financial matters as anti-professional and mindless is to adopt a blinkered approach to the problem of the public sector in general and libraries in particular. To regard libraries as being above such mundane matters as finance and politics is naive in the extreme and is not in the long term interests of the library service, librarians nor library users. Similarly it is not realistic to argue that library expenditures are so small that there are no grounds for charges. This claim could be made on behalf of many other services provided by local government which, considered together, impose significant financial demands on limited resources.

Fifth, it is important to see user charges not just as a means of raising additional revenue to overcome financial constraints and permit service expansion. Rather, user charges may have to serve a multitude of objectives including promoting the desired array of service provision, promoting efficiency and so on (Bailey, 1986). To argue that there will be little, if any, financial benefit brought about by the introduction of charges is to see their role in narrow accounting terms. Pricing services has the much wider role of promoting efficiency and good management. Except in cases of 'market failure' (i.e. the existence of externalities, public goods, merit goods and economies of scale) full cost charging for consumption of a good or a service will improve efficiency in both production and consumption. A service which is free at the point of consumption will be over-utilised and consumption will increase until the benefit at the margin is zero. If all demand is met, production will be excessive. Pricing can also be used to purposively direct service provision to particular groups, reorganise service orientation and so on.

Sixth, many of the fears concerning the potential deleterious effects of charges on libraries are based on a simplistic 'before-and-after' basis for the current array of service provision. This views library services from a static viewpoint. Except in very special circumstances, it is indisputably true that a given service which was previously free will experience reduced demand if a charge is suddenly levied. The simple laws of supply and demand show that in general as price rises demand falls, *ceteris paribus*. But this is too simple a view of both economics and of library provision. The fall in demand may only be temporary, returning to near former levels after an interval of time as the idea of charges is accepted. In other words the degree of sensitivity of demand to changes in the price or charge is itself a function of the time period considered. Furthermore, library services should be seen in a dynamic rather than static context. It is highly unlikely that only prices or charges will change. Charges are most likely to be implemented at a time of service reorganisation or expansion, for example where a new service is being introduced and part-financed by user charges. In this 'with-and-without' basis of comparison it is clear that charges do not necessarily reduce usage of the service.

Hence, it is not self-evident that the introduction of charging on a *selective* basis will have an irreparably damaging effect on public libraries and their users. Indeed in certain cases quite the opposite effect may be achieved and the correct identification of such cases is crucial. Revenue from appropriate charges could be used carefully and positively to widen (rather than narrow) the concept of the public library; new services could provide positive outlets for curiosity and blanket claims of reduced inter-library cooperation and ensuing administrative problems should not be used as a volte-face to deter further consideration of charges. As noted earlier, it is unlikely that a limited policy of user charges would cause excessive dependence on this source of finance. As for the claim that charges, in reducing usage, would exacerbate the problems of the publishing industry, the latter organisation argues that it is precisely the free provision of books by libraries which reduces their markets!

A PRACTICAL CHARGING POLICY

In the context of public library services the question is about the appropriate balance between the use of subsidy and of revenue from charges. Charges are administratively feasible: individual users can be identified and charges can be enforced for the service delivered (e.g. books borrowed, bibliographic assistance, etc.). Nonpayers can be excluded from many aspects of library service. Whether 'ability-to-pay' is important or not depends on the precise array of charges. Charges should also be set in the context of the objectives of library provision. In addition, 'before a pay or charge system can be instituted there must be an intelligent valid foundation supporting it' (Fikes, 1978, p. 13).

By way of warning, Lunden (1982, p. 471) argues that 'charging fees and accounting for costs require a very conscientious approach to user-orientated services and to public relations'. Moreover, Stayes (1980) notes that the direct library budget is usually a significant understatement of the true costs involved in providing a library service. For example, besides salaries, true costs include building maintenance, charges for heating and lighting, use of the computer centre, materials, business services, building asset costs, administrative overheads, etc. As for the relative contribution of revenue from charges, even in the USA 'despite an intensive search, we were able to locate only one library system that recovered more than 10 per cent of its total costs from fees and only one other that approached a 5 per cent recovery rate (McCarthy *et al.*, 1984, p. 30).

The total cost of UK public libraries is only about 15 pence per head of population a week. Of that amount only 0.78 pence is financed by libraries' own income sources. In its Green Paper *Financing our public library service* (Cm 324, February 1988) the government suggests that English library authorities could more than double their own income from £21.6 m (in 1985/86) to over £50m per annum. This would be about an eighth of total costs.

The government's objectives are to preserve and support the provision of the free basic library service at public expense and at the same time to enlarge the scope for library authorities to generate increased revenues by joint ventures with the private sector and charging for specialised services (Cm 324, para. 1.2).

It is clear that the government is not proposing a radical 'charge for almost everything' approach as advocated in the past by such writers as Herbert (1962), Ilseric (1963), and Harris and Seldon (1976). Rather it is attempting to increase the role of charging on a more discretionary basis by defining the free basic library service, leaving library authorities to themselves decide whether or not to charge for non basic services. Librarians totally opposed to any form (or extension of) charging will see this proposal as only the first step towards a more comprehensive charging system. Others may be willing to judge the proposal on its merits and this is the approach now adopted.

The first task is to define 'basic service'. The Green Paper states that the free basic service should 'provide individuals with access to literature and information which will enable them to play their part in the country's cultural, political and economic affairs; and to promote reading at a time

M

when there is much justified concern about educational standards and literacy' (Cm 324, para. 1.6). Consistent with these laudable objectives, it proposes that the basic service should comprise the borrowing of print materials and provision of reference services for people living, working or in full-time education within a library authority's area.

Charging could be used to finance all other services. Under the 1964 Public Libraries and Museums Act libraries can already levy charges on any person not living, working or in full-time education in the area. They can also charge for use of non print items (including printouts from an electronic database), for notification of the availability of reserved items, for late returns, for supplying book catalogues, etc., and for any facilities in excess of those ordinarily provided. In addition the Green Paper suggests charges for new services such as a premium book-subscription service (for newly published novels and biographies which are available on demand), for services supplied by specialist libraries or by subject-trained librarians, for consultancy services (e.g. on family genealogy, local market research, background research for a book) etc.

Whilst there is no obligation to provide such non basic services, nor to charge for them if provided, the government hopes that library authorities will, in fact, adopt full cost charging for such services. The government's view is that the subsidisation of chargeable services from grant and rate revenues is at the expense of the basic service. In other words, given constrained public finances, they are mutually exclusive and rival. By contrast, the Library Association see many of these non basic services as complementary to basic (print and non print) lending services, so adding to the value of basic provision. It also regards the attempt to distinguish between print and non print materials as unhelpful. The Association's view is that, in addition to the borrowing of print materials and provision of general reference services, free services should also include the lending of new novels and biographies, video tapes, compact discs, other non print items, the inter-library loan system, the provision of subject-specific assistance and expertise and any other services which library professionals consider contribute directly to the educational and cultural functions of the library or which relate to the social economic and recreational needs of library users. These could include children's story-telling sessions, meetings, exhibitions, events, etc. and especially those tailored to the needs of disadvantaged groups, mentally and physically handicapped people and ethnic minority groups. 'The question of charges should be left to the discretion of the appropriate librarians when determining their local priorities' (Library Association, 1987, p. 145).

There is obviously a major disagreement here over the definition of free basic services and other chargeable services. The government is attempting to minimise discretion over the financing (rather than provision) of library services. The Library Association is trying to maximise that discretion. The only area of agreement seems to be the validity of charges for 'publication programmes, client specific information services, consultancy, and the organisation of conferences and other special events' (Library Association, 1987, p. 144). Even here, however, the Library Association does not necessarily recommend full cost charging and where marginal costs (i.e. user-related additional costs) are low then free provision is preferred. This is the case for example for end-user direct database searching on CD-ROM discs, which provide a service comparable to online database searching via an intermediate (librarian) searcher. In the latter case the library's costs are a direct function of time taken so that marginal cost is high for online searching. CD-ROM discs are leased at fixed cost so that the marginal cost of use is near zero. In this case the Library Associations' preference is for a free information service whereas the government's preference is to charge the user.

Given that the Green Paper explicitly recognises the value of public library services, the question is resolved to one of who should pay, library user or (national and local) taxpayer? The answer depends upon how charges affect both the supply and use of particular services. Remembering the confusion between freedom of access and free provision, charges can either stimulate or deter use of library services.

Charging for all existing services with no change in service provision would undoubtedly reduce library usage (on a simple before-and-after basis) resulting in a better quality service (i.e. less congested) for a smaller number of high-income users. The precise impact would depend on the sensitivity of demand to charging which in turn would depend on the characteristics of library users before charges were introduced.

To charge for all services is clearly unrealistic given the considerations discussed earlier. A more realistic approach is to follow suggestions by Linford (1977). He suggests a practical rationale to use when deciding whether or not to charge library patrons for services, materials or whatever. First, libraries should generally not charge for use of materials, facilities or services which are made available for general use, *or* for which patron-specific out-of-pocket costs are not incurred or cannot be identified. Second, any charges to patrons should be limited to those for materials, facilities or services provided for primary or exclusive use by individual patrons *and* for which patron-specific costs are incurred by the library.

Third, libraries should provide, at no charge to patrons, a reasonable level of service which can be said to be fair and effective for most patrons. Fourth, any charges to patrons should be limited to patron-specific costs beyond the subsidised minimum established by each library.

The first of these criteria would appear to entirely exclude charges for library cards and for entrance (A1 and A2 in Table 2). The second of these criteria would appear to exclude anything but nominal charges for the lending of materials (B3 to B12 in Table 2) since they are only temporarily available for exclusive use by individual patrons (i.e. whilst out on loan)

TABLE 2. *List of services that may be charged for, depending on legislation*

A. Access to the use of services
   1. Library card
   2. Entrance (turnstile chage)
 	
B. Lending of materials
   3. Books (rental and subscription)
   4. Periodicals and pamphlets
   5. Films 16 mm and 8 mm
   6. Video tapes
   7. Art prints and paintings
   8. Sound recordings
   9. Sheet music
  10. Toys and games
  11. Film strips and slides
  12. Multi-media kits
	C. Access to information, material and
	     search services
	  13. Reservations and/or notification
	  14. Interlibrary loan
	  15. Reference service (not
	     computer based)
	  16. Computer based reference service
	  17. Bibliographies
	
	D. Lending of audiovisual equipment
	  18. Projectors 16 mm and 8 mm
	  19. Screens
	  20. Overhead and slide projectors
	  21. Record and cassette players
	
	E. Copying services
	  22. Photocopying
	  23. Microform copying
	  24. Printing on-line or off-line from
	     machine-readable databases
	  25. Typewriters
	
	F. Programming and use of buildings
	  26. Programs and events
	  27. Meeting rooms and auditorium

Source: Bassnett (1981).

and the only patron-specific costs incurred by the library are general wear-and-tear costs. Hence a nominal flat-fee could be justified but a study by Leicestershire County Council (reported in Taylor, 1976, pp. 286–290) suggests that administrative costs would be sufficiently high to make such charges impractical. If exclusive use whilst on loan was seen to be a problem the period of loan could be shortened in preference to a charge being levied. The third and fourth criteria would appear to justify some level of subsidy but also permit charges related to costs for most other services (categories C, D, E and F in Table 2).

'It is imperative that librarians clearly distinguish between those activities which are fundamental to the library identity and those services that derive from it' (Gell, 1979b, p. 172). The approach adopted in this paper will be to follow Linford's criteria and to maintain the current policy of not charging for services except where they are specifically designed for the convenience of individual users and which are therefore avoidable without foregoing access to normal library services. These charges could be classified as fees for time-saving services (Van House, 1983, pp. 115–119) which would in fact make libraries more accessible to the extent that many people are deterred from using libraries simply because they 'don't have the time' to do so. Existing users would be undeterred by such a policy and, in fact, may be encouraged to use libraries more intensively by taking advantage of new time-saving services.

By way of a practical example, a library user using reference material could copy out by hand the relevant information. Alternatively that information could be photocopied if the user wished to save time and effort. It is reasonable to charge the library user for the costs of photocopying and possibly, over and above those costs, charge in relation to the benefit gained (approximated by charges levied for private sector photocopying). In fact, the 1956 Copyright Act requires libraries to charge for photocopying costs.

More generally, it has been suggested that 'to charge for a service, some sort of added value must be given' (Biddiscombe, 1988). This recognises the fact that the provision of public services often has private attributes and it may be possible to charge for certain of the purely private value-added aspects of public provision whilst continuing to finance the bulk of service provision through tax revenues. This is a rather more sophisticated approach than that adopted by the Green Paper in attempting to delineate between free basic services and chargeable non basic services. The latter does not allow for varying levels of subsidy between services. This value-added principle will now be applied to a range of library services.

Library membership

The only charge that could be justified is for nonresidents' use of the library. Presumably such use benefits non-resident patrons either because the library is close to their place of work, and therefore more convenient to use than libraries in their own areas, or because this particular library has material unavailable in the non-residents' own library and which would entail delayed access through interlibrary loan. Hence non-residents could be required to pay a library membership fee. The charge would be based on equity grounds, being set at the average contribution by ratepayers to library services and rising in line with that contribution each year (suggested by Bassnett, 1981). According to Leckie (1980) such a charge would appear to be acceptable to both residents and nonresidents but American experience suggests a substantial decline in non residents' use of facilities (WLB, 1981; LJ, 1982). Reciprocal membership arrangements could possibly be used instead of non-resident membership charges, but it is unlikely that reciprocation would be directly offsetting. Central cities, in particular, are likely to have relatively more library use by non-residents who commute into the urban core on a daily basis. Such a membership charge could be efficient, fair and have very low administrative costs. Non-residents would then be entitled to use library services on the same basis as residents. On the basis of the foregoing figures (and assuming about half of expenditures are funded by grant) the membership fee would have averaged about £4 a year in 1986/87.

Book reservation

Library users could be charged to cover the administrative costs of reserving books, etc. and for any subsequent mailing costs if postal notification is used to inform the user of availability of reserved items. This service is purely for the convenience of the user in terms of reducing waiting time (waiting for other library users to finish with the items and to gain priority over other potential users of those items) and dispenses with the need to visit or telephone the library to see if the material is available. It is administratively feasible if users buy stamped reservation cards and fill in the details themselves, as already happens in many libraries.

Extended loan periods

Fines for overdue items are not normally defined as a charge on the basis that they are meant as a deterrent; they are neither related to benefit nor to service provided. However, the library user perceives a fine for overdue items as a form of rental fee for the period in excess of the usual loan period. Hence the distinction between fines and charges is not as clear-cut as is often supposed and it may be possible to redefine fines as a rental charge payable by library users who wish to retain an item for a period in excess of the standard loan period. The rationale for this would be that such an extended loan affords the user a higher standard of service and, in retaining the item, the user is imposing a cost on other library users in reducing the availability of the item and increasing their waiting time. Hence extended loan is both rival and exclusive and, by definition, must be of particular benefit to the user in terms of the convenience of retaining the book for a longer period. The stigma attached to fines could therefore be dispensed with by redefining them as 'extended loan charges' and using them as a positive (rather than a negative) tool of management. The extended loan charge could be progressive, rising more than in proportion to the period of loan, in recognition of the cumulative impact of the reduced availability to other potential users and, given that retention of the item is voluntary, the obviously progressive nature of the benefits received by the user of the item. Administrative feasibility would depend on computerisation of checking-in and checking-out, with charges being calculated automatically upon return of the item. Manual calculation would be costly and cause delays in processing returns.

Increased borrowing facilities

In addition to charging for extended loan periods libraries could also charge users for borrowing more items than normally allowed. The library users' consumption of the service is rationed by administrative means (e.g. limits on the number of books that can be borrowed in a given period), by queueing (e.g. for reference service) or by charging. A user wishing to borrow more items than provided for in the normal standard of service could be allowed to do so, but at a progressive charge reflecting the benefit received by the user, the convenience of having to make less frequent trips to the library to fuel a voracious reading appetite and reflecting either the reduced availability of items afforded to other library users or some of the extra costs imposed on the library in providing a larger stock of material. Administrative feasibility would again depend upon computerisation of the lending process.

Rental of items in heavy demand

Where an item is in particularly heavy short-term demand by adults (e.g. a popular work of fiction) the library may feel unwilling to commit scarce funds to purchasing multiple copies of the title, particularly when it may be purchased at commercial bookstores and when its value is obviously primarily recreational, for example newly published novels and biographies. In such a case the library could purchase multiple copies which would be for rental (as distinct from the usual 'free' loan), This is the premium book subscription service described in the Green Paper. The justification for such a policy would have to be clearly explained to library users to avoid resentment at the use of charges. Ultimately, however, the charge does not have to be paid since the reader could wait to get access to the material once it is no longer 'newly published'; payment of the charge is voluntary. It should be recognised that rationing will occur even if such a scheme is not adopted, although this may be more morally acceptable to users and librarians than explicit rationing by price. An alternative rationing mechanism would be simply to reduce the length of the loan period for these newly published items so that a smaller stock with higher turnover (and charges for extended loan periods) can be maintained.

Inter-library loans (ILLs)

The tradition of free ILLs was based on the moral obligation that librarians felt to share their resources with other libraries and so increase accessibility to users. However DeGennaro (1980) argues that the ILLs service is becoming too important to be continued as a free service. A free ILLs service was feasible as long as it was voluntary and as long as the volume of requests was limited, largely by the inefficiencies of traditional manual location, request and delivery systems. However, computerisation of ILLs location and communication functions through OCLC and other online networks and the growing use of online bibliographic search services have greatly increased the demands on the service (e.g. see LJ,

1980). Requests for ILLs are now received from distant libraries with little affinity to the lending library and which are in competition with the library's own users for use of materials. Hence charges for ILLs may be necessary to compensate the lending library for the cost of the service, to ration demand by price (rather than by administrative means) and to measure the value of the service. If the service is highly valued then user charges will remove financial constraints on ILLs and increase accessibility to the service user by financing expansion of the service (Prentice, 1979).

There could be problems due to variations between libraries in the levels of charges (referred to above) but charges for ILLs are already implemented in certain cases so as to cover postage and other costs. Another justification for charging the user is that time is saved by avoiding the need to visit other libraries in search of the item. Furthermore, users would probably accept as equitable the passing on of charges levied by the source library since it is clear that they are directly responsible for the costs incurred and benefit exclusively from the service. Given the large administrative costs already incurred, the extra administrative burden of requiring payment would be insignificant.

Photocopying and microform copying services

Reference has already been made to the private nature of photocopying. The user is not charged for access to library materials but can reasonably be charged for photocopying services. This is equitable and efficient since the user clearly imposes an additional cost on the library and retains exclusive use of the photocopy. It saves the user the time required to copy the information by hand. Microform copying, unlike photocopying, is usually not on a self-service basis and so the charge should be higher to cover the labour costs involved.

Computer based reference service

User charges can be justified firstly, because this service reduces the user's time in undertaking bibliographic enquiry by computerised rather than by manual means. Second, the computerised search service is of a higher standard than manual searching in providing more sophisticated access to a larger database. Third, the product of an online search is highly customised, being tailored to the user's precise needs and so has added value. Fourth, use of the service has significant, identifiable costs in terms of staff time required to undertake the search and the charge from the search service vendor (which provides the database) to the library. Hence it has been suggested that there would be public acceptance of user charges for use of highly specialised computer search services for the benefit of a very few, many of whom earn money from them (Leckie, 1980).

Even in what appears to be a clear cut case for charging there are those opposed to the idea. 'As more online databases replace print resources, any type of fee for service will become a barrier to the individual's access to essential information' (Kranich, 1980, p. 1048). 'Setting the precedent of information for a fee for charging for online search services has far reaching consequences because the potential of machine readable databases and online technology suggests that electronics will progressively replace paper' (Huston, 1979, p. 1814). In other words such a charge sets a precedent which, once accepted, could see the widespread introduction of charges in tandem with technological advances. 'Further innovations in information services will probably come from the application of technology to the storage, retrieval and dissemination of information. They will have significant and identifiable costs. The products will be highly specific to the individual client's needs. And many will be aimed at making more effective use of the end-user's time' (DeWath, 1981, p. 31).

As noted earlier, opponents of charges argue that information is a public good to which every citizen has a right of access, regardless of ability to pay. However, 'it is important to distinguish between knowledge itself and the various forms in which knowledge is found, e.g. in the mind and in print' (King, 1979, p. 49). Knowledge or information has many of the attributes of a public good being nonrival in consumption and exclusion is very difficult if not impossible. However, copies of manuscripts and of computer printouts are like private goods so that a charge can be justified. 'The service has private good characteristics, the users can be identified and they could hardly be considered a disadvantaged group' (Buckle, 1980, p. 26). Others argue that this service should be incorporated into the generality of free public services (Knapp, 1980).

By way of comparison, charges for online search services are already widespread in America. Lynch (1982b) reports a survey by the American Library Association showing that 72 per cent of publicly supported libraries charge fees to some or all of those using their online search services. The usual practice is to set the user charge so as to cover vendor bills. Three quarters of those libraries so charging include the cost of communication, connect time and off line printing in their fees. Only 14 per cent charge for the searchers' time, 12 per cent for general operating expenditures and overheads and 4 per cent for start up costs, for example costs of terminals, telephones, manuals and staff training. There is a general view that public funds may be used to finance the costs of making the service available to all (particularly start up and overhead costs) but that private funds should be used to cover those direct costs related to a service from which one person benefits (communication charges, connect time and offline printing).

Initially this service was viewed entirely as an add-on service, but the number of indexes available *only* on online is increasing so that it is now an essential component of the totality of library services. In initially viewing this service as an add-on facility, libraries were not averse to charging, users valued the service highly and charges (passed on from search vendors) were easily understood and easy to administer. In addition, it was thought that libraries could only absorb a gradual increase in the number of searches provided, given current financial constraints. In fact the service expanded rapidly because of the users' willingness to pay for the service as it provides dramatically improved access to information. Furthermore, the uncertainty with respect to costs also encouraged charges for the variable costs of online and searcher time. Libraries were more willing to cover the predictable fixed costs of training fees, terminals and manuals from their operating budgets (Lynch, 1982a). Charging for such direct costs was also seen as acceptable in that it does not 'exploit' the user, i.e. the charge is not a function of benefit received from the service and hence not a function of demand.

This approach also encouraged expansion of the service in which libraries were keen to be seen to participate. In particular they were keen to fully exploit available technologies in providing a full and professional service to library patrons (both actual and potential) in comparison with information services provided by corporate libraries and information brokers (Maranjian and Boss, 1980; Felicetti, 1979). 'With the advent of the commercial computer-based data banks a lot of the information business is being eroded away from libraries' (Kibirige, 1983, p. 94). Hence 'the only real alternatives to charging fees appear to be to cut back still further on existing services or to discontinue online services altogether. Faced with choices such as these the question to be answered will not be whether to charge but rather how much to charge for online searching' (Cogswell, 1978, p. 278).

This assumes that libraries should provide such a service. However, 'it is not obvious that online information retrieval service should necessarily be provided by public libraries. This service has the characteristic of a private good which enables it to be provided by the private sector. In view of its expertise in the field of information services, however, the library profession has a responsibility to ensure that the service provided is adequate, easily accessible, and avoids unnecessary duplication' (Buckle, 1980, p. 27).

It should, however, be recognised that provision of such a chargeable service does affect the orientation of other library services. 'In the libraries where fee charging was an established policy, the librarians *were* more responsive to their online search service clients' (Neilson, 1987, p. 35). Cooper and DeWath (1977) found that it took longer to do all the search related tasks when a charge is levied but that the actual searcher time at the terminal declined, presumably in an attempt to minimise charge costs to the patron. 'Shifts in library resources were found to have taken place with the librarian spending relatively more time preparatory to and subsequent to the search and less time at the terminal during the pay period than during the free period (Cooper and DeWath, 1977, p. 304).

Hence there is some evidence that libraries increase the efficiency of charged-for services and that the standard is higher than for a free service. The drawback is that where a fee is charged, librarians undertake more clerical work than when a fee is not charged so that they are less responsive to the totality of service demands. This perhaps suggests a reallocation of purely clerical duties to lower grades of staff. Besides, 'the economics of the new technologies will make it difficult, if not impossible, for many public libraries to offer services at no charge' (Drake, 1984, p. 634).

It is for this reason that computerised reference and information services are the most promising source of additional revenue from charges. The previous seven options discussed are unlikely to raise much revenue in excess of administrative costs. (In these cases charges are primarily a management tool, assessing demand for services.) In some cases value can best be added to basic public information resources by joint enterprise between public libraries and private commercial information brokers. This will usually involve some form of charging to provide the private firm with a return on its investment (PUPLIS, 1987).

It remains to question the nature of the charge. It has been noted that charges are usually set equal to the costs directly imposed by the user. This may be acceptable for bibliographic databases, but Jaervelin (1986) argues it is inappropriate for numeric databases which consituted half of all databases in 1982 and which contain information that can be used directly rather than simply providing bibliographic references which require further searching by the user. For numeric databases 'because information is what is being sold that is what should be charged for. Alternatively, or complementarily, the value added by the online service and/or the query processing costs, should also be charged for, but not connect hours, because that is counter productive' (Jaervelin, 1986, p. 66). Such charges would be a function of demand and relate to benefit received rather than to cost. Charges levied by independent, private sector information brokers could be used as a guide in determining levels of charges. This is realistic given that half of the commercially available databases are in the field of science and technology (Huston, 1979).

CONCLUSIONS

Whilst there are rational grounds for an increased use of charges for library services, the Green Paper adopts too simplistic a division between free basic services and other chargeable services. At best it appears to be a crude and simplistic revenue raising exercise. At worst it could be an attempt to narrow the range and quality of public library services by pricing them beyond the reach of a majority of library users. Taking a more balanced view, it provides the stimulus for renewed debate over the appropriate range of public library services and the mix of public and private financing.

The rationale suggested in this paper would be to charge where added-value services are primarily provided for the personal convenience of the library user, saving the time, expense and effort of searching for materials, checking bibliographies, etc. It may be desirable to distinguish between categories of user, for example business and commercial users, private individuals, societies and clubs (e.g. booking rooms for meetings, etc.), elderly people, unemployed people, students, etc.

A more practical justification of such charges is that without their revenue the library may not be able to make adequate provision of innovative services. This is particularly the case in the current period of fiscal restraint. The alternative to not charging for such services may be no service at all. Hence charges can be used to further the objectives of public library provision in terms of facilitating the provision of a full range of modern library services, not being restricted to a narrow range of traditional services due to lack of finance. Furthermore, such an approach to charging policy would be efficient where costs and benefits incurred by individual library users are of a purely private nature. Charges can also serve as a management tool, indicating which added-value services are demanded.

There will undoubtedly be problems and anomalies to overcome, but in general the careful introduction of charges could be used to promote the wider objectives of library provision. Revenue from charges could not fully finance library services, most of which will continue to be tax-financed. Only certain highly specialised or personalised services could reasonably be charged for and even they will often be partly subsidised, charges possibly only covering direct operating costs. Revenue from charges could support provision of a wider range of partially subsidised, specialised or personalised services compared with a much reduced number of fully subsidised services. In this way the library, the individual and the community all benefit. The library has increased funding to finance expansion (assuming revenue from charges is retained by the library and is in addition to tax-financed support); the individual can choose from a wider array of library services and the community benefits from having a progressive dynamic library service and all the external benefits that it entails.

In practice the choice may not even be between a slowly growing tax-financed service and a more progressive tax and charge-financed service. Even if public libraries make no changes in present operations and policies, use is likely to continue to decline over the long term. Libraries must continue to be innovative and progressive in service provision to increase the productivity of library users' time through provision of specialised and personalised services which can justifiably be financed in part from user charges. Reducing library costs by shifting activities from library staff on to individual users is not a feasible long term solution to constrained tax finances. It will merely lead to a deterioration of library patronage, particularly for informational services, leaving public libraries concentrated on the traditional functions of lending, archiving and holding out-of-print items.

Adoption of a charging policy based on the considerations noted above would allow library users to have more influence on the standard and type of service afforded to them by the library. For example, users could effectively determine their own borrowing requirements in terms of types of material (newly published items), number of items (charges being levied on items in excess of the standard number) and length of loan period (charges for extended loan periods). Libraries would, however, continue to make a much wider range of provision than that dictated by the demands of a majority of users. Such charges should be seen as aids to management as much as revenue raisers.

To some extent the increased use of charges is inevitable as traditional library delivery systems are replaced by new formats. For example, the development of document delivery systems allows the instantaneous provision of copies of journal articles on demand and the direct costs can be passed on to the user. Also, as computer-based bibliographic services expand, libraries will be able to justify passing on the database and operating costs to the user. If such costs are not passed on the library will find it cannot afford the increasing costs of developing information series and delivery systems, particularly as tax-based finance is tightly constrained. The increasing sophistication of reference services, in terms of their range and automation, provides users with a much improved service at a greater monetary cost but at a reduced non-monetary cost (i.e. time) than earlier service delivery methods.

Charges for the new and innovative added-value services directed specifically at individual users could (as the Green Paper suggests) lead to improvements in service. However, given constrained resources, the government may have to provide pump-priming funds before new kinds of information services can be developed. Poor public library services are more a result of constraints on public expenditure than they are of absent market forces. The judicious use of charges for added-value services can lead to service improvements but they are not a panacea for the current problems of public libraries.

ACKNOWLEDGEMENTS

This paper is based on research undertaken at the Centre for Urban and Community Studies, University of Toronto, during the period May to August 1987, supported by The Public Finance Foundation, The Leverhulme Trust, The Carnegie Trust for the Universities of Scotland and The British Academy.

REFERENCES

Bailey, S. J. (1986) 'Paying for local government: charging for services', *Public Administration,* Vol. 64 No. 4, Winter, pp. 401–419.

Bassnet, P. J. (1981) 'Implications: charges for public library services', *Canadian Library Journal,* Vol. 38, April, pp. 57–63.

Berry, J. (1976) 'Double taxation', *Library Journal,* Vol. 101 No. 20, November, p. 2321.

Berry J. (1982) 'How to lose (or win) an election' (Charge or not charge, library fines as in Albuquerque) (Editorial), *Library Journal* Vol. 107, 15 May, p. 921.

Biddiscombe, R. (1988) 'The academic dilemma', *Proceedings of a British Institute of Managers Conference* held at the City Conference Centre, London, 26 May.

Blake, F. M. and Perlmutter, E. L. (1977) 'The rush to user fees: alternative proposals', *Library Journal* Vol 102 No. 17, 1 October, pp. 2005–8.

Buckle, R. A. (1980) 'User charges for library services', *New Zealand Libraries,* Vol. 43, June 1980, pp. 25–27; Discussion Vol. 43, September, p. 50.

Casper, C. A. (1978) 'Estimating the demand for library services', *American Society of Information Science Journal,* Vol. 29 No. 5, September, pp. 232–237.

Casper, C. A. (1979) 'Pricing policy for library services', *American Society of Information Science Journal,* Vol. 30 No. 5, September, pp. 304–309.

Cm 324 (1988) *Financing our public library service: four subjects for debate,* London: HMSO.

Cogswell, J. A. (1978) 'On-line search services: implications for libraries and library users', *College and Research Libraries,* Vol. 39, J u Iy, p. 278.

Cooper, M. D. and DeWath, N. A. (1977) 'The effect of user fees on the cost of on-line searching in libraries', *Journal of Library Automation,* Vol. 10 No. 4, December, pp. 304–319.

Crompton, J. L. and Bonk, S. (1980) 'Pricing objectives for public library services', *Public Library Quarterly,* Vol. 2 No. 1, Spring, pp. 5–22.

De Gennaro, R. (1975) 'Pay libraries and user charges', *Library Journal,* 15 February, pp. 363–367.

De Gennaro, R. (1980) 'Resource sharing in a network environment', *Library Journal,* Vol. 105, 1 February, pp. 353–5.

DeWath, N. V. (1981) 'Fees for on-line bibliographic search services in publicly-supported libraries', *Library Research,* Vol. 3, Spring, pp. 29–45.

Dougherty, R. M. (1979) 'Fees and subsidies', *Journal of Academic Librarianship,* Vol. 5, July, p. 123.

Drake, M. (1984) 'User fees: aid or obstacle to access', *Wilson Library Bulletin*, Vol. 58 No. 9, May, pp. 623–635.

Felicetti, B. W. (1979) 'Information for fee and information for free: the information broker and the public librarian', *Public Library Quarterly*, Vol. 1, Spring, pp. 18–20.

Fikes, R. (1978) 'User charges: a debate in search of a premise', *News Notes of California Libraries*, Vol. 73 No. 2, Spring, pp. 11–14.

Gell, M. K. (1979a) 'User fees I: the economic argument', *Library Journal*, 1 January, pp. 19–23.

Gell, M. K. (1979b) 'User fees II: the library response', *Library Journal*, 15 January, pp. 170–173.

Harris, R. and Seldon, A. (1976) 'Pricing or taxing' *Hobart Paper No. 71*, Institute of Economic Affairs, pp. 24–25.

Herbert, A. P. (1962) 'Libraries: free for all?', *Hobart Paper No. 19*, Institute of Economic Affairs.

Hicks, D. A. (1980) 'Diversifying fiscal support by pricing public library services: a policy impact analysis', *Library Quarterly*, Vol. 50, October, pp. 453–474.

Huston, M. M. (1979) 'Fee or free: the effect of charging on information demand', *Library Journal*, Vol. 104, 15 September, pp. 1811–14.

Iliseric, A. R. (1963) 'Relief for ratepayers', *Institute of Economic Affairs*, p. 48.

Jaervelin, K. (1986) 'A straightforward method for advance estimation of user charges for information in numeric databases' *Journal of Documentation*, Vol.42 No. 2, June, pp. 65–83.

Kibirige, H. M. (1983) *The information dilemma: a critical analysis of information pricing and the fees controversy*, pp. 93–104, London: Greenwood Press.

King, D. W. (1979) 'Pricing policies in academic libraries', *Library Trends*, Vol. 28, Summer, pp. 47–62.

Knapp, S. D. (1980) 'Beyond fee or free', RQ, Vol. 20, Winter, pp. 117–120.

Koefoed, I. (1981) 'All library service should be free of charge', *Scandinavian Public Library Quarterly*, Vol. 14 No. 3, Winter, pp. 82–84.

Kranich, N. (1980) 'Fees for library service: they are not inevitable!', *Library Journal*, Vol. 105 No. 9, 1 May, pp. 1048–51.

Leckie, P. (1980) 'A dangerous quest for certainty: fee for service and the public library', *Canadian Library Journal*, Vol. 37 No. 5, October, pp. 317–318.

Library Association (1979) 'The case against charges', *Library Association Record*, Vol. 81 No. 9, September, pp.431–433.

Library Association (1987) 'Public and private sector relationships: LA guidelines', *Library Association Record*, Vol. 89 No. 3, March, pp. 142–145.

Linford, J. (1977) 'To charge or not to charge: a rationale', *Library Journal*, Vol. 102 No. 17, 1 October, pp. 2009–10.

LJ (1980) 'Columbus to charge for ILL' Library Journal, Vol. 105, 1 April, p. 767.

LJ (1982) 'State/county pact provides $$ to make Denver public fee free', *Library Journal*, Vol. 107, 1 November, p. 2034.

Lunden, E. (1982) 'Library as a business: Conference on fee-based research in academic libraries finds cost recovery mandatory in serving off-campus users', *American Libraries*, Vol. 13, July, pp. 471–472.

Lynch, M. J. (1982a) 'Financing online services', RQ, Vol. 21 No. 3, Spring, pp. 223–226.

Lynch, M. J. (1982b) 'Libraries embrace online search fees', *American Libraries*, Vol. 13, March, p. 174.

McCarthy, K. *et al.* (1984) *Exploring benefit based finance for local government services: must user charges harm the disadvantaged?*, US Department of Health and Human Services, July, Washington DC.

McMullen, H. L. (1978) 'History of charging for services in American libraries that have traditionally been free', In *Charging for computer-based reference services,* Chicago: Reference and Adult Services Division American Library Association, pp. 3–16.

Maranjian, L. and Boss, R. W. (1980) *Fee-based information services: a study of a growing industry,* New York; Bowker.

Neilson, B. (1987) 'Do user fees affect searcher behaviour?', In B. F. Pasqualini (ed.) *Dollars and sense: implications of the new online technology for managing the library,* Chicago and London: American Library Association.

Prentice, A. E. (1979) 'Money from within the library', *Public Library Quarterly,* Vol. 1 No. 2, Summer, pp. 129–137.

PUPLIS (1987) *'Joint enterprise: roles and relationships of the public and private sectors in the provision of library and information services,* (PUPLIS), Office of Arts and Libraries, Library Information Series No. 16, London: HMSO.

Rettig, J. (1981) 'Rights, resolutions, fees, and reality', *Library Journal,* Vol. 106, 1 February, pp. 301–304.

Rice, J. G. Jr. (1979) 'Fee or not to fee', *Wilson Library Bulletin,* Vol. 53, May, pp. 658–659.

Ronnie, M. A. (1984) 'User charges in public libraries', *New Zealand Libraries,* Vol. 44 No. 6, June, pp. 99–101.

Skrzeszewski, S. (1985) 'User fees: the time has come to face the issue', *Canadian Library Journal,* Vol. 42 No. 3, June, pp. 137–141.

Smith, J. (1981) 'A conflict of values: charges in the publicly funded library', *Journal of Librarianship,* Vol. 13 No. 1, January, pp. 1–8.

Stayes, S. (1980) 'What does it really cost to run your library?', *Journal of Library Administration,* Vol. 1 No. 2, Summer, pp. 1–10.

Stoakley, R. (1977) 'Why should users pay twice?', *Library Association Record,* Vol. 79 No. 4, pp. 170 and 185.

Taylor, L. J. (1976) 'A Librarian's Handbook Vol. 1', *Library Association,* pp. 286–290.

Taylor, L. J. (1980) 'A Librarian's Handbook Vol. 2', *Library Association,* pp. 420–429.

Van House, N. A., (1983) *Public library user fees: the use and finance of public libraries* (Contributions in Librarianship and Information Science, No. 43), Westport, Connecticut and London, England: Greenwood Press.

Waldhart, T. J. and Bellardo, T. (1979) 'User fees in public funded libraries', *Advances in Librarianship,* Vol. 9, pp. 31–61, Academic Press.

WLB (1981) 'Denver nonresidents to pay fees' *Wilson Library Bulletin,* Vol. 56, December, pp. 253–254.

The Privatizing of Government Information – Economic Considerations

Calvin A. Kent

Director, Center for Private Enterprise,
Baylor University, Waco, TX 76798, USA

ABSTRACT

This article discusses the privatization of government information. It begins by delineating the cases for and against privatization and the various forms that privatization can and has taken, both in the United States and in other countries. The theory behind the government's provision of information services is presented. It concludes that the economic case for government activity in the information services area is to be found in the concept of merit goods. Since government information is a merit good providing external benefits that the market will not consider, government activity is justified. Major studies and positions taken regarding the privatization of government information are evaluated, including those of the National Commission on Libraries and Information Science and the Information Institute of America. A critique of the current government policy as contained in OMB Circular A–130 is provided. Finally, the article presents 10 conclusions and recommendations for further action and discussion.

The last decade has seen an increased interest on the part of governments, both in the United States and worldwide, in the privatizing of government activities. Privatization is viewed as a means of reducing costs, increasing efficiency, and better satisfying consumer demand. In 1987, President Reagan created a 12-member commission that reported in March 1988[1] on ways to turn over parts of the government to the private sector. The President's Commission made no recommendations regarding privatizing government information. Budget Director James Miller has indicated that the administration is considering proposals to privatize a wide range of federal activities such as the postal service, prisons, customs service, tax courts, veterans health care services, Coast Guard, National Institutes of Health, Amtrak Passenger Service, and federal wastewater treatment facilities.[2] In the past years there has been a trend toward increased privatization of government information which has been a concern to some[3] and hailed by others.[4]

The purposes of this article are: a) to discuss the concept of privatization: what is it? what forms does it take? what are its claimed advantages; b) to discuss the economic theory of privatization: when should government provide goods or services in lieu of, or in competition with, the private sector; and c) to apply the theory of privatization to the current controversy between government and private firms in the information industry.

THE THEORY OF PRIVATIZATION

Privatization is a concept without precise definition. It covers a wide range of governmental activities which can be turned over, in total or in part, to the private sector. In nations such as Britain, privatization has meant the selling off of government enterprises to the private sector. Madsen Pirie has noted at least nine variants employed in Britain for privatizing state-owned industries:[5]

Selling a profitable operation to the private sector.

Selling profitable parts of an otherwise unprofitable public operation.

Selling controlling interest (51 per cent) of the operation to the public while the government maintains a strong minority position.

Selling the operation to its employees.

Giving the enterprise away to its employees or customers at either zero or below market price.

Privatizing financing under which user fees are charged by the government operation at a sufficiently high level to cover costs.

Contracting with the private sector. The operation is still publicly funded, but is privately produced.

Dilution of public ownership. Private capital is used to finance new projects with the private sector replacing public ownership over time.

Creating 'bolt holes', which removes government monopolies as providers and allows private individuals to elect whether to purchase from a public or private vendor.

There is relatively little public enterprise in the United States when compared to other nations.[6] Most of the privatization discussion concerns option seven – contracting. Particularly at the state, and local level, more and more governments are contracting public functions to be performed by private contractors.[7]

It is important to make a very clear distinction between the two economic activities that government performs. Either one or both could be privatized. The first government activity is to provide a service. The government takes the responsibility for making sure that the good or service is made available to the citizens within its jurisdiction under the terms, price, and at the service levels considered by the political process to be satisfactory. The second economic activity of government is to produce a service. It may do so either directly through a government enterprise or agency, or indirectly by contracting with the private sector.

Kolderie has developed a very useful four-part taxonomy to explain the different types of privatization.[8] For purposes of discussion, assume a government decides to provide a library for its constituents. In case one, the government both provides and produces. An example would be a public library, where the government establishes the library, provides the money for its operation and has a specific government agency which runs the library. In this case, neither function is privatized. Most public libraries follow this model, including the Library of Congress and Presidential libraries. Case two is where production is private, but provision is public. The government determines that the library is to be provided, specifies the terms and conditions of that provision and provides the funding, but contracts with a private entity to build and operate the library. In case three, provision is private but production is public. Under this option the government sells a good or service in the marketplace to private buyers. In this case, the government would run and operate the library but would rent its books and materials and sell its services rather than making it available to the public at no charge. Examples of this situation abound in the information industry where private firms purchase or obtain from the government the information they use for their databases or include in their reports and studies. An example would be the National Technical Information Service (NTIS). Kolderie's case four has both functions private. In this situation, a private firm builds and maintains the library and sells its services in the market. This situation describes private video stores and many law libraries.

The privatization debate in the USA focuses primarily on cases two and three. The questions which this case presents are what information should be generated, on what terms should it be made available to private users, and what type of packaging of information services should the public producer provide in competition with private organizations.

THE RATIONALE FOR PRIVATIZATION

The rationale for privatization is based on four economic principles:

1. Those who want the goods or services provided by the government should pay the full cost of having those goods and services provided for them.
2. Production in the private sector is governed by competition and is, therefore, likely to be more efficient and less costly than government production.
3. The consumer is likely to be more satisfied when presented with a variety of alternative providers of services from which to choose.
4. The innovative genius of the entrepreneur will provide new and innovative service delivery systems and technologies.

Each of these contentions deserves elaboration.

FULL COST PRICING

Those who support privatization of government activities contend that public agencies have cultivated support for public provision by under-charging for what they provide. People like low rates for water and sewage. They resist increased rates for garbage collection and are most vigorous in advocating expansion of what appears to be free or low-cost governmental services for which they are not fully charged. This resistance is particularly intense for essential services which must be used regardless of the cost.

Waters mentions three reasons why government services tend to be underpriced.[9]

1. Current government accounting systems do not adequately assign the cost of capital to government enterprises. A private firm must either borrow or use equity financing (the selling of shares) to raise money for its start-up and continued expansion. Both interest and depreciation are then part of the cost that a private firm must recover with the fees that it charges. These capital costs are rarely calculated or allocated to projects in the public sector.

2. General overhead costs are rarely allocated to specific governmental functions. Although there are techniques for doing this, the widespread practice in government is to charge administrative and other overhead expenses to some general expense account without assigning the cost to a specific government activity.

3. The government agency has no real concept of what market demand is for what is being provided. Since there are not competitive price signals, consumers use the government service at whatever price the government is charging. The government has no way to compensate for its lack of information about consumer demand. The tendency is to charge a low fee while subsidizing the service from general revenues. A low fee insures high usage that can then be presented to the policy makers as evidence of high demand.

Economics teaches that prices should be set equal to full cost. If they are not, productive resources are diverted from more highly valued options to those that give consumers less satisfaction. Under government provision individuals pay for the service whether they value it little or use it extensively. When specific functions are subsidized out of general taxes, a transfer is made from the taxpaying group to the service recipients. Individual preferences for the good are distorted. Demand appears to be high, when in reality it is merely being subsidized by the low cost provision.

COMPETITION

A second reason advanced for privatization concerns the advantages of competition. Ever since the days of Adam Smith, economists have discussed the role of competition as an *invisible hand* in the marketplace that causes self-seeking producers and consumers to maximize the welfare of all even though they did not intend to so do. Competition is seen as assuring the highest quality, lowest prices, and the introduction of new technology. The private entrepreneur is motivated by the desire for profit to find the best ways of satisfying the variety of consumer demands presented in the marketplace. The entrepreneur knows that by introducing a less costly method he can gain a competitive cost advantage over rivals. Private providers can often lower costs because it is easier for them to hire, transfer, fire, promote, and reward employees as they may not be covered by union contracts or civil service rules. Sometimes a private company can purchase new equipment more quickly by avoiding the bidding process.

It is also true that private firms that operate in more than one governmental jurisdiction are able to spread the costs of major capital purchases over a much wider customer base. They can also more fully utilize the equipment and technology that they have. They can engage in centralized purchasing systems and are more likely to be able to cover the costs of management information systems and training programs for their employees.

The government agency does not face competition and is motivated primarily by the desires for security and expansion.[10] Prestige and power are both related to the size of an agency's budget and the number of its employees, not to how well the consumer has been satisfied or how efficiently the service is provided. For that reason, it is contended that government provision of goods and services mitigates against economic efficiency.

CONSUMER SATISFACTION

In the market, if a consumer is dissatisfied with either price or quality, the consumer can turn to another provider. Consumers' preferences and tastes vary widely. A market economy is structured to accommodate these variations in tastes and desires for service levels. By casting dollar votes in the market, consumers tell producers what variety they desire. The political process does not reflect this variety of preferences. The product or service is usually provided in a politically established format that may not reflect consumer tastes.

INNOVATIVE ENTREPRENEURSHIP

There is evidence that the privatizations of local government functions in Europe, the United States, and less developed nations have unleashed innovative creativity on the part of private entrepreneurs. Entrepreneurs have developed new technologies and service delivery systems for functions as diverse as sanitation, mail service, air traffic control, emergency medical service, fire protection, prison systems, schools, mass transit, and park maintenance.[11] There is not the same type of incentive in the government sector. Entrepreneurship does occur in the public sector, but only rarely, as the incentive to innovate (gain to the innovator) is absent. Also, large bureaucracies (both public and private) tend to resist change. One of the unintended but real benefits of the trend towards privatization has been noted by Hatry: 'Competition by the private sector encourages public employees to become more innovative and to improve public employee efficiency'.[12]

One of the major issues in the delivery and production is the extent to which the public presence has discouraged private entrepreneurial activity.

ISSUES IN PRIVATIZATION

The trend towards privatization is not without its critics.[13] Those objections may be grouped as follows:

1. *Unemployment*. Concern over loss of jobs has led to strong opposition from organized labor to privatization.[14] Public enterprises may be overstaffed. The more labor-intensive the function being privatized, the greater the unemployment problem may be. Several governments have dealt with this problem by requiring private contractors to hire existing employees or have assumed the obligation to retrain and relocate those workers whose jobs have disappeared because of the privatization. Even so, it is to be anticipated that those who may lose their jobs will oppose privatization. While the burden of redundant workers in government agencies is reduced through privatization, a new problem may appear in the form of unemployment.

2. *Increased prices*. The consumer may experience an increase in prices due to privatization. While privatization usually results in a more efficient operation, it does not always result in a lower price to the consumer. If the government has been providing a service on a zero or below full-cost basis, changing to private provision may result in a price increase. Butler has commented that contracting as a form of privatization will not necessarily guarantee lower prices because contracting strengthens the public/private coalition, which can lobby for expanded spending on the service.[15]

3. *Lack of capital*. Privatization requires that the private sector be able to mobilize sufficient capital to assume and continue the activity. Both Britain and the United States have achieved a great deal of privatization because these nations are the world's financial capitals and are able to draw on substantial domestic savings and export earnings to raise necessary funds. But functions that are candidates for privatization may not in the short run appear to be financially attractive enough to entice private investors. Thus, the government must either subsidize the

function or see the scope of the service reduced to bring costs in line with revenue.

4. *Loss of control*. There are many who oppose privatization because they believe that when a function is privatized, responsible public control of that function ceases. This loss of control is a concern voiced by the American Library Association.[16] This loss of control manifests itself in two ways. First, only information may be gathered that is profitable, or at least potentially so, by private firms. Other information that serves a useful propose or has a benefit to society at large may not be provided. A second way in which control is lost is by having the private sector decide what information will be available to the general public. This is viewed as private censorship and as antithetical to the ideals of a democratic society. It should be noted, however, that when information is solely in the hands of the government this problem is not absent. Government agencies become the gatekeepers of public information and whether they do or do not exercise that responsibility in a more socially responsible fashion than would private firms is certainly open for debate. This problem can be minimized, if not eliminated, through a well-crafted and rigorously enforced contract.

5. *Competition*. If privatization amounts to nothing more than trading a public monopoly for a private one, little has been accomplished. Much of the benefit claimed for privatization depends upon competition being present to lower prices and to improve product quality. With a private monopoly the customer still faces a sole source arrangement. If privatization results in trading a public monopoly for a private one, then the government has an obligation to regulate that private monopoly in accordance with the public interest. If the government privatizes through a sole, source supplier, it is incumbent that the government entity regulate both the prices and the quality of the service provided. It is also essential that the franchise be of limited duration and the bidding for the franchise be completely open to all possible service providers.

6. *Creaming*. One of the more frequently mentioned complaints about privatization is that it results in the service being provided only for the profitable customers and those who are easiest to serve. This practice is called creaming. In the days before regulation electric utilities creamed their markets by not serving remote areas and not extending lines into low-income sections of a city. Private firms may have an incentive not to service clients who are unlikely to pay or those to whom the cost of providing the service may be high. Kolderie points out that this argument reflects a failure to distinguish between government providing and producing. The government can always require that the service be made available to any and all classes of potential customers at whatever price the government deems to be appropriate. Or, the government may, as has been done in the case of public utility regulation, force the private producer to provide the service at low cost to certain groups of consumers

while collecting above average costs from other groups to pay the difference. This requires that the government be diligent in specifying exactly what it expects from a privatized operation. As a third alternative, the government could subsidize the consumption by target consumer groups.

7. *Interruption of service.* Critics also complain that private organizations are more likely to curtail, interrupt, or cease operations due to circumstances such as financial problems, strikes, or the re-bidding of contracts. In 1987, such a situation slowed the distribution of government documents in microform to depository libraries, which was contracted out to a private sector deliverer. It is surprising to note that this argument is also used by advocates of privatization who claim that such interruptions are less likely under a private system where the private provider can subcontract around work stoppages. In an era in which public unions are becoming more militant, interruptions by public employees may have the same effect, as has been the case in many European nations.

THE ROLE OF GOVERNMENT IN PROVIDING INFORMATION SERVICES

It has become accepted in public finance theory to make the case for government activity in the economy on grounds of market failure.[17] The standard public finance theory begins with the assumption that the free market will produce what consumers want at the lowest possible cost using the most efficient techniques while insuring a stream of innovations as profit-minded entrepreneurs rival each other. But economists are quick to point out that if there are imperfections or failures in the market system, the system does not always produce the salutary results mentioned above. When the system does not operate as the competitive model dictates, it is called market failure and these failures are what give rise to the case for government activity.

There are four failures of the market system that cause government to function in the economy:

Allocation

Government moves resources from the private sector, where they are under the control of market forces, to the public sector, where political decision-making dominates. The government is called upon to do this, as the market will not produce a good or service that the public wants.

Redistribution

Income and/or wealth are redistributed to assure conformity with what society considers a fair or just state of distribution, as opposed to the distribution that results from the market where some individuals will be worth less than others. This involves the process of taxing one group and reducing its disposable income and transferring that income to another group.

Regulation

The market mechanism is usually viewed as being self-regulatory so long as there is sufficient competition and both producers and consumers possess sufficient information upon which to make rational choices. If there is no competition, then there is no assurance that consumers will get what they want at the lowest possible prices or that the most effective production techniques will be used.

It may be necessary for the government to perform its regulatory function when either consumers or producers lack necessary information to make rational decisions or cannot obtain it at a sufficiently low cost. This is the case with some licensing activities. Consumers, given enough time and knowledge, would determine which doctors were qualified, but it is unlikely that they would have either. Licensing is both more certain and cost effective.

Another cause for regulation arises from monopoly when one or a few firms can supply a market at a lower cost than can many, as is the case of public utilities. Since the market force of competition is absent, the government must step in, set rates, and regulate quality of service.

A final justification for regulation exists when there are externalities. An externality is a cost or a benefit that is not reflected in the price the consumer pays. Air pollution is a cost that must be borne by someone, but it lies outside, or is external to, the market. Competition may actually force producers to dump their effluent into the air or water supply as the least costly means of disposal. A positive externality exists when there are benefits that the market does not record. Individuals may wish to have everyone inoculated against a dreaded disease. There are benefits to others than just those who are receiving the inoculations, since the others face a lower possibility of catching the disease and are spared the potential costs involved of paying the medical expenses of those who would otherwise have contracted it.

Stabilization

The economy has fluctuated periodically between periods of recession with unemployment and periods of inflation with full employment. Government should use tax, expenditure, and monetary policy as a means of maintaining high employment and to achieve a reasonable degree of price stability insuring an appropriate rate of economic growth as well as to secure stability in the nation's foreign trade balance. The great contribution of the English economist John Maynard Keynes[18] was to demonstrate that a market system is inherently unstable and government correctives are justified.

The case for government intervention in the information marketplace can be found in both the allocation and regulation functions. So far as the allocation function is concerned, there are certain information services and products that would not be produced in the marketplace at all by profit motivated firms, yet the public desires to have these goods and services available to them. These goods are called by various titles, either public, social, or collective goods.[19] The classic example is the lighthouse. Those who own boats may desire very much to have a lighthouse available to give them information about the dangerous rocks which lie in their paths and to serve as a reference point for navigation. Why would the owners of the boats not pay someone to build and man the lighthouse? The reason is simple. The lighthouse shines for all whether they pay or not. Therefore, all will seek to pay either nothing or very little because there is no way that they can be excluded from the beneficial effects of the light. Each will wait, hoping to free ride on the others.

This simple example illustrates the essential characteristics of public goods. First, public goods are consumed by all people in the same amount at the same time. One boat captain's consumption of the lighthouse's beam does not reduce the amount of light available to others. Economists say that there is no rivalry in the consumption of a public good. One person's consumption of it in no way limits another's. Second, non-payers cannot be excluded from the benefits of a public good, or if they can be excluded, it is at an extremely high expense which would render exclusion economically unjustifiable. Even though all boat owners would benefit from the lighthouse, only some form of collective provision with compulsory payment will make it feasible for the lighthouse to operate.

Government information rarely meets the test of a pure public good. Non-payers can be excluded, usually at a fairly minimal cost. The product is divisible into units that could be sold in the marketplace. The market would provide information services. The economic justification for governmental information generation and distribution must be found elsewhere.

INFORMATION AS A MERIT GOOD

The economic theory that justifies government in the information business can be found in the concept of merit goods.[20] These are goods that the private sector would provide, but in insufficient quantity to satisfy the demands of society. In the market, goods and services are made available to those who are both willing and able to pay for them. This means that those who are either unwilling or unable to pay go without. The market system also requires that consumers pay the full cost associated with the production of the good. If the business is foolhardy enough to price its product below cost then it will either quickly have to raise its price or go out of business. In an attempt to cover costs, businesses raise prices and thus exclude some who might desire or benefit from the product due to an insufficient income.

At first this situation may seem to be a question to be assigned to the redistributive function of government. Raise everyone's income to the point where they can purchase those goods and services which are essential and then leave it to the market to respond to their enhanced incomes. This would not always be the appropriate approach, since some goods or services are deemed by society (as manifested through elected representatives) to be so meritorious because of their positive externalities that all should consume them or at least be able to consume them, as is the case of inoculations mentioned previously. Merely redistributing income so that all could afford the inoculations would not insure that all would be inoculated. Some might choose to spend the money elsewhere. Because of the positive externalities of a healthier society, the reduced threat of disease, and lessened probability of public health expenditures, society may want all to be inoculated.

Herein lies the case for government activity in the area of information services. Certain information may be so vital and so important that society feels access to it should be subsidized so that all can consume. In fact, some information may be deemed so meritorious that society may compel, or at least try to compel, individuals to partake of a minimal amount of it. The latter case describes compulsory public education.

The National Commission on Libraries and Information Science noted that, 'the citizens need ready access to information about our society if our democratic system is to continue to function'.[21] Smith has commented '. . . the concept of selling certain types of information runs counter to the social policy of government information as a public good . . . the policy is firmly officed in the American free educational system, in the belief in academic freedom and information exchange, in the First Amendment guarantee of free speech and in the Freedom of Information laws dealing with government actions'.[22]

Economists express this concept in a more formal way. Figure 1 shows a demand curve for a particular type of information. The market demand curve (D_m) shows the amount that would be purchased in the market at all possible prices by all potential consumers. The market demand curve is downward sloping because at lower prices consumers will purchase more and new consumers will enter the market. Perhaps the most certain law in economics is that more of virtually any commodity will be sold at lower prices.

The market demand curve is the sum of the demand of all consumers in the market reflecting the amounts at all possible prices, but there is a second demand curve, called the social demand curve (D_s), which lies to the right of the first demand curve. That demand curve includes the external benefits to be received by other than the direct consumers. While the individual curves record the benefits that the individual consumers receive, the social

FIGURE 1. Market for information. P_1, X_1 are the price and quantity of information services produced by the market because only the demands of individual consumers are recorded. P_2, X_2 are the price and quantity of information services produced when the external benefits of increased information services to those who are not direct consumers are included also.

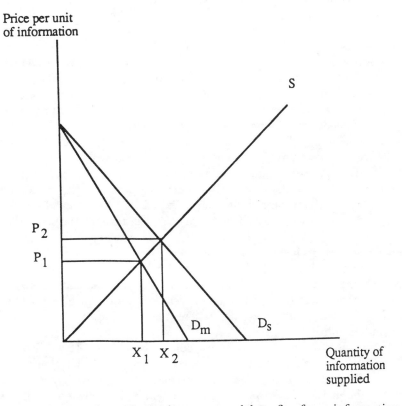

demand curve also reflects those external benefits from information. When positive externalities are present, the total social demand is greater than the sum of all demands of individual consumers. As can be seen from the diagram, if left to the marketplace only X_1 information would be consumed and the price would be P_1. When the external or social benefits are considered, the desired equilibrium would be a higher amount, X_2, which would necessitate a higher price, P_2, to insure provision.

An example will illustrate: economic historians[23] recognize that one of the reasons the United States became a prosperous and economically advanced nation after the American Civil War was the wide dissemination of information to farmers, which was facilitated through the land grant colleges, the agricultural research and experimentation stations, and the system of county agents affiliated with them. Not only was the USA the first nation to attempt to improve scientifically the productivity of farms through systematic research, but it was also the first nation to recognize the benefits to society of having that information as widely distributed as possible. The farmers benefited from the information and would have been willing to have paid something for it, but the nation benefited as well. Higher farm productivity not only meant that Americans were better fed and healthier at a lower cost, it also freed the farm labor force to go to the cities and to participate in the industrial economy.

There is little doubt that today is the information age. A century ago easy access to low-cost information made it possible for advances on the farm to lead to the industrial age and subsequent prosperity. The extent to which information can be generated and disseminated in the next century will determine the economic fate of the nation. Since information is a merit good, one that the market will not produce in sufficient quantity or disseminate widely enough on its own, there is a case that can be made for government activity in the information services area.

Having established that there is a role for government in the provision of information, several formidable questions arise. First, it can be determined with fair precision what individuals' private demands are for information. They reveal these in the marketplace through the prices that they are willing to pay for the information they receive. While it may be known that there is even a greater demand for information (the social demand), there is no way of measuring with any degree of precision just how great that demand is. While it is known that demand curve D_s in the model above exists, there is no way of precisely determining how great the external benefit is, and therefore, where it lies. Both price and quantity are indeterminate.

Thus the political process must replace the market. It will be the political decisionmakers' estimates of the benefits that will determine how much information should be generated and distributed beyond that which the market would provide. It is inevitable that everyone will be unhappy. Those who value information highly will say the government has not gone far enough, and those who value it less will see the government being wasteful and spending excessively. There is a case for government intervention in the market for information, but economics alone cannot define the justifiable scope of that intervention.

The other major question that governmental activity in the area of information raises is, once the government has determined the amount of information that would be supplied, in excess of what the market will generate, how is it to be supplied? Should the government both provide and produce the information? The government could choose to generate the information itself and distribute it through the bureaucratic process. On the other hand, it could subsidize private firms that gather and distribute information, and contractually lower costs and increase availability to the public. As a third alternative, the government could directly subsidize the beneficiaries, as it has done in the case of food stamps and rent subsidies, allowing them to obtain the information while at the same time insuring that their vouchers are only spent on information. Just because there is a role for government in the generation and distribution of information, it cannot be concluded that any one of the three alternatives mentioned above (or a hybrid of them) is the economically preferable way of meeting that objective. As noted later, there is no definitive means which economists can supply to answer these questions.

THE NCLIS RECOMMENDATIONS

In February 1982, the National Commission on Libraries and Information Science (NCLIS) Task Force, composed of representatives from government, not-for-profit organizations, and for-profit organizations, issued a detailed analysis regarding privatization of government information.[24] Seven principles and 24 recommendations to implement those principles were listed. There was nearly unanimous agreement on the principles and on 22 of the 24 recommendations. NCLIS's views can be summarized as follows:

1. The Task Force favored easy and open access to the information that was generated by the federal government. Recognizing that most government information is generated for the use of public decision makers and policy implementers, the task force recognized that this information would have value for users outside of the government. Information is a valuable resource, not only to the government, but to others. Government should insure public access.[25]

2. The Task Force felt that libraries and private organizations (both for-profit and not-for-profit) should be the primary conduits for making information available that the government generates. The Task Force was particularly concerned that ability to pay not create barriers that would deny access to information on the part of potential users. On the other hand, it supported efforts by the private sector to develop and market a multiplicity of information services. The value of those services would be determined by private purchasers in the marketplace.[26]

3. The Task Force saw a leadership rather than a management role for government in the information industry. While the government should foster the use of information as a social and economic resource, its leadership role would be to encourage development by the private sector of information resources, products, and services designed to meet market demand.[27]

4. The Task Force wished to limit direct government intervention in the marketplace for information. While the federal government was not to be arbitrarily excluded from providing information services that were deemed socially desirable, it was felt that the government should not enter the marketplace unless there were clearly defined and compelling reasons for so doing. If the government did enter the marketplace with those services,

those services should be subject to periodic review to insure that continuation was warranted.[28]

On the whole, the Task Force recommendations supported increased privatization of government information, by both non-profit and for-profit entities. At the same time it sought to insure that the government would generate useful information and provide relatively easy and inexpensive access to it through the existing library systems.

The greatest controversy in the Task Force evolved over its third principle: 'The federal government should not provide information products and services and commerce except when there are compelling reasons to do so, then only when it protects the private sector's every opportunity to assume the function(s) commercially'.[29] To implement that principle, several recommendations were advanced. One of these was Recommendation 23, which was the most controversial and passed on a 9–7 vote. It states: 'Do not arbitrarily restrict the federal government from enhancement of information products and services, even if solely to meet the needs of constituencies outside the government itself'.[30] This was adopted over the original wording, which read, 'The federal government should refrain from enhancement of information products and services solely to meet the needs of constituencies outside of the government itself'.[31]

The recommendation directly recognizes that the government may, under certain circumstances, compete with the private sector in the dissemination of information to those not inside the government. The key term here is *arbitrarily restrict*. The implication is that the government is to be restricted, but not arbitrarily, so if there is a compelling reason, however defined, the government could provide information services to those outside government. The majority believed that the review process provided for in other of the Task Force's recommendations would sufficiently restrict the government from unfairly competing with the private sector.

Recommendation 10 was the only other recommendation not unanimously agreed upon. It reads, 'Encourage federal agencies to regard the dissemination of information, especially through the mechanism of the private sector (both for-profit and not-for-profit) as a high priority responsibility'.[32] This recommendation suggested that the government was not to be merely passive but was to actively encourage an interface with private providers of information services. Some of the Task Force members opposed to the recommendation felt that this would merely perpetuate government bureaucracies while others felt that this recommendation was superflous as its intentions were covered in other recommendations.

Other recommendations also tended to support private efforts in the area of government information.[33] The Task Force recommended that the government:

Provide an environment that will enhance competitive forces of the private sector so the market mechanism can be effective in allocating resources in the use of information and directing innovation into market determined areas. (Recommendation 1)

Encourage the setting and use of voluntary standards which do not inhibit the further development of innovative information, products, and services. (Recommendation 5)

Conduct a periodic economic assessment of the impact of federal government information products and services. (Recommendation 9)

Identify and evaluate alternatives to existing federal information dissemination services. (Recommendation 11)

Identify and eliminate legal and regulatory barriers to the introduction of new information, products, and services. (Recommendation 13)

Encourage private enterprise to add value to government information, that is, to repackage it, to provide further processing services, and otherwise enhance the information so that it may be sold at a profit. (Recommendation 14)

Provide incentives to existing organizations, such as libraries and book stores, that will encourage them to expand their activities in the dissemination of governmentally distributed information. (Recommendation 15)

Establish procedures which will create a realistic opportunity for private sector involvement in the planning process for information activities. (Recommendation 16)

Involve the private sector in the process of formulating federal standards relating to information activities. (Recommendation 17)

The Commission also provided four specific recommendations that were designed to help determine what the compelling reasons would be which would allow the government to provide information services to parties outside the government. These were:

1. Announce plans sufficiently ahead of time to provide an opportunity for private sector involvement when a government agency, for reasons it regards as compelling, should plan to develop or market an information product, or service. (Recommendation 19)

2. Review and approve before implementation any plans for the government to develop and/or market an information product or service, the review to be carried out by an agency appropriate to the branch of government (such as OMB, GAO, and CBO). (Recommendation 20)

3. Include an information impact and cost analysis as part of the process of review, evaluation, and approval of any plans for the government to

develop and/or market an information product or service, the analysis to cover economic and social effects; effects on any existing products or services; effects on potential products and services; an evaluation of the benefits to the public. (Recommendation 21)

4. Review periodically to evaluate the desirability of continuation of any product or service as a governmental activity. (Recommendation 22)[34]

Taken together these recommendations were designed to insure that there would be adequate opportunity for the private sector to make its input before any decisions were made on the provision of government information services prior to their being instituted. These would reduce the uncertainties to private vendors in making investments in information services that might later become redundant and unprofitable should the government produce a competing or substitute product. In addition, the economic burden of proof would be transferred to the government to demonstrate that there were compelling reasons why the service should be offered to nongovernment constituencies and that the private sector was not capable of meeting or was unwilling to meet the needs.

THE POSITION OF THE PRIVATE SECTOR

Nongovernmental organizations are concerned about government activities in the area of information production and dissemination. This is not surprising since the information industry now generates some $400 billion a year in income.[35] The Information Industry Association (IIA) represents over 500 firms involved in the production and dissemination of information products and services, often in direct competition with the government. In 1983, the IIA issued a policy statement.[36] It outlines three basic concerns about government involvement in the information marketplace and makes proposals for procedures that the government should follow. The focus of the industry's effort was to encourage the Office of Management and Budget to develop a policy on federal information management. The three problems which were of concern to IIA were: no single policy regulating government information activities and when policies did exist they were often vague and inconsistent; the detrimental effects of unfair government competition, principally in the dissemination of information; and the prices the government charged for information products and services which were below cost, preempting private activity.

Lack of Policy

In its point about the lack of consistent government policy regarding the pricing of information, the IIA cites the conflict in legislation regarding the fees to be charged for users of government information. The statute authorizing the Government Printing Office provides authority for charging for publications sold '. . . the price . . . shall be based on the cost as determined by the public printer plus 50 per cent',[37] while at the same time, intermediate products in the printing process are to be sold 'at a price not to exceed the cost of composition, the metal and making to the government plus 10 per cent'.[38]

On the other hand, the National Archives authorization allows the administrator to charge 'a fee not in excess of 10 per cent above the cost of expenses for making or authenticating copies or reproduction of materials transferred to his custody'.[39] By way of contrast, since it was established in 1901 the National Bureau of Standards (NBS) has been authorized to charge 'a reasonable fee according to a schedule submitted by the director and approved by the Secretary of the Treasury'.[40] In 1932 that provision was amended to read that nongovernmental recipients of NBS Services should be charged 'a fee sufficient in each case to compensate the National Bureau of Standards for the entire cost of services rendered'.[41] Similar language can be found in the legislation authorizing the Bureau of Labor Statistics, the National Technical Information Service, and the National Library of Medicine. Suffice it to say that the complaint of the industry seems justified that the government has never established a uniform comprehensive policy regarding the pricing of government information.

Competition with the Private Sector

It has become the policy of the government, as stated by the Office of Management and Budget, not to compete with the private sector.

In the process of governing, the government should not compete with its citizens. The competitive enterprise system characterized by individual freedom and initiative is the primary source of national strength. In recognition of this principle it has been, and continues to be, the general policy of the government to rely on commercial sources to supply the products and services the government needs.[42]

In keeping with this general philosophical position, the IIA has suggested that the government not be allowed to develop products or services that duplicate those available in the private sector. This is particularly true in the area of information dissemination where the government has disseminated information in a format that competed with already existing products developed by private industry. Among the numerous examples of alleged unfair competition cited by the industry is the GPO's distribution of documents to depository libraries in free microform, thus substantially reducing the potential market for the private producer, Congressional Information Service, Inc. The Office of the *Federal Register* distributed the *Federal Register* on a daily basis in a microform edition at a price approximately 40 per cent less than the paper edition in direct competition with several private publishers of the *Federal Register* in microform format. After announcing that it would not be able to produce a file based on the 1980 census and after a private company announced that it would make the investment necessary to produce the file, the Census Bureau reversed its decision and made the file available, even though the private firm offered to make the file available to the entire federal government at no cost.[43] The position of the IIA on this issue is unequivocal.

Government should not develop and disseminate new information products, or services that compete with all of those already available from or planned by, or which could be provided by, private sector sources, nor should new formats for existing government information, products or services be developed by the government when private sector sources are equipped to offer or are already offering such formats.[44]

The IIA also called upon the government to periodically review government information services currently being offered to make sure that their continued production and dissemination are not being done in a way that would diminish potential competition with the private sector. The IIA is concerned that private firms not make investments in new methods of disseminating information without some assurance that the government will not, at a future date, undercut those efforts by issuing duplicate services at lower costs. The IIA proposal was that the government turn to the private sector first, and that public agencies be required to provide public notice of their intention to develop or discontinue an information product or service so that the industry could comment. The IIA does believe the government might provide new information products, or services when there is a 'genuine, demonstrable and critical need for the product and that the private sector is not now providing or is not capable of providing'.[45] When this situation occurs, the IIA recommends that a four-step process be followed. The government should encourage the private sector to meet the need; provide secondary inducements to the private sector to meet the need (subsidies, tax credits, etc.); contract out with the private sector to provide the product or service; and only as a last resort, produce the information product or service itself, in a way and at a price that keeps competition with the private sector to a minimum.

The industry's position is that the private sector has a distinct comparative advantage in the production and dissemination of information since it can disseminate the information more quickly and in a variety of formats designed specifically to meet the various needs of the consuming public.

The Pricing Issue

The information industry has also been very concerned about the pricing policies followed by government. The IIA's basic position is that all government information and products should be priced to recover all of the costs associated with developing, producing, and disseminating the information. This is particularly true for information services that compete with the private sector. A price less than the full cost is viewed by the industry as a barrier to potential private entrants into the field. The posture of the IIA is that users of information should be free to choose who will provide them with any information service, but that if the government is subsidizing the cost or charging a price that does not capture all the cost of providing a service the ability of the market to efficiently allocate resources will be adversely affected. A government price that is below cost keeps private sector participants out of the market, since in order to compete the industry would have to charge a price below cost. From an economic standpoint the industry is correct when it contends that a government subsidized price sends a signal to the users of information that the information is less valuable than it really is. This situation also makes it difficult for private sector firms to pursue full cost recovery pricing policies. In defining full cost, the IIA advocated this definition:

The term 'full cost' includes the direct and indirect costs (including overhead), applying generally accepted cost accounting principles to the United States associated with (i) the administrative and intellectual preparation of information products; (ii) the creation and maintenance of systems for the storage, retrieval and dissemination of these products, (iii) the storage and retrieval of these products; and (iv) the dissemination of these products.[46]

The industry recognizes that such full-cost pricing may create barriers to some individuals whose financial means would not allow them to purchase or use the information. However, the IIA believes that government policy should be to devise ways to aid those meritorious users with low ability to pay through subsidies or credits rather than lowering the price of information to all users regardless of their financial means.

CURRENT GOVERNMENT POLICY

The current policy regarding privatization of government information is contained in OMB Circular A–130, which was issued on December 24, 1985. The Office of Management and Budget has interpreted the Paperwork Reduction Act of 1980 as placing the responsibility for developing a federal information policy.[47] This circular only covers information generated by the executive branch of the government and executive agencies. It does not apply to the Congress, the federal courts, or the agencies that appertain to them. As a result, a consistent and comprehensive policy for all government information has not yet been developed. Prior to the issuance of this circular the OMB's efforts had been primarily focused on information resources management, including technological aspects of information, in addition to the sharing of information and technology between government units. Circular A–130 includes these concerns but goes well beyond them.

The circular supersedes five previous OMB circulars that have little to do with the question of privatization. It was the intention of Circular A–130 to provide an overall policy framework for management of federal information resources. The major privatization provisions of Circular A–130 can be distilled into several major topics.

How should the government's role as a producer and disseminator of information be balanced against the private sector's willingness and ability to perform these functions?

How should the cost issues raised by the Congressional mandate to minimize the cost of government information activities while maximizing the usefulness of government information be answered?

Who should be responsible for the establishment of an agency's information management practices?

The circular recognizes the value of government information. 'Government information is a valuable resource . . . the free flow of information from the government to its citizens and vice versa is essential to a democratic society'.[48] At the same time, the circular strongly advocates privatization:

Certain functions are inherently governmental in nature being so intimately related to the public interest as to mandate performance by federal employees. The government should look first to private sources where available to provide the commercial goods and services needed by the government to act on the public's behalf, particularly when cost comparisons indicate the private performance will be the most economical.[49]

The circular states that government agencies are to generate and disseminate information only when they can do so at a lower cost than what could be accomplished in the private sector. The OMB requirement that the federal agencies rely on the private sector as much as possible for the provision of government information services is detailed in the circular. 'Agencies shall . . . disseminate such government information, products and services . . . in the manner most cost-effective for the government, including placing maximum feasible reliance on the private sector for the dissemination of products and services in accordance with OMB Circular A–76.'[50] The circular further provides for agencies not to duplicate information systems and services that are available either from other governmental agencies or from the private sector.

It is also the responsibility of each agency to publish its intent to either initiate or terminate any information product or service.[51] The purpose of this notice is to allow the private sector or other government agencies to comment as to whether or not there is a need for this product or service so as to avoid duplication. This requirement is only applicable to 'significant' products or services. Which products are significant is left to the discretion of the agency head.

Circular A–130's guidelines regarding cost recovery and user fees are unclear, at best. Agencies are to recover the costs of generation and dissemination where appropriate. The OMB discusses those situations where the government is the sole possessor and supplier of certain information which has commercial value.[52] If the specific users of information can be identified as receiving value, they should be subject to user charges. Whether or not user charges are appropriate depends in principle on whether identifiable recipients will receive special benefits for the information products, or services.[53] The circular does not define what those special benefits are.

To further compound the confusion, A–130 requires that 'agencies must balance the requirement to establish user charges and the level of fees charged against other policy, specifically the proper performance of agency functions and the need to insure that information, products, and services reach the public for whom they were intended'.[54] If user fees inhibit the agency's responsibility to generate and disseminate information, then the user charges may be properly reduced or eliminated. These guidelines are sufficiently vague to make them virtually non-usable. The circular allows discretion to the agency heads who are given the sole responsibility for making such determinations.

The circular also contains a discussion of the recovery of those costs associated with the generation and dissemination of government information. Full costs are to be charged to all users including other government agencies when they make use of information generated or disseminated elsewhere within the federal structure. Full costs are defined to mean 'all significant expenses incurred in the operation of an information technology facility'.[55] This includes:

Personnel salaries and benefits
Equipment, including depreciation
Software
Supplies
Contracted services
Space occupancy charges
Intra- and interagency support services.[56]

The section on cost recovery is unsatisfactory, as it does not address the issue raised above about what the appropriate charge should be by a government agency for information generated for its own use or for the use of another agency. An economic case can be made that if the information is for the making or execution of public policy, then the full costs of generating the information should be charged to the agency or agencies making use of it. Since the initial costs of generating and disseminating the information are fully covered, the only costs that are appropriate to charge to the general public are the additional, marginal, or incremental costs associated with that dissemination. The full costs of the method of dissemination to nongovernmental users including extra copies should be covered in any charges levied, but not the original cost of generation.

While the industry tends to resist any government provision of information services and advocates government subsidization of the private sector rather than generating the information in-house, many of the recommendations of the IIA have been adopted. The IIA supported the concept of public notice in advance of commencing or terminating information products or services, but Circular A–130 does not close the door on further contention in this area. The circular only requires that advance notice be given in the event of significant products or services, leaving it to the agency head to determine which products and services are significant. Also, the giving of notice in no way prohibits the agency from developing the new information or dissemination service.

While the IIA would have required all government information dissemination programs be enacted with sunset provisions to terminate them if they were not specifically reauthorized after congressional review, this suggestion was not adopted. Circular A–130 strongly supports the depository library system and leaves the decision as to whether or not a program should or should not continue in the hands of the head of the appropriate agency. It can be predicted that controversy in this area will continue as the industry favors less use of the depository system and more direct sale such as done through NTIS.

While Circular A–130 has answered many of the questions raised by private industry regarding federal information policy and has put the government on the side of privatization, it has not gone as far as the industry would have wanted and probably further than those outside of private industry would have liked. The burden of proof in the future will be upon government agencies to demonstrate why information generation and dissemination should not be further privatized.

CONCLUSIONS

This article has looked at the process of privatization, the economics of privatization, and the issue of privatization of government information services. From an economic point of view, what conclusions is it possible to draw based on this analysis and review of the literature?

1 . The two extreme positions must be rejected. There is no economic case that can be made either for completely public generation and dissemination of government information or for leaving the generation and dissemination of government information solely in the hands of the private sector.

2. Governmental activity can be justified on the basis of the positive externalities that are associated with government information services. These positive externalities make government information a merit good. As is the case for all merit goods, the private sector will not supply the socially desired amount if left on its own.

3. Government information is primarily generated for use inside the government by legislators and bureaucrats. The use of this information by those outside the government constitutes the external benefit.

4. The government should continue to generate information for its own

use. This generation of information may be done in-house or through a private contractor. From an economic standpoint, private contracting is to be preferred unless either the nature of the data, such as military secrets, or the comparative cost dictates otherwise. The government has a responsibility to provide itself with information, but not necessarily to produce it in-house.

5. The government needs to have a consistent and constant policy regarding privatization of government information. A single government entity should be responsible for promulgating and enforcing the rules. These rules should be generated on the basis of a private/public dialogue to insure that all interested parties can be heard.

6. The area of greatest controversy concerns government dissemination of information to nongovernmental users. There is a conflict between access and efficiency. Those who favor privatization argue that privatization would improve efficiency and provide information in a greater variety of formats to meet consumer needs. Those who oppose privatization feel that its commercial dissemination would limit access and exclude some individuals from the use of that information. Economics cannot resolve this debate.

7. As a general rule, the government should price the information it generates and disseminates in such a way as to cover the full costs associated with its generation and distribution. For information generated for the use of the government, the costs for development of that data should not be included in the cost passed on to outside consumers, but only the marginal or additional costs involved in preparing and transmitting the information to the private sector for further manipulation and packaging. In all other instances, the price the government charges for its information should cover the full costs including development, overhead costs, and depreciation. If government sells an information service below cost, it not only limits private entrepreneurial activity but necessitates that the taxpayers subsidize the difference. The current array of government pricing policies and practices is not satisfactory.

8. There needs to be established a consistent and universally used system of cost accounting for the generation and dissemination of government information. Without such a policy, current statements regarding costs and pricing are meaningless and are subject to various and arbitrary interpretations. Since the pricing issue lies at the heart of the privatization debate, this system is crucial.

9. The government should not compete with private firms that manipulate and package government information unless there is a compelling reason for them to so do. The compelling reason should relate to the external benefits to be derived from government competition and a clear cost advantage.

10. Government information should be made widely available at low cost through the depository library system as the most efficient means of

capturing the external benefits to society. For other forms of dissemination below cost, competition with the private sector is not warranted. If the government wishes to encourage wider access to information products it can do so either through subsidies to private providers or by subsidies to groups of consumers who are deemed worthy or meritorious.

There may be no way of resolving the tensions between the IIA and the American Library Association and other groups which are worried about the privatization trend. These disagreements involve values which economics cannot reconcile. Nor should economic considerations be the only ones considered in the debate. This article has indicated what economists can contribute to the debate and which issues can be clarified and more precisely defined by economic analysis. Economic analysis is a tool to be used in developing public policy. When considering privatization of government information economists have something to say which is valuable, but their voices are not the only ones to be heard.

REFERENCES

1. US President's Commission on Privatization, *Privatization: Toward More Effective Government, Report on the President's Commission on Privatization* (Washington: Government Printing Office, March 1988).
2. Alan Murray and David Wessel, 'Proposals to Privatize Many Operations Are Being Considered by the White House,' *Wall Street Journal*, December 17, 1987, 54.
3. Diane Smith, 'The Commercialization and Privatization of Government Information,' *Government Publications Review* 12(January/February 1985): 45–63.
4. Robert S. Willard, 'Whose Information Is It Anyway?' *Government Publications Review* 13(May/June 1986): 323–35.
5. Madsen Pirie, *Dismantling the State* (Dallas: National Center for Policy Analysis, 1985).
6. Calvin A. Kent, 'Privatization of Public Functions,' in *Entrepreneurship and the Privatizing of Government*, ed. C. A. Kent (New York: Quorum Books, 1987), 6.
7. Robert Poole, Jr., *Cutting Back on City Hall* (New York: Universe Books, 1980). C. F. Valente and L.D. Manchester. *Rethinking Local Services* (Chicago: International City Managers Association, 1984); E.S. Savas, *Privatizing the Public Sector: How to Shrink Government* (Chatham, NJ: Chatham House, 1982); D. Fisk *et al.*, *Private Provision of Services—An Overview* (Washington: The Urban Institute, 1978); Harry Hatry, *A Review of Private Approaches for Delivery of Public Services* (Washington: The Urban Institute, 1983).
8. Ted Kolderie, 'Two Different Concepts of Privatization,' *Public Administration Review* 13 (July/August 1986): 285–90.
9. Alan Rufus Waters, 'Privatization: A Viable Policy Option,' in *Entrepreneurship and the Privatizing of Government*, ed. C. A. Kent (New York: Quorum Books, 1987). 35–66.
10. William Niskanen, *Bureaucracy and Representative Government* (Hawthorne, NY: Aldine, 1971).
11 R.Q. Armington and W.D. Ellis, *This Way Up: The Local Officials Handbook for Privatizing and Contracting Out* (Chicago: Regnery Gateway,

1984); Poole, *Cutting Back on City Hall;* E. S. Savas, *Privatizing the Public Sector: Hoe to Shrink Government.*

12. Harry Hatry, 'Privatization of Public Services: A Cautionary Note,' *The Urban Institute, Policy and Research Report* 18(Winter 1988): 9.

13. Robert Poole, Jr., 'Objections to Privatization,' Policy Review (Spring 1983): 105–121; Joan Allen, *et al., Opportunities for Greater Use of the Private Sector in Delivering State Services* (Washington: Council of State Governments and The Urban Institute, 1988); Harry Hatry, *et al., Analysis of Service Delivery Alternatives: Building Innovation into Program Reviews* (Washington: The Urban Institute, 1988).

14. American Federation of State, County, Municipal Employees, *Passing the Buck,* (Washington, DC: AFL–CIO, 1984).

15. Stewart Butler, *Privatizing Federal Spending: A Strategy, to Eliminate the Deficit* (New York: Universe Books, 1985).

16. Smith, 'The Commercialization and Privatization of Government Information,' op. cit., 55–6.

17. Richard Musgrave and Peggy Musgrave, *Public Finance in Theory and Practice* (New York: McGraw-Hill, 1976), 3–20.

18. J.M. Keynes, *The General Theory of Employment, Interest and Money* (New York: Harcourt Brace, 1936).

19. Paul A. Samuelson, 'Pure Theory of Public Expenditures and Taxation,' in *Public Economics,* ed. J. Margolis and H. Lutton (London: Macmillan, 1969).

20. Musgrave and Musgrave, *Public Finance in Theory and Practice,* 56–9.

21. US National Commission on Libraries and Information Science (NCLIS), *Public Sector/Private Sector Interaction in Providing Information Services* (Washington: GPO, 1982).

22. Smith, 'The Commercialization and Privatization of Government Information,' 47.

23. Gilbert Fite and Jim E. Reese, *An Economic History of the United States* (Boston: Houghton Mifflin. 165), 413–33; Wayne D. Rasmussen, 'Agriculture' in G. Porter, ed., *Encyclopedia of American Economic History* (New York: Scribners, 1980), 344–60; Fred A. Shannon, *America's Economic Growth* (New York: Macmillan, 1951), 394–96.

24. NCLIS, *Public Sector/Private Sector Interaction.*

25. NCLIS, 9.

26. NCLIS, 9–10.

27. NCLIS, 7.

28. NCLIS, 8.

29. NCLIS, 43–5.

30. NCLIS, 67.

31. NCLIS, 67.

32. NCLIS, 62.

33. NCLIS, 55–71.

34. NCLIS, 65.

35. Letter from Robert S. Willard, Vice President of Governmental Relations of Information Industry Association, to J. Timothy Sprehe, Office of Information and Regulatory Affairs, Office of Management and Budget dated November 28, 1983 as part of comments submitted regarding the development of a policy circular on Federal Information Management.

36. Information Industry Association (IIA), *Meeting Information Needs in the New Information Age,* October, 1983.

37. 44 *U.S.C.* 1708.

38. 44 *U.S.C.* 505.

39. 44 *U.S. C.* 2111(c).

40. 'An Act to Establish the National Bureau of Standards,' *Statutes at Large,* 31, sec. 10, 1450(1901).

41. Information Industry Association (IIA), *Development of An OMB Policy on Federal Information Management,* A Statement of the Information Industry Association to the Office of Management and Budget, November 28, 1983, 22.

42. US Office of Management and Budget. *Circular No. A–76,* Section 4.a.

43. IIA, *Development of An OMB Policy,* 9.

44. IIA, *Meeting Information Needs in the Nee Information Age,* 5.

45. IIA, 6.

46. Congress, House of Representatives, Committee on Government Operations, *Electronic Collection and Dissemination of Information by Federal Agencies: Hearings,* 99th Cong., 1st sess., April 29, 1985, 159.

47. 44 *U.S.C.* 35, Section 3504.

48. Office of Management and Budget (OMB). *Circular No. A–130,* 7b.

49. OMB, Section 7e.

50. OMB, Section 8.B

51. OMB, Appendix 4(10).

52. OMB, Appendix 4(11)(c).

53. OMB, Appendix 4(8.a(11)(c)).

54. OMB. Appendix 4(8.a(11)(c)).

55. OMB, Appendix 2(4b(1–8)).

56. OMB, Appendix 2(4b(1–8)).

The Information Industry

The Information Industry – Introductory Notes

Blaise Cronin

The formative years, growth dynamics and contours of the information industry have been amply documented. [1,2,3,4,5] Suffice to say that there is a (more or less) definable information industry, which exhibits (selectively) high growth rates, reveals a tendency to oligopoly, and is driven by the profit maximisation principle.

Our opening paper (*Marketing electronic information*) looks at some of the major players, their strengths and strategies, and identifies some of the content, packaging, pricing and delivery features which will be the determinants of future industry success. As the market matures and customers become more sophisticated and demanding, a larger proportion of industry expenditures will be channelled into marketing: 'Given the increasing number of look–alike services available to the consumer of electronic information, it is hardly surprising that there has been in recent years an increase in expenditures on marketing. Customer satisfaction engineering is now an important consideration for vendors in an overcrowded market and the trend to customised products and added–value utilities will surely continue in the foreseeable future'.

Stephen Arnold (*End–users: dreams or dollars*) sees the online bibliographic database industry as 'an elephant balancing on its trunk'. That is to say, a great deal of effort is required (in terms of marketing and sales) to woo the majority of customers. Arnold's paper is useful for the consumer typology and market segmentation insights it offers. For some, online information is a licence to print money, but despite the journalistic hype, it is a small minority who boast hefty revenues: deep pockets, cash rich parents and patience are necessary for long–term survial in this industry. [6,7,8,9] Anne Field' short article (*The data dealers: turning a mountain of information into gold*) presents a few cases of electronic alchemy and concludes optimistically that 'with a healthy dose of imagination, a little tenacity, and a good understanding of the business, almost anyone can make a go of it as an information entrepreneur.'

A more balanced assessment of the industry and its prospects is provided (again) by Stephen Arnold (*Stormy weather in the datasphere: the problems of pricing and marketing electronic information*). His main focus is the difficulty of pricing EIPs (electronic information products) given that we 'do not understand the exact nature of EIP life cycles'. His paper is also noteworthy for its literary style: 'In a country where cruising the shopping mall is one of life's most meaningful moments for Joe Average, shopping by PC is a shot on goal from midfield. Mega–hyper–slam dunk marketing can pull off this stunt'. Mega–hyper–slam dunk marketing may not feature in any of Philip Kotler's textbooks, but we ignore the concept at our peril.

Another upbeat account of the information industry comes from Andrew Gross (*The information vending machine*). Information is a peculiar commodity; it is 'reusable, portable, expandable, compressible and sharable. Its real value derives from organization; when properly arranged, it becomes knowledge, a most saleable commodity'. What Gross offers that is new, is a spatial map of the product–price interface in the computer services industry, which could be applied, with a little modification, to the library/information services arena.

How and why customers select particular database services and hosts is the subject of Crawshaw's paper (*Online buying behaviour – how customers choose hosts and databases*). He provides a plausible conceptual model of the steps involved in taking a potential customer from a position of awareness/need appreciation to eventual trialling, purchase and sustained adoption. As a general rule, however, success will depend upon producers and hosts developing 'the solution oriented systems and marketing communications which the user requires'.

Quality control and assurance were featured topics in the section on *Mainstream Marketing*, and their relevance to the database industry is illustrated in Tom Aitchison's reprinted lecture (*Aspects of quality*), which features concepts such as quality–improvement plans, zero defects, first time right, just–in–time (JIT) scheduling and PEET (Program for Ensuring that Everyone's Thanked).

REFERENCES

1. CSP INTERNATIONAL Ltd. *The global structure of the electronic information services industry*. London: British Library Research Paper 1, 1986.

2. McLAUGHLIN, J. F. and ANTONOFF, A. L. *Mapping the information business*. Cambridge, MA: Harvard University, 1986.

3. HARTLEY, J., NOONAN, A. and METCALFE, S. *New electronic information services: an overview of the UK database industry in an international context*. Aldershot: Gower, 1987.

4. SCHILLER, H. I. *Who knows: information in the age of the Fortune 500*. Norwood, NJ: Ablex, 1981.

5. CRONIN, B. The information industry in AD2000. In: WHITEHEAD, J. (ed.). *Information management and competitive success*. London: Aslib, 1988, pp. 222–250.

6. HARRIS, C. L. This 'Maid' specializes in market research. *Business Week*, November 24, 1986, p. 72.

7. GANNES, S. Dun & Bradstreet redeploys the riches. *Fortune*, August 19, 1985, p. 38.

8. KELLY, K. and TREECE, J. B. EDS. How sweet it is to have a sugar daddy. *Business Week*, September 18, 1989, pp. 64–65.
9. BREMNER, B. and ROTHFEDER, J. Dow Jones's $1.6 billion baby is hardly a bundle of joy. *Business Week*, September 10, 1990, pp. 40–42.

Marketing Electronic Information

Lizzie Davenport and Blaise Cronin

Lizzie Davenport, MA, MLitt, is a research student in the Department of Information Science, Strathclyde Business School, University of Strathclyde Glasgow
Blaise Cronin is Professor of Information Science and Head of the Department of Information Science, Strathclyde Business School, University of Strathclyde, Glasgow

INTRODUCTION

In an earlier article[1] we surveyed the convergence and integration of major players in the information industry. The trend towards vertical integration, which can be observed in the macromarket, is also evident in the operations of individual online hosts – the micromarket. In this article we look at the vending of online business data, a sector in which commercial bias is strong and where market patterns mimic those of the larger theatre.

Electronic publishing (excluding real-time financial information services) is one of the few areas of the information industry relatively untouched by IBM and AT&T – the latter was originally banned for seven years from this sector at the time of divestiture (1984), a move intended to protect the production of Yellow Pages, but with wider implications. The big battalions are, however, poised for penetration, with IBM, BT, financial conglomerates and the Japanese (who have recently launched a CD-ROM business database through OSD)[2] in a position to enter the market, while AT&T in May 1986 was given the green light by the FCC (Federal Communications Commission) to provide advanced information services, such as computer communication networks, without first setting up an arms-length company.

THE INTEGRATED INFORMATION CHAIN

The field is far from level, with, for example, Dialog and Mead Data Central in the dominant roles enjoyed by IBM and AT&T in the larger arena. In addition to the advantage of historical precedence, both companies have benefited from strategic marketing. Other features of the information macromarket can be observed in the electronic publishing sector – concentration and increased competition, bundling of services, and flexible packaging to meet individual needs and enhance competitive edge. As information is now recognised as a key weapon, commercial companies are prepared to pay for the right service – or integrated information chain, supplying hardware, transmission and data, offered in one package to facilitate what have been called 'SIS' or strategic information services.[3]

The provision of online business data (as opposed to bibliographic files or realtime commodity/currency data) is a useful area of comparative study, as it is largely unsubsidised, and producers and hosts must implement realistic costing policies. The genealogy and ethology of the more important hosts show a strategic deployment of classic business strategies: consolidation of assets (by vertical integration, or buying-out of rivals) must be matched with differentiation of products. With an increasing number of hosts offering the same bases, value-added services become an important distinguishing feature.

High capital costs are involved in maintenance of these services (backfiling and updating), in the provision of dedicated transmission and in the supply of idiomatic front-end systems, and, not surprisingly, many of the leading players in the host section are linked to larger companies: Dialog/Lockheed, MDC/Mead, BRS/ Thyssen, Datasolve/Thorn EMI. Some providers (McGraw Hill, Dun & Bradstreet) have jettisoned traditional products, 144 years of printed output in the case of the latter, to supply a comprehensive electronic portfolio of financial files which can be processed and matched to individual needs.[4]

DIALOG–A SUCCESSFUL PHENOTYPE

One of the most successful operators, in terms of databases offered, client base and turnover is Dialog. It did not originate as part of a vertically integrated group, and its umbrella, Lockheed's Information Services Group, appears to be a purely administrative creation. Dialog is a phenotype of the United States' information industry: started in the 1960s in-house at Lockheed Missile & Space Research Division to provide access to bibliographic data, journal and report literature; encouraged by a contract from NASA – won in the face of competition from SDC – in 1968 to develop its interactive computer facilities further; launched as a commercial company within Lockheed in 1972, and fully fledged as an independent, Dialog Information Services Inc., in 1982.[5]

To date the company's main rivals in the United States have been SDC and BRS, and in Europe, DataStar, InfoLine and ESA/IRS. It has provided continuously innovative front-end services to maintain its leading position, and the company has thrived where rivals have atrophied: SDC, for example, has recently been rescued in a takeover by Pergamon.[6] Dialog Version 2 offers the client the capability to create a tailor-made package with data provided with tagged output, online editing of saved searches and SDIS, and a 'Report' feature which formats numeric data. Dialmail offers current awareness searches and offline prints; all can be delivered via Dialnet, a dedicated wire. In addition to such convergent services, Dialog offers frills – Dialorder (complete texts may be ordered online), and Dialindex. The company is anxious to develop the provision of full-text information, including adequate half-tone graphics.[7] Precedence in R & D has been an important factor in the company's success.

When BRS introduced its non prime-time service (After Dark) in 1982, Dialog was prompt in its riposte (Knowledge Index): both services exploit spare computing capacity (host advantage) while catering for the private or poorly funded client. The company's own software (Dialog-link) is designed for IBM's smaller range (and its compatibles) – most access software in the business data field bears witness to IBM's dominant status in the hardware market.

COPING WITH COMPETITION

With such a secure market niche, Dialog presents a challenge to competitors. DataStar and ESA/IRS, Dialog's rivals in Europe, derive their advantage from their locale, they are much cheaper to use within the continent, but compare favourably even when accessed from the United States. The search languages offered by these hosts show a contrast of competitive emphasis: ESA/IRS adopted an early version of Dialog and exploited the family resemblance to a parent that has been used by so many for so long that it has become a *de facto* standard. BRS Search software, however, enjoys the advantage of simplicity.

BRS aims for 'customised interfaces and online documentation anticipating a variety of applications and user concerns', and has followed an innovative policy to achieve this: After Dark in 1982,[8] BRS Colleague, which is targetted at the medical community, BRS Brk Thru, which offers a simple menu-driven search strategy more accessible to the untrained user than Dialog's – an approach followed by other commercial gateway packages, such as SciMate from the ISI stable, and access via its own international network in addition to common carriers.

The company's position in a large information conglomerate (part of the Thyssen Bomemisza Group) provides financial security and strategic alliances with a network of parental contacts – the development of CD-ROM medical presentation with the Saunders group is a case in point (Mead is also poised to enter this sector). The company trails Dialog in Europe, with a lack of local offices and training courses, and it has recently been deprived of the marketing advantage (non-competition and non-duplication) offered until 1985 by DataStar, under its foundation contract.

AGGRESSIVE NICHEMANSHIP

Mead Data Central dominates the online non-realtime business and legal sector, through a combination of aggressive marketing and pugnacious acquisition. Where Dialog has pursued a generalist strategy, Mead's history shows intense concentration in a specialist sector, initially using dedicated equipment and relying on a captive audience who may have been unaware of the overall potential of personal computing. Many users have been alienated by this policy (in particular, professional searchers with their own existing equipment), and Mead has recently allowed access through commercial Software – PC networks on IBM PCs, and Lotus' Jazz software offers access via the Macintosh Apple.

Mead has paid little attention to the complaints of information professionals: the original emphasis of Lexis was on lawyers themselves, not intermediaries. But Nexis, with its more general applications, has altered this policy, as the system has to compete with offerings (Datasolve, Textline) from other hosts.[9]

The company overlooked the convenience of its clients in its presentation of the newly acquired New York Times Information Service (July, 1983). Two particular issues were raised – access via Nexis dedicated terminals, and reduction of indexing to conform with Mead's historical support of free text searching on the grounds that indexing was too sophisticated for the untrained user, Mead's original clients.[10]

Mead originated in the efforts of the Ohio Bar Association to computerise state legal records in the 1960s, and was taken over by Mead Corporation in 1970. Lexis was commercially launched in 1974, and was joined by Nexis in 1980 – a period during which the company invested millions of dollars to nurture its fledgling services, in the face of sustained competition from Westlaw. In 1983, two controversial moves were made: the newly acquired New York Times database (an acquisition coveted by Dialog), was made available only through MDC; and the European database, Eurolex, was closed after purchase by Butterworth (a Reed subsidiary). Mead's marketing agent in Britain, Butterworth, enjoys royalties on the English part of Lexis in the United States , and provides marketing, training and customer support for Lexis in Britain; and Mead's own London office was intended to do the same for Nexis in respect of its European sales drive. Mead has diversified with other bases – Lexpat, NAARS (National Automated Accounting Research System), Lextrack (a private library service) and Infobank, and all can be carried on Meadnet, a dedicated line.

Mead's training programme is distinctive: the company has, from the start, captured its market young with a comprehensive law school programme, recently extended to high schools; and plans have been made to expand into business schools. Public policy statements have revealed a move from a product-oriented to customer-oriented strategy. Services now include Exchange (a financial data processing system which qualifies marketing leads) aimed at Merrill/Lynch, Paine Webber and similar corporations, and Eclipse (an off-peak electronic clipping service which creates and sustains a customised file) intended to give Nexis additional competitive edge.

The system can support 500 simultaneous users, and the company claims that it is 'working with the terminal and PC vendors to ensure the most optimal user interface'. The tyranny of the 'red terminal', Mead's original dedicated interface, has ended, with many of these UBIQ's recalled and used for training purposes, the traditional pasture for used company workhorses.

With a five year contract to supply Lexis and Nexis and equipment to the United States' Federal Courts in its bag,[11] the company is in a strong position to divert resources into new ventures: it recently launched (May 1986) Mead Micromedex medical base on CD-ROM (a development from Mead's existing Medis service).

Mead's main European rival, Datasolve, is a wholly owned subsidiary of Thorn/EMI, and enjoys the advantages of European coverage, simple search strategies, and local marketing and training services. But these may be offset by Mead's current European sales drive.

MARKET SEGMENTATION AND PRODUCT DIFFERENTIATION

DRI and Pergamon provide further illustration of commercial data chains sustained by a strategic balance of consolidation and differentiation. Pergamon InfoLine's hosting of Dun & Bradstreet's bases makes it prominent in the business sector. The conditions of the company's recent acquisition of SDC will squeeze the maximum strategic advantage from the move: five key files (and presumably their client base) have been retained, and Pergamon will acquire the rights to SDC's Orbit software.[12]

DRI's original remit was economic forecasting, and it offers consultancy services which enable clients to make effective use of models and training in different industrial sectors (an offshoot of the focussing which resulted from McGraw's reorganisation and splitting of DRI into six parts). Software staff work with individual clients to solve specific problems, and industry profiles can be linked to macroeconomic models for two-way data transfer.

DRI's target audience is the large corporation,[13] and the company offers a downloading and local analysis facility, performed by themselves (with tapes or disks mailed to the customer), or by the client. A joint venture with Visicorp has produced the Datakit, offering access to fixed cost preformatted segments of DRI data for manipulation in Visicalc sheets. Access is through DRINET (dedicated) or common carrier.

A more baroque array of customer services might seem hard to find, but Dun and Bradstreet's offerings may be described as rococo. In the last two years, the company has made over 33 acquisitions (financed partly by the sale of television, broadcasting and book publishing divisions), and policy is aimed at squeezing the resulting databanks till the pips squeak.[14] Dun & Bradstreet is not a converged operation, and does not offer hardware: bases must be accessed by the client's own system, though they are transmitted on Dunsnet. Pergamon, the host, has developed user-friendly features – SDI; copyline (delivering the complete text of articles, reports and patents referred to in the bases); easily operable commands (it will be interesting to see if the newly acquired Orbit software will be deployed on existing bases), and private file services for clients wishing to load in-house databases. Teething troubles in 1981 shortly after takeover by Maxwell were solved by the acquisition of a DEC Vax/11780 and Battelle's Basis software. As a general host, Pergamon can offer prices which compare favourably with its rivals (Dun & Bradstreet's *Who Owns Whom*, however, costs $125/hour); it has not over-capitalised on the fact that many of its bases are exclusive. Its training courses are in-house and company oriented.[15]

It is clear that hosts are offering polymorphously friendly features and value-added services on the assumption that such differentiation will attract clients. The position of clients who can only afford basic data has become insecure. For them, SDI, downloading, spreadsheeting, and so on may be considered as secondary features, and they may prefer to see their primary needs satisfied by reasonable pricing, precision of retrieved information and convenience.

PRICING STRATEGIES

In academic and public institutions suffering budget constraints, pricing may dictate the choice of system, and when Gurnsey claims that the online market is largely price insensitive,[16] he may be dismissing this group as being insignificant in revenue terms. Outside most public sector institutions, increased affluence coupled with product differentiation enable the consumer to consider other factors. Muller observes that oligopoly diverts the market from price competition; the polymorphous front-end packages described above confirm this.[17]

Price differentiation does not depend on hosts in many instances, but results from the different costing policies of producers and the terms on which they negotiate: 'Key British Enterprises' on Pergamon is three times as expensive as on other hosts. Inter-host comparisons quoting average prices, a common feature of promotional and press features, are meaningless unless the comparison is restricted, like Muller's, to shared bases on hosts, when some attempt can be made to isolate the processing, marketing, and telecommunication costs. These will not be constant across hosts, but depend on the characteristics of individual files: some are sought and others are brought to the host; some will require reformatting and editing (particularly those from small publishers – Pergamon performs this function for Maid), and some will require basic keyboarding and processing.

Royalties may be paid in different ways – upfront charges depending on usage; percentage of price paid for data; payment on a fixed time schedule with monthly statistics on usage, or the application of a one-time only global fee. Revenue may be based on the number of searches, a flat amount per hit, or a percentage revenue from the contracted hours of use. Where market share is established (e.g. Dialog), pricing appears to be cost/demand-oriented; where there is still competition for market share (DataStar and Dimdi), pricing can be loss-leading or competitive – DataStar, one of the hosts most often in competition with others, is also one of the cheapest.

The interaction of cost-oriented (benefits host) and demand – oriented (benefits client) pricing can be explored in Mead's revamping of Nexis prices in June 1984. Previous policy based prices on online time, plus complexity of search (the number of times a term appeared in the database); new prices were based on online time, plus charges for each search, depending on the file used. Though Mead claimed that this was more in tune with user needs, reaction has not been favourable. One writer suggests strategies for 'beating' the new structure (search as small a file as possible; modify an existing search rather than start another[18];) another concludes that Mead is 'reconsidering the profitability of the library sector' in a deprecatory article on contracts, which reinforces the suggestion that producers and vendors of commercial data are not interested in performing a 'welfare' role, in the provision of basic information [19].

ONE-STOP SHOPPING

Hosts of online commercial data vie with each other to provide the most complete service for their clients. This inevitably involves chaining of resources, and some maintain that such integration of services is an adverse development, as it locks the client to one organisation. But others claim that too much choice may be as commercially paralysing as too little. In any event, the advantages of 'one-stop shopping' are likely to be no less obvious to the customer of electronic information than the weekend shopper at the hypermarket.

Given the increasing number of look-alike services available to the consumer of electronic information, it is hardly surprising that there has been in recent years an increase in expenditures on marketing. Customer satisfaction engineering is now an important consideration for vendors in an overcrowded market and the trend to customised products, bundled services and added-value utilities will surely continue in the forseeable future.

REFERENCES

1   L. Davenport and B. Cronin, 'Vertical Integration: Corporate Strategy in the Information Industry,' *Online Review*, 10, 4, August 1986, pp. 237–47.

2   D. Green, 'The Online Explosion,' *Business*, August 1986, p. 129.

3   C. Wiseman, 'Strategy and Computers: Information Systems as Competitive Systems,' Homewood: Dow Jones-Irwin, 1985.

4   S. Gannes, 'Dun & Bradstreet redeploys the riches,' *Fortune*, August 1985, pp. 38–47.

5   CSP International Ltd, 'The Global Structure of the Electronic Information Services Industry,' London British Library R&D Department, 1986.

6   *Monitor*,' September 1986, p. 1.

7   J.K. Pemberton and J.-P. Emard, 'Dialog in '84', *Online*, March 1984, pp. 13–20.

8   R.V. Janke, 'BRS/After Dark: The Birth of Online Self-service,' *Online*, September 1983, pp. 12–29. For a detailed comparison with Dialog's Knowledge Index see *Online*, January 1983, p. 10.

9   J.K. Pemberton and J.-P. Emard, 'What's happening at Mead Data Central?' *Online*, July 1984, pp. 13–19 and *Business Week*, August 1986, p. 53.

10 M. Corcoran, 'Mead Data Central and all the news that's fit to print,' *Online*, July 1983, pp. 32–5.

11 Micromedex, *Online*, May 1986, p.75 and Lexis, *Online*, January 1986, p. 102.

12 *Monitor, op. cit.*

13 CSP International Ltd., *op. cit.*

14 S. Gannes, *op. cit.*

15 G. Smith and A. Foster, 'Online Business Directory,' Hartlepool: Headland Press, 1985, pp.88–90.

16 J. Gurnsey, 'The Information Professionals in the Electronic Age,' London: Bingley, 1986.

17 P. Muller and R. Wilson, 'Pricing Policies for Parallel Publishing,' *Elsevier International Bulletins*, 1985.

18 J.-P. Lomio, 'The High Cost of Nexis and what a searcher can do about it,' *Online*, September 1985, pp.54–6.

19 'Open Letter to the Members of the Southern California Online Users Group on the, subject of the Mead/Nexis Acquisition of New York Times Information Service,' *Online*, July 1983, p.4.

End-users: Dreams or Dollars

Stephen E. Arnold

Vice President UMI Data Courier

The phrase end-user has been bandied about the online industry for years. Online services, database producers, software companies, modem manufacturers, and most recently the compact disk prophets have pursued this elusive creature with increasing sophistication, agressiveness, and zeal. How many of them are there?

The August 12, 1986, *USA Today* compared the size of the computer industry in 1981 and 1986. One staggering forecast is that the value of personal computers shipped to all market segments in 1986 will approach $14.6 billion, compared with $1.9 billion in 1981. In 1986, 6.6 million PCs will move from manufacturers to business, science, education, and home customers. Business customers bought 362,000 PCs in 1981. This year the number of units will approach 3.25 million. Even the home market which most online information companies have written off seems strong. In 1981, only 151,000 PCs were purchased for home use. Contrast this with 1986's estimated 2.2 million. One week before the *USA Today* article, the *Wall Street Journal* reported that shipments of personal computers for the home-use buyer are likely to rise 28 per cent this year, to $2.77 billion.

Last year, *Personnel Journal* offered an observation which reminds us to view such heady statistics with caution. In its July 1985 issue, Philip Harris reported that only about 3 per cent of the 25 million managers and white collar professionals in the United States used computer workstations. The August *PC World* summarized a nationwide survey conducted by Dataquest, an American consultancy. Suzanne Purnell, an analyst for the firm, said, 'PCs are not as ubiquitous as many assume'. Ten per cent of the companies with 1000 or more employees had no PCs, 37 per cent had fewer than 11, and PCs were 'nowhere to be found in 19.2 per cent' of the companies with IBM mainframes.

Mead Data Central's success offers convincing evidence that users outside the law library can be hooked on online. According to the August 1, *IDP Report*, 25 timesharing services have more than 1.6 million customer passwords. These password holders represent a market of companies and individuals who do search or plan to search online.

Judy Wanger, Vice President, Cuadra Associates, believes that end-users can and will make use of online. She says, 'The trend for companies building their own internal databases and the increasing awareness of external databases are feeding one another. Customers of our STAR database are learning to use Boolean logic. But the marketing techniques for reaching end-users are not crystal clear'.

In the pages which follow, I offer a fresh look at attracting new users to online bibliographic information. Online access of textual databases has migrated from the special library and librarians to other parts of organizations and professionals in non-library disciplines. The ideas presented here are my preliminary effort to look at non-librarian online searchers in an objective way.

WHAT IS AN 'END-USER?'

At ONLINE '81, sponsored by Online, Inc., Steve Goldspiel, Vice President of Marketing, Disclosure, said, 'There are end-users out there all right. They just don't know who they are'.

For bibliographic database producers and online services, an end-user market means online searchers who are not special librarians. Special librarians comprise a market consisting of skilled searchers with a degree in library science or extensive online training. The $300 million online bibliographic industry derives the bulk of its revenue from about 3,000 firms, with large organizations contributing the bulk of the revenue.

Although the potential market is huge, the online bibliographic industry is like an elephant balancing on its trunk. The massive effort to get end-users online is the elephant's body, and the special librarian, the trunk that supports the industry. The animal trainer hopes the trunk holds out, or the creature will come crashing down.

The special library market is sharply defined and well-known. The search for the other market of end-users has become for database producers and online services a modern day Manifest Destiny. The dream of large numbers of end-users frequently accessing bibliographic information offers hope to the database producer, seduces the venture capitalist, and promises profits to the timesharing companies. It is the information industry's American Dream: There's gold in the next valley where the end-user lives.

End-users play a role in the computer industry, which has gathered some facts about them. For example, the August 1986 *Information Center* ran an advertisement which said, 'End-users want today's skills yesterday', and, '... your end-users [can] learn just about anything, except patience'.

The June 1986 *MIS Information Quarterly* reported the results of a survey by Tor Guimaraes and Vasudevan Ramanujam of data processing managers' ten most urgent concerns:

1. Lack of user education regarding company-wide and long term planning for personal computing.
2. User requests for assistance overwhelming the MIS department.
3. Lack of user knowledge or concern about microcomputer data-integrity control measures such as backup.
4. Lack of integration in micro/mainframe data exchange and control.
5. Poor maintainability of user developed systems.
6. Mismatching of user problems and computing alternatives for systems development.
7. Lack of centralized management over corporate data resources to support user personal computing.
8. Lack of integration in MIS management of personal computing and mainframe user computing.
9. Lack of user concern about personal computing equipment security.
10. Lack of user-friendly mainframe software packages to compete successfully with micros.

To my knowledge there is no comparable study for the end-user of online bibliographic information, so I have recast these findings for the online bibliographic industry:

1a. Lack of searcher education regarding company-wide and long term planning for internal and external online information.
2a. Searcher requests for assistance overwhelming the special library.
3a. Lack of searcher knowledge or concern about copyright.
4a. Lack of integration in micro/mainframe data exchange and control.
5a. Poor maintainability of searcher developed retrieval systems.
6a. Mismatching of searcher problems and computing alternatives for systems.
7a. Lack of centralized management over corporate information resources to support online searchers.
8a. Lack of integration in personal and mainframe searching.
9a. Lack of searcher concern about personal searching equipment security.
10a. Lack of user-friendly software for searching on the mainframe or personal computer.

What struck me when I completed this exercise was that these are the same issues which come up when bibliographic database producers and online services discuss their end-user experiences. This list of ten items omits two special bibliographic challenges: (1) the cost of online, and (2) the frequency of bibliographic file use.

In one of our conversations about getting end-users to come to our joint training seminars, Steve Goldspiel recently said to me, 'End-users are people who ask questions. They take action on the information someone gets for them. Online is for the people who get the information and present it to an end-user. These 'getters' are really *end-user patrons*'.

'There are two problems associated with these new users', he continued. 'First, they hate the library because it is too much work to explain what they need. And, second, these end-user patrons are hard to locate. Our problem is that we don't know who they are'.

An observation by Donald Baker, managing director of ICC Information Group Ltd., is worth noting: 'In the world of discretionary databases, that is, ones people don't absolutely have to have, the end-user is a bit of a myth. A more proper term is *distributor*, and this person is rarely an executive'.

I agree with these observations, but I would for the purposes of this essay like to translate *end-user patron* and Donald Baker's *distributor* into the term *new intermediary*. I reserve the phrase *end-user* for the person who asks the questions, and I use the term *special librarian* to refer to the librarians who now search online. The market the online bibliographic industry seeks is one which, if it exists, will consist of *new intermediaries*. These people will perform many of the same functions as special librarians, but they will have non-library backgrounds and such titles as 'market researcher', 'analyst', 'corporate planner', 'consultant', 'administrative assistant', etc.

WHY DOES SOMEONE BECOME A NEW INTERMEDIARY?

There are five reasons why someone will become a new intermediary.

First, someone is told he has to learn how to search online. His superior allows no choice.

Second, online searching puts money in the new intermediary's pocket. Thus, a small consultant will use online information to prepare proposals faster or create reports to sell to his clients.

Third, the individual likes to work with a computer. I have a friend who takes great pride in his rapid advancement from an Apple II to an IBM AT. On his AT, he personally maintains information about his company's inventory of fasteners. Though this man owns the company, he does this work himself because he loves personal computing.

Fourth, peers pressure one another to master word processing, spreadsheets, and online information retrieval. At large consulting firms it is not uncommon to hear MBAs say, 'Everyone in my class at Harvard did it, so I did it too'. Peer or career pressure forces people into learning bibliographic retrieval when they would rather be merging and acquiring, or whatever MBAs do for fun.

Fifth, someone has a problem and an online computer application solves it. A new intermediary is created when a 'compelling need' – a phrase used by Loene Trubkin, the former president of Data Courier – is satisfied. For example, a medium-sized trucking company cannot calculate freight rates manually because of growth, and online information offers a way to do this work more rapidly without adding additional staff.

WHY PEOPLE DON'T BECOME NEW INTERMEDIARIES

A chilling rumor circulates every year at Comdex. For every 100 personal computers sold, 75 sit unused. *Computer Decisions,* September 10, 1985, reported that high-ranking executives are the employees most likely to resist the computer. Part of the fix, according to Robert Becker of Rabeck Inc., is that systems must duplicate the way managers work, not force the managers to adapt to the computer. Computers do not yet work like executives. I have gathered six other reasons and added a marketing corollary to each.

First, the person does not have a strong need. Just because a marketer requires a new crop of prospects each month doesn't mean that person needs online to get them. Online marketing rule 1: Any need, no matter how powerful, is always met the easiest way without taking into account time and money.

Second, the prospective new intermediary has a habit which he does not want to break. Online marketing rule 2: Once an information gathering habit is established, it is tough to change without dropping a ton of money on the head of the prospect. Even then, the old habit may persist. Third, without understanding online and without the ability to differentiate among databases, the online customer will never: (a) spend the time to learn how to be an effective searcher, and (b) be able to grasp the nuances of digitized information. The reasoning goes 'This work can be done by my secretary. Let him learn'; or 'This stuff is never exactly what I want'. Online marketing rule 3: Online searching is always pushed downward in the organization.

Fourth, online information does not fit a prospect company's financial practices. When I worked for a nuclear and environmental consulting firm, I marveled at the sophisticated computer monitoring equipment we installed at client locations, yet there wasn't a single computer in our building. The president of the company explained it to me this way, 'We only buy capital equipment when the client pays. I don't want those asset expenditures on my balance sheet'. Online marketing rule 4: If a company has neither equipment nor a willingness to pay for information, there is no prospect, no sale.

Fifth, the person who will search may not have the aptitude for the task. Online marketing rule 5: You can talk to a Cocker Spaniel all day, but it won't learn Boolean logic.

Finally, the prospect objects to that which he finds easiest to complain about. When asked in the course of a market research product about online bibliographic databases, the interviewee responds, 'It is too hard to use. Make it easier to use, and I'll buy it'. When the researcher or salesman says that online is easy to use, the new intermediary replies, 'It is too expensive. Make it cheaper, and then I'll use it'. What this individual really means is 'I haven't any reason to use this stuff. Go away'. People like this spark new product concepts in the online industry; for example, user-friendly front ends and deep discounts. Online marketing rule 6: Uninformed prospects cannot explain their problems; others lie.

MAPPING USERS – SPECIAL LIBRARIANS, NEW INTERMEDIARIES, AND OTHERS

In the last five years I have spent considerable time trying to make sense out of the crazy quilt of online services, types of users, and markets.

What are the principal markets, what do they buy, and what type of searcher is in each? For the online bibliographic industry I have identified three general markets – Libraries, Professions, and Business. Each of these has several segments:

The Library Market

Public libraries (little online searching)
Special/corporate libraries (special librarians)
Academic libraries (some online searching)

The Professional Market

Doctors (good PC penetration, little online)
Lawyers (pockets of online searching)
Consultants (online in major firms)
Finance/Accountants (online to internal data only)

The Business/Technology Market

Corporate planners (starting to accept online)
Sales/Marketing (little online searching)
Research/Technical (pockets of online searching)

What databases enjoy substantial market success? Each year Martha Williams drops hints at online shows about what companies in the online industry are leading the revenue race. Industry gossip and trade show chatter suggests what files are used and by whom. Figure 1, Business information market, illustrates a competitive profile.

Based upon my experience in the online industry, I have indicated the penetration of specific databases into particular markets. A quick glance

FIGURE 1: Business information market (Hypothetical)

Five types of information products	Libraries			Professional				Business/Technology		
	Pub	Spec	Acad	* Dr	● Law	* Consult	* Fin	* Plan	* Sales	● Research/Tech
Index databases/ pointer files										
• Magazine Index (IAC)	Y	O	S	O	O	O	O	O	O	O
• WilsonLine (Wilson)	B	O	B	O	O	O	O	O	O	O
• OCLC	Y	S	Y	O	O	O	O	O	O	O
Abstract databases/ informative abstracts										
• ABI/INFORM (Data Courier)	O	Y	S	O	B	Y	Y	B	O	Y
• Promt (Predicasts)	S	Y	S	O	O	Y	Y	B	O	Y
• Claims (Plenum)	O	S	O	O	Y	Y	O	O	O	Y
Text & numbers										
• Disclosure (Disclosure)	O	Y	O	O	Y	Y	Y	B	O	O
• Investext (Business Research)	O	Y	O	O	Y	Y	Y	O	O	O
Statistics										
• DMI (D&B)	O	O	O	O	O	S	Y	Y	O	O
• I.P. Sharp	O	O	O	O	O	S	Y	Y	O	S
• Stock quotes (DJN/R)	O	S	O	S	O	O	S	S	O	O
Full text										
• Business Dataline (Data Courier)	O	Y	S	O	B	Y	Y	B	O	Y
• LEXIS (Mead)	O	S	O	O	Y	Y	Y	S	O	O
• Wall Street Journal	O	Y	O	O	B	S	S	O	O	O
• MEDIS	O	O	O	O	O	O	O	O	O	S

O — Never   Y — Yes   S — Sometimes   B — Beginning   * End users   ● New intermediaries

FIGURE 2: Online customers profile

reveals that more than 90 boxes have a 0, which indicates little online usage for particular files. The pattern of file usage shows the origin of my assertion that a few dedicated users in specific segments support the online bibliographic industry.

What characteristics do online users share? To help answer this difficult question, I cross tabulated frequency of searching with the searcher's general role in an organization. At one end of the spectrum is the person who asks questions, the decision maker. At the other end is the individual who gets answers, an order taker.

Figure 2, Online customer profile depicts relationships between different market segments. I have mapped several markets, including truck rate estimators, automobile parts dealers, chemists, special and public librarians, accountants, data processing professionals, attorneys, marketers, and executives. What Figure 2 shows is that online revenue flows from Quadrant I segments where online is job related.

Quadrants II, III, and IV promise opportunities and problems. For example, public librarians do not use significant amounts of online information, but there are several hundred thousand of them who could. Accountants and data processing professionals do not use online to obtain external information either. Although accountants do use computer services for internal analyses, they are not now searchers of external bibliographic data. Which of the seven barriers is most important for each group? How can one economically make them online consumers of bibliographic information?

Based on my experience, I have ranked each of these four quadrants in terms of the amount of online revenue they yield:

QUAD	MARKET SIZE	BARRIERS	REVENUE
I	Very small	Applications	High
II	Smallest	None exist	Little
III	Largest	No need, money	None
IV	Small	Time, interest	Small

The implications of these two figures are:

Each market has different online information needs which must be researched and analyzed before a product is offered. Failure to understand the factors influencing use can lead to product failure.

Online users have some distinct characteristics; therefore, likely market segments must have them too. Segments without these characteristics are more difficult, if not impossible, to sell.

Specific applications seem more attractive than broad sweeping information services.

It is more difficult to sell large numbers of new intermediaries because they have diverse needs and are harder to support.

MAKING NEW INTERMEDIARIES INTO HEAVY CONSUMERS

Building usage is a problem which can be approached from a variety of viewpoints. The most common line-of-attack is to rely upon marketing to increase usage, but marketing online requires money and time to pull a number of different strings. The revenue return, if any, is not easily traced to a specific promotion the way a department store can measure its January White Sale. What sells online bibliographic information?

One way to answer this question is for the organization to pick a market segment populated with prospects who need online information to do their job. The segment cannot be so large that appropriate support is impossible. Too many poorly qualified prospects create hidden marketing costs; for example, printing and mailing newsletters, billing and collections, or exhibiting at trade shows which do not reach potential users.

An alternative market approach is to offer a private file. Prospects are individuals who have a need for the information, and users are restricted to specific individual groups who may have to pay an upfront fee to obtain access to the information.

Somewhere between these two approaches is a public file offered to a restricted user base. Two examples are Interactive Market Systems, the advertising expenditure data service and Mead Data Central's LEXIS. Prices are usually higher than those of other systems in order to discourage password proliferation. Direct selling cultivates big spending accounts.

Based upon estimated revenues and the number of passwords each has issued, we can speculate about some online services' per password revenue. First, consider a databank with online revenues of about $2 million and 185,000 passwords. If 20 per cent of these passwords return 80 per cent of the firm's revenue, 37,000 passwords annually yield about $40 per password. The other 80 per cent of the users contribute about $2 per year in revenue yet must be supported. Billing and routine communications will erode the financial resources of the databank.

Contrast that with a databank who has revenues of about $121 million and approximately 9,500 passwords. Twenty per cent of this company's customers yields revenue of about $97 million, or an average annual return per password of $51,200. The smaller customers which comprise 80 per cent of the passwords contribute approximately $3,000 each per year.

These examples suggest that online services should seek fewer, larger customers. Selling a big account may be harder but simplifies customer support and increases revenue.

FIGURE 5: Corporate niche strategy

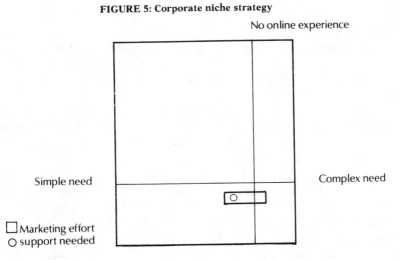

No online experience

Simple need

Complex need

☐ Marketing effort
○ support needed

Online expert

To develop new customers and grow usage, these marketers use direct sales calls, demonstrate an essential application, ignore requests for technical user support, and restrict the number of customers with high prices.

FIGURE 6: The expert strategy

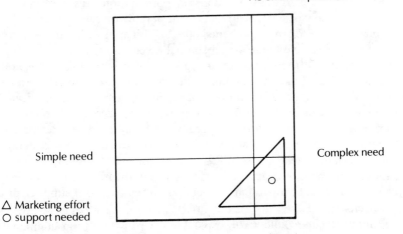

No online experience

Simple need

Complex need

△ Marketing effort
○ support needed

Online expert

To find new users, these marketers casually seek customers from Quadrants B and C, emphasize technical support, develop a diverse market of experts who need a supermarket of specialized databases, and have an international market.

Figure 3: Market segment profile offers a simplified way to visualize the implications of these two examples. The x axis represents a prospect's online needs from the simplest to the most complex. The y axis presents the online experience range, from no experience with online to online mastery. Each of the four quadrants has been labeled. The boxes represent the relative number of each group of prospects in that market.

The A quadrant (the general segment) shows that the general market is larger than any other universe. To reach a mass market requires consumer selling-benefits, sizzle, brand identity, etc. Each time a password is sold in the general market, education about online is required. Such educational support is expensive and, at best, equips the customer to decide if online is something he needs. For some consumer-oriented online companies, the general market is anyone with a computer. Since marketing cost will be high and non-usage predominates, online usage alone cannot repay this investment.

The B quadrant (the high expectation segment) represents an easier sale but a more difficult support problem because of the prospect's high expectations for online bibliographic information. This individual wants results yesterday. The challenge is to capitalize on this interest in a cost-effective way without killing it. Marketers who oversell online to motivated yet unsophisticated people run the risk of losing customers if the support is not on target. Different companies do this in strategically different ways. Services with a consumer orientation stress an easy-to-use system and low prices. Mead Data Central relies on sales representatives who teach and sell in their clients' offices. This approach requires a small customer base able to return substantial revenues.

Quadrant C (the corporate or organizational segment) is a desirable target because it has a population with some computer capability, money, and needs online information. Marketing focuses upon applications because the prospects may use a computer for one dedicated function, for example, word processing or spreadsheet analysis. The sales program should be need-oriented and pivot on education about online, database differentiation, features, applications, and benefits. Organizations employing the prospects are not hard to find, but the individual prospect is. Decisions about how much to spend are often made on supplier price, reputation, and service. This group requires broad-based support. Winners in this segment will be companies which take advantage of the market's tendency to use one or two databases for particular applications.

Online services and database producers sell most effectively to Quadrant D (the expert segment). People in this segment know online so well they seem as if they work for the database producers and timesharing companies. They are information sensitive, interested in complex applications, and respond to technical information. Unfortunately, this is a static, select group of professionals which many companies pursue hotly.

FIGURE 3: Market segment profile

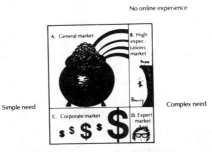

No online experience

A. General market

B. High expec- tations market

Simple need

Complex need

C. Corporate market

D. Expert market

Online expert

A. General segment

Sales approach—
Consumer sales tech-
niques and missionary
marketing

• Extensive support
needed

• Low and infrequent
usage

• High overhead

**B. High expectation
segment**

Sales approach—React to
customer inquiries with
password sales

• First online experience
critical

• Training and tutorials
necessary

• Potential large users

• High likelihood of
customer dissatis-
faction

**C. Corporate/organi-
zation segment**

Sales approach—Direct
sales/professional ser-
vices sales

• Formal proposal and
contract sometimes
required

• Frequent use

• Usage concentrated in
an application area

• Fast customer support
required

D. Expert segment

Sales approach—Tech-
nical sale

• Detailed documen-
tation required

• Technical seminars,
newsletters, data
sheets increase usage

• Several thousand large
users who use 5 to 10
databases heavily and
supplement with spe-
cialized files

• Desirable market sub-
ject to overselling
and confusion about
products and services

Selling a big account may be harder but simplifies customer support
and increases revenue.

FIGURE 4: Consumer strategy

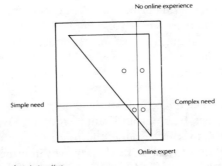

No online experience

Simple need

Complex need

Online expert

△ Marketing effort
○ support needed

To sell new users, these marketers use consumer product campaigns, try to
pull customers from the four market segments, incur high customer support
overhead, and base their unique selling proposition on economical data with
wide interest and an easy-to-use system.

Figures 4, 5 and 6 illustrate the marketing strategies of three hypothetical timesharing services.

Figure 4: A Consumer strategy presents an unsuccessful marketing approach for selling. The sales effort is skewed toward a market drawn from all four quadrants. This strategy promises a large user base but attracts people who will (a) never use the service or (b) use it infrequently for very short periods of time. When an online company sells passwords, it is in the credit collection, not the online business. Eventually hundreds of thousands of inactive accounts must be maintained, billed, added, and deleted. The technical group, which usually provides customer support in the form of telephone help and documentation, is overwhelmed. The market's needs are all over the map, making support impossible.

Figure 5: A Corporate niche strategy illustrates a marketing winner. The sales objective is to build big accounts. Direct sales is the foundation of customer support for its largest clients. If some high expectation customers or some expert searchers contribute revenue, that is okay, but they receive minimal support from the direct sales force. A handful of companies employ this strategy because most online services and database producers do not have information tailored to this type of market.

Figure 6: The expert strategy depicts a marketing effort aimed at the special librarian. Marketing explains technique, not applications. Expert customers have diverse needs which require a supermarket of databases. Pricing follows a normal distribution with expensive, economical, and moderately priced databases. There is less price flexibility than enjoyed by the company illustrated in Figure 5. Like the consumer online service, periodic sales forays to Quadrants B and C (the high expectation and corporate segments) are made to attract new intermediaries. These efforts also contribute to holding prices down. But shotgun marketing gradually increases the number of passwords and the costs of carrying a larger password base. Training and customer support are geared to the technical needs of the experts. This strategy yields approximately one-tenth the return of the winning strategy because of lower dollar return per password.

One consequence of the industry's effort to reach end-users and new intermediaries has been an anti-online reaction. When a prospect in Quadrant B tries to search online, they are frustrated and disappointed. We are not sure how to market to a happy, new intermediary, let alone one who says, 'I've tried this, and I don't like it. Go away'.

THE PRICING ISSUE

The online industry believes that the cost of online is one of the greatest barriers to increased usage. The barrier is finding someone to pay. The LEXIS approach is interesting, maybe unique, because the cost of the search is passed on to the lawyer's client. 'When a search is not billable to the client, we use books', observed one Louisville attorney. 'Online's just too expensive'.

In these terms, price is only relevant when the money comes from your own pocket. The Mead Data Central model works in consulting firms, some special libraries where a budget allocation is debited or a charge back to the patron occurs, researchers funded by government grants, etc.

The stockbroker's use of online presents an interesting case. Online information services increase the broker's turnover, and turnover equals commissions. In this case, the cost of the service is not an issue when online yields money to the user. The marketing job is to ensure that the searcher understands the profit generated by online usage, not the costs of using the service. The payoff to the user can be real or imagined.

A third pricing twist is now taking shape. Large banks' commitment to online electronic banking sets the stage for a pricing innovation. Banks and their partners can easily offer a range of information services to consumer and business customers. Electronic banking can pay for itself if it helps reduce paper handling.

As an incentive for customers to bank online, 'free' online business information can replace coffee pots, gift certificates, and calendars. Banks can offset the costs of this free information by deducting a service fee.

One thread which runs through these three pricing variations is that the money to pay for online information appears not to come from the user's pocket. They are, what I call, *masked pricing*. It suggests that the charges for online service are not paid by the person doing the search.

Services with masked pricing techniques have captured the most revenues. Contrast this with the struggles of online services with overt pricing. Although some information companies have tens of thousands of potential customers, these companies sell to individuals – and individuals are price sensitive when it comes to non-essential information. Dollars spent online must compete with buying shoes for the baby. As Loene Trubkin former President of Data Courier, puts it, 'The person doesn't have a big enough incentive to get information online'.

The misconceptions about price continues to put downward pressure on online access charges. As we have seen, price cuts do not yield greater volume. When the number of passwords goes up, the online service spends more than comes in. One key to online success is marketing through masked pricing. People who want free or low cost online information can use bulletin boards or the emerging bank services. Price cutting will erode the earnings of many companies.

HAVE WE FORGOTTEN THE SPECIAL LIBRARIAN?

In the late 1970s, the nerve center of the online industry was the librarian responsible for technical information in large US corporations. From this core group, today's online bibliographic industry has grown.

The special librarian was the only person who linked the information with the person who wanted it. If one considers the technical information function, it was often a single person like Ben Weil (former Director, Exxon Engineering Research Center, now a consultant in the information industry) who was the catalyst for online action. In a number of information-sensitive organizations, online searching spread from the special library to the chemist or engineer when that person expressed an interest in conducting the search himself.

The watershed for the special librarian was 1980, the year which marked the industry's discovery that without more online searchers, revenue and growth predictions could not be met. Until 1980, the industry – regardless of segment – knew who its customers were, where they went to school, and where they worked. The online searcher had these characteristics:

Library background
Technical search instruction in system commands and file content by timesharing companies and database producers
Information sensitivity
Technological awareness
Service orientation

In short, it was marketing heaven – a homogeneous, close-knit, well-educated community with loyalty to their profession, particular data-bases, and databanks.

BOOM. The computer revolution and its myths and dreams about end-users swept over the information industry. The online services began drifting from this heartland, seeking a new user community which would be hundreds, maybe thousands of times larger than the universe of special librarians. The special library market consisted of several thousand online searchers who used online to answer questions. In contrast, the markets outside the special library had hundreds of thousands of potential customers in advertising, law, personnel, data processing, corporate planning, accounting, management, purchasing, product development, and other disciplines.

In 1980 – and in some information companies today – the reasoning was that if just 10 per cent of the people in marketing or corporate finance searched databases, online companies could make millions upon millions of dollars. As we have seen, reality and the dream are not the same.

To catch the new intermediary, the information industry continues to rely upon the 'customer as fish' model. We have dangled our bait in the water, but not many fish have bitten. When that does not work, some companies use a Seventh Avenue strategy – cutting prices to build demand. Price cutting devalues information.

To net different markets, database producers make new files. The number of databases has risen from several hundred in 1980 to more than

3,000 today. Few people are able to keep up with the confusing array of online products and services.

In 1983, the online industry realized that the available systems were too difficult for the new markets. The crusade for user-friendliness started. The innovators have included Menlo Corporation, EasyNet, Dialog, Mead Data Central, BRS, Business Computer Network, InnerLine, and Dialcom. In addition, the new users cannot differentiate one database from another. In response, the online industry is making the source of information generic with homogenizing front end software. Among the consequences of these actions are the:

Diluting of the special library market with individuals who are untrained and lack an information commitment.

Alienating expert searchers with marketing programs that say, 'You are not important to us any longer'.

Reducing technical support to improve sagging profitability caused by the addition of customers who do not spend money, *and the*

Weakening of database brand identity.

Undermining file loyalty through heightened competition for the available dollars.

The big question still remains, 'Where are the end-users and new intermediaries?' I believe that a small percentage of these people will integrate online into their work. However, they will use one or two files and not as frequently as special librarians. I agree with Eric Bradshaw, Assistant Director of Marketing for Dow Jones News/Retrieval, who says, 'People are not conditioned to using online sources as the primary means of gathering information. They don't think online first. They use other ways to which they're accustomed. This is complicated by a generation/technology gap, case of use considerations, and a feeling of intimidation. Also, online products themselves as a group are not geared to end-users'.

New online users will make increasing use of the information industry's products and services. The journey, however, will be a long one, and we will probably lose our way, spend more time than we want, but eventually we get beyond the next hill to more markets and new users.

The Data Dealers Turning a Mountain of Information into Gold

Anne R. Field

Hulbert Financial Digest Inc. in Alexandria, Va, harnesses the power of computers to rate how the portfolios of some 120 investment newsletters fare each month. In Atlanta, Dataman Information Services electronically stores 85 per cent of the 3.7 million home purchases in the USA and sells the data to a variety of subscribers. The eight-year-old company is now the world's largest compiler of real estate and mortgage data. Telepraisal Inc., a New York company, sells information on 90,000 artists to art dealers tracking what they've sold and for how much.

Information. It is the hot commodity. And for these companies, as well as many others, it is proving to be the ticket to a highly profitable business. Some 4,000 firms now sell computerized information – everything from stock quotes and litigation histories to horoscopes and shipping schedules – aimed at a vast array of traders, market researchers, librarians, and media executives, to name a few. And industry experts predict a lot more to come.

For now, the biggest chunk of the $4.5 billion information business is in financial data, chiefly securities and commodity quotes and company credit histories. The reason: People in the fast-paced world of investing and finance, particularly brokers and traders, have clamoured for up-to-the-minute information.

But that is sure to change. Indeed, as more and more companies computerize their operations, industry observers say that demand for electronic information services will proliferate in all industries. Already, there is an astounding variety of customers. Lawyers, for example, depend on LEXIS, an information service from Mead Data Central, to do legal research. Shipping executives use Lloyd's Maritime Information Services to track the movements of 75,000 commercial vessels. Marketing executives study their company's newspaper, magazine, and television coverage by subscribing to Burrelle's electronic clipping service. Still, while the information business holds plenty of opportunity for entrepreneur, success is no cinch. Company founders and industry observers warn that the market is deceptively easy to enter. Because the industry is new – and the product intangible – you've got to be prepared before you make your move. 'If you skip the basic steps, you'll never get to market', says H. Skip Weitzen, author of *Infopreneurs*, a study of information entrepreneurs.

GETTING STARTED

Your starting place should be the information itself: deciding what to sell and who will buy it. Take a tip from 25-year-old Daniel Wagner. Doing a ton of market research isn't always necessary. The best source of inspiration often is your own experience. Wagner got the idea for his M.A.I.D Information Systems from his work at a London advertising agency. His job was to draw up detailed marketing plans for prospective clients. Much of his time was spent wading through research from publications around the world.

After a few years, Wagner got to thinking that there had to be a better way. His solution was to computerize all the research, allowing him to get the latest information in a matter of seconds over a personal computer. 'It seemed such a good idea,' recalls Wagner. 'I left my job to do it'.

Now, with offices in London, New York, Log Angeles, Tokyo, and Melbourne, M.A.I.D allows access via personal computers to over 40,000 marketing reports and daily updated news bulletins culled from over 700 publications. Cost: $10,000 a year, plus $180 for every hour of use. Revenues are about $2 million.

FINDING A FOCUS

As a rule, the most successful ideas involve niches. The more targeted your market – market researchers in the pharmaceutical industry, for example – the better your chance of attracting interested customers. But that is not enough. Make sure you're not dumping material into a computer that subscribers could just as easily find in a book or another publication. You have to offer a capability or a kind of information that has never been available before.

Consider Hulbert Financial. In 1980, founder Mark Hulbert surveyed the market for investment newsletters and decided there wasn't room for another one. But after studying the hundreds of publications available and their often contradictory recommendations, the then 24-year-old philosophy major came to another conclusion: He could create a successful business with a very specialized service that only a computer could make possible.

He decided to electronically store the model portfolios listed in every newsletter, rate the success of their selections, and print the results in his own newsletter. After one year, Hulbert and the two college friends with whom he started the company signed on 3,000 subscribers, each paying $135 a year. Today, he has about 15,000 subscribers. Revenues are an estimated $1.2 million, and the company is profitable.

James Kollegger, CEO of Tele/Scope Networks Inc., offers a service called Tele/Scope. It presents a daily news wrap-up for telecommunications executives, with about 60 headlines, each featuring a 25-line summary or a longer analysis. Clients also have an option that would be impossible without a computer: They just define the specific news they want – Justice Department rulings, for example. Then, throughout the day, the service pulls out only those summaries that pertain to the subject. After four years, Tele/Scope has about 7,000 users, and rakes in over $1 million. Kollegger is planning to expand the concept to other industries.

PARCELING THE DATA

When choosing the data you'll sell, think about future products. The name of the game is repackaging. That means gathering together a core of information that you can split in parts and recombine in many different ways. For an extra fee, you might customize the product for clients, so they receive their own proprietary sets of data.

Ruth Stanat, founder of Strategic Intelligence Systems, may be the queen of repackaging. Her information service helps strategic planners keep tabs on the competition. A team of 15 specialists analyze 300 research reports covering 18 industries and 50 market segments, such as financial services, health care, and consumer goods. If a client wants information about the rental market for compact-sized cars, Stanat's staff searches through the automobile database and comes out with a list of research summaries. On top of that, she offers a custom service that will track specific competitors for a client and will not be sold to anyone else.

Customers are willing to pay big bucks for Stanat's information. The base service costs from $5,000 to $20,000 a year and the custom product runs from $25,000 on up. Company revenues of well over $1 million have been growing at 40 per cent a year.

Stanat also knows another important rule: When it comes to delivery of the information, you have to be flexible. Allow customers the option of receiving the data over their computers, stored on a floppy disk, or in written form. It all depends how quickly the client needs the information. Remember that many people still prefer to see information on paper.

BUILDING THE BASE

After you decide what kind of information you want to sell, start gathering the data. What's the first thing you'll need? Patience. Putting together a database of information that has never before been collected in one place is time-consuming work. But once the initial effort is over, rivals won't be able to touch your business, since they'll have to go through the lengthy task of creating their own database.

James Monaco, founder of Baseline, is one entrepreneur who spent a long time building his database. The 46-year-old former film critic and New York University professor took about six years before even introducing his entertainment-industry information service in 1986. He and a staff of editors spent a good part of that time poring through films, videos, and press materials, and telephoning industry players to design the database. It now includes all 70,000 movies and television programs made, along with over 20,000 entertainment companies, and over 300,000 active industry participants.

Today, Monaco's slow-paced gamble is paying off. His basic service is profitable and pulling in revenues 'well in excess' of $1 million. Entertainment companies now regularly call him with additions to the database. 'If someone wanted to compete with Baseline, how would they do it?' he asks.

SELLING THE IDEAS

Creating the database isn't the only part of the process that takes perseverance. Monaco discovered that marketing is also a delicate job. Forced to open up a marketing niche that never existed before, he has devoted many hours to educating potential customers about the benefits of information services. The result: Monaco has been as much a missionary as a businessman. 'We had to talk our customers into a new way of doing business', he explains.

For that reason, Monaco spent a lot of time of the key ingredient in any information entrepreneur's marketing campaign. He slowly nurtured relationships with important people in the industry through meetings, telephone conversations, and visits to trade shows. It was only last year, after he was satisfied that he'd won over the influential trendsetters, that he started a full-scale marketing effort with a 10- person sales force and a major advertising campaign.

Building a database and an effective marketing campaign also takes a lot of money. 'You've got to have deep pockets to help you through in the early years', says Stanat of Strategic Intelligence. At least 35 cents of every dollar you earn should be plowed back into marketing, she says. And often you have to reinvest your earnings in order to expand your database and marketing force.

Still, there are ways around the money dilemma. You can start out by acting as a consultant for a few big clients, and then branch out from there. Charles Cleveland, who launched Communication Development in West Des Moines, Iowa, did just that. He developed a unique method of analyzing consumer attitudes using computers while working as a professor in the 1960s and soon started to do consulting, using the system.

When a local newspaper accused Cleveland of being in cahoots with the CIA, he was flooded with phone calls from major companies seeking his help. Anyone working with the CIA had to be a real professional, they assumed. With demand soaring, Cleveland left teaching in 1977 to become an entrepreneur. Customers pay from $50,000 and up for his advice. Company revenues for 1988 are projected at $8.5 million.

That kind of success can be had by enterprising people who familiarize themselves with the tricks of the trade ahead of time. With a healthy dose of imagination, a little tenacity, and a good understanding of the business, almost anyone can make a go of it as an information entrepreneur. 'This industry abounds with opportunities,' says Kollegger of Tele/Scope Networks. 'The ground floor's opening up all the time'.

OPPORTUNITY KNOCKING

So, you want to start a database company. There are lots of opportunities, as long as you pick the right market. Here are a few possibilities, according to Margaret T. Fischer, a vice president of LINK Resources Corp., a New York market research firm:

Financial services

It is one of the hottest sectors of the information industry. And there is still plenty of room for newcomers, particularly if you focus on the increasing number of customers who'll need international financial data. That includes everything from up-to-the-minute currency rates to stock performances of individual companies and lists of corporate directors.

Marketing specialists

Their jobs are getting more and more complex. As a result, researchers in virtually every industry will need better and more precise demographic information, telling them who is buying their products, for what purpose, and in what part of the country.

Consumers

Most successful database companies target businesses. But now that many consumers have easier-to-use personal computers at home, they are more likely to use their PCs for tapping into electronic services. Your best bet is to aim at busy two-career families. One new venture will let subscribers order groceries over their PCs.

Stormy weather in the datasphere: the problems of pricing and marketing electronic information

Stephen E. Arnold

7202 Iron Gate Court,
Louisville, K7 40241, USA

A specter is getting fat and sassy in the United States, and he's planning a trip to your homeland soon, maybe tomorrow.

As one young American industrial design student said 'There is now a computer-generated world, a hyperworld, that does not exist in the normal sense but is challenging our definitions of *real* and *physical*'.[1] Electronic information recreates reality. Furthermore, information and technology are prolific collaborators. Together they breed new digital gizmos and lots of data at an ever-accelerating rate like microchip rabbits.

My topic is pricing electronic information products, to which I shall refer as EIPs. My specialty is text databases, and I will narrow my comments about EIPs to files which contain words, numbers, facts, and images. Although my focus is sharp, I believe that many of my observations apply to a range of electronic media – online, CD-ROM, and facsimile. (Facsimile real-time publishing is sending information to a customer via facsimile. Group III machines made this possible. McGraw-Hill was one of the early leaders in this field, and now other publishing companies are using the technology. The real explosion in this technology will occur when Group IV machines are available. Though estimates of throughput vary, six to eight pages a minute of text will be possible.)

Let me warn you. I will touch on issues which are usually discussed without reference to pricing EIPs. Technology, epistemology, and business voodoo conjoin in poorly-understood ways. An awareness of this complex environment can be the difference between EIP success or failure.

THE DATASPHERE

The EIP environment is difficult for many to see. We are like a goldfish trying to know more about the water in which we swim. But as we look through our atmosphere we see a world shimmering in the distance. Electronic publishers generally agree that the environment for EIPs has an elusive surreal quality.

We have all heard that 'the medium is the message'. EIPs are, of course, media. In America's highly-developed *datasphere* (its total electronic media environment), EIPs release gigabytes of data that have considerable force. My trying to predict the impact of a new EIP makes me into a weather forecaster of sorts. There is one difference, though: weather forecasters are correct more often than I am. I cannot explain why one product thrives as a better one withers. Nor do I know what twists and turns EIPs will follow. Information responds to forces which we understand in a superficial way at best. I do know that a single factor like pricing has little, if anything, to do with an EIP's success or failure. But all products must have a price, so I will try to highlight a few of the major issues a publisher must resolve before going to market.

We need to know more about the datasphere in America, how EIPs behave in it, and what is on the horizon. So armed, we improve the odds that our EIPs will succeed. The first step is to understand what is happening in the USA on the threshold of the 1990s.

AMERICA – THE FIRST ODC

As I was editing this essay, the current issue of *PC Week* arrived by post.[2] One of the secondary articles reported on an erasable optical drive with 35 millisecond access time, which is almost ten times faster than the CD-ROM drives currently available. Storage Dimensions, a unit of Maxtor, says the drive can accept 650 Mb and 1 Gb cartridges. A single-drive system will cost about $8,000 and a two-drive system, about $15,500. The drive has been engineered to operate as a network file server.

This is an important breakthrough. WORM technology of this speed and capacity makes it possible for corporations to put massive databases online easily. But technology trade journals report many innovations every week. Joe and Jean Average will greedily consume what these stepping stones make possible, including real-time simulations for business, image databases, and nifty games rated R for relaxation.

WORM developments are now coming quickly. They promise to make optical storage a strong weather system in the datasphere. And simultaneously US businesses are getting serious about real-time facsimile publishing: Group III facsimile machines delivering personalized newsletters to subscribers anywhere in the world – fast. When Group IV machines arrive, hundreds of fax publishers will pop up almost overnight. Concurrently Dialog Information Services and Mead Data Central, two dominant timesharing companies, are trying to put every published document's full text online. And distributed image databases are multiplying rapidly. What will be the role of each of these EIPs? Who will emerge as the *big* winner?

These are examples of what is brewing in America's datasphere. Consider what can happen when we stir into this technological hot house electronic banking via PC, fiberoptic networks, free databases and timesharing services, 24-hour HV religious programming, low-cost video rentals, beach movies, boom boxes with digital sampling, and audio CDs clipped to jogging shorts. America's datasphere is lashed by hurricanes of electronic information and downpours of data, the environment endlessly changing and evolving. Like any force of nature, it can be dangerous for the ignorant or arrogant.

The USA, I believe, is the first over-developed country or ODC. After an ODC loses its manufacturing base, business embraces an economy based on EIPs. Considerable effort and energy go into shifting assets and making data, not manufacturing things. Other characteristics of an ODC include:

- The country's intellectual resources are exploited the way under-developed and lesser-developed countries' natural resources are exploited.
- A two-class society emerges, which in the USA consists of the YuppiElite and a granular underclass.
- No consistent set of beliefs unifies society.
- The infrastructure rots.
- Education is ineffective, producing graduates who cannot read but who can consume electronic media.
- There is a precipitous drop in the number of scientists and engineers and an increase in people trained in law, finance, and other 'soft' disciplines.

America, according to Professor Neil Postman, is 'amusing itself to death'.[3] He suggests that the marketing lessons in the USA teach 'that short and simple messages are preferable to long and complex ones; that drama is to be preferred over exposition; that being sold solutions is better than being confronted with questions about problems'.

What does this have to do with pricing electronic information? Well, what marketing says about a product may be more important than the product itself. In many instances, the hype is the EIP.

WHY THE OLD LAWS DON'T WORK ANYMORE

My first employer took pity on me when I was a college student; to help me, he shared his business secrets with me. This gentleman sold soft drinks and hot dogs for a living, and he said:

- 'The learning curve for a new product is expensive, so you have to set a price high enough to stay in business but not so high that your customers will beat a path to your competitor's door.'

- 'The more you make, the cheaper your production costs will be. You can cut prices to gain market share or you can raise prices to increase your profit.'
- 'High prices mean that you will get a smaller share of a market. Low prices mean you will get a bigger share of the market. You can't have both. You have to pick a strategy.'[4]

When I went to university, I found out that he had taught me exactly what the textbooks said. Let's look at each of these Golden Rules in terms of EIPs, not frankfurters.

My mentor's first tip was that the theory of the learning curve says that I must charge a high price for my product. The idea makes some sense for traditional manufacturers. Machines have to be designed, work mapped, raw materials located, and so on. These require large capital investments. But many EIPs are often preceded by a printed version. The data factory is already built and operating. A new EIP can be created by processing a typesetting tape. To be sure, we cannot ignore the cost of this intellectual work, but the EIP's cost structure is radically different from that of the traditional manufacturing operation. Setting a learning curve-based price is a dubious suggestion at best.

Secret 2: the idea that mass production lets me reduce prices as I crank out more widgets has a seductive charm. But the well-publicized success of some Far East manufacturing facilities is based upon the companies' ability to make changes rapidly. Thus, aggregate volume sales come from moving many different versions of the product. *Mass* then does not mean selling millions of the same thing. Many US and Western European electronic publishers confuse *mass* and *aggregate volume*. Mass production of a single item does not necessarily encourage lower prices.

His final business nugget promises that high prices reduce the size of the market; low prices expand it. Let's consider two EIPs: Knowledge Index (KT) and the Alde software CD-ROM. If low price increased market share, both of these products would be among the largest, most successful of their kind. KI is excellent value. The service allows access to exceptional databases at comparatively low prices. Best of all, customers pay a flat rate and no per-record hit charges.

The Alde CD-ROM costs about $100 and contains hundreds of tested, high-value shareware software programs ready to copy and use. As I understand it, neither KI nor the Alde CD-ROM has captured tens of thousands of buyers. On the other hand, comparatively expensive databases like Promt, InvesText and ABI/INFORM enjoy large shares of the online market.

Some products capture market share, but they don't do it by price cutting. I chuckle when inexperienced EIP managers either raise or lower the price of their product as soon as they can. Neither action has a significant short-term revenue impact. In fact, sudden price shifts disturb the datasphere igniting a chain of reactions far beyond what a comparable move in the carpet business would trigger.

Can you see the wrongness for EIPs of these three pearls of hot-dog wisdom? What you may not know is that the ideas hidden in such concepts as market share, segmentation, product portfolio, distribution channels, strategic planning, competition, and pricing itself need to be revisited in terms of the datasphere's hyperworld.

EIP LIFE CYCLES AND PRICING

One of the most cherished ideas in marketing is the product life cycle. Put simply, the idea means that a product has several stages, ending with the product's death. Most business consultants would agree that the four major stages are:

- Product introduction
- Growth
- Maturity
- Decline.

The problem is that EIPs seem to be long-lived and hard to kill. They linger. Some of them disappear for a short time and then creep back onto disc packs with the encouragement of different publishers. We do not · understand the exact nature of EIP life cycles.

Consider the printed telephone directory. We can use the data in the telephone book in a few predefined ways. Our access is enabled and constrained by its alphabetical listing. The bigger the city, the less usable the telephone book. When we put the same data online, the telephone book becomes a different product entirely because the medium of online transforms the data by allowing us to manipulate it in many ways. We can make a list of everyone on a particular street or generate a mailing list with a few keystrokes. The electronic version of the telephone book is a 'new' product. The costs of this 'new' product are generally less than the cost of making the paper directory. Thus, the cost of an EIP is *incremental*.

Our new telephone listing product starts its own life cycle. Obviously the printed directory keeps living and moves through its life cycle. If we were to put the data on a CD-ROM, we would have another 'new' product. Now we have three separate media and three life cycles. We have given our customer three product choices: paper, online, or CD-ROM.

What do we charge for each? The printed telephone directory has been a low- or no-cost item for the customer. The telephone company in the USA gives them away to build usage of the system and reduce the need for operator-assisted calls from people who want telephone numbers. Maybe our online directory should be free? To my knowledge, most commercial directory databases cost money. Dun & Bradstreet, for example, charges

$85 for a single financial company record which is an expanded directory listing with credit information.

If we are going to set the price for our printed directory and EIPs, these three products are both different and the same simultaneously. Before we can set a price, we must weigh such factors as:

- Ways to protect our revenue from each product from cannibalization by our own EIPs.
- How to make a pricing structure 'look good' or 'make sense' among the three products that we sell.
- Tactics which allow us to gain an advantage over our competition.
- What our revenue target is for each product.

We can expand this list of factors. But I think you can see that pricing gets tied to strategic issues.

MEDIA MIGRATION

Each new EIP technology gives customers a chance to migrate from one medium to another. And who migrates to the new technology first? The most sophisticated customers! They reason: 'If I can reduce my costs for the information by using this product on (a) CD-ROM, (b) online, (c) via facsimile, (d) in-house tape, (e) other, I save x amount of money and become a corporate superstar'. If the customer can choose between an unwieldy paper directory and an online database, the customer may migrate to online. The customer can log on and pay only for specific information. The online query may last less than a minute. If the EIP is easier, more precise, more cost effective, or some other combination of benefits, customers may drop the print directory subscription. The EIP's price must compensate for lost subscriptions.

US timesharing companies, as I noted in my March 1989 essay in *Online*, have considerable control over the pricing.[5] For example, vendors can offer discounts to large organizational customers. Vendors offer support for high-speed modems which reduce the database producer's connect hour royalties. What takes 20 minutes with a 1200 baud modem can be accomplished in 2.5 minutes with a 9600 baud modem. This means that a connect hour royalty of $40 becomes $5. Timesharing companies perceive the customer as 'theirs.' Thus, the electronic publisher may not know why revenues are falling nor have the information necessary to counter the downward trend.

If and when a CD-ROM replaces an online product, some electronic publishers discover that the CD-ROM revenue does not make up for lost online and print subscription income.

PRAGMATIC PRICING

Some publishers have found a way out of the datasphere's pricing jungle.

The trick is to examine pricing in terms of:

- Segment identification. To whom are we going to sell our EIP? Where are these people? What do they now spend for other versions of this information?
- Equivalency with a competing product. What is the range of prices in the market now for comparable or competing products being delivered with this technology? What is the pricing history of these products?
- Product benefits. At what stage of our marketing campaign does pricing come into play? How are we positioning the product? What importance does pricing play in terms of the overall campaign?
- Capturing customers and building market share. What specific steps do we have to take to get usage and expand that base?
- Generating revenue immediately, regardless of volume. What can we do to make cash flow?

Electronic publishers have to publicize prices and keep them stable in the midst of rapid change. However, each customer values data *situationally*. When the need for the information increases, the value of the data goes up. Blue-chip consulting firms can charge tens of thousands of dollars for information obtained from online or CD-ROM sources. Consulting firms package the information and deliver exactly what the customer wants. EIPs, at this time, cannot deliver information with this kind of added value. Electronic products necessarily warrant more modest prices in the eyes of the customer. Information producers, on the other hand, want more money.

All data are not created equal. Visualize a pyramid with three layers. The base is 'data'. *Data* are facts, opinions, numbers, and any other material which flow over an electronic distribution channel. Data are commodities. Examples of data are stock quotes and wire service feeds. Data age at different rates and are plastic.

Information is the middle layer of the pyramid. Information is organized, structured data. Value has been added in the form of indexing, abstracting, compilation, graphic representation, etc. Think of a wire service feed as data and the indexed, edited, and structured full-text record in a database as information. Information often costs more than raw data.

At the top of the pyramid is *wisdom*. It is scarce and expensive. Wisdom is distilled and processed information, and it seems to be something that only a few humans can generate. But code stokers in the USA, England, France, Germany, Japan and Tibet are trying to make computers turn an alchemist's trick: information into wisdom.

Pragmatic pricing requires a close study of the five factors summarized above and a judgment based on the value the customer will assign to the EIP's content.

PRICING BEHAVIORS

The prices charged for EIPs behave in several interesting ways. First, the prices for EIPs have a specific gravity; that is, they find a level and hover about that point. Even though the cost of information technology drops, the publishers nudge prices up. The two cancel one another out.

Second, online databases, reference CD-ROMs, and facsimile publications are not mass market products even though some are virtually free. It takes time, money, need, and brains to use EIPs. Effective use of EIPs requires a conceptual aptitude that is often ignored or dismissed with the quip, 'Any fool can use this CD-ROM'.

One day the EIP publisher accepts that the 'real' market for the EIP is smaller than his 1–2–3 forecast predicted, and a marketing arms race begins. In addition to head-to-head comparisons in advertisements, pricing is now a deadly instrument. An EIP publisher introduces a lower-cost service and says that it is 'new and improved'. Then an EIP's price is raised slightly to allow the publisher to claim 'higher quality'. We can shift the battle to a different medium and start again. As a last resort, the weakest publisher can sell his product out to a competitor who wins. Merger mania and acquisition fever are two results. And where's the customer in all this? I once heard a proverb attributed to an African seer: 'When elephants fight, the grass is trampled'.

We need to understand that marketing warfare accelerates change in the datasphere. The USA has the dubious distinction of leading the world in making and remaking EIPs with greater velocity than any other country.

A PRICING EXERCISE

Let's take a hypothetical EIP and price it. In the interests of making the model workable, let me outline the assumptions. First, we have a printed technical reference book which allows identification of drugs by their brand and generic names, addresses of the companies manufacturing and marketing the pharmaceuticals, and tabular data which gives the dollar value of drug imports and exports for 24 countries.

Second, we sell 500 copies of the book each year at $1,000 each, so we have revenues of $500,000 and costs of $400,000. We want to take some of this $100,000 surplus and make a CD-ROM.

Third, we do our research and determine that we can manufacture 100 discs twice a year for about $80,000. We allocate $20,000 for marketing to libraries. We hope to sell 50 discs.

How do we price the product? Let's assume that we have conducted the analyses suggested above in Pragmatic pricing and can select from these approaches:

- Relevant range pricing. This means that certain products can only be sold within a specific pricing range regardless of the cost of producing the product. One example would be charging for soft drinks. Six cans of Coca-Cola have to sell between $2.50 and $3.50 per pack, or they gather dust.
- Competitive pricing. We do what the other guy does. This is sometimes called 'me too' pricing.
- Undercutting. We price lower than our competitor. Some think that. the Japanese hold black belts in this sport. When they capture market share, prices rise.
- Demand-oriented pricing. We charge whatever the market will pay. This is how products on the black market are priced.
- Cost-mark up pricing. We figure out cost and then mark it up a specific amount. We always get our margin.
- Predatory pricing. We charge as little as possible. This is the marketing equivalent of terrorism.
- Skimming. We charge as much as we can. This is cherry picking unrestrained by season.[6]

We do some research for this hypothetical product and find that no CD-ROM competitor exists. The closest electronic competition is from Dialog Information Services, Data-Star, and Mead Data. Each company has a disc farm of pharmaceutical data. We examine the pricing of other CD-ROM products, of course, but we know that the pharmaceutical industry is one which values information and has money. Drug companies are data addicts. We can set whatever price we want.

Well, we are conservative and test *penetration pricing* and *skimming*. After we set this strategy, we analyze our costs, add 20 per cent extra to cover surprises, make sure our sums were correct, check against the competition, and put the pedal to the metal.

We offer the disc at $6,000 per year, without any hardware, and $17,000 per year with a drive, PC, etc. Our internal accounting policies allow us for the one-year test to exclude software licensing fees and certain overhead costs like salaries of our sales force whose principal job is to sell books.

Our marketing campaign sells five units immediately and pulls 50 requests for an on-site demonstration. Although we did not budget for live on-site demonstrations, we send salespeople to visit as many of the 50 inquirers as possible. We sell ten machines in eight weeks. We receive a slightly better response from the $6,000 promotion and decide to go with the higher ticket.

After six months of effort, we have sold 50 units, place an additional 25 on approval and are in the midst of producing the second disc for the subscribers. Meanwhile we are attempting to modify the disc to respond to customer suggestions. We get a report that renewals to the print directory have begun to falter. We cross-check the list of print subscribers and EIP buyers. The two lists overlap. We reach for the Maalox.

A 30-SECOND CASE ANALYSIS

At this point, let's stop the case and examine the situation the EIP created. First, our cost analysis did not – and in all fairness could not – predict all the expenses associated with redirecting the sales force, funding the trial installations, providing customer support, and modifying the software. These costs are hard to estimate for a known product – nearly impossible for a new one.

Second, we spent more money than budgeted trying to respond to what the customers told us. Listening costs money.

We did not anticipate having to make any CD-ROM design changes, but the customers did.

Third, our marketing program has become more important than the EIP. We have to generate more revenue which means we make more visits, offer training, cut deals, give away samples, and support expensive, free 30-day trials. We have to spend more to get more, right?

Would we be in a stronger position if our price had been higher – say, $50,000? Maybe. One unexpected development was the loss of renewal revenue when subscribers froze their decision until they examined the CD-ROM. The cost of making each sale astounds us; each sale is a long, expensive process, not tidy like direct mail or tool-free ordering. With 20/20 hindsight a higher price may have pumped up cash flow and increased our print directory sales.

Another factor was the 'noise' generated by the promotion of the EIP. The new product got high visibility, which unintentionally rendered our print directory invisible.

Finally, we underestimated the need for post-sale telephone support and on-site service.

Although hypothetical, this case hints at a few of the more obvious traps which await the electronic publisher who see EIPs as just another product.

TECHNOLOGY AND MARKETING SHIFTS

With each EIP created by a technology shift, a marketing shift also occurs. As the pace of change accelerates, some consumers may resist innovative products or services because an innovation may disrupt their routines or conflict with their beliefs.[7]

EIPs are self-perpetuating. The more information available electronically fuels innovation in delivery technology which, in turn, creates more ways for information to grow. We are suffering from information pollution in our datasphere.

Bear in mind that successful EIPs are vulnerable to technology shifts. Protecting an EIP is a job for marketing. When technology shifts reduce an EIP's revenue-producing life by 50 per cent – for example, a two-year cycle becomes a one-year cycle – the cost of marketing increases by a factor of two. In other words, what would have cost $100,000 over a period of two years costs $200,000 in twelve months. The increased costs come from two factors:

- Rush charges add to the cost of printing, production, writing, and design. Redos are, as we all know, increasingly likely when time is short.
- High-visibility techniques are required to get attention in a short period of time. With a longer time horizon, 'free' publicity in the form of news releases, bylined articles, and word-of-mouth advertising are viable. With a short timeline, bundles of bucks are needed to buy attention through advertisements, direct mail, and marketing collateral.

When a product has its life cycle shortened, the EIP becomes less important than the merchandising of the EIP's concept. Marketers are quite good at building expectations and then delivering products which disappoint. When customers crash into reality, they become more cautious. I think online's slowing growth is a result of overselling the benefits of the medium.

PRODIGY OR DUNCE?

Can marketing alone make an EIP successful?

Consider the Prodigy service, which is a joint venture of a large retail store and a computer company.[8] Prodigy Services Co. (White Plains, New York) began in 1984 as Trintex, a joint venture of IBM Corp., Sears, Roebuck & Co., and CBS. CBS pulled out in 1986, but the other two partners remain solidly behind the Prodigy network project. Sears and IBM have invested around $600 million in Prodigy. The Prodigy system is an online service that, for about $10 per month, allows subscribers access to over 500 services including American Airline's reservation service, grocery shopping, weather forecasts, and banking – via their personal home computer and a modem.

Estimates are that Prodigy will require around 2.5 million homes, or over 25 per cent of the present basic market population, to recover its investment. Already 1.3 million people subscribe to other videotex systems. Prodigy is one of the few videotex services to carry advertising. Typically, companies pay Prodigy each time an advertisement is viewed or a sales lead generated, as well as a percentage fee for each product sold using the service. So far, some 170 companies have signed up to advertise.

The marketing push for Prodigy consists of a low-cost modem and password, print media advertisements, and a public relations blitz. What Prodigy offers is also available on CompuServe, a consumer timesharing service with 600,000 live passwords. CompuServe, based in Columbus, Ohio, has responded to Prodigy with more advertising, acquiring a faltering competitor (The Source), and introducing a less-hostile software interface.

Can Prodigy win the Nobel Prize?
It is doubtful.

In a country where cruising the shopping mall is one of life's most meaningful moments for Joe Average, shopping by PC is a shot on goal from midfield. Only mega-hyper-slam dunk marketing can pull off this stunt.

After the roll-out, Prodigy's marketing tasks are differentiating itself from CompuServe and pumping up usage. When the product doesn't live up to the customer's expectations, nothing – including giving the product away free – will sell the product in a volume sufficient to earn a profit. Again: price has become irrelevant.

In conclusion, pricing is an important part of EIP marketing. But we do not fully understand how pricing and the other events in the datasphere impinge on the success or failure of the EIP. Pricing cannot be ignored. But it is not the only factor. Now, right or wrong, it is one of the causes for publishers' insomnia.

The people with EIP winners think about pricing somewhat differently. Their secret is not marketing. Success has come from data integrity, accuracy, consistency, and excellence. When an excellent product meets a specific need, the customer can tell you what the product is worth. Publishers with EIP winners listen to these people because they are always right. They speak in dollars, not data-dreams.

REFERENCES

1   R.S. Wurman, *Information Anxiety*, Doubleday, 1989, p. 294.
2   K.B. Sullivan, 'LaserStor Erasable-Optical Drives Offer Performance Levels Equal to Winchester,' *PC Week*, 31 July 1989, p. 10.
3   N. Postman, *Amusing Ourselves to Death: Public Discourse in the Age of Show Business*, Viking, 1985, p. 5.
4   These tenets come from W.R. Hilker and E. P. Gee, *The MBA Toolkit*, Chilton 1985, one of the best summaries of American business beliefs, formulae and precepts that I have found.
5   S.E. Arnold, 'Online Pricing: Where It's at Today and Where It's Going Tomorrow,' *Online*, March 1989, pp. 6–9.
6   W.R. Hilker and E.P. Gee, *The MBA Toolkit*, pp. 85–86.
7   S. Ram and J.N. Sheth, 'Consumer Resistance to Innovations: The Marketing Problem and Its Solutions,' *Journal of Consumer Marketing*, [bo]6, 2, Spring 1989, pp. 5–14.
8   S.N. Chakravarty and E. McGlinn, 'This Thing Has to Change People's Habits,' *Forbes*, 26June 1989, pp. 118, 122.

The Information Vending Machine

Andrew C. Gross

Cleveland State University

The information vending machine will become busier and busier, as more and more businesses find their need for information growing. The author presents evidence that there are major opportunities for entrepreneurs in the field of information delivery.

In today's business world, information is becoming the most-needed resource. It may be information about a competitor, or the state of the economy, or something that at first may seem completely unrelated; but decision makers have found that they can't fly by the seats of their pants anymore, and information is their flight map.

To find that information, these savvy business leaders turn to the information vending machine. Not the type of machine from which you can buy soft drinks and candy, this machine is really composed of the companies that deliver information through the computer, or in the mail, or in person – however the customer wants it.

Entrepreneurs searching for an undiscovered niche could do worse than to enter this industry. Informational activities are increasing in all types of business, and the types of information needed are growing all the time as well. This article will look at those trends and suggest some marketing strategies for those entering this fast-growing industry.

INDICATORS IN THE NON-TECHNICAL ENVIRONMENT

It is a cliché that in the modern economy, everything is related to everything else. It is equally accepted that computer hardware and software permit us to construct giant models with hundreds of equations. But in practice, we must choose relatively simple relationships. Businessmen, economists, market researchers, and corporate planners tend to tie shipments of their particular product or sales of their particular service to a few widely used indicators, such as those in Figure 1 and Table 1. The actual choice among indicators depends on the particular business or enterprise, the segments served, and the product's or service's end use (see Figure 2).

But the inquisitive entrepreneur seeks a competitive edge, the niches or pockets of profitability that grow far faster than the average. It does not matter if we speak of the demand for refrigerators for new households or

FIGURE 1. THE MOST WIDELY USED ECONOMIC INDICATORS

Demography	*Business Sector*
Population	Manufacturers Sales
Households	Plant & Equipment Expenditures
Births/Deaths	Construction Activity
Marriages/Divorces	Producer Durable Expenditures
	R & D Expenditures
General Economics	*Government Sector*
Gross National Products	Federal, State, Local Spending
Index of Industrial Production/	Defense Expenditures
Employment/Unemployment	Transfer Payments (Social Security)
Business Formations	
Consumer Sector	*Other*
Disposable Income	Health Expenditures
Housing Starts	School Enrollment
Recreation Expenditures	Motor Vehicles in Use

TABLE 1. *General Demographic, Economic and Industrial Indicators – U.S., 1970–1980*

Item	1970	1972	1974	1976	1978	1980	Annual growth
Population (mil persons)	205	209	212	218	223	228	1.1%
Immigrants, total (000 persons)	373		395	399	601		6.2
Divorces (000s)	708	845	977	1083	1130	1191	6.7
Gross National Product (bil '75 $)	1363	1489	1567	1633	1804	1859	3.1
Personal Consump. Expend. (bil '72 $)	672	737	764	823	903	931	6.4
Indust. Production Index (1967 = 100)	108	120	129	131	146	147	3.3
Iron ore production (mil 1g tons)	89.8	75.4	84.4	80.0	81.6	69.6	−2.5
Woodpulp production (mil m tons)	37.3	40.0	41.4	40.6	42.9	45.8	2.1
Wheat production (mil bushels)	1352	1596	1782	2142	1776	2374	4.2
Elec. power prod'n (bil kwhr)	1492	1750	1867	2038	2204	2286	5.1
Passenger car prod'n (000 units)	6547	8824	7331	8498	9165	6400	−1.3
Passenger cars in use (mil units)	89	97	105	110	117	124	3.4

1. Annual growth rate refers to 1970–1980, except for immigration.
SOURCES: 1. *Statistical Absttract of the U.S., 1981 and 1982* (Washington: USGPO, annually).
   2. *Survey of Current Business* (Washington: U.S. Dept. of Commerce, monthly)
   3. *Basebook, 1982* (Cleveland: Predicasts, annually).
   4. *World Development Report, 1983* (Washington: World Banks, annually).

FIGURE 2. HOW TO CHOOSE INDICATORS

Nature of Demand	*Segment of Market*	
Original Equipment	*General Indicator*	*Specific Segment*
Aftermarket or		
Replacement		
	Housing Starts	1-Family Starts
Population	Population over 18	
Major End Use	Plant & Equipment	Chemical Industry P&E
	Expenditures (P&E)	
Consumer Sector	Personal Consumption	Recreation Expenditures
Business/Industry	Expenditures	
Government	Index of Industrial	Nondurable Goods
Export	Production	Prod. Index

AN EXAMPLE – REFRIGERATORS

For New Sites	*For Replacement*	*Other Considerations*
Housing Starts	Number of Households	Imports
Mobile Homes	Households with	Exports
Recreation Vehicles	Refrigerators	

TABLE 2. *Count of Entities – Organizations, Projects, Operations – U.S., 1970–1980*

Item	1970	1972	1974	1976	1978	1980	Annual growth
Local government units (000s)		78.8			80.0		0.3%
Federal food stamp areas	1747	2126		3035			9.6
Defense contract awards (000s)				52.8	61.1	76.4	13.0
Hospitals	7123	7061		7130	7015		−0.3
Major opera companies	35		53	65	78	109	12.0
Urban symphony orchestras	24		43	56	76	85	13.5
Commercial FM stations	464	590	678	713	777	904	6.9
Business phones in use (mil)	33	36	39	41	44	48	4.1
Residl. phones in use (mil)	87	96	105	114	125	133	4.7
Mobile & spcl. radio station (mil)	1.9	1.8	2.0	6.8	15.7	15.5	23.5
Franchd. rstrs., co.-owned (000s)	4.9	6.3	10.1	12.6	15.5	17.8	13.8

1. Local govt. units – figure shown for 1978 is actually for 1977.
2. Defense contract awards – figure shown for 1976 is actually for 1977.
3. Annual growth rate refers to span between two most distant years.

SOURCES: 1. *Statistical Abstract of the U.S., 1081 and 1982* (Washington: USGPO, annually).
2. *Survey of Current Business* (Washington: U.S. Dept. of Commerce, monthly).
3. *Basebook, 1982* (Cleveland: Predicasts, annually).
4. *World Development Report, 1983* (Washington: World Banks, annually).

the replacement market; both appear to be quite mature. The same holds true for hundreds of other consumer and industrial products. So where are the lucrative opportunities? Many point to high-technology and service industries, but the solution is not all that simple, and traditional economic and demographic indicators tell only part of the story.

Organizations and projects

A second useful set of indicators comes from a systems count of the number of organizations, projects, agencies, or programs in an area that exist or are about to be established. Table 2 provides a small but representative sample. Of course, many entities – including governmental units at various levels and not-for-profit institutions, ranging from churches to labor unions – have low growth rates; indeed, some declined in number in the 1970s. But others have displayed rather healthy increases.

Consider the following two examples:

The number of defense contracts awarded rose from 52,800 in 1976 to 76,400 by 1980; *and*

The number of food-stamp participating areas grew from 1,747 to 3,035 between 1970 and 1976.

The annual growth rates in both cases approach 10 per cent (9.7 per cent and 9.6 per cent, respectively), solid increases in a mature economy. The first example represents a dispersal of contracts among vendors and signals a rise in the information-processing needs of the Pentagon and in the contracting organizations. The second example means more necessary coordination among federal, state, and local authorities; this, in turn, signals an increased level of data handling at all three levels. In both instances, marketing opportunities arise for vendors in information-processing services and related areas.

One of the most encouraging signs for the economy in general and for vendors of information services in particular is the rise of the entrepreneurial spirit.[1] This is shown in the number of new business formations. The number of proprietorships rose from 9.4 million in 1970 to 12.0 million by 1978; that of partnerships increased from 0.9 million to 1.2 million during this time; the count of corporations went from 1.7 million to over 2.0 million. New business ventures rose from 264,000 in 1970 to 534,000 in 1980, an annual growth rate of 7.3 per cent. Put differently, the size of the average business declined, but the total number of businesses increased. Since each new business is an entity, it requires data processing, information handling, and knowledge generation. It is unwilling to share these activities with other firms, for obvious competitive reasons. We see once again definite opportunities for many types of vendors, ranging from data processors to consultants.

TABLE 3. *Count of Transactions – Frequent Events on Annual Basis – U.S. 1970–1980*

Item	1970	1972	1974	1976	1978	1980	Annual growth
Business incorporations (000s)	264	317	319	376	478	534	7.3%
Consumer install, debt outstnd (bil $)	102	127	155	194	274	314	11.9
No. of bonds listed, new issues	1729	2105	2380	2708	2895	3057	5.9
Stocks traded, reg. stock exch. (bil sh)	4.5	6.3	4.9	7.0	9.6	15.5	13.1
Auto intercity travel (bil pas-mi)	1026	1129	1071	1215	1317	1263	2.1
Domestic air transprt. (bil pass-mi)	119	133	147	164	189	204	5.6
Air cargo (bil miles)	3.3	3.7	3.6	4.5	5.2	4.5	3.1
Foreign travel by US ctzns (000 dep)	6499	8312	8306	7755	8883	9971	4.4
Arrival by foreign ctzns (000 arr)	4060	5190	5940	6260	7860	11250	10.7
Local telephone calls (mil)	167		210	219	248	262	4.6
Long distance phone calls (bil)	9.9		14.2	16.4	20.4	25.6	10.0
U.S. Postal Serv., 1st cl. mail (bil)	48.6	48.9	51.6	52.1	56.0		1.6
Hospital admissions (mil)	31.8	33.3	35.5	36.8	37.2	38.9	2.0
Master degrees awarded (000s)	208	252	277	312	312	298	3.7
Foundation grants (000s)				12.1	15.4	21.6	15.6
Operas performed	341		403	427	448	497	3.8
Opera attendance (mil pers)	4.6		8.0	8.9	9.8	10.7	8.8
Symphony orch. concerts played	4349		4723	5314	5851	5520	2.5
Symph. orchestra attend. (mil pers)	9.0		11.8	13.4	13.7	13.9	4.5
Road show/theatre/box off. recpts (mil $)	48		46	53	106	181	4.2

1. Annual growth rate refers to 1970–1980, except for USPS-1st cl. mail.
SOURCES: 1. *Statistical Abstract of the U.S., 1981 and 1982* (Washington: USGPO, annually).
2. *Survey of Current Business* (Washington: U.S. Dept. of Commerce, monthly).
3. *Basebook, 1982* (Cleveland: Predicasts, annually).
4. *World Development Report, 1983* (Washington: World Banks, annually).

Actions and transactions

Beyond demographic-economic forces and the count of entities lies a third set of data, that of actions and transactions. Actions and transactions occur hundreds, thousands, and millions of times each day: artistic performances; hospital admissions; telex messages; automobile accidents; buy and sell orders on financial markets; credit-card purchases of all types; and many other types. A representative, if very much incomplete, set of transactions is given in Table 3. As corporate planners, government statisticians, and market researchers express their need for such data, more series will be developed. Others may never become available, because of low interest, insignificance, or the impossibility of collecting them. (For example, there is a series for the number of performing-arts organizations, and statistics on the number of performances; but while data on massage parlors may exist, no one has yet suggested collecting data on the number of massages given).

Some actions and transactions are growing slowly; others are easily measured and do not require extensive analysis. Included in this category are such items as long distance calls made per day per household, airport departures, and picture postcards mailed. The number of shirts laundered daily in a home or a small commercial laundry may be of little interest; the same is true of fire drills held. On the other hand, life-insurance policies written; motor-vehicle accidents; hospital admissions in a metropolitan region; credit-card purchases in department or specialty stores; and electronic-mail messages are significant and require subsequent reporting by private and public agencies (for record-keeping, credit rating, and other purposes). In this sense, then, the growth of such transactions has a definite ripple effect.

TRENDS IN THE INFORMATION-TECHNOLOGY ENVIRONMENT

Over two decades ago, the Austrian-born economist Fritz Machlup noted that the production and distribution of knowledge in the USA had become big business and that such activity was also growing fast in other economies.[2] Since that time, the evidence has been mounting that the information explosion is no short-lived phenomenon. Investigators have noted the growth in the number of information specialists, the doubling of journal articles every decade, and the rapid rise of literature searches from computer-readable databanks. Online searches were estimated at a few thousand in 1968, 1.2 million in 1976, and more than 3 million in 1983, while data banks grew from 100 in 1973 to 2,500 in 1984. This was made possible by changes in computer equipment and software and technological development in communication and data processing.[3]

Machlup's pioneering effort included an examination of industrial categories and occupations. He was able to show that certain industries and jobs were heavily information-laden. For example, he found that about one-half of the doctor's work during an office visit consisted of informational activities; a physician deals as much in information as in medicine. The percentage is even higher for accountants and financial officers. Machlup was able to offer some broad data on industries, as well, and ultimately determined that many professionals, managers, and sales-clerical staff were engaged in heavily information-laden activities in a variety of fields. Finally, Machlup alerted readers to opportunities for new business ventures and new occupations. It remained for others, however, to define the specific characteristics.

Information content

Several years after Machlup's groundbreaking volume, Marc Porat wrote a doctoral dissertation at Stanford University on the same subject; it was published later as a nine-volume US Government document.[4] Relying

FIGURE 3. SPATIAL MAP OF INFORMATION CONTENT

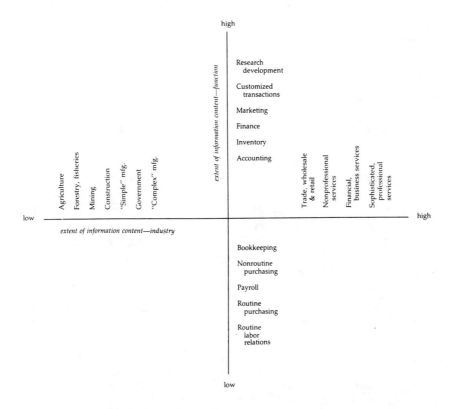

on several costly studies in the intervening years and his own primary research (which utilized countless time series and a wide variety of databases), Porat was able to document more accurately the information content (the amount of information-related activity) of a larger number of specific industries and occupations. He also paid tribute to his predecessor by showing that Machlup's rough estimates of the information content of a given occupation or industry were accurate – and that Machlup's research cost far less than others' subsequent investigations.

This writer did similar research, but on specific business functions. Their natures were examined and information content ranked. This ranking, combined with the Porat ranking of industries, is shown in Figure 3. The rankings for both categories are accurate as of the early 1980s. The less information-laden industries and activities are moving from the low to the high end of the scale; even those at the middle or the high end are inching further upward. By the end of the 1980s, and certainly in the 1990s, there should be much more clustering at the high end. The informational aspect of primary industries (agriculture, forestry, fisheries) and manufacturing is gaining significance; the role of

Q

information in services is, of course, well understood. Examples will be cited to show how these represent marketing opportunities.

Information delivery

Technological developments and significant cost decreases in electronics (computer hardware, software, and telecommunication) enable many organizations and individuals to easily carry out tasks previously done at great expense or not even attempted. Market researchers now conduct indepth searches by querying many databanks and files. Medical specialists use computers to better diagnose patients' illnesses; the computer's enormous manipulative ability allows comparison and contrast of symptoms and presentation of meaningful alternatives (still subject to human interpretation). Economists, financial planners, and managers at all levels can construct planning models using well-known spreadsheets such as VisiCalc and Lotus 1–2–3. Those at home can shop or bank electronically. Videotex is being promoted as an interactive delivery system through which a broad range of informational/transactional services can be provided to users either in the home or the office.[5]

Problems remain, of course, ranging from disagreement on a videotex standard to well-documented failures in automating banking transactions. Previously, management/marketing information systems were envisioned making decisions; now a more modest view sees them as supporting decision-makers. Regardless, computer equipment, related services, and communication or information delivery will play a major role in the USA in the 1985–1995 period.

Users want two things from computers:

1. Computing power, especially sufficient memory and handling capability; *and*
2. Access to that power, regardless of the mode of such access.

Personal computers should be able to function as free-standing units or as terminals capable of reaching larger computers, major mainframes, and vast databanks. Computer services, in turn, should provide users with assurance that they can carry out two distinct kinds of operations (although in practice, these overlap): number-crunching or processing of many data points in vast quantities; and customized solving of unique problems.

The manner in which information is delivered to users must be considered in light of the wide diversity that exists in mode of delivery, characteristics of users, and type of information or knowledge demanded. The two crucial questions that must be asked are:

How urgently do users wish access to the information? *and*
How fast can the information be delivered?

FIGURE 4. SPATIAL MAP OF INFORMATION DELIVERY

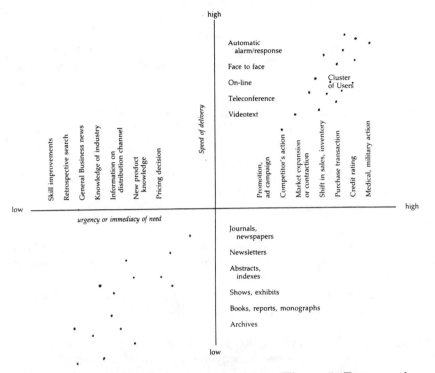

The situation is illustrated on a spatial map (Figure 4). For example, the archivist or classical scholar is willing to undertake an investigation that is leisurely, or at least has a long horizon; and, not surprisingly, he or she is also willing to wait some time for a response. In contrast, the medical or military team demands instant data processing and immediate feedback; the answer about patient symptoms or troop positions should come almost simultaneously. In Figure 4, users will tend to cluster along a diagonal line from lower left to upper right.

APPLICATIONS AND OPPORTUNITIES FOR MARKETERS

We have sketched the key dimensions of the information-technological environment and recognized the importance of new indicators in the business-economic environment. Now, we are ready to discuss some new horizons open to entrepreneurs.

Primary Industries

In agriculture, small and medium-sized farms are threatened; the name of the game is agribusiness. But regardless of the size of the operation, farmers and agriculture managers are keenly interested in such things as crop yields, livestock-breeding results, irrigation patterns, and the proper use of fertilizer and pesticides. The forestry and fishing industries are considered very low in information content. But new lumber companies and trawler-fleet operators find that they can obtain higher yields from timberlands and fishing grounds if they engage experts who can assist them in mapping, calculating potential harvest results, and comparing actual with projected figures. These entrepreneurs are following in the footsteps of the oil-drilling firms, which have used seismographic analysis for many years. In mining and construction, cost estimating, material ordering, and project scheduling could not be done without sophisticated computer programs and the proper massage of statistics. This means keeping tabs not only on total revenues and expenditures, but on projects or programs and specific transactions (delivery of a certain material to the site).

Manufacturing

Industrialized economies, such as those of the USA, Canada, Japan, and Western Europe, are witnessing a pronounced switch from sunset to sunrise manufacturing. The more basic and more-polluting industrial activities are being shifted to developing countries or eliminated. Emphasis is on high-tech, cost cutting, quality control, and streamlining fabrication, while keeping inventories at a low level. Consider just one example, that of monitoring energy savings and the level of pollutants in a given factory. Numerous measurements must be made, not just on throughput volume, but on a host of other parameters as well, ranging from temperature and pressure to the specific level of pollutants, whether water or airborne. These statistics then need to be interpreted, with varying speed, so plant operators can make decisions, on the spot or in the long run. Innovative vendors are designing sophisticated packages that offer just such capabilities. Some marketers have gone so far as to offer genuine hand holding, for example, assuring the client that the organization is in compliance with government standards (up to and including the completion of legal forms).

Services

This segment has become the dominant one in the Western world, with retailing, wholesaling, and financial, transportation, and communications services leading the way. Regardless of which sector is examined – banks or supermarkets, colleges or airlines – the opportunities have never been greater. Funds-transfer, shelf-stocking, enrollment, and passenger load factors are of crucial importance in daily and in long-run decisions. By keeping tabs on which saving instruments, food packages, or schedules are popular, companies can make decisions almost instantaneously. Once again, it is important that detailed data be kept not just on total volume, but on specific items as well; not just on passenger miles, for example, but also on the load or occupancy ratio of each particular flight, the credit-card purchase of airline tickets, and so forth. There are major social issues (privacy, transborder data flow, public access, and quality standards) and legal considerations (antitrust, taxation, copyright, standardization, and security) that must be resolved, but they should not pose insurmountable barriers.

RECOMMENDED MARKETING PRACTICES FOR INFORMATION PROVIDERS

While it is simplistic to recommend one strategy as best for all types of firms engaged in delivering information, there are several practices that can be recommended for most firms. They center around the four P's of marketing – product, price, promotion, and place.

Product

Information is a most unusual resource, whether it comes as text or numbers, whether it is public or private. It is reusable, portable, expandable, compressible, and shareable, real value derives from organization; when properly arranged, it becomes knowledge, a most saleable commodity. Information is valuable, however, only when properly managed – not because there is so little of it, but because there is now so much of it. Vendors must deal with information as an almost pure service, rather than as a tangible product. Successful firms show a clustering toward one of two extremes. Several companies offer highly standardized, low-priced, but 'nutritional' menu items to thousands of clients. In this cafeteria mode, they have gone beyond the slogan 'vanilla is our only flavor'. Instead, they properly 'portion and precook' their offerings. Examples range from payroll processing to rearranged census data. As the other extreme, we see customized, high-priced, sophisticated services, such as one-on-one market-research reports, software packages, or turnkey systems. In either case, follow-up and maintenance are essential features.

Price

The 1980s will be a decade of tight budgets, lean staffing, and cost/performance ratio emphasis, and information providers must sharpen their pencils. Still, price wars are not likely in this industry, because even the commodity offerings are hard to compare with each other. As is the case with the type of product provided, two major pricing alternatives seem to dominate. Those who wish to be information wholesalers (the giant data-bank vendors with their hundreds of files) are likely to ask for an hourly rate plus a per-item charge. In effect, price is related to volume.

FIGURE 5. SPATIAL MAP OF PRODUCT-PRICE INTERFACE IN THE
COMPUTER-SERVICES INDUSTRY

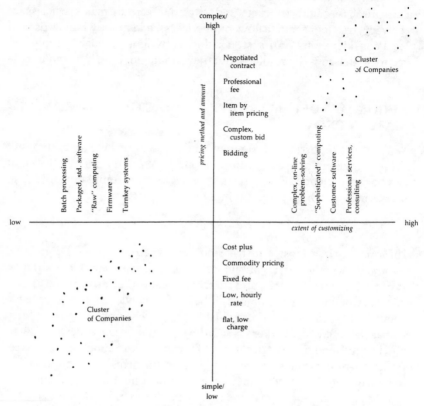

In information retailing, on the other hand, there may be an up-front fee
as well as a variety of charges related to what is being processed and how it
is processed. In this case, price is related to value perceived by the client,
rather than to volume provided by the vendor. Consulting, custom-
designed software, and tailor-made market-research reports belong in
this category. The spatial map for the product-price interface and the way
in which vendors are clustered is shown in Figure 5.

Promotion

The traditional methods of promoting information services range from
word-of-mouth to direct mail, from discreet telephoning to the printing
of business cards in journals and, of course, personal selling. But newer,
though not necessarily better, approaches are surfacing. Examples include:

Appearing at trade shows;
Encouraging staff members to write articles for highly technical or
    academic journals;

Providing a variety of live or electronic demonstrations;
Offering guarantees or warranties;
Citation of rankings by independent rating services; *and*
Soft selling at half-day or full-day seminars, offered on a complimentary or low-fee basis.

There is a possibility that consumer-goods techniques will invade the field; information providers may yet dazzle business clients with coupons, discounts, and sweepstakes as well as gather them for focus-group sessions.

Place

Policies in this field have changed little, and they are not likely to be substantially altered except to follow promotional practices. Many firms have their own sales forces, while others rely on distributors. As a general rule, though, vendors are reluctant to let others distribute information without their control., Corporate protocol also dictates that vice presidents get involved when a major account is on the line. We expect that sellers of information will rely on their own sales forces, rather than on others such as independent distributors, agents, or brokers (exceptions, of course, exist, such as Find/SVP of New York and many small information retailers in other metropolitan locations.) It is conceivable that information will be sold on busy corners or lobbies by vendors and vending machines – much like hot dogs, soft drinks and newspapers. And, of course, selling can take place in the home, along the lines of at-home banking or shopping, given the proper equipment.

Key considerations

In the years following World War II, the idea of catering to clients' needs became pervasive and came to be known as the marketing concept. The judicious blending of the four P's of marketing to implement this concept became accepted and has been labeled as the appropriate marketing mix. Both are still valid considerations, but the astute vendor of information services must define his own strategy in specific terms. Call it *positioning*, call it a strategic *planning* with tactical implementation, or call it competitive *combat* readiness, it must be done before the marketing plan has a chance of succeeding.[7]

Three major facets must be looked at:

1. Recognition of the firm's own strengths and weaknesses in existing technology, its cost situation, corporate culture, geographic location, and so forth.

2. The product (service)-market interface, the specific features now demanded and likely to be wanted in the future; *and*

3. The manner in which threats, constraints, and barriers can be turned into opportunities.

FIGURE 6. SPATIAL MAP OF THE COMPUTER SERVICES IN-
DUSTRY (USA)

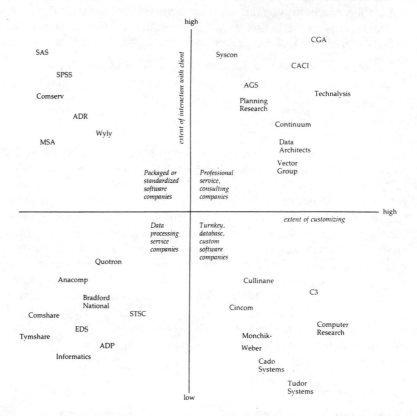

In short, a proactive stance must be assumed, with constant interaction
between the external and internal environments. In many cases, users
may not know what they want now; it is the marketer's task to anticipate
them.[8] Conversely, users may suggest new uses to vendors for existing
products.[9]

The imaginative vendor of information services will take into account
all the indicators suggested in the first part of this article – not only the
traditional demographic-economic signposts, but also the count of
entities and transactions and their growth rates. Transactions are
especially worth watching, as they are likely to pinpoint fast-changing
fields. An examination of the information-technology situation should
reveal which industries, occupations, and functions are high in information content. Marketers must then probe how speedily the information
needs to be delivered and to what extent it can be either standardized or
customized. As a general rule, users will tend to cluster along an axis,
from low speed/low cost/standard to high speed/high cost/ custom
features.

After considering these factors, companies will find their own positions on the information map. One way of looking at such a map is shown as Figure 6, where the two axes are the extent of customization and the extent of interaction with the client. The situation is illustrated for one particular industry, computer services, and specific vendors in it. This industry is made up of four segments: data processing, software, consulting and turnkey.[10] It is possible to develop similar maps for other branches of the information industry. The map is even applicable to a large, diversified company that markets information in a variety of ways to a diverse client base. Such firms, by definition, will be conglomerates and will span more than one quadrant with their offerings. For the vast majority of companies, however, it will make sense to stick to one of the four quadrants and to carve out a strong profile in that particular sector.

REFERENCES

1. See: G. Gilder, *The Spirit of Enterprise* (New York: Simon & Schuster, 1984); J. Naisbitt, *Megatrends* (New York: Warner Books, 1982).
2. F. Machlup, *The Production and Distribution of Knowledge in the United States* (Princeton, N.J.: Princeton University Press, 1962).
3. See: R. Goldberg and H. Lorin, *The Economics of Information Processing* (New York: Wiley & Sons, 1982, 2 vol.); J. Martin, *The Wired Society* (Englewood Cliffs, N.J.: Prentice-Hall, 1978); W. Phister, Jr., *Data Processing Technology and Economics*, 2nd ed. (Maynard, Mass.: Digital Press, 1979); W. Senn, *Information Resources in Management* (Belmont, Cal.: Wadsworth, 1982); *Infotech: State of the Art Reports,* selected volumes (Elmsford, N.Y.: Pergamon Press, 1968–1983).
4. M. U. Porat, *The Information Economy* (Washington, D.C.: U.S. Department of Commerce/Office of Telecommunications, 1977, 9
5. J. Tydeman et al., *Teletext and Videotext in the United States* (New York: Data Communications/McGraw-Hill, 1982).
6. For example, in December Dun & Bradstreet brought pressure on Dialog Information Services (a subsidiary of Lockheed) to deny availability of credit information to labor unions, but professional information brokers offered to help unions.
7. See: P. Bloom, 'Effective Marketing for Professional Services,' *Harvard Business Review,* September-October 1984, pp. 102–110; C. Lovelock, *Services Marketing* (Englewood Cliffs, N.J.: Prentice-Hall, 1984); D. Maister, 'Balancing the Professional Services Firm,' *Sloan Management Review,* Fall 1982, pp. 15–29; M. Porter, *Competitive Strategy* (New York: The Free Press, 1980).
8. R. Bennett and R. Cooper, 'The Misuses of Marketing: An American Tragedy,' *Business Horizons,* November-December 1981, pp. 51–60.
9. E. von Hippel, 'Successful Industrial Products from Customer Ideas,' *Journal of Marketing,* January 1978, pp. 39–49.
10. This fourfold classification is the one adopted in the annual report of ADAPSO, the Association of Data Processing Service Organizations.

Online buying behaviour – how customers choose hosts and databases

S. Crawshaw

BIS Infomat, UK

ABSTRACT

Analysis of buying behaviour is essential to successful marketing. The model analyses the steps taken and the influences involved in purchasing electronic database services. Starting with the information need through to host selection and database trial. Three types of users are examined: the novice, the regular user and the expert. For each category the host and the database users need to adopt the appropriate tactics. For the novice this involves easier front-ends and ensuring initial success, for the expert sophisticated command languages and high quality of service. To be successful in the long run the hosts and producers must work closely together to develop familiarity with their respective services.

INTRODUCTION

For the online industry to be successful we require clear marketing strategies. Such strategies are dependent on branding, positioning and market segmentation. These can only be developed by detailed analysis of buyer behaviour. How customers actually select databases and hosts and what influences them.

The buyer behaviour model is merely a tool which forces the clarification of assumptions, raising questions for evaluation and hopefully prompting comment and discussion within the industry. The model grew from an examination at BIS Infomat of the database purchase process. Initially, the models for selecting hosts and databases were separate. With further development and revision a single host/database purchase model emerged. I am indebted to many of our colleagues within the information industry for their contribution and comments. I do not expect the model of itself to be particularly contoversial; after all it should be a consolidation of the implicit assumptions on which we have all been working. What it does, however do is make those assumptions explicit. Thereby providing the mechanism for developing the clear marketing strategies referred to earlier.

After considering the model, I will examine the implications for the database producers and hosts in their marketing approaches.

FIGURE 1

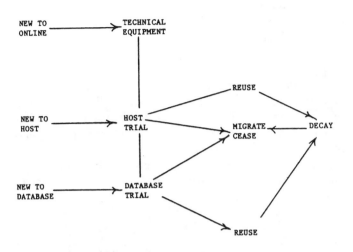

MODEL OVERVIEW

Figure 1 is a summary of the model. Given a basic information need someone new to online services first has to have the appropriate technical equipment, passwords, etc., then try a host. Implicit in the host trial is the selection and use of a specific database or databases. Judging from the satisfaction obtained from such use the new user will be satisfied and potentially reuse, or will find that the need(s) are not met and will cease using entirely, migrate to another database or indeed to another host. It is clearly the objective of the hosts and databases to encourage all new users to develop from uncertain trialists to convinced users as quickly as possible.

Two points emerge very clearly from this overview. Firstly, it is impossible to utilise online services without the appropriate technical equipment. This involves the modem, the terminal, gaining the appropriate PSS codes and of course may be subject to internal budgetary constraints. Similarly the host has to issue passwords and obtain billing addresses. Compared with the process of purchasing many other services, this question of technical access and password collection makes online services an exceptionally difficult service to try. In some respects it is remarkable that there are so many users to the services already.

The second vital point is that the user can only gain satisfaction from a host by being satisfied with the information provided within a specific database or combination of databases. This is especially important when considering the development of new users (though it becomes less important with the regular online user who is already loyal to a particular host). It is a key inter-relationship, The host is fully dependent on the database producer. Equally the database producer, unless it is self-hosting, is totally dependent on the host for the communication services, help desk, etc. The implications of this will be discussed later.

THE MODEL IN DETAIL

Information Need

All users of online services must have a basic information need. The type of information they require varies according to their role, their current activity. If they are information brokers, it is a combination of all of their internal or external customers' needs. The type of information required could be credit ratings, current marketing information, mergers and acquisitions, details of company results, etc. This type of information has a substantial influence on the type of host and equally the type of database they find most useful.

Search

Where there is an unsatisfied need, the user seeks information to enable evaluation of the possibilities. Having obtained sufficient information about the options available to meet that need the users can then make their selection and trial the various services. Search is therefore, the intermediary process which raises awareness to the various stimuli which exist.

Stimuli

The range of stimuli affecting a user or potential user is enormous. Some of these are controlled by the host or databases, e.g. mailshots, PR, exhibitions, seminar presentations, special promotions or indeed direct telephone contact. Others are more diffuse; press articles, industry association meetings, some form of personal contact and word of mouth or recommendations from other users. Traditionally word of mouth contact is one of the most powerful influences of behaviour. For the first time users it is almost certainly a strong influence since the perceived risk and the complexity of purchase is so high.

Awareness

For people to purchase services they must normally be aware of them. This implies that some knowledge exists within active memory of those products or services. For this to be achieved requires exposure to stimuli, some attention to them and eventually reception of such information so that it is available for active recall. For the first time user this could be any of the exhibitions, presentations, PR, or word of mouth influences. Repetition of messages either directly with advertising or mailshots helps build the awareness and influences the confidence.

Perceived Content

The user must believe that the online host or database has a reasonable probability of meeting his information needs. The users' perception of content is dependent on the various publicity materials, marketing and other stimuli discussed above. Once a host or database has been used the perceived content will be strongly influenced by that prior experience. Indeed, as seen below, if satisfaction is not obtained immediately the perception of a database or host content may be damaged irrevocably.

Confidence

Confidence is closely allied with the elements of perceived risk. Users bring to the situation their own personality, their keyboard skills and their technical competence. Confidence is also influenced by the nature and the length of exposure to various marketing stimuli discussed above, as well as the perceived content of the host or database.

Perceived Risk

In using online databases there is a very high perceived risk. Costs are substantial and mount by the minute. There is no guarantee of success. Unlike other products, you certainly cannot examine the goods before you buy them as they are held electronically possibly many continents away. In the model, there are two steps through which the perceived risk area has to be penetrated. Firstly, in selecting the host and secondly once actually logged into a host in selecting the database of their choice.

Host Selection

Host selection for the initial user will be most influenced by awareness, personal recommendation and attendance on a training course, and most importantly the perceived content of the databases which will enable the user to answer their specific information problem.

The model shows a linkage through obtaining a password and gaining technical access before host trial. Where another department has already gone through that hoop, host trial can take place very much more easily. Where a new user cannot benefit from somebody else's experience the barrier of technical access (referred to in the overview) may deter a huge number of potential users. There may be some budgetary constraints. More importantly the time commitment required to resolving such issues demands a very high commitment to this form of information delivery.

Host Trial

The user has finally overcome all the barriers, obtaining passwords, technical access, PSS numbers and actually tries the service. Assuming there are no telecommunication difficulties the host's system software is then a key determinant in providing guidance and service to move to the next step. Before moving to database selection the user has to go through a further barrier of perceived risk.

Clearly for the initial first time user there is some predetermined reason for using the host. Where however, it is a matter of a user trying a new database, there needs to be some considerable grounds for believing that the information in the new database will meet their particular information needs.

Database Selection

The new user selects the database based on their information needs and how that matches to the perceived content of the database they are selecting. They may be assisted in this process by the system prompts available on the hosts and also by the free-trial or cross-file searching and by the stimuli referred to earlier.

Database Trial

The user has finally reached the point of interest for them. They may now actually satisfy some information needs!

Database Satisfaction

Satisfaction with the database will be achieved if the information need is met. This will be a function of the information content, its pertinence, geographic coverage, length of abstracts, indexing, the comprehensiveness and size of the database, speed of update, timeliness, ease of use. Ease of use – are menus available and is the indexing useful?

Judgement of these issues will almost invariably depend on the type of information need. An outline briefing on a company may require 10 or 15 short stories to provide the flavour of recent developments. For patent searchers finding nothing is as important as finding something and comprehensiveness is vital. The success of Textline and Maid with their initially easy use demonstrates the importance of menus to their customers.

Host Satisfaction

Users can only be satisfied with the host if they are satisfied with the combination of databases available on that host. For the initial user the success on the first database is vital. Research shows that most users remain loyal to their first host unless there is some very good reason to change. The other elements affecting host satisfaction are ease of use, quality of service, system response time, the nature of the people involved and the quality of advice provided by the help desk.

Host Re-use

The most important influences in reusing a host are prior satisfaction with that host, familiarity and content. Familiarity is clearly a function of training, previous use, availability of manuals, etc. Ease of use is a combination of the availability of the menus and the flexibility and power of the command language. Negative influences may be cost and pricing and the billing processes. It is worth noting that excessive initial use may actually reduce subsequent use due to substantial initial bills.

The importance of familiarity and confidence cannot be stressed too much. The loyalty to the first host, both in terms of limited migration to other hosts and in terms of proportion of revenue spent with the first host is impressive.

Database Re-use

As with host re-use database re-use is a function of previous satisfaction, awareness and content. Obviously users will change their choice of databases according to the appropriate information needs they need to fulfill. Consequently re-use will be a function of marketing communications, especially where initial experiences have not been successful.

Dissatisfaction

Dissatisfaction or dissonance occurs wherever the database or host fails to meet the users' needs. This may be due to content, i.e. a mis-match of perception with the actual content. The content may not be suitable for that particular user's needs or it may merely be inadequate for that application.

Excessive system complexity, poor command languages and slow system response are major sources of dissatisfaction. Many of us have received unhelpful information like 'bad command syntax, illegal command' and poor host response in terms of jammed help desks and other elements.

If users are dissatisfied they will either cease using or migrate to a new host or database. Given that most users are loyal to their first host they only migrate if content is definitely better, e.g. when Medline was launched on DataStar or if there is some specific event which prompts a change in behaviour.

It is interesting to note that the factors which can cause initial success can also contribute to subsequent frustrations. Textline menus are highly praised by new/inexperienced users but often severely criticised by expert users.

Decay

Given the complexity of using databases and the learning process involved in using them effectively when such skills are not exercised decay can occur which will lead to withdrawal of use and potentially ceasing again.

MAIN CONCLUSIONS

The user selects the host first and the database second:–

1. Hosts and Database producers are dependent on each other. Users can only be satisfied if the databases provide the solution to the information needs.
2. Purchasing databases is complex, has a high perceived risk and barriers to trial are considerable.
3. Word of mouth recommendation and education about the option is vital to the new user.
4. Initial users must obtain almost immediate satisfaction or they will cease using.
5. The information need is the main determinant of database selection.
6. Experienced users purchase a different criteria from new users.

Analysis of User Types

Users can be segmented into three potential types: the novice, the regular but not expert users and the expert. The novice will require:–

- Immediate satisfaction
- Simple facilities
- Guidance on screen
- Good help desk support

The regular users will be influenced by content, of language dependent also on quality of service, cost and training. Above all they are constrained by familiarity.

The expert user will have access to a multiplicity of hosts and will be strongly influenced by the content (i.e. the multiplicity of information providers, the exclusiveness of the information providers).

- Content, comprehensiveness and timeliness of updates
- Cost
- Command language
- Manuals
- Pricing/invoicing
- Procedures
- Speed of response

FIGURE 2. DATABASE PURCHASE MODEL

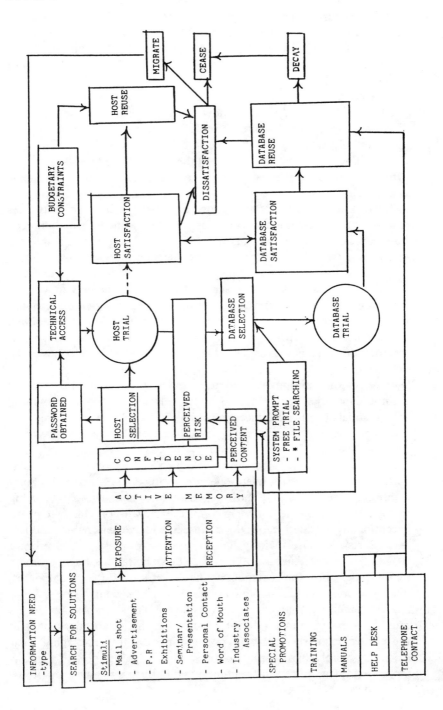

Implication for Hosts

1. To capture the so-called end user, hosts must make technical access easier. This is already happening with Mead's dial up software, Dialog's Dialink, ICC's similar package and elements like Infomaster. These packages also obviously help host loyalty since the dialing to the first host is obviously built in.

2. Secondly, make the initial system commands easier. This means MENUS, MENUS, MENUS; how often does it have to be repeated? The systems must be absolutely simple for the first time user. Few hosts yet have menu systems as flexible and genuinely as user friendly as MAID. The hosts must also dispose of the unhelpful and insulting 'illegal syntax' and other responses. Useful help instructions should be available at every single level.

3. Host literature needs to be more application/solution oriented. As shown by the model the individual user has a specific information need for which he/she requires an answer. The hosts' literature and marketing seminars need to be structured around the solutions. One particularly powerful idea is to have an online guide which provides free guidance to the most promising files, e.g. a series of menus ask the user to identify their information need (one of ten options); for each option there would then be a number of qualifying questions and then two or three online sources which may provide the answer. Typically this is the sort of information that a new user asks at a seminar or when he telephones the help desk.

4. Given the solution oriented needs the hosts could also provide just the initial materials required to solve that solution rather than providing total manuals on their services, most of which will never be used and therefore represent a frustrating, complicated and expensive waste of time.

5. Look after users. Hosts must maintain regular contact with their existing users through the telephone, prompting usage or via their regular communications. Clearly, most of them now already do this using newsletters. Telephone follow up contact for new users is likely to prove exceptionally productive, provided those users have reasonable produce.

6. Hosts must use their system to inform, advertise and to prompt usage of different databases. Just as television stations cross promote different demands, the host must do the same for the different databases. The development of cross-file searching software is vital.

7. Research the market and adjust the content. Database producers must be prepared to adjust the information which they are offering to suit the electronic market place as opposed merely to repackaging their existing possibly hard-copy products. For US producers this means increasing their European content or the Europeans will do it for themselves.

Implications for Information Providers

Since the information provider is totally dependent upon the host (except where self-hosting) the database producer must maintain very close contact with the host and ensure regular feedback about any particular problems.

The information provider needs to ensure genuine awareness among users of its service. Regular or expert users may select a database purely out of habit or awareness. The information provider has to ensure that the user has a clear perception of the database content and the solutions which that database in conjunction with other databases can deliver.

The better known the database is, the greater the confidence and the lower the perceived risk.

The database producer must deal directly with customers. However good the hosts' sales force and help desk are the customer cannot know all the products as well as the producer knows its own products. After all, we do not expect the retail assistant to be familiar with how the can of baked beans is actually manufactured. Some of you may find that analogy offensive. It is, however, important given that the range of databases available on certain hosts mirror the volume of products in a traditional supermarket. In dealing direct with the customer it is particularly beneficial for the database producer to contact users immediately after their first use. In a recent survey by BIS Infomat we contacted approximately 50 users. A large proportion of these said that they would not necessarily re-use our database. Following a conversation and an explanation of the database they then appreciated that there were additional capabilities they had not previously understood, and 75 per cent of those contacted stated that they would be likely now to retry the database. Without that prompting those users would undoubtedly not have used the database again and would have maintained an incorrect perception of the content of our database. These little steps will make a substantial difference to the usage of individual databases as the market grows.

CONCLUSIONS

The advent of the PC and the widespread distribution of computing power has substantially reduced the technofear associated with using terminals and obtaining electronic information. These changes in our environment have created new circumstances which will open the market place to a wiser usage base. In order to capture that base effectively and build a wider constituency we have got to work together as producers and hosts to develop the solution oriented systems and marketing communications which the user requires. It is no longer good enough to make data available electronically. What the customer requires is information tailored to his needs.

Miles Conrad Memorial Lecture – Aspects of quality

T.M. Aitchison

Director, INSPEC, Institution of Electrical Engineers, Station House, Nightingale Road, Hitchin, Herts SG5 1RJ, UK

Various aspects of quality in relation to database production are discussed. The absolute requirements and those of the EUSIDIC Code of Practice are related to the expectations of intermediaries and end-users. Factors which influence or inhibit the attainment of quality are considered and methods of overcoming the problems are reviewed. The importance of the people factor is stressed and this and other aspects are discussed in relation to recent management writings on the pursuit of quality.

INTRODUCTION

In choosing my title, 'Aspects of Quality', I have followed what your President, Ron Dunn, called the only formal guideline for the lecture when he wrote to invite me. This is, '. . . that it be presented . . . on a suitable topic in the field of abstracting and indexing, but above the level of any individual service'. Putting this in its most direct terms, in my case it clearly should not be a special puff for INSPEC. Equally, I can promise it will not be a special puff for me: I have a strong interest in, but claim no special knowledge of or expertise in the pursuit of quality, the control of quality, or the obtaining of quality. What I simply hope to do is to share with you some thoughts on various aspects of quality in the database-production business.

I am conscious that, later in the Conference there will be a session devoted to Quality. Initially, I felt somewhat embarrassed to be talking on a subject that would be dealt with later by other speakers, but I consoled myself with two thoughts. First the program of the Conference is so comprehensive that it was bound to cover any subject I might choose. Second, I should be talking at a level of generality – in accordance with my brief – whereas the other speakers would be talking specifically about the implementation of plans in their own organisations. In addition, ever the optimist, I felt that if their ideas and mine were similar, the similarity would reinforce any points made: if they differed, the conflict would add interest to the subsequent discussion.

I shall be talking about quality, or some aspects of it, in the light of my own experience, supplemented by two external inputs. The first is the work that our Database Editorial Manager, Gill Wheeler, has carried out in connection with a thesis on the subject. The other is, of course, the considerable literature on quality which has developed, particularly in the last ten years. Ever since I was seriously introduced to the topic, by receiving a copy of 'In Search of Excellence' from Cathy Ferrere four years ago, I have followed the various developments and the proliferation of concepts and slogans with great interest. Many of them I found thought-provoking, some inspiring, others deeply unattractive. This latter reaction may be a personal one but I believe that it reflects some differences between the US and European cultures or sensibilities.

DEFINITION OF QUALITY

The definition that I prefer is that given in the Concise Oxford Dictionary, 'Degree of excellence . . .' However, I realise that most authors in the recent literature shy away from such a value-ascribing concept and prefer:

'conformance to requirements'[1] *or*
'fitness for use.'[5]

Or, like Townsend,[7] they postulate two types of quality:

'Quality in Fact, and, Quality in Perception.'

or following Deming (Gitlow and Gitlow[3]), three types:

(1) quality of design/redesign;
(2) quality of conformance;
(3) quality of performance;

with Townsend's definition being the most comprehensive, 'doing the right thing, doing it the right way, doing it right first time, and doing it on time'.

All of these definitions could be used in the pursuit of quality or total quality, but in the database business, particularly bibliographic abstracting and indexing production, the excellence definition seems particularly suitable when one considers the qualities that are sought. In other words, the desiderata.

DESIDERATA

When I was seeking to find the best portmanteau word to use for the qualities to be sought, desiderata came to mind and blotted out any alternatives. It seemed somewhat pretentious to me, but as I could not immediately think of an alternative, I persisted and checked that it was in common use. When I found from the dictionary that it was, I was also delighted to learn that it was much more apt than I realised, since the definition is as follows:

Desideratum: thing lacking but needed or desired.

That seemed to encapsulate my view of the qualities I was going to list:

Absolute accuracy.
Complete reliability.
Unvarying consistency.
Total comprehensiveness.
Maximum timeliness.

Actually of these qualities, only one, comprehensiveness, is normally limited, in intention as well as fact, by the database producer. The producer will normally specify which class of document he covers or excludes and list those publications he makes selections from and which he covers completely. Of the remainder 'quality' is related to how closely the service can approach the ideal.

In working on its Code of Practice for Databases and Databanks, EUSIDIC, the Association of European Information Services[2], did not aim for such ideals but instead sought to encourage the best practice. The code includes the following points (which I have ruthlessly abbreviated to a few words each):

(1) Clearly-stated selection policy.
(2) Selection strictly in accordance with policy.
(3) As correct as possible.
(4) Errors reported and corrections made.
(5) Host to assist in (4).
(6) Index policy clearly stated and changes notified.
(7) Arrangements with online vendors openly stated and common to all.
(8) Vendor to state implementation procedure adopted.
(9) Withdrawal from vendor to be notified to users and alternative vendor announced.

I remember, when we started to develop the EUSIDIC Code of Practice some six years ago, it was a new idea and we did not have a model to use. We were seeking to produce a code to cover each link in the information chain. The question was whether the code of practice for a link should be drawn up, in the first place, by someone from the link before or the link after. I suggested that, instead, the first draft should be made by someone from that link in the chain, i.e. a poacher turned gamekeeper. So I took upon myself to produce the first one on databases and databanks, and did it as altruistically as possible. It was quite interesting to consider what was best for everyone else, whether or not it was good for me as a database producer, and whether or not I could easily deliver.

Although it was considerably edited and changed before the draft was published, I felt I had perhaps succeeded too well in wearing the other hat, when I observed the reaction. I found that many fellow producers, among them some that I greatly respect, were extremely upset by that code and considered it naive and unrealistic. My regret was that, as it happened, I was not present at the meeting when this view was expressed most forcibly.

Anyway, looking at the code afresh, after these years, I sit more comfortably with it than I should have expected.

Having thus exposed my lack of contrition ever the EUSIDIC Code of Practice, I should like to address the question of user expectations. In this I shall limit myself to bibliographic databases in science and technology since these are the ones I have most experience with.

USER EXPECTATIONS

In considering this question of user expectations, one must make a clear distinction between information workers as users and the rest of mankind (known as 'end-users' in our less-than-attractive jargon). In general, the end-users have a higher opinion of the performance of abstracting and indexing services than information workers have or the services deserve. Obviously, this is because they do not know any better. Thus they have a picture of a group of scholars, who receive the world's literature, and read through it to pick out the important papers for which they prepare abstracts and indexes. These are immediately published and added to an online file. Unfortunately, when the end-user finds an imperfection in this ideal world, for example when his paper is omitted from the service or his name is misspelt, he can become correspondingly disappointed and extreme in his criticism.

With information professionals, on the other hand, there is an understanding, one might say a weary acceptance – that our services are not perfect. It is for this reason that they will normally expect to search more than one database or service, even in a simple search, and to search a large number of databases if they are seeking to retrieve most of the papers published. Of course, when they come to search the indexes online they have the imperfections spread out before them and can, if they wish, check coverage, timeliness, etc. Perhaps we should ask ourselves why they are so easy-going, why the rumbles of discontent are strangely muted or communicated in such gentlemanly fashion.

It may be that everyone is still seduced by the sheer quantity of the references available, or it may be that they are aware, perhaps only subconsciously, of the imperfections or poor quality in other parts of the information chain. The seductiveness of sheer volume may be significant since it may also account for the marked reduction in interest in information retrieval studies. A decline in quality in the information chain has been considered to parallel growth in quantity. It is suggested that the volume of *significant* science and technology literature is growing at a much lower rate than that of the total, perhaps because 'the total number of scientists increases more or less as the square of the number of outstanding ones'. This, compounded by the pressures on academics to publish, cannot be expected to be conducive to high quality. If one adds the delays that occur between the acceptance of a paper and its appearance in print, the impression of patchy and somewhat tired original material could be a disincentive to strong complaints about its subsequent treatment.

A professional's view of secondary publications was given by Jewitt[4] in a paper in December 1986:

Publishers of indexing and abstracting vehicles exercise several quality controls, the first of which is in the selection of original materials covered. While a great deal of respect is paid towards the ideal of total coverage of the literature, in practice secondary publishers are actually faced with the same problems as the individual scientist. Greater resources, and the fact that this is a primary task, imply considerably better performance than the individual, but the publisher is faced with balancing the expectation of comprehensiveness against the rapidly rising costs of the service caused by the relative sluggishness of conventional print technology growth and the expansion of the literature, which also give problems of identification and absorption. The result is that indexing and abstracting services continually lag behind in their coverage, while growing, sometimes very fast.

Of course, the information professional knows the main characteristics of the databases she or he is particularly concerned with or uses regularly. These will include:

Coverage
- types of literature;
- sources within each type;
- whether coverage of compilations is complete or selective;
- selection criteria.

Classification and Indexing
- systems used;
- frequency of updating;
- types of access points or indexing;
- exhaustivity target for each type.

Bibliographic data provided
Products and services available from database
- updating or delivery schedules;
- timeliness of content;
- price.

Support
- user aids;
- HELP desk.

If he or she does not have full knowledge of these elements, the information professional will have a personal assessment – possibly inexact – of at least the main elements. Even this will only apply to the small number of databases used regularly and the products and services derived from them. For the remainder, only an impression will be held, gained from the comments of others and occasional use.

The lack of exact knowledge will apply even more to the information professional's perception of the quality of all databases except those used very regularly. As a result, since the number of alternative databases in almost every field is large and growing, it would be possible for a database to fail or receive too little usage simply because a view became widespread that it was unsatisfactory or unreliable. Even if this view were unfounded, it might be never corrected or corrected only slowly if the database were avoided as a result.

It is clear that, while an unfounded reputation for quality is likely to be of only temporary value, since it will be tested frequently, an unfounded reputation for poor quality could be a permanent disaster. It follows that the database producer must bear in mind the non-user as well as the user in seeking to. enhance the perceived quality of his database.

Having considered quality requirements and expectations, let us turn now to what stands in the way of perfect, or at least very good, quality.

INHIBITING FACTORS, TEMPTATIONS TO BACKSLIDING

The factors which inhibit the attainment of quality are, of course, manifold in any operation and particularly so in database production. The temptations are there for both management and staff in varying degrees. For the individual staff member these vary from the worker who lets an error through, in the expectation that it will be picked up elsewhere, to the indexer who settles for less than his best because it is late and he wants to go home. For the manager or 'management' there is the temptation to concentrate coverage on the most-used or most-easily-available literature rather than the full range that was promised; or to encourage cutting corners in order to obtain a higher output. These management temptations can clearly extend to enhancing profitability by simply reducing the number of items added to the database. As this gives only short-term benefit, it is only likely to tempt someone who is desperate or who expects to leave in the short term (who is perhaps retiring shortly).

Among the factors that inhibit or, at least, do not encourage a drive for quality are those that arise from the special nature of database production and use. It is interesting to contrast this with the manufacturing system model described in the literature on quality. In this manufacturing system, the most important factor is the satisfaction of the customer. This is monitored through comments and complaints received by the manufacturer and his dealers, by interaction between customers, dealers and sales staff, and by after-sales service under warranty and later. The database producer does not have the same inbuilt monitoring process available. The printed products from his database are supplied by mail, not sold face-to-face, and many may not be used for some time. For example, for retrospective searches when the volume of abstracts and indexes is bound. The electronic products are supplied to the eventual user through organisations which do not carry out quality checks and only some of whom feel any responsibility for the quality of the file. Equally, the efforts of the database producer may be frustrated by poor or limited implementation of his file by the processing organisation or online host.

Another factor in the manufacturing system described in the literature on quality is the careful control of raw materials or components input to the manufacturing process. JIT or Just-In-Time scheduling allows the inventory to remain small and ensures that the input is in small easily-identified batches. In bibliographic database production, on the other hand, the incidence of input is dependent on a multitude of publishers throughout the world and on the vagaries of foreign and local postal authorities. Thus the database producer can exert no control over the quantity of material he must deal with at any time and has to expect much bunching.

Another inhibitory or discouraging factor is the database's back file. With a database of, say, 1 million items of modest quality, it is difficult to forget that the addition of even a thousand higher-quality items will produce an average of only 0.1 per cent of the improvement in quality. To achieve any real improvement action must also be taken retrospectively, with all the very large costs that would imply for even a medium-sized database.

When I used the phrase 'inhibiting factors', I did so to make the heading more arresting and, in fact, might have used 'influencing factors' instead. This more neutral phrase would allow us to include a mention of two factors which tend to promote quality.

The first of these factors is the role which a number of database producers have brought with them from their previous experience as conventional abstracting and indexing services: a self-imposed obligation to record the total output in their subject field, without commercial, national or other bias. This obligation has been expressed recently by the management of one of the leading database producers. I would like to give one or two quotations, without identifying either it or them.

To meet these objectives, we do not limit our coverage to the economically interesting but assume the burden of a lot of small organisations that are not significant to a commercial vendor.

It is important to make this kind of research available for even the small percentage who desire it. It is indeed possible that among the papers of less prestigious research institutions there are gems of wisdom that may be valuable. If they are not captured in our database, they are probably lost forever.

We take our archival responsibilities seriously. To continue in that role we tend to be more conservative because the penalties of our taking risk are so extreme for our users. When it comes to process, for instance, there are ways to do the job cheaper and faster, such as paying less attention to those that haven't got as much money to spend. But if we chose those ways, we would no longer be a reliable, consistent, quality service.

The second of these factors is the pursuit of long-term rather than short-term considerations, since quality is an important factor for long-term success.

Whether a profit objective (or surplus generation for not-for-profit organisations) is more or less conducive to quality than a target of break-even is a matter for debate. On balance, I believe that a break-even approach can too easily encourage settling for something less than the best. On the other hand, a drive for profitability, particularly long-term, imposes the necessary discipline on all aspects of the work.

THE CONVENTIONAL PURSUIT OF QUALITY

Having discussed some of the factors which, at the very least, do not help the database producer in pursuing his quality goal, I should like to look at how most of us have sought to fulfil the goal without the tools and the formal approach offered by Deming,[4] Juran,[5] Crosby,[1,9] Groocock,[9] Townsend et al.[7]

Many of us became database producers as a consequence of computerising our conventional abstracting and indexing services which had been operating for many years. We therefore had existing markets for our printed products and had quality standards in acquisition, abstracting, indexing and classification to which we sought to adhere. There was a great deal of editorial control and checking of work to ensure consistency and accuracy, but perhaps few impartial or published records of errors or imperfections, mainly because these were extremely difficult to obtain before the advent of the computer.

For the electronic products, i.e. magnetic tape services, produced in the database system, a new market had to be established, first for batch processing and, later, for batch and online services. This market tended to be concerned with format rather than content, and it was some time before the demands of customers required further improvement in quality.

In the meantime, however, the demands of electronic processing had produced essential standardisation of input and hitherto-unheard-of levels of accuracy. Over the years this has been further enhanced as more and more elaborate validation routines have been built into all the processing, until today, changes to validation routines seem to be the major element in any software development.

Thus at the level of spelling, format and field content, the consistency and accuracy of the data has improved markedly over the years through this harnessing of the computer. The checking of the computer-flagged errors and their correction has continued to be an expensive element in the total production cost.

The information content, or value-added part of the database, including selection, abstracting and subject delineation, and indication of affiliation, bibliographic type, treatment, etc., was not amenable to similar checking by computer and has required the setting up of various quality control systems. Commonly these will range from 100 per cent checks of the work of less-experienced staff, to only occasional checks on that of experienced staff. Thus the problems of consistency and reliability in subject delineation are contained rather than completely solved by the system and still rely heavily on the dedication of the individual members of staff for their solution. Similarly in systems operations and systems development, and in marketing, in spite of the elaborate checks and balances, quality continues to depend heavily on the individual's inbuilt quality-control mechanism. This, of course, depends on the desire to make use of this self-monitoring system and thus on motivation.

The development of this motivation is, of course, one of the essential roles of management and requires a number of factors to be satisfactory before it is attained:

(1) The objectives of the organisation should be acceptable and the worker should be able to identify with them.

(2) The organisation, or the department in the organisation, should be seen as 'best' compared with other organisations or departments in its field.

(3) The system and arrangements set up and operated should seem sensible and the worker should feel free to suggest changes where he or she considers they are not.

(4) The worker should be aware that his or her performance is being monitored and be convinced that this is being done fairly.

(5) Consistent good work should be acknowledged regularly and special effort should receive early praise both from the immediate supervisor and the chief.

(6) Everything should be done to develop the worker's self-image and encourage him or her to feel part of the team and to realise that he or she is relied on and trusted to do a good job.

(7) Where performance does not match management expectations, the worker should be counselled and training given. If this does not effect the necessary improvement, the worker should be encouraged to seek other employment for his or her own sake.

In addition to the above it is, of course, assumed that the salary is satisfactory and that the conditions of work are good.

It will be realised that the list given is a mixture of Hertzberg's motivators and hygiene factors, and that it tends to MacGregor's Theory Y (happy family) with little of his Theory X (carrot and stick). Desirably the factors would be supplemented or reinforced by an appropriate style of management. This would include frequent formal and informal communication and general openness on objectives, targets and results, and regular tours of the workplace by the chief in which he or she would receive information and engage in conversation, but would *not* make decisions or give instructions.

This conventional management approach to quality probably works best with a comparatively small workforce. It is known to give results: the main query is whether some of the approaches mentioned in the recent literature would give better results. The question is whether one or other of the formal approaches to quality management would focus the attention of all staff and thus be beneficial; or whether setting up a formal project would inhibit the unselfish individual contributions that are regularly made in the best examples of the conventional approach.

The one concept that does seem to be generally missing from the conventional approaches is that of Zero Defects or Right First Time. This move away from an expectation that errors will be created which must be corrected later seems eminently desirable, but probably too radical to be adopted as an accepted view throughout an organisation without the preparation and planning that is recommended in the recent writings on quality.

It therefore seems desirable to assess how best these could be applied to the special circumstances of the database producer. As we discuss some of the special approaches and techniques, I hope you will relate these to your own organisation and picture them being applied there.

TOTAL QUALITY: QUALITY REVOLUTION: QUALITY IMPROVEMENT

There is general agreement in the literature that a fundamental change in organisational attitudes is required if the new quality goals are to be attained or even pursued effectively. The fundamental change consists of transforming quality control into quality improvement by defect prevention (Crosby[1]) or looking at the organisation as a whole in its role of providing customer satisfaction (Townsend[8]). The two approaches do not conflict and, in fact, should be combined. They could be said to reflect the two parts of Townsend's 'Quality in Fact, and, Quality in Perception'.

In the defect-prevention model the fundamental concept is Zero Defects or Right First Time. This is based on the view expressed memorably by Crosby that 'it is much less expensive to prevent errors than to rework, scrap and service them' and that 'if you don't expect errors and really are astonished when they occur, then errors just do not happen'. Others suggest that not expecting errors is folklore and that it will only succeed if so much control and checking has been introduced that errors are, indeed, unexpected.

The customer-satisfaction model starts from the premise that the sole purpose of the organisation is to satisfy its customers. Its definition of a quality product or service is one that satisfies the customer by meeting his needs and expectations. This approach has the advantage of broadening the area of concern to include the whole organisation, since the work of everyone will have impact on the satisfaction of the customer. It removes any possibility of considering quality to be the concern of the production department only and ensures that marketing, finance, fulfilment and systems departments are seen to be equally vital to success.

This emphasis on customer satisfaction is designed to avoid the situation which might arise in the defect-prevention approach, where a product or service of the highest quality is produced but is not bought since it does not meet the customer's requirements. In other words, it adds to the 'do things right' of the defect-prevention approach, another imperative, 'do the right things'.

The model is given further weight, and brought close to the defect-prevention model by expanding the concept of customer beyond that of final customer to internal customers. Thus each section or individual in the organisation has a number of 'customers' who receive a product or service and whose satisfaction must be the main aim. This has the inestimable advantage of allowing each relationship between producer or service supplier and his customer within the organisation to be discussed regularly by the parties concerned, in the knowledge that 'the customer is always right'.

The writings contain a wide range of suggested steps towards implementing a quality revolution, but seem to have a number of elements in common:

(1) Commitment by top management and middle management. This is necessary to provide the authority to start the project but equally important to ensure that the eventual involvement is seen to include all levels.
(2) A committee of senior staff drawn from all areas of the organisation, to define, plan and run the project.
(3) Data on current quality from customers, workers and management, and on cost of quality (more correctly, non-quality or doing it wrong), which will be used subsequently to measure improvement. Achievements will be displayed prominently in the appropriate areas.
(4) Awareness and training: communicating through all levels of staff about the cost of non-quality, and preparing all levels of management for the implementation of the new way of working.

(5) Implementation: through the planned involvement of all staff, possibly through Quality Teams or section or department teams, and with or without Value Analysis.

(6) Reinforcement, recognition, rewards, celebrations: achieving of goals publicised and team and individual contributions recognised.

(7) Re-start: the process repeated with new team leaders and new goals (i.e. keeping going through continuous improvement).

APPLICABILITY TO DATABASE PRODUCERS

It would seem that none of the steps outlined above could not be applied to database production. On balance, an approach on the lines suggested by Townsend might be suitable. He modified the structured approach and concentration on error prevention of Crosby's 'Quality is Free' with the emphasis on attitude and motivation from Peters' 'In Search of Excellence' and gave special weight to meeting the customer's needs and expectations.

The great strength of these approaches is the aim of encouraging all members of staff to assist in the quality-improvement process as a regular day-by-day, year-by-year commitment. In this it must commend itself to any manager who is sufficiently comfortable in his role to encourage delegation of authority and to welcome participation by all staff in decision-making.

The doubt which remains is how to avoid the encouragement of motivation lapsing into cynical manipulation. This may arise from a personal trait or from a cultural difference but it leaves me with a slight reservation.

It arises in two main areas and one subsidiary. The first is in the launching of the implementation phase of the zero defects project, where it is suggested that all employees are assembled and there are 'speeches, music and pizzaz' before they return to their work-places to sign their pledges and receive their pins. The other is in the recognition of groups meeting their goals. Crosby suggests performance plaques presented at special lunches or dinners. Townsend, on the other hand, has bronze, silver and gold pins awarded to each team member when the team reaches the appropriate level of achievement, with the opportunity to select gifts in addition for the silver and gold teams. In this case the awards were made by senior vice-presidents at the work area of the team and were designed to be light rather than formal occasions. This suits me better than the frenzied recognition ceremonies that some other companies are reported to stage frequently, in one case weekly.

The final very small reservation seemed, when I first read it, a perfect example of destroying an attractive, human activity by making it part of a management technique, and worse still, giving it an acronym. We already have MBWA or Management by Wandering Around for the estimable habit of going round the shop to keep in touch and see that all is well. I find I have to work at it to continue to do it, now that I know that what I thought was a self-indulgent habit is an approved management technique.

The new offence that has been perpetrated is a mechanisation of the simple act of saying 'thank you' for good work. This is PEET: Program for Ensuring that Everybody's Thanked. I thought that Townsend was making a joke until he explained that each of the top executives was given a PEET sheet each week with the names of two team leaders and was required to visit them. Townsend claims that there was a one-for-one correlation between areas that excelled in the quality process and bosses who incorporated MBWA/PEET in their way of doing business. I have sufficient faith in the independence and sense of the ridiculous of European staff to feel sure that there would be a negative correlation between quality excellence and departments exposed to MBWA/PEET.

However, these are extreme manifestations of a very attractive approach. Instead of these systems of mechanical goodwill, I suggest we should express, perhaps more openly than we normally do, our genuine interest in and concern for people.

If we build on this instead of some of these extreme methods of enhancing motivation, we should be able to add to our current pursuit of quality, a continuing drive for improvement by incorporating the main points of the quality revolution:

(1) Concentrating on satisfying the customer's needs and expectations.
(2) Preventing defects, through 'zero defects' or 'right first time' concepts.
(3) Setting up a quality-improvement plan.
(4) Ensuring the planned involvement of all staff.
(5) Recognising or acknowledging special contributions as they are made.

Of course, to be successful in this, we as managers must have a firm and clearly-seen commitment to quality. We must not treat it as something to be sought when conditions allow but must show by our statements, our decisions and our actions that the pursuit of quality has an absolute priority.

If we follow this course of action our customers will gain by receiving products and services which match their needs and expectation more closely. At the same time, we and all our staff will gain from having much more challenging, interesting and rewarding jobs.

It should also be fun.

REFERENCES

1   Crosby, P.B. (1980). *Quality is free*. New York: The New American Library.
2   EUSIDIC Codes of Practice, 1 (1983). *Databases and Databanks*. London: EUSIDIC.
3   Gitlow, H.S. and S.J. Gitlow (1987). *The Deming Guide to Quality and Competitive Position*. New York: Prentice-Hall.
4   Jewitt, C. (1986). Quality control in the information dissemination cycle. 10th International Online Information Meeting. London: Learned Information, 209–220.
5   Juran, J.M. et al. (1974). *Quality Control Handbook*. New York: McGraw-Hill.
6   Peters, T.J. and R.H. Waterman (1984). *In Search of Excellence*. New York: Warner.
7   Townsend, P.L. (1986). *The Journey to Excellence*. New York: Wiley.
8   Crosby, P.B. (1984). *Quality Without Tears: The Art of Hassle-Free Management*. New York: McGraw-Hill.
9   Groocock, J.M. (1986). *The Chain of Quality: Market Dominance Through Product Superiority*. New York: Wiley.
10 Peters, T. and N. Austin (1985). *A Passion for Excellence: The Leadership Difference*. New York: Random House.
11 Robson, M. (1986). *The Journey to Excellence*. New York: Wiley.

Market Research

Market Research – Introductory Notes

Blaise Cronin

Only an idiot, evangelist or intuitive genius would launch a service, develop a new product or raise prices without some kind of market analysis. My opening paper (*Approaches to market research*) is an elementary introduction to market research techniques: 'Market research is the systematic analysis of consumer characteristics, behaviours, lifestyles, needs, wants, demands and preferences . . . It furnishes data upon which a marketing plan can can be built' and provides information on which 'to make intelligent and informed decisions about corporate strategy or service philosophy.' Librarians, however, still prefer to speak of user studies or community analysis rather than market research. Even a casual perusal of the numerous surveys carried out over the last decade (whether by practitioners or academics) reveals the methodological rawness of so many studies; studies which have failed to aggregate into a useful corpus of knowledge on public behaviours and preferences. Nevertheless, there have been some notable exceptions: a number of public library services (for example, Surrey County Libraries in the UK), have applied mainstream commercial market research techniques, such as C.A.C.I.'s powerful ACORN segmentation and consumer targeting system, to the analysis of their operations.

John Myers' paper (*Consumers and markets: stimulating and fulfilling consumer demands*) reviews the results of various public opinion surveys and tries to tease out the implications for future policy: 'The library of the 1990s and the 21st century could be – and will need to be – vastly different from the libraries you know and cherish today'. In some respects not a great deal has changed in the last 10 to 20 years; skewed patterns of use are still the norm.[1,2,3] As Myers notes: 'the greatest public library use is concentrated in the AB and C1 groups, who exploit public libraries more intensively than the numerically larger C2 and DE groups'. The result is a form of distributive injustice: those with higher levels of disposable income (the bulk of library users) are being subsidised by the less affluent (the minority user population). Anthony Land's synopsis of a recent (1990) public opinion survey (*Consumer attitudes to public libraries: the Which? report*) provides further confirmation of the 'solidly middle–class subscriber profile' and raises questions about 'the air of cloistered calm quite typical of many libraries'. In his view, this suggests 'under–use of an important and expensive public asset', just the kind of thing likely to attract the attention of the Audit Commission.[4]

Market research is not simply about estimating or forecasting demand. With any service, there is a need to continuously evaluate performance and quality. Childers' paper (*Evaluative research in the library and information field*) is a helpful overview of evaluative research studies and techniques, which concludes that the quality of investigation in the field is on the whole reasonably good, but 'fragmented and noncumulative, lacking sufficient basic research'. The theme is picked up in Wilson's article (*Productivity measurements in special libraries: prospects and problems for use in performance evaluation*): 'Productivity measures do have their place in the special librarian's tool kit of evaluation measures . . . When compared with other evaluation measures that have been developed for libraries, productivity complements rather than replaces them'. Williams illustrates his points with two worked examples from federal special libraries.

The question of quality *vis à vis* online databases was addressed in the previous section: here Kathleen Eagleton looks at hospital libraries (*Quality assurance in Canadian hospital libraries – the challenge*). Despite its solidly Canadian focus, this is a useful point of departure for the literature of standards and quality assurance as applied to library services (the paper has a fine bibliography).

There are many reasons why people do not use information systems and services: lack of need, ignorance, inaccessibility, cost. Inability is another. Inability may be caused by poor or insensitive design, which, in turn, may be the result of inadequate (or zero) market research. I have included two papers which deal with human/cognitive design aspects in respect of information retrieval systems. Borgman's paper (*Human factors in the use of information systems: research methods and results*) is a straightforward review of current and likely future trends, which concludes as follows: 'If we are to advance the state of knowledge about users of information systems and make systems accessible to a broader population, we need better research methods and better means for implementing both the methods and the results into design'.

Annelise Mark Pejtersen's paper (*The 'Bookhouse': an icon based database system for fiction retrieval in public libraries*) is a delight in that it shows how with care and effort it is possible to produce a system which positively invites use. 'Traditionally classification and indexing schemes have been developed to reflect the contents of a document in terms of its relationships with the knowledge structure of the subject field to which it belongs and do not usually take the users' requests as a focus'. The 'Bookhouse' system uses a unique, multi–faceted classification system which includes the physical characteristics of the book, its readibility, format, storyline, and the author's intention.

The final paper in the volume reminds us that even if the service, systems, products and price are right, the overall effect may still be damaged by poorly trained or motivated staff. Margaret Slater's paper (*Careers and the occupational image*) confirms the low public esteem in which the profession is held ('if you want to end up as a managing director, don't enter library–information work') and raises familiar questions about recruitment and selection into the field. Nothing much, it would appear, has changed in the three years since she published her findings, as the following quotation from the *Guardian* newspaper makes all too clear:

The Government, while reaffirming its commitment to a free 'core service' believes that libraries should be doing more to generate income of their own: charging for some services; becoming information technology centres; offering computer services and so on at commercially competitive rates to local businesses . . . The sensible librarian will hide in the stacks until the Dark Angel of 1980's enterprise culture has passed overhead and exercise sandals have come back into fashion and a New Age of Post–Modernist mahogany librarianship is upon us . . .[5]

And the view from some quarters in the USA is no less encouraging:

Face it, folks. You *do* know why your pay is low and why your 'profession' gets no respect. Deep down you *know* any schlemiel can be a librarian. Once you peel away the euphemisms, librarianship boils down to fetching Mrs. Brown that latest best seller, finding Johnny the elusive fact in the *Encyclopedia Britannica* for his term paper, or showing Joe Fixit where the latest issue of Popular Mechanics is stashed. Not much brain power needed there, and you know it . . . You're a gofer. That's why your pay is low and nobody respects you.[6]

The language of marketing may have been absorbed into the professional *patois* of many librarians and information scientists in the course of the last ten years, but it is abundantly clear that much remains to be done if these kinds of perceptions and stereotypes are to be laid to rest.

REFERENCES

1. LUCKHAM, B. *The library in society*. London: Library Association, 1971.
2. ZWEIZIG, D. *Predicting amount of library use: an empirical study of the public library in the life of the adult public*. Syracuse: Syracuse University, 1973. (PhD dissertation).
3. TOTTERDELL, B. and BIRD, J. *The effective library: a report of the Hillingdon project on public library effectiveness*. London: Library Association, 1976.
4. FERGUSON, A. The limits of authority. *Management Today*, April 1989, pp. 40–41.
5. STAFFORD, D. Binding love. *Weekend Guardian*, September 1–2, 1990, pp. 9.
6. PLAISS, M. Libraryland: pseudo–intellectuals and semi–dullards. *American Libraries*, June 1990, pp. 588–589.

Approaches to market research

Blaise Cronin

Head, Department of Information Science, University of Strathclyde

ABSTRACT

The importance of market research or organizational development is stressed. Techniques for analysing and segmenting markets are discussed: demographics, life cycle/lifestyle analysis, benefit segmentation. The mechanics of user studies/community profiling are outlined and various data collection/analysis techniques assessed.

THE VALUE OF APPLIED RESEARCH

The membership of the Market Research Society has doubled to its present figure of almost 5,000 in less than a decade. Today the value of commercially available market research in the UK is in excess of £160 million. Worldwide the figure is probably of the order of £3,000 million.[1]

This growth has taken place against a backcloth of global recession. Recession heightens competitiveness. The increasing competition for domestic and foreign markets, the globalization of markets (and advertising) and the pressure to develop new or improved products/services for increasingly sophisticated consumer groups have greatly stimulated demand for applied market research in both manufacturing and service industries.

WHAT IS A MARKET?

A market is a place (literal or figurative) in which a buyer and seller, producer and consumer, supplier and receiver meet to exchange goods or services and where transfers of ownership titles occur. The market for a product or service is the aggregate of demand (actual and potential) among an identifiable consumer population. The concept of a market implies a demand for a product or service. Often, the terms 'market' and 'demand' are used interchangeably or conjoined as 'market demand'.

A market is usually defined as a population of individuals with needs and/or wants, money to spend and a preparedness to spend that money to acquire the means of satisfying those needs/wants. But not all market transactions involve monetary exchange. The consumer in some cases will be required to give time, effort or commitment rather than a cash payment for services rendered. Marketing techniques are today widely used by not-for-profit organizations (e.g. hospitals, universities, charities, churches) as well as manufacturers of consumer goods.

WHAT IS MARKET RESEARCH?

Market research is the systematic analysis of consumer characteristics, behaviours, lifestyles, needs, wants, demands and preferences. Armed with reliable data on how its actual and potential clients think and behave, a company is better placed to: (1) improve its customer-orientation and targetting; (2) reassess its product range and distribution channels; (3) refine its pricing strategies; (4) identify new product development opportunities; (5) provide customised or highly niched products; and (6) attack its competitors' market share.

Markets, whether for consumer durables or services, can be highly fragmented. Factors such as discretionary income, geographic location, family size, terminal education age, and so on, can heavily influence purchasing behaviour. The more detailed the data and information available on different market segments, the greater the likelihood of the consumer's specific requirements being met – profitably and effectively.

MARKET SEGMENTATION

A manufacturing company may choose to treat its market as a single, homogeneous entity (market aggregation) and produce one product for all potential customers. The attraction of this approach has to do with economies of scale in relation to design, production, packaging, distribution and advertising. The benefits of a product/production-centred approach of this kind to the consumer are the relatively low unit costs.

Product differentiation enables a manufacturer to respond more closely to the needs and wants of submarkets and in so doing improve competitiveness against a single-line manufacturer. As a general rule, the greater the degree of product differentiation the greater the manufacturing (and associated) costs and the higher the price charged to the consumer. It is the difference between bespoke tailoring and off-the-peg retailing.

Market segmentation is the process of slicing up a market into its constituent parts and identifying significant, discriminate features of each segment with a view to achieving a closer 'fit' between the product and customer needs. This approach may be characterised as customer- as opposed to product-oriented. With advances in computer integrated manufacturing, mass production techniques will progressively give way to individualised design and short-run, on-demand production.

NICHEMANSHIP

Market research makes it possible to go beyond mass production and 'shotgun' marketing to customised production and 'rifle-shot' marketing. The automotive industry is a case in point. Ford, for example, manufactures a wide range of models (of varying size, power and price), but the consumer can also choose between several versions of a particular marque (from the basic saloon to the expensive, 'limited edition', high-powered, top-of-the-range GT version).

A small company in a competitive market would, for instance, be well advised to identify niches or market segments on which to focus. Developing a reputation for product excellence in a clearly defined sector or submarket may prove more beneficial in the long-term than trying (and failing) to satisfy a complex, horizontal market.

Within the automobile industry both approaches can be clearly seen. Ford offers a highly differentiated range of products across a very wide price spectrum as a part of its policy to hold a significant share of the total market. Rolls Royce, by way of contrast, produces a unique product of demonstrable excellence, affordable by only a small section of the population. Ford spends vast sums advertising its products (in the press, on TV); Rolls Royce spends much less (proportionately), relying instead on word-of-mouth recommendation and reputation. Ford's customers are concerned about price; the luxury car market, by way of contrast, is basically price insensitive. Two companies in the same broad product market, but using quite different marketing strategies to achieve their corporate objectives.

DISSECTING MARKETS

A market can be segmented in many ways, to various levels of sophistication. Analytical strategies can range from the simple (univariate) to the sophisticated (multivariate), depending upon the skills, time and resources available. consumer behaviours and attitudes are complex and necessarily call for the application of powerful tools to identify key interacting variables.

Market segmentation can be approached from a number of directions. Four broad options are outlined below.

Demographics

Market segmentation based upon demographic data is commonplace and relatively easy to apply. Consumers are grouped according to age, sex, race, social class, occupation, type of residence, religion, nationality, etc., and associations between the selected variables (or clusters thereof) and such dispositions as propensity to buy verified or falsified.

ACORN is a commercial market segmentation tool (produced by C.A.C.I. in the UK) which allows consumers to be classified according to the type of residential area in which they live. Households are classified into 11 neighbourhood groups and 38 neighbourhood types. To illustrate: one of the 11 groups is 'Poorest council estates', which is further divided into 4 sub-groups: (i) new council estates in inner cities; (ii) overspill estates, high unemployment; (iii) council estates with overcrowding; and (iv) council estates with worst poverty. The ACORN classification is based upon an analysis of 40 different variables encompassing demographic, housing and employment characteristics. Value-added market data of these kinds clearly increase the chances of successful consumer targetting and product promotion for those companies willing and able to use such a facility.

Family life cycle

The concept of the family life cycle brings together a number of household features (age, marital status, presence of children) and seeks to relate behaviour at different stages in the family life cycle to purchasing patterns. Its appeal, as with the ACORN approach, is that it does not rely solely on individual variables, such as age, to pinpoint potential market segments.

The family life cycle consists of six broad phases: (i) Bachelor stage (young, single individuals); (ii) Young married couples (no children); (iii) Full nest (young married couples with children) – Full nest I (youngest child under 6) – Full nest II (youngest child over 6); (iv) Full nest III (older married couples with dependent children); (v) Empty nest (older married couples with no children at home); (vi) Solitary survivors (older single or widowed people). By classifying households along these lines, the product manufacturer has a clearer idea of spending power and priorities in relation to stages in the cycle, and can thus market his goods accordingly.

Psychographics

An individual's perceptions of a product are not simply a function of the intrinsic quality of the product, its price, utility or the effectiveness of related advertising. Consumer preferences and perceptions are influenced by cultural forces, peer group beliefs, family attitudes, received wisdom, personality factors, and so on. Effective market research requires that the consumer's psychological field is given due weighting in the overall analysis of variables. Consumer modelling based on demographic data will inevitably be deficient, if no account is taken of measures of general attitudes, interests and opinions.

Psychographic data can provide an enriched picture of consumer groups (lifestyle mapping) and allow for more focussed product marketing. The use of psychographic data has been commercially exploited in the UK by Taylor Nelson Monitor Ltd. The company monitors changes in social values and attitudes and groups individuals according to their attitudes and beliefs and classifies people into one of seven Social Value Groups: (i) Belongers; (ii) Self-explorers; (iii) Experiment-alists; (iv) Conspicuous consumers; (v) Social resistors; (vi) Survivors; (vii) Aimless.

The purchasing patterns, brand consciousness and responsiveness to advertising of these groups differ markedly. To illustrate: Self-explorers are looking for inherent quality and are not likely to be greatly influenced by product image. They will, as a rule, pay extra for quality. The Belonger, on the other hand, is extremely brand conscious and loyal, and tends not to experiment or try a new product unless endorsed and well established among his circle of friends.

Benefit segmentation

This approach to segmentation is based on the belief that people use a service or product because they wish to derive some form of benefit. If this view is accepted, it makes sense to cluster individuals or groups in terms of benefits sought. Having identified 'benefit clusters', second order classification can be carried out, using more traditional demo-graphic measures.

Why does a person buy a Rolls Royce? As a means of transport? Possibly, but there are many other automobiles which could satisfy this need for considerably less cash outlay. Other reasons for purchasing a Rolls Royce might include: product reliability; product exclusivity; image-enhancement; resale value, etc. Rolls Royce could choose to market its products on the basis of product reliability and craftsmanship; or it could choose to stress the benefits (in terms of image enhancement, business prestige) accruing to the owner – benefits which have little to do with automobile design and engineering achievements.

Different products will confer different benefits at different times to different consumer groups, but the approach has much to recommend it. Product excellence, uniqueness, reliability, value-for-money, etc. may seem like fail-safe marketing levers, but in practice this is not always the case. Benefit segmentation recognises the limitations of an exclusively product-centred approach to marketing and prefers to promote a product in terms of what it can do for, or ways in which it can benefit, the consumer.

IMPORTANCE OF MARKET RESEARCH

Studies of innovation in manufacturing and service companies have repeatedly cited an understanding of customer needs as an attribute of successful organisations. Closeness to the customer, attention to the moods of the market and a commitment to 'warm armpit marketing' are features of the successful organisation. A new product launch without detailed consumer research and feedback from the marketplace is today almost unheard of among major manufacturing enterprises.

Technical excellence, a keen price or state-of-the-art-design are not always in themselves a guarantee of a successful launch. The ill-fated Bell Videophone; Levi Strauss' less than successful entry into the formal menswear market; Prestel's uninspiring penetration of the domestic viewdata market; Sir Clive Sinclair's short-lived C5 motor-assisted tricycle. In each case, the inventor's/manufacturer's vision was not enough to ensure success. The point of investing in market research is to eliminate (or at least reduce) the risk of costly miscalculations of these kinds; to guide product development and identify segments of the market where a product is likely to establish a foothold within a financially acceptable timescale.

Market research is not simply a risk-avoidance mechanism. The use of focus groups and sensitivity panels to furnish suggestions for new products, product refinement, image development, or novel packaging and distribution mechanisms can provide the manufacturer with un-expected insights and concrete product development opportunities. Proactive market research of this kind complements the more traditional survey-based approach to consumer analysis and can be applied in a wide variety of contexts.

INVESTIGATIVE TECHNIQUES

The techniques of market research are essentially those used in social sciences research. Increasingly, qualitative methods are combined with the more classical quantitative approaches to data collection, analysis and presentation to provide deeper insights into consumer behaviour, attitudes and outlooks.

Aspects of the quantitative paradigm include the following: emphasis on facts and causes of social phenomena rather than the subjective states of individuals; employment of hard data; stress on replicability; assump-tion of a steady reality; encouragement of statistical sampling and generalisations. The qualitative paradigm incorporates the following: an understanding of human behaviour from the actor's own frame of reference; uncontrolled observation and subjective accounting; single case studies; coincidence of data collection and analysis.

Techniques from both these schools can be applied to the three main types of market research: (i) exploratory; (ii) descriptive; (iii) ex-perimental.

Exploratory research

The goal of exploratory research is to determine what needs to be known; what questions need to be posed; what hypotheses need to be tested. Exploratory research typically uses a convenience sample to crystallize early thinking and test out initial hunches before embarking on a full-scale investigation.

Descriptive research

Descriptive market research aims to find out 'what is'. Typically such questions are asked as: 'How many people use – buy – rent – own – motor cars?'; 'What are the backgrounds of those who own Rolls Royces – what is their modal income –how many miles do they drive in a year?'; 'What is IBM's reputation for aftersales service – has it improved or deteriorated in the last five years?'

Descriptive research also includes causal-comparative research. 'Is there a higher incidence of lung cancer among those who smoke 20 cigarettes per day than non-smokers?' It could include a comparative study, for example, of the effectiveness of different direct mailing techniques on a population of C2 housewives, or the impact of pricing changes on the volume use made of online information retrieval systems in an educational establishment.

Experimental research

This type of research aims to establish causal connections by careful manipulation of a key treatment variable through active intervention by the researcher. Subjects are divided into two groups – control and experimental – and the treatment (which could be a drug or the raising of anxiety levels) would be administered only to the latter. Performance differences between the matched groups would then be attributable to the manipulation of the treatment variable by the researcher.

MARKET RESEARCH AND INFORMATION PROVISION

The application of market research techniques to library and information services/products provision is well established. However, terms such as 'community profiling', 'community analysis', and 'user studies' are more commonly used in this field, particularly when talking about public sector services.

User studies

The Centre for Research on User Studies (CRUS) at the University of Sheffield has for some years acted as a focal point and clearing house for studies of this kind. According to CRUS, 'the motivation to conduct a user study often arises from a need or wish to evaluate services, in order to try to establish how far good use is being made of scarce, and often decreasing, resources, to re-assess priorities, or to justify the existence of all or part of the services offered'. The questions typically addressed in a library user study of the following kind: 'Who uses the service?'; 'Why is the service being used?'; 'Is the service being used effectively?'; 'Who does not use the service, and why?'; 'Are user needs being met – if not, why not?'; 'Are users satisfied with the services on offer?'; 'Are resources being deployed effectively?', etc.[2]

A user study can be global in character, that is to say, concerned with all aspects of current provision and needs throughout the community, or it can focus on the needs of a specific sub-group, – e.g. the business community, the elderly, the socially disadvantaged.

User studies should not be confused with use studies. The former concentrate on the needs, demands, attitudes, opinions and preferences of users, non-users and lapsed users; the latter focus on the use made of all or part of the collections and facilities on offer to the public. A use study can be conducted without any questioning of users, data being gathered on volume, frequency and intensity of use in relation to specific features of the overall service. For example, a bibliometric or citation analysis could be carried out to identify key journals in a library collection, or to monitor the use made of a short loan collection. A user study (of, say, a journal collection) would supplement the quantitative data with the subjective views of a sample of users to provide an enriched understanding of the patterns and determinants of use.

Community profiling

This technique is most commonly applied to the evaluation of public library services. Simply put, a community profile is an outline description highlighting the main features and characteristics of a particular community. The aim is not merely to describe the community-as-it-is, but to relate those data to the provision of services and to identify ways in which the 'fit' between provision and needs might be improved.

A community can be defined in terms of (i) the catchment area (i.e. the area on a local authority map notionally serviced by a particular library or library system); (ii) the residents' own conception of community – which may differ from that imagined by the library service; and (iii) census or local government boundaries.

Using official sources (e.g. census data, planning information, structure plans, etc.) it should be possible to develop a clear impression of the community in terms of such variables as population structure, household composition, economic activity, education, leisure and amenity provision, socioeconomic groupings, etc. Formal data collection can be usefully supplemented by structured observation (i.e. walking about and soaking up the local atmosphere) and interviews/discussions with opinion leaders, 'key informants' and others within the community. The overall aim is to ensure that there is alignment between the character, structure and philosophy of the service and the community being served. The purpose is to test the validity of the service's operating philosophy and to expose gaps or shortcomings in provision.

The sophistication and comprehensiveness of a community profiling exercise is a function of resources (money; expertise; time) available at any given moment. However, even with limited resources it should be possible, without a great deal of difficulty, to identify major deficiencies in service provision and determine appropriate remedial actions.

Lifestyle analysis

The value of lifestyle analysis in market research was mentioned earlier. The application of the technique calls for specialist skills not usually found in the library profession and is thus relatively untried. Two major lifestyle analyses have, however, been carried out in the USA.[3,4] Both used questionnaires containing more than 200 activity, interest and opinion items. Data on library use were then related to overall lifestyle characteristics. The findings of the two studies proved complementary. To summarize: the more active an individual tends to be, the more likely that he or she will use library facilities. To quote Madden: Library use is most highly related to activity. An individual who is active in other aspects of life, whether it be community organizations, politics, work, or sports, is also likely to be a library user. Libraries are simply a part of the lifestyle of active people – there is clear evidence that the library is simply not a potential part of the lifestyle of some people'.[5]

The attraction of lifestyle analysis applied to a particular community is that it allows for more realistic service development and targetting, based upon a rounded appreciation of how people actually lead their lives. Specific functions, collections and activities can then be constructed or remodelled to match more closely the needs and demands of the various sections of the community.

MARKETING INFORMATION PRODUCTS

The electronic information industry's revenues increase dramatically year by year. Vast sums are earned by vendors and distributors of electronic information and data. However, only a minority record after-tax profits. The market for online databases (particularly of the bibliographic variety) is oversubscribed. A number of hosts trade profitably and a number of databases produce healthy income for their parent companies, but this would appear to be the exception rather than the rule.

Consequently, new entrants to the marketplace need to gather accurate data on the scope for new products, likely customer base, and actual user requirements upon which to base realistic revenue projections. General, all-purpose databases are likely to prove less successful than those which are targetted at a specific market segment and have high added-value (e.g. are dynamic, frequently updated, integrative, supported by software for post-search data manipulation, are easy to use, etc.).

Finding a niche for a new product will be critically important if a return on investment is to be achieved. A highly niched product serving a small, homogeneous and resource-rich community (e.g. venture capitalists; exporters) with a number of exclusive features (real-time information; multi-lingual commands) will have a much higher chance of success than a lookalike product aimed at a generalist market. In the years ahead, market research and advertising expenditures will feature more prominently in the total costs of creating and launching a database onto the market. In view of the capital costs involved in competitive database marketing, investment in systematic market research is not just advisable, but essential.

This is equally true of other information products/technologies. The Library Association is considering launching LISA (Library & Information Science Abstracts) in CD-ROM format. Part of its market research has been the circulation of a self-complete questionnaire to potentially interested customers. The information gathered via the questionnaire will be used to estimate demand, determine price elasticity and ultimately to decide whether a viable market for the product (packaged and delivered in novel form) exists.

As the consumer market for information technology products becomes increasingly sophisticated, manufacturers will invest more time and money in prelaunch market research. 'Technology push' is giving way to 'demand pull' in the IT field, and manufacturers/suppliers would be ill-advised to rely entirely on technical excellence or product uniqueness as a guarantee of financial success. What are the advantages/benefits/savings to the library/information community of online access, CD-ROM, interactive videodisc and other technologies? Are these stressed in the marketing and advertising campaigns? Are the benefits claimed in the marketing literature actually perceived as such by the target consumer market?

Knowing the mood of the market or (in the case of a library) the local community is crucially important. Markets are volatile (they often undergo structural and attitudinal change over time) and need to be monitored in systematic fashion. Information on a market's current status and likely longer-term trends is needed to answer basic questions relating to an organisation's marketing strategy. Should the goal be increased penetration in existing markets; new product/service development in existing markets; promotion of the existing product range in new markets; the launch of new products/services in new markets – or a combination of these?

Pricing is another important consideration. In some cases (e.g. online searching in the business sector), use is price insensitive. If a service is essential, users will pay the asking price. In other cases (e.g. the introduction of charges for the borrowing of records and cassettes in a public library), the volume of use may be dramatically affected by a change in charging policy or pricing strategy. In a library context, charging is not an either/or issue. Charging can be blanket, differentiated or discretionary in character, but whichever option is selected there is a clear case for some preliminary market research to test likely user reaction to the practice in general and the various means of operationalization (e.g. direct cost pricing; demand-based pricing; value-based pricing; competitive pricing, etc.).

GATHERING IN THE RAW DATA

There are numerous books which describe methods of survey/market research, including several written specifically for information and library specialists. Thus, the main approaches are merely adumbrated below:

- Observation
- Questionnaires
- Interviewing
- Diaries/activity logs

Observation

This entails watching, listening and recording actions, behaviours and verbal exchanges. Observation may be overt or covert; individual or group-based; machine-supported (e.g. using a hidden camera) or 'natural'; participant (e.g. attending a committee meeting) or not. The attraction of this approach is that it gives the researcher a 'feel' for the community or problem under the microscope and may help in the formulation of subsequent research design and strategy.

Questionnaires

This is the most frequently used data collection instrument. It is especially suited to large-scale data collection with a dispersed population. The relative rigidity of the medium is both its strength and drawback. The trade-off is between structure (which allows for data aggregation and comparison) and flexibility (lacking due to preimposed formats and response options).

Interviewing

Interviewing can be carried out face-to-face, by telephone, or by using computer conferencing facilities. It can be on a one-to-one, one-to-several, several-to-one, or several-to-several basis. Questions asked can be highly structured (with or without predetermined response categories), semi-structured (i.e. a range of topics/aspects is agreed between researcher and interviewee at the outset), or unstructured (i.e. free-ranging discourse around the research topic). Successful interviewing (as with questionnaire design) requires considerable skill, and ought not to be undertaken without careful planning and (ideally) training in interview techniques.

Diaries/activity logs

This method effectively offloads the work effort to the subject under investigation, who is asked to keep a faithful record of critical incidents/ events over an agreed timespan, or log his behaviours/feelings at fixed intervals. The end-product is a narrative or natural history which can be a rich source of insight for the remote researcher.

Which method, or combination of methods, is employed will depend on the problem domain, resources available and character of data/ information sought.

CONCLUSION

Market research is a means of estimating demands, needs and levels of satisfaction among specific market segments. It furnishes data upon which a marketing plan can be built, thus enabling a manufacturer/ service supplier to align his products/services with the requirements of the marketplace. Market research does not answer the questions: 'What business are we in?'; 'Which markets should we attack?'; 'How should we prioritize our services?', but it should provide data upon which to make intelligent and informed decisions about corporate strategy or service philosophy.

REFERENCES

1. GOODYEAR, J. The UK market research industry: past, present and future. MRS Newsletter. May 1985, pp 44–48.
2. STONE, S. and HARRIS, C. Designing a user study: general research design. CRUS Guide 1. Centre for Research on User Studies, Sheffield University, 1984.
3. BOLTON, W.T. Life style research: an aid to promoting public libraries. Library Journal, May 15, 1982, pp 963–968.
4. MADDEN, M. Marketing survey spinoff: library user/non user lifestyles. American Libraries, 10(2), 1979, pp 79–81.
5. Ibid.

Consumers and Markets – Stimulating and fulfilling consumer demands

John Myers

Principal, Solon Consultants

As a prologue to my paper, let me tell you a fable. There was once a man walking in high mountains. As he was going along a path by a steep chasm, he slipped and fell into it. A little way down there was a bush growing out of the cliff face, and the man was able to grab hold of it and halt his fall. He cried out, *'Help! Is there anyone up there?'* And a voice from on high said, *'I am God, I am up here. Do you believe?'* And the man said, *'Yes! I believe, I believe!'* And the voice said, *'If you believe, let go.'* There was a long pause, and then the man asked, *'Is there anyone else up there?'*

It will call for an act of faith from those who have charge of our libraries to leap from the known into the unknown. Maybe today's papers and discussion will show more of the way ahead, and even that there could be a soft landing. Maybe, maybe not.

Mr Chairman, you kindly made mention of my earlier paper on policies and perspectives. In that paper, I drew attention to a legacy on which much of our nation's heritage is based, that is, our tradition of buccaneering private enterprise. This element of my thesis attracted some attention, and you may feel that I come with a reputation as a freebooting pirate, who does not want libraries to remain safe and secluded havens of culture. I am even told that some of you, who already know me and my reputation, feel that you could easily have written my paper for me without ever needing to come to this conference to hear what I might have to say.

But I should like to remind you that in that earlier paper I also drew attention to the parallel English tradition of fostering the liberal verities – that is, the traditions we enjoy which assign merit to social equity, balanced opportunities, representation and participation. In fact, you may recall I suggested that what we needed was to achieve a better equilibrium between these two traditions.

When preparing that paper, I thought that libraries were indeed changing, but with a devotion to the inevitability of gradualness which might be the envy of a Fabian. Today, I believe that libraries are inevitably facing metamorphosis, and that it will be impossible for those who run them to avoid the impact and interaction of the social, technological, economic and political changes which are taking place. The purpose of my earlier paper was to stimulate thought, to provoke a dialogue, to open up further debate, to prompt study of the issues. I feel it did help a little towards those ends; but it is now time to consider how far we have come, and how we might make further progress.

Thus, my paper to you this morning has a similar aim – to promote a discussion that I hope can be held outside the prison of today's measures, constraints, myths and taboos, so that you and I, and others who may read what we say, can focus on the probabilities and the possibilities of the future with more freedom.

TRADITIONAL VIEWS

With this in mind, let me therefore ask you to consider first the traditional qualities which many librarians are trying hard to preserve, and which are being put to the test by the changes which are taking place.

Librarians argue, and I would accept, that our libraries should be seen as part of our civilized heritage and social dignity, and as symbols of freedom and liberty. Admittedly, in some public libraries, what you actually see is the liberty of the date-stamp, the freedom of the book trolley, and the dignity of warmed-over tramps in the reading room. Nevertheless, the concepts are fine and we would all want to pursue them, but they do not mean that libraries should function merely as literary retreats for the cultured and leisured classes. In some parts of the country, there is a risk that libraries might be little more than that, partly because some librarians do not want to see their libraries as bustling centres of information enterprise and community activity.

Last year, an American writer on library matters, Mark Hornung, captured a view which is sometimes put to me by librarians. He wrote that, *'People enjoy libraries as a place of peace, calm and comfort'*. In this context, it is significant that LISC in Scotland, in dismissing the Institute's discussion paper on sponsorship, contended that libraries should be *'places for research, quiet reflection and intellectual development, not for a sales convention'*. Among these Scottish librarians, the law of the nostalgia quotient evidently prevails; but you will see that there is a risk in their approach – that libraries will be thought of as no more than staid, old, limited-service, neighbourhood institutions, targeted more at the literate classes than the community as a whole.

Not all our librarians are content with this image. It contradicts the ambitions of some, who are eager *'to reach the most people with the best reading at the least cost'*. These social librarians see our libraries as the repositories of vast amounts of stored knowledge and information, but they want to make these libraries a vital part of a community's cultural agenda; and they are keen to ensure that services are offered equitably to all segments, not only to those who have always used them.

THE USE OF LIBRARIES

Libraries have yet to come close to satisfying these ambitions. Use of these libraries remains biased towards certain social groups and certain age groups. Now, you may feel that the categorizing and labelling of groups of people and measuring their behaviour is how sociologists while away the long empty hours between becoming sociologists and trying to discover what that qualifies them to do. But today, everyone is at it. Marketeers, pollsters, bar room pundits, of course, politicians, and indeed librarians, are all seeking to measure, draw and quarter how people think and act.

In spite of their efforts, by and large we still lack really penetrative market research on library use – although I have seen some impressive work by the Rand Corporation, who have studied Californian libraries, and some equally impressive in-house studies by the Surrey County Library Service over here. Incidentally, may I say how pleased I am to see the Chief Librarian of Surrey, John Saunders, in the audience today.

The genuine research studies, that have been carried out, all point to the same conclusions, which have been highlighted in some work for the *Sunday Times,* carried out in December last year by the opinion research firm, MORI, and published a few weeks ago. MORI's findings confirmed that the greatest public library use is concentrated in the AB and C1 groups, who exploit public libraries far more intensively than the numerically larger C2 and DE groups. The same research demonstrated that use was much less intense among the young and the old than among the 'betweenagers'.

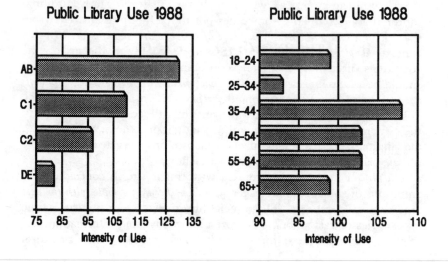

Thus, it seems that libraries – probably because of the ways they organize and deliver their services – may not be offering the unsophisticated what they want, or are presenting them with barriers to effective use of the services. Those barriers may, of course, be increased by individuals' lack of familiarity with library use and services. As MORI was able to show, the people who use libraries are mainly the same people who buy and read books, representing in total more than three-fifths of the population. The others never go into our libraries, and rarely read a book.

Library Users

Book Buyers **Non–Buyers**

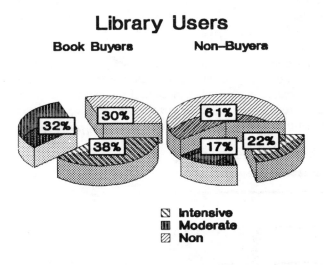

☒ **Intensive**
▥ **Moderate**
▨ **Non**

This pattern of behaviour may not persist. As others have remarked, *'the pace of events is now moving so fast that – unless we can find some way to keep our sights on tomorrow – we cannot expect to be in touch with today'*. Or as someone else put it, *'we don't want to start learning geology the morning after an earthquake'*.

SOCIAL AND TECHNOLOGICAL CHANGES

Seismic changes are already taking place in society. For example, the demographics are altering. The age distribution of the population, as it was earlier in this decade, reflected the baby boom of the 1960s; and the 1970s, the dominance of younger folk. The demographers are now predicting a shift to an ageing population over the next two or three decades.

You can also anticipate increased leisure time in certain sectors of the population, as a result of labour saving and the drop in hours worked by part of the labour force – I guess that might not include you or me. And the forecasters predict substantial movements in working patterns, with more women in the workforce, who will have a greater interest in business information.

The pundits will tell you to expect a transformation in the means of delivering this information. Decisions on broadband telecommunications and the use of fibre optics to create the 'information highways' of the future are probably the most important of all. The exciting products and services which could emerge from the power promised in the heartland technologies of information could well lead to tremendous growth in the potential of network-based services.

Many forward scenarios that have been published foresee information becoming a commodity – not only in its recognizable form in databases, videotex and value added network services, but also in more varied and sophisticated entertainment and leisure services, that will use broadcasting, cable and satellite. The forecasts for the years ahead suggest that ecological and environmental pressures could also lead to electronics being used more to substitute for paper. And these forward predictions show significant increases in the value of capital goods in households, with wider availability of education, entertainment, environment and communication facilities in the home and in the community.

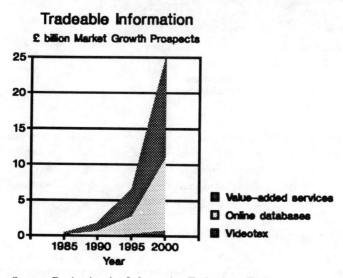

Source: Benjamin, A – Information Technology Futures

As a result, you are already seeing new developments in retailing. New types of lifestyle shops are being created, developers are refurbishing their shopping centres, and visual merchandising is becoming a competitive tool in retailing. Before long, electronic shopping is likely to influence consumer behaviour. The objectives of the retailers are similar to those which should be set for public libraries – to create an appealing environment for the client or customer.

In other words, libraries might become multi-media gathering places, acting in an expanded role as urban focal points. And, in the future, life could be enriched for those who choose to leave their cocoon-like homes to combine informal and self-directed learning with pleasure and socializing, and the social use of information-based retailing.

In this context, it is instructive to look at the findings of research carried out by Morgan Grenfell Laurie on places of public resort. For example, they highlight the importance of customer relations. Their findings suggest that we might do a better job of serving library users by developing in-house motivation programmes, such as management incentives that highlight service, and increased training of managers down to the departmental level, so that they can set examples for other library employees.

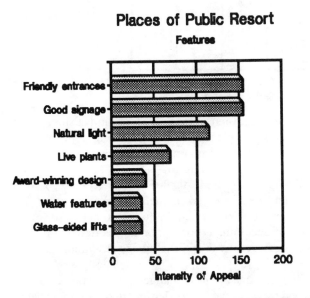

could be enriched for those who choose to leave their cocoon-like homes

Other findings from the Morgan Grenfell Laurie research are of interest. Image and accessibility are of course essential to the success of any organization, but they are of special importance to an entity that deals with intangibles, such as information services. In a complex and confusing society, the mental perceptions that an individual forms of an institution can create enduring, relatively dependable patronage patterns that ultimately determine the success of the institution.

PLANNING FOR THE FUTURE

We may also learn lessons from architects and space planners, such as James Terrell, who specializes in retailing. According to Peter Born, Terrell comments that *'Each store is a statement. Each department should be a theatre, with the feeling of individual shops tied together by architecture'*. He could have been talking about libraries.

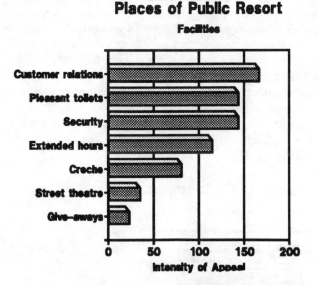

Places of Public Resort

Facilities

As changes in retailing make their impact on clients and customers, the future for libraries should involve new merchandising concepts, new physical designs, the integration of other service trade components; in short a process of constant change. The successful library will adapt to this change and will aim to provide facilities which are seen to be attractive, functional and responsive to the needs of the customer. The sucessful library will make effective use of its customer base, of the available technology, of accumulated operational experience, of a new orientation of library staff, of a fresh external image, of enhanced bricks and mortar.

I am therefore suggesting that all these changes can be expected to have long-term impacts upon the workplace, upon leisure, upon shopping habits, upon education, upon expectations, and upon public libraries – in brief, these events are likely to induce massive social change; and it seems probable that the library of the 1990s and the 21st century could be – and will need to be – vastly different from the libraries you know and cherish today.

As a result, the typical public library of today could soon be experiencing a middle-aged crisis. If it is to fit in with the society of tomorrow, librarians will need a favourable climate to allow them to make the great leap forward from an industrial economy to an information one. But it is always difficult to leap a chasm in a series of jumps; and more research will be needed to reduce the uncertainties associated with giant strides.

NEED FOR INDEPTH RESEARCH

In my view, there is a need for indepth research on the impacts of changes in lifestyles, and research on demand for library and information services among different segments within our communities. As you may be aware, the basic premise of lifestyle research is *'the more you know and understand about your customers in each of the relevant segments, the more effectively you can communicate and market to them.'*

When I am talking to my clients, they like to have a definition of what is involved in lifestyle and segmentation research, and it may be helpful if I take a moment to explain what I mean. You can carry out research to group consumers in mass or niche markets according to:

- Their activities, that is, how they spend their time;
- Their interests, that is, what importance they place on their immediate surroundings;
- Their opinions, that is, their view of themselves and the world around them;
- And some basic profiling characteristics, such as their stage in the life cycle, their income, their education and where they live.

The findings can help all of us to understand which segments of a community, or of a user population, are reacting in certain ways:

- So that you can offer them real benefits attuned to their perceptions and interests;
- So that you can pinpoint and profile key targets;
- So that you can develop a fresh view of your markets;
- So that you can position your activities in these markets, and develop appropriate new products and services;
- So that you can communicate effectively with your clients or customers;
- So that you can develop sounder marketing and media strategies;
- Overall, so that you can both explain and do something about the 'why' of the use and non-use of libraries and information services.

The findings of such research should be acted upon; and library services might be redefined, where necessary. As a result, you might well see librarians adopting a more consumer-driven approach, with more in-library services designed to be friendly to users of them. I believe that libraries by their very nature could be particularly well suited to innovative services. With forward-looking location, layout and merchandising decisions, and imaginative use of their assets, libraries could be seen as easily accessible, as reasonably non-threatening to potential users, as dedicated to providing a wide range of information services for the entire community.

CONSUMER-LED SERVICES

This implies a new approach which would need extensive education and training programmes to inculcate new skills, new attitudes, new capabilities; and you would need programmes to train library staff to act more as sales people than mere processors of transactions or lookers-up of references.

When I suggest the concept of such radical extensions to our library services you will, I imagine, raise the question of how we are to afford and deliver them. Up till now, librarians have seen themselves faced with insurmountable opportunities.

However, I suggest to you that facilities could be enhanced to uniquely qualify the public library as a key service point in the distribution network for information services directed at families, at individuals and at many businesses and professional firms.

Such an enhancement would certainly call for a strategy that is consumer-driven, in the sense that it would aim to create and serve greater expectations among library users. At the same time, librarians could take advantage of some of the changes which are beginning to affect other consumer service activities, such as retailing. As a case in point, more of the routines involved in book issue and return could be automated – helping to improve the library's efficiency and its image, using either through-the-wall or free-standing installations. In this connection, you may like to note that some banks are finding that as much as 40 per cent of their transactions are now going through machines rather than branch counters. Another phenomenon that has also been seen in some banks and building societies is customers lining up to use an automated bank cash machine while human tellers are free.

The tens of thousands of bank and building society cash machines in place today are testimony to the financial industry's acknowledgement of the role that convenience plays in customer relations. These financial institutions are responding to consumer preferences.

Not everyone likes the idea of giving library users the initiative. One information scientist I spoke to, as a general principle, dislikes too much emphasis on consumer-led provision. For one reason, he sees at present relatively little formal demand for information goods and services, which implies that for some time the initiative must lie with the supply side, to create products and stimulate demand, a notoriously capital-intensive and high-risk activity. Another of his arguments is that dependence on market pull tends to generate the lowest common denominator of service, an argument already extensively rehearsed in regard to sound and television broadcasting. To sceptics like him, there is a risk that consumers will turn into a stentorian clique or a vociferous claque at variance with his preference – and that of at least some librarians – for a tranquil environment.

These doubters make a comparison with the health service, in which they believe consumer-led provision tends to result in curative medicine. What they want to see instead from either the health service, or by analogy the public library system, is at least a degree of preventive treatment and care. In the longer term, they believe this emphasis should be more beneficial.

MEASURING PERFORMANCE

To achieve such objectives in our sector, libraries have become caught up with the trend to formalize, quantify and publish under the 'performance' label, information concerning salient aspects of their activities. As a result of Royston Brown's initiatives, we have seen the creation of library plans for areas and regions. I have looked at a number of them. The majority of the plans and performance indicators seem to be 'top-down' affairs, propelled by the interests of senior officials in controlling both expenditure and the range and types of activities engaged in by lower level officials, and the way services are delivered at the point of use.

In nearly all the Library and Information Plans so far published, consumers have been consulted only in an indirect manner. Attention to consumer interests has mainly been of the innocuous variety – what Pollitt has described as the *'charm-school-and-better-wallpaper end of the spectrum'* – a 'harmless' version of consumerism that has required little serious change but much public visibility. What has been conspicuously absent from most of the performance measurement and planning so far seen in our public library services has been direct consumer-citizen participation in the design and operation of these schemes.

SELF-GOVERNING LIBRARY TRUSTS

One way of achieving such objectives would be to transfer library authority responsibility to a self-governing library trust in which consumers would be strongly and directly represented. These bodies might continue to be funded through local authorities and concentrate on services to the community in the local government catchment area. Alternatively, they might decide to offer services to other trusts or libraries on a regional, national or international basis, in which event the prime funding might come from central government. There are substantial international opportunities in the library sector: in the European Community alone, there are 75,000 libraries of all sizes run by public authorities. Over 20,000 of these are medium to large libraries.

Library authorities or trusts will need to think and plan anew in the context of the changes taking place in local government. They will have to put more and more of their business out to competitive tender, and hand over many of their activities voluntarily to third parties. Residual responsibility will continue to lie with the authority, but the job will be done by someone else. There is, of course, a risk that – as a result – library authorities could become no more than passive intermediaries.

The challenge to these authorities is therefore to explore and exploit a broader definition. For example, they might see the direct provision of services by a library authority as one means among many of offering information and library services to the community. In other words, the authority might take on an 'enabling' role. Freed from the assumption of self-sufficiency, and the need to deliver all it does directly, the enabling authority can define its role – not by the services it provides – but by a broader agenda of concerns. The library authority can begin to think and act strategically – and to develop and implement a strategy through leadership rather than direct action. The issue of what is required should be separated from the issue of how it is to be delivered. The members of the authority can then focus their attention on whether needs are being met, rather than on the bureaucracy of meeting them.

The road ahead is paved with technological advances and changing lifestyles and new market segmentations. These advances and changes provide opportunities for public libraries and their managements to develop different strategies and different marketing thrusts for each segment. We might see full service community libraries, micro-libraries in shopping malls, mail-order public libraries – innovations that will extend the presence of libraries around the country, and build upon a strong marketing and sales capability. The objectives should be to deliver services to the client in the way the client wants it.

The task is clear. We will have to manage libraries with enterprise and skill through an unsettling period of major change. Diverse enterprises, some of which are remote from professional communities, will have to cooperate in perhaps unfamiliar ways. We will have to put aside any lingering sense of complacency that might diminish our task. We will have to adapt, compete in a tough global economy and commit ourselves to growth. The rewards at the end could be great, or they could be illusory. Which it is to be is up to all of you who take the road to the future.

REFERENCES

ANON. **Grasping the idea of enabling councils** *Municipal Journal* 26 May 1989 p 22.

ANON. **ATMs are properly a full component of any strategy for retall banking** *American Banker 9 January* 1980 pp 4–8.

BAILEY S J. **Charging for public library services** *Policy and Politics* vol 17, no 1 1989 pp 59–74.

BENJAMIN A. **Information technology futures** London City University 1 March 1989 *Third annual Rank Xerox Lecture.*

BOTTOMLEY V. *et al.* **Managing buyouts** Municipal Journal 26 May 1989 pp 18–19.

BORN P. **Creating unique spaces for selling** *Women's Wear Daily* vol 154 8 September 1987 pp 17–18.

BRAUNHOLTZ S. **Books and libraries: research conducted for the Sunday Times** London Market and Opinion Research International 1989 18 p.

COSMAS S C. **Life styles and consumption patterns** *Journal of Consumer Research* vol 8, March 1982 pp 453–455.

DARDEN W R *and* PERRFAULT W D JR. Identifying interurban shoppers: multi-product purchase patterns and segmentation profiles *Journal of Marketing Research* vol 13 1975 pp 51–60.

EUROPEAN COMMUNITY DG XIII. Plan of action for libraries In the EC Luxembourg The Community 1988.

HORNUNG M. Sizing up bids for the city's new public library *Crain's Chicago Business* 6 June 1988 pp 7–13.

LIBRARIES AND INFORMATION SERVICES COUNCIL FOR SCOTLAND. Comments on Institute of Information Scientists' paper on sponsorship Edinburgh The Council 1989.

MARTYN J. Private communication 1989.

MYERS J M. Priorities and policies: private sector involvement In our fields of Interest *Journal of Information Science* vol 9 no 1 August 1984 pp 1–6.

OFFICE OF POPULATION CENSUSES AND SURVEYS. Population projections London H M Stationery Office 1989.

POLLITT C. Bringing consumers into performance measurement: concepts, consequences and constraints *Policy and Politics* vol 15 no 2 1988 pp 77–87.

PLUMMER J T. The concept and application of life style segmentation *Journal of Marketing* vol 38 January 1974 pp 33–37.

RAND CORPORATION. Public libraries face California's ethnic and racial diversity Santa Monica The Corporation 1988 *Report R3656*.

ROBERTS J. Survey of in-town retail *Estates Times* 28 April 1989 p 16–17.

SINGH S R. Happy mall fellows: library and book stores are great neighbors in urban shopping mall *American Libraries* March 1985 p 154.

Evaluative Research in the Library and Information Field

Thomas Childers

College of Information Studies, Drexel University,
Philadelphia, PA 19104

ABSTRACT

The key characteristics of evaluative research (ER) are outlined. Raizen and Rossi's fine-grained model of ER in education is applied to the library information field. Using published and unpublished examples of ER in library and information settings, the field's strengths and weaknesses in the various types of ER are explored. It is concluded that the overall volume of ER is reasonably good in the library and information field, but that it is fragmented and noncumulative, lacking sufficient basic research and research on the impact of libraries and information services and products.

THE NATURE OF EVALUATIVE RESEARCH

In some regards, evaluative research can be distinguished from other kinds of research:

- It is usually used for decision-making (that is, it is applied – in contrast to basic – research. It is clearly a tool for problem solving).
- The research questions are derived from a program, usually a service offered to a client group.
- The research provides a basis for making a judgment about the program.
- The research occurs in the environment of the program application, not in a laboratory and not in the respondent's study (there is some disagreement over this latter characteristic).

The methodology of evaluative research usually represents a compromise between 'pure' research and the demands and strictures of the applied setting, between maintaining the integrity of the research and providing data that will be useful for decision-making (Weiss, 1972).

The differences between evaluative research and other research center on the orientation of the research and not on the methods employed. Evaluative research has a problem solving orientation, implying movement and adjustment as a program moves from ideation through testing to full implementation and subsequent correction.

In other regards, evaluative research is not very distinctive. Neither the orientation of evaluative research nor the techniques through which it is carried out are unique. For instance, evaluative research is embodied in the 'evaluation of alternative strategies' step often included as an element in a strategic planning cycle. In marketing, evaluative research is implied in any effort to evaluate the market penetration of a new product.

Is it possible that the nondistinctiveness of its orientation and techniques results in the lack of deliberate attention paid to evaluative research per se in many fields, including, in this writer's estimation, library and information science?

Program Orientation

To be evaluative research, an investigation must focus on a program (a service or a product) and on a consumer (client or customer, actual or potential). Its sole purpose is to assess the affect of a program on its consumer (Ruttman, 1977). Furthermore, evaluative research ordinarily studies actual programs in the field. While either experimentally implemented or fully implemented programs may be the subject of the evaluative research effort, laboratory experimentation, in the sense of isolating the research from environmental influence, is rarely considered within the limits of evaluative research. Field experimental research is the rule where experimental research is employed.

While some writers insist that program is the focus of evaluative research, others assert with equal strength that the evaluation of internal organizational processes (such as the efficiency of staff or the cost of providing services) is essential in a full agenda of evaluative research. In this case, everyone is correct; for in the ideal, an internal process would be studied only as it could ultimately be tied to program affect.

Impact Orientation

Evaluative research seeks to discover causal sequence or the impact of a program on its audience. It necessarily strives to determine a cause-effect relationship.

Formative-Summative Dichotomy

Evaluative research is commonly divided into two classes – formative and summative. Formative is the type of evaluative research that occurs during a program's implementation in order to make mid-course corrections; formative evaluative research may therefore put considerable stress on such interim elements as how resources are being applied to a program and on the initial response of the audience to the program. Summative research occurs at the end of the program or at the completion of one cycle of a program in order to assess the impact of the total program. It may reinvestigate much the same things as formative research but will also include measures of program effectiveness, or impact and overall program efficiency. Although not recommended as exemplary research reporting, Doelker and Toifel (1984) demonstrate formative evaluation in the library and information field. They report the development of a library instruction manual for university students; in very broad strokes they use evaluative data gathered periodically to help revise their approach during the process of development.

Evaluative Research Methodology

Within the general evaluative research orientation, any research methodology can be employed. The ideal form for evaluative research – Weiss (1972, p. 7) calls it the 'classic' form – is experimental:

- the target audience exists in a given state;
- the state is measured and described;
- a treatment or program is applied;
- that new state of the audience is measured and described; and
- measures of the old and new states are compared for differences – that is, effect attributable to the program.

However, virtually any other technique of research may be appropriated for evaluative research. Many of these will be mentioned or discussed later.

Quantitative | Qualitative

Evaluative research is normally conceived in quantitative terms, but it can be equally valid in qualitative form. For instance, information systems ethnography, an almost anthropological assessment of information exchange and transformation processes, may be used to evaluate the success of a 'program' or system of information exchange in narrative unquantified terms. For a text on the subject, see Patton's (1987) work on qualitative methods for evaluative research, one of the volumes in Sage Publication's nine-volume 'Program Evaluation Kit.'

Nonprofit Focus

Evaluative research is most concerned with the nonprofit sector. Its overriding focus is on programs that seek to better individuals or society. Strictly speaking, one can evaluate a profit venture, but the term *evaluative research* is ordinarily reserved for the public nonprofit sector. Terms like *market research* or *cost benefit analysis* would be used in the private for-profit sector to describe what might amount to evaluative research.

Fugitiveness

'In evaluation, probably the majority of study reports go unpublished'

(Weiss, 1972, p. 7). Evaluative research remains largely unpublished. Fields with a large number of consumers and substantial resources at their command – such as education and health care – have generated massive evaluation studies and many of these have been published. Even so, the published literature in these fields is probably the mere tip of the iceberg. Beneath the surface lies a mass of internal and often proprietary reports that are by accident or design not circulated beyond the confines of the program or organization evaluated.

A BROAD MODEL OF EVALUATIVE RESEARCH

Attkisson and others (1978) proposed a relatively simple model of the levels of evaluative research, the management tasks typically addressed at each level, and typical evaluation activities (methods) appropriate to the level and to those tasks. The levels of evaluation proposed were:

- systems resource management (concerning inputs to the management system, internal processes of management, and relationships with external governors and funders of the service program);
- client utilization (concerning client access to service, the quantities and quality of service delivery, and the consumption of service by clients);
- outcome of intervention (concerning effectiveness of the service program from the individual client's point of view, including satisfaction with the services used); *and*
- community impact (concerning the state of the target community both before and after service intervention).

The levels graduate from input-oriented to output-oriented, through impact on the individual, and, ultimately, impact on the larger community. Other analysts might paraphrase 'systems resource management' as 'process evaluation' and combine the other three into 'program evaluation' (Chelton, 1987).

The Attkisson model is mainly useful in that it points out the essential differences between consumption of service or product ('client utilization'), and the impact of that consumption on the individual and the community ('outcome of intervention' and 'community impact'). This will be addressed again in later sections.

A FINER MODEL

Raizen and Rossi (1981) offer a finer model of evaluative research for the field of education, its purpose being to parse the overall process of evaluative research into specific component parts (see Figure 1). Like the model of Attkisson and others, the parts are roughly in order of their occurrence. In the Raizen and Rossi instance, they appear more or less in the order of tracking a program from conception through full

FIGURE 1. *The Raizen-Rossi Model. (From Raizen, S. A., & Rossi, P. H. [Eds.] [1981]. Program evaluation in education: When? How? To what ends? Washington, DC: National Academy Press, P. 41.)*

Questions Arising During the Formation of Policy and the Design of Programs

Polity Question	Evaluation/ Social Research Procedure	Research Methods Used
How big is the problem and where is it located?	Needs assessment	Assembly of archived data (Census, NCES, etc.) Special sample surveys Ethnographic studies
Can we do anything about the problem?	Basic research	Assembly of archived research studies Specially commissioned research
Will a proposed program work under optimal conditions	Small-scale testing	Randomized controlled experiments Pilot studies and demonstrations
Can a program be made to work in the field	Field evaluation	Ethnographic studies Randomized experiments Field tests and demonstrations
Will a proposed program be efficient?	Policy analysis	Simulation Prospective cost-effectiveness studies Prospective cost-benefit analysis

Questions Arising from Enacted and Implemented Programs

Are funds being used properly?	Fiscal account-ability	Fiscal records Auditing and accounting studies
Is the program reaching the beneficiaries?	Coverage accountability	Administrative records Beneficiary studies Sample surveys
Is the program implemented as intended?	Implementation accountability	Administrative records Special surveys of programs Ethnographic surveys
Is the program effective?	Impact assessment	Randomized experiments Statistical modelling Time series studies
Is the program efficient?	Economic analysis	Cost-effectiveness studies Cost-benefit analyses

implementation. Their premise is that questions related to policy trigger particular general evaluation procedures in which particular specific evaluation procedures or research methods are used. To extend the model beyond its education application, one may interpret 'problem' to include 'opportunity,' and 'beneficiary' to constitute 'patron,' 'client,' 'user . . . nonuser,' or 'target population'.

Evaluative Research and The Model

Stated broadly, the Raizen and Rossi model requires evaluative research to utilize the results of research in order to develop a market position for a program, describe the program's efficiency, and describe the program's effectiveness. The model has considerable scope, encompassing research beyond the strict limits of the program focus – and contrary to Weiss – accepting laboratory research as a legitimate method of evaluative research.

The elements of the Raizen-Rossi model, singly or in related clusters, are discussed below as they apply to evaluative research in the library and information field. The discussion is highly selective. Since the literature of evaluative research is so large and so much of it is fugitive – often recorded in no more than intramural memos comprehending evaluative research in a given field is not feasible. Moreover, to the extent that evaluative research is methodologically indistinct from other types of social research (see the introductory discussion), aspects of it are found in a wide variety of writings – from writings labeled evaluative research; to writings labeled operations research, field experiment, statistical report, white paper, research, evaluation, measurement, and many more; to unlabeled writings.

Since it is virtually impossible even to enumerate or to comprehend the writings related to evaluative research within the field, the view will be impressionistic and based on the author's selections.

Policy Question	Evaluation/Social Research Procedure	Research Methods Used
How big is the problem and where is it located?	Needs assessment	Assembly of archived data (Census, NCES, etc.) Special sample surveys Ethnographic studies

Raizen and Rossi's questions at this stage focus on identifying and typifying the client problem or need. In the library and information field, examples of archived data are to be found in the reports on academic, public, and school libraries that have been published by the National Center for Education Statistics (NCES) and in the national data collection effort for public libraries spearheaded by the Public Library Development Project of the Public Library Association. Such data have been used to determine at the most general level the major lacunae in library services such as those libraries falling below certain collection sizes or those regions where populations do not have adequate library access.

For nearly 40 years, special sample surveys have been abundant in the library and information field with the purpose of determining the nature and magnitude of a hypothesized problem. A central core of such studies has aimed to identify clients and their library and information needs. The so-called 'user studies' have most often occurred at the local level and less often at the regional, state, or national level. The published literature holds myriad studies of perceptions of services, uses of services, users of services, and user satisfaction with services of public, school, special, and academic libraries and various types of information centers. It is certain that many more exist in unpublished form.

At the level of individual needs assessment, library and information science faces all the problems, and more, of any organization undertaking market research. Chief among these problems are identifying the client's true – as opposed to idealized or generalized – reactions to products or services; and projecting likely reaction to a proposed – rather than existing – product or service.

There are two additional problems for market research in the library and information field. They doubly confound the measurement or projection of user reaction to various library and information services. First, the field's 20 years of experience in trying to determine the value of its services suggests strongly that the perceived impact of library and information services is more subtle (less palpable) and diffuse than the perceived impact of many other services such as trash collection, meals on wheels, or, for that matter, police protection. It is inherently difficult to question a client on the value of a product or service that is subtle and diffuse. Second, the library and information world, with few exceptions, has not adequately set its service objectives, especially with regard to impact. In most library and information settings, neither managers nor clients have defined the dimension of impact and established the criteria by which to judge its achievement.

There are numerous other 'special sample surveys' which are not focused directly on the use or user but have fairly direct implications for services offered and their consequent impact. Fiske's (1968) classic study of self-censorship and book selection among librarians and White's (1986) more contemporary analysis of data on librarians' attitudes toward censorship are examples of efforts to name and locate a professional problem that will impact directly on the quality of collections in libraries. Another set of indirect examples can be found in the many unobtrusive studies, beginning in 1968, of the answers that libraries and information centers provide to unambiguous requests for factual information (Crowley et al., 1971).

A large number of user studies performed over the past 40 years, both published and unpublished, provide some degree of market knowledge. However, the knowledge provided is limited, for these studies have often tended to:

- poll only users since they are easier to poll;
- utilize only the grossest demographics as correlates of library use such as education, sex, age, occupation, and income;
- measure reaction only to existing services without attempting to project reaction to possible future services; *and*
- focus solely on the library or information unit and thus gain a particular rather than global perspective on the clients and their information states.

There are exceptions to this dismal pattern. In the years immediately following the launching of Sputnik in 1957, there was a substantial effort to explore communication patterns and information needs in the scientific and technical communities in this country. Performed often under the heading of 'information science,' the studies were global – not limited by institution or informational format – and they were generally methodologically creative. They generated broad insight into the doing of science as well as its communication and significantly advanced the understanding of information needs (Griffith, 1987).

Beginning in 1973, Dervin began developing a framework for assessing the global information need of the average adult. The framework has been improved and employed since then in a number of settings (Warner et al., 1973; Dervin et al., 1976; Chen & Hernon, 1982; Gee, 1974). Wilson used a similarly global approach in her study of the information seeking activity of community activists. Focusing on a 'critical incident' related to the subject's interest, she described the information environment surrounding that incident and the effect of the information environment on the subject (Wilson, 1977). The study can be viewed as an evaluation of the impact of a social program (the public library) on the activities of the subjects and therefore will also be considered later in this article where program impact is addressed.

On a smaller scale, conjoint measurement has been used in academic libraries to identify client reaction to specific mixes of service characteristics. In this case, employing a parsimonious means of permuting features of library services, the study provided information for the market positioning of future services (Halperin & Strazdon, 1980).

Another approach that may enrich the field's perspective on client requirements for a library or information system is ethnography. While specific ethnographic techniques – such as key informant interviews, daily logs, and participant observation – have been employed to gather data on client need, studies are almost invariably cast in the vein of the standard scientific method, addressing the study question in quantitative terms. In contrast, in information systems analysis the ethnographic approach has been espoused – and used – to determine the states and needs of system clients. Qualitative presentations such as narrative argument, chronicles, and social network analyses have long been used in the area of information systems to offer a richer, more natural view of the human elements of an information system than afforded by the heavily quantitative and rigid scientific method. A recent example is Zachary et al. (1984) who make a strong case for the use of the ethnographic approach for information systems analysis. Its application to the information system design for an office of the National Park Service is reported by Zachary et al. (1986). At the library end of the spectrum, Werking (1980) reports on two instances of qualitative evaluation (calling it 'illuminative') of user education programs in Europe.

Policy Question	Evaluation/Social Research Procedure	Research Methods Used
Can we do anything about the problem?	Basic research	Assembly of archived research studies Specially commissioned research

'Long-range support for basic research on educational processes is critical for the development of the fundamental ideas for education programs' (Raizen & Rossi, 1981, p. 43). To fulfill the obligations of this stage of evaluative research, a field seeks broad understanding of the problem and its determinants. This is the moment in the cycle of evaluative research where one seeks to relate dependent and independent variables, to establish cause and effect relationships for the phenomenon at hand – in this case a library or information service. Basic research can inspire the invention or adjustment of service programs by identifying the variables on which to concentrate organizational resources. For instance, knowing the variables that correlate with student learning of online searching may lead to the design or redesign of a specific program in an educational media center – perhaps attaching such learning to particular classes or teaching online searching through a particular modality.

The library and information field has a record of published activity for this phase of evaluative research. Perhaps the best overviews of basic research relevant to the field – whether done inside or outside the field can be found in review publications – e.g., *The Annual Review of Information Science and Technology*, *Advances in Librarianship*, *Advances in Library Administration and Organization*, *Library Trends*, and review articles in *Library and Information Science Research*.

Considerable basic research has been performed in the areas of citation and cocitation patterns in scholarly literature, collection obsolescence and overlap, information transfer among individuals, and demographic correlates of library use. The recently reported work of Saracevic (1988) and others is a good example of a major piece of basic research, in this case developing models of online searching behavior.

However, for the field at large, one would not characterize basic research as vigorous. It is pursued almost exclusively by the small academic subset of the library and information field consisting of doctoral candidates and a few persistent faculty researchers, and it attracts meagre funding. On the library side of the field, most of the research funded in the field is applied in nature, seeking to answer a specific question in a specific situation; information science and information systems seem to have a stronger tradition of basic research.

Although there have been significant basic research studies in the field, library and information science has never had the resources, either human or financial, to concentrate on studying the determinants of consumption or nonconsumption of library and information services or, especially, the determinants of library or information impact. On any particular topic, basic research is sporadic, offering the field a patchwork of knowledge about its programmatic effects.

Policy Question	Evaluation/Social Research Procedure	Research Methods Used
Will a proposed program work under optimal conditions?	Small-scale testing	Randomized controlled experiments Pilot studies and demonstrations
Can a program be made to work in the field?	Field evaluation	Ethnographic studies Randomized experiments Field tests and demonstrations

The library and information field has experienced numerous demonstrations, field tests, and pilot studies intended to assess the feasibility and likely impact of new programs. Many of these investigations have been buried in local situations and have never been published, so it is difficult to assess their impact. Many others, some of them local, others regional or national in nature, have been published. Support for this type of investigation has come from the local unit's own budget (company, school, municipality, university), the federal government (administered centrally and through state library agencies), and some state library agency budgets.

Demonstrations, field tests, and the like have been one of the two most popular forms of evaluative research in the library and information field (it is matched by studies of program reach, discussed later). Historic examples include the Knapp Project, a demonstration of excellence in school library service (Sullivan, 1968); tests of the Management Review and Analysis Program, an organizational development model in academic libraries (Webster, 1980); demonstrations of outreach services in the inner city in the 1960s and early 1970s (Lipsman, 1972); trials of information and referral services through public libraries (Childers, 1975). More contemporary examples include the Siegel et al. (1984) evaluation of two prototype online catalog systems; trials of integrating

DIALOG labs into undergraduate courses (Ward, 1985); and proto-typing an information system for the National Park Service (McCain et al., 1987).

The studies of Siegel and Ward illustrate some characteristics of this type of evaluative research activity in the library and information field. Field tests, studies of demonstrations, and the like commonly do not investigate the efficacy of one means of conducting a program versus another means, as in the Siegel report. Instead, as in Ward, one and only one solution to the problem is evaluated; alternative solutions to the client need are not explored.

Moreover, as exemplified in the Ward report, control groups are commonly not used, so the measurement of only the treatment group does not correct for the many possible sources of contamination of study results. As with many evaluations in this field, the concern seems to be with promoting a particular solution to a client need rather than rigorously testing that solution.

Properly randomized controlled experiments do exist. At a substantial level, one recalls Knapp's (1966) classic Monteith College experiment in library instruction. More contemporary and much more modest is the test of the effectiveness of a computer – versus card – form catalog (Armstrong & Costa, 1983), and Harris and Michell's (1986) assessment of the effects of gender and communication behaviors on competence at the reference desk.

Policy Question	Evaluation/Social Research Procedure	Research Methods Used
Will a proposed program be efficient?	Policy analysis	Simulation
		Prospective cost-effectiveness studies
		Prospective cost-benefit analyses
Are funds being used properly?	Fiscal accountability	Fiscal records
		Auditing and accounting studies
Is the program efficient?	Economic analysis	Cost effectivenes studies
		Cost-benefit analyses
Is the program implemented as intended	Implementation accountability	Administrative records
		Special surveys of programs
		Ethnographic surveys

For the most part, the above policy questions concern elements of internal control – i.e. cost, internal processes, and technologies employed in mounting a program. While there are published investigations of cost, processes, and technologies related to particular library and information programs, most of such investigations are probably buried in the files of the organizations for which they were performed. The more public of such investigations will be found as part of a budgeting document, a planning paper, a cost-effectiveness or cost-benefit study, an operations research exercise, or other management inquiry. They are also often evident in technological reports evaluating large service innovations. The New England Academic Science Information Center (NASIC) trial of online bibliographic search service to academics in the mid-1970s typifies one kind of analysis. It consists of a simple costing of activities engaged in during the trial period without attempting to compare alternative means of offering the service nor determining the relationship between cost and payoff to the user (Wax & Vaughan, 1977). Another example of an investigation of internal control, and one more consistent with the true orientation of evaluative research, is the report of a Canadian trial of telefacsimile transmission for interlibrary loan. While the report does not include rigorous testing of alternative means of exchanging physical documents, it does compare the telefacsimile means with the traditional postal alternative in terms of costs and benefit to the user (Anand, 1987). White (1986) offers a unique approach to evaluation which addresses at the same time marketing strategy and 'a library's ability to respond to social needs in the area of lifelong education' (p. 116). He proposes that a library examine its intentions and strategies for introducing an innovative program directed at social change (e.g. literacy or lifelong learning). To do this, one renders advertising copy for the program into the typically terse, communicative, and competitive language of the yellow pages. If one is unable or unwilling to do that, one must assume the program or its administration is in some way deficient. The method is wholly qualitative in nature, a relatively rare occurrence in the field.

There seem to be two recurring blindspots regarding evaluation and internal control elements in this field. One is that alternative means of achieving ends are rarely compared in terms of their cost and their payoff. Most often a single means is considered, and the power of comparing one means to another which, to a large extent, makes evaluative research evaluative, is lost. The second blindspot is that many of the costing exercises in the field tie costs to organizational inputs and administrative processes and fail to consider adequately the benefits to users. Thus cost, processes, and technologies are unrelated to the ultimate objective of the library or information organization and true evaluation, in the evaluative research sense, cannot occur.

Policy Question	Evaluation/Social Research Procedure	Research Methods Used
Is the program reaching the beneficiaries?	Coverage accountability	Administrative records Beneficiary studies Sample surveys

This phase, along with demonstrations, field tests, and the like, is one of the two phases of evaluative research which seems to be most often considered by library and information practitioners and researchers to be evaluative research. It is often seen as equivalent to a program's impact and substitutes for assessing how a program has bettered a person's life. More specifically, describing the reach of a library or information program is probably the most common means of assessing program impact in the field. Perhaps reach is a natural preoccupation, for most libraries and information centers assume that reaching as many of their assigned constituents as possible to be a mandate. Furthermore, it may also capture the field's attention because it is far easier to assess – being more concrete – than is true impact.

Studies of program reach have included population characteristics of users and sometimes nonusers of virtually every library and information service. These are often called community studies or community analyses. Summer reading programs, bibliographic instruction, online searching, information and referral services, selective dissemination of information services, book display trials, and every other direct user service have been subjected to demographic analysis. Common user variables include age, sex, education, occupation, status within the client group (such as socioeconomic status, student class, or organizational position), frequency of use of the library or information center, and nature of the services used.

Policy Question	Evaluation/Social Research Procedure	Research Methods Used
Is the program effective?	Impact assessment	Randomized experiments Statistical modelling Time series studies

The seminal question in evaluative research is the question of effectiveness. In the services realm, where one's ultimate objective is to make a difference in a person's or a community's life, the question may barely be answerable with existing research methodologies, or the research methodologies required may be so expensive as to preclude pursuing the answer.

In the library and information field, studies of reach far outnumber studies of impact. Perhaps it is because the former are easier to conceive and execute. Statements of reach have come to be used as statements of program impact in this field. Unfortunately, assuming impact from reach requires assuming that program consumption (e.g. a book circulated) is equivalent to program impact (improvement in the person's information base or increased decision-making facility). There is no evidence to support the assumption.

If one sees the ultimate mission of this field as optimizing the consumption of library and information services and products, impact on the person is irrelevant and true evaluative research, to the extent that it is concerned with an improved state of the individual, also becomes irrelevant. If one sees the ultimate mission of the field as improving the state of the individual, impact on the person must be considered, and one must engage in true evaluative research in order to assess the field's success or failure. Students of library and information science easily recognize that the field is quite ambivalent on this issue, its literature frequently espousing the mission of improving the person's state (decision-making ability, job performance, leisure happiness, creativity, political empowerment, etc.) yet rarely assessing the degree to which a person's state has been improved.

A major problem in evaluative research in the library and information field is that it is often not treated seriously. It is frequently added to a demonstration or full program implementation as an afterthought and without sufficient resources or sufficient expertise. It is often executed at an elementary level, contributing nothing to the field's overall understanding of the impact of its programs. This is particularly the case in evaluating a program's effectiveness or impact. Frequently, the evaluation method is not integrated into the overall project, and thus, as often happens, true experimental research (with before and after testing) is foregone. Ex post facto research, with its very limited capacity to explore before-and-after changes in a person's state, becomes the only course of action. There are sufficient examples of impact evaluation in the field to show the way but not enough to characterize the field as one overwhelmingly concerned with its impact or effectiveness.

One example, again, is the Monteith College Library Experiment, a trial and evaluation of means of incorporating library services into the instructional program of a college. This was an extensive evaluation and utilized before and after testing as well as multiple measurements of impact such as improvement in performance on assignments. Qualitative measures were used. The evaluation was of the formative type, helping the development of the library-instruction program (Knapp, 1966).

A less ambitious example is found in an evaluation of a new year-round reading program for Los Angeles children, assessing children's reading activities before the program started and remeasuring it at the program's end. Although the findings did not support the hypothesis of improved reading activities, the investigation shows that the evaluation of impact can occur (Markey & Moore, 1983; Markey, 1986).

A third example is the study of impact on library skills of a program of bibliographic instruction at several colleges in the northern midwest. Surprenant (1982) employed before and after testing and control and experimental groups in a classic experimental approach.

WHERE DO WE STAND?

For the library and information field, reviews of evaluative research literature are rare, with Powell's (1984) review of evaluations of reference services being the only one located with that label. Several tutorials on evaluative research exist, including one for children's librarians, a series in *American Libraries* for general library evaluation, and another incorporated in a book on action research (Chelton, 1985a; 1985b; 1985c; 1986a; 1986b; Swisher & McClure, 1984).

Viewed simply in terms of quantity, evaluative research in library service appears reasonably strong. A search of *ERIC* and *Library and Information Science Abstracts* during the period 1982 through 1987 yielded approximately 140 items that indicated from their title or abstract that they dealt with evaluative research. It must be assumed, based on personal contact with library practitioners and program content at national conferences, that a substantial number of evaluative research efforts are carried out in the privacy of the individual library or through a collaboration among a few. An example of a substantial internal effort, collaboratively done, is an unobtrusive study of reference service undertaken by Fairfax and Arlington counties, Virginia, and Montgomery County, Maryland (Rodger, 1984). Many such studies are never published.

The nature of the evaluative research effort in the library and information field varies from an ongoing, serious commitment (such as in the systems offices of a few major public libraries and numerous large academic libraries); to a periodic effort which relies on existing staff and is relatively simple in its methodology and limited in scope; to an occasional effort which involves existing library staff in collaboration with available local research experts; to no effort at all.

Evaluative research in the field is fragmented and noncumulative. And it is unsupported by the basic research that would permit wiser experimentation with programs, such as the value of electronic linking of networks for daily problem solving among the elderly. However, some of the basic research exists outside the field. Examples include the vast amount of research on reading and children, on adult basic education, and on organizational behavior.

Not all phases of evaluative research, as viewed through the Raizen and Rossi model, are equally attended to in the library and information field. Basic research and research on program impact constitute the most important areas of neglect – neglect which indicates that the field is not pursuing a full menu of evaluative research and that the keystone of evaluative research-program impact – is largely missing.

In the ideal, evaluative research seeks to discover how a particular program has affected people. In reality, service fields in general and libraries and information operations in particular often resort to evaluating not the effect of a program but program offerings (such as number of compact discs available for circulation in a new compact disc service) or program transactions (such as the number of circulations of the new compact discs). Of the three major evaluative research options – quantities and qualities of program (i.e. products or services) offered, quantities or qualities of program consumed, and impact of consumed program on the individual – this field has commonly opted to evaluate at the two least telling points in the service cycle – offerings and transactions and thus has opted not to learn how it has affected people.

Much of the evaluative research in the field is of the post-fact quasi-experimental variety, when it would ideally be true experimental. In the former category, two studies by this author include an evaluation of Pennsylvania public library systems and the Five Cities information and referral center evaluation (Childers, 1988). Examples of true experimental design in evaluative research are to be found in McClure and Hernon's study of reference effectiveness, wherein reference performance was measured, a treatment (training program) was applied, and performance was again measured; and in an in-progress evaluation of the effect of a technology innovation on three college libraries cooperating in its adoption (Hernon & McClure, 1987; Childers & Griffith, 1988). One of the constraints in adopting true experimental approaches is that federal and state timetables for grants and contracts have frequently disallowed sufficient time for pretest/treatment/posttest design, so that evaluation has been almost completely post-hoc or 'preexperimental' (Houston, 1972).

The practical bent of the field, too, and of many of those who have awarded funds for program and research, has resulted in there often not being a substantial effort devoted to evaluation. The result is often that persons whose desired role is executing a service program are required also to assume the role of evaluator – a conflict of interest in many cases, and a situation that one would expect to result in half-hearted and amateurish evaluation methods. (Reviews by this author of numerous papers submitted for publication and grant proposals support the latter proposition.)

To the extent that the field is inadequately developed in the Raizen-Rossi cycle of evaluative research, the field is inadequate in the mechanisms useful for problem solving; for evaluative research is fundamentally a problem solving tool. The efforts of the past 40 years are encouraging. Although moving slowly, the field does seem to be making advances on various phases of the evaluation cycle. Yet it is obvious that there is substantial work yet to be done before the mechanisms and orientations necessary for a full cycle of evaluation will be available.

ACKNOWLEDGMENT

The author acknowledges the valuable help of Kathleen H. Turner in providing bibliographic support for this article.

REFERENCES

Anand, H. (1987). Interlibrary loan and document delivery using facsimile transmission: Part II. Telefacsimile project. *The Electronic Library*, *5*(April), 100–107.

Armstrong, M., & Costa, B. (1983). Computer cat at Mountain View Elementary School. *Library Hi Tech*, *1*(Winter), 47–52.

Attkisson, C.; Hargreaves, W. A.; Horowitz, M. J.; & Sorenson, J. (1978). *Evaluation of human service programs*. New York: Academic Press.

Chelton, M. K. (1987). Evaluation of children's services. *Library Trends*, *35*(Winter), 463–484.

Chen, C., & Hernon, P. (1982). *Information seeking: Assessing and anticipating user needs*. New York: Neal-Schuman Publishers, Inc.

Childers, T. (1975). *Third year continuation of [a program to] research and design criteria for the implementation and establishment of a neighborhood information center in five public libraries: Atlanta, Cleveland, Detroit, Houston and Queens Borough*. Houston, IX: Houston Public Library [Grant No. OEG–0–72–5168, U.S. Department of Health, Education, and Welfare].

Childers, T. (1988). Do library systems make a difference? *Library and Information Science Research*, *10*(October-December), 445–454.

Childers, T., & Griffith, B. C. (1988). *Drexel Tri-College research project: A proposed research and demonstration grant*. Unpublished manuscript. Philadelphia, PA: Drexel University.

Crowley, T., & Childers, T. (1971). *Information service in public libraries: Two studies*. Metuchen, NJ: Scarecrow Press.

Dervin, B.; Zweizig, D.; Banister, M.; Gabriel, M.; Hall, E.; Kwan, C.; Bowes, J.; & Stam, K. (1976). *The development of strategies for dealing with the information needs of urban residents: Phase I – Citizen study*. Seattle, WA: University of Washington [Grant No. OEG–0–74–7308, U.S. Department of Health, Education, and Welfare].

Doelker, R. E., Jr., & Toifel, P. (1984). The development of a self-guided, library-based materials and methods manual for social work research. *Behavioral and Social Sciences Librarian*, *3*(Summer), 81–93.

Fiske, M. (1968). *Book selection and censorship*. Berkeley, CA: University of California Press.

Gee, G. (1974). *Urban information needs: A replication* [A Report of the Syracuse/Elmira Study]. Syracuse, NY: Center for the Study of Information and Education, Syracuse University [contract No. OEG–0–72–5405, U.S. Department of Health, Education, and Welfare].

Griffith, B. C. (1987). Studies of information and communication and the revolution in understanding science. Address at the New Jersey Chapter, American Society for Information Science, New Brunswick, NJ, October 21.

Halperin, M., & Strazdon, M. E. (1980). Measuring students' preference for reference service: A conjoint analysis. *Library Quarterly*, *50*(April), 208–224.

Harris, R. M., & Michell, B. G. (1986). The social context of reference work: Assessing the effects of gender and communication skill on observers' judgments of competence. Library and Information *Science Research*, *8*(January/March), 85–101.

Hernon, P., & McClure, C. R. (1987). *Unobtrusive testing and library reference services*. Norwood, NJ: Ablex Publishing.

Houston, T. R., Jr. (1972). The behavioral sciences impact-effectiveness model. In P. Rossi & W. Williams (Eds.). *Evaluating social programs: Theory, practice, and politics* (pp. 51–55). New York: Seminar Press.

Knapp, P. B. (1966). *The Monteith College library experiment*. New York: Scarecrow Press.

Lipsman, C. K. (1972). *The disadvantaged and library effectiveness*. Chicago, IL: American Library Association.

Markey, P. S., & Moore, M. K. (1983). The year-round reading program: An experimental alternative. *Top of the News, 39*(Winter), 155–161.

Markey, P. S. (1986). *Year round reading program: Research and findings*. Los Angeles, CA: Los Angeles County Public Library (typescript).

McCain, K.; Woodward, D.; Zachery, W. W.; Childers, T.; & Mallos, D. (1987). *Infobank: An information system design for the National Park Service Mid-Atlantic Regional Office Planning and Grants Division*. Philadelphia, PA: Drexel University.

Patton, M. Q. (1980). *Qualitative evaluation methods*. Beverly Hills, CA: Sage Publications.

Patton, M. Q. (1987). *How to use qualitative methods in evaluation*. Beverly Hills, CA: Sage Publications.

Powell, R. R. (1984). Reference effectiveness: A review of research. *Library & Information Science Research, 6*(January-March), 3–19.

Raizen, S. A., & Rossi, P. H. (1981). *Program evaluation in education: When? How? To what ends?* Washington, DC: National Academy Press.

Robbins-Carter, J. R., & Zweizig, D. L. (1985). Are we there yet? Evaluating library collections, reference services, programs, and personnel. Lesson One: Introduction to Evaluation. *American Libraries, 16*(9), 624–627.

Robbins-Carter, J. R., & Zweizig, D. L. (1985). Lesson two: Evaluating library collections. *American Libraries, 16*(10), 724–727.

Robbins-Carter, J. R., & Zweizig, D. L. (1985). Lesson three: Reference services evaluation. *American Libraries, 16*(11), 780–784.

Robbins-Carter, J. R., & Zweizig, D. L. (1986). Lesson four: Library program evaluation. *American Libraries, 17*(1), 32–36.

Robbins-Carter, J. R., & Zweizig, D. L. (1986). Lesson five: *American Libraries, 17*(2), 108–112.

Rodger, E. J. (1984). *Preliminary reference accuracy study report*. [Fairfax County, Virginia, Public Library]. Unpublished manuscript. Typescript.

Rutman, L. (1977). *Evaluation research methods: A basic guide*. Beverly Hills, CA: Sage Publications.

Saracevic, T.; Kantor, P.; Chamis, A. Y.; & Trivision, D. (1988). A study of information seeking and retrieving: I Background and methodolgy. *Journal of the American Society for Information Science, 39*(3), 161–176.

Saracevic, T., & Kantor, P. (1988). A study of information seeking and retrieving: II Users, questions and effectiveness. *Journal of the American Society for Information Science, 39*(3), 177–196.

Saracevic, T., & Kantor, P. (1988). A study of information seeking and retrieving: III Searchers, searches and overlap. *Journal of the American Society for Information Science, 39*(3), 197–216.

Siegel, E. R.; Kameen, K.; Sinn, S. K.; & Weise, F. 0. (1984). A comparative evaluation of the technical performance and user acceptance of two prototype online catalog systems. *Information Technology and Libraries, 3*(March), 35–46.

Sullivan, P. A. (1968). *Realization: The final report of the Knapp School Libraries Project*. Chicago: American Library Association.

Surprenant, T. T. (1982). Learning theory, lecture, and programmed instruction test: An experiment in bibliographic instruction. *College and Research Libraries, 43*(January), 31–37.

Swisher, R., & McClure, C. R. (1984). *Research for decision making*. Chicago: American Library Association.

Ward, S. N. (1985). Course-integrated DIALOG instruction. *Research Strategies, 3*(Spring), 52–64.

Warner, E. S.; Murray, A. D.; & Palmour, V. E. (1973). *Information needs of urban residents.* Rockville, MD: Westat, Inc. [Final Report, Contract No. OEC–0–71–4555, (US Department of Health, Education, and Welfare].

Wax, D. M., & Vaughan, P. E. (1977). *Northeast Academic Science Information Center final report.* Wellesley, MA: New England Board of Higher Education (Grant No. SIS–7308366, GN 37296, National Science Foundation).

Webster, D. E. (1980). Description of the management review and analysis program. In E. R. Johnson & S. H. Mann (Eds.), *Organization development for academic libraries: An evaluation of the management review and analysis program* (pp. 52–64). Westport, CT: Greenwood Press.

Weiss, C. H. (1972). *Evaluation research: Methods for assessing program effectiveness.* Englewood Cliffs, NJ: Prentice-Hall, Inc.

Werking, R. H. (1980). Evaluating bibliographic education: A review and critique. *Library Trends, 29*(1), 153–172.

White, H. D. (1986a). Majorities for censorship. *Library Journal, 111*(July), 31–38.

White, H. D. (1986b). The yellow pages test for libraries. *Public Libraries, 25*(Winter), 116–122.

Wilson, P. (1977). *A community elite and the public library: The uses of information in leadership.* Westport, CT: Greenwood Press.

Zachary, W. W.;, Strong, G. W.; & Zakland, A. (I 984). Information systems ethnography: Integrating anthropological methods into systems design to insure organizational acceptance. In H. W. Hendricks & 0. Brown, Jr. (Eds.), *Human factors in organizational design and management: Proceedings of First Symposium* (pp. 223–27). North-Holland: Elsevier Science Publishers B.V.

Zachary, W. W.; McCain, K.; Woodward, D.; Carroll, A.; & Childers, T. (1986). *An information systems analysis of the National Park Service Mid-Atlantic Regional Office Planning and Grants Assistance Division.* Philadelphia, PA: Drexel University.

Productivity Measurements in Special Libraries: Prospects and Problems for Use in Performance Evaluation

Robert V. Williams

Associate Professor, College of Library and Information Science, University of South Carolina, Columbia, South Carolina

ABSTRACT

This article examines the appropriateness and use of productivity measurements as a performance assessment tool in special libraries. The concept is defined, problems in use are discussed, and guidelines given for implementation. The use of productivity measurements in two federal special libraries is presented and data are given on the results of their work. The paper concludes with a comparison of productivity measurements with other evaluation tools used in special libraries and an assessment is made of its value as a measure of excellence.

INTRODUCTION

To say that productivity has been in the news lately would be an understatement. Indeed, some individuals have gone so far as to say that declines in productivity were at least partially responsible for the severe recession and high rates of inflation of the late 1970s and early 1980s.[1] Until recently, however, librarians (and particularly special librarians in small libraries) did not hear much about how productivity applied to their work. Productivity was something for blue collar workers to worry about and was seldom an issue for white collar information workers. Those days are gone.

Increasingly, white collar workers are being asked – or pressured – for indications of how well they match up with other workers in terms of productivity and, more importantly, to show how they have increased their productivity in recent years. These trends are taking place in private industry, nonprofit organizations, and, especially, within the federal government. Librarians are one of the groups being focused on for productivity analysis.

This paper examines the application of productivity measurements in special libraries for performance evaluation. The concept is defined and guidelines given for the development of a measurement program meaningful to management. Two examples from federal special libraries are given to show actual use of productivity measures. Productivity is then compared with other measures that have been used to evaluate library effectiveness and performance. The paper concludes with an assessment of productivity measures as valid indicators of library excellence.

Before getting into definitions of productivity a few words need to be said about the use of the term in the context of libraries specifically and the 'information society' in general. There are two predominant uses of the term in the literature. First, and most generally, are the discussions of how productivity is related to information use. There is a large body of literature that maintains that productivity in the information society will only be improved when we develop and utilize improved information systems. The adage is that 'knowledge workers' must 'work smarter, not harder'.[2] The staff of the National Commission on Libraries and Information Science (NCLIS) has called for more research in this area.[3] A 1981 study of the productivity of 'knowledge workers' showed that a central source of nonproductive use of time was searching for internal and external information.[4] This is a worthwhile and interesting topic to explore, particularly since the establishment of such relationships would be a powerful argument to those of us who are trying to get better funding of our libraries and information centers.

The second usage, and the focus in this paper, is on productivity measurements for improved performance by libraries and library staff. Specifically, we want to know what productivity is, how to measure it, how to compare ourselves with others in the organization and the profession generally, and how to use it to improve performance.

DEFINING PRODUCTIVITY

Productivity has a variety of definitions, depending on how general or specific the demands of the situation call for. At its most general level it is defined as:

$$\text{productivity} = \frac{\text{outputs}}{\text{inputs}}$$

or, also generally:

$$\text{productivity} = \frac{\text{results achieved}}{\text{resources consumed}}$$

or, a little more specifically:

$$\text{productivity} = \frac{\text{goods and/or services}}{\text{labor + energy + capital + tools + materials}}$$

Bringing it down to the level of the individual:

$$\frac{\text{personal}}{\text{productivity}} = \frac{\text{what you produce}}{\text{the \# of hours it}}$$
$$\text{takes you to}$$
$$\text{produce it}$$

Some writers, will also define productivity so that it includes terms that are usually thought to be separate. Bain, goes so far as to define it as:[5]

$$\text{productivity} = \frac{\text{effectiveness}}{\text{efficiency}}$$

The Bureau of Labor Statistics (BLS), however, considers effectiveness as having to do with accomplishment of specific goals and prefers to use a more limited definition: 'Productivity is a concept that expresses the relationship between the quantity of goods and services produced – output – and the quantity of labor, capital, land, energy and other resources that produced it – input'.[6] Using this definition, the BLS notes the two most common measurements of productivity: 1) relating the output of an enterprise, industry, or economic sector to a single input, such as labor or capital; and 2) relating output to a composite of inputs, combined so as to account for their relative importance. Which of these two definitions to use is determined by the purposes for which one engages in productivity analysis.

The most commonly used measure of productivity is the relationship between output and input of labor time, called *output per hour*. This measure, however, ignores use of other input resources, such as capital and equipment, and may not be valid for meaningful comparisons across time or situations. Multifactor productivity measures are available that take these additional inputs into account. Unfortunately for the beginner, these measures are usually quite complex.

Definitions of productivity vary depending on the kinds of programs you want measured, the degree of inclusiveness that is desired for both input and output, the level at which you wish to measure, and, probably most importantly, the objectives you need to have measured by this procedure. Generally, one would like to have both broad based and narrowly focused measurements so that an assessment can be made of individual functions and the organization as a whole.[7]

MEASURING PRODUCTIVITY: POSSIBILITIES AND PITFALLS

Productivity measurements, like any evaluation tool, can be done well or poorly and the results can be valid or invalid. Bain identifies nine separate factors that work against the development of a good measurement program. For libraries, the most important of these are:

1. measurements commonly used are too broad
2. measurements are activity oriented rather than results oriented
3. inputs are oversimplified
4. work processes are complicated and difficult to separate and measure
5. short-term results are emphasized at the expense of long-range goals *and*
6. the measurement system overemphasizes some organizational performance goals at the expense of others.[8]

The criteria for meaningful measures suggested by Bain to overcome these problems are as follows:

1. the measures should be *valid*, reflecting true changes;
2. they should be *complete*, so that input and output are completely accounted for;
3. each measure should be *inclusive* of all relevant activities;
4. get your results to management in a *timely* manner; and
5. measures should include *cost effectiveness* information.[9]

Several writers have suggested that in order to attain such criteria in a productivity measurement program a detailed goal setting program needs to be established. Bain, addressing that need, takes the process very specifically from beginning to end:

1. set goals and write them down
2. define the specific productivity opportunity
3. decide on optimal productivity indicators
4. consider in writing the obstacles to the plan
5. make the plan
6. calculate the productivity evaluation measures and indexes, *and*
7. interpret and evaluate in relation to goals.[10]

The productivity literature includes a variety of practical handbooks and manuals that can be used to develop a productivity measurement program. Lawlor provides a particularly good recent text that includes case studies and self-assessment questionnaires to aid the measurement process.[11] The American Productivity Center in Houston, Texas, will also provide useful guides and materials.

PRODUCTIVITY MEASUREMENTS IN SPECIAL LIBRARIES: TWO FEDERAL LIBRARIES

In preparation for this study, I conducted an extensive literature search for items describing productivity measurement activities in special libraries. I made an appeal via the *SpeciaList,* Special Libraries Association's monthly newsletter, for information on the use of productivity in special libraries. I was unable to locate any articles describing on-going programs, and only three libraries responded to my query in the *SpeciaList*. Of those libraries responding to my inquiry, none were using productivity as defined here.

In addition, I wrote to the BLS about the use of productivity in libraries. From the list of eight agencies they provided, I heard from three directly. Only two of those, the Library of Congress and the State Department Library, were using productivity measures of the type reported by the BLS in its 'Federal Government Productivity Summary Data' reports, which permit comparisons across agency and time. (The Department of Energy's Office of Scientific and Technical Information at Oak Ridge, Tennessee, is using some different, but very interesting, measures of productivity.) The BLS did provide a summary sheet of the types of measures that are being used in all eight participating federal libraries, but the remaining five have not been willing to make available the internal results of their work in this area.

Before presenting information on the kinds of measures being used and the results of productivity studies in the Library of Congress and the State Department Library, a reminder needs to be given of the purposes and limitations of the BLS federal government productivity measures – both in general and specifically for libraries. The primary index of productivity for federal libraries (and most of the federal government as well) is output per employee hour. This measure relates output to one input – labor time. This is an index measure, weighted to reflect differing labor requirements of portions of the output measure, and stated in terms of some desired base year data. Essentially, separate output and input indexes are calculated and then the final productivity index, output per employee hour. (The BLS measures use employee year data, based on FTES, rather than hourly data. Generally, the two measures are identical or nearly identical.)

There are also some additional indexes that usefully accompany the basic productivity measure, output per employee hour:

1. *Output index* is a quantifiable unit of service combined with base year labor weights.
2. *Compensation per employee year index* shows the trend of the average compensation per employee year.
3. *Unit labor cost index* represents the cost of labor required to produce one unit of output.
4. *Employee years index* represents changes, or trends, in employee years (direct or indirect, or both) to produce the output.

When the appropriate cost-based indexes are shown as deflated indexes they are particularly useful in determining constant dollar costs changes in output and productivity. For example, a productivity deflated compensation index may be formed by:

$$\frac{\text{output index}}{\text{deflated compensation index}}$$

which is an indicator that shows the relationship between output and constant dollar costs.

A variety of additional indexes may be formed depending on the interests of the organization and the outputs to be measured. What must be kept in mind is that decisions need to be made about which outputs are to be measured, how they will be weighted, which input costs (particularly indirect costs) will be attributed to which outputs, and, finally, how outputs will be counted. The indexes (as well as the very informative basic data figures) can then be given for individual output functions, combinations of functions, and the entire library or organization. The result is a series of informative individual and summary measures that can be compared over time, across functions as well as within and across organizations.

There are limitations. The BLS recognizes at least five major limitations to the data that are compiled for federal agencies:

1. existing techniques cannot fully take into account changes in the quality of goods and services;
2. consistency of coverage of estimates for output and input may be difficult to maintain, particularly over time;
3. organizational changes (integration, specialization, etc.) may not be reflected adequately in the measures, and productivity measures may be understated or overstated from year to year;
4. employees indirectly involved in an output function may not accurately estimate their contribution to an output function; *and*
5. the basic measure of productivity should be considered a general indicator of changes in output per employee hour and not a precise measure because of fluctuations from year to year in the index.[12]

Table 1, from data supplied by the BLS, shows examples of the types of library-related functions that are being measured for productivity in the eight federal agencies where libraries are participating in productivity studies. These have been broken down into several categories, according to complexity of the library service, in order to give some indication of the variety of types.

It should be obvious from this listing that a wide variety of activities, functions, and services are being measured for productivity analysis in these eight federal libraries. Some are routine, while others are very complex. This brief listing does not provide the really essential details on the nature of the objectives/ goals being measured. This is the critical ingredient to any program of evaluation, whether for productivity or other purposes. It does indicate that it is possible given adequate attention to goals, nature of the activities, differences in categories and

TABLE 1. EXAMPLES OF PRODUCTIVITY MEASURES IN USE IN FEDERAL LIBRARIES

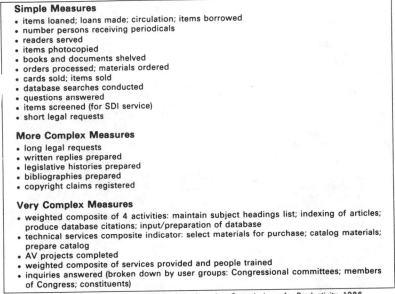

Simple Measures
- items loaned; loans made; circulation; items borrowed
- number persons receiving periodicals
- readers served
- items photocopied
- books and documents shelved
- orders processed; materials ordered
- cards sold; items sold
- database searches conducted
- questions answered
- items screened (for SDI service)
- short legal requests

More Complex Measures
- long legal requests
- written replies prepared
- legislative histories prepared
- bibliographies prepared
- copyright claims registered

Very Complex Measures
- weighted composite of 4 activities: maintain subject headings list; indexing of articles; produce database citations; input/preparation of database
- technical services composite indicator: select materials for purchase; catalog materials; prepare catalog
- AV projects completed
- weighted composite of services provided and people trained
- inquiries answered (broken down by user groups: Congressional committees; members of Congress; constituents)

Source: U.S. Bureau of Labor Statistics, Office of the Associate Commissioner for Productivity, 1986.

sub-categories of functions, and the ability to allocate labor costs correctly to perform productivity analyses for even complex library functions. If the library is willing to expend the effort to think critically through its functions, break them down into appropriate activities, keep track of employee time on these activities, and maintain adequate statistics on output, then it is possible to have good measures.

TABLE 2. BASIC DATA FOR (SELECTED) PRODUCTIVITY MEASURES, LIBRARY OF CONGRESS, 1984

Activity	Output	Employee Years	Compensation
1. Circulation	156,964	150.6	3,870,769
2. Reference	1,347,192	436.4	11,865,102
3. Copyright Reg.	502,628	683.0	15,943,486
4. Handicapped Readers Served	629,100	187.0	4,252,881
5. Cards sold	11,479,747	92.5	2,127,546
6. Congressional Res. Inquiries (Comm.)	92,836	555.0	18,261,919
7. CRS Inquiries (Mbrs)	282,327	521.3	17,152,857
8. CRS Inquiries (Cons)	67,084	73.7	2,424,624

Source: Library of Congress, Budget Office.

Given that it is possible to construct productivity measures, the question naturally arises as to the results. The State Department Library and the Library of Congress provided sufficient information for determining the results in their agencies of recent productivity studies. For the Library of Congress, table 2 shows basic data (quantities) for several activities for 1984; table 3 shows productivity (and related measures) for

TABLE 3. SELECTED OUTPUT AND PRODUCTIVITY MEASURES
FOR SELECTED ACTIVITIES, LIBRARY OF CONGRESS, 1982–1984

Activity and Output Measures		1982	1983	1984
1. Circulation				
Weighted output	(A)	149.5	191.8	205.9
Employee years	(B)	149.5	150.7	150.6
Employee year savings	(A-B)	0.0	41.2	55.3
Output/employee year	(A/B)	100.0	127.3	136.7
Unit labor cost		29.03	25.13	24.66
Deflated unit labor cost		29.03	23.80	22.24
2. Reference				
Weighted output	(A)	505.5	535.5	534.4
Employee years	(B)	505.5	426.4	436.4
Employee year savings	(A-B)	0.0	109.1	97.9
Output/employee year	(A/B)	100.0	125.5	122.4
Unit labor cost		9.02	8.49	8.81
Deflated unit labor cost		9.02	8.04	7.94
3. Cards sold				
Weighted output	(A)	224.0	191.1	167.3
Employee years	(B)	224.0	223.7	92.5
Employee year savings	(A-B)	0.0	−32.6	74.7
Output/employee year	(A/B)	100.0	85.4	180.7
Unit labor cost		.30	.39	.19
Deflated unit labor cost		.30	.37	.17
4. Cong. Res. Inquiries (Members)				
Weighted output	(A)	662.7	630.8	662.1
Employee years	(B)	662.7	502.1	521.3
Employee year savings	(A-B)	0.0	128.8	140.8
Output/employee year	(A/B)	100.0	125.6	127.0
Unit labor cost		68.77	58.68	60.75
Deflated unit labor cost		68.77	55.57	54.78
5. Cong. Res. Inquiries (Constituents)				
Weighted output	(A)	54.7	54.3	58.0
Employee years	(B)	54.7	67.5	73.7
Employee year savings	(A-B)	0.0	−13.2	−15.7
Output/employee year	(A/B)	100.0	80.4	78.7
Unit labor cost		25.36	33.80	36.14
Deflated unit labor cost		25.35	32.00	32.59

Source: Library of Congress, Budget Office.

these same activities for 1982–1984; table 4 shows the productivity
and related indexes for the entire library for 1982–84; and table 5
shows productivity, output, and employee years in graph form for the
years 1977–84. This last table is particularly effective in showing that
productivity and output at the Library of Congress are increasing very
nicely despite a severe decline in number of employee years. One would
be very proud to take this chart (and the accompanying tables) to
management!

For the State Department Library, similar data are available. The
library has productivity measures for reference requests, publications
charged, publications circulated, and external orders processed. However, instead of showing data similar to that given for the Library of
Congress, it is more useful to show changes in a series of output and
related indexes over time. Table 6 shows changes in these indexes for
selected years from 1977 to 1984.

TABLE 4. PRODUCTIVITY AND RELATED INDEXES FOR ALL OF THE LIBRARY OF CONGRESS (MEASURED ACTIVITIES ONLY) 1982–1984

Data		1982	1983	1984
Weighted output		3,075.00	3,179.62	3,276.74
Output index	(A)	100.00	103.00	106.00
Employee years		3,075.00	3,063.05	2,867.99
Employee year index	(B)	100.00	99.61	93.27
Compensation		75,353,902	81,355,676	79,818,299
Compensation index	(C)	100.00	107.97	105.93
Compensation deflator		1.0	1.06	1.11
Deflated comp. index	(D)	100.0	102.24	95.51
Calculations, Indexes				
Productivity, Empl. year	(A/B)	100.0	103.48	114.25
Productivity, Defl. comp.	(A/D)	100.0	100.82	111.57
Compensation/Emp. year	(C/B)	100.0	108.39	113.57
Unit labor cost	(C/A)	100.0	104.74	99.40
Defl. unit labor cost	(D/A)	100.0	99.19	89.63
Unit labor requirement	(B/A)	100.0	96.64	87.53

Source: Library of Congress, Budget Office.

TABLE 5. LIBRARY OF CONGRESS: PRODUCTIVITY, OUTPUT AND EMPLOYEE-YEARS, FY 1977–84 (FY 1977 = 100)

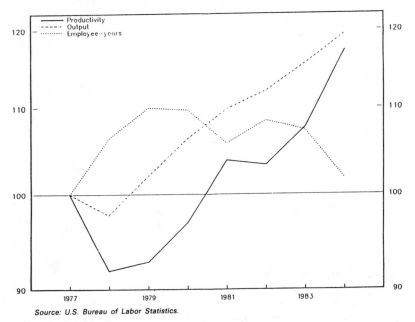

Source: U.S. Bureau of Labor Statistics.

To show changes over time, the BLS has prepared graphs for the productivity performance of the federal libraries participating in productivity studies in recent years. Table 7 shows library services productivity, output, and employee years for fiscal years 1977–84, and table 8 shows the average annual rate of change in productivity for several federal agency functions for fiscal years 1983–84. Library services are the

TABLE 6. INDEXES OF OUTPUT PER EMPLOYEE-YEAR AND RELATED DATA: STATE DEPARTMENT LIBRARY (MEASURED ACTIVITIES ONLY) – SELECTED YEARS, FY 1977–1984

Fiscal Year (1977=100)	Output per Employee Year	Output	Employee-Years	Unit Labor Cost
1977	100.0	100.0	100.0	100.0
1978	95.2	100.7	105.8	117.7
1982	122.7	113.5	92.5	131.1
1983	119.1	110.5	92.8	135.4
1984	118.3	112.7	95.3	137.3

Source: U.S. Department of State Library.

TABLE 7. LIBRARY SERVICES: PRODUCTIVITY, OUTPUT AND EMPLOYEE-YEARS, FY 1967–84 (FY 1977 = 100)

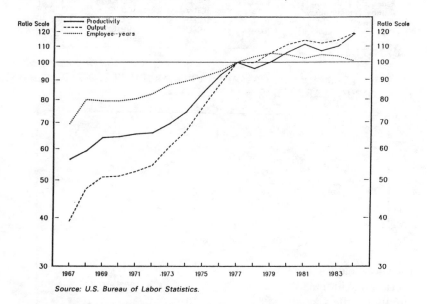

Source: U.S. Bureau of Labor Statistics.

third highest, with an average rate of 7.7 per cent. Productivity rates for library services do, however, vary in the federal government, as can be seen from table 9. The highest average annual rate of change is 3.5 per cent, the lowest is 7.1 per cent, and the function average is 2.5 per cent. (Names of participating federal libraries have been withheld by the BLS.)

PRODUCTIVITY AS AN EVALUATION TOOL: COMPARISONS WITH OTHER LIBRARY EVALUATION MEASURES

Clearly, the results for these two specific federal libraries, as well as federal libraries in general, are impressive. The real question, however, is whether productivity is a good measure of library excellence. Before venturing a response to this question, two caveats need to be made. First, it is necessary to define excellence. This is not so easily done because of

TABLE 8. AVERAGE ANNUAL RATE OF CHANGE IN OUTPUT PER
EMPLOYEE-YEAR, BY FUNCTIONAL GROUPS AND TOTAL
MEASURED SAMPLE, FY 1983–84

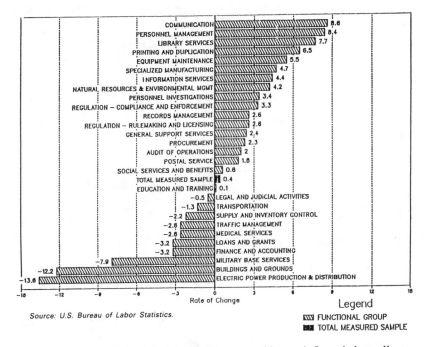

Source: U.S. Bureau of Labor Statistics.

Legend
- FUNCTIONAL GROUP
- TOTAL MEASURED SAMPLE

the variety of possible definitions. However, if one defines it broadly as
the accomplishment of goals or objectives and *if* improvement in
productivity is one of your goals, then it is a good measure of excellence.
However, it must be clear to you and your management that this is one of
the ways that the library and library staff will be evaluated. Use of this
approach to judgments of excellence should be made purposively and not
simply for the sake of having some quantitative data for show. Usually,
one would make this determination on the basis of whether it fits in
with organizational goals and organizational approaches to evaluation.
Second, productivity measures may be biased toward large libraries
where quantities of output for a particular function are greater and
statistical data are more easily maintained. In special libraries, where one
staff member may handle several functions almost simultaneously,
questions of separation of functions for record keeping and the added
expense of such procedures must be raised. There are at least five
evaluation measures that have been applied to special libraries and are at
least partially useful in comparisons with productivity. These are: user
satisfaction, cost benefit, value of information, document delivery tests,
and quality of information. Each of these will be briefly compared with
productivity as a potential measure of library excellence.

TABLE 9. LIBRARY SERVICES: AVERAGE ANNUAL RATE OF
CHANGE IN OUTPUT PER EMPLOYEE-YEAR, BY ORGANIZATION
AND FUNCTION AVERAGE, FY 1977–84

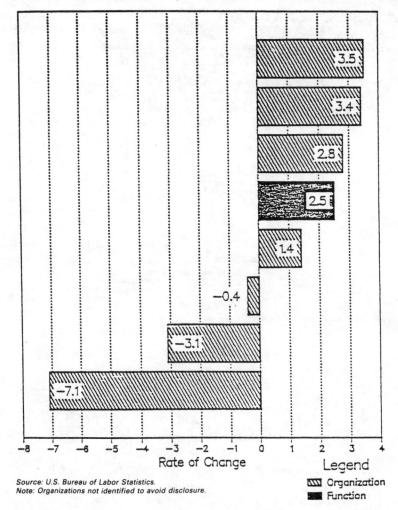

Source: U.S. Bureau of Labor Statistics.
Note: Organizations not identified to avoid disclosure.

User Satisfaction

This measure of excellence has been used to judge, for individual services
as well as for the library overall, the rating that users assign to the library
when asked how satisfied they are with the library or a library service.
Ratings are usually based on ordinal measurement scales specifying
degree of satisfaction or dissatisfaction. It is probably the most frequently
used performance measure in library evaluation studies. The measure has
both advantages and disadvantages. The central advantage is probably
the ease of collecting and analyzing the data. And, if users do share

agreement about the meaning of satisfaction, then it may be a valid measure of satisfaction.

Generally, however, we know little (or do not attempt to find out) about the extent of shared agreement about the meaning of the term. Recent research by D'Elia and Walsh on public library user satisfaction has shown that there is little agreement about what it means and, further, that beyond some unknown minimal level of service, it is very difficult to validly assess user satisfaction as it relates to library performance.[13] Despite continuing doubts about the validity of the measure, it will probably remain a useful, though limited, indicator of library excellence.

When compared to productivity as a measure of excellence, user satisfaction can only be described as measuring something entirely different. User satisfaction asks for a quality judgement from your 'customers', while productivity assesses how labor efficient you are in producing services and products for them.

Cost Benefit Analysis

Cost benefit analyses have been very popular in a variety of fields of study, particularly in business and engineering. Librarians have attempted to use them under a variety of names, but with somewhat mixed results. The major problem has been valid determination of the benefit side of the equation. The cost side is not easily determined (usually because of the difficulty of attributing precise costs to a particular service), but is much simpler than the benefits question. Manning's formula, described in a recent article by Zachert and Williams[14] is a good example of an attempt to estimate cost benefits for a special library. King Research, Inc. used a similar user-based judgement approach in a study of the value of the US Department of Energy's Energy Data Base.[15] Both studies rely on the judgments of users regarding how much time the library saved them as the critical gauge of benefits. Whether this is a valid process for estimating benefits is yet to be determined by further research.

When compared with productivity, cost benefit analysis is a useful companion measure for judging library excellence. As productivity increases, costs (at least when compared in constant dollars for labor costs) for library functions decrease. If one were to use a multifactor measure of productivity (including input costs such as capital expenditures) then it would be an even more interesting companion to cost benefit measures.

Value

Value appraisals are closely allied conceptually to cost benefit analyses, and many authors would consider them to be the same thing. Here, however, the approach is to use value measures to address the question: what would it have cost the organization if the library/service/product had not existed? King Research used this approach and estimated that the Energy Data Base saved scientists about $3 billion in time and equipment. In a follow-up study by King at DOE, it was estimated that the value of library services (in terms of willingness to pay) was $3.1 million (or $600 per professional employee) and value in terms of savings derived from reading was $28 million (or $5,400 per professional).[16] Again, both of these judgments were based on self-assessments of value by users.

Like cost benefit analyses, value of information studies are also a useful companion measure to productivity. Indeed, King Research says that *with* the Energy Data Base, research and development in energy cost $5.8 billion. Since the value of the database was $3 billion to scientists, then it would have cost $8.8 billion to achieve the same level of output *without* the Energy Data Base. This is an increase in national scientific productivity of about 52 per cent.[17] Thus, value studies, while still filled with a great number of validity problems, serve as a complementary measure to productivity when productivity is considered in the larger framework of the entire organization.

Document Delivery Tests

Document delivery tests were developed to assess the ability of a library to deliver a specified set of documents in a timely fashion.[18] These tests have three components: 1) test of the probability of ownership of a sample of documents; 2) test of the probability of availability of the documents; and 3) a capability index that takes into account ownership, availability, and speed of delivery. Research on validating the measures has not been extensive, but indications are that they do a moderately good job of assessing the usefulness of a collection. The central problem with validity is defining the population of documents from which a sample is taken. Document delivery tests may be biased toward large libraries which emphasize in-depth collections in a subject. When compared with productivity, document delivery tests should be considered a complementary measure of library excellence because they tap the concept of the quality of the collection based on (hypothetical) user document demands.

Quality

Quality is an elusive concept. Precision in definition is not aided by the different ways in which it is used in the literature where reference may be made to it in terms of a specific service or to describe the library overall. What is needed are specific definitions that can be measured. King Research, in its second study of the DOE libraries, attempts to do this by defining quality as the user's satisfaction with 20 library services and characteristics. A narrower definition of the quality of a search is also given by King as the relevance (as judged by the user) of the output.[19]

King Research, however, does not use these definitions as an overall measure of quality but considers them a part of its measures of library performance and library effectiveness, a reflection of the terminology problem in library evaluation. A similar problem exists with the measures of the quality of reference work, an area that has had a good deal of research in public and academic libraries. Crowley discusses the results of this work, noting particularly the disappointing fact that reference answers seem to be only 'half right'.[20]

The major problem, then, with measures of quality is the lack of agreement about definition of the term. It may not be possible to resolve this issue because the concept is so broad and elusive. A more useful approach may be to develop more narrowly defined evaluation measures and construct from them a general measure of quality. In reality, this is what can be done with measures of productivity, where individual functions are assessed as to productivity and from those an overall index of productivity can be constructed.

SUMMARY AND CONCLUSIONS

Productivity measures do have their place in the special librarian's tool kit of evaluation measures. Larger special libraries will probably find them more useful than small libraries because of the problems involved in constructing indexes for defined discrete output functions. They are not, however, without their uses in the small library if the librarian is willing to make the effort to construct the necessary indexes and maintain accurate records on input and output. The two keys to a successful productivity measurement program are their meaningfulness to upper-level management as a library evaluation measure and the setting of precise objectives for productivity measurement. Without successfully meeting these two criteria, the librarian is wasting his/her time in measuring productivity and might be well advised to use one or more of the general measures discussed above.

The federal librarians who provided information for this study have shown that they are successfully meeting these two essential criteria. In addition, they have developed a series of measures that show promise for imitation by other special libraries, particularly large ones. They have developed both simple and complex measures of productivity and are using these as evidence in their requests for budgets[21] and in meeting federal government requirements for productivity reporting. While results vary from agency to agency, they do effectively show that productivity of library services is increasing.

The librarian's (and particularly the special librarian's) evaluation tool kit is an exceedingly thin one because of the lack of research and development work in this area. Productivity is one useful addition to it. When compared with other evaluation measures that have been developed for libraries, productivity complements rather than replaces them. The special librarian needs and can make use of all – and more – of these evaluation measures. Hopefully, in the coming years, practitioners and researchers will join forces for the improvement, refinement, and expansion of the special librarian's evaluation tool kit.

REFERENCES

1.   Bain, David. *The Productivity Prescription: The Manager's Guide to Improving Productivity and Profits*. New York: McGraw-Hill, 1982.
2.   Marchand, Donald A. 'Managing Information as a Resource: The Key to Productivity in the Information Economy.' New York: Special Libraries Association, 1984; pamphlet, 6 pp.
3.   Bearman, Toni C., Polly Guynup, and Sandra N. Milevski. 'Information and Productivity.' *Journal of the American Society for Information Science 36:* 369–375 (November 1985).
4.   Booze, Allen and Hamilton, Inc. 'Summary Report: Booz, Allen Study of Managerial/Professional Productivity.' New York: Booz, Allen and Hamilton, Inc.; typescript, June 1980, variously paged.
5.   Bain, pp. 51–55.
6.   U.S. Bureau of Labor Statistics. *Productivity and the Economy: A Chartbook*. Washington, D.C.: U.S. Government Printing Office, June 1983 (Bulletin 2172), p. 1.
7.   U.S. Bureau of Labor Statistics. *Handbook of Methods*. Washington, D.C.: U.S. Government Printing Office, 1981 (Bulletin 2134, pp. 106–107.
8.   Bain, pp. 60–62.
9.   Bain, pp. 64–66.
10.   Bain, pp. 75–80.
11.   Lawlor, Alan. *Productivity Improvement Manual*. Westport, Conn: Quorum Books, 1985.
12.   U.S. Bureau of Labour Statistics. *Handbook of Methods*, p. 107.
13.   D'Elia, George, and Sandra Walsh. 'Patron's Uses and Evaluation of Library Services: A Comparison across Five Public Libraries.' *Library and Information Science Research 7:* 3–30 (January–March 1985).
14.   Zachert, Martha Jane, and Robert V. Williams. 'Marketing Measures for Information Services.' *Special Libraries 77* (no. 2): 61–70 (Spring 1986).
15.   King Research, Inc. *Value of the Energy Data Base*. Oak Ridge, Tenn: U.S. Dept. of Energy, Technical Information Center, 1982 (DOE/OR/11232–1). 81 pp. Available from the National Technical Information Center.
16.   King Research, Inc. *A Study of the Value of Information and the Effect on Value on Intermediary Organizations, Timeliness of Services and Products, and Comprehensiveness of the EDB*. Oak Ridge, Tenn: U.S. Dept. of Energy, Technical Information Center, Sept. 1984 (DOE/NBM–1078). 122 pp. Available from National Technical Information Center.
17.   King Research, Inc. *A Study of the Value of Information . . .*, pp. 2–3.
18.   Orr, Richard H., et al. 'Development of Methodologic Tools for Planning and Managing Library services.' *Bulletin of the Medical Library Association 56:* 242–267 (September 1968).
19.   King Research, Inc. *Study of the Value of Information . . .*, pp. 31, 39.
20.   Crowley, Terence. 'Half-Right Reference: Is It True?' *RQ 25:* 59–68 (Fall 1985).
21.   Letter to the author from Mr. John O. Hemperly, Budget Officer, Library of Congress, July 1986.

Consumer attitudes to public libraries: the *Which?* report

Anthony Land

Assistant Director of the Association for Consumer Research

The consumer magazine *Which?* publishes the results of its survey on attitudes to public libraries. Anthony Land, Assistant Director of the Association for Consumer Research, gave a sneak preview of some of the findings to the LA Conference in September 89, findings which he believes demonstrate the need to re-examine some fundamental points . . .

When I was first invited to speak today, I was inclined to think I would have to refuse, because, to my recollection, we had done no recent research on how consumers viewed public libraries and the services they provided.

An online search by our excellent in-house library showed that no similar research of consumer attitudes on a national scale appeared to have been done by anyone, at least in the last ten years. But by a happy coincidence I discovered in May, when the invitation to speak was issued, that *Which?* had just commissioned research on this precise topic for the first time in more than 30 years' publishing. I was thus able to accept your invitation to speak.

First, methodology. It has been standard practice over many years for our organisation to conduct readership surveys. We have our own professional market research staff who carry out these surveys for us. Each month a 16-page questionnaire is sent to a random sample of the one million subscribers to *Which?* In the May 1989 questionnaire, which was sent to 4,000 subscribers and included questions on public libraries, the other topics covered were: how household bills are settled; frequency of use of primary health services (GPs, dentists, opticians, etc); thefts from gardens; and marketing questions about the likelihood of subscribers to buy pre-recorded video-cassette tapes.

Typical response rates to these questionnaires are 55 per cent (2,200) (after two reminders). No incentives are offered or given for completion. The raw data are then analysed using established market research computer programmes and then reported to the project team in charge of the report.

So, what questions did we ask and what results did we get?

Table 1 shows that there was a rather higher response rate than usual. I should add, in parenthesis, that such research as we have done among non-respondents to our postal surveys has indicated that their attitudes tend to be broadly similar to respondents and that their reasons for not replying are of the too busy/don't like questionnaires type.

TABLE 1

Questionnaires dispatched	4016
Response	2389
Response rate	59%

But who are *Which?* subscribers? Table 2 gives some simple information which points to a relatively affluent membership. I must confess that we are not as sophisticated as most publishers in researching the profile of our members. Editorially, we do not find it essential to do so. And we do not have the commercial imperative of seeking to persuade advertisers to buy space in our magazine.

TABLE 2. *Profile of Which? subscriber*

Male	71%
Female	29%
16–44	52%
45 plus	48%
AB1	49%
C1	30%
Total subscribers	950,000

Table 3 answers the first question in the questionnaire 'do you or does anyone else in your household use a public library at all?' It must be a matter of judgement as to whether usage by seven households out of ten is satisfactory, bearing in mind the solidly middle-class subscriber profile of *Which?*

TABLE 3. *Use of public libraries (by household)*

Yes	69%
No	31%

Obviously, more than one person in many households uses public libraries. In our survey, there are 1,650 responding households which use public libraries and, in these households, there are 1,596 main adult users and 575 main child users, as Table 4 shows. It is on the views either of households or of the main users that the rest of the figures are based. I am assured that these are statistically significant samples.

TABLE 4

Main adult users	1596
Main child users (under 18)	575
Male adults	55%
Female adults	45%
Male children	44%
Female children	56%

How often do users in our sample make use of public libraries? Table 5 shows that two thirds use their libraries at least once a month and nine out of ten, three times a year or more. Adults and children follow very similar patterns of use. For comparison, usage in the general population, as estimated in a *Sunday Times/MORI* survey, is shown in Table 6.

TABLE 5

	Adults	*Children*
Once a week or more	13%	9%
Once a month or more	66%	72%
Three times a year or more	91%	95%

TABLE 6. *How many visits to a public library each year?*

None	34%
1–10	28%
More than 10	37%

Sunday times/MORI Survey of 1000 adults December 1987

There may be other data on the quantity of users of public libraries. No doubt there are large regional, seasonal and day-to-day variations. A personal impression would be that, while no-one would wish public libraries to resemble Saturday morning at the supermarket, the air of cloistered calm quite typical of many libraries I know could perhaps be described on occasions as under-use of an important and expensive public asset.

A question about the service most used in the past 12 months produced the results shown in Table 7. Nothing very surprising here, but certainly support for the continuation of reference services.

TABLE 7. *Service most used in past 12 months*

	Adults	*Children*
Borrowing adult books	80%	13%
Borrowing children's books	1%	77%
Using reference service	16%	10%

A separate question was asked about services not provided now which users would like to have available to them. Most respondents did not reply to this question; of the 30 per cent, who did, the three services most requested were video hire, records/tapes/CDs borrowing and specialist services or clubs for adults (films, talks, etc).

We also asked about how well librarians let people know about what services are available. With hindsight this seems to have been a somewhat ambiguous question. Within libraries, it is probably clear enough where different sections are housed. But how good are public libraries at letting their potential customers know where exactly the library is situated? We asked two questions about the convenience of opening hours. Table 8 gives the overall ratings.

TABLE 8. *Opening hours*

Very convenient	28%
Fairly convenient	56%
Not very convenient	12%
Not at all convenient	3%

Nevertheless, 42 per cent of the sample indicated they would like changes made and Table 9 shows what ideas they had. We did not specifically ask about early closing on, say, one weekday per week, which has been an irritant to my family in the past. Why is it always Wednesday afternoon that we choose to take the children to the library? Why are libraries often if not always closed on extra days over Bank Holidays? The bias in this figure is very towards opening in the evening and more at weekends, as opposed to earlier in the morning.

TABLE 9. *676 (42%) said they would like changes*

Earlier in the morning	15%
Later in the evening	48%
All weekend	28%
Longer at weekends	33%

We asked about how users rated their library overall. Table 10 shows little difference between adults and child main users. The key statistic here, it seems to me, is the rating for 'fair'. Whatever the dictionary may say about the meaning of 'fair' in this context, I would doubt that librarians who take a pride in the service they offer would regard a 30 per cent rating of 'fair' among users of their service as satisfactory.

The same point emerges in Table 11 which rates different aspects of public library service. All of us will welcome and agree with the high rate for helpfulness of staff. However, wearing both my

TABLE 10. *Overall rating of local library*

	Adults	*Children*
Excellent	7%	6%
Good	56%	58%
Fair	30%	31%
Poor	5%	3%

consumer and my publisher hats, I would not be alone in regarding the 'fair' ratings for range and updatedness of reference books and the number of new titles available for lending as less than satisfactory. I would readily acknowledge that publishers must bear some part of the blame, simply because of the sheer volume of their new title production, including reference books. It cannot be easy for librarians on limited budgets to select from the thousand or so new titles that pour out of publishers every week. That is not just a problem for librarians. Table 12 shows how many books our sample buys a year.

TABLE 11

	Excellent/Good	*Fair*	*Very Poor/poor*
Helpfulness of staff	80%	16%	4%
Condition of lending books	72%	25%	3%
Number of lending books stocked	60%	34%	6%
Range/Updatedness of reference stock	41%	41%	18%
Number of new lending books stocked	31%	49%	20%

TABLE 12. *How many books do you buy a year?*

None	4%
1–9	63%
10–19	20%
More than 20	12%

Table 13, again from *Sunday Times/MORI* evidence, shows how many books the general population buys a year. The contrast is striking, but I would not say that even the comparatively affluent *Which?* sample is buying a satisfactory number of books. Put it another way: there ought to be ample opportunity here for well-managed publishers to extend their market well beyond the limits indicated here – but that really is another subject. What is true is that librarians, booksellers, publishers and authors have a common interest in developing, with the help of modern marketing, the market for the printed word – the demise of which has far too frequently been predicted.

TABLE 13. *How many buy a book every year?*

None	37%
1–9	50%
More than 10	13%

Sunday times/MORI Survey of 1000 adults December 1987

I should like to add some comments, none of which should be taken to be anything other than my own personal thoughts; they are emphatically not the policy of my Association. But before I do so I feel I must make clear the apolitical nature of my Association. Recent publicity has led some to believe that we are anti-industry and/or anti-Government; not so. Nor are we pro-industry or pro-Government. What we are is pro-consumer and our chosen vehicle is information, factual and unbiased.

First, is it not a matter for concern that this national survey of *Which?* subscribers appears to be something of a rarity? Should not libraries, like other service providers, regularly assess the wishes and views of their customers – the book-borrowing public – and adapt their services accordingly? We certainly do so regularly and systematically.

Are libraries anyway sufficiently responsive to customer pressure? Should they establish consultative committees through which suggestions and criticisms could usefully be channelled? I recall complaining once about my local library by writing to the librarian: I was not pleased to receive a deadpan, bureaucratic reply from the Borough Councillor who was Chairman of the Libraries Committee at the time. Why did the librarian, the responsible manager, not reply? Is it ever possible to 'see the manager' as you might do in a department store?

Second, to this observer, standards of display and presentation in public libraries are variable. Do public libraries have adequate resources – both for training and marketing – to project their services effectively? I was told the other day of a bus shelter poster campaign in New York City promoting the generic use of local libraries: is such a campaign feasible in London or Birmingham or Edinburgh?

Many of you may have personal knowledge of our marketing methods. Some may dislike them. Without them we would be dead. Effective marketing is the key to the successful promotion of *all* products and services: but of course it is expensive.

Third, and inevitably, resources. As rates go and the community charge succeeds them, most believe that resources will remain tight. I was struck by the relatively high response in our survey supporting the introduction of video *hire*. If video hire, why not other income-generating services? National Trust shops, cathedral shops, art gallery and museum shops – all are commonplace these days. There is even to be a Charing Cross Hospital shop. (A publisher of popular but quality art books told me the other day he sold more English-language books in Paris than in Birmingham. Why? The shop at the Louvre Museum is the single reason). Why not library shops? Public libraries are often in good locations and many appear to be generously housed. If necessary, the development of library shops could be franchised to an established retailer – though, no doubt, more profits would be generated if you ran such shops yourselves.

Finally, and here I may be treading on very sensitive ground, is local authority control an absolutely sacred cow? In these days of self-governing hospitals and opting-out schools, would the managers of public libraries – grouped perhaps by county or larger areas – meet customer wishes more sensitively, raise income more effectively, display their books and other products more imaginatively, market their service more vigorously, indeed achieve greater job satisfaction for themselves and their staff if they were freed of local authority control? Direct funding could come, say, from a Libraries Council, established along similar lines to the Arts and Sports Councils.

I have left to the very end my continued and full-blown support for the principle of not charging for the basic lending services of public libraries. None of my personal observations should be taken as leading to the abandonment of that principle; rather, they should be regarded as supporting and underpinning it. I would like to see public libraries as independent, self-reliant, lively places – what might be called 'centres of community excellence'.

Quality assurance in Canadian hospital libraries – the challenge of the eighties.

Kathleen M. Eagleton

Director of Library Services, Brandon General Hospital, 150 McTavish Avenue East, Brandon, Manitoba, R7A 2B3, Canada

ABSTRACT

The challenge facing the provider of library services in Canadian health-care facilities in the mid 1980s is the development of a structured method of monitoring the quality of service provided. In order to explain the evolution of this process, a brief background history of the accreditation of health-care facilities in Canada is presented, together with the role of the Canadian Council on Hospital Accreditation. An account of the development of Canadian standards for the provision of library services is followed by an introduction to the philosophy of quality assurance as it is applied to the institution as a whole, and to the library in particular. A bibliography is appended.

THE HISTORY OF ACCREDITATION

The first stirrings of concern about the quality of professional services in North American hospitals emerged in the late teens of this century, when the American Colleges of Surgeons instituted a 'hospital standardization program' that was designed to provide a measure of a hospital's performance using five basic criteria.[1,2]

These criteria covered the requirements that the medical staff be competent graduates, organized into a definite group with rules, regulations and policies; that accurate and complete case records be kept; and that diagnostic and therapeutic facilities be available.

With support from the Catholic Hospital Conference and the American Hospital Association, a survey was undertaken of some 240 hospitals in the USA and Canada during the period 1919–20. So appalling were the results that the reports are said to have been burned in the furnaces of the old Waldorf Astoria Hotel in New York.[3]

Instituting a standardization and accreditation programme proved difficult. The requirements that detailed records were to be kept for all patients, and that medical staff had to organize themselves, sit on committees and hold regular meetings, proved too demanding for many a busy and independently inclined doctor.[1]

However, in 1921 the Canadian Medical Association gave its approval to the programme, and from 1919 to 1951, Canadian hospitals were 'approved', 'provisionally approved', or 'not approved' by the American College of Surgeons. The College was truly American in the larger sense, in that it had been founded by both American and Canadian surgeons.

The standardization programme was strictly voluntary, but peer pressure often led to hospital participation, once the idea was accepted by an institution in the same geographical region. The first director of the programme, a Canadian, Mr Malcolm T. McEachern, proved to be the genius needed to bring about the widespread acceptance that occurred over this 30-year period.

With the retirement of Dr McEachern in the early 1950s, the American College of Surgeons decided that the time had come to spread both the load and the cost of their accreditation programme amongst more organizations, and discussions took place between several health-related groups in the USA the result was the birth of the Joint Commission on the Accreditation of Hospitals (JCAH), which included the American College of Surgeons, the American Hospital Association, the American Medical Association and the American College of Physicians.[4]

The JCAH took over the programme in 1951–52, and Canadian hospitals continued to be surveyed by them. In 1953 the Commission invited the Canadian Medical Association (CMA) to provide a representative to the programme in order to facilitate the continued participation of Canadian facilities, and this invitation was accepted.

However, at the annual meeting of the CMA in 1950, a Committee on the Accreditation of Hospitals had been established, in response to the general feeling that Canadian facilities should carry out their own accreditation programme. As a result, the Canadian Commission on Hospital Accreditation (CCHA) had been established in 1952. The Commission consisted of representatives of the Canadian Medical Association, the Royal College of Physicians and Surgeons of Canada and l'Association des Médecins de Langue Français du Canada (AMLF). Due to financial and other restraints, surveys continued to be done under the auspices of the JCAH, but by two Canadian surveyors hired by the CCHA. Finally, in December of 1958, the CCHA received its own federal charter from the Secretary of State, and assumed total legal responsibility for the Canadian accreditation programme on 1 January 1959.[4]

From that date the programme has grown steadily, from 333 accredited facilities in 1959,[3] 525 in 1970,[1] 930 in 1981,[3] to 1186 in 1986 (M.Pill personal communication). This represents 92.18% of acute-care beds, 60% of mental health-care beds, and 43% of long-term-care beds in Canada. This is remarkable progress, considering that the programme remains voluntary, and that all costs of the survey must be covered by the health-care facilities. The general hospitals, being in the accreditation programme first, clearly lead the way, but the mental health, long-term-care and rehabilitation centres are making great strides. Ambulatory health care centres were added as a special care service in 1980. As of 1981, a representative of the Canadian Long Term Care Association replaced AMLF on the CCHA, now called the Canadian Council on Hospital Accreditation/Conseil Canadien D'Agrement des Hopitaux. The Canadian Nurses Association has been represented on the Council since 1973. The Council conducts its activities in both English and French.

The Standards used in the JCAH programme were those that had evolved over a period of 35 years' use by the American College of Surgeons, and were also used initially by the CCHA. They were based on 'minimal' achievements. Both commissions agreed to maintain a close liaison, and the standards later developed in Canada showed great similarities, including a change from 'minimal' to 'optimal' standards in the early 1970s.

The Canadian standards have seen revisions in 1972, 1977, 1983, 1985 and 1986. Separate standards are now published by the CCHA for long-term-care centres, rehabilitation centres, mental health centres and an interpretation for small acute health-care centres.

THE LIBRARY IN THE ACCREDITATION PROGRAMME

Standards for a library service were included in the JCAH standards in 1952 as a contingent service, considered 'desirable, but not absolute prerequisites to accreditation . . . Whether they must be met is contingent on the type, size and organization of the hospital, and its financial resources'. The three components were outlined.

1. Organization. There shall be a medical library directed by a competent librarian.
2. Facilities. Books and journals shall be catalogued and shall be readily accessible.
3. Personnel. Personnel shall be provided to assure efficient service to the medical staff.[5]

Separate Canadian standards for staff library services have been included since 1967, when the standard read as follows:

Medical library service

1. The Canadian Council on Hospital Accreditation does not publish an approved list of suitable text books and journals for an accredited hospital; this is a responsibility for recommendation by the medical staff acting on the best advice it can obtain.
2. The size and contents of the library should vary with the size and degree of specialism of the medical staff and the types of clinical work undertaken as well as with the location of the hospital and the types of

patients served. In all hospitals the journals regularly received should be appropriate to the types of diagnostic and treatment problems encountered in the hospital.

3. Other good libraries may be proximate but there must be an adequate basic library on site in the hospital so the physicians will be able to review medical literature during diagnostic work-up or for management of a difficult or unusual case. He should not have to run home, or to another hospital or to a central library to find the reference he needs.

4. On the other hand, full use should be made of the lending library or reference facilities of central libraries of other hospitals; indeed, an important function of the hospital librarian may be to arrange for, and facilitate prompt action on requests for such loans. The availability of useful audio and visual learning aids libraries should not be overlooked by the hospital and its medical staff.

5. With reference to the locality of the hospital, it has been said with some justice that the medical staff of a geographically isolated hospital has a relatively greater need for a comprehensive medical reference library in the hospital.

6. One of the terms of reference of the medical staff's library committee should be to recommend and support realistic budget submissions for the medical reference library on an annual basis. Both immediate and longer term goals should be evaluted in such budgetary considerations.

7. a. In small hospitals and in many special treatment hospitals, the library also should be adequate in space and furnishings to serve as a room for medical staff committee meetings, and even for general staff meetings if there is only a small medical staff.

b. In a small general hospital the basic text books should include at least texts in medicine, surgery, obstetrics and gynaecology and paediatrics, and text books in certain of the basis sciences, such as anatomy, physiology and biochemistry.

c. In chronic, convalescent and special treatment hospitals there should be text books in the basic sciences, in general medicine and surgery and in the specialties appropriate to the hospital.[6]

Looking back, it is really quite remarkable how well these very basic standards were written, and how far we still have to travel in some instances. There may well be many professionals who still must 'run home', or perhaps to their office, for information that the library does not provide.

In the 1972 Guide[4] the CCHA developed a standard format for all hospital services, which included three parts – a Principle, standards developed out of that Principle, and an interpretation of each standard. The Principle for Staff Library Services read: 'The hospital shall provide library services appropriate to the professional, technical and administrative needs of the medical and hospital staff'. A single standard dealt with the nature and scope of services. Significant, however, was a widening of the client base of the service from medical staff to all hospital and medical staff.

Comparatively rapid development has taken place in the field of library standards in health care since 1967. The early process has been well described by Flower.[7] In 1978, the Committee on Medical Library Services of the Ontario Medical Association developed a check-list for staff library services, designed to expand the brief questionnaire by which the surveyors of the CCHA evaluated the library services of a hospital. This questionnaire was officially still made available to surveyors in 1980 (A.L.Swanson personal communication), but was never a requirement. Its use apparently disappeared by 1983, when new standards and a revised questionnaire were issued. Standards of service for the staff library department of health-care facilities (in particular, acute-care facilities) are now well entrenched in the regularly revised accreditation guides.

By 1986, the Principle for Library Services read: 'Library services shall be maintained for all of the professional and ancillary staff as appropriate', and there are seven standards to be met. An accompanying questionnaire, formerly published separately, has been incorporated into the text of the standard in the 1986 revisions.

Unfortunately, in the process of revising the format of the standards, the CCHA has lost much of the quality and soundness of content that had been developed by the health library community and accepted by the CCHA in the 1970s. Consequently, the Canadian Health Libraries Association/Association des bibliothèques de la santé du Canada (CHLA/ABSC) established a Task Force on Hospital Library Standards in 1987 to prepare revised standards and to submit them to CCHA for their consideration. It is anticipated that these standards, together with their accompanying background documents, will be completed by 1989.

Unfortunately, too, in the standards for acute-care hospitals, library services to patients have never been addressed, and it has been necessary to utilize the rather brief standards from long-term care and psychiatric guidelines. This lack of patient library standards has undoubtedly resulted in the poor library service to patients that is evident in most acute-care hospitals.

QUALITY ASSURANCE

Between 1977 and 1983 the concept of quality assurance in the provision of patient care was being developed, following on the heels of the Joint Commission on Accreditation of Hospitals, which even by 1978 had a separate section in its guidelines designed to measure the quality of professional services; specifically, the quality of care provided to all patients, and the appropriate allocation of resources contributary to the quality of patient care.

In 1983 the CCHA standards stated: 'The health care facility's quality assurance program shall be emphasized in determining the accreditation of the facility'.[8]

Dr Fulvio Limongelli, executive director of CCHA, provided an explanation (quoted in reference 9):

'Quality assurance is a method for correcting identified weakness, introducing a control study following a suitable interval and reassuring the hospital board that corrective actions have been taken' . . . 'And, . . . in reassuring the board, we are in turn reassuring the public that a hospital is, in fact, making every effort to provide quality patient care'.

The CCHA definition read: 'Quality assurance is the establishment of hospital-wide goals, the assessment of the procedures in place to see if they achieve these goals and, if not, the proposal of solutions in order to attain these goals. The quality assurance program should be internal, internally-administered, ongoing, specific to the institution, structured and coordinated within the facility'.[10]

QUALITY ASSURANCE IN THE LIBRARY

Like all other hospital departments faced with this newly structured and newly emphasized requirement for accreditation, library services personnel began to agonize over the problem, pondering how to address it as it applied to the measurement of library services that they provided. Agonizing is not too strong a word, especially for library staff in hospitals that were due for an accreditation visit soon after the requirements were first published.

Many of us turned to the literature and experience of the United States, where librarians had been grappling with the problem over the previous decade. The work done in New York State[11] suddenly became very popular and very valuable, especially to those library services faced with the necessity of fast action. However, we had to mesh these qualitative and quantitative guidelines with the standards specifically laid out by the CCHA and, from this, develop a comprehensive quality assurance programme for the library services department.

As the hospital administration staff was normally working on the overall quality assurance programme at the same time, those library services departments were fortunate indeed, if they were able, whilst developing their programme, to dovetail it also with the overall hospital programme. In many instances, library services personnel experienced difficulty with this process. The entire exercise proved to be a very time-consuming task, and one not easily fitted into the already overloaded day that most hospital librarians experience.

One of the first requirements of a quality assurance programme is the development of a statement of mission, which described the purpose of the facility or department in terms such that goals and objectives may be developed from it. The four basic elements of a mission statement are: philosophy, structure and role, goals, and objectives.[12] Here again, some librarians found themselves in difficulty because their overall facility mission statement was unprepared at the time that the requirements dictated that they develop not only a mission statement for their department but also a quality assurance programme, which itself hinged on both the overall and the departmental statements of mission.

The process of developing a quality assurance programme for library services entails two steps:

Step 1

Taking the CCHA standards and expanding them into a set of criteria that will provide a measurement tool allowing description in general terms, of the optimum level of service that the library should be providing.

For example (sample statements only):

Goals and objectives. (i) Written goals and objectives, both short- and long-range, are developed for library services and are consistent with the overall goals of the health-care facility. (ii) The extent and scope of library service is appropriate to the size and responsibilities of the health-care facility. (iii) The library is capable of providing information:

(a) in support of patient care, (b) in support of the educational and continuing education programmes of professional and other staff and students, (c) to keep personnel aware of new developments in their own fields and (d) in support of any special function of the health-care facility.

Physical environment. (i) The library has a central location and is readily accessible to all potential users. (ii) There is adequate shelving to facilitate access to materials and to allow for growth. (iii) The library meets accepted standards of:

(a) physical layout, (b) floor load, (c) lighting, (d) ventilation and (e) electrical service.

Resources. (i) The selection policy is based on the functional responsibilities of the health-care facility. (ii) The collection is authoritative and meets standards laid down by the relevant accrediting bodies for formal educational programmes. (iii) Indices to the journal literature include those to professional and administrative materials. (iv) The collection is fully catalogued, labelled and arranged to facilitate use.

Services. (i) The library's collections are available at all times to meet clinical needs. (ii) Interlibrary loan service is available for books, journal articles and audio-visual materials. (iii) There is rapid document delivery for patient care. (iv) Orientation to library resources and services is provided.

Quality assurance. (i) There are written procedures outlining the methods of evaluation of library services and performance of library personnel. (ii) Evaluation methods shall assess structure, process and outcome of procedures. (iii) Quality assurance activities are conducted regularly, at least annually, and are documented. (iv) There is documentation of actions taken following the results of the quality assurance activities.

Components of the overall quality assurance statement for the department might include the following: goals and objectives, organization and administration, policies and procedures, physical environment, staff, continuing education, resources, services, co-operative arrangements, and quality assurance.

Step 2

Having developed a set of general quality assurance criteria that fit into the institution's quality assurance programme and mesh with its statement of mission, a set of 'on the ground' criteria must be developed, which will measure quality of service on a daily/weekly/monthly/yearly basis.

Here, the choice is wide, specifics are addressed, and realism sets in. Where to start? What is already measured? What is easiest to measure? What is most important to measure first?

For instance, perhaps we have copious statistics on who took what out of the library when, but do we know that what they took really answered the questions they had? How helpful were the staff in the process? Were the staff adequately trained and/or up to date in appropriate knowledge or techniques to be able to answer the question? Did they use appropriate funding tools? Does the library in fact hold up-to-date material in the area required? If not, why not, and can it be obtained quickly from another source? How quickly? How quickly is realistic?

Did a piece of audi-visual equipment break down during an educational session? Why did it break down? Had preventive maintenance been performed on it? Was the staff member able to assist the user? If not, why not? Was it within the scope of that staff member to be able to assist? Was training adequate? Did they know when to refer the problem?

Is there a larger backlog of cataloguing? If so, what is creating the backlog? Is it shortage of staff? Is it inefficient methods of producing catalogue cards? Is it lack of expertise in cataloguing? Is it unrealistic expectations of the level of cataloguing to be done?

Is there sufficient room to shelve materials? If not, is it because there is not enough floor space, or enough shelving? Can anything be done to change this? Are redundant materials withdrawn quickly enough? Is there a policy for withdrawals? Have you thought of utilising microform?

This type of question is easy to pose. What is not so easy is developing specific standards dealing with specific criteria, and attaching realistic and measurable norms to the standards. The norm may be written separately from the standard, or it may be incorporated into the standard itself. The specific monitoring technique to be used may also be separate or incorporated.

With a set of criteria and measurable standards covering some aspects of the library operation in place, the programme must be tested. Data are gathered, analysed and the outcome recorded. Does the result fall within acceptable norms? Does it fall within realistic norms for your particular library? Does it require corrective action? What corrective action will be taken? The corrective action is recorded, the standard, norm and monitoring technique are evaluated, and the criterion waits to be be tried again another time. The process is continuous.

This process is clearly not one that is developed overnight. If the institution has already laid out the prescribed format for criteria, standard, norm, evaluation and action-setting, then the library has little choice but to follow the required format. If, however, no institutional format is in place, then the librarian has the dubious pleasure of designing his/her own. Fortunately, there is already in the literature a number of methodologies available; these provide helpful, practical advice (see McFarlane, Gillespie, Self, McClure and Fredenburg in the Bibliography). A particularly helpful glossary for the uninitiated in quality assurance in general has been published,[13] and a recent bibliography[14] will assist the library staff in locating materials for other hospital departments.

Then, where do we start? With topics that are already suggested by accreditation standards? With topics that are deemed by library staff to be priority for quality service? With topics that are deemed by library users to be priority for quality service? Or, with those that are already obvious problems? Bear in mind that an aggressive quality assurance programme will aim not only to assure quality but also to improve it.

The decision is ours. It is true to say that there has been much re-invention of the wheel during the last few years in the pursuit of quality assurance in library services in Canadian health-care institutions. But this is the learning process, and a very valuable one too.

Where are we now? The impetus for quality assurance requirements has been gaining ground since its inception in 1983. All acute-care facilities in the programme have by now (1987) been surveyed at least once with the quality assurance component in operation. Certainly, the impending approach of a survey spurs the quality assurance activity within an institution. Most library services will have in place an overall quality assurance outline, basic tools such as departmental policy and procedure manuals and job descriptions, and will give some thought to designing quality assurance audits to fit their established priorities or problem areas.

Somewhere down the line, the Canadian patient may expect to be better served because of it. We have come a long way since 1952.

REFERENCES

1   Agnew, G.H. 1974. *Canadian hospitals, 1920 to 1970; a dramatic half century.* Toronto, University of Toronto Press.
2   Greeniaus, B. 1985. The Canadian Council on Hospital Accreditation: a brief history. *Bibliotheca Medica Canadiana*6, 130–133.
3   Wightman, C. 1982. Dr Arnold Swanson: 30 years of accreditation. *Dimensions in Health Service* 59, 24–26.
4   Canadian Council on Hospital Accreditation (CCHA). 1972. *Guide to hospital accreditation.* Toronto.
5   Joint Commission on Accreditation Hospitals. 1953. *Standards for hospital accreditation.* Chicago.
6   CCHA. 1967. *Hospital accreditation guide compendium.* Toronto.
7   Flower, M.A. 1978. Toward hospital library standards in Canada. *Bulletin of the Medical Library Association* 66, 296–301.
8   Canadian Council on Hospital Accreditation, Conseil Canadien d'Agrement des Hopitaux (CCHA/CCAH). 1983. *Standards for accreditation of Canadian health care facilities.* Ottawa (1815 Chemin Alta Vista Drive, KIG 3 Y6).
9   McLean, A and Winchell, J.R. 1984. New QA guidelines raise new questions. *Health Care* 26, 20–21.
10 CCHA/CCAH. 1986. *Guide to accreditation of Canadian health care facilities.* Ottawa.
11 *Manual for assessing the quality of health sciences libraries in hospitals.* 1983. Albany, NY, The University of the State of New York, The New York State Library.
12 Limongelli, F. 1985. Statement of mission – a valuable working tool.*Hospital Trustee* 9, 24–25.
13 Van Reenan, J.A. 1983. Quality assurance: an introduction to terminology and literature. *Hospital Trustee* 7, 18–21.
14 Canadian Association of Quality Assurance Professionals. 1986. *Periodical for quality assurance in Canadian health care.* Toronto (Suite 480, 151 Bloor Street West, M5S IT3).

BIBLIOGRAPHY

Accreditation

CCHA. 1976. *Voluntary hospital accreditation: what's it all about?* Toronto.

CCHA/CCAH. 1985. *An interpretation with special reference to the needs of small acute health facilities.* Ottawa.

CCHA/CCAH. 1985 *Standards for accreditation of Canadian long term care centres.* Ottawa.

CCHA/CCAH. 1985. *Long term care survey questionnaire.* Ottawa.

CCHA/CCAH. 1985. *Standards for accreditation of Canadian rehabilitation centres.* Ottawa.

CCHA/CCAH. 1985. *Rehabilitation centres survey questionnaire.* Ottawa.

CCHA/CCAH. 1986. *Guide to accreditation of Canadian mental health (psychiatric) centres.* Ottawa.

Library standards

Canadian standards for hospital libraries. 1975. *Canadian Medical Association Journal* 112, 1271–1274.

Flower, M.A. The president reports. 1978. *CHLA/ABSC Newsletter* 5, 4–6.

Checklist for staff library services. 1978. *CHLA/ABSC Newsletter* 5, 6–10.

Flower, M.A. The president reports. 1979. *Bibliotheca Medica Canadiana* 1, 39–40.

Checklist for hospital accreditation: staff library services. 1979. *Bibliotheca Medica Canadiana* 1, 48–53.

Minimum standards for health science libraries in hospitals. 1984. Chicago, Medical Library Association.

Quality assurance

Canada: health-care facilities

Proceedings of the CCHA quality assurance seminars, October 1983–May 1984. 1984. Ottawa. Canadian Council on Hospital Accreditation. Conseil Canadien d'Agrément des Hopitaux.

Quality control and appraisal and assurance for quality management in health care institutions. 1985. Developed by A.L. Swanson *et al.* Ottawa, Canadian Hospital Association (17 York Street, Suite 100, KIN 9Z9).

Van Wyck, P. 1985. An administrative overview of quality assurance. *Bibliotheca Medica Canadiana* 6, 141–145.

Australian Clinical Review. 1986. 6 June: 57–116 (whole issue deals with quality assurance in Canada).

Wilson, C.R.M. 1987. *Hospital-wide quality assurance; models for implementation and development* Toronto, W.B. Saunders.

Canada: health-care libraries

Smithies, R. 1985. Quality assurance in the health sciences library. *Bibliotheca Medica Canadiana* 6, 146–147.

Duchow, S.R. 1985. Quality assurance for health and hospital libraries: general considerations and background. *Bibliotheca Medica Canadiana* 6, 177–182.

McFarlane, L. 1985. QA: a personal perspective. *Bibliotheca Medica Canadiana* 6, 182–185.

Gillespie, S.A. 1985. QA do's and dont's: or points to consider when designing a library quality assurance program *Bibliotheca Medica Canadiana* 6, 187–191.

Kirchner, E. 1985. Quality assurance at work: improving library services. *Dimensions in Health Service* 62, 26–27.

Beckman, M. 1987. The importance of measuring library effectiveness. *Bibliotheca Medica Canadiana* 8, 180–189.

Wilson, T. 1987. Research methods for hospital libraries. *Bibliotheca Medica Canadiana* 8, 190–199.

United States: libraries

Evans, E., Borko, H. and Ferguson, P. 1972. Review of criteria used to measure library effectiveness. *Bulletin of the Medical Library Association* 60, 102–110.

Topper, J.M., Bradley, J. and Dudden, R.F. *et al.* 1980. JCAH accreditation and the hospital library: a guide for librarians. *Bulletin of the Medical Library Association* 68, 212–219.

Self, P and Gebart, K.A. 1980. A quality assurance process in health sciences libraries. *Bulletin of the Medical Library Association* 68, 288–292.

McClure, C.R. 1984. Performance measures for corporate information centers. *Special Libraries* 75, 193–204.

Fredenburg, A.M. 1984. The quality assurance issue: one hospital library's approach. *Bulletin of the Medical Library Association* 72, 311–313.

Human factors in the use of information systems: research methods and results

Christine L. Borgman

Graduate School of Library and Information Science, University of California, Los Angeles

ABSTRACT

Human factors studies of information retrieval systems have drawn their research methods from the disciplines of psychology, computer science, and industrial engineering. Among the methods commonly used are online monitoring, both in laboratory and field situations; verbal protocols; field observation; surveys; focus group interviews; and psychometric testing. Results achieved by different methods often have been contradictory, emphasizing the need for closely controlled studies.

The presentation will provide an overview of current research in the human factors of information retrieval, discuss the types of research methods applied and corresponding results, and suggest directions for future research.

INTRODUCTION

Information systems, once the exclusive domain of highly-skilled searchers, are becoming readily available to a mass audience. Commercial system vendors (e.g. Dialog, BRS) are marketing directly to end-users of these systems, by providing simpler interfaces, lower cost after-hours services, and microcomputer-based 'front-end' interfaces; Marovitz;[1] Williams.[2] The number and variety of these systems are expanding, from a few systems and dozens of databases to several hundred systems and thousands of databases; Cuadra;[3] Williams.[4,5] The databases cover the full range of bibliographic, full-text, and numeric records.

Another important trend in mass access to information systems is the adoption of online catalogs in libraries of all sizes and types. Libraries are closing their card catalogs, making online access by library patrons the only form of access to the collection. Many of the online catalogs are sophisticated retrieval systems with most of the capabilities of the commercial systems.

The broadening of the audience for information retrieval systems has brought with it not only new opportunities for research and development, but the responsibility to improve design and training. In addition, the diverse audience for these systems provides a useful testbed for analyzing human-computer interaction.

If we are to adapt systems to users instead of vice-versa, we must study the behavior of users on systems and evaluate the performance of the systems themselves. Both goals require appropriate research methods. This paper surveys the research methods commonly in use for studying information systems and presents research results on one major set of variables, user errors, as a case study in research methods for human-computer interaction. Both the surveys of methods and research results are intended to be illustrative; neither is an exhaustive review.

RESEARCH METHODS

Research in human-computer interaction may have one of two general goals. The first is the study of human behavior with computers. Such research may have the purpose of testing theory, or merely the intent of characterizing use with an eye to later theory development. The second goal is the evaluation of a specific system for the purpose of improving design. Evaluation studies often are done as part of the initial design process, but also are done on operational systems. While the two goals often become intertwined, each will be addressed individually here.

METHODS TO STUDY HUMAN BEHAVIOR WITH COMPUTERS

Human-computer interaction is a special case of problem solving behavior and one that is drawing much interest from researchers in computer science, information science, and human factors. The work done in this area usually is conducted in academic environments or research organizations and seeks to identify principles of human behavior that may be generalized to other computer systems and work environments. The human behavior research leads to theory, but also to design principles and guidelines. In this section we will discuss first the major methods that have been applied, then the variables studied.

METHODS APPLIED

Laboratory Experiments

Laboratory experiments allow tight control over variables, and hence are appropriate for the study of the behavioral aspects of human-computer interaction. Laboratory experiments typically are hypothesis-driven and use a particular system as a prototype or exemplar of the general type of system under consideration.

Behavioral studies often attempt to capture the discrete details of user-system interaction for the purpose of modeling behavior. A particularly useful technique is online monitoring, or the automatic capture of a record of each action taken by the user and each response by the system, usually with time stamps at a frequency of one second or more; Penniman

& Dominick;[6] Rice & Borgman.[7] The data then can be coded into discrete states representing classes of behavior and modeled as a stochastic process; Penniman;[8] Penniman;[9] Tolle;[10,11] Tolle & Hah;[12] Borgman.[13,14,15,16] Monitoring data also can be studied as a protocol of behavior, seeking more heuristic patterns of behavior.

Monitoring data have the advantage of being unobtrusive; a full and accurate record of user behavior is captured without interfering with that behavior. They have the disadvantage of indirect contact with the users; any motivation for the observed behavior must be inferred or captured by other means.

When it is not possible to capture data directly from a system, paper records (printouts) can be kept as a transaction log. While these records still provide a protocol of user-system interaction, they are more difficult to analyze, not being in computer-readable form. Further, paper records normally lack the discrete time-stamp data necessary to recreate the user session fully; Brindle;[17] Bellardo;[18, 19] Woelfl;[20]

A technique complementary to that of monitoring is the capturing of verbal protocols. Here, the subject is asked to 'think aloud', describing his or her thought processes throughout the interaction. These techniques were developed first for problem solving (Newell & Simon)[21] and later applied to human-computer interaction.

Online monitoring and verbal protocols often are used in tandem, but the monitored data reflects the interference effects of talking aloud. The two records may be merged to show the action taken and the user's concurrent verbal description of that action; Halasz.[22]

Pencil and paper tests sometimes are used in a laboratory environment to break online tasks down into more discrete units. When a problem point in the system is identified but its cause is not clear, the one action can be broken into several component tasks to be tested separately offline. Later the tasks may be tested again online. Egan & Gomez[23] used the paper and pencil technique quite successfully in isolating the portions of a text editing task that interacted with personal characteristics variables.

Field Studies

Laboratory experiments must be confined to a small number of subjects and artificial conditions, but they lead to well-defined results. Similarly, field experiments allow the capture of carefully-selected samples of behavior. Alternatively, broader field studies of operational systems can be conducted, controlling fewer variables but capturing much larger samples under 'normal' conditions. The latter types of studies are useful for characterizing behavior that is not yet well-understood. Hypotheses developed in field observations later can be tested in experiments.

Online monitoring is useful for gathering large samples of user behavior under true field conditions. Several problems are encountered in such use, however. One is the issue of privacy. Researchers usually must make the choice of collecting data on user identity, which allows the manipulation of personal characteristics variables but requires the users' permission, thereby limiting the sample size; or to collect a larger sample without any data on the identity of the user, thereby losing valuable correlations.

Another problem is caused by the need to delineate a user session, so that the behavior of users can be studied – individually. A continuous stream of data without distinction by user is of minimal value for studying behavior. With commercial retrieval systems, session marks are delineated clearly by logon/logoff commands. Online catalogs, however, rarely require users to logon or logoff because each terminal runs off one public account. Even when users are asked to give some sort of logon command, it is unenforceable; another user may begin a search where the last user left off.

Two known techniques exist for identifying session breaks in public online catalog sessions. The most reliable (but most cumbersome) is to post observers in the area of the terminals, collecting data on the starting and ending times of sessions at each terminal. Observation must be done cautiously if it is to remain unobtrusive. Timing of observations must be standardized carefully against the computer system clock for later reconciliation; Borgman.[13,14]

A less reliable method is to generate a statistical algorithm to assess the necessary time elapsed between commands to declare a new session. If the gap is too short, one user's session may be broken into two at a long pause (to study documentation, carry on a conversation, etc.). If the gap is too long, the sessions of multiple users will be merged. Borgman[13,14] using a combination of observation (time-in only) and statistical analysis, was able to retain about 60 per cent of the data as useable sessions. The discarded data were shown to have the same distribution of commands as that retained.

Surveys can be used to capture users' perceptions of their own behavior, which is distinctly different from the record of behavior available from the monitoring studies. Studies of other technologies have shown a low correlation between the users' behavior and the monitoring record Rice & Borgman;[7] Rice & Shook.[24] Surveys also can be useful to identify perceived difficulties in use and to capture the users' descriptions of the task.

VARIABLES STUDIED

While data on research methods applied are relatively easy to locate, it is more difficult to locate data on the variables studied. These vary greatly with the researcher's conceptualization of the problem.

A brief review of the literature suggests that the variables studied in information retrieval research can be classified into a few categories. The variable most commonly studied, especially in studies of bibliographic retrieval systems, is experience or frequency of use (defined in as many ways as there are studies). Researchers wish to know how behavior changes as people gain more experience with the system or as they use it more frequently. Variance by experience has been studied in patterns of use; Penniman;[9] Brindle;[17] Tolle & Hah[12] and in retrieval performance (typically expressed as recall and precision) Fenichel;[25] Bellardo;[18,19] Woelfl.[20]

Error behavior is widely studied also. Online monitoring data are very useful for locating frequency of errors and the points at which they occur; Borgman;[13,14] Tolle & Hah;[12] Penniman.[9] Surveys provide data on expressed problems with systems; Matthews et al.[26]

Another variable of recent interest is individual differences other than experience. Researchers have asked how information systems behavior (patterns of interaction or performance) varies by such characteristics as academic background; Borgman[27,28] or by various measures of personality type; Brindle;[17] Bellardo;[18] Woelfl.[20]

An item of interest, but without much study, is the effect of type of training. Borgman compared two methods of training (conceptual and procedural) to performance on an online catalog.[15,16] Wanger, McDonald and Berger[29] studied use of the Medline retrieval system and related performance to type of prior training received.

The effect of different interface methods (e.g. command, menu, form fill-in) on behavior has not been studied empirically for information systems, although it is an area of considerable interest in other interactive systems.

EVALUATION RESEARCH OF INFORMATION SYSTEMS

While behavioral research usually is done by academic researchers seeking general answers to questions of behavioral characteristics, evaluation research is more often done by design teams or human factors specialists in an industrial setting. The need is for answers to very specific questions about design factors, so less attention is paid to precise control of variables to the generalization of results to other systems or environments. The research methods tend to be less formal and to focus on the specific conditions under which the systems actually will be used.

Although applied methods are in use, they are poorly documented, no comprehensive text for them exists, and they are not being incorporated into university curricula in either computing or human factors engineering. The US National Research Council[30] explicitly noted the need for research on developing applied methods for system evaluation. A forthcoming text by Shneiderman[31] may alleviate the problems somewhat, but far more work is required.

EVALUATION METHODS

Due to the problems outlined above, it was difficult to identify descriptions of methods being applied to evaluate interactive systems. Further, much of the applied work is proprietary and not published. The research identified in information systems suggests either that few of these methods are being employed in that domain or else such research is not being published.

Although descriptive data of the techniques are not readily available, a listing of techniques is still of some value. The keyword lists of applied research methods outlined by Shneiderman,[31] the US National Research Council,[30] and Pew[32] are presented below as indication of techniques currently in use.

From Shneiderman:[31]

- pilot studies
- pencil & paper
- mockups
- rapid prototyping
- acceptance tests
- surveys, offline or online
- interviews & group discussions
- online suggestion box or trouble reports
- online bulletin board
- user newsletters & conference
- controlled, hypothesis-driven experiments

From National Research Council;[30] research methods as indicated by names appearing in keyword lists of Human Factors 1976–1981:

- accident studies
- attitude studies
- critical incident
- Delphi techniques
- fault tree analysis
- functional analysis
- lapse time photography
- near-accident studies
- operational sequence analysis
- requirements analysis
- activity analyses
- cost-benefit analysis
- decision analysis
- failure mode analysis
- flow analysis
- job analysis
- link analysis

- network flow analysis
- questionnaires
- task analysis

From National Research Council(30 p. 149): 'generally known applied methods categorized by purpose':

Analysis

- system analysis
- function/task analysis
- information analysis
- scenario analysis
- workload analysis
- time-line analysis
- operational sequence analysis
- failure mode analysis
- fault tree analysis
- link analysis
- function allocation
- anthropometric analysis
- decision analysis
- display evaluation index

Identification of needs

- critical incident technique
- surveys/questionnaires
- accident investigation
- interviews/group techniques
- definition of user population

Data collection

- activity analysis
- time lapse photography
- real time film/video recording
- direct observation
- physiological recording
- quantitative performance recording & analysis

Prediction

- The Human Error Rate Procedure (THERP)
- data store
- human operator simulator (HOS)
- control theory

- accuracy theory
- predetermined time analysis
- readability indices

Evaluation

- test plan evaluation
- simulation
- mock ups
- walk throughs
- check lists
- ratings

From Pew(32):

User needs/preliminary design

- scenario
- script
- interviews
- critical incidents
- task analysis
- task-theoretic analysis
- verbal protocols

Pre-experimental studies

- walk-throughs
- paper and pencil
- mock up
- Wizard of Oz
- rapid prototyping
- experimental programming

Experimental and Quasi-experimental Studies

- direct observation/activity analysis
- bench marking
- computer-based measurement
- activity analysis

Study existing systems

- user statistics
- logging and metering
- gripe file

User as analyst

- task analyst
- forms designer
- data collector
- test subject
- critic of design

As can be seen, the lists overlap considerably. The definition of methods can vary considerably by implementation, and no standardization yet exists; (US National Research Council).[30]

VARIABLES STUDIED

The above lists and descriptions of research methods, surprisingly, gave no indication of the variables studied using these methods. Shneiderman[31] is the only one to provide a general list:

- time to learn
- speed of performance
- rate of errors
- subject satisfaction
- retention over time

Each of these methods is applied by setting some benchmark goal, in terms of the conditions to be met (number and description of subjects, tasks to be performed, etc.) and by defining each of these operationally for the system being evaluated.

Evaluating 'time to learn' for example, requires a definition of 'learning'. Typically, learning requires passing some test. 'Time to learn' is the amount of training and experience required to pass the learning test. 'Retention over time' generally is done by testing the same subjects again at a later time to assess the degree of skill loss. Some refresher training may be interposed. A system may have a short 'time to learn' but a low 'retention over time' or vice versa.

'Speed of performance' usually is operationalized in terms of the number of actions or tasks that can be accomplished in some given period of time. Testing for 'error rate' requires defining precisely what is meant by an error. 'Subject satisfaction' is a subjective measure and normally is broken down into components of satisfaction with different aspects of the interaction and training processes.

As in behavioral studies, evaluation research also may consider individual differences. Here the variables tend to be defined along working group characteristics (age, sex, experience, ethnicity, handicaps), rather than behavioral characteristics such as personality and learning type (US National Research Council).[30]

RESEARCH ON ERROR BEHAVIOR

As a means of illustrating ways in which research on human-computer interaction can be performed, the rest of the paper concentrates on the research results in one important area of human-computer interaction: the study of error behavior. This section covers studies of actual errors made; the next section covers research that attempts to explain the causes of the problems. Only the results themselves are presented here. For a fuller discussion of the results and their implications, the reader is referred to Borgman.[16]

The study of error behavior is of central interest to the study of human-computer interaction. By identifying errors, we can isolate poorly engineered system factors that may be increasing the likelihood of certain types of errors. We can also identify misconceptions about the systems, thereby understanding better how people are interpreting system actions and internalizing them into their behavior. With such knowledge, both the design of systems and training for them can be improved.

We find that people encounter problems with interactive systems both at the mechanical level (typos, incorrect commands, etc.) and at the conceptual level (controlling the interaction, achieving useful results, etc.). The discussion covers both bibliographic retrieval systems and online catalogs; and both mechanical and conceptual problems. Special attention is given to the research methods applied.

PROBLEMS WITH MECHANICAL ASPECTS OF SEARCHING

Bibliographic Retrieval Systems

Problems with the mechanical aspects of searching have not proven to be a major barrier to the use of bibliographic retrieval systems, although several observational studies have found that they are a barrier for very inexperienced and infrequent users (Lancaster et al.;[33] Sewell & Bevan[34]). Fenichel,[25,35] in an experiment capturing printed search protocols, found that both moderately experienced and very experienced searchers made significantly fewer non-typographical errors per search than did novices, although the overall number of errors was small (2.8 per search for novices). Defining errors only as erasures, Penniman[9] found an average of 8 per cent of user actions as errors. Tolle and Hah[12] using the same definition in a monitoring study of the NLM Catline database, also found an average error rate of 8 per cent.

Online Catalogs

Mechanical problems have been particularly evident in monitoring studies of online catalogs. Tolle[10,11] found that errors were not isolated. Instead they tended to occur in clusters; once an error was made, the next transaction was likely to be an error as well. In the Scorpio system of the Library of Congress, given that an error was made, the likelihood that the next command was an error was 59.8 per cent; for the SULIRS system at Syracuse University, it was 28.6 per cent; for the LCS system at the Ohio State University it was 33.3 per cent. Errors were defined in Scorpio as unrecognizable search commands; in SULIRS as an unrecognizable command, an incorrectly formatted command, or an invalid item number; in LCS as partially or fully unrecognizable commands. Data from these studies also indicate that users tend to quit immediately after receiving an error message.

In a monitoring study of the Ohio State University (LCS) online catalog, Borgman[13,14] defined two types of errors: logical errors, or commands that could be partially recognized by the system, and typing errors, or commands that could not be recognized at all. Errors were roughly equally divided between the two types. Total errors averaged 13.3 per cent of all user commands; 12.2 per cent of all user sessions studied consisted entirely of errors.

Dickson[36] and Taylor[37] analyzed the monitoring record of search input on the NOTIS system that resulted in no matches on known-item searches. Dickson found that 37 per cent of all title searches and 23 per cent of all author searches resulted in no matches. She determined that 39.5 per cent of the no-match title searches and 51.3 per cent of the no-match author searches were for records that existed in the database and were not found due to user errors in searching. 15 per cent of the errors in title searches could be attributed to typos or misspellings; the remaining errors were conceptual in nature.

Taylor[37] found that only 22.4 per cent of the no-match author searches could be determined to be good author names that were not in the database; the remaining 77.6 per cent could have been for records actually in the database. She was able to attribute 22.1 per cent of the no-match author searches to misspelled words.

CONCEPTUAL ASPECTS OF SEARCHING

Bibliographic Retrieval Systems

While problems with system mechanics are rare for both experienced and inexperienced searchers of bibliographic retrieval systems, many studies have identified significant problems with search strategy and output performance.[38] Experiments using transcripts of search behavior have shown that searchers often miss obvious synonyms or fail to pursue strategies likely to be productive; Fenichel;[25,35] Martin;[39] Oldroyd & Citroen.[40] Similarly, searchers often fail to take advantage of the interactive capabilities of the system.

In a survey comparing searching problems to prior training, Wanger et al.[41] found that most respondents said they had difficulty in developing search strategies 'some' (47 per cent) or 'most' (8 per cent) of the time. Thirty-six per cent said they had difficulty in making relevance judgements some of the time.

Perhaps as a consequence of relying primarily on simple search techniques, recall scores are often relatively low, even when comprehensive bibliographies were requested; Fenichel.[25,35] In reviewing studies that computed recall measures (using a variety of research methods), Fenichel[38] shows that average recall ranges from a low of 24 per cent (novices only; 41 per cent average minimum in other cases) to a high of 61 per cent. Average precision in the same set of studies ranged from 17 per cent to 81 per cent.

Online Catalogs

The online catalog studies also have identified many problems with the conceptual aspects of searching, although they have focused more on problems related to misunderstanding of system features than to achieving high levels of performance.

Similar to Fenichel's[25,35] findings, survey data indicate that online catalog users rarely ventured beyond a minimal set of system features (Matthews et al.).[26] The majority of searches were simple, specifying only one field or data type to be searched; the advanced search features were rarely used; even when systems included the feature of scanning lists of index terms or headings, users didn't utilize the feature unless 'forced' to do so. Survey respondents also indicated that they had problems with several of the conceptual aspects of searching, including increasing search results when too little (or nothing) is retrieved, reducing search results when too much is retrieved, and use of truncation. Users reported that they experienced a lack of control over the search process and that they found many of the codes and abbreviations in the displays confusing; Matthews et al.[26]

In assessing problems with specific types of searching, the survey found that subject searching was the most problematic area. Users indicated that they had problems both with performing the subject search and with identifying the right subject terms. In several monitoring studies reviewed by Markey,[42] no-match subject searches range from a low of 35% on Melvyl Kern-Simirenko[43] to a high of 57 per cent in the BACS system; Johnson.[44]

In the monitoring study conducted by Dickson,[36] no-match searches could be attributed to misunderstanding the search structure, such as inclusion of initial articles (10.1 per cent of no-match title searches), wrong name order (12.6 per cent of no-match author searches), and the wrong forename or the incorrect inclusion of a middle initial (9.9 per cent of the no-match author searches). Taylor[37] found that 16.7 per cent of no-match author searches were due to putting the forename first, another 5.6 per cent dub to the incorrect use of a middle initial, and 5.7 per cent were due to searching title or subject terms in the author field.

SOURCES OF PROBLEMS

Having identified the nature of the problems encountered on various types of retrieval systems, we now consider the research into the sources of those problems. Sources studied fall into two categories: those due to differences among individual users and those due to specific system features.

INDIVIDUAL DIFFERENCES

Studies of various technologies, including information retrieval systems, have found a wide range in people's abilities to use them. Differences among research subjects often overshadow differences among experimental factors; Egan & Gomez.[23] Although much individual differences work has been done in other domains, we will concentrate here only on information systems.

Bibliographic Retrieval Systems

Studies of user behavior using records of searching behavior long have found high variance in usage patterns, even when the same system and database are used; Bourne et al.;[45] Fenichel;[25,35] Oldroyd & Citroen.[40] In summarizing the characteristics of the 'average' search across multiple studies, Fenichel[38] reports broad ranges in reported means for variables such as number of descriptors searched, commands used, connect time, retrieved references, recall, precision, and unit cost. Only recently have researchers begun to identify systematically the sources of some of the variance observed.

Amount of experience with the system is the variable most commonly studied in identifying performance differences. Fenichel,[25,35] classifying subjects by degree of both system and database experience, was able only to determine that novices (low database experience and low searching experience) searched more slowly and made more errors than experienced searchers. She found some evidence that searchers who had extensive experience with both the system and the database achieved higher values on the 'search effort' variables than searchers who were experienced with the system but not with the database.

Penniman,[9] in monitoring studies, found that frequent searchers of the NLM Medline system used about the same number of single terms and displays in a search as did infrequent searchers, but twice as many advanced term search entries and half again as many Boolean searches. Moderately frequent searchers used more of all types of commands than did infrequent users.

In monitoring the NLM Catline system, Tolle and Hah[12] found that frequent users were less likely (8 per cent of the time) to end the search immediately after an error (erasure), than were moderately frequent (11 per cent), or infrequent users (20 per cent). Average number of errors ranged from 4 per cent of user inputs for frequent users to 9 per cent for infrequent users.

Experience on other types of systems also may be a factor in information retrieval performance. Elkerton and Williges[46,47] studied the use of a technical database on an in-house system by users who were classified as either computer-naive or computer-sophisticated, all of whom were new to the retrieval system. Computer experience was measured by a combination of coursework, daily use of computers, and text-editing knowledge. The researchers found highly significant differences (p < 0.0001) between the computer-naive and computer-sophisticated groups on all measures of retrieval performance.

Three dissertations have explored the personality differences that may underlie searching performance. Brindle[17] studied the relationship between cognitive style and search performance in a field experiment, but found few significant differences. Bellardo[18] studied graduate library school students who had just completed a course in online searching, testing them on two measures of creativity, one measure of personality, and obtained their Graduate Record Exam (GRE) scores. Bellardo attempted to correlate these measures with search performance (precision and recall), but was unable to explain much of the variance. However, she did find a significant (p < .05) correlation between search performance and GRE quantitative scores, but no correlation with GRE verbal scores.

In a field experiment, Woelfl[20] tested skilled NLM Medline searchers on inductive and deductive reasoning and learning style. The searchers performed four predefined Medline searches, the results of which were assessed for two outcome variables (recall and precision) and five process variables. Woelfl found that searchers clustered strongly in one learning style (high active, high abstract). overall, the cognitive attributes affected search process but not search results.

Wanger, McDonald and Berger[29] assigned three predefined searches to 216 Medline searchers and analyzed the records of search performance, which were then compared to three variables: type of training, organization type, and frequency of NLM searching. Although the results indicated high variance in search performance, both in terms of recall and precision, none of the experimental variables explained a significant amount of the variance.

Online Catalogs

As with other types of information retrieval systems, we find a wide range in skills among online catalog users. Monitoring studies have identified high variance in the types of searches performed, in the length of searches, and in the patterns of errors; Borgman;[13,14] Larson;[48] Tolle.[10] Each of these were unobtrusive field studies and did not collect any data on individual users that could be compared to the search pattern data. Survey data of the same population found a comparable range of user-reported success and satisfaction levels in system use and a broad range of user background characteristics; Matthews et al.[26]

Matthews and Lawrence,[48] Lawrence and Matthews[50] reanalysed the CLR survey data in an attempt to identify relationships among the success/satisfaction variables and the user characteristics variables. They found that the most important factors in user-perceived success and satisfaction with online catalog searching were frequency of use of the online catalog, of other catalogs, and of the library itself. That is, the heaviest users of the online catalog and the heaviest users of the library were the most satisfied with the systems. Among the other findings were that those who receive some initial training and assistance in system use are more satisfied than those who do not.

The content of the training also may affect searching ability. Borgman[15,51] compared conceptually-based training to procedurally-based training, using a 'mental models' theory; Gentner & Stevens.[52] As predicted, she found no difference between the training groups on simple search tasks (one or two terms, one index), but those in the conceptually-trained condition performed better on complex searching tasks (multiple terms, multiple indexes or Boolean operators).

Demographic characteristics have been compared in both surveys and a laboratory study. Matthews and Lawrence[49] found that age, sex, and academic status have only an indirect effect on success and satisfaction in that they affect the frequency of library use (although men were heavier online catalog users than women). They did not find relationships between the success/satisfaction variables and prior computer experience, online catalog system, or library.

Borgman[15,51] found significant differences in the ability to pass a benchmark test of information retrieval skills by academic majors. Those who failed the test were predominantly social science and humanities majors, while those passing the test were science and engineering majors ($p < 0.0001$). Prior computer experience was controlled (subjects had no information retrieval experience and at most two programming courses).

Based on the above results, Borgman[27,28] pursued the hypothesis that academic major is a gross measure of individual differences and is probably a surrogate for other characteristics that are associated with major. Preliminary results of a study incorporating personality tests used by Woelfl[20] and demographic characteristics identified in studies of programming aptitude indicate that engineering majors cluster strongly around personality characteristics associated with both information retrieval and programming, while English and psychology majors show either no pattern or one opposite that of engineering majors.

DESIGN PROBLEMS

It is easy to make a general claim that many of the problems encountered by users are due to design deficiencies, but it is much harder to substantiate such a claim with data. So many variables are involved in the use of interactive systems that it is difficult to isolate individual design features.

Bibliographic Retrieval Systems

As with other technologies, very little evaluative work of commercial information systems has appeared in the open literature. The few system evaluations that appear publicly tend to be management-oriented system comparisons, focusing largely on features that contribute to cost-effective searching; Bement;[53] Krichman;[54] Ross[55;] Rouse & Lannom.[56]

One important early work in comparing systems is the features analysis of then-extant information retrieval systems done by Martin.[57] It is a useful starting point for isolating features to be studied in information systems. Hildreth's (1982) later feature analysis of online catalogs follows Martin's initial model.

Online Catalogs

The survey studies on online catalog use funded by the Council on Library Resources represent the only studies identified of online catalog design features. Included in the CLR survey were questions about what online catalog features caused problems (Matthews et al.).[26] The majority of problems cited were in search formulation and output control, but because the specific system implementation of these features varied greatly across libraries the results tell us more about perceived problems than about specific design features. The researchers do note that features that relieved one problem often created another, especially by adding to the complexity of the interface.

Although differences among online catalogs and libraries were hypothesized, Matthews and Lawrence[49] were unable to find significant correlations between specific complaints and individual systems, and found that the problems were surprisingly similar across libraries and systems.

CONCLUSIONS

The research methods available for studying human behavior on interactive information systems are well-developed and empirical. Indeed, most are simply borrowed from the social science disciplines, principally psychology. Good behavioral research is time-consuming and labor intensive, yielding valid but often narrow results. It requires a whole program of research in an area to develop useful theory, from which design guidelines can be generated.

In contrast, the research methods in use for evaluative, or applied, research in design of systems are less well-developed and poorly documented. While they may lead to constructive results for making design decisions, they may have little value for understanding user behavior in general. Applied research remains very important to the development of usable, 'friendly' systems, however. Computer users are no more predictable than any other population; without adequate testing we can never be sure how usable a system will be.

The study of error behavior is an important case in point. Gradually we are learning that users have considerable difficulties in operating information systems in spite of their expressed satisfaction with them. We are finding common results across online catalogs and bibliographic retrieval systems, suggesting that some common types of behavior exist across all types of information systems. The two classes of systems have different user populations, distinguished primarily by degree of training and experience. Further study should determine which differences in behavior can be attributed to experience, which to system features, and which to other demographic or environmental factors.

Of particular concern in the implementation of both research methods and research results is the finding that most designers do not apply them in practice; Gould & Lewis.[59] The classic human factors paradigm of iterative design and testing, involving users early in the design process, has not been adapted in most design environments. The reasons vary, but Gould and Lewis[59] generally conclude that designers have not acknowledged the diversity of characteristics in the user population, nor do they fully comprehend the minimal level of technical knowledge most users bring to interactive systems.

If we are to advance the state of knowledge about users of information systems and make systems accessible to a broader population, we need better research methods and better means for implementing both the methods and the results into design.

REFERENCES

1.   MAROVITZ, W.F. The information industry: its development and integration within a corporate organization. Keynote Address. 48th Annual ASIS Meeting. October 21, 1985, Las Vegas.
2.   WILLIAMS, M.E. Highlights of the Online database field gateways, front ends, and intermediary systems. National Online Meeting Proceedings. Medford, NJ: Learned Information, 1985a, pp. 1–4.
3.   CUADRA ASSOCIATES. Directory of online databases. Santa Monica, CA: Cuadra Associates; 1985.
4.   WILLIAMS, M.E. Electronic Databases. Science, 228(4698), 438–456, 1985b.
5.   WILLIAMS, M.E., Ed. Computer-readable databases: a directory and data sourcebook. Chicago, IL: American Library Association, 1985c.
6.   PENNIMAN, W.D. and DOMINICK, W.D. Monitoring and evaluation of on-line information system usage. Information Processing and Management,16(1), 17–35, 1980.
7.   RICE, R.E. and BORGMAN, C.L. The use of computer-monitored data in information science and communication research. Journal of the American Society for Information Science, 34(4), 247–256, 1983.
8.   PENNIMAN, W.D. Rhythms of dialogue in human-computer conversation. Columbus, OH: Ohio State University, 137–5 (Ph.D. dissertation).
9.   PENNIMAN, W.D. Modeling and evaluation of on-line user behavior. Final Report to the National Library of Medicine. Dublin, OH: OCLC Online Computer Library Center, 1981.
10.   TOLLE, J.E. Current utilization of online catalogs: transaction log

analysis. Final Report to the Council on Library Resources. (Research Report OCLC/OPR/RR–83/2). Dublin, OH: OCLC, 1983a.

11. TOLLE, J.E. Understanding patrons use of online catalogs: transaction log analysis of the search method. In: R.F. Vondran; A. Caputo; C. Wasserman; R.A.V. Diener, Eds. Proceedings of the 46th: ASIS Annual Meeting, 20, 167–171, 1983b.

12. TOLLE, J.E. and HAH, S. Online search patterns: NLM CATLINE Database. Journal of the American Soceity for Information Science, 36(2), 82–93, 1985.

13. BORGMAN, C.L. End user behaviour on an online information retrieval system: a computer monitoring study. ACM SIGIR Forum, 17(4), 162–176, 1983a.

14. BORGMAN, C.L. End user behavior on the Ohio State University Libraries' Online Catalog: a computer monitoring study Research Report OCLC/OPR/RR–83/7. Dublin, OH: OCLC Online Computer Library Center, Inc., 1983b.

15. BORGMAN, C.L. The user's mental model of an information retrieval system: effects on performance. Ph.D. dissertation. Stanford University, Stanford, CA. 1984a.

16. BORGMAN, C.L. Why are online catalogs hard to use? Lessons learned from information retrieval studies. Journal of the American Society for Information Science, 1986a, (In press).

17. BRINDLE, E.A. The relationship between characteristics of searchers and their behaviors while using an online interactive retrieval system. Syracuse, NY: Syracuse University (Ph.D. dissertatidn). DAI 8123887.

18. BELLARDO, T. Some attributes of online search intermediaries that relate to search outcome. Ph.D. dissertation, Drexel University, Philadelphia, PA, 1984.

19. BELLARDO, T. An investigation of online searcher traits and their relationship to search outcome. Journal of the American Society for Information Science, 36(4), 241–250, 1985.

20. WOELFL, N.N. Individual differences in online search behavior: the effect of learning styles and cognitive abilities on process and outcome. Ph.D. dissertation. Case Western University, Cleveland, OH, 1984.

21. NEWELL, A. and SIMON, H.A. Human problem solving. Englewood Cliffs, NJ: Prentice-Hall, 1972.

22. HALASZ, F. Mental models and problem solving using a calculator. Stanford, CA: Stanford University, 1984 (Ph.D. Dissertation).

23. EGAN, D.E. and GOMEZ, L.M. Assaying, isolating and accommodating individual differences in learning a complex skill. In: R.F. Dillon, Ed. Individual differences in cognition. Volume 2. New Yor, NY: Academic Press, 1985.

24. RICE, R.E. and SHOOK, D. Access to and usage of integrated office systems: implications for organizational communication. Presented at Western States Communication Mini Conference Association, 64(4), 382–391, 1986.

25. FENICHEL, C.H. Online information retrieval: identification of measures that discriminate among users with different levels and types of experience. Ph.D. dissertation, Drexel University, Philadelphia, PA, 1979.

26. MATTHEWS, J.R. and LAWRENCE, G.S. and FERGUSON, D.K. Using online catalogs: A Nationwide Survey. New York: Neal-Schuman, 1983.

27. BORGMAN, C.L. Individual differences in the use of technology: work in progress. Proceedings of the 48th ASIS Annual Meeting, 22, 1985, pp. 243–249.

28.   BORGMAN, C.L. Individual differences in the use of information retrieval systems: A Psychometric Analysis. Paper submitted to ACM SIGR Conference, 1986c.

29.   WANGER, J., MCDONALD, D. and BERGER, M.C. Evaluation of the On-Line Process. Santa Monica, CA: Cuadra Associates, 1980. (NTIS Report No. PB81–132565).

30.   US NATIONAL RESEARCH COUNCIL. Committee on Human Factors. Commission on Behavioral and Social Sciences and Education. Research needs for human factors. Washington, DC: National Academy Press, 1983.

31.   SHNEIDERMAN, B. Designing the user interface. Reading, MA: Addison-Wesley, 1986. (In press).

32.   PEW, R. How to study user-computer systems. Tutorial 5, CHI '85, Human Factors in Computer Systems Conference, San Francisco, April 15, 1985.

33.   LANCASTER, F.W. RAPPORT, R.L. and PENRY, J.K. Evaluating the effectiveness of an online natural language retrieval system. Information Storage and Retrieval, 8(5), 223–245, 1972.

34.   SEWELL, W. and BEVAN, A. Nonmediated use of MEDLINE and TOXLINE by pathologists and pharmacists. Bulletin of the Medical Library Association, 64(4), 382–391, 1976.

35.   FENICHEL, C.H. online searching: measures that discriminate among users with different types of experience. Journal of the American Society for Information Science, 32(1), 23–32, 1981.

36.   DICKSON, J. An analysis of user errors in searching an online catalog. Cataloging and Classification Quarterly, 4(3), 19–38, 1984.

37.   TAYLOR, A.G. Authority files in online catalogs: an investigation. Cataloging and Classification Quarterly, 4(3), 1–17, 1984.

38.   FENICHEL, C.H. The process of searching online bibliographic databases: a review of research. Library Research, 2(2), 107–127, 1980.

39.   MARTIN, W.A. A comparative study of terminal user techniques in four European countries on a large common on-line interactive information retrieval system. First European Congress on Documentation Systems and Networks. 1973, pp. 107–167.

40.   OLDROYD, B.K. and CITROEN, C.L. Study of strategies used in on-line searching. OnLine Review, 1(4), 293–310, 1977.

41.   WANGER, J. CUADRA, C.A. and FISHBURN, M. Impact of on-line retrieval services: a survey of users, 1974–1975. Santa Monica, CA: Systems Development Corp., 1976.

42.   MARKEY, K. Subject searching in library catalogs. Dublin, OH: OCLC Online Computer Library Center, 1984.

43.   KERN-SIMIRENKO, C. OPAC user logs: implications for bibliographic instruction. Library Hi Tech, 1(3), 27–35, 1983.

44.   JOHNSON, M.F. An analysis of the log of an online public access catalog. St. Louis, MO: School of Medicine Library, Washington University; 1982. Unpublished manuscript.

45.   BOURNE, C.P., ROBINSON, J. and TODD, J. Analysis of ERIC on-line file searching procedures and guidelines for searching. Berkeley, CA: University of California, Institute of Library Research, 1974.

46.   ELKERTON, J. and WILLIGES, R.C. An evaluation of expertise in a file search environment. In: A.T. Pope; L.D. Haugh, Eds. Proceedings of the Human Factors Society 27th Annual Meeting. Santa Monica, CA: Human Factors Society, 1983, pp. 521–525.

47.   ELKERTON, J. and WILLIGES, R. C. Information retrieval strategies in a file-search environment. Human Factors, 26(2), 171–184, 1984.

48. LARSON, R.R. Users look at online catalogs: results of a national survey of users and non-users of online public access catalogs. Part 2: Interacting with online catalogs. Berkeley, CA: University of California, Division of Library Automation and Library Research and Analysis Group, 1983.

49. MATTHEWS, J.R, LAWRENCE, G.S. Further analysis of the CLR Online Catalog Project. Information Technology and Libraries, 3(4), 354–376.

50. LAWRENCE, G.S. and MATTHEWS, J.R. Detailed data analysis of the CLR Online Catalog Project. Washington, DC: Council on Library Resources, 1984.

51. BORGMAN, C.L. The user's mental model of an information retrieval system: an experiment on a prototype online catalog. International Journal of Man-Machine.Studies. 1986b, (In press).

52. GENTNER, D. and STEVENS, A.L., Eds. Mental models. Hillsdale, NJ: Erlbaum, 1983.

53. BEMENT, J.H. The new prices – some comparisons. online, 1(2), 9–22, 1977.

54. KRICHMAR, A. Command language ease of use: a comparison of Dialog and orbit. Online Review, 5(3), 227–240, 1981.

55. ROSS, J.C. Searching the chemical literature via three on-line vendors: a comparison. Journal of the American Society for Information Science, 30(2), 103–106, 1979.

56. ROUSE, S.H. and LANNOM, L.L. Some differences between three on-line systems: impact on search results. OnLine Review, 1(2), 117–132, 1977.

57. MARTIN, T.H. A feature analysis of interactive retrieval systems. Stanford, CA: Institute for Communication Research, Stanford University, 1974. NTIS PB–235 952.

58. HILDRETH, C.R. Online Public Access Catalogs: the user interface. Dublin, OH: OCLC, 1982.

59. GOULD, J.D. and LEWIS, C. Designing for Usability – –key principles and what designers think. In: Janda, A. (ed.), Human Factors in Computing Systems: Proceedings of the Association for Computing Machinery Special Interest Group on Computer and Human Interaction (SIGCHI) and the Human Factors Society Conference. 1983 December 12–15, Boston. New York: ACM, 1983.

The 'BOOK HOUSE': an icon based database system for fiction retrieval in public libraries

Annelise Mark Pejtersen

Risø National Laboratory, Cognitive Systems Group, Denmark

ABSTRACT

The BOOK HOUSE, a computer-based search system for fiction aims at supporting library users in finding fiction. It is an example of a system design using a cognitive work analysis which, in turn, builds on earlier studies of the information retrieval task based on actual user-librarian negotiations. These studies lead to the identification of a set of user search strategies for retrieving literature as well as a multidimensional framework for classifying fiction. Both of these have been necessary prerequisites for the design of the BOOK HOUSE, a flexible online database system for novice users. It employs icons in the display interface in order to enhance the utility of the system for casual users (children as well as adults) in public libraries. The analytical foundation of the design together with some of the results of the evaluation of the system are discussed.

THE FICTION RETRIEVAL TASK

Today, the retrieval of fiction in libraries is based on an alphabetical classification by authors for shelving arrangements supported by bibliographical databases with author/title vantage of uniqueness in the arrangement, identification and retrieval of an individual document, but it is of little help for the users with needs related to the subject-matter contents and the other aspects of documents. Typically, there are no exact or unique answers to such needs, nor are there within the present computer-based retrieval systems any aids, which the intermediary or end user can utilize to establish a basis for their search strategies. Users face two main difficulties: first the problem of identifying the user's often subsconscious and intuitively formulated need; secondly, the problem of formulating a relevant search strategy among documents that are not indexed and represented according to needs, but according to formal, bibliographical data. Difficulties may arise here, since the main part of the request/book correlation is usually rather intuitive and it is most likely that many of the habits of the users are based on ill-defined attitudes and associations. This problem can be solved by the design of a database with access to document contents that is compatible with the users' request/need criteria, and by the design of an interface to the database that supports their choice of search strategy. This, however, requires a new notion of the information content of the problem domain of fiction retrieval, and a new kind of indexing scheme for analysis of document contents. Traditionally classification and indexing schemes have been developed to reflect the contents of a document in terms of its relationships with the knowledge structure of the subject field to which it belongs and does not usually take the users' requests as a focus. What is needed to extend this foundation is an appropriate frame of reference for indexing and searching based on a cognitive analysis focusing on the needs and capabilities of the end user. Among other things, this can lead to solutions which let the user choose search attributes which adequately cover the specific domain of interest and, at the same time, give the user the opportunity to solve his/her problem in a natural way.

FIGURE 1. *Shows the work space of fiction retrieval in libraries.*

Document Content	User Needs
Author Intention; Information; Education; Enjoyable Experience.	Reader's Ultimate Goal
Literary or Professional Quality; Paradigm; Style or School.	Value Criteria Related to Reading Process and/or Product
General Frame of Content; Cultural Environment, Historical Period, Professional Context.	General Topical Interest of Historical or Social Setting
Specific, Factual Content. Episodic Course of Events; Factual Descriptions.	Topical Interest in Specific Content
Physical Characteristics of Document; Form, Size, Color, Typography, Source, Year of Print.	Reading Ability

A CLASSIFICATION SYSTEM FOR FICTION

Pejtersen (1979) conducted field studies in the 1970s involving a series of user-librarian conversations. Among other things, these studies led to a representation of the work space illustrated in Fig.1, and it uncovered the need for a multi-faceted or multi-dimensional classification scheme reflecting user reading needs. The left column of the work space shows the attributes of the book collection, which should be retrievable in a database search, and the right column shows the features of users' needs expressed at several different levels of abstraction, including the user's overall goal with the search as well as the necessary representation of the information to meet the user's reading capability. The retrieval task is then a multi-level mapping of book attributes with attributes of users' need criteria.

The main facets of the fiction classification scheme based on this empirical analysis can be summarized as follows:

1. Author's Intention – emotional experience, information, education, promotion/stimulation of ideas (social criticism, philosophical attitudes . . .)

2. Frame/setting of the subject matter content – time and place, geographical, historical, social, professional setting.

3. Subject matter – action and course of events (plot), psychological development or description, social relationships.

4. Accessibility – physical characteristics of book/document, readability, printing characteristics, book format, publisher.

FIGURE 2. *Shows an example of a novel from the database of the Book House. The controlled keywords are displayed in a red colour (here italics), but are kept in the context of the annotation of the book. The red keywords can be searched directly from the book description, when selected with the mouse.*

Author:	Haller, Bent
Title:	Kaskelotternes sang – 1983 – 137 pages.
Front page:	*Blue – sea – whales – icebergs.*
Names:	Gamle Dick – Gylte – Tangoje.
Subject:	A *calf* of a *sperm whale's* life in the *sea.* Its *struggle* to *survive* in spite of *pollution, hunger,* and man's *killing* of the *whales.* The sperm whales *sticking together* in their *struggle* against the *dangers* of the sea.
Environment:	*Sea environment.*
Time:	*1980's*
The author's intention:	*Criticism* of man's *pollution* of the *seas* and *killing* of *animals* on the *point of extinction.*
Experience:	*Exciting – sad.*
Genre:	*Novel – animal story.*
Readability:	*Age of 11, reading aloud from the age of 7, big-sized letters – (happy ending).*

For the BOOK HOUSE designers, a natural consequence of this was that, to support access to fiction, it should be possible for the user to identify and select search terms from one or more of these facets of 'need' as the basis for a subsequent search. Therefore the contents of the database of fiction used in the BOOK HOUSE have been indexed according to the above classification system, and an example of the representation of books from this database is displayed in figure 2. Italic shows the controlled vocabulary.

SEARCH STRATEGIES

A second important ingredient of a cognitive work analysis is the identification of the strategies which are employed by users in navigating through the work space to support their decision making. Pejtersen (1979, 1980) identified several different strategies which were employed during the user-librarian negotiations for the identification of books to match users needs. Of these, three are relevant in the current context:

1. Analytical search – a rational problem-solving approach where the intermediary is in control. The dimensions of the user's needs are explored systematically; need aspects are compared with document aspects; titles are suggested.

2. Search by analogy – the intermediary is in control and explores user needs by asking for examples of earlier 'good books in order to find 'something similar'. Prototypes thus identified can also be analyzed to identify new search terms for a subsequent analytical search.

3. Browsing – the user may have a need which is so ambiguous that no search specification is possible and, instead, the bookshelves or database are scanned in order to explore possible matches between the intuitive current need and the available items.

The designers of the BOOK HOUSE made these search strategies equally easily available for library users by letting the computer provide the necessary support to the user of required mental resources during a search.

NOVICE AND CASUAL USERS

A third component in the work analysis has to do with the various levels of cognitive control which affect performance and it is at this level that psychological factors begin to become important. For this presentation, it is sufficient to say that the previous material pointed in the direction of explaining what users can do and therefore dealt with the alternatives which should be available. However, in any single situation, any particular user will choose a given way of responding which will depend on a host of factors – need, available time, training, repertoire of heuristics and skills, etc. This has implications for the design of information displays and the way the information will be used by the users. Some of this will be treated in further detail later.

A primary postulate behind the BOOK HOUSe project is that efficient navigation in a database by a casual user will be greatly enhanced if the database structure can be embedded in a context which can be represented directly on the interface display surface. This will make it possible for the user to quickly develop efficient skills in communicating through the interface without the need for complex mental juggling to convert one representation to another. One way to attempt this is to consistently recode the abstract attributes of the items in the database to positions in various spatial arrangements on the display surface. This will directly reinforce the development of manual skills involving the mouse to cope with the resulting spatial-temporal working space in what one today calls a direct manipulation mode – i.e. an efficient automated interaction with the entities on the visible surface.

A FLEXIBLE SEARCH DIALOGUE

The user – system interaction evolves through a dialogue which has four main interaction phases:

A) Select one of two dialogue forms.

The BOOK HOUSE system allows the user to choose between conducting book searches through use of the traditional keyboard-based command dialogue which all Danish public libraries have access to and experience with *or* by means of the mouse-based BOOK HOUSE system. This paper covers the latter approach only.

B) Select one of three book bases.

After choosing the mouse-based dialogue, the user is asked to select the appropriate database. There are three possibilities – the childrens' bookbase, covering literature for children up to about sixteen years of age, the adults' bookbase, or the total bookbase covering both childrens' and adults' books. A single mouse selection is required.

C) Select one of four search strategies and specify need.

At this point in the dialogue, the user must decide how the search for books will be carried out. Based on the results of the work analysis stated earlier, the BOOK HOUSE provides four alternatives:-

1. – an analytical search
2. – a search by analogy
3. – browsing in pictures
4. – browsing in book descriptions

These are been briefly described later in the section on navigation in the Book House. Further details are given in Pejtersen 1989, Pejtersen and Goodstein (1989).

D) Examine resulting book descriptions. Revise search criteria; reexamine the search results; process eventual candidates.

In a normal dialogue, this phase of the dialogue is entered from each of the above four searches: after either the analytical specification or the browse in pictures selection has been made and 'see books' has been chosen with the mouse; after a reference book title has been specified in a 'find similar books' dialogue or after the user has desired to browse in book descriptions. A host of options now becomes available independent of the search strategy selected. Firstly, a description of the first book of the current set is displayed on the screen organized in accordance with the classification system. The user can browse through the set – one after the other in both directions, or larger leaps can be taken. The number of the book in the current set is displayed in the corner of the screen. The user can now repetitively:

– save interesting candidates in the BOOK HOUSE for later browsing and/or request that hard copies of interesting descriptions be printed – e.g. for use later in finding the books on the shelves. One can also see previously saved book descriptions.

– find similar books which, if the analogical input was selected, will as a start use the reference book as the basis for finding (at least) ten other similar books in the selected book base. However, the option can always be used at this point in the dialogue in connection with any current book description on the screen.

– modify the current need which gives the user the option of adding or removing search terms from the current search profile. This is done by displaying in red the searchable index words in the current book description which the user has access to with the mouse. Each change generates an automatic search, the number of books found is displayed and the first book description in the new set is displayed. At the present time, only the current book set is retained by the system. Figure 3 shows a selection of these options displayed to the user as icons.

This description has only dealt with a 'normal' dialogue trace. Of course, the BOOK HOUSE makes it possible for users to make strategy shifts, abandon current searches, select a new database, etc. at any time.

There are also help facilities available which attempt to give the user both a context-dependent explanation of where the user is at the moment as well as more general information about the system facilities. These will not be dealt with here.

Figure 3. shows a selection of the repertoire of icons to be used to modify, revise or change a choice of search terms or to process the resulting set of retrieved books. These icons are supposed to be perceived as signs for action possibilities during navigation of the BOOK HOUSE at different stages of the search.

USE OF ICONS AND METAPHORS

Of course, in a real-life library – as for most databases – the number of dimensions in the base can be numerous, the number of stored items is high and the search attributes are not always well known to the user. In

FIGURE 3. *Shows a selection of the repertoire of icons to be used to midofy, revise or change a choice of search terms or to process the resulting set of retrieved books. these icons are supposed to be perceived as signs for action possibilities during navigation of the BOOK HOUSE at different stages of the search.*

	Delete search terms from the current search profile.The metaphor refers to object to use.
	Print book description for later use in finding books on the shelves. The pictogram refers to object to use.
	Help gives the user context dependent as well as more general information about the system facilities. The metaphor refers to object to use.
ngs fi going 1eyea	Select new search terms from the book description and generate a Boolean AND search. The metaphor refers to state to reach.
	Select the minus and point at a search term in the book description to initiate a Boolean NOT search. The metaphor refers to state to reach.
	Find books similar to any current book on the screen.The symbol refers to state to reach.

the BOOK HOUSE intermediary, an attempt was made to exploit the flexible display capabilities of computers to relate both information in and about the database as well as the various means for communicating with the database to a location in a virtual space – i.e. by creating a kind of storehouse or book house. The many dimensions were allocated locations in appropriate rooms or sections of rooms within the storehouse. This type of metaphor was felt to be easily understood and remembered – by both children and adults. This is exemplified by the poster introducing the BOOK HOUSE (Fig.4) which is a house made of books (like a pancake restaurant). The book is the reason for, the object of and the target for the acts of users during a search. The house is the symbol of the database system in which the user has to navigate.

The most important issue regarding the use of icons is of course their comprehension by the user. This is not only a function of their form and content but, more importantly, the context within which they are viewed – e.g. where in the retrieval task one is – as well as the experience level of the user. Since the BOOK HOUSE is for novices from 7 to 70 years of age, this is a critical issue. How a user interprets an icon in a given situation depends on his/her intentions/experience at the given moment.

Figure 4. A BOOK HOUSE is chosen as a metaphor for the fiction retrieval system for the support of users' memory and navigation by

FIGURE 4. *A BOOK HOUSE is chosen as a metaphor for the fiction retrieval system to support users' memory and navigation through the location of information about the functionality and content of the system in a coherent and familiar spatial representation.*

location of information about the functionality and content of the system in a coherent and familiar spatial representation.

The challenge for the designer is to provide a match between the context (of the information retrieval task) and the icons so that the user perceives the latter in the intended fashion. In the BOOK HOUSE, the design has been focused on the use of icons as:

- **signs** indicating action alternatives during a search, *and/or*
- **symbols** providing a symbolic representation of the semantic content of the database – i.e. the substance of book contents and features.

Indeed a trained expert might conceivably perceive icons as signals in a temporal-spatial metaphorical world where direct skilled manipulation is possible at all steps in the retrieval process. However, as stated, the design has been aimed particularly at the novice user where, when appropriate, the displayed icons preferably should be multi-purpose and permit a direct mapping onto effective cues/signs for action at the manipulative level and onto the semantic organization/content of the database for use in planning and decision making.

In the BOOK HOUSE, the underlying advantage of a mouse (or equivalent) instead of the usual keyboard is that the communication of spatial-temporal information in the perception-action loop is preserved intact. The selections to send to the computer are selected from the

FIGURE 5. *Shows the room for database choice in the BOOK HOUSE. In the upper left corner of the screen, the rooms visited by the user will be displayed concurrently as the search progresses. The user can enter any of the displayed rooms and thus navigate freely from room to room.*

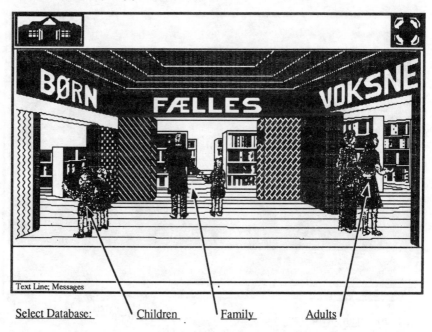

Select Database: Children   Family   Adults

repertoire on the screen by an identification based on their physical position. They are pointed at and selected ('clicked') by the mouse. If these alternate selections correspond to attributes of the database, then a very efficient spatial navigation can take place by moving the mouse followed by a selective clicking with the mouse button.

A textline at the bottom of the screen informs the first time user about the meaning of each icon. The line appears and disappears automatically along with the user's movement of the mouse on the screen.

NAVIGATING IN THE BOOK HOUSE

Thus when the user has entered the BOOK HOUSE, he/she first enters a hall connecting to three different rooms having books on shelves (Fig.5.). The left room has books for children, the right room has books for adults, while the center room has books for both. The difference is reinforced by the size of the people seen entering the three rooms.

After the user has chosen a database, a new room will appear showing people (children, adults or both – depending on the previous choice) busily searching for books in different ways (Fig. 6). The user can thus select one of four different search strategies based on the results of the empirical studies mentioned previously.

FIGURE 6. *Shows the room for choice of search strategy. From the left: search by analogy, browsing pictures, analytical searches, browsing book descriptions. When the user selects a strategy, the system supports the search accordingly by a number of heuristics used to automate many of the manipulations necessary for the performance of a database search along various strategies.*

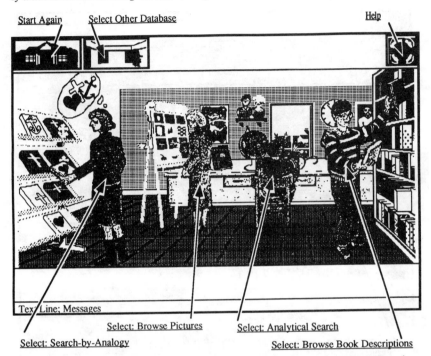

Start Again   Select Other Database   Help

Text Line; Messages
                    Select: Browse Pictures   Select: Analytical Search
Select: Search-by-Analogy   Select: Browse Book Descriptions

The direct manipulation feature allows the user to click directly on the figure executing the same strategy that he/she is interested in. A selection here leads the user to a new area where the required set of 'tools' for carrying out the chosen search strategy are made available. Each of the four strategies will be described briefly below in terms of the Book House metaphor.

Work room for analytical search

Thus Fig. 7 is one of four work rooms and is designed to support an analytic search. The user enters this room and takes the place of the figure sitting at the table in the previous picture. On and around the table are icons representing the different dimensions of the classification system. There are 13 of them. For example, the world globe represents the geographical setting of the book, the clock icon denotes the time dimension and the theatre mask refers to the emotional experience provided by the books. The user can select one of these at a time so as to get access to an open book display with the textual listing of the particular set of search terms which belong to the selected dimension (Fig 8). The

FIGURE 7. *shows the iconic display of the work space in terms of a multifaceted classification scheme based on an empirical analysis of users' search questions in libraries. When the user selects an icon, keywords are displayed and the user can specify need by clicking on one or more keywords and a subsequent search is performed. See Figure 8 for an example of an open book with display of selectable keywords.*

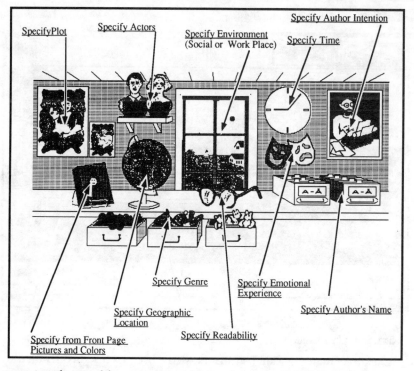

user can also combine search terms from the same or different dimensions. The Boolean operators are automatically inserted – generally with AND between dimensions and OR and AND within dimensions. This set of selected terms is the user's current search profile which he/she can revise by deleting terms, adding terms or make a NOT operation. Thereafter the user can see descriptions of the books which the BOOK HOUSE has found. These appear in an open book format (Fig. 10) and are structured according to the classification system so that the user can directly see the correspondance between his/her selected terms and the actual contents of each book.

Search by reference book

If 'find a similar book' is selected (Fig. 9), another room is entered which shows a book containing a title or author index for the database. This can be opened to help the user identify his/her reference book.

After selection of this reference book, the system will automatically attempt to find other books in the collection which include as many of the

FIGURE 8. *Shows the list of controlled keywords displayed in an open book format. When the user selects an icon from the table or wall in the work room during analytical searches, keywords will be displayed, and the user can now specify need by clicking at one or more keywords with the mouse and a subsequent Boolean search is performed. The result of the research can be seen as books in the book case in the right corner at the bottom as well as the appearance of the selected term in the left corner. If the user regrets a choice of keyword, the rubber can be used to delete the term and thus undo the search.*

SELECT KEYWORD: PLOT

Aber
Aborter
Absurditeter
Adamsæbler
Adel
Adelsfamilier
Adelsmænd
Adfærdsvanskeligheder

Administration
Adoption
Adoptivbørn
Adoptivforældre
Adoptivsønner
Advarsel mod
Advokater
Afdøde

Textline; Messages

same indexed attributes of the reference book as possible. The description of the ten most similar books will be presented one at a time in an open book format in decreasing order of relevance. The multifacetted classification scheme is used as the basis for a weighting of all books in the collection with respect to the reference book. The algorithm is quite simple and can be described as follows:

If, for a given dimension of the classification system (e.g. plot or time), c is the number of index terms common to a given book i and the reference book which itself has a index terms within this dimension, the given book's weight in this dimension is:

$$\text{wdi} = \text{wd} \times c/a$$

where *wdi* is the weight of dimension d for book i and *wd* is the collection weight for dimension d. A book's total weight is then the sum of its dimension weights.

In the BOOK HOUSE, seven of the 13 dimensions (plot, setting, place, time and impression, cognition, genre) were utilized in this calculation of similarity.

The system calculates collection similarity online after each request for 'find similar book'.

FIGURE 9. *Shows the user's model book which is used for a search for similar books. The user can identify the model book by either the name of the author or the mane of the title of the book.*

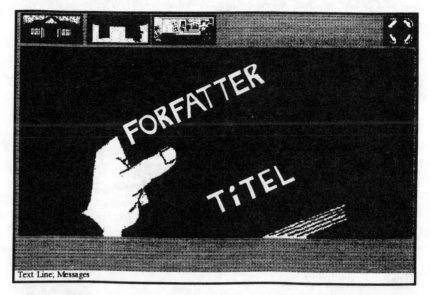

Browsing icons and books

A choice of a browsing strategy indicates that the user doesn't know the 'specific address' of a good book but would prefer to 'wander around town' until a good/familiar/interesting item is discovered. Thus after 'clicking' on this strategy, the system shifts immediately to an open book representation with a randomly chosen book description. The user can thereafter continue to step through other descriptions.

The description on a retrieved book formatted according to the classification system and displayed in an open book is shown in Figure 10. There are two default formats of display of book contents, which will depend upon the user's choice of search strategy, and is thus chosen automatically by the system. The corners of the book with arrows can be used to turn pages forwards and backwards. This is the lowest/final level of a search independent of choice of search strategy. At this level the user has access to most of the options of the system, and the user can now print books, put aside interesting books, see interesting books put aside earlier, get help, get the controlled keywords displayed in the book description as red, mouse selectable search terms, find something similar to the current book, or enter another room and shift search strategy or database.

The browsing strategy also includes an iconic version where the user can browse through small pictures describing book content (Fig. 11). This could be appropriate when the user does not have a well formulated need but would like a quick bird's eye view of what the books in the

FIGURE 10. *When the strategy of browsing books is chosen, the system displays randomly chosen books from the total database, one at a time, and the user's options are the same as mentioned below.*

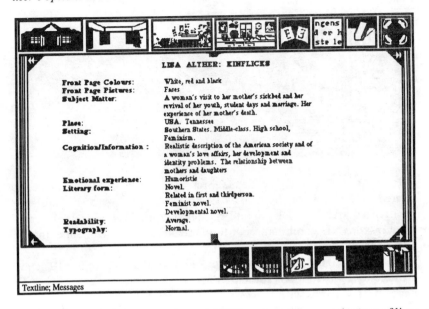

database are all about. Of course, skimming through several pages of lists of indexed terms – one for each dimension in the classification scheme – is feasible but tedious. Therefore, icons are an economic way of supporting intuitive searches since a single picture can communicate many different facets of meaning and thus can include terms from more than one dimension. In this way, apart from being effective, a skimming through icons can provide an unexpected aesthetic and emotional experience and give rise to potentially new perspectives on a topic.

FIGURE 11 A. *This icon represents the content of books that deal with* future, future society, science fiction, fantastic setting, space, pollution, industry, *etc. When a user selects this icon, the system will retrieve all the books about future OR future society OR science fiction OR fantastic setting OR space, etc.*

FIGURE 11 B. *This icon represents all the books in the database about* prison, prisoners, staff in prison, punishment, criminals *etc. When a user selects this icon, the system will retrieve all the books about prison OR prisoners OR staff in prison OR punishment OR criminals, etc.*

In Figure 11a and 11b each icon represents all the books in the database related to the topic of the icon. A combination of these two icons will result in a search for books about Prisoners OR etc. AND Future OR etc. That is, an AND combination of terms related to each icon, and an OR combination among terms assigned to each icon.

In addition to the verbal description of books as seen in figure 10, icons are used to represent book content. These pictures are implemented as six pages of small icons, with 18 icons on each page (Fig 12). The approach to constructing these icons was to use the most frequently used index terms as the basis for imagining and drawing an appropriate pictorial analogy. It was found of course that the same icon could serve as the pictorial counterpart of more than one index term. Thus the 108 icons cover more than 1,000 different index terms. The associations between keywords and icons were identified and evaluated during the design phase through a number of experiments and association tests with potential end users of the BOOK HOUSE system.

The use of icons in the BOOK HOUSE interface stands in contrast to the widely used *Desk Top Metaphor* which is nothing more than an arrangement on the display screen of some tools (files, documents, folders, trash baskets . . .) mainly depicted in terms of conventional technology without any direct support of the work situations the user could be confronted with. The icons of the BOOK HOUSE not only refer to objects to use to proceed the search. They also display alternative search routes as well as the semantic content of the database.

BOOK HOUSE EVALUATION

The BOOK HOUSE was evaluated at a public library in the town of Hjortespring over a six month period during 1988. The experimental subjects were the normal everyday users of the library and consisted of both children from 7 to 16 years and adults from 17 to over 50. The

FIGURE 12. *Shows the menu for the strategy of browsing icons. Six pages of icons represent the book content of the database. Each icon represents a semantic network of associatively related keywords belonging to several different dimensions of the classification scheme shown in figures 1 and 2. Thus each icon represents an associatively related semantic network, which can be combined with another semantic network by selection of another icon with associated keywords, which then results in a complex boolean search of a relatively high number of keywords. The result of the search is seen in the book case in the right corner at the bottom.*

Text Line; Messages

evaluation program was carefully planned and consisted of both an analytical and an empirical phase. The analytical portion concentrated on the functionality of the system and could build on the earlier studies of user-librarian negotiations which uncovered the need criteria and search strategies employed and consequently the information required to support these need criteria and strategies. This work had laid the basis for making decisions about the content of the computerized displays which thus could be verified analytically. The empirical validation was then necessary, e.g. to see how/whether users would accept the form of the displayed information as supportive of their efforts to retrieve relevant fiction.

Thus the evaluation cycle for the system consisted of a thorough verification of functionality, a set of queries to users and librarians before the system was installed, system installation and training, detailed queries and logging during/just after system use and, finally, later feedback on user satisfaction with the retrieved books. More specifically, some of the items for evaluation included:

A) subject indexing – e.g. the degree to which:

– the dimensions in the classification scheme corresponded to users' needs.

- the searchable terms were adequately specific and exhaustive.
- the indexers' representation of content was relevant and under-standable.
- users and indexers agreed on the correspondence between index words and book contents.

B) the user interface – e.g. the degree to which:

- users utilized one or more of the provided search strategies.
- users had difficulties understanding the system.
- users considered the system pleasurable to use.
- the provided 'help' facilities were utilized.
- there is a preference for 'writing' search profiles via command language or 'selecting' options with a mouse
- age and sex affect user reactions.
- the chosen metaphor is understood and accepted.
- icons support book searches, can be used to describe book contents and, in general, serve as a catalyst for finding interesting and relevant literature.

Evaluation techniques included online logging, an online question-naire, traditional questionnaires, observation and interviews.

SOME EVALUATION RESULTS AND IMPLICATIONS

In general terms, it can be said that the system received an overwhelm-ingly positive response with regard to both indexing and the user interface. A lack of space prevents any detailed presentation of results from the BOOK HOUSE evaluation. A report including this information was published 1989 (Pejtersen and Goodstein). In general terms, it can be said that the BOOK HOUSE received an overwhelmingly positive response with regard to both the classification scheme and the icon-based user interface. The following more general conclusions can be made:

The functionality of the system

– All four strategies, as well as all dimensions of the classification system, were used by both children and adults. Giving the user a choice among four different routes to exploring the contents of the database made the users feel that the system was flexible. The option of choice and shift between different strategies made help texts superfluous: when stuck in the search, users found it easier to shift to another strategy than to consult the help texts.

– The functionality of the classification system was validated; users appreciated the many alternative ways of choosing among search terms. In general, the many alternatives, together with the optional possibility for combinations from these alternatives enhanced the usefulness of the classification system. The BOOK HOUSE experiment has demonstrated that a highly structured and selective access to content keywords divided into 13 dimensions/facets helps the user to formulate his/her need more precisely and therefore leads to a better search result. The different dimensions and their related keywords were judged to be in good agreement.

– Most users prefer the 'direct manipulation' interaction provided by the BOOK HOUSE to writing their search requirements in a command language.

– The iconic approach was successful when used in combination with text: alternate search techniques such as browsing through icons can give unexpected (and gratifying) results. The iconic representation of the classification system worked according to the designers' intentions. It helped the users recognize facets of their need instead of forcing them to recall them by introspection and reformulation in order to match the data-base contents to the search enquiries (Fig. 13). The associated text descriptors supported the first-time users and satisfied the designers' intentions of easing users' acceptance and ultimate recognition of icon meanings.

– AND, very importantly, the cognitive task analysis worked.

Implications for the library:

– Other than the normally most popular books began to be borrowed. Before the BOOKHOUSE, when shelf browsing was necessary, these books were not borrowed 'because they looked boring'. The bookstock was used more efficiently and in accordance with the librarians acquisition criteria. This has economic implication for a library's costs for book acquisition.

– The librarians themselves skipped the normally utilized traditional command language search system, and used the BOOK HOUSE as an easier means of finding books when asked by users for help.

– In the long run, book reservations and other functions should be incorporated in an integrated search and delivery system to achieve an optimal automated took.

CONCLUSION

It is relevant to point out that, in common with non-fiction areas, it is impossible for librarians to be acquainted with the full scope of literature in fiction which eventually could match users' needs. Today no special tools exist to support the librarian with the task of fiction retrieval. In addition, users have sometimes difficulties in formulating these needs for

FIGURE 13. *Shows the users' responses after reading the retrieved books, based on 118 questionnaires.*

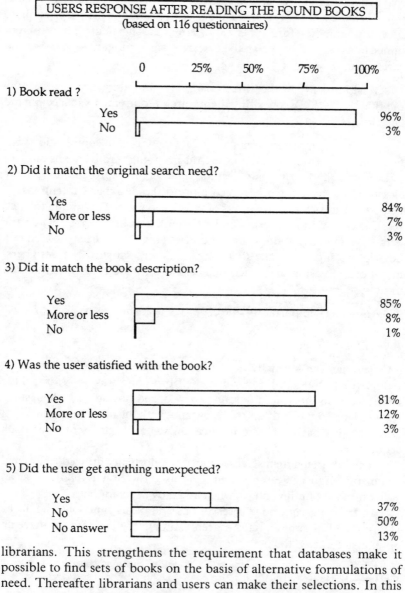

librarians. This strengthens the requirement that databases make it possible to find sets of books on the basis of alternative formulations of need. Thereafter librarians and users can make their selections. In this way, as named above, the many thousands of books, which either are not read by librarians or, from their external appearance, do not appeal to readers suddenly become as equally relevant as all the 'best sellers'. This leads to a better utilization of the collection as well as an introduction of readers to a broader spectrum of writers and their viewpoints, opinions, facts, fantasy, etc. The ultimate institutional goal for public libraries is to promote education and cultural values. The BOOK HOUSE enhances this goal.

ACKNOWLEDGEMENT

This project was supported by Denmark's Technological Council and Folkebibliotekernes Radighedssum. The project partners were Riso National Laboratory (Cognitive Systems Group), Jutland Telephone's Laboratory, Regnecentralen A.S and the Royal Art Academy's School of Architecture. The Royal School of Librarianship and Hjortespring Library. A special thanks to Inge Cramer, Jutta Austin, Finn Nielsen and Lenn P. Goodstein, who have contributed significantly to the success of this project.

REFERENCES

Pejtersen, A.M.: Design of information retrieval systems based on work analysis and supported by icons. In: Proceedings of International IFIP-HUB Conference on Information System, Work and Organization Design. Berlin, GDR, 1989.

Pejtersen, A.M.: THE BOOKHOUSE. Modelling user's needs and search strategies as a basis for system design. RISO National Laboratory. RISO-M-2794, 1989.

L.P. Goodstein and A.M. Pejtersen: THE BOOKHOUSE. Visual design. RISO National Laboratory. RISO-M-2795. 1989.

Pejtersen,, A.M. (1988) Search Strategies and Database Design, in L.P. Goodstein, H.B. Andersen and S.E. Olsen (eds): Tasks, Errors and Models, Taylor and Francis Ltd.

Pejtersen, A.M. (1980) Design of a Classification System for Fiction Based on an Analysis of Actual User-Librarian Communications; and Use of the Scheme for Control of Librarians' Search Strategies in O. Harboe and L. Kajberg (eds) Theory and Application of Information Research, London, Mansell, pp.146-159.

Pejtersen, A.M. (1979) Investigation of Search Strategies Based on an Analysis of 134 User-Librarian Conversations, in T. Henriksen (eds): Third International Research Forum in Information Research, Oslo.

Pejtersen, A.M. and Goodstein, L.P. (1988) Beyond the Desk Top Metaphor: Information Retrieval with an Icon Based Interface, in M.J. Tauber and P. Gorny (eds): Proceedings of the 7th Interdisciplinary Workshop of Informatics and Psychology on 'Visualisation in Human- Computer Interaction', Sharding, Austria 23-27 May 1988, Springer Verlag.

Rasmussen, J. (1988) A Cognitive Engineering Approach to the Control, Emergency Management, CAD/CAM, Office Systems, Library Systems, in W.B. Rouse (ed): Advances in Man-Machine System Research, Vol 4, JAI Press.

Careers and the occupational image

Margaret Slater

Information Research Group, Polytechnic of Central London, 235 High Holborn, London WC1V 7DN, United Kingdom

ABSTRACT

Drawing on material from studies conducted by the author, in the area of manpower, education and training, during the 1980s, this paper covers several linked themes. Self-actualization within the employing organization is explored, including employer and user images of library-information work. Formal and informal vocational education is also examined, in relation to curriculum development and the underlying, but largely unanswered question of 'education for what?' The emerging market and the traditional market for library-information professionals are also considered, in conjunction with the stereotype as a conditioner of acceptability in new employment venues.

In dangerous situations we are traditionally warned by the well-meaning to watch our backs – a nonsensical caution, because a physical impossibility. What our advisers really mean is that we should take measures to protect ourselves from the figurative stab in the back, or attack from an unexpected or ill-defended angle. Among these measures, mere awareness of danger from this quarter is perhaps the beginning of wisdom, and the first step on the path to survival. What I would like to do in this talk is to urge the profession to watch, not its communal 'back', but its collective occupational image, which represents a similarly vulnerable area.

Currently, like many other professions, we are at once threatened and challenged by fast-moving external change, in society and the world of work, by socio-technical and economic pressures. However, the hazards confronting us seem less those of positive attack, than of negative neglect, or being bypassed, of occupational death by attrition. Paradoxically, the present and forseeable wider future situation offers much promise as well as threat to the library-information profession. The current buzz concepts of the information society, the leisure society and of the service industry boom, seem to proffer those long-suffering marginals, those human peripherals, the library-information workers, a potential place at the core of the working world and society. Our very longstanding skills centred round information-handling ought surely to merit us some place in the sunrise, rather than the sunset industries?

Certainly in the public sector, recognition is evident that changes in work and society create greater needs for information, for community information, for employment and self-employment information, for careers and legal information. In spite of this need, what seems likely to hold back expansion in the public sector is cutting of public service provision in general – i.e. economic policy. So, further contraction may be the future norm in the public sector, rather than expansion, as one might perhaps logically expect.

In the private sector, in special librarianship and information work, what seems more likely to hold us back is our image. In particular, how we are perceived by actual and potential employers and users of our services and products may be a serious inhibitor. In this talk I'm going to confine myself to this special sector for a variety of reasons. It is in this area that the emerging markets are defining themselves most clearly. According to careers advisers, library school students (and indeed most other students) believe that 'industry and commerce is where the action is' and where the jobs will be in the immediate and forseeable future. The public and educational sectors by contrast are seen as arenas of contracting opportunity.

Not least among my reasons for concentration on this special sector is that I know it fairly well. During the last few years I've researched various aspects of it, in relation to manpower, education and training, including studies of use and non-use, staffing levels, careers guidance, career patterns and the occupational image and continuing education. In all of these investigations, the effect of the occupational image was evident. So I shall draw on this material freely, attempting to relate it to some important topics covered by the other speakers, using three recurrent and interwoven themes.

(1) Self-actualization within the employing organization: the employer and user image.

(2) Formal and informal education for the profession, which relates to curriculum development and the question: 'Education for what?'

(3) The emerging markets and the traditional market: the image as a conditioner: of acceptability in new employment venues.

Let's start with the employing organization and the profession's self-image in that context. How do library-information workers perceive this situation, particularly in terms of individual career development and collective departmental development? Poor image, low status and low profile are not uncharacteristic of the treatment and image of librarians at work. For instance, low corporate status and a bad image of libraries was believed to cause non-use of the service by 29 per cent of industrial-commercial library-information heads participating in a study of non-use published in 1981.[1]

When discussing the contribution of subjective factors to non-use, almost half their answers (49 per cent) were concerned in some way with the image and visibility of the service within the parent organization. The other 51 per cent of answers related to three main perceived characteristics of non-users themselves. These 'intrinsic' characteristics, of observed intractible non-users comprised: the DIY syndrome, peculiar to independent loners who believe that finding their own information is part of their professional expertise; low levels of information consciousness and awareness, simple failure to recognize that one's problem is information-related and soluble; lazy, apathetic, inefficient employees. In the latter case, failure to use the library is just part of a 'can't be bothered' attitude to, and at, work. Now it may occur to you that all three characteristics of non-users might be amenable to persuasion and that two of them are not totally unrelated to the library image.

To return, however, to answers directly related to the image of libraries in firms. The low profile, invisibility even, of the unit within the organization was cited. Potential users don't know what the library can do for them. Some don't even know that it exists. The generally low status and unimpressive image of librarians was also believed to lead to usage as a last resort and lack of faith in the library's ability to help. Fear, awe and apprehension of the library was also believed to exist amongst some younger, newer or lower status employees. Such potential users wonder if they are important enough or have the right to use the service.

Corporate invisibility represents an interesting facet of the whole image problem. Not only do librarians suffer from an undesirable image, susceptible to stereotypic caricature of the buns, beads and glasses variety, they also suffer from an anaemic, low profile, shallow image. In a noisy, dynamic, complex setting, like the average film, this can lead to virtual invisibility.

Concerning this invisibility, potential users (surveyed in the second stage of the non-use study, published in 1984)[2] stressed the need for librarians to be dynamic, pro-active and to get out and market their services.

An insurance operative said that the ideal librarian would be: 'Young and friendly, liking to get reasonably involved in helping others. Flexible, willing to do things beyond 'normal' work. Someone who will get up and 'dig out' information, rather than pointing to areas or giving you forms to complete'.

A chemist believed that they 'must be able to forecast users' future requirements' and 'should be more eager to 'sell' the service. They ought to do 'market research' and be aware of each department's requirements'.

An engineer imagined the ideal librarian as: 'a middle-aged man with a great deal of energy. Interested in ways in which information flows in and out of the library and the firm. Good at administration, always aware of his customers' reactions to the services provided by the library. Ready to explore new ideas and to try new developments'.

A chemist simply thought that librarians should be 'helpful to all idiots' and able to 'do most of their customer's jobs for them'.

At the same time, users seemed to realise that some mechanistic external barriers to efficiency existed, limiting the self-actualization of librarians and preventing libraries from fulfilling their potential. So failure of vision may be seen as corporate, rather than intrinsic to the library profession. A feeling that libraries in firms do as good a job as possible within the constraints imposed by lack of staff, funds, and space was expressed, as the following direct quotations from respondents may illustrate.

'Sometimes they seem out of touch either with the business in which they are employed or with life in general. This is not always their fault, it is often the fault of the business'. (Insurance operative.)

Librarians are 'most helpful. When consulted in the right way they take an enormous amount of trouble. People who think otherwise are usually those who do not have a clear idea of what information they want'. (Engineer.)

'Usually inadequately financed to do a really effective job, maybe intellectually not really equal to doing it'. (Chemist.)

'A helpful, user-oriented person prevented by administrative restrictions (i.e. funds, time, staff, space, facilities) from realising his full potential in meeting user needs'. (Chemist.)

'Busy, efficient, helpful, especially with children. Take pains, hard-working – shelving, indexing often done in their own time, after closing, without pay. (Bless 'em)'. (Chemist, obviously thinking of the public library scene rather than an industrial library.)

'A press-ganged typist who does her variable best to deal with highly technical demands. Struggles to keep abreast of computer-based systems. Easy prey for management to find 'more useful' jobs for her to do'. (Chemist.)

Librarians who provided case-histories as part of this study of non-use also mentioned mechanically imposed external barriers to visibility and hence to usage. Perhaps the most obvious of these is simply the siting of the service.

Take the case of the engineering library cum information service, which was created in 1978. By 1980 it was still little used. The founding information officer put forward the following reasons:

'Very few people seemed aware of its existence. The location was poor, being part of another department and tucked away in a corner.' The location was poor in nature as well as in siting, with little space to expand. Thus it gave an impression of being 'cramped and muddled'. Reluctance was evident on the part of some sectors of management to spend any money on the library. At the beginning of 1981, in desperation, the information officer started pushing out some pro-active services, notably current awareness and SDI.

'In May 1981 a decision was taken to move the library to a separate location. This move did more to attract attention to the library than anything that had been done before'. The information officer capitalized on this surge of curiosity by distributing promotional leaflets to all staff, describing the library in its new location and its capabilities.

This case illustrates an interplay of external and internal factors. It also emphasises the importance of entrepreneurial opportunism on the part of the library-information manager.

Not all physical moves are, however, similarly fortuitous. Consider the case of the pharmaceutical industry library. The head said ruefully: 'the unit is called the Library. No mention has ever been made of an Information Unit, which is partly the problem'. Nevertheless, 'up until a year ago, the Library was in the research block, and people popped in and out all the time. Subsequently it was moved . . . not far away, but is now in a separate building. My predecessor and assistant noticed a drop in usage following that move, albeit to a much nicer location'.

A different situation pertained in a small industrial engineering library. The head said: 'I had come from a similar library which had very heavy usage. This library, however, was lucky to have two users a day'. It was dilapidated, ill-organized, with out of date stock. Moreover, 'due to the previous librarian's deep involvement with the company's social activities, the running of the library had been mainly left to the library clerk. Also, the library was situated well away from its potential users and I never could persuade management to relocate it'.

Management-library interaction problems of this kind underline the relative invisibility of the service to management. Yet whose fault is this? The management, the librarian and the image would all seem to be culpable. All have contributed something to the creation of this Catch 22 situation or negative feedback loop. Yet if you inherit a situation of this kind, it can be remarkably hard to break the pattern. Subtle measures may be needed and timing is all important. Because of the self-effacing image, anything overtly dramatic, aggressive or unexpected that the new librarian attempts to do may only be deemed noteworthy in the 'man bites dog' sense. Such incidents are thought highly newsworthy. But the man in question is also labelled crazy – that is, indulging in behaviour unlike the accepted human template or image.

Another image-related finding of the non-user study is superficially surprising, but worth bearing in mind. Put simply, it amounts to this: potential users have a worse general opinion or image of a firm's library than they have of the generic library in society at large. Amongst a sample of 448 professional workers in industry and commerce, 43 per cent had a good opinion of libraries in general. Yet only 30 per cent held a good opinion of the typical firm's library. Perhaps they see the firm as an unsuitable setting for their concept of a library? Reasons for this difference included detrimental comment on the somewhat fuzzy focus of the firm's library or information service. Rather too generalist in nature and disconnected from the real problems and preoccupations of the firm and its employees was a not uncommon verdict. This was sometimes compared with the focused nature of non-traditional problem-solving and information providing facilities within the firm.

In this survey of users and non-users, respondents were asked to create two verbal portraits of the librarian. One was of the typical librarian (how s/he is). The other was of the ideal librarian (how s/he ought to be). Anwers were vigorous, enlightening, often amusing. They were also amenable to analysis, because common themes recurred. Results of analysis for the sample as a whole are shown in Table 1.

TABLE 1. *Whole sample summary: major characteristics of –*

A typical librarian (how they are)	The ideal librarian (how they ought to be)
Faults . . .	
35% Passive, reactive, apathetic, dull, boring	68% Helpful, approachable, accessible, service-motivated
23% Cold negative personality, aloof, superior, casual	50% Efficient, quick, professional, confident and confidence inspiring
22% Generalist – gives only superficial assistance	47% Knowledgeable, wide general knowledge, well-educated, intelligent
22% Unworldly, academic, pedantic, bookworm.	43% Dedicated, dynamic, invloved; more aggressive, lively, keen, enthusiastic
21% Wants to help, but not competent to do so	35% Warm personality, extrovert, friendly, kind, socially skilled
19% Obsessively tidy, methodical, over-conscientious, industrious	34% Possess communicative and inter-pretative skills (understand and explain)
16% Harassed, impatient, always too busy to help	34% Provide information and an active, evaluative service
16% Lacks communicative, interpretative skills	32% Know own stock and system
16% Misfit, mediocre, vague	31% Practical, down to earth, worldly-wise: knows firm and industry in this way
13% Provides only books and documents	25% Graduate or subject expert
10% Ignorant, ill-educated, ill-informed	21% Know outside sources: provide referral service
	18% Cool, calm, patient, unflappable
Virtues . . .	
24% Helpful, service-motivated	
15% Efficient, professional, confidence aspiring	
14% Knowledgeable, intelligent	
13% Cheerful, friendly, polite	
10% Knows own stock and system	

Based on responses of 448 industrial-commercial respondents. Taken from [2].

To sum up the bad side, or negative image, of actual librarians: 'passivity, incompetence, bureaucratic tendencies, unworldliness and insufficient education or subject knowledge for the job' were cited. On the credit side, real-life librarians were thought to at least possess service motivation, a sense of duty and a desire to help other people. It was sometimes said to be a shame that they were not sufficiently competent to do so. A rather pallid person seems to be delineated, slightly aloof and rather introverted, something of an amateur in a situation calling for professionalism. Alienation from the life of the firm can also lead to doing the job as an end in itself, for its own sake, rather than the firm's sake. Subsequent marginality ensues.[2]

Yet it was encouraging to note that some respondents believed that actual librarians possessed some of the qualities of the ideal librarian. Perceived actual and ideal image did overlap to a certain extent. So the librarian may be described as helpful, when carefully approached in the right way, on a good day.

The ideal librarian visualized by respondents would be much more dynamic, extrovert, well-informed and appropriately qualified (possessing subject expertise). Helpful and friendly tendencies would be more prevalent and backed up by efficiency, professionalism, competence and communicative, interpretative and evaluative skills. A more intellectually sophisticated, worldly-wise, socially skilled and practical being seems to emerge 'From descriptions of the ideal librarian. Both positive and negative images, however, indicate that potential users view the job as essentially people-related and 'up front' rather than 'back room' in nature.[2]

Regressing or back-tracking from the library in the firm, and the mature, or at least qualified practitioner, let's examine an earlier stage of career development. Let's look at the formal vocational education of the library-information workers of the future at 'library school', and at their emergence into the world of work. What do people expect to get out of library school? What do their employers expect, by way of preparation for a career in library-information work and preparation for specific jobs within the framework of that career?

As Cronin noted in 1982:[3]

Allegations of mismatch between the output of library-information schools and the requirements of employers are voiced sufficiently often as to be cause for concern.

Divergence of opinion is evident, arising involuntarily in almost any survey in any way related to staffing. It may concern mismatch between person and post in crude terms of qualification. For instance, in the ratios of staff to users study,[4] of 655 special library-information units, in only 36 per cent of cases was there no mismatch between post or grade and qualification (or lack thereof). In 23 per cent of units the mismatch was total. That is to say, everybody in the unit seemed to be in the wrong job, for which they were either under or over-qualified. So, one had managers with no formal qualifications at all and library assistants possessing subject and library-information degrees. This study was published in 1981. More recent trends indicate that the likelihood of encountering the unqualified manager or senior library executive is diminishing. The over-qualified library assistant, however, seems to be an increasingly common phenomenon, in a current period of generally higher unemployment. As one careers adviser said to me: 'Time was when you made a career choice. Now it's a compromise. Graduates have to think themselves lucky to get any old job these days'.

Crude mismatch between educational attainment and job grading probably relates directly to the occupational image. It reflects employer perceptions of the irrelevance or low status and value of library-information qualifications and indeed of the job itself.

What about more subtle degrees of mismatch between person and job, traceable back to the process of library-information education itself? In the ratios survey of 1981, qualitative inadequacy of staff, or poor performance was explored. Only 25 per cent of participating heads of special services was pleased with their staff and had no complaints at all on this score. Below this level, bare adequacy was the prevailing norm in 49 per cent of services. The remaining 26 per cent of services suffered from general inadequacy or extreme variability of staff quality and performance, of various kinds.

Factors contributing to poor performance were explored, revealing that library bosses did not necessarily blame their employees personally for inadequacy. Context-induced low morale was mentioned by 31 per cent of the sample, who cited low pay and status, unsatisfactory conditions of work, over-work, lack of career and promotion prospects as motivation reducers. Basic personality was believed to be wrong for the job by 25 per cent of service heads. This amounts to an oblique criticism of library school selection procedures and indeed of employer recruiting. More direct criticism of the formal education system came from the 15 per cent who said that formal qualifications were inadequate, irrelevant or poor preparation for the work itself.

Staff perceptions of the library-information school, of its relevance and contribution to careers and specific jobs, were examined in a current survey on informal continuing education. The 253 participants in this study were all special sector practitioners. Their verdict was that library school was rather better preparation for an overall career in the field than for any particular job within it. However, this formal vocational education did not contribute dazzlingly to either aspect of professional life. Forty per cent did not find it helped much in career development; whereas 58 per cent found it did not contribute much to discrete jobs within that career.[5]

Only 25 per cent found that it made really significant input to the wider sphere of a career, saying that it was 'really useful'. Only 14 per cent said that it contributed really usefully to execution of specific jobs and posts.

Before curriculum developers become too depressed by this finding, some of the reasons for such beliefs should be examined. Opinions of this kind are not necessarily or fundamentally hostile to the library-information schools. They do reveal, however, basic problems in the design and provision of vocational education of almost any kind. It was pointed out, for instance, that tailoring people to fit particular posts is properly the province of internal training, rather than of formal education. This was believed to be particularly applicable to a fragmented and complex occupational field like library-information work, which can be done in many contexts and for many different kinds of employer.

At the stage of entering and indeed of passing through library school, students do not necessarily know which sector they wish, or will be able, to work in. Over-specialization at library school, or rigorous streamlining to fit particular sectors is therefore undesirable, impractical, or a limitation of future employment options. Time dependency is another factor to be taken into account. Any vocational education is subject to built-in obsolescence, which particularly affects life-long careers. Short courses, as well as internal training, have a role here in updating professionals. Short courses can introduce people to necessary new skills and attitudes to information that were not current when these people were at university, and so could not be taught to them. So, logically, by implication, an academic, qualifying library-information course cannot be expected to fit anyone completely for either a lifelong career or for the jobs within it.

Incidentally, this factor of time dependency affects many other occupations. Additionally, the speed at which professional obsolescence can overtake any worker seems to be accelerating. In *Business Systems and Equipment*, September 1984, for example, Mrs. B. Cockram, a teacher of business skills, recommended 'retraining for teachers, medical staff and the like every three years'.

In this study of continuing education[5] participants were also asked directly if they thought that library schools really should or could prepare one for careers and jobs. Sixty-eight per cent thought they should definitely try to fit students for a career: 53 per cent thought that they definitely should attempt to prepare students for specific jobs. The major contributions of library schools to effective working in the field were believed to be: provision of a useful overview of the whole field and opportunities within it (mentioned by 25 per cent): acquisition of basic transferable information skills (mentioned by 24 per cent).

How common is a sense, amongst library-information professionals, of lacking skills necessary to their jobs? In particular, what skills do qualified people feel that they lack? Fifty-seven per cent of the sample were conscious of some skill gap of some kind. These skill gaps ranged widely in detailed nature, but the most frequently mentioned were in the areas of management, computing, communicative skills and subject knowledge relating to the particular service. Twenty-one per cent were also aware of what might be called basic aptitude and personality defects in relation to their work. Problems of this kind are only partly amenable to remedy by education and training. They may reflect on student selection and the occupational image rather than on the educational process itself.

A different slant on the image and on career prospects has emerged from work I've been doing recently. This has examined careers guidance in the United Kingdom, at secondary and tertiary education levels, in relation to library-information work. The report has just been published by the British Library Research and Development Department.[6]

The first chastening and somewhat sobering finding of this investigation was that the careers service appears to understand us very much better than we understand it. Probably this is as it ought to be, but it was not necessarily what we expected to find. Careers advisers (with the possible exception of that downtrodden branch represented by careers teachers) had a realistic image of library-information work. They see it as a people-related and computerate occupation. At the same time, they were not unaware of the existence of a different and unfortunate public image. In their opinion, this constitutes one of our major problems. It acts as a barrier to the entry of the right kind of people into the profession, and to career advancement once employed.

Careers advisers urged us to mount a campaign to dispel the stereotype and to promote a more positive modern image. Careers advisers themselves attempt to do this for us with employers and with potential entrants to this field of work. They point out that this is not a refugee job for the shy or anti-social but a dynamic, interactive service profession.

Changes in employment patterns have been noted by careers advisers in recent years, characterized by what they call 'a move to peripheral placement in information-related jobs'. They say that this trend is still small, but is growing and probably significant. Some modification of the employer image of the occupation has also been noticed. Employers more readily recognize the transferable nature of library-information skills. So a library-information qualification may now be listed (amongst others) as a suitable qualification in an advertisement for a job in retail management, or in advertising. A few years ago, advisers say, you would not have seen this happen.

Careers advisers themselves believe that the skills taught in library schools and acquired in library-information work itself are transferable. So they urge students to 'think wider than librarianship' and to be prepared to market themselves agressively and to be geographically mobile.

Yet students, they say, still cling stubbornly to an image of the archetypical library as a public one. They see it as just a convenience – and a public one at that – as Graham Lord tellingly said in a novel with a library setting. University entrants in general, of all kinds, also believe that industry and commerce is 'where the action is' and therefore where the jobs are occurring. Therefore bright entrants to university won't necessarily be attracted to librarianship as a career. Most assistance to the careers service apparently comes from the public library sector and this has an unfortunate compounding effect. Careers advisers would be very grateful for more help from local industry and commerce and in particular from the information sector. Such input should take the form of people willing to represent the profession at careers conventions, to give talks to groups at the careers service, to host visits and for individual student referral.

High level input to computerized careers guidance systems also seems desirable. Many of these systems work on a matching people to jobs principle. In this they rather resemble computer dating or information retrieval systems. A one-off profile of the client is matched against standard occupational profiles and good matches are retrieved as the search product, with associated information helpful to the client. The profile of the librarian in most of these systems is flattering, in that it recognizes that the librarian is a manager and that librarianship is people-related in essence. The profile of the information worker is by contrast curious. It encapsulates some loner concepts and less recognition of managerial and interpersonal skills.

Finally, let's look at what direct evidence I've unearthed on career patterns themselves and the impact of the image. Even careers advisers, with their fairly informed and sympathetic view of the profession, apparently tell students: 'if you want to end up as the managing director, don't enter library-information work'. In other words, career advisers see it as an occupation providing job satisfaction, but not power. It is not for powerful ambitious people, not for the real high fliers.

An earlier study of career patterns and the occupational image[7] published in 1980, not unexpectedly provided food for thought on the relationship between career progression and the occupational image. 1,770 library-information services of all kinds participated in this study. Heads of these services, spontaneously and unprompted, cited the image (and associated low organizational status) of library-information workers as a factor affecting staff turnover. Allegedly, staff changed jobs restlessly and unnecessarily (from the bosses' viewpoint), seeking a sector of the field or an individual employer where librarians were better respected and treated. Curiously enough, a perceived bad image seemed to cause more movement within the field (21 per cent mention) than it did desertion of the profession for other occupations (16 per cent mention). Perhaps this is because an unpalatable professional image actually inhibits escape to another occupation? If that were true, it would have great relevance to acceptance in the emerging markets.

As part of the same study of the image, organization charts were collected, to see where the library or information service was located in the corporate structure or map, and at what level of perceived importance or status. The sample consisted of 307 charts, representing some 460 library-information units. About half the participating organizations had more than one service.

If one imagines that top management represents 100 per cent status attainment, then special libraries in firms at that time were at a 29 per cent status level. This was below the average organizational status level for libraries of all kinds of 35 per cent. Libraries in the more academic fields – i.e. in societies, associations and higher education institutions – reached a 38 per cent status level. Information units in firms did rather better than industrial-commercial libraries at 38 per cent, which was also the norm for information units of all kinds. The moral here may be that in firms the service should not be called a library if it wants to be taken seriously. It should be called an information unit, or something similar.

By themselves, these figures may not mean much. It may bring them to life to cite other functions existing within the firm at the same level as the library and the information service. Prestigious equivalencies were more frequent in the case of the information service. It tended to be equated with group status, rather than sectional status. Comparable groups were publishing, personnel, finance, marketing, membership, advertising, forecasting, computer applications. Really low level parallels were conspicuously absent.

Fairly typical equivalencies for the firm's library were the press office, conference organizer, technical editors, training section, central records, visits organizer. Status tended to be that of a section rather than of a group. Lower grade parallels were, however, quite common – like print room, central typing pool, mailing, maintenance, transport, company chauffeur and even the tea lady. The status range was wide for the library. Variability and ambivalence were evident. In one company the librarian might rank with the company solicitor, in another be equated with the janitor. A tip for ambitious librarians might be to ask to see the organization chart before finally accepting the job offer.

REFERENCES

1   M. Slater, The neglected resource: non-usage of library-information services in industry and commerce, British Library Research & Development Report 5628, Aslib, London, 1981.

2   M. Slater, Non-use of library-information resources at the workplace: a comparative survey of users and non-users of onsite industrial-commercial services, Aslib, London, 1984.

3   B. Cronin, The education of library-information professionals: a conflict of objectives? Aslib, London, 1982.

4   M. Slater, Ratios of staff to users: implications for library-information work and the potential for automation, BLRD Report 5627, Aslib, London, 1981.

5   M. Slater, Ongoing research for British Library Research & Development Department into short courses and internal training-provision and needs.

6   M. Slater, Careers guidance and library/information work, Library and Information Research Report 48, British Library, London, 1986.
7   M. Slater, Career patterns and the occupational image; a study of the library/information field, Aslib, London, 1980.